# The Making of Competition Policy

# The Making of Competition Policy

*Legal and Economic Sources*

EDITED BY

Daniel A. Crane

AND

Herbert Hovenkamp

OXFORD
UNIVERSITY PRESS

**OXFORD**
UNIVERSITY PRESS

Oxford University Press is a department of the University of Oxford.
It furthers the University's objective of excellence in research, scholarship,
and education by publishing worldwide.

Oxford New York
Auckland Cape Town Dar es Salaam Hong Kong Karachi
Kuala Lumpur Madrid Melbourne Mexico City Nairobi
New Delhi Shanghai Taipei Toronto

With offices in
Argentina Austria Brazil Chile Czech Republic France Greece
Guatemala Hungary Italy Japan Poland Portugal Singapore
South Korea Switzerland Thailand Turkey Ukraine Vietnam



Published in the United States of America by
Oxford University Press
198 Madison Avenue, New York, NY 10016



Library of Congress Cataloging-in-Publication Data

The making of competition policy : legal and economic sources / edited by
Daniel A. Crane and Herbert Hovenkamp.
p. cm.
Includes index.
ISBN 978-0-19-978279-6 (cloth : alk. paper) 1. Competition—History.
I. Crane, Daniel A. II. Hovenkamp, Herbert, 1948-
HD41.M27 2013
338.6′048—dc23
2012020765

ISBN: 978-0-19-978279-6

1 3 5 7 9 8 6 4 2
Printed in the United States of America
on acid-free paper

# Contents

# Acknowledgments

Many of the works republished in this volume remain under copyright. The editors gratefully acknowledge the following reprint permissions:

Selections from Chapter IV of Edward Hasting Chamberlin's *The Theory of Monopolistic Competition* (8th ed.), which was first published in 1933, are republished with the permission of Harvard University Press.

Chapter 27 of Joan Robinson's *The Economics of Imperfect Competition*, originally published in 1948, is reprinted with the permission of Palgrave Macmillan.

John Maurice Clark, "Toward a Concept of Workable Competition," which originally appeared in Vol. XXX of the *American Economic Review*, June 1940, is reprinted with the permission of the American Economic Association.

Selections from Adolf Berle and Gardiner Means, *The Modern Corporation and Private Property*, originally published in 1932 by Harcourt, Brace & World, Inc., are reprinted with the permission of Simon & Schuster, Inc.

*Regulation of Competition Against Regulation of Monopoly* and *Shall We Abandon the Policy of Competition* are reprinted from *The Curse of Bigness* by Louis D. Brandeis, edited by Osmond K. Fraenkel, copyright 1934, by Louis D. Brandeis; renewed © 1962 by Susan Brandeis Gilbert and Elizabeth Brandeis Raushenbush, is used with permission of Viking Penguin, a division of Penguin Group (USA) Inc.

Selections from Rexford Tugwell's *The Industrial Discipline and the Governmental Arts*, originally published in 1933 by Columbia University Press, are reprinted with the permission of Russell & Volkening, Inc.

Selections from Thurman W. Arnold, *The Bottlenecks of Business*, originally published in 1940 and reprinted by Beard Books in 2000, are reprinted with the permission of Beard Books.

Richard Hofstadter, *What Happened to the Antitrust Movement*, previously published in *The Paranoid Style in American Politics and Other Essays*, by Richard Hofstadter, copyright 1952, 1964, 1965, is reprinted with the permission of Random House, Inc.

Franz Böhm, Walter Eucken, and Hans Grossmann-Doerth, *The Ordo Manifesto of 1936,* originally published in *Germany's Social Market Economy*, edited by Alan T. Peacock & Hans Willgerodt, is reprinted with the permission of Palgrave Macmillan.

Franz Böhm, *Democracy and Economic Power*, originally published as *Kartelle und Monopole im Modernen Recht*, C. F. Müller, Karlsruhe 1961, is reprinted with the permission of Verlagsgruppe Hüthig Jehle Rehm.

Kenneth Arrow, *Economic Welfare and the Allocation of Resources for Invention,* (RAND, December 15, 1959), is reprinted with the permission of the RAND Corporation.

Selections from Joseph Schumpeter, *Capitalism, Socialism and Democracy* (3d ed.), copyright 1942 and 1947, are reprinted with the permission of HarperCollins Publishers.

Chapter 10 of Joe Bain's *Industrial Organization*, copyright 1959 John Wiley & Sons, Inc., is reprinted with the permission of Elsevier Limited.

Chapter 3 of Carl Kaysen and Donald F. Turner's *Antitrust Policy*, originally published in 1959, is reprinted with the permission of Harvard University Press.

Selections from George Stigler, *The Organization of Industry*, 1983 University of Chicago Press, are reprinted with the permission of the University of Chicago Press.

Aaron Director and Edward H. Levi, *Law and the Future: Trade Regulation*, is reprinted from 51 *Northwestern University Law Review*, No. 2, by the special permission of the Northwestern University Law Review.

Selections from Robert Bork's *The Antitrust Paradox*, originally published in 1978, are republished with the permission of Perseus Books Group.

Richard A. Posner, *The Chicago School of Antitrust Analysis*, originally published in 127 *U. Pa. L. Rev.* 925 (1979), is republished with the permission of the University of Pennsylvania Law Review.

Chapter 11, *Dominant Firms and the Monopoly Problem*, pp. 208–233, of Oliver E. Williamson, *Markets and Hierarchies: Analysis and Antitrust Implications*, copyright 1975, 1983 by the Free Press, is reprinted with the permission of Free Press, a Division of Simon & Schuster. Copyright renewed 2003 by Oliver E. Williamson. All rights reserved.

F. M. Scherer, *Conservative Economics and Antitrust: A Variety of Influences*, originally published in *How the Chicago School Overshot the Mark: The Effect of Conservative Economic Analysis on U.S. Antitrust*, Robert Pitofsky, ed., is reprinted with the permission of Robert Pitofsky, F. M. Scherer, and Oxford University Press.

Herbert Hovenkamp, *Post-Chicago Antitrust: A Review and Critique*, was originally published in the 2001 *Columbia Business Law Review* and is reprinted with the permission of Herbert Hovenkamp.

Finally, we extend our thanks to Joseph Coburn, Derek Kelly, Keith Klovers, Sanjana Nafday, and Carlen Zhang, who provided excellent research assistance.

The Making of Competition Policy

# Introduction

Students today often view antitrust law as an *ex nihilo* creation of recent vintage. The received narrative understands the passage of the Sherman Antitrust Act in 1890 as a radical reformist moment that injected a new legal being into American law and political economy. This new being was, like the early earth of Genesis, "without form and void." Unbounded by precedent or concrete legislative history, the Supreme Court begin to pour meaning into the statute. Lacking any robust economic framework, the Court stumbled along for half a century with vague economic and moral intuitions concretized into legal formalisms and bolstered by vacuous rhetoric. Then, after World War II, the Court discovered economic theory, but the wrong kind. Latching onto weakly supported Harvard School structuralist assumptions, the Court created an unduly interventionist antitrust policy that thwarted efficient business practices. In the sixties and seventies the Chicago School rode to the rescue with a stronger economic theory that debunked most of the shallow preexisting thinking but pushed antitrust to the verge of extinction. Only in recent years has a post-Chicago School—the third wave of intellectual-economic thinking on competition policy—emerged to identify excesses of Chicago School theory and breathe new life into the antitrust enterprise.

This received narrative is myopic and incomplete. The Sherman Act was far from a radical or unprecedented statute, and Harvard School structuralism was far from the first economic theory of competition policy. Although 1890 serves as a useful demarcation of the beginnings of federal antitrust law, the political and intellectual issues raised by the statutes are far older than even the beginnings of the American republic. Competition policy has long been an economic issue, and it has long lent itself to economic theorizing. To reduce intellectual theories of competition policy to phenomena since World War II is to miss a deep and rich lineage of ideas.

The received narrative not only fails to understand the past but provides little help in predicting the future. Studied in historical perspective, competition policy appears less a linear progression, refinement, and cumulative development of ideas than a cyclical dialectic of attitudes, insights, and ideologies. Take, for example, the question of whether private actors or the state is more likely to contribute to entry barriers and other dislocations of competition. Or whether scale economies tend to perpetuate or diminish market competitiveness. One can find clashes on these sorts of questions not just between the Chicago and Harvard Schools but between, say, John Stuart Mill and David Ricardo, English political economists writing in the early and middle nineteenth centuries. Intellectual theories about competition policy did not originate in the twentieth century, and much of the older learning is relevant to predicting the cycling of perspectives in the future.

This book is designed to introduce the student of modern competition policy to intellectual debates that have taken place in the past and remain relevant to the present. Unlike standard law school case books that trace the development of statutes and case law, our focus here is not on legal history but on the development and clash of intellectual ideas. To that end, we have selected original intellectual contributions that introduce the contemporary reader to the arc of intellectual discourse.

Where to begin and what to include is an issue with any work of this kind. We have chosen to begin with Adam Smith. Just as easily, we might have begun with the mercantilist school against which Smith wrote and whose views have some resonance today, particularly on matters of trade policy. But lines must be drawn, and *The Wealth of Nations*' iconic status as an originator of free market ideology and its influence on the development of American political and economic ideas make it a serviceable starting place.

From Smith and his English followers, David Ricardo and John Stuart Mill, we move to the American founding and sample the clash between Federalist and Anti-Federalist ideology on federal power over monopoly and competition. Our second chapter also samples midnineteenth-century Jacksonian themes by dipping into the formidable Thomas Cooley's essay on limits to state control of private business.

Chapter Three surveys neoclassical economic thinking on competition and the monopoly problem at the time of passage of the Sherman Act. A selection from Alfred Marshall's *Principles of Economics* and Arthur Hadley's American adaptation of Marshall's ideas introduce the leading themes. We also offer Henry Hatfield's entertaining account of the 1899 Chicago Trusts Conference, which brought out the strangest assortment of intellectual, business, and political figures ever to convene at an antitrust conference.

The presidential election of 1912, which laid the political foundations for the passage of the Clayton and Federal Trade Commission Acts in 1914, provides the frame for Chapter Four. We are privileged to find speeches or essays on antitrust policy by the three major presidential candidates—William Howard Taft, Theodore Roosevelt, and Woodrow Wilson—each of whom qualified, uncharacteristically for White House seekers, as a public intellectual. Cumulatively, the candidates articulated the set of policy choices, on matters such as competition versus regulation and bureaucratic administration versus judicial governance, that would dominate competition policy for the following century.

In Chapter Five we move from the hurly-burly of electoral politics to the rarefied halls of academe with selections from the most important early-twentieth-century responses to classicism's assumption that markets are characterized by perfect competition. Joan Robinson, Edward Chamberlin, and John Maurice Clark each offered an account of market competition as far less than perfect, although their respective accounts of the mechanisms and characteristics of imperfect competition implied significantly different policy responses.

The New Deal, the subject of Chapter Six, is the moment at which the greatest dispersion of intellectual views on competition policy appears within a single political coalition. We present selections from Louis Brandeis, Adolf Berle and Gardiner Means, Rex Tugwell, and Thurman Arnold. All were prominent in the New Deal coalition, and yet their views reflect a range of preferences from atomistic competition to the displacement of competition by governmentally mediated cartelization and control. Importantly, each of the competing intellectual schools not only received a hearing in the New Deal's corridors of power but dominated policy during some period during the New Deal.

Chapter Seven contains a single selection: Richard Hofstadter's magisterial essay on the seeming disappearance of the antitrust movement. Hofstadter's essay differs from other selections in this book insofar as it engages in intellectual history directly as opposed to presenting theoretical arguments about competition that subsequently become important to the intellectual history of the field. Standing at roughly the midpoint of this book, Hofstadter's essay provides a useful moment to consolidate the reader's understanding of the intellectual currents that preceded Hofstadter and to frame the intellectual debates that follow.

Although the primary focus of this work is on Anglo-American influences on U.S. competition policy, we have not neglected the dominant postwar continental influence, German ordoliberalism. In Chapter Eight, we take an excursion across the Atlantic to consider the influence of Franz Böhm, Walter Eucken, Hans Grossmann-Doerth, and other ordoliberals on the development of German and European competition law. Ordoliberalism serves as a useful contrast and comparison to the development of English and American ideas and helps the non-continental observer understand some of the past and present ideological differences between antitrust law in Brussels and Washington.

In Chapter Nine, we introduce a pairing of selections that have become synecdoches for two ostensibly conflicting views of the relationship between competition and innovation. Drop the names Schumpeter and Arrow in any antitrust gathering, and a complex of dueling empirical and theoretical claims and policy trade-offs instantly come to mind. It does not matter that Joseph Schumpeter wrote *Capitalism, Socialism, and Democracy* more than twenty years before Ken Arrow wrote his essay on *Economic Welfare and the Allocation of Resources for Invention*, that Arrow was not directly responding to Schumpeter, or that the two works' styles are completely different—one florid and metaphysical, the other technical and mathematical. What's important is that the "Schumpeter vs. Arrow" debate has become a stylized blueprint for antitrust discourse and, alas, that many of those who engage in this discourse may never have read either Schumpeter or Arrow.

Chapter Ten picks up where most modern students of antitrust policy begin, with the Harvard School structuralism of Joe Bain, Carl Kaysen, Don Turner, and Phil Areeda. The Structure-Conduct-Performance paradigm was simple and eloquent and dominated antitrust policy the early decades of the postwar era. The paradigm ultimately collapsed under the weight of the ascendant Chicago School, with Turner even undergoing a self-described conversion experience toward a less interventionist perspective. Still, Harvard School thinking continues to exert influences, with weak structural presumptions continuing to play a role in merger analysis and a new Harvard School questioning the capacities of generalist judges and juries to decide complex antitrust matters.

In Chapter Eleven, we turn to Hyde Park and the Chicago School of antitrust analysis. Choosing the relevant selections was difficult, given the wide variety of perspectives under the Chicago School umbrella. We settled on passages from Levi and Director, Stigler, Bork, and Posner as representative of the progression and divergence of ideas within the Chicago School. Space and presentation constraints required omission of other important Chicago School pieces, such as Frank Easterbrook's *The Limits of Antitrust,* John McGee's influential article on predatory pricing, and Ward Bowman's work on intellectual property and antitrust policy. With the Chicago School, we see not only a broad theoretical attack on interventionist antitrust thinking but an effort to "get into the weeds" of antitrust law, discussing the economic assumptions underlying antitrust treatment of specific competitive practices such as tying, vertical integration, and predatory pricing. This increasingly technical shift in the intellectual literature means that it is harder to capture the thrust of the school in a few general and accessible essays. As Hofstadter both reflected and anticipated in 1964, antitrust policy is increasingly the province of specialized bureaucrats, lawyers, and economists working on discrete and technical economic and policy problems.

And that makes our job in Chapter Twelve—on transaction cost economics and the post-Chicago School—even more difficult. Unlike the simple elegance of the Harvard School, there is no comprehensive, unifying theory of post-Chicago antitrust. Post-Chicago is largely a collection of those dissatisfied with Chicago School orthodoxy and steeped in alternative frameworks (such as game theory and behavioralism) to the rational, profit-maximizing *Homo economicus*. Whether post-Chicago is yet a coherent school of thought is subject to debate. Still, the Chicago School is certainly not the end of antitrust history, and so we conclude this book in the middle of an ongoing conversation.

In order to provide context for, and continuity between, the chapters, we introduce each with a short essay. We hope that our essays do not steal the thunder of the selections that follow. Our goal is for students of antitrust to encounter original voices in the intellectual history of competition policy—and to hear in all of them themes that continue to reverberate today.

Daniel A. Crane
Herbert Hovenkamp

# 1

# Classical Theories

## Introduction

### BY HERBERT HOVENKAMP

Modern economics in the United States and much of western Europe developed through two broad and loosely defined movements. First was "classical political economy," associated most strongly with Adam Smith, whose *The Wealth of Nations* was published in 1776, and carried forward by Thomas Malthus, David Ricardo, James Mill and his son John Stuart Mill, Jean Baptiste Say, and others. The second movement, of which more later, was neoclassicism, or neoclassical "economics." Most of the classical text authors in Great Britain and the United States called their discipline "political economy," emphasizing that their thinking was mainly about policy. For Adam Smith and most of his followers, political economy was a "positive" study of actual government economic policy and "normative" recommendations about policy. In the second half of the nineteenth century economics began to become more technical and far more mathematical.[1] The incorporation of marginal utility theory into economics led to what we today call the *neo*classical revolution. This shift toward mathematical technique also led the early neoclassicists, particularly Alfred Marshall, to call their discipline "economics" in order to emphasize its scientific status and set it apart from the moral philosophy and historicism that characterized classical writing.

Classical political economy articulated the ideology of market-based capitalism and its displacement of feudalism, mercantilism, and the hierarchical economic structures that had characterized the Middle Ages. The classical political economists did not invent capitalism, however. The rise of the merchant-and-manufacturer-dominated middle class was well under way by Smith's time, transferring the economic center away from agriculture and toward industrial production and trade, and also transferring wealth away from large land owners and toward factory owners and traders. Much of what Adam Smith wrote about in *The Wealth of Nations* reflected rather than caused this fundamental change. For example, the

1. One very important early exception was Antoine August Cournot, whose highly mathematical *Researches on the Mathematical Principles of the Theory of Wealth* was published in French in 1838.

Statute of Monopolies, which severely limited the Crown's power to grant exclusive rights and has been described as one of the most important milestones in the transformation from a feudal to a capitalistic economy, was passed in 1624, a full century and a half before *The Wealth of Nations* was published.[2]

This new thinking loosened up the stranglehold that the landed classes had on the economy by emphasizing the value of production and markets and the evils of state favoritism. Thus *The Wealth of Nations* is best read as a defense of emergent but not-well-articulated doctrines of (1) free exchange and, correspondingly, hostility toward restraints on alienation or trade; (2) extreme hostility toward state created exclusive rights; and (3) the view that wealth lies in productive power and its effective use rather than ownership of a great deal of static wealth in land. Most important of all, the proposition that *The Wealth of Nations* defended so skillfully was a trust that unrestrained and largely unorganized market trading would achieve these values much more than the command and control of any king or other government leader, no matter how well intended.

The work of classical political economists in the United States was heavily, although not exclusively derivative of, the great British thinkers. None of the Americans achieved the recognition that has been given to Smith, Malthus, or Mill. Ironically, however, classical political economy influenced economic *policy* in the United States much more than England or Europe. Through most of the nineteenth century England had a large and impoverished working class that was well represented in the House of Commons, leading to many flirtations with socialism. In sharp contrast, labor was scarce in nineteenth-century America, and the allure of the West, accompanied by easy migration and at least the hope of upward mobility, provided a fertile political ground for classicism's espousal of free markets and hostility toward monopoly. Only in the very late nineteenth century did this view begin to change, driven environmentally by the rise of the large business firm and the emergence of a substantial working class, and intellectually by the gradual displacement of classicism with marginalism. By 1890, when the Sherman Act was passed, British classicism had largely been supplanted by neoclassicism. Cambridge University Alfred Marshall's great, consensus-forming *Principles of Economics* was published that same year. For economists in the United States the neoclassical revolution came later, took longer, and was attended by much more controversy. For example, the American Economic Association was formed in 1885 and immediately became a battleground of classical and neoclassical ideas.

The Sherman Act was thus passed during a time of great controversy in economic theory. The statute was controversial among economists, with more opposing it than favoring it. But that observation hardly tells the whole story. Many of the opponents were classicists, whose ideas were on the way to obsolescence. Among the rising marginalists the story was more complicated. They split into conservative and Progressive factions with strongly differing views about antitrust policy.

Had the statute been nothing more than a prohibition on cartels it would certainly have been less controversial, but both the language and the legislative history of the Sherman

2. 21 Jac. [James] I, c, 3, § 6. See Adam Mossoff, "Rethinking the Development of Patents: an Intellectual History, 1550–1800," 52 *Hastings L.J.* 1255 (2001).

Act indicated that it was intended to go much further. The language in §1 prohibiting "combinations" in restraint of trade was intended to refer not just to collusion but also to the giant trusts, to business firm mergers, and joint production. The prohibitions on "monopolizing" conduct in §2 of the statute did not refer to the state-created monopolies that were so anathema to the classicists but rather to purely private aggregations of economic power. To a classicist these were readily seen as efforts not to protect the market but rather to interfere with its natural workings.

The three excerpts from Adam Smith, David Ricardo, and John Stuart Mill provide a good platform for understanding why the more traditional political economists in the United States were so ambivalent and even hostile toward the Sherman Act.

Adam Smith (1723–1790) was a Scottish moral philosopher and political economist who is generally regarded (with David Hume) as one of the most prominent members of the Scottish Enlightenment. He was educated at Glasgow and Oxford and lectured for a time at the University of Edinburgh, although he spent most of his career back at Glasgow. His most famous book has the full title *An Inquiry into the Nature and Causes of the Wealth of Nations*, although an earlier book, *The Theory of Moral Sentiments* (1759), is widely regarded as one of the classics of Scottish psychology and moral philosophy. The passage of *The Wealth of Nations* printed below is widely regarded as the classic defense of the free, unrestrained market and of classicism's objections to state authorized monopoly. In the process Smith explains some very fundamental ideas, such as the relationship between supply and demand, why prices rise under short supply even when markets are competitive, and why monopoly produces higher prices than competition.

Reading *The Wealth of Nations* is a little like viewing the Mirror of Erised in *Harry Potter*: the person viewing it sees that thing which he or she desires most. The final excerpt includes one of its most widely quoted passages, which is on the evils of price fixing: "People of the same trade seldom meet together, even for merriment and diversion, but the conversation ends in a conspiracy against the public, or in some contrivance to raise prices" (Book I, Ch. 10, §82). Today this passage is sometimes quoted in jury instructions in criminal price-fixing cases as suggesting that a meeting alone is circumstantial evidence of a price-fixing conspiracy.[3]

In another highly influential passage Smith also expressed strong distrust of the large business corporation because the combination of shareholders being absent and managers controlling "other people's money." Smith wrote of the large "joint stock company" of his day:

> The directors of such companies, however, being the managers rather of other people's money than of their own, it cannot well be expected that they should watch over it with the same anxious vigilance with which the partners in a private copartnery frequently watch over their own. Like the stewards of a rich man, they are apt to consider attention to small matters as not for their master's honour, and very easily give themselves a dispensation from having

3. See, e.g., *United States* v. *Taubman*, 297 F.3d 161 (2d Cir. 2002) (use of this quotation in prosecutor's summation to jury was harmless error). See also *Bell Atlantic Corp.* v. *Twombly*, 550 U.S. 544, 591 (2007) (Stevens, j., dissenting).

> it. Negligence and profusion, therefore, must always prevail, more or less, in the management of the affairs of such a company. It is upon this account that joint stock companies for foreign trade have seldom been able to maintain the competition against private adventurers. They have, accordingly, very seldom succeeded without an exclusive privilege, and frequently have not succeeded with one. (book V, ch. 1, §107)

This passage has been cited countless times by antitrust activists, as well as those seeking greater government control of business corporations. It became the title of a book by Justice Louis Brandeis[4] attacking the financial industry, and it was particularly influential during the New Deal for supporting the argument based on the "separation of ownership and control" supporting greater government regulation of corporate securities.[5]

David Ricardo (1772–1823), a British businessman, speculator, and member of Parliament late in his life, did not have a university position. He was inspired to political economy by reading Adam Smith, and as an avocation he devoted much of his life to developing economic doctrine more systematically than Smith had. His primary book, *Principles of Political Economy and Taxation*, was published in 1817.

Ricardo's doctrine of "rents," developed in the excerpted passage, indicates that marginalism appeared as an economic concept much earlier than the late nineteenth century, where it is usually identified with the writings of Jevons and Marshall in England and Menger and Walras on the Continent. The theory of rents is in fact a theory about marginal production—namely, that the most efficient land will be placed into production first, and then somewhat-less-efficient land, and so on until the very last piece of land placed into production ("at the margin") will earn just enough to provide a competitive rate of return. The doctrine was widely regarded as pessimistic because it served to explain why old and wealthy landowners could amass great wealth while having no incentive to increase productivity. For example, if production on the most favorable land costs $10 per unit while that on the marginal land costs $30, the market clears at a price of $30 and the owners of the most favorable land simply pocket the difference. Karl Marx himself relied on Ricardo's theory to justify appropriation and socialism.

Ricardo's doctrine of rents was much less popular among American classicists than among the British. For example, Henry Carey, whose *Principles of Political Economy* was published in 1837,[6] flatly rejected Ricardo's theory as having no application to the United States. Rather, he said, it tended to apply to heavily developed countries whose land had all been claimed, and where population increases had driven production to subsistence levels. In sharp contrast, vast areas of the United States remained an undeveloped wilderness.

4. Louis D. Brandeis, *Other People's Money and How the Bankers Use It* (1914).

5. E.g., Adolf A. Berle and Gardiner C. Means, *The Modern Corporation and Private Property* 346 (1933) (quoting this passage).

6. 3 Henry Carey, *Principles of Political Economy* 35–40 (1837). Brown University president and prominent political economist Francis Wayland developed a similar argument. Wayland, *The Elements of Political Economy* 390 (1835). See Herbert Hovenkamp, "The Political Economy of Substantive Due Process," 40 *Stan. L. Rev.* 379, 427–428 (1988).

Other elements of Ricardo's theory remain essential to antitrust to this very day. For example, firms have differing costs, and in a competitive market the price is determined by the average costs of the "marginal" firm. Firms that have access to lower cost inputs may earn higher profits.[7] But these "rents" must be distinguished from monopoly because a firm enjoying rents has no power to raise the market price by producing less.

John Stuart Mill (1806–1873) was the son of James Mill, another political economist. His fame rivals that of Adam Smith, but mainly because of his writings on utilitarianism and political philosophy. His *Principles of Political Economy* (1848) represented the high point of classical political economy, but he also became a lightning rod that inspired the first generation of marginalists. Most importantly, his writings on philosophy, like those of Jeremy Bentham, strongly advocated a "utility" theory of value, which was a defining characteristic of marginalism. But Mill never succeeded in fusing utilitarianism with his economic theory. Rather, his *Principles* jumps ambiguously between a backward-looking theory of value based predominantly on land and previously invested labor, and the more forward-looking marginal utility theory that became neoclassical economics.

The excerpt given from Mill's *Principles* is one of the great early texts of industrial organization theory, explaining the value of organization as a business firm, the relationship between firm size and market size, economies of scale, natural monopoly, the value of a higher ratio of capital to labor, and other determinants of industry structure.

## Adam Smith

## *The Wealth of Nations*

# Of the Natural and Market Price of Commodities

There is in every society or neighbourhood an ordinary or average rate both of wages and profit in every different employment of labour and stock. This rate is naturally regulated, as I shall show hereafter, partly by the general circumstances of the society, their riches or poverty, their advancing, stationary, or declining condition; and partly by the particular nature of each employment.

There is likewise in every society or neighbourhood an ordinary or average rate of rent, which is regulated too, as I shall show hereafter, partly by the general circumstances of the society or neighbourhood in which the land is situated, and partly by the natural or improved fertility of the land.

These ordinary or average rates may be called the natural rates of wages, profit, and rent, at the time and place in which they commonly prevail.

7. All firms in a competitive market will increase output to the point that their marginal cost equals the market price, but they will earn a higher return on the fixed-cost component because they are paying less for it. For example, consistent with Ricardo's observations, if the superior land were rented, the tenant would pay a price for it such that it earned only the competitive return, and the landlord would pocket the surplus.

When the price of any commodity is neither more nor less than what is sufficient to pay the rent of the land, the wages of the labour, and the profits of the stock employed in raising, preparing, and bringing it to market, according to their natural rates, the commodity is then sold for what may be called its natural price.

The commodity is then sold precisely for what it is worth, or for what it really costs the person who brings it to market; for though in common language what is called the prime cost of any commodity does not comprehend the profit of the person who is to sell it again, yet if he sells it at a price which does not allow him the ordinary rate of profit in his neighbourhood, he is evidently a loser by the trade; since by employing his stock in some other way he might have made that profit. His profit, besides, is his revenue, the proper fund of his subsistence. As, while he is preparing and bringing the goods to market, he advances to his workmen their wages, or their subsistence; so he advances to himself, in the same manner, his own subsistence, which is generally suitable to the profit which he may reasonably expect from the sale of his goods. Unless they yield him this profit, therefore, they do not repay him what they may very properly be said to have really cost him.

Though the price, therefore, which leaves him this profit, is not always the lowest at which a dealer may sometimes sell his goods, it is the lowest at which he is likely to sell them for any considerable time; at least where there is perfect liberty, or where he may change his trade as often as he pleases.

The actual price at which any commodity is commonly sold is called its market price. It may either be above, or below, or exactly the same with its natural price.

The market price of every particular commodity is regulated by the proportion between the quantity which is actually brought to market, and the demand of those who are willing to pay the natural price of the commodity, or the whole value of the rent, labour, and profit, which must be paid in order to bring it thither. Such people may be called the effectual demanders, and their demand the effectual demand; since it may be sufficient to effectuate the bringing of the commodity to market. It is different from the absolute demand. A very poor man may be said in some sense to have a demand for a coach and six; he might like to have it; but his demand is not an effectual demand, as the commodity can never be brought to market in order to satisfy it.

When the quantity of any commodity which is brought to market falls short of the effectual demand, all those who are willing to pay the whole value of the rent, wages, and profit, which must be paid in order to bring it thither, cannot be supplied with the quantity which they want. Rather than want it altogether, some of them will be willing to give more. A competition will immediately begin among them, and the market price will rise more or less above the natural price, according as either the greatness of the deficiency, or the wealth and wanton luxury of the competitors, happen to animate more or less the eagerness of the competition. Among competitors of equal wealth and luxury the same deficiency will generally occasion a more or less eager competition, according as the acquisition of the commodity happens to be of more or less importance to them. Hence the exorbitant price of the necessaries of life during the blockade of a town or in a famine.

When the quantity brought to market exceeds the effectual demand, it cannot be all sold to those who are willing to pay the whole value of the rent, wages and profit, which must be paid in order to bring it thither. Some part must be sold to those who are willing to pay less, and the low price which they give for it must reduce the price of the whole. The market price will sink more or less below the natural price, according as the greatness of the excess increases more or less the competition of the sellers, or according as it happens to be more or less important to them to get immediately rid of the commodity. The same excess in the importation of perishable commodities, will occasion a much greater competition than in that of durable commodities; in the importation of oranges, for example, than in that of old iron.

When the quantity brought to market is just sufficient to supply the effectual demand and no more, the market price naturally comes to be either exactly, or as nearly as can be judged of, the same with the natural price. The whole quantity upon hand can be disposed of for this price, and cannot be disposed of for more. The competition of the different dealers obliges them all to accept of this price, but does not oblige them to accept of less.

The quantity of every commodity brought to market naturally suits itself to the effectual demand. It is the interest of all those who employ their land, labour, or stock, in bringing any commodity to market, that the quantity never should exceed the effectual demand; and it is the interest of all other people that it never should fall short of that demand.

If at any time it exceeds the effectual demand, some of the component parts of its price must be paid below their natural rate. If it is rent, the interest of the landlords will immediately prompt them to withdraw a part of their land; and if it is wages or profit, the interest of the labourers in the one case, and of their employers in the other, will prompt them to withdraw a part of their labour or stock from this employment. The quantity brought to market will soon be no more than sufficient to supply the effectual demand. All the different parts of its price will rise to their natural rate, and the whole price to its natural price.

If, on the contrary, the quantity brought to market should at any time fall short of the effectual demand, some of the component parts of its price must rise above their natural rate. If it is rent, the interest of all other landlords will naturally prompt them to prepare more land for the raising of this commodity; if it is wages or profit, the interest of all other labourers and dealers will soon prompt them to employ more labour and stock in preparing and bringing it to market. The quantity brought thither will soon be sufficient to supply the effectual demand. All the different parts of its price will soon sink to their natural rate, and the whole price to its natural price.

The natural price, therefore, is, as it were, the central price, to which the prices of all commodities are continually gravitating. Different accidents may sometimes keep them suspended a good deal above it, and sometimes force them down even somewhat below it. But whatever may be the obstacles which hinder them from settling in this center of repose and continuance, they are constantly tending towards it.

The whole quantity of industry annually employed in order to bring any commodity to market, naturally suits itself in this manner to the effectual demand. It naturally aims at bringing always that precise quantity thither which may be sufficient to supply, and no more than supply, that demand.

But in some employments the same quantity of industry will in different years produce very different quantities of commodities; while in others it will produce always the same, or very nearly the same. The same number of labourers in husbandry will, in different years, produce very different quantities of corn, wine, oil, hops, &c. But the same number of spinners and weavers will every year produce the same or very nearly the same quantity of linen and woollen cloth. It is only the average produce of the one species of industry which can be suited in any respect to the effectual demand; and as its actual produce is frequently much greater and frequently much less than its average produce, the quantity of the commodities brought to market will sometimes exceed a good deal, and sometimes fall short a good deal of the effectual demand. Even though that demand therefore should continue always the same, their market price will be liable to great fluctuations, will sometimes fall a good deal below, and sometimes rise a good deal above, their natural price. In the other species of industry, the produce of equal quantities of labour being always the same, or very nearly the same, it can be more exactly suited to the effectual demand. While that demand continues the same, therefore, the market price of the commodities is likely to do so too, and to be either altogether, or as nearly as can be judged of, the same with the natural price. That the price of linen and woollen cloth is liable neither to such frequent nor to such great variations as the price of corn, every man's experience will inform him. The price of the one species of commodities varies only with the variations in the demand: That of the other varies not only with the variations in the demand, but with the much greater and more frequent variations in the quantity of what is brought to market in order to supply that demand.

The occasional and temporary fluctuations in the market price of any commodity fall chiefly upon those parts of its price which resolve themselves into wages and profit. That part which resolves itself into rent is less affected by them. A rent certain in money is not in the least affected by them either in its rate or in its value. A rent which consists either in a certain proportion or in a certain quantity of the rude produce, is no doubt affected in its yearly value by all the occasional and temporary fluctuations in the market price of that rude produce; but it is seldom affected by them in its yearly rate. In settling the terms of the lease, the landlord and farmer endeavour, according to their best judgment, to adjust that rate, not to the temporary and occasional, but to the average and ordinary price of the produce.

Such fluctuations affect both the value and the rate either of wages or of profit, according as the market happens to be either over-stocked or under-stocked with commodities or with labour; with work done, or with work to be done. A public mourning raises the price of black cloth (with which the market is almost always under-stocked upon such occasions) and augments the profits of the merchants who possess any considerable quantity of it. It has no effect upon the wages of the weavers. The market is under-stocked with commodities, not with labour; with work done, not with work to be done. It raises the wages of journeymen taylors. The market is here under-stocked with labour. There is an effectual demand for more labour, for more work to be done than can be had. It sinks the price of coloured silks and cloths, and thereby reduces the profits of the merchants who have any considerable quantity of them upon hand. It sinks too the wages of the workmen employed in preparing such commodities, for which all demand is stopped for six months, perhaps for a twelvemonth. The market is here over-stocked with commodities and with labour.

But though the market price of every particular commodity is in this manner continually gravitating, if one may say so, towards the natural price, yet sometimes particular accidents, sometimes natural causes, and sometimes particular regulations of police, may, in many commodities, keep up the market price, for a long time together, a good deal above the natural price.

When by an increase in the effectual demand, the market price of some particular commodity happens to rise a good deal above the natural price, those who employ their stocks in supplying that market are generally careful to conceal this change. If it was commonly known, their great profit would tempt so many new rivals to employ their stocks in the same way, that, the effectual demand being fully supplied, the market price would soon be reduced to the natural price, and perhaps for some time even below it. If the market is at a great distance from the residence of those who supply it, they may sometimes be able to keep the secret for several years together, and may so long enjoy their extraordinary profits without any new rivals. Secrets of this kind, however, it must be acknowledged, can seldom be long kept; and the extraordinary profit can last very little longer than they are kept.

Secrets in manufactures are capable of being longer kept than secrets in trade. A dyer who has found the means of producing a particular colour with materials which cost only half the price of those commonly made use of, may, with good management, enjoy the advantage of his discovery as long as he lives, and even leave it as a legacy to his posterity. His extraordinary gains arise from the high price which is paid for his private labour. They properly consist in the high wages of that labour. But as they are repeated upon every part of his stock, and as their whole amount bears, upon that account, a regular proportion to it, they are commonly considered as extraordinary profits of stock.

Such enhancements of the market price are evidently the effects of particular accidents, of which, however, the operation may sometimes last for many years together.

Some natural productions require such a singularity of soil and situation, that all the land in a great country, which is fit for producing them, may not be sufficient to supply the effectual demand. The whole quantity brought to market, therefore, may be disposed of to those who are willing to give more than what is sufficient to pay the rent of the land which produced them, together with the wages of the labour, and the profits of the stock which were employed in preparing and bringing them to market, according to their natural rates. Such commodities may continue for whole centuries together to be sold at this high price; and that part of it which resolves itself into the rent of land is in this case the part which is generally paid above its natural rate. The rent of the land which affords such singular and esteemed productions, like the rent of some vineyards in France of a peculiarly happy soil and situation, bears no regular proportion to the rent of other equally fertile and equally well-cultivated land in its neighbourhood. The wages of the labour and the profits of the stock employed in bringing such commodities to market, on the contrary, are seldom out of their natural proportion to those of the other employments of labour and stock in their neighbourhood.

Such enhancements of the market price are evidently the effect of natural causes which may hinder the effectual demand from ever being fully supplied, and which may continue, therefore, to operate for-ever.

A monopoly granted either to an individual or to a trading company has the same effect as a secret in trade or manufactures. The monopolists, by keeping the market constantly under-stocked, by never fully supplying the effectual demand, sell their commodities much above the natural price, and raise their emoluments, whether they consist in wages or profit, greatly above their natural rate.

The price of monopoly is upon every occasion the highest which can be got. The natural price, or the price of free competition, on the contrary, is the lowest which can be taken, not upon every occasion indeed, but for any considerable time altogether. The one is upon every occasion the highest which can be squeezed out of the buyers, or which, it is supposed, they will consent to give: The other is the lowest which the sellers can commonly afford to take, and at the same time continue their business.

The exclusive privileges of corporations, statutes of apprenticeship, and all those laws which restrain, in particular employments, the competition to a smaller number than might otherwise go into them, have the same tendency, though in a less degree. They are a sort of enlarged monopolies, and may frequently, for ages together, and in whole classes of employments, keep up the market price of particular commodities above the natural price, and maintain both the wages of the labour and the profits of the stock employed about them somewhat above their natural rate.

Such enhancements of the market price may last as long as the regulations of police which give occasion to them.

The market price of any particular commodity, though it may continue long above, can seldom continue long below, its natural price. Whatever part of it was paid below the natural rate, the persons whose interest it affected would immediately feel the loss, and would immediately withdraw either so much land, or so much labour, or so much stock, from being employed about it, that the quantity brought to market would soon be no more than sufficient to supply the effectual demand. Its market price, therefore, would soon rise to the natural price. This at least would be the case where there was perfect liberty.

The same statutes of apprenticeship and other corporation laws indeed, which, when a manufacture is in prosperity, enable the workman to raise his wages a good deal above their natural rate, sometimes oblige him, when it decays, to let them down a good deal below it. As in the one case they exclude many people from his employment, so in the other they exclude him from many employments. The effect of such regulations, however, is not near so durable in sinking the workman's wages below, as in raising them above their natural rate. Their operation in the one way may endure for many centuries, but in the other it can last no longer than the lives of some of the workmen who were bred to the business in the time of its prosperity. When they are gone, the number of those who are afterwards educated to the trade will naturally suit itself to the effectual demand. The police must be as violent as that of Indostan or antient Egypt (where every man was bound by a principle of religion to follow the occupation of his father, and was supposed to commit the most horrid sacrilege if he changed it for another), which can in any particular employment, and for several generations together, sink either the wages of labour or the profits of stock below their natural rate.

This is all that I think necessary to be observed at present concerning the deviations, whether occasional or permanent, of the market price of commodities from the natural price.

## Of Wages and Profit in the Different Employments of Labour and Stock

People of the same trade seldom meet together, even for merriment and diversion, but the conversation ends in a conspiracy against the public, or in some contrivance to raise prices. It is impossible indeed to prevent such meetings, by any law which either could be executed, or would be consistent with liberty and justice. But though the law cannot hinder people of the same trade from sometimes assembling together, it ought to do nothing to facilitate such assemblies; much less to render them necessary.

A regulation which obliges all those of the same trade in a particular town to enter their names and places of abode in a public register, facilitates such assemblies. It connects individuals who might never otherwise be known to one another, and gives every man of the trade a direction where to find every other man of it.

A regulation which enables those of the same trade to tax themselves in order to provide for their poor, their sick, their widows and orphans, by giving them a common interest to manage, renders such assemblies necessary.

An incorporation not only renders them necessary, but makes the act of the majority binding upon the whole. In a free trade an effectual combination cannot be established but by the unanimous consent of every single trader, and it cannot last longer than every single trader continues of the same mind. The majority of a corporation can enact a bye-law with proper penalties, which will limit the competition more effectually and more durably than any voluntary combination whatever.

The pretence that corporations are necessary for the better government of the trade, is without any foundation. The real and effectual discipline which is exercised over a workman, is not that of his corporation, but that of his customers. It is the fear of losing their employment which restrains his frauds and corrects his negligence. An exclusive corporation necessarily weakens the force of this discipline. A particular set of workmen must then be employed, let them behave well or ill. It is upon this account, that in many large incorporated towns no tolerable workmen are to be found, even in some of the most necessary trades. If you would have your work tolerably executed, it must be done in the suburbs, where the workmen having no exclusive privilege, have nothing but their character to depend upon, and you must then smuggle it into the town as well as you can.

It is in this manner that the policy of Europe, by restraining the competition in some employments to a smaller number than would otherwise be disposed to enter into them, occasions a very important inequality in the whole of the advantages and disadvantages of the different employments of labour and stock.

## David Ricardo

## *Principles of Political Economy and Taxation*

## On Rent

It remains however to be considered, whether the appropriation of land, and the consequent creation of rent, will occasion any variation in the relative value of commodities, independently of the quantity of labour necessary to production. In order to understand this part of the subject, we must enquire into the nature of rent, and the laws by which its rise or fall is regulated.

Rent is that portion of the produce of the earth, which is paid to the landlord for the use of the original and indestructible powers of the soil. It is often, however, confounded with the interest and profit of capital, and, in popular language, the term is applied to whatever is annually paid by a farmer to his landlord. If, of two adjoining farms of the same extent, and of the same natural fertility, one had all the conveniences of farming buildings, and, besides, were properly drained and manured, and advantageously divided by hedges, fences and walls, while the other had none of these advantages, more remuneration would naturally be paid for the use of one, than for the use of the other; yet in both cases this remuneration would be called rent. But it is evident, that a portion only of the money annually to be paid for the improved farm, would be given for the original and indestructible powers of the soil; the other portion would be paid for the use of the capital which had been employed in ameliorating the quality of the land, and in erecting such buildings as were necessary to secure and preserve the produce. Adam Smith sometimes speaks of rent, in the strict sense to which I am desirous of confining it, but more often in the popular sense, in which the term is usually employed. He tells us, that the demand for timber, and its consequent high price, in the more southern countries of Europe, caused a rent to be paid for forests in Norway, which could before afford no rent. Is it not, however, evident, that the person who paid what he thus calls rent, paid it in consideration of the valuable commodity which was then standing on the land, and that he actually repaid himself with a profit, by the sale of the timber? If, indeed, after the timber was removed, any compensation were paid to the landlord for the use of the land, for the purpose of growing timber or any other produce, with a view to future demand, such compensation might justly be called rent, because it would be paid for the productive powers of the land; but in the case stated by Adam Smith, the compensation was paid for the liberty of removing and selling the timber, and not for the liberty of growing it. He speaks also of the rent of coal mines, and of stone quarries, to which the same observation applies—that the compensation given for the mine or quarry, is paid for the value of the coal or stone which can be removed from them, and has no connection with the original and indestructible powers of the land. This is a distinction of great importance, in an enquiry concerning rent and profits; for it is found, that the laws which regulate the progress of rent, are widely different from those which regulate the progress of profits, and seldom operate in the same direction. In all improved countries, that which is annually paid to the landlord, partaking of both characters, rent and profit, is sometimes kept stationary by the effects of opposing causes; at other times advances or recedes, as one or the other of these causes preponderates. In the future pages of this work, then, whenever I speak of the rent of land, I wish to be understood as speaking of that compensation, which is paid to the owner of land for the use of its original and indestructible powers.

On the first settling of a country, in which there is an abundance of rich and fertile land, a very small proportion of which is required to be cultivated for the support of the actual population, or indeed can be cultivated with the capital which the population can command, there will be no rent; for no one would pay for the use of land, when there was an abundant quantity not yet appropriated, and, therefore, at the disposal of whosoever might choose to cultivate it.

On the common principles of supply and demand, no rent could be paid for such land, for the reason stated why nothing is given for the use of air and water, or for any other of the gifts of nature which exist in boundless quantity. With a given quantity of materials, and with the assistance of the pressure of the atmosphere, and the elasticity of steam, engines may perform work, and abridge human labour to a very great extent; but no charge is made for the use of these natural aids, because they are inexhaustible, and at every man's disposal. In the same manner the brewer, the distiller, the dyer, make incessant use of the air and water for the production of their commodities; but as the supply is boundless, they bear no price. If all land had the same properties, if it were unlimited in quantity, and uniform in quality, no charge could be made for its use, unless where it possessed peculiar advantages of situation. It is only, then, because land is not unlimited in quantity and uniform in quality, and because in the progress of population, land of an inferior quality, or less advantageously situated, is called into cultivation, that rent is ever paid for the use of it. When in the progress of society, land of the second degree of fertility is taken into cultivation, rent immediately commences on that of the first quality, and the amount of that rent will depend on the difference in the quality of these two portions of land.

When land of the third quality is taken into cultivation, rent immediately commences on the second, and it is regulated as before, by the difference in their productive powers. At the same time, the rent of the first quality will rise, for that must always be above the rent of the second, by the difference between the produce which they yield with a given quantity of capital and labour. With every step in the progress of population, which shall oblige a country to have recourse to land of a worse quality, to enable it to raise its supply of food, rent, on all the more fertile land, will rise.

Thus suppose land—No. 1, 2, 3,—to yield, with an equal employment of capital and labour, a net produce of 100, 90, and 80 quarters of corn. In a new country, where there is an abundance of fertile land compared with the population, and where therefore it is only necessary to cultivate No. 1, the whole net produce will belong to the cultivator, and will be the profits of the stock which he advances. As soon as population had so far increased as to make it necessary to cultivate No. 2, from which ninety quarters only can be obtained after supporting the labourers, rent would commence on No. 1; for either there must be two rates of profit on agricultural capital, or ten quarters, or the value of ten quarters must be withdrawn from the produce of No. 1, for some other purpose. Whether the proprietor of the land, or any other person, cultivated No. 1, these ten quarters would equally constitute rent; for the cultivator of No. 2 would get the same result with his capital, whether he cultivated No. 1, paying ten quarters for rent, or continued to cultivate No. 2, paying no rent. In the same manner it might be shown that when No. 3 is brought into cultivation, the rent of No. 2 must be ten quarters, or the value of ten quarters, whilst the rent of No. 1 would rise to twenty quarters; for the cultivator of No. 3 would have the same profits whether he paid twenty quarters for the rent of No. 1, ten quarters for the rent of No. 2, or cultivated No. 3 free of all rent.

It often, and, indeed, commonly happens, that before No. 2, 3, 4, or 5, or the inferior lands are cultivated, capital can be employed more productively on those lands which are already in cultivation. It may perhaps be found, that by doubling the original capital employed on No. 1, though the produce will not be doubled, will not be increased by one hundred quarters, it may be increased by eighty-five quarters, and that this quantity exceeds what could be obtained by employing the same capital, on land No. 3.

In such case, capital will be preferably employed on the old land, and will equally create a rent; for rent is always the difference between the produce obtained by the employment of two equal quantities of capital and labour. If, with a capital of £1,000, a tenant obtain one hundred quarters of wheat from his land, and by the employment of a second capital of £1000, he obtain a further return of eighty-five, his landlord would have the power at the expiration of his lease, of obliging him to pay fifteen quarters, or an equivalent value, for additional rent; for there cannot be two rates of profit. If he is satisfied with a diminution of fifteen quarters in the return for his second £1,000, it is because no employment more profitable can be found for it. The common rate of profit would be in that proportion, and if the original tenant refused, some other person would be found willing to give all which exceeded that rate of profit to the owner of the land from which he derived it.

In this case, as well as in the other, the capital last employed pays no rent. For the greater productive powers of the first £1,000, fifteen quarters is paid for rent, for the employment of the second £1,000 no rent whatever is paid. If a third £1,000 be employed on the same land, with a return of seventy-five quarters, rent will then be paid for the second £1,000, and will be equal to the difference between the produce of these two, or ten quarters; and at the same time the rent of the first £1,000 will rise from fifteen to twenty-five quarters; while the last £1,000 will pay no rent whatever.

If, then, good land existed in a quantity much more abundant than the production of food for an increasing population required, or if capital could be indefinitely employed without a diminished return on the old land, there could be no rise of rent; for rent invariably proceeds from the employment of an additional quantity of labour with a proportionally less return.

The most fertile, and most favorably situated, land will be first cultivated, and the exchangeable value of its produce will be adjusted in the same manner as the exchangeable value of all other commodities, by the total quantity of labour necessary in various forms, from first to last, to produce it, and bring it to market. When land of an inferior quality is taken into cultivation, the exchangeable value of raw produce will rise, because more labour is required to produce it.

The exchangeable value of all commodities, whether they be manufactured, or the produce of the mines, or the produce of land, is always regulated, not by the less quantity of labour that will suffice for their production under circumstances highly favorable, and exclusively enjoyed by those who have peculiar facilities of production; but by the greater quantity of labour necessarily bestowed on their production by those who have no such facilities; by those who continue to produce them under the most unfavorable circumstances; meaning—by the most unfavorable circumstances, the most unfavorable under which the quantity of produce required, renders it necessary to carry on the production.

Thus, in a charitable institution, where the poor are set to work with the funds of benefactors, the general prices of the commodities, which are the produce of such work, will not be governed by the peculiar facilities afforded to these workmen, but by the common, usual, and natural difficulties, which every other manufacturer will have to encounter. The manufacturer enjoying none of these facilities might indeed be driven altogether from the market, if the supply afforded by these favored workmen were equal to all the wants of the community; but if he continued the trade, it would be only on condition that he should derive from it the usual and general rate of profits on stock; and that could only happen when his commodity sold for a price proportioned to the quantity of labour bestowed on its production.

It is true, that on the best land, the same produce would still be obtained with the same labour as before, but its value would be enhanced in consequence of the diminished returns obtained by those who employed fresh labour and stock on the less fertile land. Notwithstanding, then, that the advantages of fertile over inferior lands are in no case lost, but only transferred from the cultivator, or consumer, to the landlord, yet, since more labour is required on the inferior lands, and since it is from such land only that we are enabled to furnish ourselves with the additional supply of raw produce, the comparative value of that produce will continue permanently above its former level, and make it exchange for more hats, cloth, shoes, &c. &c. in the production of which no such additional quantity of labour is required.

The reason then, why raw produce rises in comparative value, is because more labour is employed in the production of the last portion obtained, and not because a rent is paid to the landlord. The value of corn is regulated by the quantity of labour bestowed on its production on that quality of land, or with that portion of capital, which pays no rent. Corn is not high because a rent is paid, but a rent is paid because corn is high; and it has been justly observed, that no reduction would take place in the price of corn, although landlords should forego the whole of their rent. Such a measure would only enable some farmers to live like gentlemen, but would not diminish the quantity of labour necessary to raise raw produce on the least productive land in cultivation.

Nothing is more common than to hear of the advantages which the land possesses over every other source of useful produce, on account of the surplus which it yields in the form of rent. Yet when land is most abundant, when most productive, and most fertile, it yields no rent; and it is only when its powers decay, and less is yielded in return for labour, that a share of the original produce of the more fertile portions is set apart for rent. It is singular that this quality in the land, which should have been noticed as an imperfection, compared with the natural agents by which manufacturers are assisted, should have been pointed out as constituting its peculiar pre-eminence. If air, water, the elasticity of steam, and the pressure of the atmosphere, were of various qualities; if they could be appropriated, and each quality existed only in moderate abundance, they, as well as the land, would afford a rent, as the successive qualities were brought into use. With every worse quality employed, the value of the commodities in the manufacture of which they were used, would rise, because equal quantities of labour would be less productive. Man would do more by the sweat of his brow, and nature perform less; and the land would be no longer pre-eminent for its limited powers.

If the surplus produce which land affords in the form of rent be an advantage, it is desirable that, every year, the machinery newly constructed should be less efficient than the old, as that would undoubtedly give a greater exchangeable value to the goods manufactured, not only by that machinery but by all the other machinery in the kingdom; and a rent would be paid to all those who possessed the most productive machinery.[1]

1. "In agriculture too," says Adam Smith, "nature labours along with man; and though her labour costs no expense, its produce has its value, as well as that of the most expensive workman." The labour of nature is paid, not because she does much, but because she does little. In proportion as she becomes niggardly in her gifts, she exacts a greater price for her work. Where she is munificently beneficent, she always works gratis. "The labouring cattle employed in agriculture, not only occasion, like the workmen in manufactures, the reproduction of a value equal to their own consumption, or to the capital which employs them, together with its owner's profits, but of a much greater value. Over and above the capital of the farmer and all its profits, they regularly occasion the reproduction of the rent of the landlord. This rent may be considered as the produce of those powers of nature, the use of which the landlord lends to the farmer. It is greater or smaller according to the supposed extent of those powers, or in other words, according to the supposed natural or improved fertility of the land. It is the work of nature which remains, after deducting or compensating every thing which can be regarded as the work of man. It is seldom less than a fourth, and frequently more than a third of the whole produce. No equal quantity of productive labour employed in manufactures, can ever occasion so great a reproduction. In them nature does nothing, man does all; and the reproduction must always be in proportion to the strength of the agents that occasion it. The capital employed in agriculture, therefore, not only puts into motion a greater quantity of productive labour than any equal capital employed in manufactures, but in proportion too, to the quantity of the productive labour which it employs, it adds a much greater value to the annual produce of the land and labour of the country, to the real wealth and revenue of its inhabitants. Of all the ways in which a capital can be employed, it is by far the most advantageous

The rise of rent is always the effect of the increasing wealth of the country, and of the difficulty of providing food for its augmented population. It is a symptom, but it is never a cause of wealth; for wealth often increases most rapidly while rent is either stationary, or even falling. Rent increases most rapidly, as the disposable land decreases in its productive powers. Wealth increases most rapidly in those countries where the disposable land is most fertile, where importation is least restricted, and where through agricultural improvements, productions can be multiplied without any increase in the proportional quantity of labour, and where consequently the progress of rent is slow.

If the high price of corn were the effect, and not the cause of rent, price would be proportionally influenced as rents were high or low, and rent would be a component part of price. But that corn which is produced by the greatest quantity of labour is the regulator of the price of corn; and rent does not and cannot enter in the least degree as a component part of its price. Adam Smith, therefore, cannot be correct in supposing that the original rule which regulated the exchangeable value of commodities, namely, the comparative quantity of labour by which they were produced, can be at all altered by the appropriation of land and the payment of rent. Raw material enters into the composition of most commodities, but the value of that raw material, as well as corn, is regulated by the productiveness of the portion of capital last employed on the land, and paying no rent; and therefore rent is not a component part of the price of commodities.

We have been hitherto considering the effects of the natural progress of wealth and population on rent, in a country in which the land is of variously productive powers; and we have seen, that with every portion of additional capital which it becomes necessary to employ on the land with a less productive return, rent would rise. It follows from the same principles, that any circumstances in the society which should make it unnecessary to employ the same amount of capital on the land, and which should therefore make the portion last employed more productive, would lower rent. Any great reduction in the capital of a country, which should materially diminish the funds destined for the maintenance of labour, would naturally have this effect. Population regulates itself by the funds which are to employ it, and therefore always increases or diminishes with the increase or diminution of capital. Every reduction of capital is

to the society." Book II, Ch. v., p. 15. Does nature nothing for man in manufactures? Are the powers of wind and water, which move our machinery, and assist navigation, nothing? The pressure of the atmosphere and the elasticity of steam, which enable us to work the most stupendous engines—are they not the gifts of nature? to say nothing of the effects of the matter of heat in softening and melting metals, of the decomposition of the atmosphere in the process of dyeing and fermentation. There is not a manufacture which can be mentioned, in which nature does not give her assistance to man, and give it too, generously and gratuitously. In remarking on the passage which I have copied from Adam Smith, Mr. Buchanan observes, "I have endeavoured to show, in the observations on productive and unproductive labour, contained in the fourth volume, that agriculture adds no more to the national stock than any other sort of industry. In dwelling on the reproduction of rent as so great an advantage to society, Dr. Smith does not reflect that rent is the effect of high price, and that what the landlord gains in this way, he gains at the expense of the community at large. There is no absolute gain to the society by the reproduction of rent; it is only one class profiting at the expense of another class. The notion of agriculture yielding a produce, and a rent in consequence, because nature concurs with human industry in the process of cultivation, is a mere fancy. It is not from the produce, but from the price at which the produce is sold, that the rent is derived; and this price is got not because nature assists in the production, but because it is the price which suits the consumption to the supply."

therefore necessarily followed by a less effective demand for corn, by a fall of price, and by diminished cultivation. In the reverse order to that in which the accumulation of capital raises rent, will the diminution of it lower rent. Land of a less unproductive quality will be in succession relinquished, the exchangeable value of produce will fall, and land of a superior quality will be the land last cultivated, and that which will then pay no rent.

The same effects may however be produced, when the wealth and population of a country are increased, if that increase is accompanied by such marked improvements in agriculture, as shall have the same effect of diminishing the necessity of cultivating the poorer lands, or of expending the same amount of capital on the cultivation of the more fertile portions.

If a million of quarters of corn be necessary for the support of a given population, and it be raised on land of the qualities of No. 1, 2, 3; and if an improvement be afterwards discovered by which it can be raised on No. 1 and 2, without employing No. 3, it is evident that the immediate effect must be a fall of rent; for No. 2, instead of No. 3, will then be cultivated without paying any rent; and the rent of No. 1, instead of being the difference between the produce of No. 3 and No. 1, will be the difference only between No. 2 and 1. With the same population, and no more, there can be no demand for any additional quantity of corn; the capital and labour employed on No. 3 will be devoted to the production of other commodities desirable to the community, and can have no effect in raising rent, unless the raw material from which they are made cannot be obtained without employing capital less advantageously on the land, in which case No. 3 must again be cultivated.

It is undoubtedly true, that the fall in the relative price of raw produce, in consequence of the improvement in agriculture, or rather in consequence of less labour being bestowed on its production, would naturally lead to increased accumulation; for the profits of stock would be greatly augmented. This accumulation would lead to an increased demand for labour, to higher wages, to an increased population, to a further demand for raw produce, and to an increased cultivation. It is only, however, after the increase in the population, that rent would be as high as before; that is to say, after No. 3 was taken into cultivation. A considerable period would have elapsed, attended with a positive diminution of rent.

But improvements in agriculture are of two kinds: those which increase the productive powers of the land, and those which enable us, by improving our machinery, to obtain its produce with less labour. They both lead to a fall in the price of raw produce; they both affect rent, but they do not affect it equally. If they did not occasion a fall in the price of raw produce, they would not be improvements; for it is the essential quality of an improvement to diminish the quantity of labour before required to produce a commodity; and this diminution cannot take place without a fall of its price or relative value.

The improvements which increase the productive powers of the land, are such as the more skilful rotation of crops, or the better choice of manure. These improvements absolutely enable us to obtain the same produce from a smaller quantity of land. If, by the introduction of a course of turnips, I can feed my sheep besides raising my corn, the land on which the sheep were before fed becomes unnecessary, and the same quantity of raw produce is raised by the employment of a less quantity of land. If I discover a manure which will enable me to make a piece of land produce 20 percent more corn, I may withdraw at least a portion of my capital from the most unproductive part of my farm. But, as I before observed, it is not necessary that land should be thrown out of cultivation, in order to reduce rent: to produce this effect, it is sufficient that successive portions of capital are employed on the same land with different results, and that the portion which gives the least result should be withdrawn. If, by the introduction of the turnip husbandry, or by the use of a more invigorating manure, I can obtain the same produce with less capital, and without disturbing the difference between the productive powers of the successive portions of capital, I shall lower rent; for a different and more productive portion will be that which will form the standard from which every other will be reckoned. If, for example, the successive portions of capital yielded 100, 90, 80, 70; whilst I employed these four portions, my rent would be 60, or the difference between

| | | |
|---|---|---|
| 70 and 100 = 30 | | 100 |
| 70 and 90 = 20 | whilst the produce would be 340 | 90 |
| 70 and 80 = 10 | | 80 |
| | | 70 |
| 60 | | 340 |

and while I employed these portions, the rent would remain the same, although the produce of each should have an equal augmentation. If, instead of 100, 90, 80, 70, the produce should be increased to 125, 115, 105, 95, the rent would still be 60, or the difference between

| | | |
|---|---|---|
| 95 and 125 = 30 | | 125 |
| 95 and 125 = 20 | whilst the produce would be increased to 440 | 115 |
| 95 and 105 = 10 | | 105 |
| | | 95 |
| 60 | | 440 |

But with such an increase of produce, without an increase of demand, there could be no motive for employing so much capital on the land; one portion would be withdrawn, and consequently the last portion of capital would yield 105 instead of 95, and rent would fall to 30, or the difference between

| | | |
|---|---|---|
| 105 and 125 = 30 | whilst the produce will be still adequate to the wants of the population, for it would be 345 quarters, or | 125 |
| 105 and 115 = 10 | | 115 |
| | | 105 |
| 30 | | 345 |

the demand being only for 340 quarters.—But there are improvements which may lower the relative value of produce without lowering the corn rent, though they will lower the money rent of land. Such improvements do not increase the productive powers of the land; but they enable us to obtain its produce with less labour. They are rather directed to the formation of the capital applied to the land, than to the cultivation of the land itself. Improvements in agricultural implements, such as the plough and the thrashing machine, economy in the use of horses employed in husbandry, and a better knowledge of the veterinary art, are of this nature. Less capital, which is the same thing as less labour, will be employed on the land; but to obtain the same produce, less land cannot be cultivated. Whether improvements of this kind, however, affect corn rent, must depend on the question, whether the difference between the produce obtained by the employment of different portions of capital be increased, stationary, or diminished. If four portions of capital, 50, 60, 70, 80, be employed on the land, giving each the same results, and any improvement in the formation of such capital should enable me to withdraw 5 from each, so that they should be 45, 55, 65, and 75, no alteration would take place in the corn rent; but if the improvements were such as to enable me to make the whole saving on that portion of capital, which is least productively employed, corn rent would immediately fall, because the difference between the capital most productive, and the capital least productive, would be diminished; and it is this difference which constitutes rent.

Without multiplying instances, I hope enough has been said to show, that whatever diminishes the inequality in the produce obtained from successive portions of capital employed on the same or on new land, tends to lower rent; and that whatever increases that inequality, necessarily produces an opposite effect, and tends to raise it.

In speaking of the rent of the landlord, we have rather considered it as the proportion of the produce, obtained with a given capital on any given farm, without any reference to its exchangeable value; but since the same cause, the difficulty of production, raises the exchangeable value of raw produce, and raises also the proportion of raw produce paid to the landlord for rent, it is obvious that the landlord is doubly benefited by difficulty of production. First, he obtains a greater share, and secondly the commodity in which he is paid is of greater value.

## On Natural and Market Price

In making labour the foundation of the value of commodities, and the comparative quantity of labour which is necessary to their production, the rule which determines the respective quantities of goods which shall be given in exchange for each other, we must not be supposed to deny the accidental and temporary deviations of the actual or market price of commodities from this, their primary and natural price.

In the ordinary course of events, there is no commodity which continues for any length of time to be supplied precisely in that degree of abundance, which the wants and wishes of mankind require, and therefore there is none which is not subject to accidental and temporary variations of price.

It is only in consequence of such variations, that capital is apportioned precisely, in the requisite abundance and no more, to the production of the different commodities which happen to be in demand. With the rise or fall of price, profits are elevated above, or depressed below their general level, and capital is either encouraged to enter into, or is warned to depart from the particular employment in which the variation has taken place.

Whilst every man is free to employ his capital where he pleases, he will naturally seek for it that employment which is most advantageous; he will naturally be dissatisfied with a profit of 10 percent, if by removing his capital he can obtain a profit of 15 percent. This restless desire on the part of all the employers of stock, to quit a less profitable for a more advantageous business, has a strong tendency to equalize the rate of profits of all, or to fix them in such proportions, as may in the estimation of the parties, compensate for any advantage which one may have, or may appear to have over the other. It is perhaps very difficult to trace the steps by which this change is effected: it is probably effected, by a manufacturer not absolutely changing his employment, but only lessening the quantity of capital he has in that employment. In all rich countries, there is a number of men forming what is called the monied class; these men are engaged in no trade, but live on the interest of their money, which is employed in discounting bills, or in loans to the more industrious part of the community. The bankers too employ a large capital on the same objects. The capital so employed forms a circulating capital of a large amount, and is employed, in larger or smaller proportions, by all the different trades of a country. There is perhaps no manufacturer, however rich, who limits his business to the extent that his own funds alone will allow: he has always some portion of this floating capital, increasing or diminishing according to the activity of the demand for his commodities. When the demand for silks increases, and that for cloth diminishes, the clothier does not remove with his capital to the silk trade, but he dismisses some of his workmen, he discontinues his demand for the loan from bankers and monied men; while the case of the silk manufacturer is the reverse: he wishes to employ more workmen, and thus his motive for borrowing is increased: he borrows more, and thus capital is transferred from one employment to another, without the necessity of a manufacturer discontinuing his usual occupation. When we look to the markets of a large town, and observe how regularly they are supplied both with home and foreign commodities, in the quantity in which they are required, under all the circumstances of varying demand, arising from the caprice of taste, or a change in the amount of population, without often producing either the effects of a glut from a too abundant supply, or an enormously high price from the supply being unequal to the demand, we must confess that the principle which apportions capital to each trade in the precise amount that it is required, is more active than is generally supposed.

A capitalist, in seeking profitable employment for his funds, will naturally take into consideration all the advantages which one occupation possesses over another. He may therefore be willing to forego a part of his money profit, in consideration of the security, cleanliness, ease, or any other real or fancied advantage which one employment may possess over another.

If from a consideration of these circumstances, the profits of stock should be so adjusted, that in one trade they were 20, in another 25, and in another 30 percent, they would probably continue permanently with that relative difference, and with that difference only; for if any cause should elevate the profits of one of these trades 10 percent either these profits would be temporary and would soon again fall back to their usual station, or the profits of the others would be elevated in the same proportion.

The present time appears to be one of the exceptions to the justness of this remark. The termination of the war has so deranged the division which before existed of employments in Europe, that every capitalist has not yet found his place in the new division which has now become necessary.

Let us suppose that all commodities are at their natural price, and consequently that the profits of capital in all employments are exactly at the same rate, or differ only so much as, in the estimation of the parties, is equivalent to any real or fancied advantage which they possess or forego. Suppose now that a change of fashion should increase the demand for silks, and lessen that for woollens; their natural price, the quantity of labour necessary to their production, would continue unaltered, but the market price of silks would rise, and that of woollens would fall; and consequently the profits of the silk manufacturer would be above, whilst those of the woollen manufacturer would be below, the general and adjusted rate of profits. Not only the profits, but the wages of the workmen, would be affected in these employments. This increased demand for silks would however soon be supplied, by the transference of capital and labour from the woollen to the silk manufacture; when the market prices of silks and woollens would again approach their natural prices, and then the usual profits would be obtained by the respective manufacturers of those commodities.

It is then the desire, which every capitalist has, of diverting his funds from a less to a more profitable employment, that prevents the market price of commodities from continuing for any length of time either much above, or much below their natural price. It is this competition which so adjusts the exchangeable value of commodities, that after paying the wages for the labour necessary to their production, and all other expenses required to put the capital employed in its original state of efficiency, the remaining value or overplus will in each trade be in proportion to the value of the capital employed.

In the 7th chap. of the Wealth of Nations, all that concerns this question is most ably treated. Having fully acknowledged the temporary effects which, in particular employments of capital, may be produced on the prices of commodities, as well as on the wages of labour, and the profits of stock, by accidental causes, without influencing the general price of commodities, wages, or profits, since these effects are equally operative in all stages of society, we will leave them entirely out of our consideration, whilst we are treating of the laws which regulate natural prices, natural wages and natural profits, effects totally independent of these accidental causes. In speaking then of the exchangeable value of commodities, or the power of purchasing possessed by any one commodity, I mean always that power which it would possess, if not disturbed by any temporary or accidental cause, and which is its natural price.

# John Stuart Mill
## *Principles of Political Economy*
## Of Production on a Large, and Production on a Small Scale

§1. From the importance of combination of labour, it is an obvious conclusion, that there are many cases in which production is made much more effective by being conducted on a large scale. Whenever it is essential to the greatest efficiency of labour that many labourers should combine, even though only in the way of Simple Co-operation, the scale of the enterprise must be such as to bring many labourers together, and the capital must be large enough to maintain them. Still more needful is this when the nature of the employment allows, and the extent of the possible market encourages, a considerable division of labour. The larger the enterprise, the farther the division of labour may be carried. This is one of the principal causes of large manufactories. Even when no additional subdivision of the work would follow an enlargement of the operations, there will be good economy in enlarging them to the point at which every person to whom it is convenient to assign a special occupation, will have full employment in that occupation. This point is well illustrated by Mr. Babbage.

"If machines be kept working through the twenty-four hours," (which is evidently the only economical mode of employing them,) "it is necessary that some person shall attend to admit the workmen at the time they relieve each other; and whether the porter or other person so employed admit one person or twenty, his rest will be equally disturbed. It will also be necessary occasionally to adjust or repair the machine; and this can be done much better by a workman accustomed to machine-making, than by the person who uses it. Now, since the good performance and the duration of machines depend, to a very great extent, upon correcting every shake or imperfection in their parts as soon as they appear, the prompt attention of a workman resident on the spot will considerably reduce the expenditure arising from the wear and tear of the machinery. But in the case of a single lace-frame, or a single loom, this would be too expensive a plan. Here then arises another circumstance which tends to enlarge the extent of a factory. It ought to consist of such a number of machines as shall occupy the whole time of one workman in keeping them in order: if extended beyond that number, the same principle of economy would point out the necessity of doubling or tripling the number of machines, in order to employ the whole time of two or three skilful workmen.

"When one portion of the workman's labour consists in the exertion of mere physical force, as in weaving, and in many similar arts, it will soon occur to the manufacturer, that if that part were executed by a steam-engine, the same man might, in the case of weaving, attend to two or more looms at once: and, since we already suppose that one or more operative engineers have been employed, the number of looms may be so arranged that their time shall be fully occupied in keeping the steam-engine and the looms in order.

"Pursuing the same principles, the manufactory becomes gradually so enlarged, that the expense of lighting during the night amounts to a considerable sum: and as there are already attached to the establishment persons who are up all night, and can therefore constantly attend to it, and also engineers to make and keep in repair any machinery, the addition of an apparatus for making gas to light the factory leads to a new extension, at the same time that it contributes, by diminishing the expense of lighting, and the risk of accidents from fire, to reduce the cost of manufacturing.

"Long before a factory has reached this extent, it will have been found necessary to establish an accountant's department, with clerks to pay the workmen, and to see that they arrive at their stated times; and this department must be in communication with the agents who purchase the raw produce, and with those who sell the manufactured article." It will cost these clerks and accountants little more time and trouble to pay a large number of workmen than a small number; to check the accounts of large transactions, than of small. If the business doubled itself, it would probably be necessary to increase, but certainly not to double, the number either of accountants, or of buying and selling agents. Every increase of business would enable the whole to be carried on with a proportionately smaller amount of labour.

As a general rule, the expenses of a business do not increase by any means proportionally to the quantity of business. Let us take as an example, a set of operations which we are accustomed to see carried on by one great establishment, that of the Post Office. Suppose that the business, let us say only of the London letter-post, instead of being centralized in a single concern, were divided among five or six competing companies. Each of these would be obliged to maintain almost as large an establishment as is now sufficient for the whole. Since each must arrange for receiving and delivering letters in all parts of the town, each must send letter-carriers into every street, and almost every alley, and this too as many times in the day as is now done by the Post Office, if the service is to be as well performed. Each must have an office for receiving letters in every neighbourhood, with all subsidiary arrangements for collecting the letters from the different offices and re-distributing them. To this must be added the much greater number of superior officers who would be required to check and control the subordinates, implying not only a greater cost in salaries for such responsible officers, but the necessity, perhaps, of being satisfied in many instances with an inferior standard of qualification, and so failing in the object.

Whether or not the advantages obtained by operating on a large scale preponderate in any particular case over the more watchful attention, and greater regard to minor gains and losses, usually found in small establishments, can be ascertained, in a state of free competition, by an unfailing test. Wherever there are large and small establishments in the same business, that one of the two which in existing circumstances carries on the production at greatest advantage will be able to undersell the other. The power of permanently underselling can only, generally speaking, be derived from increased effectiveness of labour; and this, when obtained by a more extended division of employment, or by a classification tending to a better economy of skill, always implies a greater produce from the same labour, and not merely the same produce from less labour: it increases not the surplus only, but the gross produce of industry. If an increased quantity of the particular article is not required, and part of the labourers in consequence lose their employment, the capital which maintained and employed them is also set at liberty; and the general produce of the country is increased by some other application of their labour.

Another of the causes of large manufactories, however, is the introduction of processes requiring expensive machinery. Expensive machinery supposes a large capital; and is not resorted to except with the intention of producing, and the hope of selling, as much of the article as comes up to the full powers of the machine. For both these reasons, wherever costly machinery is used, the large system of production is inevitable. But the power of underselling is not in this case so unerring a test as in the former, of the beneficial effect on the total production of the community. The power of underselling does not depend on the absolute increase of produce, but on its bearing an increased proportion to the expenses; which, as was shown in a former chapter, it may do, consistently with even a diminution of the gross annual produce. By the adoption of machinery, a circulating capital, which was perpetually consumed and reproduced, has been converted into a fixed capital, requiring only a small annual expense to keep it up: and a much smaller produce will suffice for merely covering that expense, and replacing the remaining circulating capital of the producer. The machinery therefore might answer perfectly well to the manufacturer, and enable him to undersell his competitors, though the effect on the production of the country might be not an increase but a diminution. It is true, the article will be sold cheaper, and therefore, of that single article, there will probably be not a smaller, but a greater quantity sold; since the loss to the community collectively has fallen upon the work-people, and they are not the principal customers, if customers at all, of most branches of manufacture. But though that particular branch of industry may extend itself, it will be by replenishing its diminished circulating capital from that of the community generally; and if the labourers employed in that department escape loss of employment, it is because the loss will spread itself over the labouring people at large. If any of them are reduced to the condition of unproductive labourers, supported by voluntary or legal charity, the gross produce of the country is to that extent permanently diminished, until the ordinary progress of accumulation makes it up; but if the condition of the labouring classes enables them to bear a temporary reduction of wages, and the superseded labourers become absorbed in other employments, their labour is still productive, and the breach in the gross produce of the community is repaired, though not the detriment to the labourers. I have restated this exposition, which has already been made in a former place, to impress more strongly the truth, that a mode of production does not of necessity increase the productive effect of the collective labour of a community, because it enables a particular commodity to be sold cheaper. The one consequence generally accompanies the other, but not necessarily. I will not here repeat the reasons I formerly gave, nor anticipate those which will be given more fully hereafter, for deeming the exception to be rather a case abstractedly possible, than one which is frequently realized in fact.

A considerable part of the saving of labour effected by substituting the large system of production for the small, is the saving in the labour of the capitalists themselves. If a hundred producers with small capitals carry on separately the same business, the superintendence of each concern will probably require the whole attention of the person conducting it, sufficiently at least to hinder his time or thoughts from being disposable for anything else: while a single manufacturer possessing a capital equal to the sum of theirs, with ten or a dozen clerks, could conduct the whole of their amount of business, and have leisure too for other occupations. The small capitalist, it is true, generally combines with the business of direction some portion of the details, which the other leaves to his subordinates: the small farmer follows his own plough, the small tradesman serves in his own shop, the small weaver plies his own loom. But in this very union of functions there is, in a great proportion of cases, a want of economy. The principal in the concern is either wasting, in the routine of a business, qualities suitable for the direction of it, or he is only fit for the former, and then the latter will be ill done. I must observe, however, that I do not attach, to this saving of labour, the importance often ascribed to it. There is undoubtedly much more labour expended in the superintendence of many small capitals than in that of one large capital. For this labour however the small producers have generally a full compensation, in the feeling of being their own masters, and not servants of an employer. It may be said, that if they value this independence they will submit to pay a price for it, and to sell at the reduced rates occasioned by the competition of the great dealer or manufacturer. But they cannot always do this and continue to gain a living. They thus gradually disappear from society. After having consumed their little capital in prolonging the unsuccessful struggle, they either sink into the condition of hired labourers, or become dependent on others for support.

§2. Production on a large scale is greatly promoted by the practice of forming a large capital by the combination of many small contributions; or, in other words, by the formation of joint stock companies. The advantages of the joint stock principle are numerous and important.

In the first place, many undertakings require an amount of capital beyond the means of the richest individual or private partnership. No individual could have made a railway from London to Liverpool; it is doubtful if any individual could even work the traffic on it, now when it is made. The government indeed could have done both; and in countries where the practice of co-operation is only in the earlier stages of its growth, the government can alone be looked to for any of the works for which a great combination of means is requisite; because it can obtain those means by compulsory taxation, and is already accustomed to the conduct of large operations. For reasons, however, which are tolerably well known, and of which we shall treat fully hereafter, government agency for the conduct of industrial operations is generally one of the least eligible of resources, when any other is available.

Next, there are undertakings which individuals are not absolutely incapable of performing, but which they cannot perform on the scale and with the continuity which are ever more and more required by the exigencies of a society in an advancing state. Individuals are quite capable of despatching ships from England to any or every part of the world, to carry passengers and letters; the thing was done before joint stock companies for the purpose were heard of. But when, from the increase of population and transactions, as well as of means of payment, the public will no longer content themselves with occasional opportunities, but require the certainty that packets shall start regularly, for some places once or even twice a day, for others once a week, for others that a steam ship of great size and expensive construction shall depart on fixed days twice in each month, it is evident that to afford an assurance of keeping up with punctuality such a circle of costly operations, requires a much larger capital and a much larger staff of qualified subordinates than can be commanded by an individual capitalist. There are other cases, again, in which though the business might be perfectly well transacted with small or moderate capitals, the guarantee of a great subscribed stock is necessary or desirable as a security to the public for the fulfilment of pecuniary engagements. This is especially the case when the nature of the business requires that numbers of persons should be willing to trust the concern with their money: as in the business of banking, and that of insurance: to both of which the joint stock principle is eminently adapted. It is an instance of the folly and jobbery of the rulers of mankind, that until a late period the joint stock principle, as a general resort, was in this country interdicted by law to these two modes of business; to banking altogether, and to insurance in the department of sea risks; in order to bestow a lucrative monopoly on particular establishments which the government was pleased exceptionally to license, namely the Bank of England, and two insurance companies, the London and the Royal Exchange.

Another advantage of joint stock or associated management, is its incident of publicity. This is not an invariable, but it is a natural consequence of the joint stock principle, and might be, as in some important cases it already is, compulsory. In banking, insurance, and other businesses which depend wholly on confidence, publicity is a still more important element of success than a large subscribed capital. A heavy loss occurring in a private bank may be kept secret; even though it were of such magnitude as to cause the ruin of the concern, the banker may still carry it on for years, trying to retrieve its position, only to fall in the end with a greater crash: but this cannot so easily happen in the case of a joint stock company, whose accounts are published periodically. The accounts, even if cooked, still exercise some check; and the suspicions of shareholders, breaking out at the general meetings, put the public on their guard.

These are some of the advantages of joint stock over individual management. But if we look to the other side of the question, we shall find that individual management has also very great advantages over joint stock. The chief of these is the much keener interest of the managers in the success of the undertaking.

The administration of a joint stock association is, in the main, administration by hired servants. Even the committee, or board of directors, who are supposed to superintend the management, and who do really appoint and remove the managers, have no pecuniary interest in the good working of the concern beyond the shares they individually hold, which are always a very small part of the capital of the association, and in general but a small part of the fortunes of the directors themselves; and the part they take in the management usually divides their time with many other occupations, of as great or greater importance to their own interest; the business being the principal concern of no one except those who are hired to carry it on. But experience shows, and proverbs, the expression of popular experience, attest, how inferior is the quality of hired servants, compared with the ministration of those personally interested in the work, and how indispensable, when hired service must be employed, is "the master's eye" to watch over it.

The successful conduct of an industrial enterprise requires two quite distinct qualifications: fidelity, and zeal. The fidelity of the hired managers of a concern it is possible to secure. When their work admits of being reduced to a definite set of rules, the violation of these is a matter on which conscience cannot easily blind itself, and on which responsibility may be enforced by the loss of employment. But to carry on a great business successfully, requires a hundred things which, as they cannot be defined beforehand, it is impossible to convert into distinct and positive obligations. First and principally, it requires that the directing mind should be incessantly occupied with the subject; should be continually laying schemes by which greater profit may be obtained, or expense saved. This intensity of interest in the subject it is seldom to be expected that any one should feel, who is conducting a business as the hired servant and for the profit of another. There are experiments in human affairs which are conclusive on the point. Look at the whole class of rulers, and ministers of state. The work they are entrusted with, is among the most interesting and exciting of all occupations; the personal share which they themselves reap of the national benefits or misfortunes which befall the state under their rule, is far from trifling, and the rewards and punishments which they may expect from public estimation are of the plain and palpable kind which are most keenly felt and most widely appreciated. Yet how rare a thing is it to find a statesman in whom mental indolence is not stronger than all these inducements. How infinitesimal is the proportion who trouble themselves to form, or even to attend to, plans of public improvement, unless when it is made still more troublesome to them to remain inactive; or who have any other real desire than that of rubbing on, so as to escape general blame. On a smaller scale, all who have ever employed hired labour have had ample experience of the efforts made to give as little labour in exchange for the wages, as is compatible with not being turned off. The universal neglect by domestic servants of their employer's interests, wherever these are not protected by some fixed rule, is matter of common remark; unless where long continuance in the same service, and reciprocal good offices, have produced either personal attachment, or some feeling of a common interest.

Another of the disadvantages of joint stock concerns, which is in some degree common to all concerns on a large scale, is disregard of small gains and small savings. In the management of a great capital and great transactions, especially when the managers have not much interest in it of their own, small sums are apt to be counted for next to nothing; they never seem worth the care and trouble which it costs to attend to them, and the credit of liberality and openhandedness is cheaply bought by a disregard of such trifling considerations. But small profits and small expenses often repeated, amount to great gains and losses: and of this a large capitalist is often a sufficiently good calculator to be practically aware; and to arrange his business on a system, which if enforced by a sufficiently vigilant superintendence, precludes the possibility of the habitual waste, otherwise incident to a great business. But the managers of a joint stock concern seldom devote themselves sufficiently to the work, to enforce unremittingly, even if introduced, through every detail of the business, a really economical system.

From considerations of this nature, Adam Smith was led to enunciate as a principle, that joint stock companies could never be expected to maintain themselves without an exclusive privilege, except in branches of business which, like banking, insurance, and some others, admit of being, in a considerable degree, reduced to fixed rules. This, however, is one of those over-statements of a true principle, often met with in Adam Smith. In his days there were few instances of joint stock companies which had been permanently successful without a monopoly, except the class of cases which he referred to; but since his time there have been many; and the regular increase both of the spirit of combination and of the ability to combine, will doubtless produce many more. Adam Smith fixed his observation too exclusively on the superior energy and more unremitting attention brought to a business in which the whole stake and the whole gain belong to the persons conducting it; and he overlooked various countervailing considerations which go a great way towards neutralizing even that great point of superiority.

Of these one of the most important is that which relates to the intellectual and active qualifications of the directing head. The stimulus of individual interest is some security for exertion, but exertion is of little avail if the intelligence exerted is of an inferior order, which it must necessity be in the majority of concerns carried on by the persons chiefly interested in them. Where the concern is large, and can afford a remuneration sufficient to attract a class of candidates superior to the common average, it is possible to select for the general management, and for all the skilled employments of a subordinate kind, persons of a degree of acquirement and cultivated intelligence which more than compensates for their inferior interest in the result. Their greater perspicacity enables them, with even a part of their minds, to see probabilities of advantage which never occur to the ordinary run of men by the continued exertion of the whole of theirs; and their superior knowledge, and habitual rectitude of perception and of judgment, guard them against blunders, the fear of which would prevent the others from hoarding their interests in any attempt out of the ordinary routine.

It must be further remarked, that it is not a necessary consequence of joint stock management, that the persons employed, whether in superior or in subordinate offices, should be paid wholly by fixed salaries. There are modes of connecting more or less intimately the interest of the employés with the pecuniary success of the concern. There is a long series of intermediate positions, between working wholly on one's own account, and working by the day, week, or year for an invariable payment. Even in the case of ordinary unskilled labour, there is such a thing as task-work, or working by the piece: and the superior efficiency of this is so well known, that judicious employers always resort to it when the work admits of being put out in definite portions, without the necessity of too troublesome a surveillance to guard against inferiority in the execution. In the case of the managers of joint stock companies, and of the superintending and controlling officers in many private establishments, it is a common enough practice to connect their pecuniary interest with the interest of their employers, by giving them part of their remuneration in the form of a percentage on the profits. The personal interest thus given to hired servants is not comparable in intensity to that of the owner of the capital; but it is sufficient to be a very material stimulus to zeal and carefulness, and, when added to the advantage of superior intelligence, often raises the quality of the service much above that which the generality of masters are capable of rendering to themselves. The ulterior extensions of which this principle of remuneration is susceptible, being of great social as well as economical importance, will be more particularly adverted to in a subsequent stage of the present inquiry.

As I have already remarked of large establishments generally, when compared with small ones, whenever competition is free its results will show whether individual or joint stock agency is best adapted to the particular case, since that which is most efficient and most economical will always in the end succeed in underselling the other.

§3. The possibility of substituting the large system of production for the small, depends of course, in the first place, on the extent of the market. The large system can only be advantageous when a large amount of business is to be done: it implies, therefore, either a populous and flourishing community, or a great opening for exportation. Again, this as well as every other change in the system of production is greatly favoured by a progressive condition of capital. It is chiefly when the capital of a country is receiving a great annual increase, that there is a large amount of capital seeking for investment: and a new enterprise is much sooner and more easily entered upon by new capital, than by withdrawing capital from existing employments. The change is also much facilitated by the existence of large capitals in few hands. It is true that the same amount of capital can be raised by bringing together many small sums. But this (besides that it is not equally well suited to all branches of industry) supposes a much greater degree of commercial confidence and enterprise diffused through the community, and belongs altogether to a more advanced stage of industrial progress.

In the countries in which there are the largest markets, the widest diffusion of commercial confidence and enterprise, the greatest annual increase of capital, and the greatest number of large capitals owned by individuals, there is a tendency to substitute more and more, in one branch of industry after another, large establishments for small ones. In England, the chief type of all these characteristics, there is a perpetual growth not only of large manufacturing establishments, but also, wherever a sufficient number of purchasers are assembled, of shops and warehouses for conducting retail business on a large scale. These are almost always able to undersell the smaller tradesmen, partly, it is understood, by means of division of labour, and the economy occasioned by limiting the employment of skilled agency to cases where skill is required; and partly, no doubt, by the saving of labour arising from the great scale of the transactions; as it costs no more time, and not much more exertion of mind, to make a large purchase, for example, than a small one, and very much less than to make a number of small ones.

With a view merely to production, and to the greatest efficiency of labour, this change is wholly beneficial. In some cases it is attended with drawbacks, rather social than economical, the nature of which has been already hinted at. But whatever disadvantages may be supposed to attend on the change from a small to a large system of production, they are not applicable to the change from a large to a still larger. When, in any employment, the régime of independent small producers has either never been possible, or has been superseded, and the system of many work-people under one management has become fully established, from that time any further enlargement in the scale of production is generally an unqualified benefit. It is obvious, for example, how great an economy of labour would be obtained if London were supplied by a single gas or water company instead of the existing plurality. While there are even as many as two, this implies double establishments of all sorts, when one only, with a small increase, could probably perform the whole operation equally well; double sets of machinery and works, when the whole of the gas or water required could generally be produced by one set only; even double sets of pipes, if the companies did not prevent this needless expense by agreeing upon a division of the territory. Were there only one establishment, it could make lower charges, consistently with obtaining the rate of profit now realized. But would it do so? Even if it did not, the community in the aggregate would still be a gainer: since the shareholders are a part of the community, and they would obtain higher profits while the consumers paid only the same. It is, however, an error to suppose that the prices are ever permanently kept down by the competition of these companies. Where competitors are so few, they always end by agreeing not to compete. They may run a race of cheapness to ruin a new candidate, but as soon as he has established his footing they come to terms with him. When, therefore, a business of real public importance can only be carried on advantageously upon so large a scale as to render the liberty of competition almost illusory, it is an unthrifty dispensation of the public resources that several costly sets of arrangements should be kept up for the purpose of rendering to the community this one service. It is much better to treat it at once as a public function; and if it be not such as the government itself could beneficially undertake, it should be made over entire to the company or association which will perform it on the best terms for the public. In the case of railways, for example, no one can desire to see the enormous waste of capital and land (not to speak of increased nuisance) involved in the construction of a second railway to connect the same places already united by an existing one; while the two would not do the work better than it could be done by one, and after a short time would probably be amalgamated. Only one such line ought to be permitted, but the control over that line never ought to be parted with by the State, unless on a temporary concession, as in France; and the vested right which Parliament has allowed to be acquired by the existing companies, like all other proprietary rights which are opposed to public utility, is morally valid only as a claim to compensation.

# Of Competition and Custom

§1. Under the rule of individual property, the division of the produce is the result of two determining agencies: Competition, and Custom. It is important to ascertain the amount of influence which belongs to each of these causes, and in what manner the operation of one is modified by the other.

Political economists generally, and English political economists above others, have been accustomed to lay almost exclusive stress upon the first of these agencies; to exaggerate the effect of competition, and to take into little account the other and conflicting principle. They are apt to express themselves as if they thought that competition actually does, in all cases, whatever it can be shown to be the tendency of competition to do. This is partly intelligible, if we consider that only through the principle of competition has political economy any pretension to the character of a science. So far as rents, profits, wages, prices, are determined by competition, laws may be assigned for them. Assume competition to be their exclusive regulator, and principles of broad generality and scientific precision may be laid down, according to which they will be regulated. The political economist justly deems this his proper business: and as an abstract or hypothetical science, political economy cannot be required to do, and indeed cannot do, anything more. But it would be a great misconception of the actual course of human affairs, to suppose that competition exercises in fact this unlimited sway. I am not speaking of monopolies, either natural or artificial, or of any interferences of authority with the liberty of production or exchange. Such disturbing causes have always been allowed for by political economists. I speak of cases in which there is nothing to restrain competition; no hindrance to it either in the nature of the case or in artificial obstacles; yet in which the result is not determined by competition, but by custom or usage; competition either not taking place at all, or producing its effect in quite a different manner from that which is ordinarily assumed to be natural to it.

§2. Competition, in fact, has only become in any considerable degree the governing principle of contracts, at a comparatively modern period. The farther we look back into history, the more we see all transactions and engagements under the influence of fixed customs. The reason is evident. Custom is the most powerful protector of the weak against the strong; their sole protector where there are no laws or government adequate to the purpose. Custom is a barrier which, even in the most oppressed condition of mankind, tyranny is forced in some degree to respect. To the industrious population, in a turbulent military community, freedom of competition is a vain phrase; they are never in a condition to make terms for themselves by it: there is always a master who throws his sword into the scale, and the terms are such as he imposes. But though the law of the strongest decides, it is not the interest nor in general the practice of the strongest to strain that law to the utmost, and every relaxation of it has a tendency to become a custom, and every custom to become a right. Rights thus originating, and not competition in any shape, determine, in a rude state of society, the share of the produce enjoyed by those who produce it. The relations, more especially, between the landowner and the cultivator, and the payments made by the latter to the former, are, in all states of society but the most modern, determined by the usage of the country. Never until late times have the conditions of the occupancy of land been (as a general rule) an affair of competition. The occupier for the time has very commonly been considered to have a right to retain his holdings, while he fulfils the customary requirements; and thus become, in a certain sense, a co-proprietor of the soil. Even where the holder has not acquired this fixity of tenure, the terms of occupation have often been fixed and invariable.

In India, for example, and other Asiatic communities similarly constituted, the ryots, or peasant-farmers, are not regarded as tenants at will, nor even as tenants by virtue of a lease. In most villages there are indeed some ryots on this precarious footing, consisting of those, or the descendants of those, who have settled in the place at a known and comparatively recent period; but all who are looked upon as descendants or representatives of the original inhabitants, and even many mere tenants of ancient date, are thought entitled to retain their land, as long as they pay the customary rents. What these customary rents are, or ought to be, has indeed, in most cases, become a matter of obscurity; usurpation, tyranny, and foreign conquest having to a great degree obliterated the evidences of them. But when an old and purely Hindoo principality falls under the dominion of the British Government, or the management of its officers, and when the details of the revenue system come to be inquired into, it is usually found that though the demands of the great landholder, the State, have been swelled by fiscal rapacity until all limit is practically lost sight of, it has yet been thought necessary to have a distinct name and a separate pretext for each increase of exaction; so that the demand has sometimes come to consist of thirty or forty different items, in addition to the nominal rent. This circuitous mode of increasing the payments assuredly would not have been resorted to, if there had been an acknowledged right in the landlord to increase the rent. Its adoption is a proof that there was once an effective limitation, a real customary rent; and that the understood right of the ryot to the land, so long as he paid rent according to custom, was at some time or other more than nominal. The British Government of India always simplifies the tenure by consolidating the various assessments into one, thus making the rent nominally as well as really an arbitrary thing, or at least a matter of specific agreement: but it scrupulously respects the right of the ryot to the land, though until the reforms of the present generation (reforms even now only partially carried into effect) it seldom left him much more than a bare subsistence.

In modern Europe the cultivators have gradually emerged from a state of personal slavery. The barbarian conquerors of the Western Empire found that the easiest mode of managing their conquests would be to leave the occupation of the land in the hands in which they found it, and to save themselves a labour so uncongenial as the superintendence of troops of slaves, by allowing the slaves to retain in a certain degree the control of their own actions, under an obligation to furnish the lord with provisions and labour. A common expedient was to assign to the serf, for his exclusive use, as much land as was thought sufficient for his support, and to make him work on the other lands of his lord whenever required. By degrees these indefinite obligations were transformed into a definite one, of supplying a fixed quantity of provisions or a fixed quantity of labour: and as the lords, in time, became inclined to employ their income in the purchase of luxuries rather than in the maintenance of retainers, the payments in kind were commuted for payments in money. Each concession, at first voluntary and revocable at pleasure, gradually acquired the force of custom, and was at last recognised and enforced by the tribunals. In this manner the serfs progressively rose into a free tenantry, who held their land in perpetuity on fixed conditions. The conditions were sometimes very onerous, and the people very miserable. But their obligations were determined by the usage or law of the country, and not by competition.

Where the cultivators had never been, strictly speaking, in personal bondage, or after they had ceased to be so, the exigencies of a poor and little advanced society gave rise to another arrangement, which in some parts of Europe, even highly improved parts, has been found sufficiently advantageous to be continued to the present day. I speak of the métayer system. Under this, the land is divided, in small farms, among single families, the landlord generally supplying the stock which the agricultural system of the country is considered to require, and receiving, in lieu of rent and profit, a fixed proportion of the produce. This proportion, which is generally paid in kind, is usually, (as is implied in the words métayer, mezzaiuolo, and medietarius,) one-half. There are places, however, such as the rich volcanic soil of the province of Naples, where the landlord takes two-thirds, and yet the cultivator by means of an excellent agriculture contrives to live. But whether the proportion is two-thirds or one-half, it is a fixed proportion; not variable from farm to farm, or from tenant to tenant. The custom of the country is the universal rule; nobody thinks of raising or lowering rents, or of letting land on other than the customary conditions. Competition, as a regulator of rent, has no existence.

§3. Prices, whenever there was no monopoly, came earlier under the influence of competition, and are much more universally subject to it, than rents: but that influence is by no means, even in the present activity of mercantile competition, so absolute as is sometimes assumed. There is no proposition which meets us in the field of political economy oftener than this—that there cannot be two prices in the same market. Such undoubtedly is the natural effect of unimpeded competition; yet every one knows that there are, almost always, two prices in the same market. Not only are there in every large town, and in almost every trade, cheap shops and dear shops, but the same shop often sells the same article at different prices to different customers: and, as a general rule, each retailer adapts his scale of prices to the class of customers whom he expects. The wholesale trade, in the great articles of commerce, is really under the dominion of competition. There, the buyers as well as sellers are traders or manufacturers, and their purchases are not influenced by indolence or vulgar finery, nor depend on the smaller motives of personal convenience, but are business transactions. In the wholesale markets therefore it is true as a general proposition, that there are not two prices at one time for the same thing: there is at each time and place a market price, which can be quoted in a price-current. But retail price, the price paid by the actual consumer, seems to feel very slowly and imperfectly the effect of competition; and when competition does exist, it often, instead of lowering prices, merely divides the gains of the high price among a greater number of dealers. Hence it is that, of the price paid by the consumer, so large a proportion is absorbed by the gains of retailers; and any one who inquires into the amount which reaches the hands of those who made the things he buys, will often be astonished at its smallness. When indeed the market, being that of a great city, holds out a sufficient inducement to large capitalists to engage in retail operations, it is generally found a better speculation to attract a large business by underselling others, than merely to divide the field of employment with them. This influence of competition is making itself felt more and more through the principal branches of retail trade in the large towns; and the rapidity and cheapness of transport, by making consumers less dependent on the dealers in their immediate neighbourhood, are tending to assimilate more and more the whole country to a large town: but hitherto [1848] it is only in the great centres of business that retail transactions have been chiefly, or even much, determined, by competition. Elsewhere it rather acts, when it acts at all, as an occasional disturbing influence; the habitual regulator is custom, modified from time to time by notions existing in the minds of purchasers and sellers, of some kind of equity or justice.

In many trades the terms on which business is done are a matter of positive arrangement among the trade, who use the means they always possess of making the situation of any member of the body, who departs from its fixed customs, inconvenient or disagreeable. It is well known that the bookselling trade was, until lately, one of these, and that notwithstanding the active spirit of rivalry in the trade, competition did not produce its natural effect in breaking down the trade rules. All professional remuneration is regulated by custom. The fees of physicians, surgeons, and barristers, the charges of attorneys, are nearly invariable. Not certainly for want of abundant competition in those professions, but because the competition operates by diminishing each competitor's chance of fees, not by lowering the fees themselves.

Since custom stands its ground against competition to so considerable an extent, even where, from the multitude of competitors and the general energy in the pursuit of gain, the spirit of competition is strongest, we may be sure that this is much more the case where people are content with smaller gains, and estimate their pecuniary interest at a lower rate when balanced against their ease or their pleasure. I believe it will often be found, in Continental Europe, that prices and charges, of some or of all sorts, are much higher in some places than in others not far distant, without its being possible to assign any other cause than that it has always been so: the customers are used to it, and acquiesce in it. An enterprising competitor, with sufficient capital, might force down the charges, and make his fortune during the process; but there are no enterprising competitors; those who have capital prefer to leave it where it is, or to make less profit by it in a more quiet way.

These observations must be received as a general correction to be applied whenever relevant, whether expressly mentioned or not, to the conclusions contained in the subsequent portions of this treatise. Our reasonings must, in general, proceed as if the known and natural effects of competition were actually produced by it, in all cases in which it is not restrained by some positive obstacle. Where competition, though free to exist, does not exist, or where it exists, but has its natural consequences overruled by any other agency, the conclusions will fail more or less of being applicable. To escape error, we ought, in applying the conclusions of political economy to the actual affairs of life, to consider not only what will happen supposing the maximum of competition, but how far the result will be affected if competition falls short of the maximum.

The states of economical relation which stand first in order to be discussed and appreciated, are those in which competition has no part, the arbiter of transactions being either brute force or established usage. These will be the subject of the next four chapters.

# 2

# Federalism, Antifederalism, and Jacksonianism

## Introduction

BY DANIEL CRANE

The founders of the American Republic and framers of the American Constitution clashed vigorously over matters of economic philosophy. In broad terms, the framers fell into two camps: Federalists, who supported active involvement by the federal government in stimulating a national commercial economy; and Anti-Federalists (who eventually morphed into Democratic-Republicans or just Republicans), who preferred states' rights and localized agrarian economies. The Federalists became identified with Alexander Hamilton and his vision for muscular national supremacy, a national bank, creditor rights, and commercial ties with England. The Republicans became identified with Thomas Jefferson and his vision for a strictly limited federal government, individual and debtor rights, the yeoman farmer as the archetype of American virtue, and the egalitarian ideals of the French Revolution.

Although deeply versed in the political economy literature of their European contemporaries, the American founders (Jefferson perhaps excepted) had relatively little time for writing works of abstract theory. They were too heavily involved in creating and managing a new political order. Their writing—although often of the highest intellectual caliber—was directed toward pressing political controversies and hence deployed rhetoric and ideological argumentation rather than an academic analytical mode. Nonetheless, many of the framers' hastily written pamphlets, such as the Federalist and Anti-Federalist papers, came to be known as classics of political theory.

Among the framers' most heated disputes was the power of the federal government to grant charters of incorporation. At the time of the American founding, corporate charters originated with special acts of British Parliament or, after independence, the state governments. As part of their charter, corporations often received exclusive manufacturing, importing or exporting, or trading privileges. Corporations were thus associated with royal prerogative and monopoly. Whether the federal government should have the power to grant charters of incorporation—and hence to create monopolies—was one of the key economic and political debates of the founding generation.

The dispute began in the Constitutional Convention in Philadelphia in the summer of 1787. Ironically, given subsequent events, it was a motion by the young and talented Virginia planter James Madison that set up a controversy that would dominate American politics for the next forty years. In response to a motion by Benjamin Franklin to allow the federal government to charter companies to cut canals, Madison introduced a broader proposal to grant the federal government the power to charter corporations. The proposal failed, but under ambiguous circumstances. Anti-Federalist delegates protested that the provision would allow the federal government to create commercial monopolies. Federalist delegates responded that the provision was unnecessary, since Congress would have the power to incorporate under the commerce clause of the Constitution's eventual Article I Section 8. This only made the Anti-Federalists even more opposed to the entire Constitution, since the Federalists were already admitting their intention to give the federal powers a broad construction.

After ratification of the Constitution, Hamilton, George Washington's former aide-de-camp and now his treasury secretary, proposed legislation that would create a national bank with the immediate purpose of servicing Revolutionary War debts but with the longer-term purposes of cementing national unity and creating a commercial economy. Madison, now a congressman from Virginia and increasingly suspicious of Hamilton's commercial and nationalist designs, led the charge against the bank. Madison argued that the bank would be unconstitutional since Madison's own proposal for such an express power in the Constitution had been defeated. Nonetheless, the measure passed in Congress and went to Washington's desk for signature. Washington consulted Hamilton and Jefferson (his secretary of state) on the bill's constitutionality and sided with Hamilton over Jefferson. The bank came into effect in 1793, with a twenty-year charter.

In 1813, on expiration of the first charter, Madison was now the president of the United States. The American political scene had evolved dramatically during the intervening years. Intramural bickering within the Federalist party during Washington's second term, John Adams's rigidity as president, Washington's death in 1799, Jefferson's election in 1800, and Hamilton's death from a duel with Aaron Burr in 1804 had finished off the Federalist party. From Jefferson's election to Andrew Jackson's in 1828, the American political scene was dominated by the Republican Party and hence the progeny of the Anti-Federalist tradition. And yet—as is often the rule in politics—time, place, and expediency rather than pure ideology dominated outcomes. Jefferson's Louisiana Purchase from Napoleon in 1803 violated every anti-expansionist, anti-imperialist tenet of Republicanism and yet was an opportunity that Jefferson could not have rejected without destroying his legacy as an American icon.

So too for Madison in 1813. Here was the opportunity that he had been awaiting for the last twenty years: the chance to kill off the vestiges of Hamiltonianism and mercantile monopoly by refusing to reincorporate the bank. And yet, like Washington earlier, President Madison had war debts (this time from the War of 1812) to service and needed his bank. Congress renewed the bank's charter at Madison's direction.

The battle over the bank and its supposed monopolistic tendencies set up one of the most important decisions of American constitutional law, *McCulloch v. Maryland*.[1] In 1819, the U.S. Supreme Court upheld the bank's constitutionality under a broad reading of the "necessary and proper" clause of Article I, thus creating not only conclusive legal authority for federal chartering of commercial corporations but also the foundations for dramatic expansion of federal powers in the twentieth century. The Hamiltonian vision prevailed in constitutional law.

Yet *McCulloch* proved far more important to the long-term constitutional authority of the federal government and to constitutional jurisprudence than it did to the immediate success of a federal incorporation power. The charter of the second bank of the United States was due to expire and National Republicans sought a third charter in 1833, during the presidency of Andrew Jackson. Jackson, a war hero from Tennessee—then western frontier territory—embodied a new ideological wave in American politics. The Jacksonians distrusted the eastern elite as corrupt, feared excessive concentration of power in the federal Congress, and loathed the commercial and monetary culture of the eastern states, which they believed enslaved western farmers. Objecting to the monopolistic power of the "monster bank," Jackson vetoed the bank's third charter in 1833.

Jacksonianism brought down the bank but set in motion an equally momentous development in American economic regulation that would eventually lead to reorganization of the American business firm. Jacksonians objected to corporate chartering by special act of Congress or state legislatures because it fomented corruption and cronyism, but they had no general objection to incorporation. Indeed, Jacksonians believed that the cure to the monopolistic and corrupting tendencies of corporate chartering was to make the corporate form available to all entrepreneurs without special act of the legislature.[2] Thus, Jacksonian influences propelled liberalization of corporate law in the middle of the nineteenth century and led to the broad availability of the corporate form by the time of the Civil War.

By the late nineteenth century, the easy availability of corporate charters would create complications for federal and state regulators trying to restrain the growing power of industrial trusts. The Jacksonians, however, were more concerned about the power of the legislature to grant monopoly than the power of business firms to achieve monopoly through anticompetitive devices. As late as 1878, Thomas Cooley opened his seminal essay on limitations on state control of private business with the morals of the Yazoo land grant scandal of the late eighteenth and early nineteenth century, in which the Georgia legislature corruptly sold massive tracts of land to favored interests. Cooley's essays (surveyed here) show awareness of the potential for purely private anticompetitive behavior, but they remain most concerned with the corrosive power of state interference in the market.

More than a century of controversy over the meaning and implications of monopoly and the role of the federal and state governments in managing the economy thus set the stage for debates over the Sherman Act in 1890 and the subsequent evolution of U.S. competition law and policy.

1. 4 Wheat 316, 4 *L.Ed.* 579 (1819).

2. Herbert Hovenkamp, *Enterprise and American Law: 1836–1937* 37 (1991).

## Max Farrand, ed.

## *Records of the Federal Convention of 1787*

## Notes of James Madison, Friday Sepr. 14th 1787, In Convention

[*Editor's note: The following notes from Madison concern debate in the Convention that begins with a proposal by Benjamin Franklin to add a federal power to cut canals, to the already proposed power to build post roads.*]

Docr. Franklin moved to add after the words "post roads" Art I Sect. 8. "a power to provide for cutting canals where deemed necessary"

Mr Wilson 2ded. the motion

Mr Sherman objected. The expence in such cases will fall on the U—States, and the benefit accrue to the places where the canals may be cut.

Mr Wilson. Instead of being an expence to the U. S. they may be made a source of revenue.

Mr. Madison suggested an enlargement of the motion into a power "to grant charters of incorporation where the interest of the U. S. might require & the legislative provisions of individual States may be incompetent." His primary object was however to secure an easy communication between the States which the free intercourse now to be opened, seemed to call for—The political obstacles being removed, a removal of the natural ones as far as possible ought to follow. Mr. Randolph 2ded. the proposition.

Mr King thought the power unnecessary.

Mr Wilson. It is necessary to prevent a State from obstructing the general welfare.

Mr King—The States will be prejudiced and divided into parties by it—In Philada. & New York, It will be referred to the establishment of a Bank, which has been a subject of contention in those Cities. In other places it will be referred to mercantile monopolies.

Mr. Wilson mentioned the importance of facilitating by canals, the communication with the Western Settlements—As to Banks he did not think with Mr. King that the power in that point of view would excite the prejudices & parties apprehended. As to mercantile monopolies they are already included in the power to regulate trade.

Col: Mason was for limiting the power to the single case of Canals. He was afraid of monopolies of every sort, which he did not think were by any means already implied by the Constitution as supposed by Mr. Wilson.

The motion being so modified as to admit a distinct question specifying & limited to the case of canals.

N-H—no—Mas. no. Ct. no—N-J—no—Pa ay. Del. no—Md. no. Va. ay. N-C—no—S-C. no—Geo. ay. [Ayes—3; noes—8.]

The other part fell of course, as including the power rejected.

# Ratification of the Constitution by the States

## Massachusetts

## Agrippa VI

## *Massachusetts Gazette*, 14 December [1787]

### *To the People*

To prevent any mistakes, or misapprehensions of the argument, stated in my last paper, to prove that the proposed constitution is an actual consolidation of the separate states into one extensive commonwealth, the reader is desired to observe, that in the course of the argument, the new plan is considered as an intire system. It is not dependent on any other book for an explanation, and contains no references to any other book. All the defences of it, therefore, so far as they are drawn from the state constitutions, or from maxims of the common law, are foreign to the purpose. It is only by comparing the different parts of it together, that the meaning of the whole is to be understood. For instance—

We find in it, that there is to be a legislative assembly, with authority to constitute courts for the trial of all kinds of civil causes, between citizens of different states. The right to appoint such courts necessarily involves in it the right of defining their powers, and determining the rules by which their judgment shall be regulated; and the grant of the former of those rights is nugatory without the latter. It is vain to tell us, that a maxim of common law requires contracts to be determined by the law existing where the contract was made: for it is also a maxim, that the legislature has a right to alter the common law. Such a power forms an essential part of legislation. Here, then, a declaration of rights of inestimable value. It contains those principles which the government never can invade without an open violation of the compact between them and the citizens. Such a declaration ought to have come to the new constitution in favour of the legislative rights of the several states, by which their sovereignty over their own citizens within the state should be secured. Without such an express declaration the states are annihilated in reality upon receiving this constitution—the forms will be preserved only during the pleasure of Congress.

The idea of consolidation is further kept up in the right given to regulate trade. Though this power under certain limitations would be a proper one for the department of Congress; it is in this system carried much too far, and much farther than is necessary. This is, without exception, the most commercial state upon the continent. Our extensive coasts, cold climate, small estates, and equality of rights, with a variety of subordinate and concurring circumstances, place us in this respect at the head of the union. We must, therefore, be indulged if a point which so nearly relates to our welfare be rigidly examined. The new constitution not only prohibits vessels, bound from one state to another, from paying any duties, but even from entering and clearing. The only use of such a regulation is, to keep each state in complete ignorance of its own resources. It certainly is no hardship to enter and clear at the custom-house, and the expense is too small to be an object. The unlimitted right to regulate trade, includes the right of granting exclusive charters. This, in all old countries, is considered as one principle branch of prerogative. We find hardly a country in Europe which has not felt the ill effects of such a power. Holland has carried the exercise of it farther than any other state; and the reason why that country has felt less evil from it is, that the territory is very small, and they have drawn large revenues from their colonies in the East and West Indies. In this respect, the whole country is to be considered as a trading company, having exclusive privileges. The colonies are large in proportion to the parent state; so that, upon the whole, the latter may gain by such a system. We are also to take into consideration the industry which the genius of a free government inspires. But in the British islands all these circumstances together have not prevented them from being injured by the monopolies created there. Individuals have been enriched, but the country at large has been hurt. Some valuable branches of trade being granted to companies, who transact their business in London, that city is, perhaps, the place of the greatest trade in the world. But Ireland, under such influence, suffers exceedingly, and is impoverished; and Scotland is a mere bye-word. Bristol, the second city in England, ranks not much above this town in population. These things must be accounted for by the incorporation of trading companies; and if they are felt so severely in countries of small extent, they will operate with ten-fold severity upon us, who inhabit an immense tract; and living towards one extreme of an extensive empire, shall feel the evil, without retaining that influence in government, which may enable us to procure redress. There ought, then, to have been inserted a restraining clause, which might prevent the Congress from making any such grant, because they consequentially defeat the trade of the out-ports, and are also injurious to the general commerce, by enhancing prices, and destroying that rivalship which is the great stimulous to industry.

## Alexander Hamilton
## *The Continentalist No. V*
## [Fishkill, New York, April 18, 1781]

The vesting Congress with the power of regulating trade ought to have been a principal object of the confederation for a variety of reasons. It is as necessary for the purposes of commerce as of revenue. There are some, who maintain, that trade will regulate itself, and is not to be benefitted by the encouragements, or restraints of government. Such persons will imagine, that there is no need of a common directing power. This is one of those wild speculative paradoxes, which have grown into credit among us, contrary to the uniform practice and sense of the most enlightened nations. Contradicted by the numerous institutions and laws, that exist every where for the benefit of trade, by the pains taken to cultivate particular branches and to discourage others, by the known advantages derived from those measures, and by the palpable evils that would attend their discontinuance—it must be rejected by every man acquainted with commercial history. Commerce, like other things, has its fixed principles, according to which it must be regulated; if these are understood and observed, it will be promoted by the attention of government, if unknown, or violated, it will be injured—but it is the same with every other part of administration.

To preserve the ballance of trade in favour of a nation ought to be a leading aim of its policy. The avarice of individuals may frequently find its account in pursuing channels of traffic prejudicial to that balance, to which the government may be able to oppose effectual impediments. There may, on the other hand, be a possibility of opening new sources which, though accompanied with great difficulties in the commencement, would in the event amply reward the trouble and expence of bringing them to perfection. The undertaking may often exceed the influence and capitals of individuals; and may require no small assistance, as well from the revenue, as from the authority of the state.

The contrary opinion, which has grown into a degree of vogue among us, has originated in the injudicious attempts made at different times to effect a REGULATION of PRICES. It became a cant phrase among the opposers of these attempts, that TRADE MUST REGULATE ITSELF; by which at first was only meant that it had its fundamental laws, agreeable to which its general operations must be directed; and that any violent attempts in opposition to these would commonly miscarry. In this sense the maxim was reasonable; but it has since been extended to militate against all interference by the sovereign; an extreme as little reconcileable with experience, or common sense, as the practice it was first framed to discredit.

The reasonings of a very ingenious and sensible writer[1], by being misapprehended, have contributed to this mistake. The scope of his argument is not, as by some supposed, that trade will hold a certain invariable course independent on the aid, protection, care or concern of government; but that it will, in the main, depend upon the comparative industry moral and physical advantages of nations; and that though, for a while, from extraordinary causes, there may be a wrong ballance against one of them, this will work its own cure, and things will ultimately return to their proper level. His object was to combat that excessive jealousy on this head, which has been productive of so many unnecessary wars, and with which the British nation is particularly interested; but it was no part of his design to insinuate that the regulating hand of government was either useless, or hurtful. The nature of a government, its spirit, maxims and laws, with respect to trade, are among those constant moral causes, which influence its general results, and when it has by accident taken a wrong direction, assist in bringing it back to its natural course. This is every where admitted by all writers upon the subject; nor is there one who has asserted a contrary doctrine.

1. Hume, *Of the Jealousy of Trade.*

Trade may be said to have taken its rise in England under the auspices of Elizabeth; and its rapid progress there is in a great measure to be ascribed to the fostering care of government in that and succeeding reigns.

From a different spirit in the government, with superior advantages, France was much later in commercial improvements, nor would her trade have been at this time in so prosperous a condition had it not been for the abilities and indefatigable endeavours of the great COLBERT. He laid the foundation of the French commerce, and taught the way to his successors to enlarge and improve it. The establishment of the woolen manufacture, in a kingdom, where nature seemed to have denied the means, is one among many proofs, how much may be effected in favour of commerce by the attention and patronage of a wise administration. The number of useful edicts passed by Louis XIV and since his time, in spite of frequent interruptions from the jealous enmity of Great Britain, has advanced that of France to a degree which has excited the envy and astonishment of its neighbours.

The Dutch who may justly be allowed a pre-eminence in the knowledge of trade, have ever made it an essential object of state. Their commercial regulations are more rigid and numerous, than those of any other country; and it is by a judicious and unremitted vigilance of government, that they have been able to extend their traffic to a degree so much beyond their natural and comparative advantages.

Perhaps it may be thought, that the power of regulation will be left placed in the governments of the several states, and that a general superintendence is unnecessary. If the states had distinct interests, were unconnected with each other, their own governments would then be the proper and could be the only depositaries of such a power; but as they are parts of a whole with a common interest in trade, as in other things, there ought to be a common direction in that as in all other matters. It is easy to conceive, that many cases may occur, in which it would be beneficial to all the states to encourage, or suppress a particular branch of trade, while it would be detrimental to either to attempt it without the concurrence of the rest, and where the experiment would probably be left untried for fear of a want of that concurrence.

No mode can be so convenient as a source of revenue to the United States. It is agreed that imposts on trade, when not immoderate, or improperly laid, are one of the most eligible species of taxation. They fall in a great measure upon articles not of absolute necessity, and being partly transferred to the price of the commodity, are so far imperceptibly paid by the consumer. It is therefore that mode which may be exercised by the federal government with least exception or disgust. Congress can easily possess all the information necessary to impose the duties with judgment, and the collection can without difficulty be made by their own officers.

They can have no temptation to abuse this power, because the motive of revenue will check its own extremes. Experience has shown that moderate duties are more productive than high ones. When they are low, a nation can trade abroad on better terms—its imports and exports will be larger—the duties will be regularly paid, and arising on a greater quantity of commodities, will yield more in the aggregate, than when they are so high as to operate either as a prohibition, or as an inducement to evade them by illicit practices.

It is difficult to assign any good reason why Congress should be more liable to abuse the powers with which they are intrusted than the state-assemblies. The frequency of the election of the members is a full security against a dangerous ambition, and the rotation established by the confederation makes it impossible for any state, by continuing the same men, who may put themselves at the head of a prevailing faction, to maintain for any length of time an undue influence in the national councils. It is to be presumed, that Congress will be in general better composed for abilities, and as well for integrity as any assembly on the continent.

But to take away any temptation from a cabal to load particular articles, which are the principal objects of commerce to particular states, with a too great proportion of duties, to ease the others in the general distributions of expence; let all the duties whether for regulation or revenue, raised in each state, be creditted to that state, and let it in like manner be charged for all the bounties paid within itself for the encouragement of agriculture, manufactures, or trade. This expedient will remove the temptation; for as the quotas of the respective states are to be determined by a standard of land, agreeable to the article of the confederation, each will have so much the less to contribute otherwise as it pays more on its commerce.

An objection has been made in a late instance to this principle. It has been urged, that as the consumer pays the duty, those states which are not equally well situated for foreign commerce, and which consume a great part of the imports of their neighbours, will become contributors to a party of their taxes. This objection is rather specious, than solid.

The maxim, that the consumer pays the duty has been admitted in theory with too little reserve; frequently contracted in practice. It is true, the merchant will be unwilling to let the duty be a deduction from his profits if the state of the market will permit him to incorporate it with the price of his commodity. But this is often not practicable. It turns upon the quantity of goods at market in proportion to the demand. When the latter exceeds the former, and the competition is among the buyers, the merchant can easily increase his price and make his customers pay the duty. When the reverse is the case, and the competition is among the sellers, he must then content himself with smaller profits, and lose the value of the duty or at least of a part of it. Where a nation has a flourishing and well settled trade this more commonly happens than may be imagined, and it will, many times, be found that the duty is divided between the merchant and the consumer.

Besides this consideration, which greatly diminishes the force of the objection, there is another which intirely destroys it. There is strong reciprocal influence between the prices of all commodities in a state, by which they, sooner or later, attain a pretty exact ballance and proportion to each other. If the immediate productions of the soil rise, the manufacturer will have more for his manufacture, the merchant for his goods; and the same will happen with whatever class the increase of price begins. If duties are laid upon the imports in one state, by which the prices of foreign articles are raised, the products of land and labour within that state will take a proportionable rise; and if a part of those articles are consumed in a neighbouring state, it will have the same influence there as at home. The importing state must allow an advanced price upon the commodities, which it receives in exchange from its neighbor in a ratio to the increased price of the article it sells. To know then which is the gainer or loser, we must examine how the general ballance of trade stands between them. If the importing state takes more of the commodities of its neighbour, than it gives in exchange, that will be the loser by the reciprocal augmentation of prices—it will be the gainer, if it takes less—and neither will gain, or lose, if the barter is carried on upon equal terms. The ballance of trade, and consequently the gain, or loss, in this respect will be governed more by the relative industry and frugality of the parties, than by their relative advantages for foreign commerce.

Between separate nations, this reasoning will not apply with full force, because a multitude of local and extraneous circumstances may counteract the principal; but from the intimate connections of these states, the similitude of governments, situations, customs, manners—political and commercial causes will have nearly the same operation in the intercourse between the states, as in that between the different parts of the same state. If this should be controverted, the objection drawn from the hypothesis of the consumer paying the duty must fall at the same time: For as far as this is true it is as much confined in its application to a state within itself, as the doctrine of a reciprocal proportion of prices.

General principles in subjects of this nature ought always to be advanced with caution; in an experimental analysis there are found such a number of exceptions as tend to render them very doubtful; and in questions which affect the existence and collective happiness of these states, all nice and abstract distinctions should give way to plainer interests and to more obvious and simple rules of conduct.

But the objection which has been urged ought to have no weight on another account. Which are the states, that have not sufficient advantages for foreign commerce, and that will not in time be their own carriers? Connecticut and Jersey are the least maritime of the whole; yet the sound which washes the coast of Connecticut has an easy outlet to the ocean, affords a number of harbours and bays, very commodious for trading vessels. New-London may be a receptacle for merchantmen of almost any burthen; and the fine rivers with which the state is intersected, by facilitating the transportation of commodities to and from every part, are extremely favorable both to its domestic and foreign trade. Jersey, by way of Amboy has a shorter communication with the ocean, than the city of New York. Princes bay, which may serve as an out port to it, will admit and shelter in winter and summer vessels of any size. Egg-harbour on its southern coast is not to be despised. The Delaware may be made as subservient to its commerce as to that of Pennsylvania, Gloucester, Burlington, and Trenton, being all conveniently situated on that river. The United Provinces with inferior advantages of position to either of these states, have for centuries held the first rank among commercial nations.

The want of large trading cities has been sometimes objected as an obstacle to the commerce of these states; but this is a temporary deficiency that will repair itself with the encrease of population and riches. The reason that the states in question have hitherto carried on little foreign trade, is that they have found it equally beneficial to purchase the commodities imported by their neighbours. If the imposts on trade should work an inconvenience to them, it will soon cease by making it their interest to trade abroad. It is too much characteristic of our national temper to be ingenious in finding out and magnifying the minutest disadvantages, and to reject measures of evident utility even of necessity to avoid trivial and sometimes imaginary evils. We seem not to reflect, that in human society, there is scarcely any plan, however salutary to the whole and to every part, by the share, each has in the common prosperity, but in one way, or another, and under particular circumstances, will operate more to the benefit of some parts, than of others. Unless we can overcome this narrow disposition and learn to estimate measures, by their general tendency, we shall never be a great or a happy people, if we remain a people at all.

## Thomas M. Cooley
## *Limits to State Control of Private Business*

It was a new departure in government when the people of the American States planted their institutions on fundamental principles which embodied a distrust of their own representatives. Distrust of irresponsible power may indeed be accepted as one of the conditions of liberty; and from the days of King John there had been no want of it among English speaking people. Representative institutions had grown out of it, and these had taken such root and expanded with such vigor that their branches at length overshadowed all else, and liberty was supposed to be secure in proportion as the representatives of the people were powerful. All this time, however, distrust had the crown for its object, not the legislature; and while it was not doubted that hasty or extravagant action on the part of the legislature was possible, the restraining influence of the two houses on each other, and the undefined checks which the kingly authority might in certain ways impose, were supposed to be ample to protect against serious evils. With the crown under due restraint, the people felt no alarm: it might be said that the sovereignty was still in them, and that the legislature held by delegation a trust only; but it was, nevertheless, a trust conferred in such boundless confidence, that the beneficiaries were content to retain, in respect to it, only such ultimate control as is implied in the right of revolution. The theoretical compact of government between the people on the one hand and their rulers on the other, though supposed to be conditioned on a just exercise of the powers conferred, was really one under which the only means of enforcing the condition must be such as an oppressed people might find in the implements of war. But what need of any condition whatever when those to be protected were the very persons delegating the trust, and who selected the recipients from their own number, limiting the delegation to a brief period, at the end of which time they were at liberty to recall and dismiss in disgrace the agent who proved unfaithful?

The American people, however, even for the brief period of a representative's term, conferred no unlimited authority. From the first, they separated the judicial from the law-making authority, and in creating a legislative department they made it the depository of a special trust, in the execution of which it was to act as a special agent only. In the new fabric of government, legislative omnipotence was no more allowed a place than was executive irresponsibility; and for the period, however brief, of representative authority, the delegated function must be exercised within limits previously defined, and subject to which the delegation had been made. If, therefore, in England, the representative for the time being might be said to hold a general letter of attorney, the American, on the other hand, held a special and limited authority: with the former, the act done would stand as its own justification; the latter, at the peril of having whatever he might do disregarded and annulled, must keep within the letter of his warrant.

It must be conceded, nevertheless, that in the original establishment of American constitutions no special distrust of legislative bodies was manifested. On the contrary, these bodies were from the first the chief depositaries of power, and the restraints imposed resulted as a consequence of a written charter of government and of the division of power under it, instead of having been an object in view in creating the government. Legislative powers were granted by the first American constitutions in very general terms, and the doctrine that the representative was subject to any other than a political responsibility, or that legislative acts might be questioned elsewhere, did not readily take root in American soil. It was the judges, not the legislature, who first became subject to popular mistrust, and those who first refused to obey an unconstitutional law were proceeded against as offenders. Disregard of legislative action seemed to popular apprehension an affront to the people, and was punished accordingly.

But the country was not slow to discover the need of some other check upon representatives than that which was afforded in frequent elections. The Yazoo grant of 1795, in Georgia, brought about by fraud and deception, was so enormous in magnitude and interested so many persons, that it attracted the attention of the whole country, and presented in clear light the possibility that fraud might infect the whole legislative body, and that corrupt inducements might incline the representative to connive at or assist in the robbery of his constituents. From that time to the present, the number of constitutional restrictions imposed for the express purpose of keeping the law-making department in close restraint within prescribed limits and under prescribed forms of action, have been steadily increasing in number, until in some States the presumption that the legislature possesses a general power to make laws in its discretion has almost passed away. The general power has now so many limitations, and must be exercised under such carefully prescribed conditions, that the experienced legislator is excusable if he sometimes stumbles into difficulties, and finds to his surprise that something in his legislation will not bear the test of all the rules that have been prescribed for his observance. To prove this, let the reader examine almost any of the new or recently revised constitutions. An inspection will show the following state of things: First, That a number of subjects are removed altogether from legislative cognizance. Second, That upon a still larger number of subjects the legislature is forbidden to act, except by general law. Third, That when acting upon any subject, certain set forms must be observed, which are imposed for the purpose of forcing upon the legislature a care, caution, and deliberation not otherwise likely to be secured. These forms are thus made a condition to valid legislation, and the necessity of observing them is imperative. The principal of these are, that each act shall embrace but a single object, which shall be expressed in its title; that the bill shall have several readings on different days, and shall be passed only on a recorded vote by yeas and nays. Peculiar provisions, are made in some States which are even more stringent.

It would, however, be a mistake to suppose that constitutional restraints have really narrowed the field actually occupied by legislation. On the contrary, excepting a few years immediately following the Peace of 1783, when the terrible oppression of public and private debt impelled to public disorder, and led to the legislative abuses usually accompanying the acts making paper a legal tender in the payment of debts, the early legislation was in general more careful, more circumspect, and less open to criticism as encroaching on private rights or sound principles, than much of that more recent. In late years the channel of legislation has been narrowed, but the stream has risen in proportion, and by far the larger part of all the doubtful legislation which the history of the country presents has taken place since the year 1846, when radical ideas began to be characteristic of State constitutions, and the theory that officers of every department should be made as directly as possible responsible to the people after short terms of service was accepted as a political maxim. The one may not be a consequence of the other, but the times have invited legislative experiments, and the invitation has been freely accepted.

Evidences of this may be found in abundance. The legislation in aid of private individuals and corporations would first attract attention, not only because of its magnitude, but because around it has clustered much that was questionable, and not a little that proved to be corrupt. The grants made for these purposes within the last thirty years have been of all sorts and under all pretences, and compared with some of them the Yazoo grant sinks into insignificance. They were made by the nation and by the States; and majorities of local communities were permitted to assume burdens, not for themselves merely, but also for the non-assenting minorities, to purchase stock in business enterprises. On all hands it will be conceded that the legislation pressed hard upon the implied limits of legislative power; but the reasons favoring it were always plausible, because the nominal purpose in view was always one in which the community was more or less concerned. This was particularly the case when the assistance was given to railroad enterprises; and it was often asserted by the projectors that railroads were public highways, and assistance was demanded on that ground. The evils that have resulted from such legislation, equally with the incidental benefits, are foreign to the present discussion, but the grants themselves and the ground on which they have been made may have some bearing. Questionable legislation can never stand by itself: if it is accepted, whatever is within the principle underlying it must be accepted also, and so must all that necessarily pertains and is incidental to it.

The present purpose is to inquire whether, in the matter of the regulation of property rights and of business, legislation has not of late been occupying doubtful, possibly unconstitutional grounds. The discussion in the main must be limited to fundamental principles, aided by such light as legal and constitutional history may throw upon them since the express provisions of the constitutions can give little assistance. They always contain the general guaranty of due process of law to life, liberty, and property, but in other particulars they for the most part leave protection to principles which have come from the common law. And what is due process of law can never be settled as an abstract question: it has a new phase with every new case, and judicial history shows that judges differ concerning it at the present day when peculiar cases arise, as radically as they did when ship-money was in question, and when the king's warrant was supposed by some to be sufficient justification for an arrest, though it specified no cause.

The general right of the state to prescribe rules for the regulation of property and business is so plain, that no one disputes it. The right is a necessary one in government: a man could securely have nothing and safely enjoy nothing if the limits of interference by others were not prescribed by law. The laws of property are in themselves regulations, and the rules which give remedies for the invasion of rights are what render civilization and orderly society possible. Bentham, in his Principles of the Civil Code, has expressed this with great force and clearness. "Law," he says,

> has accomplished what all the natural feelings were not able to do; law alone has been able to create a fixed and durable possession which deserves the name of property. The law alone could accustom men to submit to the yoke of foresight, at first painful to be home, but afterwards agreeable and mild; it alone could encourage them in labor, superfluous at present, and which they are not to enjoy till the future. Economy has as many enemies as there are spendthrifts, or men who would enjoy without taking the trouble to produce. Labor is too painful for idleness, it is too slow for impatience, cunning and injustice underhandedly conspire to appropriate its fruits; insolence and audacity plot to seize them by open force. Hence security, always tottering, always threatened, never at rest, lives in the midst of snares. It requires in the legislator vigilance continually sustained and power always in action to defend it against his constantly reviving crowd of adversaries. The law does not say to a man, "Work, and I will reward you," but it says to him, "Work, and by stopping the hand that would take them from you, I will insure you the fruits of your labor, its natural and sufficient reward, which without me you could not preserve." If industry creates, it is the law which preserves; if at the first moment we owe every thing to labor, at the second and every succeeding moment we owe every thing to the law.

This is a strong statement, but it is literally true and exact. Every man's rights are necessarily relative, and they are measured by means of the limits which are set to the rights of others. It is vain to say, except in the most general and popular sense, that every man has supreme dominion within the boundaries of his own freehold; for his lands are not only charged with servitudes for the benefit of his neighbor, but his management of his lands is restrained in various ways by rules prescribed for the benefit of others. Whatever he does upon his premises that would be offensive to his neighbor, and that the laws of good neighborhood would not sanction or excuse, may render him liable to prosecution for creating a nuisance. His lawful calling he is entitled to pursue at discretion, but if the calling he has chosen be one whose tendency is to disturb the peace or destroy the comfort of the immediate neighborhood, he might be driven from any thickly settled district as a malefactor if he should attempt to establish it there; and the importance and usefulness of his trade would not protect him. The state leaves the rites of sepulture and the manner of disposing of the bodies of the dead to the affections and the sense of propriety and decency of surviving friends, but, not wholly without supervision; for if these were to import into any Christian state the custom of some savage tribes of exposing their dead on scaffolds to foul birds of prey, the law would assuredly visit them with condemnation and punishment. Indeed, every item of individual property, real or personal, every kind of business, every movement of the living person where he may come in contact with others, the conduct of the living and the disposal of the dead, are all brought within the control of regulations established by the state, or by customs which the state adopts, and which thus become its regulations. Men cannot escape from these if they would, and they would fall back into a state of savagery if they could and did.

But while this is asserted in very positive terms, it is affirmed with equal positiveness that there ought to be and are some limits to the right to establish such regulations. An unlimited power in the state to control and regulate private property and private business would make freedom and content as precarious as would an unlimited power in every individual to interfere at will in the concerns of his neighbor. The latter would arm every man against his neighbor; the former would be liable at any time to direct with crushing force the power of the state against any interest which for the time had the popular feeling arrayed against it. To-day the unpopular interest may be the professional or mercantile class, to-morrow it may be corporations, and the day following the laborers upon railroads or in mines. Security can only be found in general principles, the same general principle that will protect one must protect all. If any general principle can be put aside in order that the state may reach one interest, it may also be put aside when any other interest seeks its protection. Constitutional law can know no favoritism; if principles are not fixed and permanent they are not constitutional, and may be suspended or overridden to suit the passion or caprice of the moment. And as security and content can only repose in settled principles, the question of the relative advantage of republican and autocratic institutions will be very much narrowed if it be conceded that the state may exercise in respect to private property and private business the powers an autocrat assumes. Indeed, it may almost be said to be narrowed to this: Whether many persons, having the powers of sovereignty intrusted to them for exercise, would probably exercise them with more wisdom, discretion, impartiality, and justice than would a single person with similar powers. Upon such a question the most ardent republican might well hesitate before expressing a definite opinion; for the advantages of government are not to be found in its forms exclusively: they must be perceived also in its results.

That there are some limits to state interference will probably be denied by no one. Those who go farthest in the direction of what is sometimes called paternal government by state or nation would claim some exemptions on their own behalf, and would be compelled to concede some to others. What the limits are and how they are to be found, is the question. Where they are not prescribed by the constitution of a state, probably it will be said they must be sought in the common law and in the constitutional history of the people. This is the common and necessary resort when questions arise concerning the proper functions of government....

It has also been thought that the limits of state authority in restricting the profits of business may be determined by a solution of the question whether the property by means of which the business is carried on is "affected with a public interest," whereby it ceases to be *juris privati*, and is brought, like all public interests, within the special supervision and control of the state. But in the attempt to ascertain what it is that affects private property with a public interest one seems to be feeling his way in the darkness, and at the best is compelled to accept and be satisfied with such uncertain light as the instances of state interference can afford. Certain occupations are named which from time immemorial have been subjected to exceptional legislative regulations, and it is assumed that the property employed in these is affected with a public interest, and that in this fact is found the justification for the control exercised. Starting with these as unquestioned and unquestionable cases, the conclusion is drawn that the same authority must exist in certain other cases which are so far analogous as not to be distinguishable in principle.

The phrase "affected with a public interest" is important in this discussion, and as it comes from the treatise "De Portibus Maris" of Lord Hale, it is needful to know in what sense he employed it. The important passage from that treatise is the following:

> A man, for his own private advantage, may, in a port or town, set up a wharf or crane, and may take what rates he and his customers can agree for cranage, wharfage, housellage, pesage; for he doth no more than is lawful for any man to do, viz., makes the most of his own. If the king or subject have a public wharf, unto which all persons that come to that port must come and unlade or lade their goods as for the purpose, because they are the wharfs only licensed by the queen—or because there is no other wharf in that port, as it may fall out where a port is newly erected; in that case there cannot be taken arbitrary and excessive duties for cranage, wharfage, pesage, etc., neither can they be enhanced to an immoderate rate; but the duties must be reasonable and moderate, though settled by the king's license or charter. For now the wharf and crane and other conveniences are affected with a public interest, and they cease to be *juris privati* only; as if a man set out a street in new building on his own land, it is now no longer bare private interest, but is affected by a public interest.

To appreciate the exact force of this language, it is necessary to understand that the erection of a wharf on navigable water in Great Britain was never a matter of right, but always of privilege. In the first place, the ports were creatures of the prerogative; no man at will could run his vessel into a haven and land his goods where he pleased, but the haven must first be made a port, and officers of the customs assigned to it. In the second place, the title to the soil of all tide waters below high-water mark pertained to the crown, and any wharf erected there without lawful permission was a purpresture, and liable to be removed as such. A wharf must therefore be specially and expressly licensed; and if not licensed expressly, it was only in existence by the tolerance of the crown, and on or adjacent to land belonging to the crown, and without the use of which the property could not be made available. Whether, therefore, the wharf was licensed and thereby given special and exclusive privileges, or had been set up without license, Lord Hale had for his assertion that it was affected with a public interest this justification—that it was erected by express or implied public permission, on or in connection with public property, and for the accommodation of the public by means of a private business. This is all that can be claimed from this passage from Lord Hale; and it seems quite reasonable for him to declare that one who under such circumstances had a monopoly of the business might justly be compelled to deal with the public on reasonable terms....

The rule may be said to be general, that whenever a special privilege is conceded to private parties, the enjoyment of which requires an exceptional use by them, or in connection with their business, of the public highways, either by water or by land, and the privilege is conferred for some accommodation they are to supply to the public, the property in their business is affected to some extent at least, with a public interest. This rule will embrace several of the cases in which legislative regulations and restrictions are customarily made. The case is all the stronger where the privilege conferred is in the nature of a monopoly. That was the fact in the warehouse case of Allnutt *vs.* Inglis decided by the Court of King's Bench in 1810. The warehousemen whose rights were then in question were permitted to receive wines directly from the importing vessels, before the duties were paid; it was an exclusive and valuable privilege, and was given and received in view of common-law rules, which would obligate them to receive the wines for a reasonable compensation. They undertook to appropriate the privilege, and to repudiate any corresponding obligation; in other words, which taking the benefit of the privilege, they practically asserted the prerogative of compelling the public to submit to any charges they might see fit to impose: a monstrous proposition, in view of the fact that the public had no privilege of dealing with others. The controversy is thus stated by Lord Ellenborough:

> The question on this record is whether the London Dock Company have a right to insist upon receiving wines into their warehouses for a hire and reward arbitrary and at their will and pleasure, or whether they were bound to receive them there for a reasonable reward only. There is no doubt that the general principle is favored both, in law and justice, that every man may fix what price he pleases upon his own

> property or the use of it; but if, for a particular purpose, the public have a right to resort to his premises and make use of them, and he have a monopoly in them for that purpose, if he will take the benefit of that monopoly, he must, as an equivalent, perform the duty attached to it on reasonable terms.

Such a case seems to require no comment: the conclusion of the court is so reasonable and just, that the only wonder is that the doctrine which Lord Ellenborough put aside as untenable could ever have been advanced.

There may also be rejected, as not requiring special discussion or consideration, the case of every employment, the following of which is not of right, but of favor. The case of an auctioneer may be instanced: he performs a public function, and is only allowed to take it upon himself by license. Wherever the business is a privilege, and the taking out of a license is required, the state may impose conditions upon the privilege. The case of hackney-coachmen and draymen may be classed in the same category: their avocations have always been licensed and restrained; and one of the most usual and perhaps most necessary restraints is that which is imposed in respect to their charges. Moreover, these persons are allowed to establish a business in the public highways; they stand there with their conveyances, occupying the streets to the inconvenience, more or less, of the general public, and in ways that would not be permitted but for the special conveniences they afford. Their privileges give them special opportunities for extortion and for practising frauds upon strangers, and the police supervision is required to be exceptionally active and strict. It is not of right that they shall have the privileges which are conceded to them: they might be required to stand for business on private grounds instead of in the streets, just as the merchant awaits his customers at his store, and the mechanic at his shop. The exceptional use which by law or by custom they are permitted to make of the public streets for the conveniences they afford is quite sufficient to affect their vehicles with a public interest; and they can reasonably no more contest the conditions than could a huckster who should be allowed on special terms to set up a booth on the public market-ground. Moreover, it may be said of this case as of usury, that the regulations are from time immemorial.

Whether the regulation of the business of carriers of persons and goods may extend to the fixing of prices, is a question which has received no little attention, and been the subject of much earnest controversy for the last three or four years. The right in the state to make exceptional regulations of some sort for the case of common earners is not disputed; the common law itself made some, the most important of which was the requirement that persons in this business should receive and carry, for all who offered, with impartiality. The Congressional Civil Rights Act of 1875 has supplemented this by a provision forbidding discriminations in the carriage of persons, based on race, color, or previous condition; and many of the States have regulations to further secure impartiality in the dealings of these persons with the public. But a regulation to secure impartiality is so different in principle from one limiting prices, that the power to establish the one affords no presumption in favor of the authority to do the other.

The first is only in furtherance of, and supplementary to, the common-law requirement of fairness; but the common law is put aside and reversed when the statute undertakes to prescribe what a man shall charge for his services.

When carriers are corporations, so much depends upon their contract with the state that their cases are very apt to be exceptional. It has been decided by a great weight of authority, that where a railway charter reserves to the state an unlimited right of amendment, this right may be exercised in restricting charges for transportation. In the able opinion of the Chief Justice of Wisconsin to that effect, it is intimated that, independent of this reserved power of amendment, the same thing might be done under the power of police. The idea underlying such a suggestion may perhaps be formulated as follows: 1. Railways, by general concession, are such public conveniences that the sovereign power of eminent domain is allowed to be exercised in their favor in the appropriation of lands of non-assenting parties. 2. It has been claimed, and generally conceded, that the public have such a general interest in railways, that taxes may be levied and paid over to the projectors to aid them in constructing and equipping their road. 3. The argument will then be made that if the state may bring its sovereign power to their assistance, because of the public benefits they are expected to confer, and if it may and does invest its own money in their property, they must, by accepting such assistance, be held estopped to dispute the claim of the state that their property is affected with a public interest. The subject is one having many sides, and so important that any court called upon to consider it would not venture to express any but the most mature and carefully considered opinion. The discussions hitherto have elicited nothing very conclusive or authoritative on the main question.

The case of innkeepers is sometimes said to be one in which the right of the state to limit charges is indisputable; but if an attempt should be made to exercise it, it would probably be contested with vigor. Like common carriers, innkeepers are subject to special regulations at the common law, and the Civil Rights Act also includes them among the persons who are forbidden to discriminate because of race, color, or previous condition. But these regulations, as in the case of carriers, are in the interest of impartiality, and they are not supposed to be burdensome to the business in any sense. Possibly the notions on this subject may have come from the fact that places of entertainment for travellers have generally been places for the sale of intoxicating drinks, and such places are usually required to be licensed, and the number is purposely or indirectly limited. Sufficient reason for this is found in the fact that the business brings many evils upon society, and is so likely to breed disorders and tumult, that exceptional police supervision is imperative. It is, at best, only a tolerated business, and is always subjected to special restraint when not altogether prohibited. But the business of entertaining travellers has no necessary connection with this; and it is not only a commendable and useful, but it is also a necessary business.

It is safe to classify, in the following manner, the cases in which usage will warrant one in saying that private property, invested and managed for the benefit of the owners, is affected with a public interest.

1. Where the business is one the following of which is not matter of right, but is permitted by the state as a privilege or franchise. Under this head would be ranged the business of setting up lotteries; of giving shows, etc.; of keeping billiard tables for hire; and of selling intoxicating drinks, when the sale, by unlicensed parties, is forbidden. Also, the case of tollbridges, etc.

2. When the state on public grounds, renders to the business special assistance by taxation or otherwise.

3. When, for the accommodation of the business, some special use is allowed to be made of public property or of a public easement.

4. Where exclusive privileges are granted in consideration of some special return to be made to the public.

In each of these cases the public interest is manifest. If there are any not coming under these heads, the interest ought to be equally capable of being pointed out.

Passing now to the nature of the control the state may exercise in the regulation of business within the limits of its authority, the following may be suggested as fundamental rules:

1. The state should restrain and seek to prevent whatever would impede its people in making free disposal of their wares or their services on the best terms a free market may offer.

2. The state should abstain on its own part from interposing impediments to its people reaping the advantages of competition in all lawful employments.

As to these rules, there ought to be and probably will be no disagreement. Indeed, those who have gone farthest in demanding state intervention to limit the profits of business have justified the demand on the ground that the business they desired to have regulated and restrained was a virtual monopoly, so that the regulation was needed to give competition, not to prevent it. In the Warehouse Cases already referred to, this was said; and it was strongly urged that unless the charges of Chicago warehousemen were limited to a maximum, the public had no protection against the extortions of a monopoly.

The word monopoly has an ominous sound to American ears, and whenever the appellation fairly attaches itself to any thing, it is already condemned in the public mind. Monopolies are heard of with great frequency in English history, and at some periods they have played a very important part in public affairs. It must be conceded, however, that those against which the complaints have been loudest were monopolies the government itself had set up; not monopolies of individual establishment, which the government was called upon to curb or to destroy. An instance may be taken of a monopoly in alum, granted by King Henry VI. The king had received a quantity of that article for £4,000, which he sold for £8,000, granting in the sale an exclusive privilege to the vendees of dealing in alum within the realm for a term of years. King Henry VII created a similar monopoly in this same article, by conferring upon a Tuscan merchant the privilege of importing a certain quantity, and prohibiting the importation by anyone else until he had sold this off. To grant such a monopoly was a favorite resort of the crown when money was needed for personal uses, and as a consideration of some sort was generally received for it, this was equivalent to levying a tax and farming out the collection of it to parties who had paid in advance. But monopolies were not always granted for money. In 1245, Henry III, to spite the London traders, ordered all shops in London to be closed for fifteen days for the benefit of fairs proclaimed by him at Westminster. Similar orders were repeatedly issued afterwards, but it is some satisfaction to be informed by the chronicles that the monopolists profited little, for the rains of heaven sometimes destroyed goods of greater value than all the profits. Queen Elizabeth dealt largely in monopolies, and Sir Walter Raleigh, over whose sad fate men sometimes mourn, did not scruple to find his profit in them. In the great debate upon them in 1601, Sir Robert Wroth said there were then in being patents of monopoly for "currants, iron, powder, cards, ox shinbones, train oyl, transportation of leather, lists of cloth, ashes, anis seed, vinegar, seacoals, steel, aqua vitae, brushes, pots, saltpeter, lead, accidences, oyl, calamin stone, oyl of blubber, fumachoes or dried pitchers in the smoak, and divers others." "Upon reciting the patents aforesaid, Mr. Hakewell stood up and asked thus: Is not bread there? Bread, quoth one; bread, quoth another; this voice seems strange, quoth another; this voice seems strange, quoth a third. No, quoth Mr. Hakewell, but if order be not taken for these, bread will be there before the next Parliament." And the queen was pleased to take order concerning these, and to repeal them, protesting that "never did I put my pen to any grant but that upon pretence and semblance made unto me that it was both good and beneficial to the subjects in general, though a private profit to some of my ancient servants who had deserved well; but the contrary being found by experience, I am exceeding beholding to such subjects as would move the same at first." The evil, however, did not stop here, even for this reign; but it rose to enormous magnitude under the first Stuart, and prior to 1623 nearly all the foreign trade of the kingdom was in the hands of a few people in London, who, under their royal grants, were enabled to fix the prices both of imports and exports. In that year the king was forced by the Commons to give his assent to a law which declared monopolies by royal grant illegal, and the most of those in existence were repealed. Of those which escaped repeal was that to the East India Company, which grew to such proportions afterwards. Charles I revived monopolies, and in 1640, in debate in Parliament, Sir John Colepeper said of them:

> I have but one grievance more to offer unto you; but this one compriseth many; it is a nest of wasps, a swarm of vermine, which have overcrept the land; I mean the monopolers and polers of the people: these, like the frogs of Egypt, have got possession of our dwellings, and, we have scarce a room free from them: they sip in our cup, they dip in our dish, they sit by our fire; we find them in the dye-vat, washbowl, and powdering tub; they share with the butler in his box, they have marked and sealed us from head to foot. Mr. Speaker, they will not bate us a pin: we may

> not buy our own cloathes without their brokage. These are the leaches that have sucked the commonwealth so hard that it has almost become hectical. And, Mr. Speaker, some of these are ashamed of their right names; they have a vizard to hide the brand made by that good law in the last Parliament of King James; they shelter themselves under the name of a corporation; they make byelaws which serve their turns to squeeze us and fill their purses; unface these, and they will prove as bad cards as any in the pack.

The House not only resolved against monopolies, but it resolved that no monopolist or patentee should be allowed to sit in that House; and several were turned out under this vote, Charles I even assumed to himself the prerogative of limiting the growth of the city of London, and levied fees for the privilege of building houses in extension of its limits. His assumptions were of course illegal; indeed, monopolies by royal grant to the prejudice of trade had been judicially declared void in 1602, and in their most odious forms they disappeared when Charles I lost his head. Meantime America was only suffered to be colonized under the permission of trading monopolies.

It was certainly not this kind of monopoly that was brought under condemnation in the Warehouse Cases, for no giant of special privilege had been given, nor, under the constitution of Illinois, could any have been given. There is another sort known to the English law which has been more or less obnoxious namely, the monopoly of provisions, effected usually by combination, wit a view unnaturally to raise prices. This was a common-law offence, but with several kindred common-law offences has been abolished in England. It is possible that it may in early times, when the means of transportation were imperfect, have been a serious evil, but it is inconceivable that it can be so now, except where it is accomplished through means which are no part of any regular business. If means are employed which public policy cannot sanction, it is competent and proper for the state to interfere.

A monopoly, where the term is employed with the care and accuracy proper in judicial decisions and legal proceedings, must be understood as some exclusive power to dispose of something of value, either generally, or for some definite time, or within certain limits. The method in which it may be secured has nothing to do with its exclusive character, and it is equally a monopoly whether obtained by sovereign grant or secured by individual management. If the exclusive right to dispose of their services in any given capacity at an important business centre were secured in any way by a few persons, those persons would have a monopoly, whether the right were obtained by sovereign grant, by combination, or by employing violence and terror to drive away all who might be competitors. The sovereign grant of monopolies in trade was declared unlawful in England, on the ground that "the sole trade of any mechanical artifice, or any other monopoly, is not only a damage and prejudice to those who exercise the same trade, but also to all other subjects, for the end of all these monopolies is for the private gain of the patentees." There may doubtless be exclusive privileges that would not be subject to this condemnation, but they must clearly be in cases not coming within the reasons assigned. An author or inventor is given for a certain term an exclusive right in that which his talent or ingenuity has produced; but the right here is in something which he himself has created, and which ought to be his property, as much as the wheat he has grown, or the cattle he has raised or bought. Exclusive franchises are sometimes given where in no other way can some public interest be accomplished; but the reasons ought to be of the most conclusive nature, and the state grant ought to be construed with the utmost strictness. To whatever extent special privileges are conferred upon one, he is favored, and equality of right under the government is disturbed. Nevertheless special privileges are sometimes defensible, and sometimes a grant of them may be supported on grounds of necessity.

If the mere fact that a business has or may become a monopoly can give to the legislature an authority to interfere and restrain it, it must be because a monopoly is in itself so manifestly and necessarily opposed to public policy as to be wholly inadmissible. But when any thing is wholly inadmissible, the legislature itself must be without the power to create it. A thing cannot be wrong when growing up independently, and right when set up under a special statute. Therefore, if by enterprise or management a virtual monopoly is created at any point, it must be subject to no more and no other condemnation than would be a monopoly of precisely the same sort expressly created. But in this country men are precluded from claiming that monopolies of legislative creation are subject to special restraints because of their exclusive features. A short provision inserted in the Federal Constitution to prevent the general repudiation of debts has been found to embrace within its protection the grants of exclusive privileges made by the state. Whatever grant, therefore, is made by the state is protected, if the grant was within the legislative competence. Queen Elizabeth might recall the vicious monopolies she had granted, and Parliament might at any time repeal them or bring them under control, but no future Coke in this country can wage the same exterminating war upon them which was waged by the great Chief-Justice in England. It would not be enough for him to show that the object of his attack was a monopoly; he must go farther and show some additional vice, or the legislative grant would be shielded from his attack behind the aegis of the Federal Constitution. Prima facie all legislative grants are made for conclusive reasons; and with the utmost propriety it is always assumed that all laws, whether public or private, have been adopted from honest motives and on sufficient grounds. Therefore, though the benefits may apparently all be of individual and personal nature, the law implies and the judiciary and the executive must hold that public considerations governed the legislative action. In general, however obnoxious the special privilege may seem to be, objectors will be required to show how and in what language it is forbidden in the State Constitution before they can effectually assail it. A few illustrations will give some idea of the extent of State power in the grant of monopolies. Some of the early railroad charters were exclusive, and gave a complete monopoly within certain prescribed limits; and it is notorious that those in New Jersey have caused the country much annoyance. In two or more of the States there have been grants of the exclusive right to navigate public waters, and these have been sustained where they did not come in conflict with the regulations of commerce established by Congress. The Binghamton Bridge case is worthy of special mention. The Legislature of New York at an early day created an incorporation to construct a toll-bridge across the Chenango River, and in the opinion of the Federal Supreme Court the terms of the grant, though not very clear and explicit, were such as to give an exclusive privilege to maintain a bridge across the river for a length of four miles. The growth of towns along this part of the river in time made other bridges essential, and the legislature created another corporation, which it undertook to authorize to build a second bridge within the same limits. The new grant was held to be a violation of the Constitution of the United States, and therefore void. It was in vain that Mr. Justice Grier expressed the opinion that "the power of one legislature to bind themselves and their posterity, and all future legislatures, from authorizing a bridge absolutely required for public use, might well be denied by the courts of New York;" the Court did not concur in this view, and considered themselves bound by the precedents to the contrary. The New Orleans Slaughter House Case deserves at least a passing mention. In the troublous days immediately following the war, when the passions of the people were so inflamed on questions growing out of the civil conflict as to preclude any careful supervision of legislation by the general public, the Legislature of Louisiana granted to a corporate body the exclusive privilege for twenty-five years of slaughtering cattle in New Orleans and its immediate vicinity, limiting their charges it is true, but making them sufficiently liberal. This grant the courts have felt compelled to sustain. If the legislature could lawfully create this monopoly, why not create a similar monopoly of warehousing? And if they did create one, what should prevent their fixing the rates as high as they have ever been fixed by individual warehousemen? It is notorious that the tolls taken on numerous bridges through the country are such as could not be sustained for a day if the legislative protection were taken away, and the tolls were left to competition. A single other illustration of exclusive grants will suffice. In Alabama and Missouri the grant of a lottery franchise has been held irrevocable. It would seem that all the way between the building of railways and the setting up of lotteries there must be room for monopolies almost as numerous as those in England, the schedule of which was given by Sir Robert Wroth. Whatever exist will generally be found now, as in King James's time, "to shelter themselves under the name of a corporation."

But the following question is worthy of serious consideration by legislators: If the state in respect to any particular occupation may prescribe prices, may it not also, on the same reasons and in the same occupation, set up a monopoly? The question is of vital interest, and its consideration requires an examination of the grounds on which exclusive privileges in the nature of monopolies are supposed to be granted. The following may be suggested:

1. The grant of an exclusive privilege may seem to be necessary to the accomplishment of some important public object which, with the privilege, private parties would

undertake to accomplish, when without it they would not. The familiar instance is that of a bridge across a river where a highway for teams, etc., is greatly needed. Such a bridge constructed with the privilege in the proprietors to take toll might perhaps be expected to be unprofitable for a considerable period. The state at the time might be unwilling or unable to construct it, but perfectly willing to clothe individuals with the proper franchise for the purpose. These might be quite ready to accept the franchise if they could be protected against ruinous competition by the privilege being made exclusive, when otherwise they would refuse it. Under such circumstances, making the franchise exclusive may seem to the legislature the only condition upon which the needed public convenience may be obtained, and public considerations may apparently preponderate in favor of conceding it.

2. An exclusive privilege may be granted for a consideration received or to be received by the state, and which by adding to the resources of the state would diminish taxation, and thus compensate for any incidental inconvenience or loss felt or suffered by the people in consequence of the grant. Thus a railroad company having a charter with exclusive features may accept it on condition of paying a certain proportion of its earnings to the state; another corporation may pay a certain bonus for its charter; a third may consent to pay an annual license fee in addition to the regular taxes; and so on. Many grants have been made on this principle, and in some cases the profit to the state has been large.

3. An exclusive privilege may be granted as a measure of regulation. Thus, in the case of some particular business it may be thought that it is so susceptible of abuses, so liable to be engaged in for the purposes of fraud or extortion, and furnishes such facilities for the one or the other, that the good of the community requires it to be either prohibited altogether or put in the hands of one or of a few persons, who shall first take out a state license under stringent conditions, and afterwards be subjected to a supervision which could not be extended if the business were open to every one. Taking the case of lotteries for an illustration, it might well be said, if lotteries are to be allowed at all, the opportunities they furnish for fraud are so great and so numerous, that the interest of the community would be better subserved by allowing a few persons only, of good reputation, to set up a lottery once a year, paying a reasonable license fee for the privilege, than to allow any man or combination of men to set up one at discretion. So in the case of slaughtering cattle for the markets of a large city, it might be said that if any considerable number of persons made this a business it might prove difficult if not impossible to prevent many nuisances, and since each person must have a separate place of business, there could be no such economy of labor and expense as might be possible with a concentration of the business in one or in a few establishments. Therefore it might be urged that to give an exclusive privilege to a single company or corporation, with a reasonable limitation of the charges which might be made to the dealers in meats, would on the one hand be a matter of general economy and public utility in that it would tend to reduce the cost of one of the necessaries of life, and on the other would assist in the preservation of the public health.

These, apparently, are two principal grounds which must be advanced in support of the grant of an exclusive privilege when the purpose is one of regulation merely: to obtain more perfect and effectual police supervision and protection against disorders and nuisances, and to effect a general saving to the people in some matter of general or customary expense. The first ought generally to be subordinate, if the business regulated is a necessary and useful business. The police power of the state is so pervading and ample, and it is so plainly the duty of the state to exercise it in such a manner as to protect every man in following any lawful calling he may select, so long as he violates no public law and no rights of others, that for the state to give monopolies as a substitute for such protection, would be to make its own delinquency an excuse for invidious distinctions.

Can, then, a monopoly be granted where the sole or chief purpose is to effect a saving in the cost to the people of something which is an article of public and general need? For the moment putting aside the consideration of the cases in which any exclusive privileges would be inadmissible, and conceding the right in some cases, let the grounds which must support them be examined. If a saving of individual expense can be a sufficient ground, it must be because the state has devolved upon it a duty to so shape its legislation as to effect such a saving, and the special privilege is a suitable means to the end. This brings us at once upon the ground which must be occupied by the legislature in limiting prices of wares or the charges for services: the reduction is the principal thing, and the legislature in accomplishing this will judge of the available and suitable means, and selecting these will employ them. In one case a direct act of legislation restricting charges might seem the most suitable and effectual, as it would certainly aim most directly at the end sought. In another case the more practical mode might seem to be to authorize a monopoly. One city might perhaps grant an exclusive privilege in slaughtering cattle; another, to accomplish the same end, might fix maximum prices by the carcass or the pound of the cattle slaughtered. Each would justify the regulation on the same ground.

It would seem, therefore, that those who claim a right in the state to control prices in certain cases should concede the power to create monopolies in the same cases, and whoever denies the one may deny the other. And if this be so, the question of the rightfulness of special privileges may perhaps be found so intimately connected with the question of state interference to regulate prices as to be incapable of separation.

Of the cases in which the legislature has sometimes granted special and exclusive privileges the following remarks may be made:

1. The right to grant these in certain cases not very distinctly classified by any authority is generally conceded. They are always supposed to be granted on public grounds and justifiable occasions, and as it is proper to grant them, so also it is proper to receive them, and the grantees could not, because of their exclusive nature, be subject to reproach or to invidious regulations.

2. Where the grant is to take up some employment which is not of general right, or to exercise some franchise, the authority in the state to make it exclusive cannot be

disputed. The state grants the right or the franchise to one man or body of men, and refuses to grant it to others; it stops with the one grant, as it may lawfully do. This remark assumes that the state constitution contains no express prohibition of exclusive privileges, as some of them do, and that the legislature is left unhampered in that regard.

3. The authority of the state to grant exclusive privileges in the ordinary occupations of life it must be quite safe to deny. If such an authority existed, there would be such a legislative supremacy over the business of the people as could at any time be employed to the destruction of any particular interest; and this would be inconsistent with regulated liberty. As has already been stated, exclusive privileges of this sort were judicially declared unlawful and void in the time of Elizabeth, and have been so held and understood ever since. The cases in which exclusive privileges may be granted would therefore seem to be those which, on grounds already stated, are affected with a public interest.

Some remarks regarding licenses and license fees seem to be called for in this connection. An idea seems to prevail in some quarters that to require persons following any particular occupation to take out a license is all that is essential to subject them to special regulations. This idea has no foundation. Taxes, in the form of license fees, may undoubtedly be imposed on all occupations, but a free state has no power to compel the taking out of a license as a condition precedent to the following of the ordinary pursuits of life. No despot ever claimed or exercised such a power, and no people not absolute slaves would tolerate its exercise for a single day. It will be remembered that the statutes enacted in the Southern States in 1865–6, which required freedmen to take out licenses for ordinary occupations, and to pay license fees therefor, were set aside, as establishing regulations which in effect compelled this class to submit to involuntary servitude.

Licenses may doubtless be required to be taken out by those employed in occupations the following of which is not a matter of right, and those which are "affected with a public interest" under the principles hereinbefore stated. But in the case of the ordinary and necessary avocations of the day, a license can cut no figure, and to require one to be taken, unless for the purpose of taxation, would be wholly inadmissible. It may be assumed that this statement requires no proof. To suggest the requirement that the farmer or the mechanic shall take out a license, unless for taxation, is sufficient to put before the mind the absurdity of any pretence of such authority.

Of monopolies not created by the legislature, the following may possibly exist:

1. One secured by threats or violence or other unlawful means. Temporary control of the labor market is sometimes secured in this way; but this is of course illegal, and may be dealt with by the law. The temporary monopoly of the grain market of a particular town, accomplished as a means in gambling operations, may perhaps be classed under this head, inasmuch as it would be competent to make the means illegal by statute, if they are not so at the common law.

2. The monopoly which circumstances give to one by reason of the exceptional location and special advantages of his business, or by reason of his having lawfully acquired an exclusive ownership in something for which there is a public demand. In this, of course, there is nothing wrongful, nothing illegal. Does, then, the mere fact that one owns the whole supply of any thing, whether it be of a certain kind of property or of a certain kind of services, confer upon the state the authority to interfere and limit the price he may set upon his wares or his services? To illustrate with a strong instance: Suppose in some state a single individual should own the only mine in the country of some metal important for use in the mechanical arts; would it be competent for the state, on the ground that competition with him was impossible, to restrict at discretion the price he should be allowed to charge for it? These questions, it will be perceived, present no problem concerning the authority of the state to appropriate exclusive rights, however acquired, under the eminent domain; they raise only the question of the right to limit the prices which individuals may charge for that which is conceded to be their own. Whoever shall undertake to answer these questions in the affirmative should be expected to show how the power may be harmonized with the general principles of free government.

3. The monopolies effected by combination of all who have the required wares or services for sale is of still a different nature. These exist in every part of the country, and it is generally assumed that the state is powerless to interfere and break them up when they limit their action to fixing prices by peaceable means, and when the business is not one over which the state may exercise exceptional power. Whatever may be thought of the wisdom or usefulness of trades-unions, the state, so long as they undertake only to regulate their own charges, is expected to abstain from interference. Letting others alone, these unions must be let alone by others. The state cannot say that their members shall take less than they will voluntarily consent to take; neither, on the other hand, can it compel others to pay more than they will voluntarily consent to pay. And the principle which must apply to them is general.

4. The case of "virtual" monopolies effected by superior industry, enterprise, skill, and thrift, it would seem, might be passed over in silence. When the person who by such means has secured special advantages has done so without the aid of any peculiar privileges, and with every other person at liberty under the law to compete with him, it is a misuse of terms to call his advantages a monopoly. Moreover, such a person is under the condemnation neither of the law nor of public sentiment. The qualities he has displayed in achieving his success are likely to bring him applause rather than censure, and he could not be put under restraint because of them, except upon grounds which would authorize the industrious, the enterprising, and the successful to be held in check whenever it was discovered that they were outstripping their fellows.

It seems plain, then, that there are limits which the state cannot overstep in interfering with private business under the pretence of regulation. The rules by which these limits may be determined are, from the nature of the case, incapable of being precisely indicated so as to preclude mistake or controversy, but the following ought to be unquestioned:

1. Whatever in modern times has generally been looked upon as being outside the sphere of legislation, should be regarded as finally eliminated from state authority. To do this is only to take notice of the steady growth of the free principles which have come from common-law rules and usages, and of their gradual expansion with the general advance in intelligence and independent thought and action among the people. The gradual transition from despotism to freedom has been mainly accomplished by the dropping out one by one of obnoxious and despotic powers, and by the recognition of the chances effected as permanent modifications of the constitutional system. Under this head may be classed the power in the state to create monopolies at will. For nearly three hundred years this power has been generally denied to the state, and to exercise and sustain it now is to discard whatever in freedom of industrial effort and competition has been gained in that period.

2. Wherever an extreme power has been supported by special and exceptional reasons, it should be regarded as gone when the reasons have ceased to exist. Thus, if in the founding of a colony it should be found necessary to employ the power of taxation to assist in the establishment and support of mills, yet as the power is an extreme power and only called into use by the extremity of the case, the power should be considered recalled when the necessity has ceased. And when the power to aid mills by taxation is gone, such exceptional power to regulate as must have sprung from it should be considered recalled also.

3. A questionable power, long disused, should be considered abandoned or recalled. Under this head may be instanced the power to fix the price of labor. Such a power belongs to barbarous and despotic times; it is inconsistent with genuine liberty, and it may be exercised to reduce men to virtual slavery. In the American States it has not been exercised since they passed from the colonial condition, and this of itself ought to be accepted as conclusive against the existence of the power. The American constitutions, in providing that no man shall be deprived of life, liberty, or property without due process of law, should be understood as protecting the liberty of employment with the same jealous care with which they protect against unlawful confinement behind bolts and bars.

It is not the purpose of this article to discuss the rulings of any court or to enter upon the examination of any decision. The discussion is upon general principles, and not upon particular cases. The discussion, however, may justify the cautionary remark, that it is a very dangerous thing to make by a precedent an inroad upon one of the fundamental principles of liberty, because precedents tend to beget a habit of thought and action which leads insensibly in the direction in which they point. Every doubtful precedent should therefore be carefully considered, and never accepted when it will not stand the test of settled rules of right. It has recently been said in a case in which a strong exercise of legislative power was under discussion, that the legislature may constitutionally restrict the charges which may be made for the use of property, because profits are not property, and, therefore, constitutional protection cannot be claimed for them. That is as much as to say, the constitution protects a man in his property, but not in the enjoyment of his property; he may have his farm, but the state may take away his profits by limiting his sales to the cost of production. A constitutional protection of this sort is a mere mockery. "The idea of property," says Mr. Bentham, "consists in an established expectation; in the persuasion of power to derive certain advantages from the object, according to the nature of the case." It is true that possible future profits are not property; they cannot be handled or enjoyed, and they may never be realized; perhaps if one were wrongfully deprived of the opportunity to earn them, he might, because of their uncertainty, not be able to secure suitable redress; but the capability of property, by means of the labor or expense or both bestowed upon it, to be made available in producing profits, is a potential quality in property, and as sacredly protected by the constitution as the thing itself in which the quality inheres. He who denies this may on the same grounds say that while the right to labor is a constitutional right, yet that the profits of labor before they are realized are under legislative control, and may be kept down to prevent, as the early Massachusetts statute had it, "oppression" by "excessive wages."

# 3

# Classicism, Neoclassicism, and the Sherman Act

## Introduction

### BY HERBERT HOVENKAMP

As the introduction to Chapter One indicated, when the Sherman Act was passed in 1890 economic theory was in turmoil, with the classicism of Adam Smith gradually giving way to the marginal utility school and the "neoclassical" theory that continues to dominate Western economic thinking to this day. By and large the economists that we identify with American Progressivism from the 1890s to the 1920s were all marginalists,[1] but the older and more established generation tended to be classicists.[2]

The first selection in this chapter is from Cambridge University economist Alfred Marshall's magnum opus *Principles of Economics* (1890). Marshall's book was a consensus-forming work that laid out the basic elements of neoclassical price theory, industrial organization, and the theory of the firm. Marshall (1842–1924) was preoccupied with giving economics status as a science. He was also taken with the notion of "equilibrium," which he borrowed from mechanics and engineering. His *Principles* stated in mathematical terms many of neoclassical economics' most influential theories about how resources flow—for example, that in a competitive market prices tend toward marginal cost, that economic actors substitute among different goods until the marginal value of each is equalized, that price imbalances in a single market will lead to a flow of goods from the lower-priced area to the higher-priced until the two are balanced. Marshall's work was so important that industrial economists over the next half-century devoted themselves to the implications of his work.

At the same time, however, neoclassicism opened up many questions that had been thought resolved by the classicists and created some new ones. One question with very

1. E.g., Henry Carter Adams, Lester Frank Ward, John Bates Clark, Richard T. Ely, John R. Commons, and Arthur Twining Hadley.

2. E.g., William Graham Sumner and George Gunton.

serious implications for antitrust policy was how fixed costs fit into the equilibrium model. If competition forced market prices toward marginal cost, which is the incremental cost of producing the next unit, then how could firms in competitive markets recover their fixed costs? One characteristic of industrial development in the late twentieth century was more capital-intensive industry, which by definition had significant fixed costs. The railroads were a particularly strong example, but heavy manufacturing industries exhibited the same problem.

The second selection is from Arthur Twining Hadley (1856–1930), an economist who was also president of Yale University for two decades. Hadley represented the view of many early marginalists in the United States that competition and high fixed costs were incompatible. In high-fixed-cost industries competition would become "ruinous," as firms cut prices to a level sufficient to cover their operating (variable) costs but without enough left over to pay their fixed-cost indebtedness. The strongest version of this position held that either merger to monopoly or else collusion was inevitable in such industries if they were not to be driven into bankruptcy. By contrast, the emergent Progressive economists made two quite different arguments. One was that competition would be ruinous only in a small subset of industries, such as the railroads, for which fixed costs were extremely high. The other was that to the extent competition and fixed costs were incompatible, the government must intervene by rate making and other forms of regulation. Thus the rise of Progressive-era rate regulation, mainly in the railroads, and eventually the broad regulatory mandates of the New Deal.

This "fixed cost controversy" raged simultaneously with early Sherman Act enforcement and serves to explain the division among American economists on antitrust policy. Indeed, the first entry of neoclassical economics into judicial decision making occurred when the courts confronted and rejected the "ruinous competition" defense for cartels or mergers. Prior to World War II some eighty federal court decisions discussed ruinous competition in antitrust and regulatory settings, but the courts consistently held that ruinous competition could not defend against an anticompetitive practice.[3] Indeed, an avowed purpose of the early trade association movement was to enable firms in a particular industry to avoid ruinous competition by coordinating output.[4]

Hadley's 1896 text on economics used marginalist analysis extensively, although most of it was derivative of Marshall's book. However, Hadley repeatedly warned about the dangers of overproduction, and that "the larger the fixed capital involved in an industry, the greater is the danger of such over-production" (*Economics*, 294). As a result, Hadley argued, "combinations of capital" were essential to balancing output with demand at a remunerative price (152–153).

The selection on the "Chicago Trust Conference" was reported by University of Chicago Professor Henry Rand Hatfield in the *Journal of Political Economy*, which was started in 1892 by his upstart university's increasingly influential economics department. The conference was organized in 1899 by the Chicago Civic Federation, a public service

3. E.g., *Addyston Pipe & Steel Co.* v. *United States*, 175 U.S. 211, 213–214 (1899); *United States* v. *Joint-Traffic Assn.*, 171 U.S. 505, 576 (1898).

4. E.g., *Standard Container Manufacturers' Ass'n.* v. *FTC*, 119 F.2d 262 (5th Cir. 1941).

organization focused mainly on issues of taxation and government efficiency. The invitees to the conference represented government leaders, economists, and both management and labor. The deliberations revealed a number of things, notably that the majority of economists were either opposed to the Sherman Act or deeply skeptical, and that the biggest supporters of antitrust legislation tended to be small businesses. It is worth noting, however, that at the time there was no labor exemption from the antitrust laws, and during this early period the Sherman Act was widely used as a union-busting device.[5]

The fixed-cost problem gradually came under control as economists developed fuller models about firm behavior and the relationship between scale economies and market size. One important development was John Maurice Clark's pathbreaking *Studies in the Economics of Overhead Costs* (1923), which found that pricing behavior among firms with high fixed costs was very complex and characterized by a great deal of price discrimination. Further, the existence of ruinous competition was really a consequence of economies of scale, and these dictated ruinous competition only in cases where the market could not accommodate two or more firms of minimum efficient size. That is to say, the ruinous competition problem became relegated to natural monopoly. Other parts of the puzzle were filled in with the development of monopolistic competition theory in the 1930s (see Chapter Five) and the theory of noncooperative oligopoly shortly thereafter (see Chapter Ten).

The result of these developments was a great deal of complexity and change in the theory of competition. Classicism had tended to see markets in terms of competition or monopoly, but neoclassicism began to recognize various gradations of competition. The debate also revealed that rather small differences in one's assumptions could lead to profoundly different conclusions. "Perfect" competition in concentrated capital-intensive markets came to be regarded as highly exceptional or nonexistent, but the case for intermediate positions that were socially more desirable than outright collusion or merger to monopoly became far stronger as well.

## Alfred Marshall
## *Principles of Economics*

## Conclusion. Correlation of the Tendencies to Increasing and to Diminishing Return.

§1. At the beginning of this Book we saw how the extra return of raw produce which nature affords to an increased application of capital and labour, other things being equal, tends in the long run to diminish. In the remainder of the Book and especially in the last four chapters we have looked at the other side of the shield, and seen how man's power of productive work increases with the volume of the work that he does. Considering first the causes that govern the supply of labour, we saw how every increase in the physical, mental and moral vigour of a people makes them more likely, other things being equal, to rear to adult age a large number of vigorous children. Turning

5. See Herbert Hovenkamp, "Labor Conspiracies in American Law," 66 *Tex.L.Rev.* 919 (1988).

next to the growth of wealth, we observed how every increase of wealth tends in many ways to make a greater increase more easy than before. And lastly we saw how every increase of wealth and every increase in the numbers and intelligence of the people increased the facilities for a highly developed industrial organization, which in its turn adds much to the collective efficiency of capital and labour.

Looking more closely at the economies arising from an increase in the scale of production of any kind of goods, we found that they fell into two classes—those dependent on the general development of the industry, and those dependent on the resources of the individual houses of business engaged in it and the efficiency of their management; that is, into external and internal economies.

We saw how these latter economies are liable to constant fluctuations so far as any particular house is concerned. An able man, assisted perhaps by some strokes of good fortune, gets a firm footing in the trade, he works hard and lives sparely, his own capital grows fast, and the credit that enables him to borrow more capital grows still faster; he collects around him subordinates of more than ordinary zeal and ability; as his business increases they rise with him, they trust him and he trusts them, each of them devotes himself with energy to just that work for which he is specially fitted, so that no high ability is wasted on easy work, and no difficult work is entrusted to unskilful hands. Corresponding to this steadily increasing economy of skill, the growth of his business brings with it similar economies of specialized machines and plant of all kinds; every improved process is quickly adopted and made the basis of further improvements; success brings credit and credit brings success; credit and success help to retain old customers and to bring new ones; the increase of his trade gives him great advantages in buying; his goods advertise one another, and thus diminish his difficulty in finding a vent for them. The increase in the scale of his business increases rapidly the advantages which he has over his competitors, and lowers the price at which he can afford to sell. This process may go on as long as his energy and enterprise, his inventive and organizing power retain their full strength and freshness, and so long as the risks which are inseparable from business do not cause him exceptional losses; and if it could endure for a hundred years, he and one or two others like him would divide between them the whole of that branch of industry in which he is engaged. The large scale of their production would put great economies within their reach; and provided they competed to their utmost with one another, the public would derive the chief benefit of these economies, and the price of the commodity would fall very low.

But here we may read a lesson from the young trees of the forest as they struggle upwards through the benumbing shade of their older rivals. Many succumb on the way, and a few only survive; those few become stronger with every year, they get a larger share of light and air with every increase of their height, and at last in their turn they tower above their neighbours, and seem as though they would grow on for ever, and for ever become stronger as they grow. But they do not. One tree will last longer in full vigour and attain a greater size than another; but sooner or later age tells on them all. Though the taller ones have a better access to light and air than their rivals, they gradually lose vitality; and one after another they give place to others, which, though of less material strength, have on their side the vigour of youth.

And as with the growth of trees, so was it with the growth of businesses as a general rule before the great recent development of vast joint-stock companies, which often stagnate, but do not readily die. Now that rule is far from universal, but it still holds in many industries and trades. Nature still presses on the private business by limiting the length of the life of its original founders, and by limiting even more narrowly that part of their lives in which their faculties retain full vigour. And so, after a while, the guidance of the business falls into the hands of people with less energy and less creative genius, if not with less active interest in its prosperity. If it is turned into a joint-stock company, it may retain the advantages of division of labour, of specialized skill and machinery: it may even increase them by a further increase of its capital; and under favourable conditions it may secure a permanent and prominent place in the work of production. But it is likely to have lost so much of its elasticity and progressive force, that the advantages are no longer exclusively on its side in its competition with younger and smaller rivals.

When therefore we are considering the broad results which the growth of wealth and population exert on the economies of production, the general character of our conclusions is not very much affected by the facts that many of these economies depend directly on the size of the individual establishments engaged in the production, and that in almost every trade there is a constant rise and fall of large businesses, at any one moment some firms being in the ascending phase and others in the descending. For in times of average prosperity decay in one direction is sure to be more than balanced by growth in another.

Meanwhile an increase in the aggregate scale of production of course increases those economies, which do not directly depend on the size of individual houses of business. The most important of these result from the growth of correlated branches of industry which mutually assist one another, perhaps being concentrated in the same localities, but anyhow availing themselves of the modern facilities for communication offered by steam transport, by the telegraph and by the printing-press. The economies arising from such sources as this, which are accessible to any branch of production, do not depend exclusively upon its own growth: but yet they are sure to grow rapidly and steadily with that growth; and they are sure to dwindle in some, though not in all respects, if it decays.

§2. These results will be of great importance when we come to discuss the causes which govern the supply price of a commodity. We shall have to analyse carefully the normal cost of producing a commodity, relatively to a given aggregate volume of production; and for this purpose we shall have to study the expenses of a representative producer for that aggregate volume. On the one hand we shall not want to select some new producer just struggling into business, who works under many disadvantages, and has to be content for a time with little or no profits, but who is satisfied with the fact that he is establishing a connection and taking the first steps towards building up a successful business; nor on the other hand shall we want to take a firm which by exceptionally long-sustained ability and good fortune has got together a vast business, and huge well-ordered workshops that give it a superiority over almost all its rivals. But our representative firm must be one which has had a fairly long life, and fair success, which is managed with normal ability, and which has normal access to the economies, external and internal, which belong to that aggregate volume of production; account being taken of the class of goods produced, the conditions of marketing them and the economic environment generally.

Thus a representative firm is in a sense an average firm. But there are many ways in which the term "average" might be interpreted in connection with a business. And a Representative firm is that particular sort of average firm, at which we need to look in order to see how far the economies, internal and external, of production on a large scale have extended generally in the industry and country in question. We cannot see this by looking at one or two firms taken at random: but we can see it fairly well by selecting, after a broad survey, a firm, whether in private or joint-stock management (or better still, more than one), that represents, to the best of our judgment, this particular average.

The general argument of the present Book shows that an increase in the aggregate volume of production of anything will generally increase the size, and therefore the internal economies possessed by such a representative firm; that it will always increase the external economies to which the firm has access; and thus will enable it to manufacture at a less proportionate cost of labour and sacrifice than before.

In other words, we say broadly that while the part which nature plays in production shows a tendency to diminishing return, the part which man plays shows a tendency to increasing return. The law of increasing return may be worded thus:—An increase of labour and capital leads generally to improved organization, which increases the efficiency of the work of labour and capital.

Therefore in those industries which are not engaged in raising raw produce an increase of labour and capital generally gives a return increased more than in proportion; and further this improved organization tends to diminish or even override any increased resistance which nature may offer to raising increased amounts of raw produce. If the actions of the laws of increasing and diminishing return are balanced we have the law of constant return, and an increased produce is obtained by labour and sacrifice increased just in proportion.

For the two tendencies towards increasing and diminishing return press constantly against one another. In the production of wheat and wool, for instance, the latter tendency has almost exclusive sway in an old country, which cannot import freely. In turning the wheat into flour, or the wool into blankets, an increase in the aggregate volume of production brings some new economies, but not many; for the trades of grinding wheat and making blankets are already on so great a scale that any new economies that they may attain are more likely to be the result of new inventions than of improved organization. In a country however in which the blanket trade is but slightly developed, these latter may be important; and then it may happen that an increase in the aggregate production of blankets diminishes the proportionate difficulty of manufacturing by just as much as it increases that of raising the raw material. In that case the actions of the laws of diminishing and of increasing return would just neutralize one another; and blankets would conform to the law of constant return. But in most of the more delicate branches of manufacturing, where the cost of raw material counts for little, and in most of the modern transport industries the law of increasing return acts almost unopposed.

Increasing Return is a relation between a quantity of effort and sacrifice on the one hand, and a quantity of product on the other. The quantities cannot be taken out exactly, because changing methods of production call for machinery, and for unskilled and skilled labour of new kinds and in new proportions. But, taking a broad view, we may perhaps say vaguely that the output of a certain amount of labour and capital in an industry has increased by perhaps a quarter or a third in the last twenty years. To measure outlay and output in terms of money is a tempting, but a dangerous resource: for a comparison of money outlay with money returns is apt to slide into an estimate of the rate of profit on capital.

§3. We may now sum up provisionally the relations of industrial expansion to social wellbeing. A rapid growth of population has often been accompanied by unhealthy and enervating habits of life in overcrowded towns. And sometimes it has started badly, outrunning the material resources of the people, causing them with imperfect appliances to make excessive demands on the soil; and so to call forth the stern action of the law of diminishing return as regards raw produce, without having the power of minimizing its effects. Having thus begun with poverty, an increase in numbers may go on to its too frequent consequences in that weakness of character which unfits a people for developing a highly organized industry.

These are serious perils: but yet it remains true that the collective efficiency of a people with a given average of individual strength and energy may increase more than in proportion to their numbers. If they can for a time escape from the pressure of the law of diminishing return by importing food and other raw produce on easy terms; if their wealth is not consumed in great wars, and increases at least as fast as their numbers; and if they avoid habits of life that would enfeeble them; then every increase in their numbers is likely for the time to be accompanied by a more than proportionate increase in their power of obtaining material goods. For it enables them to secure the many various economies of specialized skill and specialized machinery, of localized industries and production on a large scale: it enables them to have increased facilities of communication of all kinds; while the very closeness of their neighbourhood diminishes the expense of time and effort involved in every sort of traffic between them, and gives them new opportunities of getting social enjoyments and the comforts and luxuries of culture in every form. No doubt deduction must be made for the growing difficulty of finding solitude and quiet and even fresh air: but there is in most cases some balance of good.

Taking account of the fact that an increasing density of population generally brings with it access to new social enjoyments we may give a rather broader scope to this statement and say:—An increase of population accompanied by an equal increase in the material sources of enjoyment and aids to production is likely to lead to a more than proportionate increase in the aggregate income of enjoyment of all kinds; provided firstly, an adequate supply of raw produce can be obtained without great difficulty, and secondly there is no such overcrowding as causes physical and moral vigour to be impaired by the want of fresh air and light and of healthy and joyous recreation for the young.

The accumulated wealth of civilized countries is at present growing faster than the population: and though it may be true that the wealth per head would increase somewhat faster if the population did not increase quite so fast; yet as a matter of fact an increase of population is likely to continue to be accompanied by a more than proportionate increase of the material aids to production: and in England at the present time, with easy access to abundant foreign supplies of raw material, an increase of population is accompanied by a more than proportionate increase of the means of satisfying human wants other than the need for light, fresh air, etc. Much of this increase is however attributable not to the increase of industrial efficiency but to the increase of wealth by which it is accompanied: and therefore it does not necessarily benefit those who have no share in that wealth. And further, England's foreign supplies of raw produce may at any time be checked by changes in the trade regulations of other countries, and may be almost cut off by a great war, while the naval and military expenditure which would be necessary to make the country fairly secure against this last risk, would appreciably diminish the benefits that she derives from the action of the law of increasing return.

## The Theory of Monopolies.

§1. It has never been supposed that the monopolist in seeking his own advantage is naturally guided in that course which is most conducive to the wellbeing of society regarded as a whole, he himself being reckoned as of no more importance than any other member of it. The doctrine of Maximum Satisfaction has never been applied to the demand for and supply of monopolized commodities. But there is much to be learnt from a study of the relations in which the interests of the monopolist stand to those of the rest of society, and of the general conditions under which it might be possible to make arrangements more beneficial to society as a whole than those which he would adopt if he consulted only his own interests: and with this end in view we are now to seek for a scheme for comparing the relative quantities of the benefits which may accrue to the public and to the monopolist from the adoption of different courses of action by him.

In a later volume a study will be made of the Protean shapes of modern trade combinations and monopolies, some of the most important of which, as for example "Trusts," are of very recent growth. At present we consider only those general causes determining monopoly values, that can be traced with more or less distinctness in every case in which a single person or association of persons has the power of fixing either the amount of a commodity that is offered for sale or the price at which it is offered.

§2. The prima facie interest of the owner of a monopoly is clearly to adjust the supply to the demand, not in such a way that the price at which he can sell his commodity shall just cover its expenses of production, but in such a way as to afford him the greatest possible total net revenue.

But here we meet with a difficulty as to the meaning of the term Net revenue. For the supply price of a freely-produced commodity includes normal profits; the whole of which, or at all events what remains of them after deducting interest on the capital employed and insurance against loss, is often classed indiscriminately as net revenue. And when a man manages his own business, he often does not distinguish carefully that portion of his profits, which really is his own earnings of management, from any exceptional gains arising from the fact that the business is to some extent of the nature of a monopoly.

This difficulty however is in a great measure avoided in the case of a public company; where all, or nearly all, the expenses of management are entered in the ledger as definite sums, and are subtracted from the total receipts of the company before its net income is declared.

The net income divided among the shareholders includes interest on the capital invested and insurance against risk of failure, but little or no earnings of management; so that the amount by which the dividends are in excess of what may fairly be allowed as interest and insurance, is the Monopoly Revenue which we are seeking.

Since then it is much easier to specify exactly the amount of this net revenue when a monopoly is owned by a public company than when it is owned by an individual or private firm, let us take as a typical instance the case of a gas company that has the monopoly of the supply of gas to a town. For the sake of simplicity the company may be supposed to have already invested the whole of its own capital in fixed plant, and to borrow any more capital, that it may want to extend its business, on debentures at a fixed rate of interest.

§3. The demand schedule for gas remains the same as it would be if gas were a freely-produced commodity; it specifies the price per thousand feet at which consumers in the town will among them use any given number of feet. But the supply schedule must represent the normal expenses of production of each several amount supplied; and these include interest on all its capital, whether belonging to its shareholders or borrowed on debentures, at a fixed normal rate; they include also the salaries of its directors, and permanent officials, adjusted (more or less accurately) to the work required of them, and therefore increasing with an increase in the output of gas. A monopoly revenue schedule may then be constructed thus:—Having set against each several amount of the commodity its demand price, and its supply price estimated on the plan just described, subtract each supply price from the corresponding demand price and set the residue in the monopoly revenue column against the corresponding amount of the commodity.

Thus for instance if a thousand million feet could be sold annually at a price of 3s. per thousand feet, and the supply price for this amount were 2s. 9d. per thousand feet, the monopoly revenue schedule would show 3d. against this amount; indicating an aggregate net revenue when this amount was sold, of three million pence, or £12,500. The aim of the company, having regard only to their own immediate dividends, will be to fix the price of their gas at such a level as to make this aggregate net revenue the largest possible.

§4. Now suppose that a change takes place in the conditions of supply; some new expense has to be incurred, or some old expense can be avoided; or perhaps a new tax is imposed on the undertaking or a bounty is awarded to it.

First let this increase or diminution of the expenses be a fixed sum, bearing on the undertaking as one undivided whole and not varying with the amount of the commodity produced. Then, whatever be the price charged and the amount of the commodity sold, the monopoly revenue will be increased or diminished, as the case may be, by this sum; and therefore that selling price which afforded the maximum monopoly revenue before the change will afford it afterwards; the change therefore will not offer to the monopolist any inducement to alter his course of action. Suppose for instance that the maximum monopoly revenue is got when twelve hundred million cubic feet are sold annually; and that this is done when the price is fixed at 30d. per thousand feet: suppose that the expenses of production for this amount are at the rate of 26d., leaving a monopoly revenue at the rate of four pence per thousand feet, that is £20,000 in all. This is its maximum value: if the company fixed the price higher at, say, 31d. and sold only eleven hundred million feet, they would perhaps get a monopoly revenue at the rate of 4.2 pence per thousand feet, that is £19,250 in all; while in order to sell thirteen hundred millions they would have to lower their price to, say, 28d. and would get a monopoly revenue at the rate of perhaps 3×6d. per thousand feet, that is £19,500 in all. Thus by fixing the price at 30d. they get £750 more than by fixing it at 31d., and £500 more than by fixing it at 28d. Now let a tax of £10,000 a year be levied on the gas company as a fixed sum independent of the amount they sell. Their monopoly revenue will become £10,000 if they charge 30d., £9,250 if they charge 31d., and £9,500 if they charge 28d. They will therefore continue to charge 30d.

The same is true of a tax or a bounty proportioned not to the gross receipts of the undertaking, but to its monopoly revenue. For suppose next that a tax is levied, not of one fixed sum, but a certain percentage, say 50 percent. of the monopoly revenue. The company will then retain a monopoly revenue of £10,000 if they charge 30d., of £9,625 if they charge 31d., and of £9,750 if they charge 28d. They will therefore still charge 30d.

On the other hand a tax proportional to the amount produced gives an inducement to the monopolist to lessen his output and raise his price. For by so doing he diminishes his expenses. And the excess of total receipts over total outlay may therefore be now increased by a diminution of output; though before the imposition of the tax it would have been lessened. Further, if before the imposition of the tax the net revenue was only a little greater than that which would have been afforded by much smaller sales, then the monopolist would gain by reducing his production very greatly; and hence in such cases as this, the change is likely to cause a very great diminution of production and rise of price. The opposite effects will be caused by a change which diminishes the expense of working the monopoly by a sum that varies directly with the amount produced under it.

In the last example, for instance, a tax of 2d. on each thousand feet sold would have reduced the monopoly revenue to £10,083 if the company charged 31d. per thousand feet and therefore sold eleven hundred millions; to £10,000 if they charged 30d. and therefore sold twelve hundred millions, and to £8,666 if they charged 28d. and therefore sold thirteen hundred million feet. Therefore the tax would induce the company to raise the price to something higher than 30d.; they would perhaps go to 31d., perhaps somewhat higher; for the figures before us do not show exactly how far it would be their interest to go.

On the other hand, if there were a bounty of 2d. on the sale of each thousand feet, the monopoly revenue would rise to £28,416 if they charged 31d., to £30,000 if they charged 30d., and to £30,333 if they charged 28d.: it would therefore cause them to lower the price. And of course the same result would follow from an improvement in the method of making gas, which lowered its cost of production to the monopolist company by 2d. per 1,000 feet.

§5. The monopolist would lose all his monopoly revenue if he produced for sale an amount so great that its supply price, as here defined, was equal to its demand price: the amount which gives the maximum monopoly revenue is always considerably less than that. It may therefore appear as though the amount produced under a monopoly is always less and its price to the consumer always higher than if there were no monopoly. But this is not the case.

For when the production is all in the hands of one person or company, the total expenses involved are generally less than would have to be incurred if the same aggregate production were distributed among a multitude of comparatively small rival producers. They would have to struggle with one another for the attention of consumers, and would necessarily spend in the aggregate a great deal more on advertising in all its various forms than a single firm would; and they would be less able to avail themselves of the many various economies which result from production on a large scale. In particular they could not afford to spend as much on improving methods of production and the machinery used in it, as a single large firm which knew that it was certain itself to reap the whole benefit of any advance it made.

This argument does indeed assume the single firm to be managed with ability and enterprise, and to have an unlimited command of capital—an assumption which cannot always be fairly made. But where it can be made, we may generally conclude that the supply schedule for the commodity, if not monopolized, would show higher supply prices than those of our monopoly supply schedule; and therefore the equilibrium amount of the commodity produced under free competition would be less than that for which the demand price is equal to the monopoly supply price.

One of the most interesting and difficult applications of the theory of monopolies is to the question whether the public interest is best served by the allotment of a distinct basin to each great railway, and excluding competition there. For the proposal it is urged that a railway can afford to carry two million passengers, or tons of goods, cheaper than one million: and that a division of the public demand between two lines will prevent either of them from offering a cheap service. It must be admitted that, other things being equal, the "monopoly revenue price" fixed by a railway will be lowered by every increase in the demand for its services, and vice versa. But, human nature being what it is, experience has shown that the breaking of a monopoly by the opening out of a competing line accelerates, rather than retards the discovery by the older line that it can afford to carry traffic at lower rates. There still remains the suggestion that after a while the railways will combine and charge the public with the expense wasted on duplicating the services. But this again only opens out new matters of controversy. The theory of monopolies starts rather than solves practical issues such as these: and we must defer their study.

## Arthur Twining Hadley

## *Economics: An Account of the Relations Between Private Property and Public Welfare*

## Chapter VI.

## Combination of Capital.

### Modern Tendencies Toward Monopoly Their Effect on Prices Limitation of Profits Laws Fixing Rates Enforcement of Responsibility.

165. The investment of fixed capital described in the preceding chapter has wrought much more radical changes in manufactures and transportation than in agriculture.

There are several reasons for this difference. In the first place, the productiveness of factories has increased faster than that of farms. No means has been found for indefinitely enlarging the amount of food which can be obtained from a given area. We can perhaps double it or treble it; but no investment of capital, wise or unwise, is likely to increase it a hundred-fold. Therefore no one farm, however large, is likely to supply more than a very small fraction of the world's consumption. Until there is some radical change in the art of food production, we shall continue to have competition between different producers. Nor has the investment of fixed capital in agriculture gone so far that its interest and maintenance constitute the chief elements in the cost of food products. They form an important, but not a dominant factor. Under these circumstances, the theory of normal price, though hindered in its operation, is by no means rendered inapplicable. There is a slight delay in the adjustment between price and cost; there is a certain margin between the price which will induce new competitors to enter the field, and that which will drive out the old ones. But, in the majority of cases, we can still rely on competition to protect the consumers and do no gross injustice to the producers.

166. In manufactures the case is different. The units of capital are much larger. Each producer can extend his output with a gain rather than a loss in economy. If he

can increase his sales, there will be only a slight increase, perhaps none at all, in the expense for wages and materials and a decided decrease in the share of the charges on fixed capital, which each unit of product must pay. There is no fixed standard of cost which we can treat as the normal price; for the cost per unit of product depends on the quantity sold, falling as sales increase.

The price which will induce new competitors to enter the field is also much higher than that which will lead old ones to withdraw. No concern will quit competition as long as it can pay an appreciable part of its interest charges. It is better to lose part of your interest on every piece of goods you sell, than to lose the whole of it on every piece you do not sell. As long as the price received more than covers the expense for wages and materials each of the old factories will continue to compete.

Even if it changes ownership by foreclosure it will remain in operation. But, on the other hand, no new competitor will be called into being unless the price is high enough to afford a liberal profit, after paying interest, maintenance, and other charges on fixed capital invested under modern methods. Thus prices, instead of constantly tending to gravitate toward an equitable figure, oscillate between two extremes. The rate of production, at figures which give a fair profit, is usually either much larger than the rate of consumption, or much smaller. In the former case, prices are unremunerative and unjust to the producer; in the latter case, they are oppressive to the consumer. The average price resulting from such fluctuations may perhaps be a fair one; but the wide changes of price are disastrous to all parties concerned.

167. The failure of competition to secure fair or stable rates gives additional force to the pressure toward combination which always exists among certain classes of business men.

Many writers on combination treat it as a new thing, peculiar to the present stage of commercial and industrial development. This is a mistake. Efforts at trade combination have always been made, and have not infrequently been successful. The more we study the past history of any line of business, the more we are impressed with the extent of such efforts at combination. The distinctive feature of the present age lies in the existence of certain added causes peculiar to this stage of commercial development, which work in favor of those who advocate combination, and make it harder for independent competitors to resist it, or for the law to prohibit it on grounds of public policy.

168. The economy, to the public as well as to the individual, of concentrating capital as much as possible, always furnishes a pretext, and sometimes a real reason, for substituting combination for competition. In some cases the industrial units which are necessary for proper utilization of labor have become so large as to produce actual monopoly. This is especially true of distributive services, like water, gas, telegraphs, or railroads. The attempt to have two independent agencies perform any of these services for a single community is apt to result in loss to the producer and inconvenience to the consumer. So much of the expense of delivery of water or gas is connected with the laying of mains, that a system which duplicates these mains is a public burden. So

much of the advantage of the telephone service to each subscriber lies in the power of reaching all the other subscribers, that the existence of two competing exchanges in the same city destroys the usefulness of both. In railroad transportation a single organized company can put lines just where they are needed, and run trains at the time when the public wants them. If the same service is performed by two companies, there will be unnecessary duplication of lines in some places, and failure to build needful ones in others; while the train times and train connections will be arranged, not with regard to the maximum convenience of the public, but with a view to increase the business of one competitor at the expense of the other. Even in cases where the necessity for concentrated management is not quite so marked as in those just described, the competition of different concerns always involves a loss, from the need of maintaining too many selling agencies, the expense of unnecessary advertising, and the lack of proper utilization of fixed capital.[1]

169. The simplest form of combination is an agreement to maintain rates, where the several competitors promise not to reduce their prices below a scale fixed by common consent, with a view to giving producers a fair profit. But such an arrangement rarely proves effective. Each company is at the mercy of its agents. They will try to steal business from rival concerns by cutting rates. If they are allowed a commission on sales, they will divide it with the buyer; if they are not allowed such a commission, they will find a hundred different ways, less obvious but hardly less effective, of rendering a rate agreement nugatory. It is so profitable for one concern to steal business from another, and so disastrous to its rival to lose the business, that the latter will always suspect the former of bad faith when any irregularities of its agents are discovered or surmised. A contest will be inaugurated which tends to drive prices far below the normal rate; usually to the advantage of those who least need and least deserve such reductions. The honest and straightforward business man is content with the one-price system. He is not seeking to gain an unfair advantage over his neighbor, but to be treated squarely. Fluctuating and uncertain rates are not what he desires, for he knows that his less scrupulous rival will be the first to gain the benefit of such changes. It is better for A to be paying 30 cents and be sure that his competitor B is also paying 30 cents, than for A to pay 25 cents when

1. The increasing profit when we enlarge the output of a factory is often contrasted with the diminishing profit when we attempt to do the same thing on a farm; and some writers say that industries with large fixed capital are subject to a "law of increasing return" which contrasts with the law of diminishing return that prevails in agriculture. This statement hardly goes to the root of the matter. The distinction is not so much between kinds of industry as between kinds of capital. With a given amount of fixed capital, whether invested in agriculture or in manufactures, any increase of output diminishes the charges on such capital per unit of product. The current expenses per unit of product do not thus tend to diminish as the output increases; in fact, when a certain relation has been established between output and fixed capital, the current expenses per unit of product increase very rapidly. Whether, with an increase of output, the gain from fuller use of fixed capital offsets the loss from increased current expenses, depends partly on the amount of the fixed capital, but chiefly on the degree to which it was previously utilized. If it was not fully utilized we shall see the phenomena of increasing return; if it was already fully utilized, we shall see those of diminishing return. The apparent contrast between agriculture and manufacturing in this respect is chiefly due to the fact that population habitually approaches a limit set by the arts of food production, so that its agricultural improvements are always employed nearly to the limit of profitable output; while in manufactures there is no such increase of demand, and fixed capital is often quite inadequately employed.

B pays 20. Wars of rates, though they produce very low prices, generally work to the disadvantage of the honest purchasing public and to the advantage of the shrewder speculators.

170. A single instance will serve to illustrate the difficulty of maintaining rates by agreement. Twenty-five years ago a fair rate for cattle from Chicago to New York was about $110 a carload. If the large shippers of cattle wished to break this rate, they would drive all their steers to one of the competing lines and would spread a rumor in the commercial columns of the newspapers that this line was not maintaining rates. This rumor, combined with the fact that the line in question was getting all the shipments, would make the other lines think there was foul play, and lead them to order a reduction in rates to meet the supposed cut. As soon as any such reduction was announced the shippers would all divert their cattle to the lines that had made it. The road that was carrying everything yesterday received nothing to-day; and indignant at the bad faith on the part of its rivals it would meet their reduction by a yet larger reduction. To this process there was no limit as long as the price paid for the carriage of cattle more than covered the expenses of loading and hauling. Under the excitement of the contest the railroad agents sometimes went even lower than this, and carried cattle at an actual loss in order to prevent rivals from making a profit.

171. When competing concerns are thus at the mercy of their agents or of outsiders, a resort to closer forms of combination is inevitable. If it proves that an agreement to maintain rates is not enough, they will arrange a pool or division of traffic. Pools take three distinct forms. Sometimes rival concerns divide the field; as when competing gas companies agree, to serve different streets in the same city, or when competing railroads agree not to build branch lines into one another's territory. Sometimes they divide the traffic itself. If three railroads find that each has done an approximately equal amount of business during the year preceding, they may arrange to divide the competitive business equally, and let each company take one-third. If more than one-third of the shippers desire to use one of the three lines during the coming month, that line agrees to turn over a part of its business to one of its rivals. If the different railroads are not of equal importance, the traffic can be divided on the basis of the percentages actually carried during the previous period of competition. Sometimes the railroad which is less favorably situated has to make concessions in rates in order to secure any traffic at all. In this case it is allowed to charge a lower price than its rivals, and receives a percentage of traffic at this lower rate. Such a concession is called a differential rate in favor of the weaker line, and is used as a means of inducing it not to enter into cutthroat competition. Sometimes, instead of dividing the traffic, the competing concerns may divide the earnings from that traffic, having a common accounting office and perhaps a system of joint agencies connected with it.

These divisions of traffic or earnings are far harder to arrange than agreements as to rates, but, when once established, they are much more effective. For when such a division exists, any irregularities of the agents in the matter of rates hurt the company which they represent far more than its rivals. This arrangement, therefore, substitutes mutual confidence for mutual suspicion.

172. Pools have not been regarded with favor by the law.[2] In the United States they are treated as contracts in restraint of trade, and therefore void as a gambling contract would be void. The courts say that they are against public policy and will not aid in their enforcement.

In certain kinds of business, notably railroad transportation, such pools or combinations are treated as misdemeanors, and attempts are made to punish their promoters by fine or imprisonment. But these efforts to do away with pools have conspicuously failed of their object. There are many ways of evading them. A joint accounting office may take the form of a clearing house established for the convenience of the public, and yet may serve all the purposes of a pool. If competing companies are forbidden to divide traffic by contract, they may secure a permanent understanding by putting a majority of their stock into the hands of a common board of trustees. Such an arrangement is known as a trust. The stockholders, in thus putting their securities in trust, part with the voting power, that is to say, the power of directing the policy of the concern, retaining the right to receive whatever may be earned on their stock, while it is held in trust by a board that secures harmony of management between the different companies engaged. If trusts are prohibited, it is always possible to resort to actual consolidation; the only serious difficulty being that a large consolidated company is liable to be taxed on the whole of its capital stock in a number of different states. It was this difficulty which the trust agreement was primarily designed to evade. As tax legislation becomes more systematic, the trouble from this source becomes less, and the possibility of consolidation is decidedly increased.

173. The attempt to prohibit combination has proved futile, and has simply driven the competing concerns into closer consolidation. Had it been successful, it must either have retarded the development of modern business and the utilization of modern methods requiring concentrated management of capital, or it must have subjected all of our large industries to constant fluctuations in their scale of prices, which would have been hardly less disastrous to the consumer than to the investor.

But the advantages of industrial combination, when it comes to include all competitors, are frequently balanced by the evils of commercial combination. The economy connected with the use of concentrated capital is in some measure offset by the loss of that stimulus which competition alone seems able to give; and the resulting monopoly makes it uncertain whether the consumers will get the benefit of the economy which is actually obtained.

174. If a monopoly is managed by inexperienced hands the effort to put prices up is usually more noticeable than the effort to put expenses down. It seems so easy to make a profit at the expense of society, that managers are apt to neglect the more

2. In England the legal decisions are much more favorable to pools than in the United States; while in most parts of Continental Europe they are accepted as matters of course; the governments themselves entering into pooling contracts with private companies with which they find themselves brought into competition in the management of state railroads or other industrial enterprises.

laborious method of making a profit by service to society. When business men have been all their lives accustomed to face immediate competition, they think that the combination of all competitors removes the only effective restriction upon charges. But this is a short-sighted view of the matter which has wrecked most of the enterprises run on such a basis, and has made the average trade combination a means of hindering rather that helping its members.

If the managers of a combination make it their chief concern to suppress competition rather than to realize economies in production, their policy toward trade rivals results in violation of commercial morality, if not of commercial law. Not content with obtaining unfair advantages in the way of discriminating rates for transportation of its goods, the combination tries to exclude its rivals from their accustomed markets by methods of boycotting and intimidation, which, when they are used by trades-unions, provoke fierce denunciation from the same men who have been ready to practise them for their own advantage.[3]

Even among those combinations which, like the Standard Oil Company, have realized economies and reduced rates for their product, this unscrupulous policy toward competitors has been carried to such an extent as to create a just prejudice against them; a prejudice which is enough to explain, and in one sense to justify, the tendency on the part of the public to ignore or depreciate the industrial services which they have actually rendered.

175. There is one case, and one only, where a monopoly has almost unlimited power to make high charges. If a number of contracts must be fulfilled within a specified time, a combination which controls the matter which is made the subject of these contracts can fix prices to suit itself, limited only by the danger of driving the contracting parties into bankruptcy.[4]

If operators have sold for future delivery stock which they did not own, or have contracted to deliver wheat during a certain month without assuring themselves of their sources of supply, the owners of the stock or of the wheat can, by a sufficiently extensive combination, force the operators to pay what price they please. Such a combination is known as a corner. Its managers have a great advantage in not being compelled to control the supply for more than a limited period, and of being assured of a fixed demand during that time. But the number of successful corners is less than is commonly supposed. Though the apparent profits of such an operation are often large, the expenses of securing control of the whole supply, and the difficulty of selling it to advantage upon the expiration of the corner, make the real gains less than the apparent ones.

176. If the article is to be sold to consumers instead of to speculators who have made fixed contracts, the chance for financial success by a policy of exorbitant prices

3. It is interesting to see how combinations of capital and combinations of labor are subject to the same possibilities of abuse or mismanagement; and how the same violation of commercial right looks excusable to the party benefited, but monstrous to the party injured.

4. Or by special rules of particular exchanges framed to avoid such a result.

is very small indeed. We have seen in chapter iii that the demand for an article falls as the price rises. In the case of almost everything except necessary food supplies, this fall in demand is very rapid, so that the gross receipts of the sellers under a high charge are less than those which they obtain with the lower scale of prices. Under these circumstances the maximum gross income is obtained by making rates low enough to develop a good volume of traffic, instead of by raising them so high as to reduce that traffic to a small amount. If a concern uses a large amount of fixed capital, it will rarely happen that the most money can be made by a policy of high charges with small volume of business. Experience has shown that the opposite method is the one which has proved permanently profitable, even to the concerns whose monopoly seemed most assured. It pays in the long run to bring rates down very near to the limits of actual cost, if such reductions are followed by a large development, of traffic.

177. Where a monopoly is of such precarious character that it may be subjected to direct competition at almost any moment, this truth is sufficiently obvious. If a concern in this situation attempts to do a small business at high rates and make large temporary profits by such a policy, new capital will come into the business in the hope of securing the good-will and custom of the community by lower rates. High charges invite duplication of plant in all cases where such duplication is possible. If, on the other hand, the original concern adopts a policy of doing a large business at low rates, the promoters of a rival enterprise will soon see that they cannot hope either to do the business cheaper, or to make a satisfactory profit on that moderate fraction of the existing business which it is possible for a new competitor to secure without special concessions in rates.

178. Even where a monopoly does not fear direct competition, there are many cases where it is subjected to similar restraints in an indirect manner. If there is but one railroad in a certain section of country, and this has a monopoly of available routes for reaching the market which the producers of the district naturally seek, the shippers are apparently at the mercy of that company and its agents. But if there is another railroad line which supplies the same market with goods from another section, it is all but inevitable that the competition of the two districts with one another should regulate the price which the railroads can charge.[5] We cannot have two different prices for similar goods in the same market. If the supply and demand of wheat at Liverpool fixes the price of wheat in the Liverpool market at a certain rate per bushel, the railroad and steamship lines in every direction must make their charges such that the wheat producers, in the sections which they can serve, can ship their supplies at a profit. Some of the transportation agents may disregard this necessity for a year or two, but not permanently. The penalty for such disregard is the destruction of the traffic on which the transportation route makes its living. The railroads of the United States, of Russia, and of British India feel one another's competition in determining the prices which they can charge on their international traffic.

5. When permanent monopoly rights are guaranteed by law in all the competing districts, as on French railroads, we are apt to find a system of high charges which no nominal powers of public supervision prove adequate to control.

179. There are a few cases where the monopoly of the sources of supply is so complete that even this possibility of indirect competition is absent. A private company may thus control all the available water within reach of a large city. A great industrial combination like the Standard Oil Company may become the sole means of supplying certain grades of oil to the United States, or even to the world. Here it might seem as though the power to make high charges were absolutely unlimited. Yet, even in these cases, the self-interest of the producers dictates the adoption of a relatively low scale of prices. Such monopolies can, as a rule, only be secured by very large investments of capital. Adequate profit on these investments involves correspondingly large public consumption. A man whose facilities are so rude that he makes only a few articles in the course of a year and supplies but a small part of the public demand, is interested in having the price of those articles as high as possible. But the man who makes a great many articles in the course of a year and meets a large part of the public demand is primarily interested, not in getting a maximum price for a few things, but in getting the public to take a great many things. Among those trusts and other combinations that have had apparently a complete monopoly, a large number have made conspicuous failures, simply because they thought of high prices rather than large sales, and did not see that such a policy was suicidal.

180. Perhaps the most striking illustration of this truth is furnished by the history of the French copper syndicate of 1888. By a series of brilliant financial operations, this syndicate obtained control of the copper product of all the best mines of the world. It attempted to raise the price of copper from nine cents a pound to sixteen cents. Everything was apparently favorable to the success of these operations. Copper was a necessity for use in the arts; the sources of supply where copper could be produced cheaply were few in number, and the syndicate had exclusive contracts with them all. The demand for copper was constantly tending to increase, owing to the new uses of electricity. The syndicate itself had very large capital, and was supported by many of the strongest financial houses of Europe. Yet with all these things in its favor it failed disastrously, because the consumption of copper at the advanced prices shrunk to such a degree that all the calculations of the syndicate were deranged and its financial resources put to a strain which they could not stand. Even the strongest of monopolies must make its price low enough to cause the public to buy its goods or services to a sufficient extent to utilize its capital, and this price will usually be found to be nearly the same as that which would have been fixed by free competition.

181. If a large industrial combination uses the advantages given by concentration of capital to render labor more efficient and obtain a good profit at low rates, it has excellent chances of success. But if it makes such economy of labor a pretext instead of an object, and uses its monopoly to put prices up, the danger of failure is wholly disproportionate to the chances of success. Such a policy may succeed for a few years, but sooner or later it seems bound to ruin those who adopt it.

Can we trust the managers of our large industrial enterprises to see this for themselves? Can we treat their mistakes as a self-correcting evil, and wait quietly for the time when they shall learn that their own permanent interests are best served by doing good public service? To this question it is impossible to return a general answer. Our decision in any particular case will depend partly upon the character of the business involved, partly upon the intelligence of those who manage it, and most of all, perhaps, on our own habits of mind.

182. If we are in the habit of looking at direct consequences, and disregarding indirect ones, we shall see grounds for active public interference in almost all cases of industrial combination. The managers of a monopoly have it in their power to do a great deal of harm before they begin to feel the loss to themselves which arises from the adoption of a short-sighted policy. Even if the trouble corrects itself in the long run, a great many legitimate interests are sacrificed in the process. A railroad ultimately finds it suicidal to kill the local shippers who are its best permanent customers; but it is small comfort to the shippers to know that their deaths are to be slowly avenged by the operation of economic laws. The shippers demand some immediate control over the railroad agent; something which will prevent the evil in the beginning, instead of simply sufficing to prevent its indefinite repetition. They will be prone to adopt the socialistic solution of the problem, and insist that the government should own the railroad, as the surest means of avoiding such abuses.

But the man who is in the habit of looking at indirect consequences will see that the undiscriminating attempt to prevent evil often results in preventing an even greater amount of good. He will be prone to take the individualistic view of the matter. He will be disinclined, except as a last resort, to put the business into the hands of a government whose agents are almost always chosen on other grounds than those of industrial efficiency, and whose methods are much less flexible than those of a private corporation. He will be indisposed to see stringent regulations put in force until he is convinced that milder remedies are inadequate to protect the interests of the public as a whole.

183. The industrial and political conditions which determine whether the conduct of a business may advantageously be entrusted to the government instead of being delegated to the property owners, are discussed at length in chapter xii. We have here to consider the merits of various methods of regulation of such industries, where government ownership proves undesirable or impracticable. These may be grouped under three heads:

1. Limitation of profits.
2. Fixing of rates by public authority.
3. Enforcement of far-sighted methods of management.

184. The first of these methods looks much better than it really is. It is a favorite remedy with people who have had no practical experience of its working. They say that it is very unjust for a monopoly to obtain a much higher dividend than would be possible under free competition; and they think that if we limit the dividend we shall remove the motive for extortion. In practice the matter does not work in this way. Laws limiting profits, if obeyed, tend to keep rates high instead of low; if evaded, they substitute a crooked method of distribution for a straight one.

If a company is selling gas at $1.50 a thousand feet, it indicates that this is the price which furnishes the maximum profit. A higher rate would lessen this profit by limiting consumption; a lower rate would lessen it by making the margin above expenses too narrow. If the cost of making the gas is $1.00 a thousand feet, and the consumption will be 10,000,000 at $1.75, 20,000,000 at $1.50, and 30,000,000 at $1.25, the profit at $1.75 would be $7,500, at $1.50 it would be $10,000, and at $1.25 it would be $7,500. If the company were forbidden to divide $10,000 the price would be quite as likely to be kept up at $1.75 as to be reduced to $1.25. In fact, the higher figure would be very much the more probable one; first, because it is on the whole easier for the officials of a company to handle a small business on a liberal margin of profit than a large business on a close one; and second, because the actual rates charged almost always represent the result of a process of reduction which has been going on for years, for the very purpose of obtaining a maximum profit. If our large corporations were trying to raise their charges, limitation of profits might readily remove the temptation to such a policy. But this is not what they are habitually doing. They are lowering their charges for the sake of possible profits. Take away the chance for increased profit and we destroy the motive for reductions in charge. We invite corporations to pursue a conservative policy when a progressive one means better public service at cheaper rates.

Lord Farrer, whose long experience as secretary of the Board of Trade gave him unique opportunities for observing the effects of various methods of regulation practiced in England, says that limitation of profits does not cause reduction in rates; and that in trying to apply this principle Parliament has gone on a wrong tack and involved the country in a "maze of absurdities."

185. Besides hindering reductions of rates, limitation of profits also prevents the increased investment of capital which is the best guarantee of efficient public service. If it is impossible for a concern to make more than an ordinary rate of profit, there is no adequate motive offered to the investor to develop new facilities and introduce new methods. These experiments may turn out badly and involve loss. If the company is to be deprived of the special profit in case they turn out well, the motive for their introduction is taken away, and the public fails to secure the service which it might otherwise enjoy.

186. If laws limiting profits are evaded instead of being obeyed, the effects, though different in kind, are equally undesirable. It is easy to reduce profits by extravagance in management, or by giving officials large salaries. This does no good to the consumer, and positive harm to the investor. Such laws may also be evaded by inflating the company's capital account: a practice known as stock-watering. If a corporation is allowed to divide all the money that it makes, there is no temptation to honest managers to create a fictitious capital account. But if the dividends are arbitrarily limited to eight percent when the company is really earning twelve, the directors are tempted to pretend that there has been an investment of capital one and one half times as great as has actually been expended. On the basis of this supposed investment they issue a stock dividend of fifty percent. This is in common language, "water." It does not represent money actually paid in. By dividing eight percent on the watered stock, they can put the real earnings

of the company into the hands of the investors without direct conflict with the law, and sometimes without public knowledge of the actual nature of the transaction.

The worst of the matter is that when the practice of stock-watering once becomes tolerated, it is indefinitely abused by those who are in a position to do so. If companies begin to issue fictitious capital, there is no limit to such issues. A false capital account gives opportunity for every kind of stock-speculation and for all sorts of illegitimate methods of control by financial operators. Many attempts have been made to prohibit stock-watering; but as long as limitation of profits is attempted, there are enough honest men who are interested in the more defensible forms of stock-watering to render it almost impossible to detect and punish the indefensible ones. The evil from this source alone far outweighs any good that has ever been obtained by trying to limit dividends.

## Henry Rand Hatfield
## *The Journal of Political Economy*
## December—1899
## The Chicago Trust Conference.

The Chicago Trust Conference of September 13–16 met in response to a call issued by the Civic Federation. This is an organization designed originally to correct abuses in local politics. Its success in securing the enactment of the civil service act, in establishing the Municipal Voters' League, and in other enterprises connected with the welfare of the city led it to try its powers in dealing with questions of national rather than local significance. Four national conferences have been held under its auspices. The first in 1894, at Chicago, dealt with industrial arbitration; the second in January 1898, at New York City, with primary election reforms; the third in August 1898, at Saratoga, with the foreign policy of the United States; and the latest, just held at Chicago, considered the trust problem in its political, economic and social aspects.

Being thus called by a local political organization, it was questioned whether the conference was not inspired by some partisan motive. By some it was construed as an attempt on the part of shrewd politicians to get the trust out of national politics so that the campaign of next year might be fought on other lines; others thought it was rather an attempt to sound public sentiment, so as to enable party managers to shape their platforms accordingly. Whatever the motive may have been, it at least did not prevent free discussion, and while individual politicians did not forget their calling when they entered the assembly hall, partisan politics were disbarred, and the managers endeavored to limit the debate to the consideration of the economic problem now so prominently before the public.

To secure an expression of sentiment from all parts of the country the Federation asked the governor of each state and territory to appoint seven delegates. In addition to this quasi-public representation, members of congress, governors, attorneys-general, and various private individuals supposedly interested in the subject, were invited directly by the Federation, while national associations of workingmen and other organizations, such as manufacturers' associations, boards of trade, reform clubs, and universities, were asked to send delegates.

The delegates appointed by the governors constituted about one half of the membership. In some cases—as Texas—they came as a solid body, instructed to maintain the views of the dominant political faction, and confessedly not open to conviction by any argument which the debate might unfold. In other cases the appointments were made with more impartiality, Governor Roosevelt, for instance choosing not only politicians of each party, but also a labor leader, a merchant, and scholars from the two great universities of the state.

The four hundred delegates who responded to the call were varied enough to satisfy the demand for diversity of sentiment. Coming from thirty states, all sections and almost every class of society were represented. Capitalists, manufacturers, unskilled laborers, trade unionists, grangers, lawyers, professional reformers, skilled mechanics, labor commissioners, single taxers, economists, commercial travelers, and anarchists, all were officially represented through some organization, while the gubernatorial appointees showed every shade of political belief—an assembly whose diversity gave promise of many-sided discussion and proof of widespread interest in the subject. The trusts them selves were, however, not directly represented. Several corporation lawyers and some others whose interests were allied to trusts were there, but the officers and managers did not appear, although a few had been appointed or invited. This was the only defect in representation.

The call for the conference having been general in terms, no one could predict the character of the assembly. Though the professed purpose was impartial discussion, it was by many styled the "anti-trust" conference, while others thought its leaders would attempt to force an endorsement, rather than a criticism, of consolidation. The press had alternately ridiculed the enterprise and made vague insinuations as to the motives of its promoters. The extreme opponents of the trust were especially suspicious of some sinister design. They feared lest the trusts would again indulge their penchant for buying up everything in sight, and that the conference would itself prove to be the latest purchase of some syndicate. Semi-secret cabals were held to plan against being overwhelmed by a packed house. On the opening days this mutual suspicion was curiously manifest, and it was difficult to arrange for the necessary committee on organization and program. Each scheme for representation on this committee was opposed by some clique which dreaded the dominance of some other faction. How votes should be cast, how many should be on the committee, by whom they should be appointed, were all wrangled over until the compromise of Mr. Cockran was adopted. This provided that each national organization should choose one member of the committee, and that each state should have one representative, to be selected by a joint vote of the delegates from all local organizations within the state, and of the delegates appointed by the governor. Another dispute arose as to the treatment of resolutions, and again it needed Mr. Cockran's influence to check a wrangle which threatened to be interminable. A similar committee was appointed, to which all resolutions were referred and from which none ever emerged.

While the control of the conference was thus vested in its own committee, the program adopted was practically what had been prearranged by the Civic Federation, whose wise selection of speakers deserves much praise. While the dangers of heated partisan discussion were avoided, nearly every shade of belief was given a liberal hearing. As was inevitable in a body composed largely of politicians, much time was wasted in mere buncombe and rhetoric, which contributed neither facts nor argument to the discussion. The shifty finesse of the demagogue attempting to be all things to all men, and the turgid eloquence of the professional orator, with his stock of patriotic properties, were, of course, not lacking, but many of the fifty addresses were able and deserve careful study; some of them merely as showing the viewpoint of various classes, others because of scientific treatment of the subject discussed.

Professor John B. Clark presented the ablest economic discussion, captivating the audience alike by his impartiality and his scholarship. A more extreme wing was represented by George Gunton who delivered a panegyric on centralization, seeming to ignore any possibility of abuses. He showed boldness in presenting views distasteful to many of his auditors, dogmatism in his statements, and eloquence unusual in economic discussion. Striking, too, were the speeches of B. R. Tucker, the anarchist, and T. J. Morgan, a socialist of local reputation, both of whom defended industrial consolidation. Even Chicago prejudice against the term anarchy did not prevent appreciation of the rugged logic which carried the principles of industrial freedom to its extreme limit; in contrast the socialist, with more of the demagogue and less of the philosopher, pushed the claims made for the trust to the logical outcome of a socialist regime where all industry would be operated by one all-embracing public trust.

The radical anti-trust views were best represented by Dudley Wooten, of Texas. Despite the crudity of his views, his speech was enthusiastically received, his "breezy rhetoric," as it was termed by Mr. Cockran, being accepted in place of weightier qualities.

The interest of the conference centered, however, in the addresses of Mr. Bryan and Mr. Cockran. To these alone was given the privilege of unlimited time. The prominence of the men, the possible political significance of their utterances, the expectation of personal tilting, and the reputation for oratory held by each, all gave added importance to their addresses. Mr. Cockran's speech easily outranked all others as an exhibition of oratorical powers. Appearing as a supporter of trusts, he made unexpected concessions to the other side, some of which might, perhaps, logically damage his main position. His address was an advocate's plea, grounded on economic principles, couched in an orator's rhetoric, and tinged, possibly, with a politician's craft. Mr. Bryan made a less striking speech, distinctly inferior to Mr. Cockran's in economic reasoning, and not equal in eloquence to his own best efforts. With much direct appeal to the prejudices of his hearers, he yet was more moderate in his program than many had anticipated. It was, on the whole, a strong, thoughtful plea, but inconsistent in detail, and clearly the expression of an adroit politician rather than a philosopher.

On every point of theory divergence of opinion was to be expected from such a body with different interests and varying degrees of candor. It is impossible even to summarize all these conflicting doctrines, but it may be profitable to consider some of the views more frequently expressed in regard to the chief topics: the nature and origin of trusts, the merits or demerits of the system, the remedy for evils, the interrelation of competition and monopoly, and the attitude of labor towards trusts.

1. *The nature and origin of trusts.*—At the start one is troubled by the absence of any clear definition of the fundamental concept. The printed reports show only one definition of trusts, that of Professor Clark: "Any combination so big as to be menacing." Other speakers did not always have this definition in mind; indeed, in many cases, had no clear concept, but discussed the growing tendency towards consolidation without stopping to consider how large the business must be or what other attributes it needed to be dubbed a trust.

The weight of evidence, however, supported the view that the modern system of large business establishments was the outgrowth of natural industrial evolution. This was necessarily the view of those who advocated trust methods, but it was also advanced by all save one of the professional economists, by the leading labor representatives, and even by some who were avowed anti-trust men. Professor H. C. Adams, the unique dissentient among economists, distinguished between industries like railroads, which would naturally consolidate, and many manufacturing industries, whose recent trusting was caused by abnormal economic or juridical conditions. With him though less reserved in their statements, were all the more radical wing, who held that trusts were ever the evil product of unnatural conditions. In specifying these conditions many items were mentioned. The most common were the tariff and railroad discrimination. It must, however, be borne in mind that "trust" was used in very different senses by different speakers, and that one who described the trust as originating in some specific condition may not have meant the same thing that the economist attributed to natural evolution.

2. *Is the trust harmful?*—Here again we find a confusion of tongues even greater than the discrepancy of opinions. No one can tell whether a trust is beneficial or not unless he knows what a trust is. No two men can agree as to its merits and defects save as they agree in its definition. Under this one question, then, several are properly included. The fundamental one is whether production on a large scale is of itself advantageous. This may be considered aside from the question of probable coercion of labor, of extortion toward consumers, of corruption of politics. It involves two distinct questions: (1) whether consolidation cheapens production, and (2) whether the accompanying transformation of self-directing artisans, shopkeepers, and petty manufacturers, into employees of a great concern, works ill to society. In this form the question needs to be answered by socialists as well as by individualists. In general there was agreement in answering affirmatively as to cheapened production, although here again Professor Adams varied the monotony—at least to the extent of intimating that there was a limit to profitable consolidation. Whether this limit was an organization larger or smaller than the modern trust, Professor Adams unfortunately did not state. Whether consolidation in itself degraded mankind was a more mooted question. Some evaded

it; some—as Mr. Cockran and Mr. Gunton—boldly declared that large production necessarily and inevitably meant a higher type of man, a fuller degree of liberty; the socialists an ambiguous answer, declaring that the laborer was neither harmed by consolidation in itself, nor necessarily benefited by the resulting increase in product; while the popular orator, the small proprietor, the commercial traveler all agreed in declaring that the injury done by turning a man into a cog-wheel far and away outweighed all possible gains from increased production.

Granting that the industrial gain from consolidation outweighs the sacrifice of individuality, the evaluation of trusts involves a second question: Can private ownership be safely trusted with the power which comes from the control of a vast industry? As publicists admit the greater efficiency of a benevolent despotism, yet oppose the granting of absolutism to any individual, so economists may admit the advantages of production on a large scale, yet fear the effect of industrial absolutism. The centering of industry in a few hands may mean only greater power to grind the laborer and to rob the consumer. It is of little avail that production is larger, if the increased gain goes only to swell the capitalist's luxuries. Here, too, diversity of opinion was heard. One held that the industrial advantage was not vitiated by private ownership and control, for "even the capitalist, who from the most sordid motives seeks to raise the rate of interest from 5 percent. to 6 percent., must serve his fellows in doing it." This view, which was upheld by Professor Clark and Mr. Cockran, was directly opposed by western radicals, by socialists, by Mr. Bryan and others. These argued that the possession of such great industrial power meant also the possession of political power, which would result in the corruption of legislatures and the overthrow of democracy. The political objections thus urged were not met frankly by the extreme pro-trust speakers.

One question remains. Granting that consolidation is economically beneficial, and that the force of competition tends to distribute the benefits even against the selfish desires of capitalists; granting that the legitimate use of consolidation is advantageous, are not the abuses and perversions of trusts so common as to require rigid control? Even their defenders admitted some such evils, while their opponents adduced a long catalogue, which it is not necessary to repeat in full. The subjects of most frequent complaint were the watering of stock, the displacement of labor, extortion—especially when aided by the tariff or by railroad discrimination—and corruption.

A significant point in this discussion is that the gist of each speaker's accusation was the injury inflicted by the trust on the peculiar interests of his own class. Those whose interests were allied to capital complained of the financial mismanagement so often found in large corporations; the commercial traveler thought trusts evil because 35,000 of his class were thrown out of employment; the retailer, because he could no longer compete; the agriculturalist, because the price of raw products was low; the consumer of trust goods, because prices were high; the displaced artisan, because new processes were introduced; and the patent lawyer, because invention was discouraged. If it is true that each class is thus injured by the trust, even the Texan vituperation seems not altogether inappropriate. Such a general enemy of mankind may well be called robber, monster, or octopus.

The diversity of accusations, however, raises a suspicion as to their validity. This suspicion is increased on recalling the American proclivity for finding some convenient scape-goat on which any and all evils may be laid. A bank charter, a coinage act, a change in the tariff have in turn been used to explain serious industrial ills, although it was impossible that such far-reaching results should flow from a single source. This tendency may be fostered by politicians who hope to unite the unfortunate and disaffected by proclaiming a crusade against a popular bugaboo. The trust—so striking a feature in modern industry—is well suited to serve as the object of such an attack.

Many of the evils charged against trusts are not peculiar to trust organization. Abuses which are common to other forms of enterprise are brought into prominence because of their connection with trust operations. The large scale on which modern business is conducted acts as a magnifier, and popular clamor is excited against trusts because evils are there disclosed which elsewhere exist unseen.

This may be made clear by a hypothetical illustration. It is conceivable that in the case of some commodity ill-suited to American resources a tariff might keep prices above the European level without giving abnormal profits to competing American manufacturers. The high price paid by consumers would merely repay the high cost of production under the wasteful system of small establishments. If a trust should combine these warring factories, and introduce improved methods, the cost would be lowered, but not necessarily the price, since foreign competition—a force which would otherwise compel the monopoly to lower prices—would be barred out by tariff. In such a case the high profits would be made the basis of an attack on the trust. But the real evil, namely, that consumers are forced to pay a higher price for American goods than the foreign article would bring, existed equally under the old system. Clearly the trust did not cause the evil; it merely profited by it. In a similar way the watering of stock is not an evil peculiar to large corporations. It is only one manifestation of the tendency to swindle gullible investors. To condemn trusts as the cause of this phenomenon would resemble holding the legal-tender law responsible for every "green-goods" swindle. Again, granting that the displacement of labor is an evil, it would be an evil independent of trusts, one that would recur with each new invention, with each improvement introduced by the individual manufacturer. And, finally, corruption, emphasized—perhaps facilitated—by the concentration of capital, was surely not unknown in the days of private enterprise.

3. *The remedies suggested.*—The admission that the accusations are exaggerated, and that trusts suffer vicariously for common misdeeds does not at all deny the validity of some of the complaints nor the seriousness of some of the abuses. The practical question then is: What can be done to remedy these evils? The answer to this depends on the position one takes on the question suggested in a preceding paragraph. To one who believes that consolidation is in itself evil, the only remedy is to strike at once at large enterprises; to one dreading the vesting of great power in private hands, the remedy is either more individualistic industry or else more thorough socialism; to one finding the cause in some external condition various specific reforms are desirable.

The simplest program was to destroy or prevent all large aggregations of capital. Some of "the methods suggested for carrying out this program were: to prohibit outright corporations with more than a given limited capital; to make each stockholder liable without limitation for all the corporation debts, and thus hinder the consolidation of small capitals; to tax the income, stock, or franchise of corporations, and thus check their growth by limiting their profits."

The criticism of these plans is obvious. Many who cried for extermination failed to state how it could be accomplished. To make stockholders liable without limitation would strike a blow at the chief merit of corporations, and harm society rather than the capitalist. Even Mr. Bryan's more systematic plan lacks definiteness. Regulation by both state and Federal government is an imposing demand, but purely formal. The detail that no licenses should be given corporations exercising or attempting a monopoly is impracticable in view of Mr. Bryan's own statement that there is no real monopoly as yet, and because every business enterprise is an attempt to monopolize some trade or some market. The clearest point in the program of those who would annihilate large corporations is the declaration by Mr. Bryan that some action is needed and any attempt to legislate reform is preferable to supine inaction. But this proposal is rather an outline for a politician's campaign than an economic policy. The economist would argue that, because a shifting policy is so disastrous, no steps should be taken unless it be shown beyond cavil that beneficial results will follow.

Slightly less drastic than such proposals were those designed to prevent misconduct by the trusts rather than to prevent consolidation. Almost every form of control was suggested, including the direct legislative determination of prices for trusted goods, and of wages for trust employees. The most popular plan, indeed almost the only proposal which met with no direct opposition, was for greater publicity of public accounts, designed to prevent stock-jobbing. Some thought this should be seconded by direct prohibition of stock watering; others, notably Mr. Cockran, thought that mere publicity would be a panacea.

Besides legislation dealing directly with the trusts, there was much emphasis placed on indirect methods of effecting the desired control. The burden of these plans was: destroy the artificial monopoly which law has erected around the trusts, and with the destruction of special privilege much of the evil of trusts will disappear; modify the patent laws so as to lessen or destroy the monopoly of invention; modify the tariff so that trusts may not lurk within its shelter; prevent railroad discrimination, and thus give every competitor equal opportunity. Such changes were widely proposed; while some thought them insufficient, none thought them objectionable.

Another class of proposals recognized that trust evils were merely symptoms of some general complaint. While this or that abuse might, perhaps, be bettered by some local application, a thorough cure could come only from a remedy which went to the root of the evil. To secure such a re-ordering of society, socialism, anarchy, public ownership, single tax, and the referendum were, each in turn, recommended as the one thing needful. Mr. Seymour's paper was one of the most suggestive on this line. Finding an identity between the corrupt practices of corporations and of individuals, he traced them both to the low moral tone of the business world. Perfectly to solve the trust problem, he held, involved the discovery of some method of raising the moral standard of a race.

4. *The interrelation of competition and monopoly.*—The foregoing discussion has shown the importance of the theory of monopoly to the trust problem. It is true that not all the evils charged to trusts are dependent on monopoly. The dehumanizing effects of centralization would remain were there two competing combinations instead of a single one; the displacement of labor would be almost as great; political corruption might be even greater. But, in general, trusts are criticised because they are held to destroy competition. The critics use trust and monopoly as synonyms; their corrective measures are aimed at the monopolistic features. The discussions in the conference, accordingly, turned much on monopoly, yet there was no general agreement in the use the term. When Professor Clark declared the evil of monopoly he meant something quite different from that which Mr. Bryan condemned. One speaker would describe monopoly as the antithesis, another as the perfect fruit, of competition. Behind this apparent disagreement there was, however real unanimity. If a monopoly be defined as the power on the part of producers arbitrarily to maintain high prices, all agreed that such power could not wisely be vested in private control. Even Mr. Cockran agreed to this. There was further agreement that any form of governmental favoritism which indirectly gave this power would be as unjustifiable as would the direct enactment of a corporate monopoly. Disagreement arose as to whether, in the absence of such government favoritism, the force of competition was adequate or whether, in addition to such negative action, government should take positive measures to secure competition. Subordinate to this was the question whether certain government regulations were of such a nature as to establish monopoly which would otherwise exist. Thus, while all agreed that government favoritism was unjustifiable, it might be debated whether a tariff law really gave monopoly powers to an American trust.

As shown above there was much agreement that in order to prevent such an artificial monoply [sic] some changes should be made in the tariff and patent laws, and railroad discrimination should be prevented. Both Professor Clark and Mr. Cockran argued that natural competition would prevent extortion. Perhaps, after all, this is the crucial point of the whole conference: whether in a free market the force of competition is adequate to prevent extortion? The radicals generally ignored the power of latent competition. The usurpation of a market by the goods of a single concern was held by them to be tantamount to wholesale robbery of the consumer. Mr. Bryan was emphatic on this point, at the cost of being inconsistent. Even in the more extreme case of a capitalist monopolizing land in a given neighborhood, Mr. Bryan argued that competition would check his greed; how, then, can a manufacturing combination, where there is much less friction in competition, hold undisputed sway over customers? But Mr. Cockran may have erred on the other side. Theoretically-free competition does not exist in actual life. The abstractions of the economist are valuable in making deductions, but there is danger when an unskilled hand applies them as working models in practical politics. As the mechanic does not start his machine and trust to the physicist's abstraction of inertia and persistence of force to keep it moving, so the politician should not trust to the abstraction of free competition to keep society in its course. To say that free competition will prevent extortion would be to beg the question: Does free competition, in any proper sense, exist as between a small producer and a great trust? Latent competition is certainly a mighty force wherewith corporate greed may be kept in check; that it is ever-present and all-sufficient needs to be demonstrated. Professor Clark, though a professional economist, was at once more philosophical and more practical. He recognized that something more was needed to secure the benefits of competition than the mere repeal of legislative privileges. The power of the corporation itself might create privileges almost as potent as a governmental patent. The repeal of objectionable tariff measures and the cure of railroad discrimination are in the line of securing greater freedom of competition, but are insufficient if the action of the corporations themselves can effectually destroy rivals. Hence Professor Clark urges the need of preventing trusts from killing off competition by showing discrimination against certain rivals. Uniform prices should be required of all corporations equally with uniform rates in transportation. Perhaps the realization of such a program would be a difficult task, but the recognition of the evil is at least an advantage.

While several speakers emphasized latent competition by possible producers, only one speaker, and he the representative of a labor union, brought out the competition of substitution.

Mr. Garland said:

> There is not an article produced in these modern times but there are, or can be adopted, several substitutes for it; and the cost as a rule will not vary enough to permit any greater or long lasting extremity to our needs.

The importance of this is great. Even a city gas company, which can have no direct rival, is constantly restrained by such competition. In such a case there is no chance, should prices go too high, for rival capital to come into the field and build a new plant; that is prevented by the exclusive franchise. But the ever-present competition of oil and electricity set a very definite limit to the extortion of the gas company. Similarly, natural and artificial gas, oil, wood, soft coal (raw and coked) briquettes, even corn and twisted hay act as a bar to the extreme extortion which might otherwise be practiced by a monopoly of anthracite-coal barons. It is true this form of competition may at times be insignificant; but to speak of trusts as being able to establish prices on their own terms is oratorical hyperbole. Linseed oil, sugar, glucose, whisky, cordage, strawboard, biscuits, cereal preparations, beer, all trusted products have substitutes whose competition can be met only by keeping down prices. It is surprising that the conference paid so little attention to this phase of competition.

5. *The relation of trusts to labor.*—The debates of the conference are most significant on this point than on any other. The aggressions of the trust on the rights of the laborer and the lowering effect on wages make fine subjects for public harangues, and the politicians of the conference used them freely. The starving employee is an excellent

bit of oratorical property not to be slighted by any stump speaker. But it is a significant fact that it was not the laborer who was the most bitter complainant. The small producer and the traveling man were the extremists. To be sure, the representative of the Knights of Labor could not well be exceeded in virulence, but the trade unionists all spoke with moderation. Mr. Gompers said that wages were continually rising, and that trusts will increase; Mr. Garland conceded that trusts may have some advantages to the workman; Mr. White, in a paper which for impartiality and clear reasoning was scarcely surpassed in the conference, claimed no friendship for the trusts, and hinted at probable abuses, but indulged in no general denunciation. Mr. Morgan, of course, took the socialistic attitude of encouraging trusts as a step towards socialism.

The more bitter foes of the trusts intimated that organized labor was not altogether disinterested in holding these conservative views. Trade unions were accused of having leagued with capital to form a more gigantic trust for the joint spoliation of the consumer; they had been bribed by high wages to become a party to a conspiracy against their fellow-workmen and against society. In support of this view it was urged that the rate of wages would be immaterial to such a combination, since a monopoly could always recoup itself by increasing the price of its products. Granting this, though the force of substitutional competition denies it, it is difficult to see why an unrestrained power to raise prices should wait on higher wages, or why additional profits are not as much sought for at the expense of labor as at that of the consumers. Whatever the price, higher wages mean, *ceteris paribus*, lower profits. The only way in which juggling with prices could affect the problem is on the assumption that the monopoly has some maximum rate of gain, beyond which it is not desirous to go. But this is an hypothesis which the critic of monopoly would hardly accept.

Another explanation of the attitude of organized labor is more reasonable. While it is true that disinterested students of social and economic problems have recognized and criticised the dangerous tendencies of modern centralization, yet it is the small manufacturer who has constituted the backbone of at least the popular attack on trusts. Others whose interests have been injured have joined in the campaign, and politicians, for one reason or another, have espoused the cause. But it is the small producer, whose business has been destroyed by fair means or foul, who supplies the virulence of the attack. The general public has been asked to come to the support of the small proprietor, whom the octopus threatens to swallow. Now, in this conflict the laborer is not primarily interested. Complaints enough he has against the employing class, but he sees that the small proprietor, equally with the trust, is an employer of labor; and he does not see that it is incumbent on him to fight one employer for the benefit of another. Recognizing that the centralization of industry gives a few men dangerous power which may be used to oppress the laborer, he also sees that the power may result in immensely better conditions for labor. The sufferings under the regime of small proprietorship by no means lead labor to champion the old as against the new system, which at least offers hope of some benefit through higher wages and lower prices. Being thus neutral in the fight between the small proprietor and the trust, the labor-leader sees both the merits and the dangers of consolidated industry. In the

Chicago conference the labor-leaders ranked next to the professional economists in the disinterestedness of their position.

Both enemies and friends of the trust made strenuous efforts to secure the active support of the labor class. On one side a picture was shown of the oppression of the wage-earner which would follow when the trusts gained absolute power; and rhetorical appeals were made to the laborer's prejudices against the employing class. One who would make a popular appeal in favor of trusts has a more difficult role. It is hard to awaken sympathy or excite enthusiasm for the wealthy capitalist. To offset this handicap seemed to be part of the policy of Mr. Cockran. His extreme courtesy to the labor representatives, as shown by two motions to grant them unusual privileges on the floor, his compliments to their wisdom and economic learning, his eloquent eulogy of labor, the consultations reported to have been held with the labor delegates, and their expressed hope "that he might be able to do something" for them—all these would seem to indicate that behind the economic discussion, the fervor, and the eloquence there was an undercurrent of shrewd political policy. If this political foresight was apparent in the case of Mr. Cockran, it without doubt was present with many another. Politics could not be entirely kept out, even by the diligence of the management, and to some extent the conference was less valuable because of this element of finesse.

Perhaps one of the most gratifying features of the conference was the deference paid to acknowledged economic principles and the respect accorded to professional economists. Since the days when Webster vented his scorn of all economists "from Adam Smith to Professor Dew" it has been customary for politicians to treat them, at least, with complacent disdain. The economist has not been looked up to with any marked respect, the laws of the last forty years witness. Little of this spirit appeared in the conference. In one instance a western politician declared that the academic element never was friendly to practical freedom. The only other instance (save some remarks made in an irrelevant discussion of the tariff) came, strangely enough, from one who is himself an eminent economist, and was an insinuation of professional venality. The conference, composed largely of practical politicians, listened to the seven economists on the program with more than average attention, and press and public alike recognized that the impractical theorist had a message of real import. It was evident to many that neither the scheming politician, nor the unbalanced enthusiast, nor the unfortunate victim of industrial changes was the best judge of conditions, nor the wisest guide for legislation. The calm, measured, disinterested propositions of the professional economist appeared all the better for the background. No speaker created a better impression on the public than did Professor Clark.

Nor was the courtesy shown economists the only gratifying sign. Despite much wild talking there was evidence that many of the speakers had made careful study of the underlying principles. That any politician, speaking on a subject of so many emotional phases, could appeal to economic reasoning rather than to passion is encouraging. Mr. Cockran's speech is a good example of this. His skill as a politician, his power as an orator are well known, yet he did not merely appeal to prejudices, nor rely solely on the spell of his eloquence. Without agreeing to all his propositions, one must admit that his argument was based on economic principles, and that it could have been made only by one who was a student as well as a brilliant orator. The leavening of the body politic with economic doctrine at times seems hopeless. The members of the academic circle are too often unfitted by their training and disposition to make popular appeals, and they are often disheartened by having their logic put to rout in the arena by the clever sophisms of some master speaker. To find an orator such as Mr. Cockran dealing in economic wares is a more hopeful sign than even the fact that a dozen economists sat in a public convention. It perhaps presages a closer union of politics and economics, a bridging of the chasm which has separated the academy from the forum.

# 4

# Progressivism and the 1912 Election

## Introduction

### BY DANIEL CRANE

The 1912 Presidential election among William Howard Taft, Theodore Roosevelt, and Woodrow Wilson[1] roused more interest in antitrust issues than any other election in American history. This in itself would be an insufficient reason to include the campaign's political rhetoric in a book of intellectual history. But Taft, Roosevelt, and Wilson fit the public intellectual mold far better than most presidential candidates. Taft was a former state and federal judge and future chief justice of the U.S. Supreme Court and wrote an academic book on antitrust policy.[2] Wilson was a political scientist and the former president of Princeton University. Roosevelt was... well, where to begin? Easily the most prolific writer since Thomas Jefferson, TR wrote a mountain of books, articles, and essays on such varied subjects as natural history, ornithology, naval strategy, the taming of the west, African large game animals, the geography of the Amazon river, art criticism, Greek philosophy, and of course political theory.

From the centennial perspective, 1912 is loaded with dramatic story lines. The former larger-than-life president battles his now-alienated protégé for the Republican nomination. A summer convention in Chicago crowns Taft the nominee. TR charges fraud and bolts the party. Running as a Bull Moose Progressive, TR engages Taft in a bitter and personal contest in the general election. A would-be assassin's bullet pierces TR's chest in Milwaukee outside a campaign event, yet he staggers into the venue where, bloodied and rasping, he delivers over an hour of political invective before staggering off to a near-death swoon.[3] Wilson, the cool Presbyterian academic, stands aloof of the Taft-Roosevelt personality politics, waiting for

1. A fourth candidate, Socialist Eugene Debs, received almost 6 percent of the popular vote—the strongest electoral showing for a Socialist candidate in American presidential contests.

2. William Howard Taft, *The Anti-Trust Act and the Supreme Court* (1914).

3. Edmund Morris, *Colonel Roosevelt* 243–247 (2010).

the erstwhile friends to destroy each other. Yet, upon TR's premature death in 1919, it is Taft who lingers by the graveside weeping.[4]

Many of the election headlines include an extraordinary contest over antitrust law. The straw that breaks the camel's back and prompts TR to challenge Taft for the nomination is the Taft administration's antitrust lawsuit against U.S. Steel, in which it alleges that U.S. Steel misled TR into approving an anticompetitive deal in the midst of the 1907 financial panic.[5] Roosevelt saves his bitterest words for Wilson in a response to Wilson's supposed mischaracterization of TR's remarks about the "the 'inevitable' rise of monopolist corporations."[6]

In battling over antitrust, the candidates were reacting to one of the great issues of the day. The year prior to the election, the Supreme Court had handed down its landmark *Standard Oil* decision.[7] Although finding that Rockefeller had violated the Sherman Act and ordering the Standard's dissolution, the Court also embraced a rule of reason to govern the legality of the trusts. Many Progressives saw this as the creation of a legal loophole through which the robber barons would continue their ride toward industrial despotism. Already before the *Standard Oil* decision, a widespread political consensus had emerged that the Sherman Act was proving an insufficient foil to the trusts. Demand for a major overhaul of the antitrust laws and enforcement institutions was in the air.

Hence, the three major candidates scrambled to articulate a vision for enhanced scrutiny of the trusts. Taft, the conservative, argued that the existing legal and institutional framework was sufficient and that more aggressive enforcement by the executive would do the trick. His recent cases against U.S. Steel, American Sugar, General Electric, the meat packers, and the transcontinental railways served as prominent exhibits.[8] A former and future judge, Taft embraced the judiciary and its common law incrementalism, proclaiming (in the passage that follows) "I love judges and I love courts." Roosevelt's barbed attacks on the Supreme Court justices and proposals for judicial recall and the Progressives' proposals to replace judicial decision making with technocratic administrative bodies offended Taft's increasingly conservative sensibilities. The prosecutors and courts would see to it that America got back to competition as its organizing industrial principle.

Roosevelt had too many run-ins with courts to count judges his friends. TR, the man of action who clove the Panama Canal through the jagged force of his will, saw courts as too passive and reactive to meet the pressing needs of the day. But nor did TR deserve the "trustbuster" moniker he obtained for challenging the Rockefeller and J. P. Morgan interests during his presidency. Roosevelt did not want to "bust" the trusts; he wanted to subordinate them to the authority of the chief executive. In private correspondence, TR

4. Id. at 558.

5. Id. at 148–151.

6. Id. at 249.

7. *Standard Oil Co.* v. *U.S.*, 221 U.S. 1 (1911).

8. Martin J. Sklar, *The Corporate Reconstruction of American Capitalism: 1890–1916*, 354–382 (1987).

lamented the *Standard Oil* dissolution remedy, noting, "I do not myself see what good can come from dissolving the Standard Oil Company into forty separate companies, all of which will still remain really under the same control. What we should have is a much stricter governmental supervision of these great companies."[9] Hence, Roosevelt's Square Deal would call off attempts to break up the trusts, which TR viewed as historically inevitable, and instead seek to manage them through executive and administration regulation and superintendence.[10] Roosevelt's New Nationalism exposed him to criticism from the right that he was a covert socialist and from the left that he was abandoning a policy of industrial competition and mollycoddling the trusts. Ironically, neither charge was completely spurious. At moments, the vision articulated by Roosevelt came close to calling for comprehensive management of the trusts by the government. (Recall, as we saw in the preceding chapter, that at the Chicago Trusts Conference some socialists favored the trusts as paving the way for an eventual move toward socialism.) On the other hand, as Taft's antitrust prosecutions progressed and Wilson called on Louis Brandeis to articulate his antitrust vision, many on Wall Street began to see Roosevelt as the least of the evils seeking the White House.

Greater subtlety marked the antitrust vision of Woodrow Wilson.[11] One who slotted himself somewhere on the continuum between Hamiltonianism and Jeffersonianism, Wilson also marked himself as falling somewhere on the continuum between capitalism and socialism. And on antitrust issues, between Roosevelt and Taft. Drawing on the intellectual firepower of his antitrust "brainstrust" in the person of Louis Brandeis (whom we shall encounter in Chapter Six), Wilson articulated a snappy slogan to differentiate himself from Roosevelt. Roosevelt wanted to regulate monopoly, whereas Wilson wanted to regulate competition. Of course, Taft also proposed to reinvigorate competition rather than to jump in bed with the trusts. But, per Wilson, Taft was too committed to slow-moving judicial methodologies. The courts had proven themselves inept at solving the trust problem. Some administrative agency with greater expertise and investigatory and remedial powers was needed. Two years later, that body would be born as the Federal Trade Commission. But, even on questions of institutional design, Wilson proved to be a compromiser. Many Progressives longed for a powerful and independent regulatory body with the mandate to reign in the trusts free from judicial interference. But Wilson rejected the unfettered technocratic vision of Progressivism: "I don't want a smug lot of experts to sit behind closed doors in Washington and play providence to me."[12] On antitrust, as on many other issues, Wilson lacked the purity of vision of Taft and Roosevelt. And, yes, he won the election.

9. Letter from Theodore Roosevelt to Arthur B. Farquhar (Aug. 11, 1911), in *Theodore Roosevelt: Letters and Speeches* 652 (Louis Auchincloss ed., 1951).

10. Sklar, at 333–364.

11. Id. at 383–430.

12. 25 Woodrow Wilson, "A Campaign Address in Sioux City, Iowa," in *The Papers of Woodrow Wilson* 148, 154 (Arthur S. Link ed., 1978).

## Editorial by Theodore Roosevelt
## *The Trusts, the People, and the Square Deal*

The suit against the Steel Trust by the Government has brought vividly before our people the need of reducing to order our chaotic Government policy as regards business. As President, in Messages to Congress I repeatedly called the attention of that body and of the public to the inadequacy of the Anti-Trust Law by itself to meet business conditions and secure justice to the people, and to the further fact that it might, if left unsupplemented by additional legislation, work mischief, with no compensating advantage; and I urged as strongly as I knew how that the policy followed with relation to railways in connection with the Inter-State Commerce Law should be followed by the National Government as regards all great business concerns; and therefore that, as a first step, the powers of the Bureau of Corporations should be greatly enlarged, or else that there should be created a Governmental board or commission, with powers somewhat similar to those of the Inter-State Commerce Commission, but covering the whole field of inter-State business, exclusive of transportation (which should, by law, be kept wholly separate from ordinary industrial business, all common ownership of the industry and the railway being forbidden). In the end I have always believed that it would also be necessary to give the National Government complete power over the organization and capitalization of all business concerns engaged in inter-State commerce.

A member of my Cabinet with whom, even more than with the various Attorneys-General, I went over every detail of this trust situation, was the one time Secretary of the Interior, Mr. James R. Garfield. He writes me as follows concerning the suit against the Steel Corporation:

> Nothing appeared before the House Committee that made me believe we were deceived by Judge Cary.
>
> This, I think, is a case that shows clearly the difference between destructive legislation and constructive legislation. I have not yet seen a full copy of the Government's petition, but our papers give nothing that indicates any kind of unfair or dishonest competition such as existed in both the Standard Oil and Tobacco Cases. As I understand it, the competitors of the Steel Company have steadily increased in strength during the last six or seven years. Furthermore, the percent of the business done by the Steel Corporation has decreased during that time. As you will remember, at our first conference with Judge Gary, the Judge stated that it was the desire and purpose of the Company to conform to what the Government wished, it being the purpose of the Company absolutely to obey the law both in spirit and letter. Throughout the time that I had charge of the investigation, and while we were in Washington, I do not know of a single instance where the Steel Company refused any information requested; but, on the contrary, aided in every possible way our investigation.
>
> The position now taken by the Government is absolutely destructive of legitimate business, because they outline no rule of conduct for business of any

> magnitude. It is absurd to say that the courts can lay down such rules. The most the courts can do is to find as legal or illegal the particular transactions brought before them. Hence, after years of tedious litigation there would be no clear-cut rule for future action. This method of procedure is dealing with the device, not the result, and drives business to the elaboration of clever devices, each of which must be tested in the courts.
>
> I have yet to find a better method of dealing with the anti-trust situation than that suggested by the bill which we agreed upon in the last days of your Administration. That bill should be used as a basis for legislation, and there could be incorporated upon it whatever may be determined wise regarding the direct control and supervision of the National Government, either through a commission similar to the Inter-State Commerce Commission or otherwise.

Before taking up the matter in its large aspect, I wish to say one word as to one feature of the Government suit against the Steel Corporation. One of the grounds for the suit is the acquisition by the Steel Corporation of the Tennessee Coal and Iron Company; and it has been alleged, on the authority of the Government officials engaged to carry on the suit, that as regards this transaction I was misled by the representatives of the Steel Corporation, and that the facts were not accurately or truthfully laid before me. This statement is not correct. I believed at the time that the facts in the case were as represented to me on behalf of the Steel Corporation, and my further knowledge has convinced me that this was true. I believed at the time that the representatives of the Steel Corporation told me the truth as to the change that would be worked in the percentage of the business which the proposed acquisition would give the Steel Corporation, and further inquiry has convinced me that they did so. I was not misled. The representatives of the Steel Corporation told me the truth as to what the effect of the action at that time would be, and any statement that I was misled or that the representatives of the Steel Corporation did not thus tell me the truth as to the facts of the case is itself not in accordance with the truth. In *The Outlook* of August 19 last I gave in full the statement I had made to the Investigating Committee of the House of Representatives on this matter. That statement is accurate, and I reaffirm everything I therein said, not only as to what occurred, but also as to my belief in the wisdom and propriety of my action—indeed, the action not merely was wise and proper, but it would have been a calamity from every standpoint had I failed to take it. On page 137 of the printed report of the testimony before the Committee will be found Judge Gary's account of the meeting between himself and Mr. Frick and Mr. Root and myself. This account states the facts accurately. It has been alleged that the purchase by the Steel Corporation of the property of the Tennessee Coal and Iron Company gave the Steel Corporation practically a monopoly of the Southern iron ores—that is, of the iron ores south of the Potomac and the Ohio. My information, which I have every reason to believe is accurate and not successfully to be challenged, is that, of these Southern iron ores the Steel Corporation has, including the property gained from the Tennessee Coal and Iron Company, less than 20 percent—perhaps not over 16 percent. This is a very much smaller percentage than the percentage it holds of the Lake Superior ores, which even after the surrender of the Hill lease will be slightly over 50 percent. According to my view, therefore, and unless—which I do not believe possible—these figures can be successfully challenged, the acquisition of the Tennessee Coal and Iron Company's ores in no way changed the situation as regards making the Steel Corporation a monopoly.[1] The showing as to the percentage of production of all kinds of steel ingots and steel castings in the United States by the Steel Corporation and by all other manufacturers respectively makes an even stronger case. It makes the case even stronger than I put it in my testimony before the Investigating Committee, for I was scrupulously careful to make statements that erred, if at all, against my own position. It appears from the figures of production that in 1901 the Steel Corporation had to its credit nearly 66 percent of the total production as against a little over 34 percent by all other steel manufacturers. The percentage then shrank steadily, until in 1906, the year before the acquisition of the Tennessee Coal and Iron properties, the percentage was a little under 58 percent. In spite of the acquisition of these properties, the following year, 1907, the total percentage shrank slightly, and this shrinking has continued until in 1910 the total percentage of the Steel Corporation is but a little over 54 percent, and the percentage by all other steel manufacturers but a fraction less than 46 percent. Of the $54\frac{3}{10}$ percent produced by the Steel Corporation $1\frac{9}{10}$ percent is produced by the former Tennessee Coal and Iron Company. In other words, these figures show that the acquisition of the Tennessee Coal and Iron Company did not in the slightest degree change the situation, and that during the ten years which include the acquisition of these properties by the Steel Corporation the percentage of total output of steel manufacturers in this country by the Steel Corporation has shrunk from nearly 66 percent to but a trifle over 54 percent. I do not believe that these figures can be successfully controverted, and if not successfully controverted they show clearly not only that the acquisition of the Tennessee Coal and Iron properties wrought no change in the status of the Steel Corporation, but that the Steel Corporation during the decade has steadily lost, instead of gained, in monopolistic character.

So much for the facts in this particular case. Now for the general subject. When my Administration took office, I found, not only that there had been little real enforcement of the Anti-Trust Law and but little more effective enforcement of the Inter-State Commerce Law, but also that the decisions were so chaotic and the laws themselves so vaguely drawn, or at least interpreted in such widely varying fashions, that the biggest business men tended to treat both laws as dead letters. The series of actions by which we succeeded in making the Inter-State Commerce Law an efficient and most useful instrument in regulating the transportation of the country and exacting justice from the big railways without doing them injustice—while, indeed, on the

1. My own belief is that our Nation should long ago have adopted the policy of merely leasing for a term of years mineral-bearing land; but it is the fault of us ourselves, of the people, not of the Steel Corporation, that this policy has not been adopted.

contrary, securing them against injustice—need not here be related. The Anti-Trust Law it was also necessary to enforce as it had never hitherto been enforced, both because it was on the statute-books and because it was imperative to teach the masters of the biggest corporations in the land that they were not, and would not be permitted to regard themselves as, above the law. Moreover, where the combination has really been guilty of misconduct the law serves a useful purpose, and in such cases as those of the Standard Oil and Tobacco Trusts, if effectively enforced, the law confers a real and great good.

Suits were brought against the most powerful corporations in the land, which we were convinced had clearly and beyond question violated the Anti-Trust Law. These suits were brought with great care, and only where we felt so sure of our facts that we could be fairly certain that there was a likelihood of success. As a matter of fact, in most of the important suits we were successful. It was imperative that these suits should be brought, and very real good was achieved by bringing them, for it was only these suits that made the great masters of corporate capital in America fully realize that they were the servants and not the masters of the people, that they were subject to the law, and that they would not be permitted to be a law unto themselves; and the corporations against which we proceeded had sinned, not merely by being big (which we did not regard as in itself a sin), but by being guilty of unfair practices towards their competitors, and by procuring unfair advantages from the railways. But the resulting situation has made it evidence that the Anti-Trust Law is not adequate to meet the situation that has grown up because of modern business conditions and the accompanying tremendous increase in the business use of vast quantities of corporate wealth. As I have said, this was already evident to my mind when I was President, and in communications to Congress I repeatedly stated the facts. But when I made these communications there were still plenty of people who did not believe that we would succeed in the suits that had been instituted against the Standard Oil, the Tobacco, and other corporations, and it was impossible to get the public as a whole to realize what the situation was. Sincere zealots who believed that all combinations could be destroyed and the old-time conditions of unregulated competition restored, insincere politicians who knew better but made believe that they thought whatever their constituents wished them to think, crafty revolutionaries who wished to see on the statute-books laws which they believed unenforceable, and the almost solid "Wall Street crowd" or representatives of "big business" who at that time opposed with equal violence both wise and necessary and unwise and improper regulation of business—all fought against the adoption of a sane, effective, and far-reaching policy.

It is a vitally necessary thing to have the persons in control of big trusts of the character of the Standard Oil Trust and Tobacco Trust taught that they are under the law, just as it was a necessary thing to have the Sugar Trust taught the same lesson in drastic fashion by Mr. Henry L. Stimson when he was United States District Attorney in the city of New York. But to attempt to meet the whole problem not by administrative governmental action but by a succession of lawsuits is hopeless from the standpoint of working out a permanently satisfactory solution. Moreover, the results sought to be achieved are achieved only in extremely insufficient and fragmentary measure by breaking up all big corporations, whether they have behaved well or ill, into a number of little corporations which it is perfectly certain will be largely, and perhaps altogether, under the same control. Such action is harsh and mischievous if the corporation is guilty of nothing except its size; and where, as in the case of the Standard Oil, and especially the Tobacco, trusts, the corporation has been guilty of immoral and anti-social practices, there is need for far more drastic and thorough-going action than any that has been taken, under the recent decree of the Supreme Court. In the case of the Tobacco Trust, for instance, the settlement in the Circuit Court, in which the representatives of the Government seem inclined to concur, practically leaves all of the companies still substantially under the control of the twenty-nine original defendants. Such a result is lamentable from the standpoint of justice. The decision of the Circuit Court, if allowed to stand, means that the Tobacco Trust has merely been obliged to change its clothes, that none of the real offenders have received any real punishment, while, as the New York "Times," a pro-trust paper, says, the tobacco concerns, in their new clothes, are in positions of "ease and luxury," and "immune from prosecution under the law."

Surely, miscarriage of justice is not too strong a term to apply to such a result when considered in connection with what the Supreme Court said of this Trust. That great Court in its decision used language which, in spite of its habitual and severe self-restraint in stigmatizing wrong-doing, yet unhesitatingly condemns the Tobacco Trust for moral turpitude, saying that the case shows an "ever-present manifestation ... of conscious wrongdoing" by the Trust, whose history is "replete with the doing of acts which it was the obvious purpose of the statute to forbid, ... demonstrative of the existence from the beginning of a purpose to acquire dominion and control of the tobacco trade, not by the mere exertion of the ordinary right to contract and to trade, but by methods devised in order to monopolize the trade by driving competitors out of business, which were ruthlessly carried out upon the assumption that to work upon the fears or play upon the cupidity of competitors would make success possible." The letters from and to various officials of the Trust, which were put in evidence, show a literally astounding and horrifying indulgence by the Trust in wicked and depraved business methods—such as the "endeavor to cause a strike in their [a rival business firm's] factory," or the "shutting off the market" of an independent tobacco firm by "taking the necessary steps to give them a warm reception," or forcing importers into a price agreement by causing and continuing "a demoralization of the business for such length of time as may be deemed desirable" (I quote from the letters). A Trust guilty of such conduct should be absolutely disbanded, and the only way to prevent the repetition of such conduct is by strict Government supervision, and not merely by lawsuits.

The Anti-Trust Law cannot meet the whole situation, nor can any modification of the principle of the Anti-Trust Law avail to meet the whole situation. The fact is that many of the men who have called themselves Progressives, and who certainly believe that they are Progressives, represent in reality in this matter not progress at all but a kind of sincere rural toryism. These men believe that it is by strengthening the Anti-Trust Law to restore business to the competitive conditions of the middle of the last century. Any such effort is foredoomed to end in failure, and, if successful, would be mischievous to the last degree. Business cannot be successfully conducted in accordance with the practices and theories of sixty years ago unless we abolish steam, electricity, big cities, and, in short, not only all modern business and modern industrial conditions, but all the modern conditions of our civilization. The effort to restore competition as it was sixty years ago, and to trust for justice solely to this proposed restoration of competition, is just as foolish as if we should go back to the flintlocks of Washington's Continentals as a substitute for modern weapons of precision. The effort to prohibit all combinations, good or bad, is bound to fail, and ought to fail; when made, it merely means that some of the worst combinations are not checked and that honest business is checked. Our purpose should be, not to strangle business as an incident of strangling combinations, but to regulate big corporations in thoroughgoing and effective fashion, so as to help legitimate business as an incident to thoroughly and completely safeguarding the interests of the people as a whole. Against all such increase of Government regulation the argument is raised that it would amount to a form of Socialism. This argument is familiar; it is precisely the same as that which was raised against the creation of the Inter-State Commerce Commission, and of all the different utilities commissions in the different States, as I myself saw, thirty years ago, when I was a legislator in Albany, and these questions came up in connection with our State Government. Nor can action be effectively taken by any one State. Congress alone has power under the Constitution effectively and thoroughly and at all points to deal with inter-State commerce, and where Congress, as it should do, provides laws that will give the Nation full jurisdiction over the whole field, then that jurisdiction becomes, of necessity, exclusive—although until Congress does act affirmatively and thoroughly it is idle to expect that the States will or ought to rest content with non-action on the part of both Federal and State authorities. This statement, by the way, applies also to the question of "usurpation" by any one branch of our Government of the rights of another branch. It is contended that in these recent decisions the Supreme Court legislated; so it did; and it had to; because Congress had signally failed to do *its* duty by legislating. For the Supreme Court to nullify an act of the Legislature as unconstitutional except on the clearest grounds is usurpation; to interpret such an act in an obviously wrong sense is usurpation; but where the legislative body persistently leaves open a field which it is absolutely imperative, from the public standpoint, to fill, then no possible blame attaches to the official or officials who step in because they have to, and who then do the needed work in the interest of the people. The blame in such cases lies with the body which has been derelict, and not with the body which reluctantly makes good the dereliction.

A quarter of a century ago, Senator Cushman K. Davis, a statesman who amply deserved the title of statesman, a man of the highest courage, of the sternest adherence to the principles laid down by an exacting sense of duty, an unflinching believer in democracy, who was as little to be cowed by a mob as by a plutocrat, and moreover a man who possessed the priceless gift of imagination, a gift as important to a statesman as to a historian, in an address delivered at the annual commencement of the University of Michigan on July 1, 1886, spoke as follows of corporations:

> Feudalism, with its domains, its untaxed lords, their retainers, its exemptions and privileges, made war upon the aspiring spirit of humanity, and fell with all its grandeurs. Its spirit walks the earth and haunts the institutions of to-day, in the great corporations, with the control of the National highways, their occupation of great domains, their power to tax, their cynical contempt for the law, their sorcery to debase most gifted men to the capacity of splendid slaves, their pollution of the ermine of the judge and the robe of the Senator, their aggregation in one man of wealth so enormous as to make Croesus seem a pauper, their picked, paid, and skilled retainers who are summoned by the message of electricity and appear upon the wings of steam. If we look into the origin of feudalism and of the modern corporations—those Dromios of history—we find that the former originated in a strict paternalism, which is scouted by modern economists, and that the latter has grown from an unrestrained freedom of action, aggression, and development, which they commend as the very ideal of political wisdom. *Laissez-faire*, says the professor, when it often means bind and gag that the strongest may work his will. It is a plea for the survival of the fittest—for the strongest male to take possession of the herd by a process of extermination. If we examine this battle cry of political polemics, we find that it is based upon the conception of the divine right of property, and the preoccupation by older or more favored or more alert or richer men or nations, of territory, of the forces of nature, of machinery, of all the functions of what we call civilization. Some of these men, who are really great, follow these conceptions to their conclusions with dauntless intrepidity.

When Senator Davis spoke, few men of great power had the sympathy and the vision necessary to perceive the menace contained in the growth of corporations; and the men who did see the evil were struggling blindly to get rid of it, not by frankly meeting the new situation with new methods, but by insisting upon the entirely futile effort to abolish what modern conditions had rendered absolutely inevitable. Senator Davis was under no such illusion. He realized keenly that it was absolutely impossible to go back to an outworn social status, and that we must abandon definitely the *laissez-faire* theory of political economy, and fearlessly champion a system of increased Governmental control, paying no heed to the cries of the worthy people who denounce this as Socialistic. He saw that, in order to meet the inevitable increase in the power of corporations produced by modern industrial conditions, it would be necessary to increase in like fashion the activity of the sovereign power which alone could control such corporations. As has been aptly said, the only way to meet a billion-dollar corporation is by invoking the protection of a hundred-billion-dollar government; in other words, of the National government, for no State Government is strong enough both to do justice to corporations and to exact justice from them. Said Senator Davis in this admirable address, which should be reprinted and distributed broadcast:

> The liberty of the individual has been annihilated by the logical process constructed to maintain it. We have come to a political deification of Mammon. *Laissez-faire* is not utterly blameworthy. It begat modern democracy, and made the modern republic possible. There can be no doubt of that. But there it began its limit of political benefaction, and began to incline toward the point where extremes meet.... To every assertion that the people in their collective capacity of a government ought to exert their indefeasible right of self-defense, it is said you touch the sacred rights of property.

The Senator then goes on to say that we now have to deal with an oligarchy of wealth, and that the Government must develop power sufficient enough to enable it to do the task.

Few will dispute the fact that the present situation is not satisfactory, and cannot be put on a permanently satisfactory basis unless we put an end to the period of groping and declare for a fixed policy, a policy which shall clearly define and punish wrong-doing, which shall put a stop to the iniquities done in the name of business, but which shall do strict equity to business. We demand that big business give the people a square deal; in return we must insist that when any one engaged in big business honestly endeavors to do right he shall himself be given a square deal; and the first, and most elementary, kind of square deal is to give him in advance full information as to just what he can, and what he cannot, legally and properly do. It is absurd, and much worse than absurd, to treat the deliberate lawbreaker as on an exact par with the man eager to obey the law, whose only desire is to find out from some competent Governmental authority what the law is, and then to live up to it. Moreover, it is absurd to treat the size of a corporation as in itself a crime. As Judge Hook says in his opinion in the Standard Oil Case: "Magnitude of business does not alone constitute a monopoly... the genius and industry of man when kept to ethical standards still have full play, and what he achieves is his... success and magnitude of business, the rewards of fair and honorable endeavor [are not forbidden]... [the public welfare is threatened only when success is attained] by wrongful or unlawful methods." Size may, and in my opinion does, make a corporation fraught with potential menace to the community; and may, and in my opinion should, therefore make it incumbent upon the community to exercise through its administrative (not merely through its judicial) officers a strict supervision over that corporation in order to see that it does not go wrong; but the size in itself does not signify wrong-doing, and should not be held to signify wrong-doing.

Not only should any huge corporation which has gained its position by unfair methods, and by interference with the rights of others, by demoralizing and corrupt practices, in short, by sheer baseness and wrong-doing, be broken up, but it should be made the business of some administrative governmental body, by constant supervision, to see that it does not come together again, save under such strict control as shall insure the community against all repetition of the bad conduct—and it should never be permitted thus to assemble its parts as long as these parts are under the control of the original offenders, for actual experience has shown that these men are, from the standpoint of the people at large, unfit to be trusted with the power implied in the management of a large corporation. But nothing of importance is gained by breaking up a huge inter-State and international industrial organization *which has not offended otherwise than by its size*, into a number of small concerns without any attempt to regulate the way in which those concerns as a whole shall do business. Nothing is gained by depriving the American Nation of good weapons wherewith to fight in the great field of international industrial competition. Those who would seek to restore the days of unlimited and uncontrolled competition, and who believe that a panacea for our industrial and economic ills is to be found in the mere breaking up of all big corporations, simply because they are big, are attempting not only the impossible, but what, if possible, would be undesirable. They are acting as we should act if we tried to dam the Mississippi, to stop its flow outright. The effort would be certain to result in failure and disaster; we would have attempted the impossible, and so would have achieved nothing, or worse than nothing. But by building levees along the Mississippi, not seeking to dam the stream, but to control it, we are able to achieve our object and to confer inestimable good in the course of so doing.

This Nation should definitely adopt the policy of attacking, not the mere fact of combination, but the evils and wrong-doing which so frequently accompany combination. The fact that a combination is very big is ample reason for exercising a close and jealous supervision over it, because its size renders it potent for mischief; but it should not be punished unless it actually does the mischief; it should merely be so supervised and controlled as to guarantee us, the people, against its doing mischief. We should not strive for a policy of unregulated competition and of the destruction of all big corporations, that is, of all the most efficient business industries in the land. Nor should we persevere in the hopeless experiment of trying to regulate these industries by means only of lawsuits, each lasting several years, and of uncertain result. We should enter upon a course of supervision, control, and regulation of these great corporations—a regulation which we should not fear, if necessary, to bring to the point of control of monopoly prices, just as in exceptional cases railway rates are now regulated. Either the Bureau of Corporations should be authorized, or some other governmental body similar to the Inter-State Commerce Commission should be created, to exercise this supervision, this authoritative control. When once immoral business practices have been eliminated by such control, competition will thereby be again revived as a healthy factor, although not as formerly an all-sufficient factor, in keeping the general business situation sound. Wherever immoral business practices still obtain—as they obtained in the cases of the Standard Oil Trust and Tobacco Trust—the Anti-Trust Law can be invoked; and wherever such a prosecution is successful, and the courts declare a corporation to possess a monopolistic character, then that corporation should be completely dissolved, and the parts ought never to be again assembled save on whatever terms and under whatever conditions may be imposed by the governmental body in which is vested the regulatory power. Methods can readily be devised by which corporations sincerely desiring to act fairly and honestly can on their own initiative come under this thoroughgoing administrative control by the Government and thereby be free from the working of the Anti-Trust Law. But the law will remain to be invoked against wrongdoers; and under such conditions it could be invoked far more vigorously and successfully than at present.

It is not necessary in an article like this to attempt to work out such a plan in detail. It can assuredly be worked out. Moreover, in my opinion, substantially some such plan must be worked out or business chaos will continue. Wrong-doing such as was perpetrated by the Standard Oil Trust, and especially by the Tobacco Trust, should not only be punished, but if possible punished in the persons of the chief authors and beneficiaries of the wrong, far more severely than at present. But punishment should not be the only, or indeed the main, end in view. Our aim should be a policy of construction and not one of destruction. Our aim should not be to punish the men who have made a big corporation successful merely because they have made it big and successful, but to exercise such thoroughgoing supervision and control over them as to insure their business skill being exercised in the interest of the public and not against the public interest. Ultimately, I believe that this control should undoubtedly indirectly or directly extend to dealing with all questions connected with their treatment of their employees, including the wages, the hours of labor, and the like. Not only is the proper treatment of a corporation, from the standpoint of the managers, shareholders, and employees, compatible with securing from that corporation the best standard of public service, but when the effort is wisely made it results in benefit both to the corporation and to the public. The success of Wisconsin in dealing with the corporations within her borders, so as both to do them justice and to exact justice in return from them toward the public, has been signal; and this Nation should adopt a progressive policy in substance akin to the progressive policy not merely formulated in theory but reduced to actual practice with such striking success in Wisconsin.

To sum up, then. It is practically impossible, and, if possible, it would be mischievous and undesirable, to try to break up all combinations merely because they are large and successful, and to put the business of the country back into the middle of the eighteenth century conditions of intense and unregulated competition between small and weak business concerns. Such an effort represents not progressiveness but an unintelligent though doubtless entirely well-meaning toryism. Moreover, the effort to administer a law merely by lawsuits and court decisions is bound to end in signal failure, and meanwhile to be attended with delays and uncertainties, and to put a premium upon legal sharp practice. Such an effort does not adequately punish the guilty, and yet works great harm to the innocent. Moreover, it entirely fails to give the publicity which is one of the best by-products of the system of control by administrative officials; publicity, which is not only good in itself, but furnishes the data for whatever further action may be necessary. We need to formulate immediately and definitely a policy which, in dealing with big corporations that behave themselves and which contain no menace save what is necessarily potential in any corporation which is of great size and very well managed, shall aim not at their destruction but at their regulation and supervision, so that the Government shall control them in such fashion as amply to safeguard the interests of the whole public, including producers, consumers, and wageworkers. This control should, if necessary, be pushed in extreme cases to the point of exercising control over monopoly prices, as rates on railways are now controlled; although this is not a power that should be used when it is possible to avoid it. The law should be clear, unambiguous, certain, so that honest men may not find that unwittingly they have violated it. In short, our aim should be, not to destroy, but effectively and in thoroughgoing fashion to regulate and control, in the public interest, the great instrumentalities of modern business, which it is destructive of the general welfare of the community to destroy, and which nevertheless it is vitally necessary to that general welfare to regulate and control. Competition will remain as a very important factor when once we have destroyed the unfair business methods, the criminal interference with the rights of others, which alone enabled certain swollen combinations to crush out their competitors—and, incidentally, the "conservatives" will do well to remember that these unfair and iniquitous methods by great masters of corporate capital have done more to cause popular discontent than all the orations of all the Socialist orators in the country put together.

I have spoken above of Senator Davis's admirable address delivered a quarter of a century ago. Senator Davis's one-time partner, Frank B. Kellogg, the Government counsel who did so much to win success for the Government in its prosecutions of the trusts, has recently delivered before the Palimpsest Club of Omaha an excellent address on the subject; Mr. Prouty, of the Inter-State Commerce Commission, has recently, in his speech before the Congregational Club of Brooklyn, dealt with the subject from the constructive side; and in the proceedings of the American Bar Association for 1904 there is an admirable paper on the need of thoroughgoing Federal control over corporations doing inter-State business, by Professor Horace L. Wilgus, of the University of Michigan. The National Government exercises control over inter-State commerce railways, and it can in similar fashion, through an appropriate governmental body, exercise control over all industrial organizations engaged in inter-State commerce. This control should be exercised, not by the courts, but by an administrative bureau or board such as the Bureau of Corporations or the Inter-State Commerce Commission; for the courts cannot with advantage permanently perform executive and administrative functions.

## William Howard Taft

# "We Must Get Back to Competition," Declares Mr. Taft

## In Speech at Pocatello, Idaho, President Again Applauds Decisions of Supreme Court and Asserts That Prosecutions of Trusts Must Continue—Hopes That We May Yet Return to a "Legitimate and Independent Competition"—State Socialism Only Alternative[1]

Competition has found an ardent supporter in President Taft. The president's western tour has disclosed him as a defender of the supreme court decisions against the trusts and as an earnest advocate of competition as against monopoly. This has been shown by telephony in two of the president's speeches. Another delivered at Pocatello, Idaho, emphasizes the matter still further. The three are conclusive as to determining exactly the conviction of the administration and promise much for the future.

"Now we can get back to competition," said Mr. Taft. "We must get back to competition as an element in this country. If it is impossible, then let us go to socialism, for there is no way between. I, for one, am not discouraged as yet in the hope that we may return to a legitimate and independent competition. I am an individualist and not a socialist."

Mr. Taft bitterly assailed the critics of the supreme court. "I love judges and I love courts," said the president. "They are my ideals on earth that typify what we shall meet afterward in heaven under a just God. And when a court is doing its duty, when it is trying to interpret the law as it ought to be, to have it condemned and attacked and its motive questioned for mere political purposes, without solid ground for attack, goes to my heart, and I resent it with deep indignation."

Mr. Taft spoke with far greater feeling than he put into his Detroit and Waterloo speeches, but along the same lines. He said he had received many criticisms, but had failed to receive an answer to his challenge to W. J. Bryan and other publicists to cite one instance of a combination in restraint of trade which ought to be condemned and which would not be condemned under the supreme court's interpretation of the antitrust law in the Standard Oil and tobacco cases.

"What distinguishes this country from any other," said the president, "is the supreme court that we have in Washington, that oft has stood between us and errors that might have been committed which would have been greatly injurious to this country. To turn upon that court and question its motive and to attack it seems to me to lay the ax at the root of the tree of our civilization."

Mr. Taft referred to the court's disposal of the Standard Oil and tobacco cases as "two great decisions."

1. This address to the Pocatello, Idaho, Chamber of Commerce was reported in the *New York Evening Post*, Oct. 6, 1911. The full article was reprinted in *Telephony: The American Telephone Journal*, which consisted of speeches and other news events that were phoned in by correspondents—apparently a novelty at the time. 61 *Telephony* 447 (Oct. 14, 1911).

"They were two of the greatest trusts that existed," he said, "and in the working out of the decree the court had to make a remedy. The Standard Oil company presented all the phases of illegality and criminality necessary to establish a monopoly at a time when it did not feel the necessity for concealing its methods or its motives. The tobacco trust represented an organization made in anticipation of the operation of the law, helped out by the advice of cunning lawyers in order to avoid its operation. But against them both the decree of the supreme court has been pronounced."

Mr. Taft said it was unfortunate that the country had got into a condition that required a remedy like this. A remedy of any evil, he added, was bound to produce for a time not business disaster, but a difficult situation that might make business slow. But after the solution had been worked out he saw no reason why the country should not go on to greater prosperity.

"To one in my place," said the president, "there is no discretion with reference to the trial of cases brought to the attention of the executive as violations of the law. The prosecutions must go on. It is not for the executive to say he can withhold criminal prosecutions, or any kind of prosecutions, just to help business. Business must reform itself, and these executive duties must be performed under the oath of office that I took and under the oath that those under me took.

"But when that part of the business community that thought that the antitrust statute did not mean anything understands that it is to be enforced we may reach a solution that will enable the business community to settle down on a proper and legitimate basis. I hope the time is near when we must get together for prosperity. We must eliminate, so far as we can, this desire to attack wealth earned by thrift and gathered by foresight, attention and industry, because that is to set up a feeling that bodes no good for the result. When a man attempts that he ought to be marked by the patriots of the country who understand that he is attempting to use some disaster to the country to benefit himself.

"I believe we are going on to a greater future. If we had allowed these combinations to go on and develop the only remedy would have been to change by force the power thus concentrated in the hands of a few individuals to the state, and then we would have had state socialism. It was the inevitable result of the movement toward trusts unless broken up."

## Woodrow Wilson
## *The Tariff and the Trusts*

## Address Delivered at Nashville, Tennessee, February 24, 1912. From Pamphlet in the Library of Princeton University.

Found about this core of all questions which lies in the tariff, lie all these other questions, many of which we sum up under the general term of the corporation question, the trust question.

Nobody can fail to see, no matter how clearly you perceive the evils that have come upon the country by the use of them,—nobody can fail to see that modern business is going to be done by corporations. *The old time of individual competition is probably gone by.* It may come back; I don't know; it will not come back within our time, I dare say. We will do business henceforth when we do it on a great and successful scale, by means of corporations. But what we are afraid of, as we have said in the Sherman Act, is such use of corporations as will be in restraint of trade; that is, such use as will establish monopoly. Very well, we have got to know what particular things do establish monopoly; because if we merely say "this concern is so big that it looks to us like monopoly" that isn't satisfactory. I am not afraid of any corporation, no matter how big. I am afraid of any corporation, however small, that is bad, that is rotten at the core, whose practices and actions are in restraint of trade. So that the thing we are after is not reckoning size in measuring capacity for damage, but measuring and comprehending the exact damage done. Very well, we are getting details. For example, in the Stanley investigation, in the investigation connected with the trial of the meat packers, and in the investigation I hope will be pushed forward in connection with the so-called money trust (great applause) we are going to find out how the thing is done.

For example, take the meat men, I have some friends connected in a subordinate way as employees of that great industry, some college men who are quick to see and intelligent to comprehend, and once or twice when I have made remarks that did not seem complimentary to the meat trust these gentlemen have written to me and asked if I was aware of the fact that the operations were as a matter of fact yielding this concern only a very minute fraction of profit, and there would be no profit in it at all if they didn't command so large a proportion of the product as to make the sum total considerable. And I didn't know what to say until I read the testimony taken in the trial of the meat packers at Chicago, and then I found out that these gentlemen buy cattle on the hoof, as everybody knows, and they charge up all the expenses of all their operations to the meat; and they sell the hides and the hoofs, and the parts, whatever they may be, that yield very valuable glue, and all the byproducts, which in their sum total are extremely profitable, without any charges being entered against them in their books. So that we are paying for meat in order to enable them to sell hides and determine the price of shoes. (Applause.) Now that is a valuable inside piece of information. They can't any longer impose upon us by showing us their books upon fresh meat (or meat that isn't fresh that comes out of cold storage). That is what I call one of the items in the bill of particulars. We know also by their own testimony it isn't necessary for them to combine themselves in a corporation in order to fix prices; it is only necessary to have a gentleman's understanding, and have correspondence through a secretary agreed upon, and that this secretary, once every so often, shall send out a circular suggesting a price for meat, and this suggestion be taken kindly and acted upon. (Laughter.) That suggestion is perfectly arbitrary; they can establish the price of meat upon an absolutely non-competitive basis.

Very well, we know what the meat packers are doing and what the steel men are doing, and what all these other men are doing. We have got now some of the transactions and the form in which they are carried through. It seems to me that now, therefore, we are ready to proceed to business, so far as we see what we are about. We are not going to lay about us in any blind and vague way, but we are going to do something like this, not proposing this as a measure but merely as an illustration. If you want to cure men of joy riding you won't break up their automobiles, but catch the men that do the joy riding and see that these very useful and pleasant vehicles of our modern life are left for legitimate uses. If you want to stop joy riding in corporations—for that is what is being done (laughter and applause)—you will not break up the corporations; we may need to use them; but you will break up the game, namely, that use of corporations. I dare say the judge and other lawyers present,—if it is true that judges are still lawyers (laughter) will agree with me that this is at any rate feasible; with the necessary legislation, we can say that a corporation, so long as it acts within its charter, or is within the limits of the law, is something we won't look inside of. We will regard it as long as it is within its legitimate uses as a body corporate that has its own separate entity, and into the details of whose organization we won't pry. We will hold it responsible so far only as a body, an unbroken body, but the minute somebody inside begins to use it for purposes he has no right to use it for, then we are going to turn it inside out and see who is inside. And we are going to establish this principle that with regard to breaches of the law we will deal not with corporations but with individuals, that we don't know corporations, that we never heard of them, when we are dealing with breaches of the law. We can oblige every corporation to file with the proper officer of the law a sworn analysis of the way its business is done, which will be conclusive—not merely presumptive evidence—upon any trial, an analysis which it cannot controvert upon trial; which will show that such and such transactions are ordered by the president, such and such transactions are ordered by a committee of its board, certain other transactions are ordered by the board as a whole, others by its first vice-president, and so on down through the analysis. Then when a wrong is committed we will turn to the analysis and find the officer who according to that analysis ordered that particular thing done, and we will indict him *not as an officer of the corporation but as an individual who used that corporation for something that was illegal*. Then you say, we will find out he was a dummy. Very well, go on, push the trial, draw in all the collateral evidence and find whose dummy he was, then amend the indictment and include the gentlemen whose dummy he was, whether it happens to be an official connected with that corporation or not, because in this process we have nothing to do with corporations, we are finding men. You know the old cynical French maxim, when any man is running an incalculable course *"cherchez la femme"* (find the woman). Now we must establish the maxim "find the man." Anything that is wrong must have originated with some person in particular. When you have found that person and given him a season to think it over in the penitentiary (applause) the thing will be stopped, and business will be relieved of the embarrassment of breaking up its organization in order to stop these practices.

Do you see any other way to avoid interrupting the natural and normal processes of American business? If you will do this then all the prohibitions of your law will work, no man will use corporations in restraint of trade; and item by item we can put in *our statutes what constitutes restraint of trade*, not leaving it to courts for generalizations which may fit some cases and not others. Then we shall have a programme which need disturb no honest man, and will begin to see the map of the thing. I want to see the map of our corporate life. You don't know the highways of it, you don't know any of the intricacies of it. The difficulty in this country is not altogether that we have big corporations, but that these big corporations are combined with one another, not by law, but by the fact that their directorates interlace in every direction and that the same combinations of men control the majority of the stock in corporation after corporation.

No corporation can ever get big enough to make the Government of the United States afraid, but all of them combined might in some sinister and fateful day make the Government of the United States subserve them. So that you have got to disentangle this puzzle; you have got to find where the lines of personal responsibility interlace; you have got to lift these persons up and put them under cross-examination as to what they are doing with the business of the country, not for the purpose of gibbeting them, not for the purpose of putting them under contempt and mortifications, but for the purpose of saving the country and saving its business.

I am not aware that I cherish in my heart any bitter feelings toward any individual concerned in these matters. Many of these men do not see the consequences of the thing they are doing. They are just as patriotic so far as they have examined their own consciences as either you or I. They don't comprehend. We have got to wake them to the things that are to be feared, and then devise the particular methods by which they are to be corrected. We are not vindictive, but determined men, with open eyes.

For in the meantime what is going on? When I hear gentlemen say that politics ought to let business alone, I feel like inviting them to first consider whether business is letting politics alone. It is a two-sided matter; if you will quit, we will. If you will stop trying to determine elections by campaign contributions; if you will stop encouraging bi-partisan political machinery, so that it is worth your while to contribute to both campaign funds; if you will stop making the control of legislatures a business proposition, then you will find that in the most complete and only effectual way you have disentangled business from politics.

The initial steps are taken in lobbies, they are not taken in the councils of statesmen; they are taken in those secret and whispered conferences that go on in almost every legislative lobby in this country, where men are shown that it is to their material interest—whether directly or indirectly—that they shall vote as interested parties desire them to vote. These great leagues of business, in other words, are not merely leagues to command markets, but they are often also leagues to command legislation.

And so the view widens, does it not? So the country is asking itself, who is represented in our representative assemblies? In some states the people are represented, thank God, but in some states they are not represented. In some states the legislatures are secretly and privately controlled. Now, are you going to stir the blood of those people in those states by preaching a eulogy on representative institutions? If they have found out election after election that to vote one ticket or the other is to choose between tweedledum and tweedledee; if they know no matter how they vote things don't get better at the State capital, how are you going to stir their patriotism with the tradition of the great representative institutions in this country? They will laugh in your face, they will say: "Are you so young, so unsophisticated as to suppose you know what you are talking about? Show us representative institutions to worship and we will be the first to fall on our knees, but we want to know who are represented."

There are two or three theories of government in this country. Don't deceive yourself by supposing all the people in this country believe in democratic government, because they do not. You have only to listen to the utterances of very distinguished Republican speakers to see that they do not believe and do not pretend to believe in popular government. They will tell you they do not believe the judgment of the people can be trusted. Are you going to take counsel from these gentlemen as to the preservation of our representative institutions when they don't want them to represent the great body, the rank and file of the people? I don't know whether I was born so, or learned so, or what happened to me, but I know this, that the deepest conviction I have, arising out of observation and experience is this, that I would rather take the judgment of the rank and file than the judgment of the men who have become absorbed and successful as the leaders in great undertakings. (Applause.)

I want to ask these gentlemen this query: What sustains business in the United States? What is it that makes the United States prosperous? Is it that we have great captains of industry? What would they do without the cunning and skill, the muscle and the indomitable aspiring hope of the American people? If these people were to find hope dying out of their hearts, they will be dumb-driven beasts, and your enterprises will fall for lack of the very breath that sustains them. (Applause.)

If you want to find whether a nation is prosperous or not, ask the men who are on the make what they hope and what they fear. Go to the country districts and ask anxious fathers who are looking for openings for their sons where they expect to get them in, where they find doors open and where they find doors shut. Go to the places where men are making earnings and see whether they dread or confidently look forward to the future, and then you will find whether America is waxing or waning, for if these men are confident, full of hope, if they know they are going to have free chances, if they know that the doors of opportunity are open to them, if they know they are going to get fair treatment wherever they go, then America can conquer the world of enterprise by means of their hope. But if you find, what you do find, men everywhere asking themselves whether the doors of opportunity have not been locked in their faces, then you will have to take a new reckoning as to the future of America.

What was it that they proposed to investigate in Congress the other day? Not a money trust in the ordinary sense that anybody is hiding or hoarding money anywhere. Men who have money are not fools enough not to want to use it, because it does not yield them anything if it is not used. What is suspected is this: that nobody can get large loans in this country to start those large enterprises by which alone our industry thrives, unless he will consent to take certain gentlemen in with him who furnish the money; that the privileged circle is closed, and that while you can get all the little credits you please in your local banks you can't get your big credits where the reserves of the country are kept, except on the terms of the gentlemen who stand guard over these reserves. (Applause.) That is what is charged. And it is not charged without evidence.

It is not charged without abundant evidence. Therefore, if only those who are chosen at the top have the right of way in, what is going to happen to America? Did you ever hear of a nation that was renewed from the top? Did you ever hear of a nation that was not made virile, that did not account for its youth by renewal from the bottom? Did you ever hear of a tree that drew its sap from its flowers? Does it now draw it from the dark and silent places of the soil? Does not a nation draw its power of renewal and enterprise, and all its future, from the ranks of the great body of unnamed men? And if you are going to discourage these men; if you are going to put the chill of fear in their hearts, then American captains of industry can whistle for their future, and they will whistle in a wilderness. (Applause.)

# 5

# Imperfect, Monopolistic, and Workable Competition

## Introduction

BY HERBERT HOVENKAMP

As was developed in the introduction to Chapter Three, the "ruinous competition" debate of the turn of the twentieth century tended to follow the classical bifurcation of markets into competition and monopoly. Seeing no room for competition in industries with high fixed costs, many economists of this period saw collusion, trade association organization, merger, or monopoly as the only viable alternatives. As a result many of them believed that the Sherman Act would be economically harmful.

But over the next four decades the theoretical landscape of competitive markets became much more complex, acquiring many of the features it retains to this day, although the relevance and impact of most of them remains controversial. These attributes include oligopoly, product differentiation, monopolistic competition, price discrimination, and barriers to entry. Economists began to see that perfect competition and absolute monopoly (aside from exclusive state franchises) were relatively uncommon features of the industrial landscape. Most firms lived somewhere in between.

The implications for antitrust policy proved to be disturbing, as the selections in this chapter reveal. First, as Cambridge economist Joan Robinson (1903–1983) pointed out, most large firms and even small firms in smaller markets did not face flat demand curves as the perfect competitor did. As a result they were not "price takers" but had some power to meter price by varying output. This made strategic behavior possible. Second, it quickly became apparent that price discrimination was a much more ubiquitous phenomenon than previously acknowledged, particularly for firms with high fixed costs and excess capacity, which compelled them to make as many sales as possible in order to keep output up. By every measure, Robinson ranks with Marshall, Pigou, and Keynes as one of the great economists of the first half of the twentieth century.[1] However, she was not made a full professor until

1. See Nahid Aslanbequi and Guy Oakes, *The Provocative Joan Robinson: The Making of a Cambridge Economist* (2009).

she was sixty-two and was denied a Nobel Prize, very likely because she was a woman. Her *Economics of Imperfect Competition* remains one of the classic studies of price and output behavior of the single firm under imperfect competition. Fundamentally, Robinson's book was *not* about oligopoly theory or about interactions among firms. Rather it was about how firms facing moderate competition maximized their earnings by equating marginal cost and marginal revenue (a concept that Robinson herself largely developed), or by reducing inputs in order to suppress the purchase price ("monopsony," another term that she invented).

Edward H. Chamberlin (1899–1967) wrote *The Theory of Monopolistic Competition* (1933), the second selection in this chapter, as his doctoral dissertation. On its strength he obtained a position in the Harvard economics department. Chamberlin was much more concerned than Robinson was with how firms in a market for manufactured products interact with one another. Unlike Augustin Cournot, however, Chamberlin did not assume a market with a small number of sellers making identical products, where the decision variable for every firm was output. Rather, there could be any number of sellers, but the tool for blunting competition was product differentiation. That is, each seller maximized profits by differentiating its product from that offered by its rivals and claiming sales over customers attracted to a particular variety. Chamberlin was generally unconcerned about entry barriers and assumed that new entry was easy. This was in contrast to emergent oligopoly theory, with its assumption of high entry barriers. Under monopolistic competition theory, firms were driven into long-term situations where returns were no higher than the competitive level even though prices were higher than marginal cost. Further, they generally had excess capacity, and there was too much product differentiation for cost-effective production.

Coming out of the 1930s, the leading theory offered three competing and overlapping models of business firm behavior. Imperfect competition was concerned with the price and output strategies of firms that had at least some market power. Orthodox Cournot oligopoly theory was concerned with firms making more-or-less-identical products, but in markets where the number of firms was relatively small and entry barriers were high. More complex versions of Cournot took product differentiation into account as well. Monopolistic theory was concerned with firms making differentiated products; there could be any number of firms and entry was assumed to be easy.

Problematically, real-world markets often displayed some characteristics of all three sets of theories. This led to a great deal of uncertainty about the appropriate role of antitrust policy in markets for manufactured products, although it led to a certain amount of consensus as well. One element in the consensus was that the number of firms in a market was very critical, with the threat to competition increasing as the number declined. A second was that high entry barriers were bad, in particular those barriers that were "artificial" in that they could be created by strategic behavior. A third principle was that product differentiation was likely to be "excessive" and led to poor economic performance.

This is where John Maurice Clark's consensus-building 1940 article on "workable competition," the final excerpt in this chapter, comes in. Clark (1884–1963) was the son of John Bates Clark, probably the most influential technical American marginalist of the Progressive period. By 1940 Clark was an influential "elder statesman" in industrial organization economics and antitrust policy. Clark's argument was elegant and easily stated. First, in a world of manufactured products and large-scale industry "perfect" competition is neither possible nor desirable. Second, the numerous theories of firm interaction in such markets were based on different assumptions and applied in different situations; none of them supplied a global theory of competitive behavior. Third, many of the attributes of modern industry that make competition something less than perfect are a consequence of the inherent structures of firms and markets and are beyond effective government control. Fourth, some attributes that we might identify as imperfections can actually serve to make markets more competitive. Fifth, the goal of competition policy should not be to force markets toward a model of perfect competition, but rather to ensure that specific practices do not hinder competition in their particular environment. For example, price discrimination is inconsistent with perfect competition, but it should not be condemned on that basis; in fact, in an oligopoly industry firms often compete by price discriminating—that is, by offering lower prices to buyers that are in greater competitive play. As a result, condemning price discrimination can actually make the situation worse. Clark's essay on workable competition set the tone for much of the antitrust policy debate from World War II through the rise of the Chicago School.

## Edward Hastings Chamberlin

## *The Theory of Monopolistic Competition: A Re-orientation of the Theory of Value*

## Chapter IV

## The Differentiation of the Product: Monopolistic Competition

### I. The Meaning of Differentiation

The interplay of monopolistic and competitive forces now to be considered is of a different sort from that described in the previous chapter. It arises from what we shall call the differentiation of the product. This chapter introduces the subject by explaining what differentiation means, and how and in what relationship it involves both monopoly and competition.

A general class of product is differentiated if any significant basis exists for distinguishing the goods (or services) of one seller from those of another. Such a basis may be real or fancied, so long as it is of any importance whatever to buyers, and leads to a preference for one variety of the product over another. Where such differentiation exists, even though it be slight, buyers will be paired with sellers, not by chance and at random (as under pure competition), but according to their preferences.

Differentiation may be based upon certain characteristics of the product itself, such as exclusive patented features; trade-marks; trade names; peculiarities of the package or container, if any; or singularity in quality, design, color, or style. It may also exist with respect to the conditions surrounding its sale. In retail trade, to take only one instance, these conditions include such factors as the convenience of the seller's location, the general tone or character of his establishment, his way of doing business, his reputation for fair dealing, courtesy, efficiency, and all the personal links which attach his customers either to himself or to those employed by him. In so far as these and other intangible factors vary from seller to seller, the "product" in each case is different, for buyers take them into account, more or less, and may be regarded as purchasing them along with the commodity itself. When these two aspects of differentiation are held in mind, it is evident that virtually all products are differentiated, at least slightly, and that over a wide range of economic activity differentiation is of considerable importance.

In explanation of the adjustment of economic forces over this field, economic theory has offered *(a)* a theory of competition, and *(b)* a theory of monopoly. If the product is fairly individual, as the services of an electric street railway, or if it has the legal stamp of a patent or a copyright, it is usually regarded as a monopoly. On the other hand, if it stands out less clearly from other "products" in a general class, it is grouped with them and regarded as part of an industry or field of economic activity which is essentially competitive. Thus, although patents are usually classed as monopolies, trade-marks are more often looked upon as conferring a lesser degree of individuality to a product, and hence as quite compatible with competition (sometimes even as requisite to it). By this dispensation, the value of patented goods is explained in terms of the monopolist's maximizing his total profit within the market which he controls, whereas that of trade-marked goods is described in terms of an equilibrium between demand and supply over a much wider field. All value problems are relegated to one category or the other according to their predominant element; the partial check exerted by the other is ignored.

This procedure has led to a manner of thinking which goes even further and denies the very existence of the supposedly minor element. Monopoly and competition are very generally regarded, not simply as antithetical, but as mutually exclusive. To demonstrate competition is to prove the absence of monopoly, and vice versa. Indeed, to many the very phrase "monopolistic competition" will seem self-contradictory—a juggling of words. This conception is most unfortunate. Neither force excludes the other, and more often than not both are requisite to an intelligible account of prices.

## 2. Patents and Trade-Marks

The general case for a theory which recognizes both elements concurrently may be presented by inquiring into a particular problem: does any basis really exist for distinguishing between patents and trade-marks? Patents (and copyrights) are ordinarily considered as monopolies. They are granted under the authority vested in Congress by the United States Constitution to secure "for limited times, to authors and inventors, exclusive rights to their respective writings and discoveries." The privilege granted is *exclusive*—the inventor has the sole right to manufacture and sell his invention for seventeen years. The monopoly nature of this privilege is generally recognized both in the literature of patents and in that of general economics. To be sure, the issue is usually not sharply drawn, but one gains the impression that here are instances where the principles of monopoly value are true without qualification.

On the other hand, the competitive element has been pointed out, and it has even been claimed that patents are, in their essence, competitive rather than monopolistic.

Vaughn argues that "Patented products may be in competition both with patented and unpatented goods. In fact, the patent law is conducive to competition in that it stimulates individual initiative and private enterprise." Seager points out that "a large number of them [patents] are for the protection of rival processes and serve to stimulate rather than to diminish competition among those employing the different methods." The Committee on Patents in the House of Representatives reported in 1912 that before the era of trusts and combinations in restraint of trade "the monopoly granted by the patent law, limited as it was, in time tended to stimulate competition. It incited inventors to new effort, and capitalists and business men were encouraged to develop inventions. Under these conditions a patent, while granting a monopoly in a specific article, had rarely a tendency to monopolize any branch of the trade, because few inventions were so fundamental in character as to give the owner of the patent a monopoly in any branch of the trade, and every great financial success arising from an individual patent was sure to result in rival inventions." The report goes on to demonstrate the competition normally present if patents are separately held, in the following words: "Capital seeking to control industry through the medium of patents proceeds to buy up all important patents pertaining to the particular field. The effect of this is to shut out competition that would be inevitable if the various patents were separately and adversely held." Evidently, when they are so held, the fact that they are monopolies does not preclude their being in competition with each other. Every patented article is subject to the competition of more or less imperfect substitutes.

It is the same with copyrights. Copyrighted books, periodicals, pictures, dramatic compositions, are monopolies; yet they must meet the competition of similar productions, both copyrighted and not. The individual's control over the price of his own production is held within fairly narrow limits by the abundance and variety of substitutes. Each copyrighted production is monopolized by the holder of the copyright; yet it is also subject to the competition which is present over a wider field.

Let us turn to trade-marks. Their monopolistic nature has not been entirely ignored. Says Johnson, "Somewhat analogous to the profits arising from a patent are the profits arising from the use of a trade-mark or from the 'good-will' of a concern." These returns "fall under the general head of monopoly profits." The tone of hesitancy should, however, be noted, for it is characteristic. These profits are not *the same* as those arising from a patent; they are only "somewhat analogous." Ely classifies trade-marks as "general welfare monopolies," and, although "it may be questioned whether they ought to-be placed here," he argues that they should be. "They give the use or monopoly of a certain sign or mark to distinguish one's own productions.... Of course, another person may build up another class of goods, and may establish value for another trade-mark." He therefore concludes that "it is a monopoly only in a certain line, marking off the goods of one manufacturer." Veblen speaks of monopolies "resting on custom and prestige" as "frequently sold under the name of goodwill, trade-marks, brands, etc." Knight puts "in the same category of monopoly...the use of trade-marks, trade names, advertising slogans, etc., and we may include the services of professional men with established reputations (whatever their real foundation)." The list might be extended further.

On the other hand, trade-marks and brands are commonly regarded in the business world as a means of enabling one seller to compete more effectively with another—as congruous with and even necessary to competition. The view is implicitly sanctioned in economic literature by a common failure to take any cognizance of trade-marks whatever. They are simply taken for granted as a part of the essentially competitive regime. Frequently patents and copyrights alone are mentioned as monopolies; the implication is that trade-marks are not. A positive stand is taken by the late Professor Young in Ely, *Outlines of Economics,* where the elaborate classification found in Ely, *Monopolies and Trusts,* is reproduced with the significant change that trade-marks are omitted. "Trade-marks, like patents, are monopolies in the strictly legal sense that no one else may use them. But, unlike patents, they do not lead to a monopoly in the economic sense of giving exclusive control of one sort of business." By means of a trade-mark a successful business man "may be able to lift himself a little above the 'dead level' of competition...he is able to obtain what might be called a quasi-monopoly. But because his power to control the price of his product is in general much more limited than that of the true monopolist, and because competition limits and conditions his activities in other ways, his business is more properly called competitive than monopolistic." Against this position it may be urged, first, that single patents, as has been shown, do not ordinarily give exclusive control of one sort of business and do not confer a monopoly in this sense of the term; and secondly, that, even granting that patents do give *more* control, this is simply a matter of degree, reducible to relative elasticity of demand. Both patents and trade-marks may be conceived of as *pure* monopoly elements of the goods to which they are attached; the competitive elements in both cases are the similarities between these goods and others. To neglect either the monopoly element in trade-marks or the competitive element in patents by calling the first competitive and the second monopolistic is to push to opposite extremes and to represent as *wholly* different two things which are, in fact, essentially alike.

An uncompromising position as to the competitive nature of trade-marks is found in Rogers, *Goodwill, Trade-Marks and Unfair Trading.* "These things [patents and copyrights] are monopolies created by law.... A trade-mark is quite a different thing. There is no element of monopoly involved at all.... A trade-mark precludes the idea of monopoly. It is a means of distinguishing one product from another; it follows therefore that there must be others to distinguish from. If there are others there is no monopoly, and if there is a monopoly there is no need for any distinguishing." Here explicitly is the dialectic behind the attitude widely prevalent in economic and legal thinking, to which reference has already been made, that monopoly and competition must be regarded as alternatives. Evidently, it applies equally well to patents, for, to paraphrase the argument, no matter how completely the patented article may be different from others, there are always others and therefore no monopoly. Monopoly becomes, by this reasoning, a possibility only if there is but one good in existence. What is the difficulty? Assuredly, two things may be alike in some respects and different in others. To center attention upon either their likeness or their unlikeness is, in either case, to give only half of the picture. Thus, if a trademark distinguishes, that is, marks off one product as different from another, it gives the seller of that product a monopoly, from which we might argue, following Rogers, that there is no competition. Indeed, Rogers himself falls into the trap and refutes his own argument a few pages further on, where, speaking of a buyer's assumed preference for "Quaker Oats," he says, "It is a habit pure and simple, and it is a *brand* habit, a *trade-mark* habit that we and others like us have, and that habit is worth something to the producer of the goods to whose use we have become habituated. It *eliminates competition,* for to us there is nothing 'just as good.'" If trade-marks "preclude monopoly" and "eliminate competition," one may well ask the nature of the remainder.

Are there any bases, after all, for distinguishing between patents and trade-marks? Each makes a product unique in certain respects; this is its monopolistic aspect. Each leaves room for other commodities almost but not quite like it; this is its competitive aspect. The differences between them are only in degree, and it is doubtful if a significant distinction may be made even on this score. It would ordinarily be supposed that the degree of monopoly was greater in the case of patents. Yet the huge prestige value of such names as "Ivory," "Kodak" "Uneeda" "Coca-Cola," and "Old Dutch Cleanser," to cite only a few, is sufficient at least to make one sceptical. It would be impossible to compute satisfactorily for comparison the value of the monopoly rights granted by the United States Government in the form of patents and copyrights, and the value of those existing in the form of trade-marks, trade names, and good-will. The insuperable difficulty would be the definition (for purposes of deduction from total profits) of "competitive" returns, and of profits attributable to other monopoly elements. Allowance would also have to be made for the difference in duration of patents and trade-marks, for the enhanced value of patents in many cases by combination, and for other factors. But merely to suggest such a comparison is to raise serious doubts as to whether the monopoly element in patents is even quantitatively as important as that in trade-marks. Let us apply the reasoning to the second phase of differentiation mentioned above,—that with respect to the conditions surrounding a product's sale. An example is the element of location in retail trade. The availability of a commodity at one location rather than at another being of consequence to purchasers, we may regard these goods as differentiated spatially and may apply the term "spatial monopoly" to that control over supply which is a seller's by virtue of his location. A retail trader has complete and absolute control over the supply of his "product" when this is taken to include the advantages, to buyers, of his particular location. Other things being equal, those who find his place of business most convenient to their homes, their habitual shopping tours, their goings and comings from business or from any other pursuit, will trade with him in preference to accepting more or less imperfect substitutes in the form of identical goods at more distant places; just as, in the case of trade-marked articles and of goods qualitatively differentiated, buyers are led to prefer one variety over another by differences in their personal tastes, needs, or incomes.

In this field of "products" differentiated by the circumstances surrounding their sale, we may say, as in the case of patents and trade-marks, that both monopolistic and competitive elements are present. The field is commonly regarded as competitive, yet it differs only in degree from others which would at once be classed as monopolistic. In retail trade, each "product" is rendered unique by the individuality of the establishment in which it is sold, including its location (as well as by trade-marks, qualitative differences, etc.); this is its monopolistic aspect. Each is subject to the competition of other "products" sold under different circumstances and at other locations; this is its competitive aspect. Here, as elsewhere in the field of differentiated products, both monopoly and competition are always present.

Speaking more generally, if we regard monopoly as the antithesis of competition, its extreme limit is reached only in the case of control of the supply of all economic goods, which might be called a case of pure monopoly in the sense that all competition of substitutes is excluded by definition. At the other extreme is pure competition, where large classes of goods being perfectly standardized, every seller faces a competition of substitutes or his own product which is perfect. Between the two extremes there are all gradations, but both elements are always present, and must always be recognized. To discard either competition or monopoly is to falsify the result, and in a measure which may be far out of proportion to the apparent importance of the neglected factor.

Hence the theory of pure competition falls short as an explanation of prices when the product is (even slightly) differentiated. By eliminating monopoly elements (i.e., by regarding the product as homogeneous) it ignores the upward force which they exert, and indicates an equilibrium price which is below the true norm. The analogy of component forces, although not exact, is helpful. Actual prices no more approximate purely competitive prices than the actual course of a twin-screw steamship approximates the course which would be followed if only one propeller were in operation. Pure competition and pure monopoly are extremes, just as the two courses of the ship, when propelled by either screw separately, are extremes. Actual prices tend towards neither, but towards a middle position determined with reference to the relative strength of the two forces in the individual case. A purely competitive price is not a normal price; and except for those few cases in the price system where competition is actually pure, there is no tendency for it to be established.

It might seem that the theory of monopoly would offend equally in the opposite sense by excluding the competitive elements. This would be true, however, only in the case of *pure* monopoly, as defined above—control of the supply of all economic goods by the same person or agency. The theory of monopoly has never been interpreted in this way. It applies to particular goods, and as such always admits competition between the product concerned and others. Indeed, we may go so far as to say that the theory *seems* fully to meet the essential requirement of giving due recognition to both elements, and the interesting possibility is at once suggested of turning the tables and describing economic society as perfectly monopolistic instead of as (almost) perfectly competitive. Subsequent chapters will carry the refutation of this view. Meanwhile the issues are clarified by displaying the large element of truth it contains. Let us see upon what grounds it may *not* be refuted.

## 3. The Economic Order as Perfectly Monopolistic

The essence of monopoly is control over supply.[1] May not the entire field of differentiated product therefore be described in terms of perfect monopolies, one for each seller? The first objection which may be made is that substitutes exist for many products which are, in fact, virtually the same product; whence it would appear that the element of monopoly, instead of being absolute and perfect, is almost non-existent.

Now, of course, the owner of a trade-mark does not possess a monopoly or any degree of monopoly over the broader field in which this mark is in competition with others. A monopoly of "Lucky Strikes" does not constitute a monopoly of cigarettes, for there is no degree of control whatever over the supply of other substitute brands. But if, in order to possess a perfect monopoly, control must extend to substitutes, the only perfect monopoly conceivable would be one embracing the supply of everything, since all things are more or less imperfect substitutes for each other. There is no reason to stop with the supply of cigarettes any more than with the supply of cigarettes within a certain quality or price range (which would be narrower) or with that of tobacco in all forms (which would be broader). The term "monopoly" is meaningless without reference to the thing monopolized. A monopoly of diamonds is not a monopoly of precious stones, nor, to go still further, of jewelry. Differentiation implies gradations, and it is compatible with *perfect* monopoly of one product that control stop short of some more general class of which this product is a part, and within which there is competition.

Although the idea has never been developed into a hybrid theory of value, it represents, so far, no departure from currently accepted doctrine. Two writers only need be cited. According to Taussig, "Copyrights and patents supply the simplest cases of absolute monopoly by law." Yet he is explicit that "the holder of such a monopoly must reckon with the competition of more or less available substitutes, and thus is compelled to abate his prices and enlarge his supplies more than he would otherwise do." Ely points out that "the use of substitutes is consistent with monopoly, and we nearly always have them. For almost anything we can think of, there is some sort of a substitute more or less perfect, and the use of substitutes furnishes one of the limits to the power of the monopolist. In the consideration of monopoly we have to ask, what are the substitutes, and how effective are they?"

To the conception of economic society as perfectly monopolistic it may be objected, secondly, that, if differentiation is slight, even perfect control over *supply* may give a control over *price* which is negligible or non-existent. This is the ground upon which Professor Young, choosing between alternatives, preferred to call trade-marks

1. An able defense of a broader definition of monopoly to include all cases of scarcity appears in Dobb, *Capitalist Enterprise and Social Progress,* pp. 105ff., together with references to prove that such a definition has "the sanction of usage." To the writer this seems misleading and dangerous. Mr. Dobb distinguishes three kinds of monopoly (scarcity)—natural, institutional, and deliberate, the latter referring to control of the supply by one person or group of persons. Clearly the third type must be distinguished from the other two, and even though qualifying adjectives are employed, the distinction is weakened and confused analysis invited by broadening the definition to include all cases of "restriction," or scarcity. The Greek derivation of the word (μόνος, alone + πωλεῖν, to sell), as well as the *preponderance* of economic usage, is definitely against such extension.

competitive rather than monopolistic. Seager also makes control over price an important element in his definition of monopoly. Now a monopolist's control over price may be limited for either of two reasons: first, because his control over the supply is only partial, or secondly, because the demand for his product is highly elastic. If control over the supply is not complete, clearly the monopoly is not perfect, and control over price is only partial. But a highly elastic demand is a limitation of another sort. A monopolist's control over price is never complete in the sense that he can set it without regard for the conditions of demand for his product. It is to his advantage that the demand be inelastic, to be sure, but it is not in accord with general usage to measure the perfection of his monopoly by the degree of its elasticity.

The demand for a good may be so elastic that the seller's best price is little different from that of others selling products almost identical. It may be lower instead of higher, or it may conform to a commonly accepted price for the general class of goods. But the fact that all the producers set the same price does not indicate absence of monopoly, for, as will be shown later, this price will be higher than it would be if the commodity were perfectly homogeneous and sold under conditions of pure competition. Of course, prices might be higher yet if, instead of a monopoly of each different brand, there existed a monopoly of the entire class of product. The more substitutes controlled by any one seller, the higher he can put his price. But that is another matter. As long as the substitutes are to any degree imperfect, he still has a monopoly of his own product and control over its price within the limits imposed upon any monopolist—those of the demand.[2]

Thirdly, it may be objected that distinctive features often give profits which are not excessive, unreasonable, or above the "competitive level." This is, of course, true, but it has no bearing on the question. Most patents come to nothing; but they are not for this reason competitive. They are worthless monopolies—things nobody wants. Many copyrighted books are unsuccessful, and others, although sold at prices higher than they would be under pure competition, are sold in such small volume that the profits are nominal or wholly absent. It is quite possible for the preferences of buyers to be distributed with rough uniformity among the products of a number of competing sellers, so that all have about the same profits. Monopoly necessarily involves neither a price higher than that of similar articles nor profits higher than the ordinary rate.

2. There is an apparent difficulty in the case where, the differences between products being very slight, the seller might be unable to dispose of anything at all above the generally accepted price for that type of goods, the demand schedule for his product being perfectly elastic—the horizontal line which has been identified with pure competition. Buyers might prefer his goods at the same price, whereas they would go *en masse* to his competitors if there were the slightest difference.

The difficulty would not appear if the monetary unit were infinitely divisible. For if buyers had a preference for one product over another at the same price, it would require at least a slight divergence in price to eliminate it. The amount of this divergence would vary with individual buyers, and hence, if there were many of them, the demand schedule for each product would be continuous and tipped slightly from the horizontal. Actually, however, let it be granted that, at the next price above the one asked, sales may fall to zero. Monopoly is not thereby eliminated, for profits may be high through a large volume of sales as well as through a high price. Where this is the case, extra profits must be attributed to differentiation, for if the product were perfectly homogeneous, buyers would have no basis whatever for choice and would trade with different sellers at random, giving them each approximately the same volume of sales. Any excess of actual profits over what they would be under pure competition must be regarded as due to monopoly.

In summary, wherever products are differentiated, the theory of monopoly *seems* adequately to describe their prices. Competition is not eliminated from the explanation; it is fully taken into account by the recognition that substitutes affect the elasticity of demand for each monopolist's product.

## 4. Monopolistic Competition

It may now be asked in what respect monopolistic competition differs from this. Is it anything more than a new name, designed to soften a much wider application of the theory of monopoly than has heretofore been made? And if it is more, wherein lies the deficiency of the theory of monopoly, which has just been defended as adequate?

The answers to these questions are fully developed in the chapters to follow. Monopolistic competition is evidently a different thing from either *pure* monopoly or *pure* competition. As for monopoly, *as ordinarily conceived and defined,* monopolistic competition embraces it and takes it as a starting point. It is possible to do this where it would not be possible to take competition as a starting point, for the reason which has just been set forth at such length: that the theory of monopoly at least recognizes both elements in the problem, whereas the theory of competition, by regarding monopoly elements as "imperfections," eliminates them.

The theory of monopoly, although the opening wedge, is very soon discovered to be inadequate. The reason is that it deals with the isolated monopolist, the demand curve for whose product is given. Although such a theory may be useful in cases where substitutes are fairly remote, in general the competitive interrelationships of groups of sellers preclude taking the demand schedule for the product of any one of them as given. It depends upon the nature and prices of the substitutes with which it is in close competition. Within any group of closely related products (such as that ordinarily included in one imperfectly competitive market) the demand and supply conditions (and hence the price) of any one are defined only if the demand and supply conditions with respect to the others are taken as given. Partial solutions of this sort, yielded by the theory of monopoly, contribute nothing towards a solution of the whole problem, for each rests upon assumptions with respect to the others. Monopolistic competition, then, concerns itself not only with the problem of an *individual* equilibrium (the ordinary theory of monopoly), but also with that of a *group* equilibrium (the adjustment of economic forces within a group of competing monopolists, ordinarily regarded merely as a group of competitors). In this it differs both from the theory of competition and from the theory of monopoly.

The matter may be put in another way. It has already been observed that, when products are differentiated, buyers are given a basis for preference, and will therefore be paired with sellers, not in random fashion (as under pure competition), but according to these preferences. Under pure competition, the market of each seller is perfectly merged with those of his rivals; now it is to be recognized that each is in some measure isolated, so that the whole is not a single large market of many sellers, but a network of related markets, one for each seller. The theory brings into the foreground the monopoly elements arising from ubiquitous partial independence. These elements have received but fragmentary recognition in economic literature, and never have they been allowed as a part of the general explanation of prices, except under the heading of "imperfections" in a theory which specifically excludes them.[3] It is now proposed to give due weight to whatever degree of isolation exists by focusing attention on the market of the individual seller. A study of "competition" from this point of view gives results which are out of harmony with accepted competitive theory.

# Joan Robinson

## *The Economics of Imperfect Competition*

## Chapter 27

## A World of Monopolies

### 1

It is customary, in setting out the principles of economic theory, to open with the analysis of a perfectly competitive world, and to treat monopoly as a special case. It has been the purpose of the foregoing argument to show that this process can with advantage be reversed and that it is more proper to set out the analysis of monopoly, treating perfect competition as a special case. We have been concerned, however, only with the problem of price and output for a single industry considered in isolation, and it must be conceded that for problems connected with the distribution of resources between

3. Several instances of fragmentary mention given to the idea of a separate market for each seller may be cited. Fisher points out *(Elementary Principles of Economics,* p. 323) that "the slight undercutting of prices by one grocer will not ruin the trade of another in another part of the same town for the reason that the two are not absolutely in the same market. Each has a sphere which the other can only partially reach, not only because of distance, but also because each has his own 'custom,' i. e., the patronage of people who, from habit or from other reasons, would not change grocers merely because of a slight difference in price." Marshall *(Principles,* 8th ed., p. 458; also Mathematical Appendix, note xiv) speaks of "industries in which each firm is likely to be confined more or less to its own particular market," but seems to regard this as entirely a short time phenomenon. The particular demand curve of the producer's own special market, he thinks, "will generally be very steep," probably on this account. No doubt it will be less elastic for a short period than for a long period, but, the differentiation of product remaining, it will never become horizontal, as under pure competition. The following passage is found in Dobb, *Capitalist Enterprise and Social Progress,* p. 88: "In any fairly-established line of business... each firm will probably possess a 'private market' of its own, composed of a fairly regular clientele which in various ways it has attached to itself." The accompanying brief discussion as to the effect on prices is in the vein of Chapter V, below.

J. M. Clark, in explaining his conception of a qualified monopoly as necessary to competition, says that "to a limited extent, each producer has his own individual market, connected more or less closely with those of his competitors, so that discrepancies are limited in amount and in duration, becoming narrower and briefer in proportion to the standardized character of the goods" *(Economics of Overhead Costs,* p. 418). But he develops the idea no further, and thinks of competition as taking place in one large market. A. B. Wolfe points out the fallacy of treating retail merchants in different cities as if they were in the same market, and finds that even in the same city there are "distinct, though not absolutely independent, markets, defined by location and by class of custom" ("Competitive Costs and the Rent of Business Ability," *Quarterly Journal of Economics,* Vol. XXXIX [1924], p. 50). But he never reaches the logical conclusion of the argument—a "distinct, though not absolutely independent," market for each seller. To him, "each town or locality constitutes a market," though with many qualifications and adequate recognition of its imperfections. F. H. Knight ("Cost of Production and Price over Long and Short Periods," *Journal of Political Economy,* Vol. XXIX, at p. 332, reprinted in the *Ethics of Competition and Other Essays,* see p. 213) states clearly the case for applying the theory of monopoly rather than that of competition to the "partial monopoly" resulting from differentiated products.

It is unnecessary to extend the list further.

different uses, and the distribution of the proceeds of industry between the factors of production, the assumption of competition forms a more useful starting point. For instance, we have already found it necessary to appeal to perfect competition in order to find a criterion of exploitation. But if our theory of value is to be based upon the conception of monopoly it is obviously necessary to discover what becomes of the theory of distribution upon the basis of monopoly. It is therefore necessary to attempt the analysis of a world in which every commodity is produced under monopoly. Moreover, this problem obviously has some practical relevance in the present age. We see on every side a drift towards monopolization under the names of restriction schemes, quota systems, rationalisation, and the growth of giant companies.

Our question can only be answered precisely if it is precisely stated and the assumptions underlying it clearly set out, but when we have answered it upon the most abstract terms, some moral may be drawn from it which may be applicable to the actual situation.

## 2

In order to solve the theoretical problem in its simplest form a number of assumptions must be made which will be removed as we examine various aspects of the problem.

The most convenient assumptions at the first stage are these:

There are $n$ industries producing $n$ commodities for each of which the conditions of demand and supply are exactly similar. Each commodity will be to some extent a substitute for every other, but none will be a perfect substitute. Thus, if a certain volume of incomes is being spent on commodities, so that the elasticity of demand for all taken together is equal to unity, the elasticity of demand for each considered separately will be greater than unity.

There is a fixed total amount of each factor of production. This entails that there are a given number of workers of given efficiency, who always work equally hard for the same number of hours throughout the story; and that there is no net addition to capital throughout the story. The existing stock of capital is kept intact by replacement but can be changed in form if it is profitable to do so.[1]

The supply of each factor to every industry considered separately is perfectly elastic, and there are no economies of large-scale industry. Thus each of our $n$ commodities is produced under constant returns, and the proportions of the factors employed do not alter with changes in output. The supply of each commodity taken separately is perfectly elastic, and of all taken together perfectly inelastic.

We take as the basis for the comparison a world in which there is perfect competition in every way.

The community which we are considering is a closed system.

1. The problem of measuring the stock of capital presented no difficulty as long as we were concerned only with a single industry, for then it was possible to measure capital in money value (assuming the general rate of interest to be constant), but when we have to deal with the total stock of capital the problem presents difficulties which no attempt is here made to solve.

We treat only of positions of full equilibrium, that is to say, of positions in which there is no spontaneous tendency towards any alteration in the existing state of affairs.

The monopolists who come into the story have no function except the control of output. Each consists of a controlling agency which has negligible running costs and is capable of an indefinitely large output. When such an agency comes into command of an industry the general structure of the industry in separate firms is maintained, though the constitution of outputs of the firms may be altered if it is profitable to do so. The head of the firm is retained as a manager, and is paid as a salary whatever sum would have constituted his transfer profit to a competitive industry. The profits of the monopoly may be divided up in any sort of way we please to imagine, after they have been secured. Management, in the sense of the managers of the firms, must be treated on the same footing as the other factors, but it may be the same individuals who were the entrepreneurs under competition who share in the spoils of the monopolists. This assumption about the nature of the monopolists will not be removed throughout the argument.

There is no collusion between monopolists. Each tries to maximize his own profits without regard to the interests of the others.

## 3

Now, starting from the position of perfect competition, suppose that each of these n commodities comes into the hand of a monopolist, everything else remaining the same. At first sight we might be inclined to suppose that the monopolists would reduce the output of everything; for instance, that if all the demand curves were straight lines half of the former output of each commodity would be produced. But this is obviously absurd. Half of the supply of each factor of production would be unemployed, and there would not be equilibrium—the wage of a factor is less than the value of its marginal physical product, and we have distinguished two types of exploitation, monopolistic exploitation which arises when the demand curve for the commodity is not perfectly elastic, and monopsonistic exploitation which arises when the supply curve of the factor is not perfectly elastic to the individual employer. We are at present assuming that the supply curves of the factors are perfectly elastic to the separate industries, that is to say, to each monopolist; thus it is only with monopolistic exploitation that we are for the moment concerned.

Under perfect competition the factors received their marginal physical product multiplied by the price of the commodity they produce. Thus if we take the price of the commodity in each industry as an index number of all prices, the factors received in real wages their marginal physical product. Under the regime of the monopolists their money wages are equal to their marginal physical product multiplied by marginal revenue. Thus their real wages may be represented as marginal physical product multiplied by $\frac{\text{marginal revenue}}{\text{price}}$ in each industry. Under the conditions that we are at present assuming, the marginal physical productivity will be unchanged by the advent of the monopolists. Thus the earnings of the factors have been reduced in the ratio of marginal revenue to price. For instance, suppose that the money wages or all factors of production remain the same when the monopolies are set up. The costs of all commodities will then be unaltered, and in order to ensure full employment the prices of all commodities must rise until the new marginal revenue from each commodity is equal to its old price,[2] so that the output of each commodity under monopoly (at which marginal revenue is equal to cost) is equal to its former output under competition (at which price is equal to cost). The price level will then have risen in the ratio of price to marginal revenue in the new position, and the real earnings of the factors will be reduced in the same ratio, since their money earnings remain unchanged.

The extent to which the factors are exploited will depend upon the elasticity of demand for the commodities. The ratio of marginal revenue to price is equal to $\frac{\varepsilon - 1}{\varepsilon}$ where $\varepsilon$ is the elasticity of demand. It follows that the smaller the elasticity of demand for the separate commodities the greater will be the degree of exploitation. Thus, if the elasticity of de mand is, say, 20, the factors receive as real wages $\frac{19}{20}$ of their marginal products, but if the elasticity of demand is equal to 2 they receive only half of their marginal physical products.

## 4

Already from this highly abstract case, we can draw a moral for the real world. First, it is worth while to notice that in the position just described each monopolist would be earning normal profits, for the normal profit in each industry is the profit which can be earned elsewhere, and the reward of enterprise would be no higher in any one industry than in any other. The wages of labour would be fair in the sense that work of equal skill would receive the same reward in all industries.[3] If we looked at each industry separately, we should see that the wages of the factors were equal to average as well as to marginal net productivity, for in calculating average net productivity we should be obliged to subtract from the gross product the normal profits of the entrepreneur, which are now everywhere swollen by monopoly gains. Any arbitrary rise of wages in a single trade would lead to unemployment. The wage would then be "uneconomically high," and it would be generally considered desirable to lower it again. No ordinary touchstone would be able to tell us that anything was amiss. Yet the factors of production would all be exploited, and the monopolists would be keeping the spoil.

Secondly, our abstract case has shown that the factors of production are more likely to be exploited the larger is the unit of control which employs them. As we have

2. We must suppose that the quantity of money can be freely increased in order to support the new price level. In equilibrium the total money value of the national dividend (which is unchanged in physical magnitude) will be greater than before by the amount of the total incomes of the monopolists.

3. *Economics of Welfare*, p. 549. Professor Pigou's definition of *fair* wages includes the absence of exploitation, for he envisages a world of perfect competition.

seen, the degree of exploitation is greater the smaller the elasticity of demand for the commodities. And the elasticity of demand is likely to be less the greater is the unit of control in industry. When the unit of control is one firm selling in competition with others the elasticity of demand for its particular output is likely to be very high, even if the market is not so perfect that the elasticity is infinite. The output of each firm in the same line of business will be a close substitute for the output of every other, and the elasticity of demand for each of them will be great. But if the unit of control consists of a combination of all the firms producing some well-defined commodity for which the substitutes are different articles rather than different brands of the same article, the elasticity of demand must be considerably less. Moreover, the smaller the number of firms producing any one commodity the smaller will be the elasticity of demand for the output of any one of them.[4]

Our abstract analysis must therefore lead to the reflection that the prevalence of imperfect competition in the real world sets up a tendency to exploitation, and that this tendency must be greatly strengthened by the formation of large combines absorbing a large number of formerly competing firms. As we have seen, the degree of exploitation due to imperfect competition may be very great. Even with an elasticity of demand as great as two, the factors receive only half the perfectly competitive real wage.

## 5

We must next examine the effect of removing the third assumption, that the supply of the factors is perfectly elastic to each industry, while retaining the assumption that there are no economies of large-scale industry.

We found in Chapter 14 that when the elasticities of supply of various factors to a particular industry are not all alike a monopolist will alter the competitive proportions of the factors and produce a given output at lower average cost. It might at first sight appear, therefore, even if we start from a position of perfect competition, that when the industries are working under rising costs our monopolists will be able to improve upon the competitive method of production and that the national dividend would be increased. This, however, would be a false inference. We cannot deduce results applicable to all industries taken together from results applicable to one industry in isolation by a simple process of multiplication.

Let us suppose that the industries are alike, but that the supply of some factors is less elastic, and of some more elastic, to every industry. Then, looking at the matter from the point of view of one industry, we can see that the monopolist will restrict his use of the factors which are in less elastic supply. The effect will be to lower the price of these factors and to cause part of them to become unemployed. But this will lower the transfer cost of these factors to all other industries, and their reward will be

4. Further, the elasticity of demand for the output of anyone firm is likely to be less the smaller is the total number of firms in all industries. If the unit of control is everywhere large, so that the total number of firms is small, then a rise in price by any one firm will cause an appreciable rise in the prices charged by all other firms. And if a rise in the price of the commodity produced by one firm raises the price of rival commodities the elasticity of demand for the commodity whose price is raised will be less than it would be if the prices of other commodities were unaltered.

reduced in each industry, until they are absorbed into employment. The proportions of the factors, in each industry, will be the same as before, and the same national dividend as before will be produced. The only effect will be that the relative rewards of the factors will be altered. Those which are in less elastic supply will be worse off than those which are in more elastic supply. In short, by postulating an imperfectly elastic supply of factors to an industry, we have admitted the possibility of monopsonistic exploitation.

The marginal cost of each actor will be equal to its marginal physical productivity multiplied by marginal revenue. Since the proportions are unaltered, marginal physical productivity is the same as before, and the real wage is reduced (below the competitive wage) first in the ratio of marginal revenue to price, and secondly in the ratio of average to marginal cost of the factor to each industry. Now the average cost of the factor (the money wage) can be expressed as $M\frac{E}{E+1}$ where M is the marginal cost and E is the numerical value of the elasticity of supply.[5] Thus the real wage of each factor under the monopolists will be equal to the competitive wage multiplied by $\left(\frac{\varepsilon-1}{\varepsilon}\right)\left(\frac{E}{E+1}\right)$, where $\varepsilon$ is the elasticity of demand and E is the numerical value of the elasticity of supply of the factor. Thus those factors whose supply is relatively less elastic will be most exploited.[6]

Moreover if the supply of a factor is less than perfectly elastic to a particular industry, it is possible that the monopolist may discriminate in buying it, so that the factors of production may be deprived of the rents which they earned under competition.

Thus we may add to the moral which we draw from the abstract analysis that perfect competition not only in selling commodities, but in buying the factors of production, is advantageous to the factors, and that any increase in the size of the unit of control, by reducing the elasticity of supply of the factors to the employing agency, will increase the degree of exploitation.

## 6

So far we have been concerned with the effect of monopoly upon the distribution of the national dividend. In order to isolate this problem we have assumed that all industries are alike. We must now examine the effect of monopoly upon the distribution of resources between various uses, and to do so we must remove our simplifying assumption. This can be done most conveniently in three stages. We shall first retain the assumption that the elasticities of demand are all equal and examine the case in which there are no economies of large-scale industry, but in which the elasticity of supply of each factor is different to different industries. Then, supposing that there are

5. The formula is modified in this way because the elasticity of a rising curve is treated as negative.

6. The existence of economies of large-scale industry would have the same effect as an increase in the elasticity of supply of the factors, and would reduce the degree of exploitation.

no scarce factors (from the point of view of an individual industry) we shall examine the effect of economies of large scale. And finally we shall remove the assumption that the elasticities of demand are all alike.

First, suppose that to some industries the supply of any one factor is more elastic than it is to others. Then (assuming that the monopolists pay some rent for the factor) the use of it will be restricted in those industries to which its supply is least elastic. Its reward will therefore fall, and its use in those industries to which its supply is more elastic will increase. There will thus be a change in the composition of the national dividend. The factors will be diverted from those uses to which their supply is relatively less elastic to those where it is relatively more elastic. Now, it can be shown that the optimum distribution of resources between industries is achieved under conditions of perfect competition,[7] for, under perfect competition, the value of the marginal physical product of resources is equal in all uses, so long as there are no economies of large-scale industry. Therefore (so long as we retain the assumption of no economies) the distribution brought about by monopoly will be different from the optimum, and the national dividend will be reduced.

But when there are economies of large-scale industry the optimum distribution of resources is not achieved under competition, since the value of the marginal physical product of resources is greater (under competition) in those industries which are subject to economies than in those which are not. Suppose that there are no scarce factors, and that different industries are subject to economies of large scale to varying degrees. Then, under the monopolists, the output of commodities most subject to economies will be increased, and the output of commodities subject to less degree of economies will be contracted until the marginal productivity of resources is everywhere the same,[8] and the optimum distribution of resources will be brought about by the monopolists. Thus we find that in respect of rising costs the monopolists do harm and in respect of falling costs they do good. When both are present together the net effect of monopolization may be either to improve upon the competitive distribution of resources or the reverse, and on balance the national dividend may be either increased or diminished.

## 7

We have so far retained the assumption that the elasticities of demand are all equal. The effect of removing this assumption can be isolated by reverting to the assumption that all commodities are produced under constant cost. We may now suppose that though

7. The argument of the *Economics of Welfare* is the basis of the above analysis. But it is clearly necessary to ignore Professor Pigou's references to an "archetypal industry" which need not exist in fact and to interpret his analysis as applying to a world in which the generality of industries are conducted under perfect competition. The optimum distribution of resources will be attained provided that the marginal cost to the individual employer is equal to the marginal cost to society and this will, in general, be attained (in the absence of economies of large scale) under perfect competition. Exceptions occur (even when there are no economies of large scale) in the case of costs (such as the smoke nuisance or industrial disease) which are not borne by the employer.

8. The assumption that all elasticities of demand are equal is necessary to this conclusion, for it is only then that the equality of marginal productivities entails the equality of the values of marginal physical productivities.

the elasticity of demand for each commodity is the same before and after the advent of the monopolists,[9] The elasticities of demand of different commodities are different.

Now in a world of absolutely perfect competition without economies of large-scale industry, the marginal cost to society of every commodity is equal to its price. And the price of each commodity is equal to its marginal utility to the individual buyer. Thus we may say (leaping a dangerous chasm into which we must peer in a moment) that under perfectly competitive conditions the marginal utility of every commodity is equal to its marginal cost to society. Resources are thus distributed so that a unit of resources will yield the same marginal utility in every direction, and the maximum of satisfaction is obtained from a given supply of resources. But under conditions of monopoly it is not price but marginal revenue which is equal to marginal cost. Under the monopolists resources will be distributed so that the marginal revenue obtained by employing a unit of resources is everywhere the same, and marginal revenue is not equal to marginal utility. If the elasticities of demand of the commodities are not all equal, the ratio of marginal utility (measured by price) to marginal revenue will be different in different industries and the marginal utilities (from an increment of resources) will not be everywhere equal. The output of commodities for which the demand curves are relatively more elastic will be expanded, and there will be a further reason to expect that the composition of the national dividend will be changed. If the national dividend in the first position under perfect competition yields the maximum satisfaction from the given resources, the national dividend under monopoly will yield less than the maximum.

But is this picture of the ideal distribution of resources under competition really justified? We leapt over a very doubtful step in the argument when we supposed that it was. To a strictly logical mind any discussion of utility to more than one individual is repugnant. It is not really justifiable to talk about maximum satisfaction to a whole population. But common sense protests that if we treat all individuals as being exactly alike it is then permissible to sum their satisfactions, and that human beings, in their economic needs, are sufficiently alike to make the discussion of aggregate satisfaction interesting. Upon this basis we may say that if any two individuals have the same real income they derive the same satisfaction from it. We may further say that if one individual has a larger real income than another the marginal utility of income to him is less. Now in the world of perfect competition, with constant cost for each commodity, all marginal costs are equal to prices, and prices are equal to marginal utilities, measured in terms of money. If income is perfectly equally distributed its marginal utility is equal for every individual. Therefore the distribution of resources is then such that

9. The advent of the monopolists alters the distribution of incomes and so would be likely to change the elasticity of demand of many commodities. And this would have some further repercussions. If the things consumed by the monopolists are mainly produced under increasing cost, and the things consumed by the exploited factors under decreasing cost, the position of the factors will be still worse. If the things consumed by the monopolists are produced under decreasing cost they will gain a further advantage, but there will be no offset to the exploited factors. We can abstract from this effect either by supposing that the monopolists consume all commodities in the same proportions as the rest of the community, or by supposing that the profits of the monopolists are taxed away from them and distributed as a bonus to the rest of the community.

satisfaction is at a maximum. Thus to represent the competitive world as an ideal state we have had to introduce the highly unreal assumption that wealth is equally distributed. If it is not equally distributed, there is no reason to suppose that the satisfaction obtained from given resources is at a maximum in a perfectly competitive world.

Our world of monopolists therefore has not after all such a very high standard with which to compete. But even when we abstract from the change in distribution of wealth brought about by the monopolists, it seems on the whole justifiable to say that the composition of the national dividend under monopoly will be even further from the ideal than it was under competition, since both will be subject to the maldistribution of resources due to unequal wealth, and the dividend under monopoly will be subject to a further maldistribution due to the different divergences of marginal revenue from price.

The monopolists would be freed from this charge, and might even improve upon the competitive distribution of resources, if it were the case that the demand for commodities consumed by richer classes of consumers was generally less elastic than for commodities consumed by poorer classes. The production of goods consumed by the poorer owners of the factors would then be expanded, and their prices lowered, relatively to those of goods consumed by richer owners of the factors. There may be some reason to suppose that this is the case. But it is probable that demands tend to be more elastic when the market is made up of a larger number of income groups, and to be less elastic both when the market is composed entirely of rich individuals and when it is composed entirely of poor individuals. If there are two equally homogeneous markets the demand in the poorer market is likely to be the more elastic, but if the poorer markets are the more homogeneous the elasticity of demand for goods consumed by poorer individuals may be less than for goods consumed by richer individuals. The change in the composition of the national dividend brought about by the monopolists would then enhance and not mitigate the maldistribution of wealth.

One further point remains to be considered. We have seen that some factors will be exploited more than others. The individuals who provide the factors for which the supply to individual industries is relatively less elastic and which are therefore most exploited may be richer than those which provide the less exploited factors. This would tend to mitigate the maldistribution of wealth. For instance, if land is relatively more exploited than labour, and if landlords are richer than workmen, there will be a tendency in this direction. In so far as labour is strongly organised in trade unions while the supply of land to a particular industry is often imperfectly elastic, it is probable that land is more exploitable than labour. But the factor of production which is at once the poorest and the most exploitable is unorganised unskilled labour. It is therefore unlikely that monopolists can claim much credit for a-beneficial redistribution of wealth between the factors of production.

## 8

In comparing the world of monopolies with a world of perfect competition we have found that monopoly may have an unfavourable effect upon the distribution of resources between different uses and must have an unfavourable effect upon the distribution of wealth between individuals. But we cannot conclude that the spread of monopolistic combinations in the real world must be harmful until we have compared monopoly with imperfect competition, for in the real world competition is not perfect. Let us suppose, once more, that the demand curves and cost curves for each of the *n* commodities are alike, but let us suppose that, before the arrival of the monopolists, the market within each of the *n* industries is imperfect.

There are then *n* groups of firms; the individual demand curve of each firm will be more elastic than the demand curve for the commodity, but not perfectly elastic, and if profits are normal for each group, the firms are all of less than optimum size. When the group of firms comes into the hands of a monopolist he will be able to organise the industry more efficiently. If, as we have supposed, the supply of each factor to the industry is perfectly elastic, the monopolist will reproduce exactly the methods of production that would obtain in a perfect market, efficiency will be increased, and costs of production will fall.

The reorganisation of the industries may bring about the specialisation of firms by the process of lateral and vertical disintegration, and there may be a very great increase in efficiency. But even if there are no possibilities of reorganisation of this sort there may be an increase in efficiency. If each firm in the world of imperfect competition was producing a homogeneous commodity (so that there is no possibility of lateral disintegration) by a single process (so that there is no possibility of vertical disintegration), then there may still be economies for the monopolists to introduce, for in the world of imperfect competition the firms would be of less than optimum size. If technical economies could be gained from growth in the size of the firms the monopolists would reorganise industries in fewer and larger productive units and the average physical productivity of the factors would be increased.[10]

But even if the average physical productivity of the factors is raised it does not necessarily follow that their marginal physical productivity will be raised, since marginal physical productivity must begin to fall (as the output of firm increases) before average physical productivity. It is only if the firms, under imperfect competition, were

10. The saving in cost brought about by a growth in the size of the firms may be divided into two parts: technical economics due to the larger scale of production, and the economy of spreading the fixed cost of the entrepreneur over a larger output. Thus even if the firms in the world of imperfect competition were of such a size that there were no technical economies to be gained from growth, they would still be of less than optimum size. There would be a tendency for the monopolist to increase the size of the productive units in order to reduce cost by spreading the reward of the entrepreneur (who takes service under the monopolist as a manager) over a larger output. But we have supposed that the supply of entrepreneurs is perfectly inelastic to industry as a whole. The attempt of the monopolists to increase the size of firms and dismiss some entrepreneurs would therefore be countered by a reduction in the reward of the entrepreneurs. This would reduce the optimum size of the firms, and if all the entrepreneurs are employed by the monopolists their reward will be reduced to the point at which the new optimum size of the firms is equal to their former actual size. Thus the size of the firms will be unaltered.

But if there are technical economies to be gained from a growth in the size of firms the monopolists would not employ the full number of entrepreneurs even if their reward was reduced to zero. The firms would then be larger in size and some of the entrepreneurs would be permanently unemployed or would be obliged to seek some other occupation, such as unskilled labour.

so small that marginal physical productivity was rising that there is any possibility of a gain to the factors of production from a mere growth in the size of the firms.[11]

Thus a growth in the size of the firms may increase the marginal physical productivities if the firms were sufficiently small under imperfect competition, and the reorganisation of the industries by vertical and lateral disintegration is likely to increase them. There may thus be some offset against the additional exploitation, and, on balance, the factors may even gain from the advent of the monopolists. In both positions the factors receive as real wages their marginal physical product $\times \frac{\text{marginal revenue}}{\text{price}}$. In the new position the ratio of marginal revenue to price is less than before, since the demand curve for the commodity is less elastic than the demand curve for the output of the individual firm, but it is possible that marginal physical productivity will have increased (because of the increase in efficiency) to an extent sufficient to balance or overbalance this loss. The absolute real income of the factors may therefore be increased, and they may have cause after all to be grateful to the monopolists.

But there is a strong presumption that the factors will not gain. Marginal physical productivity will only be increased by the mere growth of the firms if competition was very imperfect, and the firms very small, before the monopolists reorganised the industries. And though it is probable that the disintegration of firms will increase marginal physical productivity it is only when marginal physical productivity increases by more than the increase in the ratio of price to marginal revenue that the factors can gain from the advent of the monopolists.

By removing the assumption that the market in each commodity was perfect in the first position we have put fresh powers into the hands of the monopolists. If the conditions which made the markets imperfect persist, the monopolists will be able to discriminate in selling each commodity, in a way which was impossible in the first case when we took perfect competition as the basis of the comparison, since the same causes which make the market imperfect make discrimination possible.

If the monopolists can discriminate their profits will be larger, and they will gain at the expense of the factors of production not only in paying them a lower wage but also in allowing them a smaller consumer's surplus on their purchases.[12] At the same time, although taken as a whole consumers are worse off, some members of the community will be better off than under a system of simple monopoly. It is impossible to set the damage to those individuals who have to pay higher prices against the gains of those who pay lower prices. But since there is a presumption that those to whom

11. The relative positions of the factors may be altered by a growth in the size of the firms.

12. We found when we were considering a single monopoly in isolation that the power to discriminate in selling will sometimes lead to a larger output, sometimes to a smaller output, and sometimes to the same output as would occur if the monopolist could only sell at a single price. If our *n* industries in the monopolised world conform to the conditions of those cases where the output for one industry tends to increase, the difference between marginal revenue and price to the monopolists will be less than under simple monopoly. The degree of exploitation will therefore be less, but it will not be sufficiently less to offset the loss of consumers' surplus, since the monopoly profit must in any case be larger under discrimination than under simple monopoly.

higher prices are charged will be on the whole richer than the rest, the monopolists, in playing the part of Robin Hood, may once more be conceded to have some redeeming features.

## 9

If we remove our second assumption that no capital accumulation occurs, the other factors of production will enjoy a further offset against the damage done to them by the monopolists. It may be assumed that the class sharing in the monopoly gains consists of fewer individuals than the owners of the factors of production, and since their earnings will be increased by all that the other factors are forced to forgo, the distribution of wealth will have become more unequal than it was before. If capital accumulation is to be allowed into our scheme, it is therefore on the whole probable that it will go on faster than before, although the lower rate of interest may reduce the volume of saving coming from those who were providing new capital under the competitive regime. The lower return to capital will be a disadvantage to former capital owners, but the increase in the amount of capital will increase the national dividend, and it will tend to increase the real wages of labour progressively through time. The fact that an unequal distribution of wealth promotes saving is not, of course, a justification for inequality (if saving can be secured in any other way), but it is a redeeming feature of inequality, and to this extent our monopolists may be given credit for it.

## 10

It may appear rash to draw any conclusion applicable to the real world from the highly abstract analysis which we have made. But one general result appears to emerge from it. We find in comparing a world of monopolised industries with a world of imperfect competition that there may be very considerable improvements in the technique of production when the unit of control in industry increases in size. But we find that an increase in the size of the unit of control will lead to an increase in the inequality of the distribution of wealth. The problem of the world of monopolists thus resolves itself into the familiar dilemma between efficiency and justice. In order to form a judgment upon the present-day movement towards monopoly we must decide whether it is worth while to put power into the hands of large concerns for the sake of the increase in productivity which they promise to bring about. This is a problem which no amount of abstract analysis can help us to solve. It resolves itself into two questions. The first is a question of fact. How great will the economies of monopolisation actually be—how great is the improvement in the organisation of industry that we may expect from an enlargement of the unit of control? It is clearly of the utmost importance to evaluate the gains which may be expected from monopolisation, before we can decide whether it is worth while to submit to the possible dangers which it entails. The second question is one of judgment. What gain in the efficiency of production would be sufficient to make us consider that monopolisation was desirable?

The first question is outside the scope of a theoretical treatise. A great and detailed knowledge of the exact technical situation in many industries would be necessary before any estimate could be formed of the economies to be expected from monopolisation. But it is legitimate, even for the theorist, to suggest that different types of monopoly hold out very different hopes of technical reorganisation. When a scheme takes the form of machine-wrecking pure and simple, as in the case of the National Shipbuilders' Security, Limited, or of restriction of output by quotas without any concentration, as under the Coal Mines Act of 1930, there seems little reason to expect any increase in efficiency; whereas an organisation which exercises a detailed control over a large number of productive concerns may have very great possibilities of technical improvement.

The second question involves a matter of personal judgment upon which everyone must have his own opinion. But it is important to remember that a question does arise, the question of balancing the possible efficiency of monopoly against the dangers of an increased maldistribution of wealth. It is not sufficient to show that monopolisation will increase efficiency in order to show that it is desirable.

## 11

Three of the assumptions necessary to the most abstract case remain to be discussed.

First, there remains the assumption that the world of monopolies consists of a closed system within which the supply of factors is perfectly inelastic, each taken as a whole. If this assumption is removed it becomes probable that the advent of the monopolists will reduce the national dividend. If labour, for instance, is strongly organised in trade unions which stand out for a certain real wage the advent of the monopolists, by reducing real wages, will cause unemployment. And if capital can be invested abroad in countries where it can earn a higher reward there will be (in the long period) a reduction in the amount of capital available for the monopolised industries. In either case the national dividend will be reduced when the real reward of the factor in question is lowered by the introduction of the monopolies. Secondly, we have not discussed the assumption that full equilibrium is maintained with full employment of the factors of production. An examination of this subject would carry us outside the sphere of this book. But the study of a world of monopolies cannot be completed until we know, first, whether the introduction of monopolies is likely in itself to upset equilibrium, and secondly, whether there would be at least as good a chance of maintaining equilibrium under a system of monopolies, once they have been established, as there is in the actual world. It may be that a sudden and widespread introduction of restriction schemes will lead to very prolonged and perhaps permanent unemployment. And it may be that the very imperfect mechanisms by which full employment can be re-established under competitive conditions would be even less effective under a regime of monopoly. In either case a very important item would have to be added to the list of the disadvantages of monopolies which must be set against the possible improvements in technique that they may introduce.

Finally, there remains our last assumption, that there is no collusion amongst the monopolists. If they were to make common cause the wages of the factors might sink to almost any level, since the supply of each factor, taken as a whole, is highly inelastic. The powers of the monopolists would then be so great that they would only be restrained from exercising them by the fear of provoking a revolution on the part of the owners of the factors of production, and no precise analysis is possible of what would occur.

## Conclusion

The purpose of this book has been to provide a box of tools for the analytical economist. The area within which these tools can work is very narrowly bounded. A number of unsolved problems lie behind and before the problems with which they are adapted to deal. Behind lie the fundamental problems on whose solution depends the validity of the whole supply-and-demand-curve analysis. To these general questions the tools, in the nature of the case, can have no contribution to make. But even within their own sphere the tools can do no work unless they are given some materials to work on. The imaginary examples of the shapes and movements of demand curves and costs curves, constructed in order to display the apparatus, serve to show the kind of results that the tools could produce if they were given some realistic matter on which to exercise their ingenuity. Ahead lie a number of problems for which fresh tools may be required, but which are soluble at the same level of abstraction as the problems here discussed. Beyond them again lie the problems which require some more complicated technique, such as could survive at a lower level of abstraction.

The level of abstraction maintained in this book is distressingly high. The technique can only survive in an atmosphere rarefied by the adoption of very severe simplifying assumptions. The reader who is interested in results immediately applicable to the real world has every right to complain that these tools are of little use to him. The knives are of bone and the hammers of wood, only capable of cutting paper and driving pins into cardboard. But the analytical economist who is prepared to work stage by stage towards the still far-distant ideal of constructing an analysis which will be capable of solving the problems presented by the real world may perhaps find in this tool-box some implements which will serve his turn.

# Chapter 16

# The Moral of Price Discrimination

It is now possible to inquire how far price discrimination is harmful or advantageous to the customers of the monopolist and to society as a whole. First of all, it is clear, since average revenue is greater under price discrimination than under simple monopoly, that there may be cases in which no output would be produced at all if price discrimination were not possible. If the average cost curve of a certain product lay above the demand curve for it throughout its length no profit could be made by producing it under any one-price system. But if the average cost curve, though above the demand curve, lay at some point below the average revenue curve under price discrimination, a profit could be made and some output would be produced provided that discrimination was possible.[13] It may happen, for instance, that a railway would not be built, or a country doctor would not set up in practice, if discrimination were forbidden. It is clearly desirable that price discrimination should be permitted in such cases, for the average revenue of the monopolist cannot be greater than average utility to the consumers.[14] If average revenue is greater than average cost, average utility will also be greater, and the investment will lead to a gain to society.

But this fact must not be considered to justify (from the point of view of the community) price discrimination on the part of a concern in which very long-lived investment (such as the permanent way of a railway) has been made in the past and which discovers that, owing to a decline in demand, normal profits can only be made in the present if price discrimination is possible. From the point of view of society it is only necessary that the concern should make sufficient profit to maintain the efficiency of the plant, and not a profit which would have been sufficient to justify the original investment.

## 2

When some output would be produced even if discrimination were forbidden, it is only possible to say definitely whether price discrimination is damaging to the interests of the customers, as compared with a single price monopoly, if we identify ourselves with one or other group of customers. As compared with simple monopoly, discrimination must always be disadvantageous to those buyers for whom the price is raised, and advantageous to those for whom the price is reduced, and it is impossible to set the gains of one group against the losses of the other. But we may have some reason to prefer the interests of one group above those of the other. For instance, members of the more elastic markets (for whom price is reduced) may be poorer than members of the less elastic markets, and we may consider a gain to poorer buyers more important than a loss to richer buyers. In this case price discrimination must always be considered beneficial. On the other hand, the less elastic market may be at home and the more elastic market abroad, so that the interests of the members of the stronger market are considered more important than the interests of the weaker market.

But in this case price discrimination need not always be disadvantageous, for, as we have seen, when the conditions are such that output under discriminating monopoly is larger than under simple monopoly then, if marginal costs are falling, discrimination may actually be beneficial to the members of the less elastic market, since the

13. Professor Pigou [referring to Arthur C. Pigou, *The Economics of Welfare* (4th ed., 1932)—eds.] has worked out the conditions of this problem under perfect discrimination Under perfect discrimination the marginal revenue curve is given directly by the demand curve, and Professor Pigou points out that if the demand curve lies below the marginal cost curve throughout its length no output would be produced even under perfect discrimination. And he shows that the more rapid the rate of fall of average cost the more likely is the demand curve to lie above the marginal cost curve for a sufficient distance to ensure that some output will be produced: to ensure, in our terms, that the monopolist's average revenue curve at some point shall be cut by the average cost curve.

14. For the purposes of discussions of this type it is necessary to attach some meaning to utility as a measure of economic welfare.

marginal cost of the total output will be reduced, and the price which they are required to pay may be lowered. It must be lowered (provided that marginal costs are falling) if the conditions are such that the simple monopolist would sell no output in the weaker market. For then output is necessarily increased by the introduction of discrimination, and consequently marginal cost is reduced; but for the simple monopolist marginal cost is equal to marginal revenue in the stronger market; hence it follows that marginal revenue, and consequently price, in the stronger market are necessarily reduced by the introduction of discrimination.[15]

We have seen that the condition in which output will be much increased by discrimination is that the demand curve in the more elastic market shall be highly concave. This is probably a common case where the more elastic market is an export market in which the exported goods are in competition with those produced locally. It will often happen that only a small amount can be exported at relatively high prices but that as the price of the exported goods approaches and falls below the price of the local rival goods the demand for them increases very rapidly—in short the demand curve is highly concave.[16] Thus there are likely to be many cases in which the "dumping" of a commodity (that is, selling at a lower price in the export market than in the home market) is likely to reduce its home price, provided that marginal costs are falling with increases of output.

It is sometimes argued (for instance by railway officials anxious to justify the practice of discrimination) that the members of the high-price markets must in any case benefit from the fact that other markets are served at a lower price. The argument runs as follows: If a single price were charged the output sold in the weaker markets would be less; a larger share of the total cost of the concern would then have to be borne by the stronger markets alone, and the price charged to them would therefore be higher than when discrimination occurred. This argument would be valid if the monopolist was limited to earning a certain fixed profit, although the conditions of demand were such that he could make a larger profit. But so long as the monopolist acts upon the principle of maximising his profits (as he is assumed to do throughout

15. Professor Pigou points out that discrimination may some times be beneficial to the members of the stronger market, but he only considers the case in which no output at all would be sold in the weaker market under simple monopoly. Professor Pigou's analysis is limited to this case because he is only able to reach exact results for the case in which the separate demand curves are straight lines. When no output would be sold in the weaker market under simple monopoly, the introduction of discrimination will leave the price in the stronger market unchanged if marginal costs are constant, and raise it if marginal costs are rising. But Professor Pigou's statement is ambiguous, for he talks of supply price in place of marginal cost). Professor Viner (*Dumping,* p. 103) states, without proof, that the price in the stronger market will always be unchanged and challenges his readers to find a case in which it will be altered. This challenge was taken up by Professor Yntema who reaches the same conclusions as Professor Pigou, by a method in some respects similar to that employed in the last chapter. Neither Professor Viner nor Professor Yntema seem to have been aware of Professor Pigou's simple treatment of this problem. [The references are to Jacob Viner, *Dumping: A Problem in International Trade* (1923); and Theodore O. Yntema, "The Influence of Dumping on Monopoly Price," 36 *J.Pol.Econ.* 686 (1928).—eds.]

16. As we have seen, in the limiting case there is a certain price above which no output at all can be sold in the weaker market, and the demand curve takes on the limiting degree of concavity. The case considered above, in which price in the stronger market must necessarily fall if marginal costs are falling, is thus seen to be an extreme example of the general case.

the analysis of this book), discrimination can only benefit members of the high-price markets in the situation described above.

From the point of view of society as a whole it is impossible to say whether price discrimination is desirable or not. It is obviously wasteful, from the point of view of society, if any commodity fails to be produced up to the point where its marginal utility (shown by its demand price) is equal to its marginal cost. But under simple monopoly marginal revenue is equal to marginal cost; monopoly output is therefore undesirably small. From one point of view, therefore, price discrimination must be held to be superior to simple monopoly in all those cases in which it leads to an increase of output, and, as we have seen, these cases are likely to be the more common. But against this advantage must be set the fact that price discrimination leads to a maldistribution of resources as between different uses, a subject which would take us too far afield to discuss. Before it is possible to say whether discrimination is desirable or not, it is therefore necessary to weigh up the benefit from the increase in output against this disadvantage. In those cases in which discrimination will decrease output it is undesirable on both counts.

## 3

One further point remains to be considered. In Chapter 13 we discussed the question of price control, but we assumed that only a single price could be imposed. We must now consider whether it would be preferable to impose a system of discriminating prices.

Under a single price the maximum output will be achieved, when average costs are falling, if the imposed price is that at which demand price and average cost are equal. This, however, involves a waste, since there would be a considerable range of output, beyond that at which demand price was equal to average cost, over which demand price exceeded marginal cost; and since demand price is presumed to measure marginal utility, it is desirable that this additional output should be produced. This waste could be partly eliminated and a larger output could be achieved if it were possible to impose discriminating prices. The average revenue under uncontrolled price discrimination is greater than under uncontrolled simple monopoly, and the largest possible output will be that for which the average revenue of a discriminating monopolist would be equal to his average cost. With any given system of markets, in order to induce the monopolist to produce the maximum possible output, it is necessary to impose a system of prices such that the marginal revenues in all markets are equal, and such that average total revenue is equal to average cost. The required output will then be produced. No larger output could be sold without involving the monopolist in a loss.[17]

17. The difference between average revenue under discrimination and under simple monopoly will be greatest in those cases in which the difference between output under discrimination and under simple monopoly is greatest. The same conditions, therefore, which make discriminating output large as compared to simple monopoly output (relative concavity of the more elastic demand curve) will make the output obtainable by the above method large relatively to the output obtained by a single imposed price.

This method would ensure that the largest possible output should be produced, but it is subject to the general objection to price discrimination referred to above. It might therefore be considered desirable to sacrifice some part of the increase in output which could be obtained by this method, and to indulge in a smaller degree of price discrimination, but some degree of discrimination will almost certainly be desirable.[18]

## John Maurice Clark

## *Toward a Concept of Workable Competition*

## *The American Economic Review*

## Vol. XXX (30) June, 1940 no. 2

[Note: The paper of which this is an enlarged and revised version was read at a joint Round Table of the American Economic Association and the Econometric Society, during the meetings at Philadelphia, December, 1939.]

Where one of the conditions of perfect competition is absent, the presence of others may lead to greater rather than less imperfection. Long-run curves of individual demand and cost are flatter than commonly represented, and the imperfections of competition correspondingly less. Industry subject to fluctuating demand requires prices in excess of short-run marginal cost. Favorable conditions appear to include a sloping individual demand curve, and some uncertainty whether a reduction of price will be promptly met.

With standardized products, a chaotic market tends toward ruinous competition. Pure oligopoly is seldom found; the important case being that of openly quoted prices with varying amounts of deviations on actual sales. Standard products with sloping individual demand curves are also possible.

While extreme quality differentials approach monopoly, more moderate ones may be workably competitive, especially with further growth of closer substitutes and better knowledge of qualities on the part of buyers.

18. Professor Pigou, having established the fact that perfect competition is generally preferable to discriminating monopoly, proceeds to argue (*Economics of Welfare*, chap. xviii.) that it is desirable that railway rates should be fixed at the level appropriate to simple competition, which, as he shows, would entirely eliminate price discrimination. But his argument is extremely obscure. Under competition price is equal both to average and to marginal cost for the individual concern. It would only be possible to impose such a price upon a railway if it so happened that it was working just at its optimum capacity, so that average cost was at a minimum and equal to marginal cost. But, as Professor Pigou himself points out, railways are very likely to be working under falling average costs, and when average cost for the individual concern is falling there is no such competitive price, since marginal cost must be less than average cost. Professor Pigou may, however, be interpreted to mean that it is desirable to impose the price at which demand price is equal to average cost. This, as we have seen, will involve a waste of output which might be secured by the method here suggested, which appears to have been overlooked by Professor Pigou. In order to justify price discrimination in favour of the weaker markets he introduces the fact that demand price may not be as great as the marginal social utility of the commodity, for instance when cheap workmen's tickets enable workers to live healthily in the country (*loc. cit.* p. 314). But in order to establish the fact that there is a waste of potential output it is only necessary to consider that, for a greater output than that which would come about under a single imposed price, the demand price (which is taken to measure marginal utility) is greater than the marginal cost.

## I. Introduction

Theories of imperfect and "monopolistic" competition have for some time been current, in an unformulated state, in the field of economic policy; and important beginnings have been made at formulation by economic theorists. As a necessary step in this last development, the conception of "perfect competition" has itself for the first time received really specific definition and elaboration. With this has come the realization that "perfect competition" does not and cannot exist and has presumably never existed, for reasons quite apart from any inescapable tendency toward collusion, such as Adam Smith noted in his familiar remark on the gettings-together of members of a trade. What we have left is an unreal or ideal standard which may serve as a starting point of analysis and a norm with which to compare actual competitive conditions. It has also served as a standard by which to judge them.

I am not quarreling with proper use of this standard as an ideal. However, it has seemed at times to lead to undesirable results, in that it does not afford reliable guidance to the factors which are favorable to the closest available working approximation to that ideal, under actual conditions. With this problem the present paper is concerned.

The theory of the subject has defined for us the results of various forms of imperfect competition—some of the results being still debatable. It has defined these results in abstract terms which might be quantitative if the controlling functions could be measured, but which in the absence of such measurement remain qualitative, indicating to most minds chiefly the *direction* of departure from the standard of "perfect competition." There has been some speculation as to the amount and seriousness of these departures, but no very definite conclusions. And there has been speculation as to ways of reducing the imperfections, chiefly in specific cases.

It seems that a contribution might be made to this process, of an orienting sort, by attempting to formulate concepts of the most desirable forms of competition, selected from those that are practically possible, within the limits set by conditions we cannot escape. This would at least be an antidote to mere "historic homesickness"; but might render a more positive service. For some of the features listed as "imperfections" in our present theoretical scheme may turn out to have some positive use in actual situations. It would be a truism to say that the most effective forms of competition we have, or can have, are imperfect forms, since there are no others. But it will mean something if we can find, after due examination, that some of these forms do their jobs well enough to be an adequate working reliance—more serviceable, on the whole, than those substitutes which involve abandoning reliance on competition. And it will be useful if we can learn something about the kinds and degrees of "imperfection" which are positively serviceable under particular conditions.

One central point may be put abstractly. If there are, for example, five conditions, all of which are essential to perfect competition, and the first is lacking in a given case, then it no longer follows that we are necessarily better off for the presence of any one of the other four. In the absence of the first, it is *a priori* quite possible that the second and third may become positive detriments; and a workably satisfactory result may depend on achieving some degree of "imperfection" in these other two factors.

Suppose the first requisite is perfect two-way mobility of the factors of production, with no specialized and irrecoverable fixed capital. Granted this, an industry can stand the most rigorous conditions in all other respects. It may have a multitude of small producers, who produce a supply and then place it on a market for what it will bring instead of quoting a price and seeing how much they can sell at that price; and it may produce a standardized commodity, so that individual demand curves are infinitely elastic: but efficient producers will still cover their total costs of production. Take away the saving grace of perfect two-way mobility and leave the other conditions; let demand decline, and competition becomes too strong: you have a "sick industry" on your hands. Reduce the number of producers and let them sell on quoted prices and anticipate one another's reactions and you have a form of "oligopoly." Change one more condition, substituting a chaotically imperfect market in which irregular, temporarily secret and discriminatory pricing is the rule rather than the exception and you have (whenever demand decreases or fails to grow as anticipated) a situation tending strongly to degenerate into a cut-throat price war, driving prices below an efficient producer's total cost of production, though, if producers are few and large, this condition is not likely to be permanent.[1]

These examples are merely illustrative. They point toward a thesis, which finds reflection in the apparent confusion of our present policies (trying to raise some prices and lower others)—namely, that imperfect competition may be too strong as well as too weak; and that workable competition needs to avoid both extremes.

## II. Competition and Its Forms

By way of a generic definition of competition in price between business units and sellers, we might consider the following.

> Competition is rivalry in selling goods, in which each selling unit normally seeks maximum net revenue, under conditions such that the price or prices each seller can charge are effectively limited by the free option of the buyer to buy from a rival seller or sellers of what we think of as "the same" product, necessitating an effort by each seller to equal or exceed the attractiveness of the others' offerings to a sufficient number of sellers to accomplish the end in view.

This is not a complete definition, but brings out certain features crucial to the following argument. Specifically, it is not limited (as are some current implied definitions) to cases in which one seller succeeds in excelling the offerings of others; and it focuses attention on a crucial point which is sometimes neglected—namely the nature of the option actually open to the buyer.

The specific character of competition in any given case depends on a surprisingly large number of conditions—so many, in fact, that the number of mathematically possible combinations runs into the hundreds or thousands—and suggests the

1. These conditions are sufficiently familiar to permit the reader to fill in the gaps in the above shorthand statement of the conditions necessary to these various results.

possibility that every industry may be in some significant respect different from every other, or from itself at some other stage of development. At least ten conditioning factors appear worth noting, within each of which there are a number of variants or gradations.

1. *The standardized or unstandardized character of the product.* Standardization may be so complete that an open market tolerates no price differential between different sellers at any one point of purchase, or it may tolerate moderate quality differentials which are in effect subject to competitive forces, or the differentials may be large and subject to little or no competitive check. The commodity may be standardized while services rendered in connection with it permit some price differential, or it may be standardized by segregation of "seconds."

2. *The number and size distribution of producers.* There may be many, all small, or few, all large, or a few large and numerous small, in which case the large producers may or may not be the "dominant" factor in the market.

3. *The general method of price making.* The producer may create a supply and then sell it at whatever the market will bring ("supply-governed price"); or he may quote a price and sell what he can at that price until he sees fit to change it ("quoted price"). In the latter case, he may produce to stock or to order. Or he may sell on sealed bids.

4. *The general method of selling.* Sale may be by brokers in a produce market, by exclusive agents, through general dealers or direct *via* traveling salesmen or by mail.

5. *The character and means of market information.*

6. *The geographical distribution of production and consumption.* This is important where transportation cost is a material factor.

7. *The degree of current control of output.* Production may be seasonal, or non-seasonal with a significant lag between the initiation of a change in the rate of production and the resulting change in supply available for sale, or inventory changes may be sufficient to cushion the effect of this lag and so minimize its importance.

8. *Variation of cost with varying size of plant or enterprise.*

9. *Variation of cost with short-run fluctuations of output.*

10. *Flexibility of productive capacity.* Increase may be easy and rapid, or difficult and slow; while rapid decrease may be virtually impossible, owing to fixed capital investment.

The following outline, which is tentative and admittedly incomplete, attempts to take account of some of the more important conditioning factors, selecting as the basis for the main heads those which appear to have more effect on price behavior. The distinction between "quoted" and "supply-governed" prices has already been defined, and appears to deserve an important place. The term "quoted" is used instead of "administered" because the latter term carries implications of some degree of discretionary control, which may not always accompany the mere quoting of a price. For "supply-governed" the phrase "market-made" might be used to indicate that the making of the price quotations is literally *done by* the market machinery (as on a produce exchange) instead of being merely conditioned or controlled by it; but it seemed desirable to avoid any possible implication that the only real markets are those of the produce-exchange type, and to use terms consistent with a more inclusive concept of a market. A producer who does not sell his goods on a produce exchange or the equivalent might be surprised to be told that he had no market for them at all. The outline is herewith presented, with apologies for the amount of familiar material it contains. Its indebtedness to Professor Chamberlin is obvious.

I. *Pure (rigorous, unmitigated) competition.* Requisites: standard product, known price, many sellers available at any locality, free entry. Price may be quoted or supply-governed. Price tends to equal marginal cost.
  A. *Perfect competition.* Probably the outstanding requisite, in addition to the above, is perfect two-way mobility of the factors of production; also assumptions as to cost behavior and relationships consistent with the continued presence of many sellers. Current control of output is probably implied. Price covers average cost, which equals marginal cost.
  B. *Imperfect pure competition.* Lacking perfect mobility, marginal cost is less than average cost when demand at average-cost prices falls below capacity.
    1. Output currently controllable by each producer.
      a. Capacity such that price exceeds average cost at peaks of demand, and covers cost on average of fluctuations.
      b. Conditions such that average price is less than this. ("Sick industry" problem; ex., bituminous coal mining.)
    2. Output not currently controllable (ex., agriculture). This includes the problems giving rise to the "cobweb theorem," and related problems. Sub-heads a and b as above. (Under b, "sick industries"; ex., unregulated agriculture.)

II. *Modified, intermediate or hybrid competition.* ("Monopolistic competition" in the broader sense.)
  A. Standard products, few producers. The most important cases involve formally free entry, but no exit without loss.
    1. Quoted prices, horizontal individual demand schedules if others' prices unchanged, and variants.
      a. Open price, perfectly conformed to (rarely found): first species of oligopoly.
      b. Imperfectly known price and chaotic discrimination.
        (1) Enduring ignorance: local near-monopolies.
        (2) Temporary ignorance: tendency to "cut-throat competition."
      c. Open price with limited departures, all or part of the time: secrecy temporary. Probably the most important case.
    2. Supply-governed prices (implies an open market). Individual demand schedules sloping, but more elastic than general demand schedule: *second main species of oligopoly.*
    3. Quoted prices, sloping individual demand schedules.

a. Demand schedules definite and calculable (spatially separated producers with uniform mill prices). May result in a third species of oligopoly.
b. Demand schedules indefinite (ex., above condition with limited freight absorption).

B. Unstandardized or quality products: If *monopolistic competition.* Individual demand schedules sloping, but more elastic than general demand schedule.[2] Importance of competitive element hinges largely on extent to which quality differences are open to free imitation. Schedule of response to selling outlay a complicating factor.
1. Quoted prices; single producer's product usually standardized or graded, with separate disposal of "seconds."
2. Supply-governed prices; price differentials for quality made directly in market. For agricultural products number of suppliers usually nullifies any monopoly element.

Certain competitive categories cross the divisions of this outline. For example, "imperfect competition" covers headings I.B. and II. What may be called "atomistic competition" covers heading I, and an undivided share of the cases under II.B., though it may be noted that the outline suggests some reservation as to whether atomistic competition in the sale of quality products deserves the designation "monopolistic competition."

Among the omissions from the outline are the effects of durability *versus* perishability of products; and most of the complications of cost behavior, including the problem of joint *versus* separable costs. And it may be that a separate set of headings should have been devoted to retail selling, which presents special problems. For instance, even physically identical commodities need not sell at identical prices in neighboring stores. This fact could be forced into the headings of the outline, but might better be separately dealt with. Most important, perhaps, the outline makes no note of differences between long-run and short-run adjustments. This is vital, since it seems probable that one of the criteria of workable competition is that there shall not be too gross discrepancies between the action of short-run pressures and long-run tendencies.

## III. Long-Run Considerations

At the risk of being convicted of an optimistic bias, I should like to point to certain ways in which long-run forces serve to mitigate the seriousness of the effects of imperfect competition. These considerations center largely in the proposition that long-run curves, both of cost and of demand, are much flatter than short-run curves, and much flatter than the curves which are commonly used in the diagrams of theorists. In fact, it may appear that much of the apparent seriousness of Professor Chamberlin's results derives from what I believe to be the exaggerated steepness of the curves he uses to illustrate them. This, of course, is a matter of degree only; but in the field of imperfect

2. For this purpose the "general demand schedule" would presumably have to be defined in terms of the response of sales to simultaneous and proportionate changes in the prices of all the grades or sub-species of "the commodity" in question.

competition, and especially in the search for workable adjustments, these matters of degree are of the essence of the problem.

In the first place, the more attention centers on the imperfections of active competition, the more important become the forces of potential competition and substitution (both of which find a place in Chamberlin's system). Neither is a perfect check; but both together may come near it under favorable conditions.

As to potential competition, it is this, or the materializing of it, on which Chamberlin relies for the tendency to wipe out monopoly profits in the production of quality goods, and to bring individual demand curves and cost curves into tangency. But there seems to be a tendency to regard the businessman as having too little foresight to anticipate the materializing of potential competition, and as following an unduly grasping policy in regard to price, and an unduly restrictive policy as to output, until potential competition becomes actual, and the industry is burdened with too many producers, whose individual output is restricted short of the optimum. This undoubtedly has some truth. It would be expecting a great deal of businessmen that they should generally have perfect foresight of the emergence of potential competition, and on that account should avoid unduly restrictive policies. Nevertheless, there is apparently a tendency of somewhat similar effect on the part of some or many businesses, even if not guided by such impossibly perfect foresight. There is a tendency to strive to maintain and increase output, as if this were an end in itself, aside from the resulting net earnings and perhaps at a short-run sacrifice of net earnings which a more grasping policy might secure. In such cases, business, whether putting its reasoning in this form or not, acts as if it were governed by anticipations of potential competition, and by the desire to forestall its materializing.

As to substitution, it is a commonplace that the triumphs of modern industrial chemistry have vastly increased its range and flexibility; and it is increasingly spoken of as one form of competition. Indeed, it seems that the differences between substitute products, in cost of production and service value, are nowadays often no more serious than similar differences between different varieties of what we think of as the "same" product. This fact is so much in the businessman's consciousness that there is no need to emphasize it. Both potential competition and substitution have the effect of flattening the slopes of individual demand curves.

To develop the full importance of this it is necessary to take account of the time dimension of these curves. The abstraction of a timeless demand schedule has tended toward the neglect of this factor. Yet in actual elasticities of demand a crucial element is the time required for a given change of price to bring about a given effect on volume of sales. In some instances the full effect may be felt in a matter of hours, while in others it may require a generation. In the latter case, of course, the effect of the price factor will be inextricably tangled with that of a complex of other changes.

One feature of this relationship might be expressed by a skewed surface or contour-map in which the vertical dimension measures price—or possibly price minus optimum selling expenses, if such a quantity could be given a usable definition.[3] The

3. It would presumably vary with price, and also be complicated by the time factor.

price should be that of one producer's grade of the product, those of others' grades being held constant. What we may call the west-east dimension would represent the length of time during which a given price relationship remains in effect; and the north-south dimension would represent physical volume of sales of this producer's grade of the product. The intersection of the surface with any vertical north-south plane would be a demand schedule representing the sales under various price differentials, each being assumed to remain in effect a length of time represented by the distance of the plane from the west end of the diagram, where time equals zero. These curves would grow less steep from west to east. The horizontal contour lines would be growth curves (positive or negative) each representing the increasing effect, with time, of a given price differential on volume of sales.

Such a surface would, however, represent only a beginning of analysis. Action by one producer would provoke responses by others which, if the original action had gone some distance, would act on a modified set of growth curves. Changes in quality are, of course, not represented. Actual demand-curves may depend, not only on the price factor represented, but also on the relation between the price range of the various grades of this commodity and those of various substitutes; and on the profits made by this producer and by others in the industry, as an incentive to the materializing of potential competition. Even this affords an unduly simplified picture, and the whole functional relationship is probably so complex as to defy mathematical plotting.

The chief proposition remains—namely, that the long-run effects of a high-price policy on the part of any one producer would tend to a much larger falling-off in sales than would occur in the short run. The long-run schedule might in numerous cases approach the horizontal so closely that the slope would not be a matter of material moment, in the light of all the uncertainties involved. And this fact may be roughly represented by the attitude of some businesses, that it is "good business" to maintain and expand their sales volume, even at some sacrifice of immediate profits.

Long-run cost curves also tend toward the horizontal. There are two quite distinct types of cost curve for a given productive unit in relation to volume of output. One has to do with changes in output within the physical capacity of an existing plant, and the other with changes in the amount of plant capacity without change in the percentage which is utilized. Long-run cost curves are apparently dominated by the second factor; and I shall take it for present purposes as representing the long-run function. Evidence of its character is difficult to secure, some of the best indications being derived from simultaneous comparisons of costs in considerable numbers of plants of different size, with the effect of percentage utilization eliminated where possible. Such evidence of this sort as I have analyzed points to the conclusion that it is likely to be only the very small plants which show materially higher costs causally traceable to their small size, while most plants are in a range of size which shows little or no downward or upward trend with increased size, while other factors account for much greater differences in cost between plant and plant than those due to size itself.

The indicated conclusion is that there is typically no definite "optimum size," but rather a wide optimum range of size, within which most plants fall; and that economies due to size are far from being such a vitally important factor as is suggested by the type of theoretical cost curve now in general use. A further conclusion is that imperfections in competition arising from the slopes of the long-run curves of cost or demand may, so far as these curves affect actual policy, be relatively unimportant. So far as immediate price policies are governed by long-run demand curves, or behave as if they were so governed, they are likely not to differ materially from those of perfect competition (this would have little application to the problem of unduly expanded selling costs). And even if the long-run scale of production is somewhat restricted, cost of production, as distinct from selling, is not likely to be thereby materially increased.

## IV. Short-Run Conditions

The most serious problems of imperfect competition seem, as already noted, to center in the fact that the immediate short-run pressures are out of harmony with the conditions of long-run equilibrium. And the starting point of a search for the conditions of workable competition seems to be the search for ways and means of reducing these discrepancies, under the conditions actually encountered. One approach to this question is by way of some of the paradoxes or conflicts in prevalent ideas as to the symptoms of a satisfactory competitive condition.

Perfect competition requires a market with such full knowledge that a standard commodity cannot sell at two prices at the same time at the same point of purchase and delivery. Actually, at least in large-scale industry, such a condition of "identical prices" is frequently taken as an indication of a monopolistic condition And a state of less perfect market knowledge, permitting differences in price, is sometimes spoken of as causing active price competition to arise, where presumably there had been none previously. This attitude implies a theory that one kind of imperfection requires another to take part of the curse off it. And there would be no paradox about it if the same persons did not at other points maintain the attitude that any departure from any of the conditions of pure or perfect competition is evidence of a monopolistic tendency.

The above implied theory suggests that the standard character of the product is not in itself favorable to workable competition between few and large producers, and that in such cases effective competition requires some uncertainty whether a reduction in price will be met or not. This in turn points toward a search for the least undesirable form of remedial "imperfection" (uncertainty).

Among the apparent inconsistencies of prevailing attitudes is the position that discrimination is a non-competitive symptom, coupled with the view that, when buyers invite sealed bids, unless they get a price lower than the general market affords, this result proves monopoly. In part, this seems to be a manifestation of the fairly general psychology of buyers, who do not object to discrimination so long as they get the benefit. So far as there is a real economic theory involved, it seems to imply the abandonment of the idea that competition and discrimination are mutually inconsistent. There is *prima facie* ground for the hypothesis that some forms and degrees of discrimination have a place in a scheme of workable, as distinct from perfect, competition. And as part of this problem, the theory of sealed-bid competition stands out as an unworked field for economists.

Perfect competition requires operation at full capacity, which is sometimes defined as the point of minimum cost, or as the point where marginal and average cost are equal. Actual competition has to make terms with the fact that, when demand fluctuates, industry must inevitably be operating short of full capacity much of the time. Workable competition must be workable under these conditions. Some of the requirements of such a result may be briefly indicated.

A price which at all times covers only short-run marginal cost would lead to large operating deficits whenever demand is short of capacity, and would bankrupt most industries, no matter how shock-proof their capital structures. And since the horizontal individual demand curve of pure competition leads to a price that covers only marginal cost, it is not one of the conditions of workable competition. Instead, the requirement is an individual demand curve with sufficient slope to bring price, on the average, far enough above marginal cost so that average cost may be covered, over the run of good times and bad. Along with this should go, presumably, enough price flexibility to afford a stimulus to demand in dull times, and the reverse in boom times. These are not easy requirements, but at least they mean that workable competition has some positive use for the sloping individual demand curve.

This will be disputed by some on the ground that competition can be trusted automatically to limit capacity at such a point that even under pure competition profits in good times will compensate for losses in bad times; and that this is the desirable adjustment. A realistic view of this objection seems to involve the whole theory and practice of maintaining stand-by units (usually of inferior quality) to handle peak demands. Without going into this matter at length, it may be sufficient to indicate that, in the ordinary course of modernization and replacement, the stand-by units (the best units which are just not good enough to justify keeping them at continuous or nearly continuous operation) are not likely to be sufficiently obsolete and inefficient to bring their marginal costs of operation up to a point that would yield large profits for the plant as a whole: large enough to offset operating deficits incurred most of the time, and to make the average represent an attractive return on investment. Hence the indicated result is extremely unlikely to follow.

Cost curves for varying output with a fixed plant probably fall into two main groups or types. In one, physical capacity has fairly rigid limits, and marginal cost appears to remain approximately uniform, nearly or quite up to the limit of physical capacity. This type may provisionally be taken as characteristic of continuous-process industries, dependent on heat or chemical action, which cannot be substantially speeded up beyond the ordinarily economical rates. The other type would include processes which can be speeded up or worked overtime. Here it may be possible to produce considerable amounts beyond the point of lowest average cost, with marginal cost above average operating expenses, though possibly not far enough above so that a price equal to marginal cost would yield a fair return on the fixed investment.

The use of stand-by units might bring the first type a little nearer the second. But in the instances of steel and cement, this factor does not appear to modify the pattern of costs materially—possibly for the reasons already briefly indicated. In either case, it seems fair to conclude that the industry could not survive under prices which were always limited to marginal costs of the short-run variety, unless it deliberately destroyed its superseded units instead of leaving them to serve as stand-by capacity, and thus created an artificial bottleneck on industrial expansion. And that may be dismissed as a possibility, for reasons hardly necessary to state. Under these circumstances, certain types of competitive situations may be distinguished and briefly analyzed.

First we may consider the standardized product, sold in a chaotic market in which discrimination is possible; any sale may be a subject for special bargaining, and special prices will permit the producer making them to gain a volume of business of material size, relative to his total sales, before these special prices are discovered and met by his competitors. This condition has been represented in the outline by a time lag in the spread of market knowledge, which may be longer or shorter; but this is not the only controlling factor. A few hours during which the price cutter can make fast one very large future order may be as good as a much longer period in an industry where there are no very large buyers or where firm long-term contracts cannot be secured. The size of the price cutter relative to that of his rivals also has a bearing on the outcome. Variants are possible; but the general conclusion of a tendency to drive prices below cost seems justified.[4]

The reason for this may be suggested by an abstract limiting case, which does not, however, accurately express the operation of actual cases. If a particular bit of business can be secured by a special reduced price, applicable to it exclusively, and will be lost if this special price is not made, and if this transaction is expected to have no effect at all on other business, then it is a source of increased net revenue at any price above marginal cost. Actually, such reductions would not have the general effect indicated above unless they did spread to other business; and if this is their usual result, rational businessmen would naturally come to expect it. But the deterrent effect of this expectation may be partially counteracted in a number of ways. Most important, perhaps, is the likelihood that someone will hope to "get away with it this once," coupled with the suspicion that others will start the process, or have already done so, and that the first seller will not succeed in protecting the price structure by refraining, but will merely lose business. Then there are the sellers who are so hard-pressed for cash that they may disregard all but immediate effects on net income. The result is a nibbling process which can almost always go a little farther than it has gone. This may be mitigated by intermittent attempts to introduce more open and uniform prices.

At the other extreme comes the standardized product, with prices completely open and uniform for each purchasing locality. Here a reduction is sure to be met almost instantaneously, so long as price is above marginal cost; and the producer initiating it may, in the extreme case, hope to gain only his *pro rata* share of the general increase in sales of all producers resulting from the reduction in price. His sales would then be expected to increase in the same proportion as if he had a complete monopoly;

4. This might be modified by adopting schemes of cost accounting with heavy allocations of capital overhead to peak output. Such allocations represent a mixture of short-run and long-run considerations, and may fairly be disregarded here.

and if this were the whole story, the incentive to reduce prices might be expected to stop at the same point as if a monopoly existed. However, the incentive to raise prices, if they get below this point, is a different matter, since an increase will not be automatically met; and thus the conclusion that this situation yields results identical with complete monopoly, is not warranted.

Among numerous modifying circumstances, there is still the possibility of securing a few large forward contracts, or at least some valuable goodwill, by taking the initiative in a general price reduction. In the second place, the market is governed by whichever among the several producers has the lowest price policy. If one of them is keenly alive to the desirability of forestalling potential competition, he may fix a price close to the long-run normal, and the others will have to follow. There is much room in such a situation for the personal equations of different producers to modify the result. Or an increase of wages or prices of materials may, without changing the selling price of the product, bring it nearer the competitive norm; and if for this or any of the other reasons mentioned, it gets below the monopoly level, there is no force tending to bring it back up, and it may remain there for a considerable period. The generally indicated result is, not so much a monopoly price as a decidedly sticky price, somewhere between the levels of pure competition and monopoly.

All this is on the assumption that the open prices are perfectly adhered to; and this is probably an extremely rare case. In fact it would not be very rash to assume that in most cases some degree of irregular pricing is chronic, and that there are hardly any in which occasional fits of it do not occur. The pure case may prove to be almost entirely limited to instances of open-price systems with waiting periods and otherwise implemented; and it is probable that even these should not be expected regularly to result in 100 percent uniformity.

Thus it seems that the really important problem is not so much the case of pure "oligopoly," but the case in which the existence of openly quoted prices exercises some degree of restraint on more or less chronic "chiselling" which is irregular, temporarily secret, and usually more or less discriminatory. Such a situation contains no guarantee of ideal prices; but it is something intermediate between pure oligopoly and the ruinously low prices likely to result from unlimited market chaos: more strongly competitive than the first, and more workable than the second. And something intermediate appears to be well nigh a necessity. Incidentally, such limited "chiselling" seems likely in a general way to become more active in times of slack demand, and thus to tend to some degree in the direction of price flexibility.

Economic theory has not attacked the special problem of this form of pricing; and perhaps it cannot shed much light on it. But it appears to be one of the most important forms of imperfectly competitive pricing, and might under favorable conditions prove to be fairly "workable." These conditions may be rather subtle and intangible matters; and the facts bearing on them are certainly not easy to secure. Nevertheless, it seems rather important to know more about them than we do.

As an approach to such analysis, a few tentative propositions may be considered. First, the actions of businessmen in such a situation may be interpreted in the light of a complex of motives and considerations, among which the following might be mentioned. (1) The immediate effect on net earnings. (2) The effect with some account taken of the probable early reactions of others. (3) Long-run effects, chiefly reflected in effects on volume of sales. (4) Intangibles, including effects on goodwill and on the satisfaction or dissatisfaction of customers, bearing largely on the expediency of setting limits to discriminations and discrepancies between actual and openly quoted prices. This may lead to a desire to make openly quoted prices "fairly representative" of prices actually received, which may mean "equal to the prices actually paid by those customers who have no exceptional bargaining leverages," or may have somewhat different shades of meaning. There are obvious reasons for not wishing one's openly quoted prices to give one the reputation of charging more than one is actually charging.

Reductions in openly quoted prices may be classified according to the proportion of actual sales that the reduction is expected to affect. The intention and expected effect may be to reduce the whole scale of prices actually charged. Or the openly quoted prices may apply to a considerable part of the business, and the intent may be to bring these prices down without reducing the lower ones, and thus reduce the spread. Or the reductions may occur at a time when the openly quoted prices have come to apply to little or no business; and the intent may be simply to make them more "representative." Increases would presumably be intended to bring about an increase in the general scale, and would occur naturally at a time when demand was strong and competitive pressures toward irregular departures were therefore relatively weak. Or they might occur after a period of ruinous price cutting had made producers ready to follow an upward lead—preferably one substantial enough to afford real relief, but not so large as to make the industry too invitingly prosperous. The preceding price war would need to have driven home the bad effects of irregular pricing sufficiently to keep it temporarily in abeyance, or within narrow limits.

Special departures from openly quoted prices are made for obvious reasons; and the large customer has an obvious advantage in securing such special prices. Such prices are not likely, however, to go close to the theoretical limit of marginal cost unless the whole price scale has become demoralized to an extent that would bring it into the class of the chaotic market, already discussed. In typical large-scale industries, if the whole price scale is such as to yield anything approaching a normal return on investment, special prices could not go close to short-run marginal cost without creating such discrepancies as a market of the sort we are now considering is not likely to tolerate. Special prices are, however, likely to be made without full recognition of their ultimate effects in dragging the whole price structure downward, and to be lower than they would be if these ultimate effects were accurately forecast and fully taken into account.

Particular cases may be influenced by a number of specific pricing practices, including probably the looser forms of open-price arrangement, which, as already indicated, are not likely to bring about complete elimination of irregular pricing. Advance announcements of price changes may facilitate increases by enabling the initiator to learn whether others are following suit, without losing too much business in the interval. The practice appears likely to have less effect on price reductions. Protection of customers against price declines subsequent to the giving of orders is a practice of some significance, largely neglected by students. It seems to have little applicability except in cases of quoted prices in industries with a limited number of sellers and a fairly well organized price structure. Its effects would be different according as it was applied in an industry in which orders are given at a particular time of year for the coming season (for example, retail sale of oil for household heating) or an industry in which there are always some outstanding orders which would be affected by a price reduction. These are only a few instances of special practices which a more complete study would need to take into account.

A standard product is consistent with a sloping individual demand curve, chiefly in the case of few sellers and a supply-governed price. The slope of the curve is a function of the output of the producer in question, relative to the total output; and the resulting excess of price above marginal cost, while worth study, may not be a real "imperfection," from the standpoint of workable competition. Price flexibility with fluctuating demand would theoretically depend on the nature of the fluctuation as affecting elasticity near the existing price range. But these problems need not detain us here.

Another special case is that of a standardized product, with sloping individual demand curves which are definite and knowable—the case of spatially separated producers selling at uniform mill prices. As a first approach, we may assume the marginal costs of the various producers to be equal, and known. Here there would be a point, above marginal cost, below which price would not go. If the slopes of the individual demand curves were just the right ones, this point might be the long-run normal price, but it seems more likely that it would be below it. These slopes would depend on the spatial distribution of demand; and one difficulty is that, with large consuming centers, the curves would be discontinuous. Another difficulty is that, if prices were above this stopping point, there would be no incentive to lower them, since a reduction would be sure to be met. If the marginal costs of the producers were different and uncertain, there might be a range instead of a point, within which active price competition might prevail. But there would still be a higher range within which there would be no reliable force tending to reduce prices. Thus the conditions of a tendency toward equilibrium would not be present. "Chiselling" would, by definition, be eliminated and the conditions leading to it (incentive plus opportunity to do it undetected) would be limited to the boundary points between different producers' selling areas.

A variant permitting limited freight absorption would make the individual demand curves steeper and more indefinite and uncertain, leading to uncertainty whether a price reduction would be met. It might also leave substantial room for "chiselling." In both this and the preceding case, the outcome would vary with the geographical facts of each particular industry. Neither can safety be regarded as a universally workable, *a priori* formula.

Finally, we may turn to quality products, where there are sloping individual demand curves and considerable uncertainty whether, or to what extent, a given reduction of price will be met. Here it is worth while distinguishing degrees of quality differential. There is the extreme degree, in which the individual producer's product has a rather steep demand curve and will stand a very considerable price differential for a long time. This approximates the condition of monopoly. In some cases, where the customer is a poor judge of quality, this kind of situation can apparently be built up by sheer advertising.

But there is also the case of more moderate quality differentials, or those of which the consumer is better informed. Here the individual demand curve is flatter, especially if a moderate time is allowed for the consumer to find out what quality is being offered in return for any given price differential. It seems that some of the healthiest cases of workable competition in large-scale industry are of this type. Automobile production is generally regarded as a fairly workable example. And in the case of tires, price competition appears to be even stronger, though tires are a quality product, and therefore come under the head of "monopolistic competition."

As to directions in which to look for possible improvement in the future, it may be worth considering the possibility that technical progress may bring about still closer and more general substitution; and also that the increased use of specifications, and more widespread knowledge of them, may help to bring more of these substitutes, or price-insensitive quality differentials, within the range of moderate and price-sensitive differentials. This would increase the number of industries which, despite large-scale production, have the characteristics of fairly healthy and workable imperfect competition, rather than those of slightly qualified monopoly. In such cases, one may hope that government need not assume the burden of doing something about every departure from the model of perfect competition.

# 6

# The New Deal and the Institutionalists

## Introduction

BY DANIEL CRANE

The landslide election of Franklin Delano Roosevelt in 1932 marked a momentous shift in the American political landscape. Foundering in the Great Depression since 1929, the American people were prepared to accept changes in the political and constitutional order of a magnitude not seen since the Reconstruction amendments of the 1870s. Although the Constitution was never formally amended, the New Deal represented what the constitutional historian Bruce Ackerman has called a "constitutional moment"—a moment of intensified public consciousness on foundational political principles.[1]

FDR had the political capital to achieve transformative change, and he did so on a number of scores—from securities and banking regulation to the creation of the social security system. But how would he spend his capital to address the microeconomic foundations of the Depression? How would he understand the role of competition in an economy increasingly dominated by federal regulatory power?

The answer is, equivocally. For all his certainty that the country needed fundamental political and economic change, FDR was remarkably uncertain of what sort of policy to follow on competition issues. Rather than invoking a coherent set of guiding principles on competition, Roosevelt empowered different wings of his broad coalition to run the show on competition at certain points during his four-term administration.

The New Deal answer to the competition problem was a play in three acts, each act corresponding to one wing in the New Deal coalition. As historian Ellis Hawley has shown in his masterful work on competition policy during the New Deal,[2] three factions populated the top levels of the administration. Each faction prevailed in running administration policy toward competition during one period of the administration.

1. Bruce Ackerman, *We the People: Foundations* (1991).

2. Ellis W. Hawley, *The New Deal and the Problem of Monopoly: A Study in Economic Ambivalence* (1995 [1966]).

First, a "collectivist democracy" faction rejected the capitalist, free-market order and advocated a centrally planned economy.[3] This faction blamed the Depression on corporate greed and easy-money Wall Street policies. The solution to the Depression lay in rationalizing economy under technocratic governance. This governance would not be managed centrally from Washington but decentralized into local planning committees populated with representatives of business, labor, and consumer groups: "The typical proposal called for the detailed planning... to be undertaken by a system of industrial councils, composed of representatives of each of the special interests involved; and once formulated, the plans would then be perfected, coordinated, and enforced by a central board of technicians, economists, engineers, and other 'qualified experts.'"[4]

The collectivist democracy crowd grew inspiration from economists such as Rex Tugwell, whom we survey in this chapter, as well as other public intellectuals such as the historians Charles A. Beard and Will Durant and the philosopher John Dewey. Drawing on the work of Adolf Berle and Gardiner Means, they argued that, because capitalism had already resulted in the separation of ownership and control of industry, the locus of control might be shifted to the government without effecting widespread redistribution of wealth.[5]

The collectivist democrats held sway from FDR's inauguration in 1933 until the middle of 1935. Their signature legislation was the National Industrial Recovery Act, which mandated partial repeal of the antitrust law and its displacement with industrial management by local committees. These committees were to establish industry codes regulating every facet of production and distribution—prices, output levels, quality standards, etc.

In 1935, an old world shock knocked the collectivist democracy crowd out of power. In two controversial decisions—*Schechter Poultry*[6] (the "sick chickens" case) and *Panama Refining*[7]—the Supreme Court invalidated NIRA's cornerstones on commerce clause and nondelegation grounds. FDR publicly fumed against the Supreme Court's decisions as the worst since *Dred Scott*. Privately, he was relieved at the opportunity to abandon the increasingly unpopular NIRA experiment, blame its failure on the Supreme Court, and turn over competition policy to another wing of his coalition.

Next in power were the competitionists aligned with the classical political-economic tradition of Adam Smith, John Stuart Mill, Alfred Marshall, and John Bates Clark.[8] Perhaps no one better captured their views than Louis Brandeis, the Progressive intellectual and Supreme Court justice famous for his attacks on Wall Street in *Other People's Money* and monopoly in *The Curse of Bigness* (surveyed ahead). Like the collectivist democrats, the competitionists threw the Depression at the feet of big business. But unlike the

3. Id. at 43–46.

4. Id. at 45.

5. Id. at 175.

6. *A.L.A. Schechter Poultry Corp.* v. *U.S.*, 295 U.S. 495 (1935).

7. *Panama Refining Co.* v. *Ryan*, 293 U.S. 388 (1935).

8. Hawley, at 47–51.

collectivist democrats, they did not believe that governmental planning was the answer. Rather, the answer lay in a return to atomistic competition. Far from effectively cartelizing all of industry as the NIRA had attempted to do, governmental policy would be focused on tearing down the cartels and monopolies that stood in the way of effective competition.

No one better encapsulated the competitionist perspective than Thurman Arnold, a Yale Law professor and mainstay of the legal realist movement.[9] In 1938, Arnold succeeded Robert Jackson as assistant attorney general in charge of the Antitrust Division. In *The Bottlenecks of Business*, which we survey in this chapter, Arnold argued that only an aggressive antitrust policy could pull the country out of depression and ensure that the benefits of the national wealth reached ordinary men and women. Under Arnold, antitrust prosecutions increased dramatically, including prosecutions of firms and individuals who had closely cooperated with the government during the NIRA period.[10]

Arnold's career at the Justice Department ended when yet a third wing of the New Deal coalition swept into power. In 1943, when he attempted to indict Averill Harriman and the railroads for price fixing, Arnold was removed from the Justice Department and given a seat on the U.S. Court of Appeals for the D.C. Circuit. With war rather than Depression the headline, the administration had lost its appetite for aggressive trust busting. (Arnold would later become a defender of accused communists during the McCarthy era and a founder of the Washington D.C. powerhouse law firm Arnold & Porter).

The war elevated a "business commonwealth" wing to power.[11] Unlike the other two wings, the business commonwealthers were sympathetic to big business. They believed that excessive competition—deep price cutting by "chiselers"—was responsible for the Depression and that paternalistic, public-minded cooperation by business leaders was the way forward. The business commonwealth faction was dominated by "men of action" rather than the intellectuals and academics who dominated the other factions; hence we focus in this chapter on writers from the other two wings.

The New Deal is a remarkable microcosm of competing intellectual theories and practices about competition and antitrust policy—all played out within a single political administration.

## Adolf A. Berle and Gardiner C. Means

## *The Modern Corporation and Private Property*

## Chapter I: The Traditional Logic of Property

The shifting relationships of property and enterprise in American industry here described, raise in sharp relief certain legal, economic, and social questions which must now be squarely faced. Of these the greatest question is whose interests should the

9. See generally Spencer Weber Waller, *Thurman Arnold: A Biography* (2005).

10. See Daniel A. Crane, "The Story of United States v. Socony-Vacuum: Hot Oil and Antitrust in the Two New Deals," in *Antitrust Stories* 91 (Eleanor M. Fox and Daniel A. Crane, eds., 2007).

11. Hawley, at 36–43.

great quasi-public Corporations (now representing such a large proportion of industrial wealth) be operated. This problem really asks in a different form the question, who should receive the profits of industry?

It is traditional that a corporation should be run for the benefit of its owners, the stockholders, and that to them should go any profits which are distributed.[1] We now know, however, that a controlling group may hold the power to divert profits into their own pockets. There is no longer any certainty that a corporation will in fact be run primarily in the interests of the stockholders.[2] The extensive separation of ownership and control, and the strengthening of the powers of control, raise a new situation calling for a decision whether social and legal pressure should be applied in an effort to insure corporate operation primarily in the interests of the "owners" or whether such pressure shall be applied in the interests of some other or wider group.

The lawyer answers this question in no uncertain terms by applying to the quasi-public corporation the traditional logic of property. The common law, extended to meet the new situation, logically demands the award of the entire profit to the security holders, and in particular to the stockholders. According to this logic a corporation should be operated primarily in their interests.

The legal argument is largely historical; but it has been built up through a series of phases which make this conclusion inevitable. From earliest times the owner of property has been entitled to the full use or disposal of his property,[3] and in these rights the owner has been protected by law. Since the use of industrial property consists primarily of an effort to increase its value—to make a profit—the owner of such property, in being entitled to its full use, has been entitled to all accretions to its value—to all the profits which it could be made to earn. In so far as he had to pay for the services of other men or other property in order to accomplish this increase in value, these payments operated as deductions; the profit remaining to him was the difference between the added value and the cost of securing these services. To this difference, however, the owner has traditionally been entitled. The state and the law have sought to protect him in this right.

From earliest times, also, the stockholder in the corporation has posed both as the owner of the corporation and the owner of its assets. He was removed slightly from legal ownership in the assets in that he did not have legal "title" to them—that was vested in the corporation; but collectively the stockholders, through their participations were entitled to the whole of corporate assets and to the whole of any corporate profits which could be made. The corporation was theirs, to be operated for their benefit.

1. Bonus schemes are usually undertaken with an aim of increasing the profit remaining and available to be distributed as dividends. For this reason they must, in general, be regarded as a cost to the stockholders rather than as a sharing or distribution of profit.

2. While there are other possible groups,—the employees, the consumers, etc., in whose interest a corporation might be run, discussion of them can best be delayed.

3. Except as impaired by the exercise of police power by the state.

In the development of the corporation, constantly widening powers over the management of the enterprise have been delegated to groups within the corporation. At first these powers concerned mainly the technical (profit-making) activity of the enterprise. Later, powers were delegated which had to do with the distributions of profits and interests among security holders. With the separation of ownership and control, these powers developed to a stage permitting those in control of a corporation to use them against the interests of ownership. Since powers of control and management were created by law, in some measure this appeared to legalize the diversion of profits into the hands of the controlling group.

Following the traditional logic of property, however, it is clear that these powers are not absolute. They are, rather, powers in trust. The controlling group is, in form at least, managing and controlling a corporation for the benefit of the owners. While insertions might be made in corporation statutes and in corporate charters apparently giving power which could be used against the interests of the owners, these were, in the light of the common law, only grants of power to the controlling group, the better to operate the corporation in the interests of its owners. The very multiplication of absolute powers, including power to shift interests in the corporate assets and profits from security holders to those in control threw into bold relief the tacit (but by no means fictitious) understanding that all these powers were designed for the benefit of the corporation as a whole, and not for the individual enrichment of the management or control. While the law fumbled in application of this principle, and developed through a series of rules, sometimes inconsistent and often not clear in application, not a single case on record denies the ultimate trusteeship of the controlling group, nor even faintly implies that such a group may use its power for its individual advantage. Fact-situations can be "rigged" whereby the individual profit of this group is made to appear an advantage to the corporation as a whole; advantage may be taken of emergencies in which the management and control present the security-holding group with the alternative of permitting profit to the "control" on the one hand or inviting disaster of the other. Sometimes the courts, shielding themselves behind a consideration of the advantage of the "corporation as a whole," have overlooked the fact that apparent advantage to the mythical corporate entity may mean staggering loss to its separate owners; and that it is often necessary to trace *what group within the corporation* receives the ultimate advantage. Despite these situations, in many of which the controlling group is able, first, to seize a portion of the corporate profits and, second, to hold them against legal attack, the theory of the law seems clear. All the powers granted to management and control are powers in trust.

Tracing this doctrine back into the womb of equity, whence it sprang, the foundation becomes plain. Wherever one man or a group of men entrusted another man or group with the management of property, the second group became fiduciaries. As such they were obliged to act conscionably, which meant in fidelity to the interests of the persons whose wealth they had undertaken to handle. In this respect, the corporation stands on precisely the same footing as the common-law trust. Since the business problems connected with trusts were relatively restricted, a series of fairly accurate regulations could be worked out by the equity courts constraining the trustee to certain standards of conduct. The corporation, which carried on any and every kind of business, raised a set of problems of conduct infinitely more varied, and calling for expert business judgment which courts were not equipped to render. Fixed standards of conduct, therefore, became impossible of development in the corporate situation; such rigid standards as were worked out, (for instance, the standard that no stock must be issued unless first offered preemptively to existing shareholders) became arbitrary or inapplicable in the complex corporate structure of today. But though definite rules could not be laid down, the courts have maintained a supervisory jurisdiction; the fundamental principle of equitable control remains unimpaired; and the only question is how it should be applied in each case. Inability to answer these questions has given ample latitude to the control to absorb a portion of the corporate profits. This does not mean, however, that the law concedes them a right to such absorption. It merely means that legal machinery may not be sufficiently developed to accomplish a remedy.

Underlying all this is the ancient preoccupation of the common law with the rights of property. Primarily, the common law did not undertake to set up ideal schemes of government. It aimed to protect men in their own. Only where the property interests conflicted with some very obvious public policy did the law interfere. Its primary design was protecting individual attributes of individual men,—their right to property, to free motion and locomotion, to protection of individual relationships entered into between them. In this aspect the corporation was merely one more bit of machinery by which the property of individuals was managed by other individuals; and the corporate management took its place in the picture alongside of agents, trustees, ship captains, partners, joint adventurers, and other fiduciaries. As the power of the corporate management has increased, and as the control of the individual has sunk into the background, the tendency of the law has been to stiffen its assertion of the rights of the security holder. The thing that it has not been able to stiffen has been its regulation of the conduct of the business by the corporate management. And this omission has resulted, not from lack of logical justification, but from lack of ability to handle the problems involved. The management of an enterprise is, by nature, a task which courts can not assume; and the various devices by which management and control have absorbed a portion of the profit-stream have been so intimately related to the business conduct of an enterprise, that the courts seem to have felt not only reluctant to interfere, but positively afraid to do so.

The result accordingly is that the profits of the enterprise, so far as the law is concerned, belong to the security holders *in toto.* Division of these profits among the various groups of security holders is a matter of private agreement, but they, between them, have the complete right to all of the profits which the corporation has made. Not only that: they are entitled to those profits which the management in reasonable exercise of its powers ought to make. They have further a right that no one shall become a security holder except upon a suitable contribution to the corporate assets—that is, that the security holding group shall be a group of persons who have committed actual property to the administration of the management and control of the corporation.

Such is the view which the law has developed by extending to the new situation the traditional logic of property. The control group is not in a position openly to combat this logic. Constant appeals are made both to this ideology and to its legal basis when corporations go into the market seeking capital. The expectation of the entire profit is the precise lure used to induce investment in corporate enterprises. The possibilities of the situation are continuously stressed by investment bankers who, in turn, act for the corporate management and control when the latter are bidding for the public investor's savings. Whatever their private views or actual practice, the control groups within corporations have estopped themselves from maintaining any other view. The legal hypothesis has been too much the basis of the financial structure of today.

Yet, while this conclusion may result inevitably when the traditional logic of property is applied to the new situation, are we justified in applying this logic? In the past, the ownership of business enterprise, the only form of property with which we are here concerned, has always, at least in theory, involved two attributes, first the risking of previously collected wealth in profit-seeking enterprise; and, second, the ultimate management of and responsibility for that enterprise. But in the modern corporation, these two attributes of ownership no longer attach to the same individual or group. The stockholder has surrendered control over his wealth. He has become a supplier of capital, a risk-taker pure and simple, while ultimate responsibility and authority are exercised by directors and "control." One traditional attribute of ownership is attached to stock ownership; the other attribute is attached to corporate control. Must we not, therefore, recognize that we are no longer dealing with property in the old sense? Does the traditional logic of property still apply? Because an owner who also exercises control over his wealth is protected in the full receipt of the advantages derived from it, must it *necessarily* follow that an owner who has surrendered control of his wealth should likewise be protected to the full? May not this surrender have so essentially changed his relation to his wealth as to have changed the logic applicable to his interest in that wealth? An answer to this question cannot be found in the law itself. It must be sought in the economic and social background of law.

## Chapter II: The Traditional Logic of Profits

The economist, approaching the problems growing out of the shifting relationship of property and enterprise which we have examined, must start from a different background and with a set of interests differing essentially from those of the law. His interest is not primarily in the protection of man in his own, but in the production and distribution of what man desires. He is preoccupied, not with the rights of property, but with the production of wealth and distribution of income. To him property rights are attributes which may be attached to wealth by society and he regards them and their protection, not as the inalienable right of the individual or as an end in themselves, but as a means to a socially desirable end,[4] namely, "a plentiful revenue and subsistence" for the people.

The socially beneficent results to be derived from the protection of property are supposed to arise, not from the wealth itself, but from the efforts to acquire wealth. A long line of economists have developed what might be called the traditional logic of profits. They have held that, in striving to acquire wealth, that is, in seeking profits, the individual would, perhaps unconsciously, satisfy the wants of others. By carrying on enterprise he would employ his energy and wealth in such a way as to obtain more wealth.[5] In this effort, he would tend to make for profit those things which were in most demand. Competition among countless producers could be relied upon in general to maintain profits within reasonable limits while temporarily excessive profits in any one line of production would induce an increase of activity in that line with a consequent drop of profits to more reasonable levels. At the same time it was supposed that the business man's effort to increase his profits would, in general, result in more economical use of the factors of production, each enterprise having to compete with others for the available economic resources. Therefore, it has been argued that by protecting each man in the possession of his wealth and in the possession of any profits he could make from its use, society would encourage enterprise and thereby facilitate the production and distribution of goods desired by the community at reasonable prices with economic use of labor, capital, and business enterprise. By protecting property rights in the instruments of production, the acquisitive interests of man could thus be more effectively harnessed to the benefit of the community.

It must be seen that under the condition just described, profits act as a return for the performance of two separate functions. First, they act as an inducement to the individual to risk his wealth in enterprise, and, second, they act as a spur, driving him to exercise his utmost skill in making his enterprise profitable.[6] In the case of a private enterprise the distinction between these two functions does not assume importance. The owner of a private business receives any profits made and performs the functions not only of risk-taking but of ultimate management as well.[7] It may be that in the past

4. Adam Smith treated property as a "natural right" (following the teachings of Locke) and its protection as a "law of nature." At the same time he analyzed the beneficent results which might be expected to flow from making actual conditions conform to this "law of nature," i.e., from protecting property. The Nineteenth Century has seen the atrophy of the idea of "natural law" and the shift of emphasis to the advantages of the protection of property. See Adam Smith, "Wealth of Nations," Book I, Chapt. X, Pt. II.

5. Since this study is concerned with property rights in the instruments of production, we need not here consider the process of acquiring wealth in the form of wage and salaries or in the form of interest.

6. These two functions have been recognized by the current literature on profits. Some writers have maintained that profits are primarily a return for the taking of risk while others have maintained that they are primarily a return for exercising business judgment and enterprise. See S. H. Nerlove, "Recent Writings on Profits," *The Journal of Business of the University of Chicago*, Vol. II (1929), p. 363.

7. Even though he employs a manager to carry on the immediate activities of the business, his desire for profits presumably induces him to select the most efficient manager available and to require of him a high standard of performance.

when industry was in the main carried on by a multitude of small private enterprises the community, through protecting property, has induced a large volume of risk-taking and a vigorous conduct of industry in exchange for the profits derived therefrom.

In the modern corporation, with its separation of ownership and control, these two functions of risk and control are, in the main, performed by two different groups of people. Where such a separation is complete one group of individuals, the security holders and in particular the stockholders, performs the function of risk-takers and suppliers of capital, while a separate group exercises control and ultimate management. In such a case, if profits are to be received only by the security holders, as the traditional logic of property would require, how can they perform both of their traditional economic roles? Are no profits to go to those who exercise control and in whose hands the efficient operation of enterprise ultimately rests?

It is clear that the function of capital supplying and risk-taking must be performed and that the security holder must be compensated if an enterprise is to raise new capital and expand its activity just as the workers must be paid enough to insure the continued supplying of labor and the taking of the risks involved in that labor and in the life based on it. But what if profits can be made more than sufficient to keep the security holders satisfied, more than sufficient to induce new capital to come into the enterprise?[8] Where is the social advantage in setting aside for the security holder, profits in an amount greater than is sufficient to insure the continued supplying of capital and taking of risk? The prospect of additional profits can not act as a spur on the security holder to make him *operate* the enterprise with more vigor in a way to serve the wants of the community, since he is no longer in control. Such extra profits if give to the security holders would seem to perform no useful economic function.

Furthermore, if all profits are earmarked for the security holder, where is the inducement for those in control to manage the enterprise efficiently? When none of the profits are to be received by them, why should they exert themselves beyond the amount necessary to maintain a reasonably satisfied group of stockholders? *If* the profit motive is the powerful incentive to action which it is supposed to be, and *if* the community is best served when each enterprise is operated with the aim of making the maximum profit, would there not be great social advantage in encouraging the control to seize for themselves any profits over and above the amount necessary as a satisfactory return to capital? Would not the prospect of this surplus profit act as an incentive to more efficient management by those in control? Certainly, one cannot escape the conclusion that if profits have any influence as a motivating force, any surplus which can be made over a satisfactory return to the investor would be better employed when held out as an incentive to action by control than when handed over to the "owners" who have surrendered control.

8. "Profits sufficient to keep the security holders satisfied," etc., is a vague expression and not easily defined. In practice, however, it is not necessarily so vague. Dissatisfaction among stockholders is presumably not important if it does not make itself known; and inability to raise new capital with ease is likely to be all too evident to a controlling group.

This conclusion is somewhat modified by the fact that the separation of ownership and control has not yet become complete. While a large body of stockholders are not in a position to exercise any degree of control over the affairs of their corporation,[9] those actually in control are usually stockholders though in many cases owning but a very small proportion of the total stock. It may be that the prospect of receiving one or two percent of the total added profit which could be produced by their own more vigorous activity would be sufficient inducement to produce the most efficient operation of which the controlling group are capable. It remains true, however, that profits over enough to keep the remaining stockholders satisfied and to make possible the raising of new capital would still involve an economically wasteful disposal. Only the one or two percent of profits going to the controlling group would perform both roles traditionally performed by profits.

The traditional logic of profits, when thus applied to the modern corporation, would indicate that *if profits must be distributed either to the owners or to the control*, only a fair return to capital should be distributed to the "owners"; while the remainder should go to the control as an inducement to the most efficient ultimate management. The corporation would thus be operated financially in the interests of control, the stockholders becoming merely the recipients of the wages of capital.

This conclusion runs directly counter to the conclusion reached by applying the traditional logic of property to precisely the same situation—and is equally suspect.

## Chapter III: The Inadequacy of Traditional Theory

When such divergent results are obtained by the application of the logic of two major social disciplines to a new fact situation, we must push our inquiry still further back into the assumptions and concepts of those disciplines.

Underlying the thinking of economists, lawyers and business men during the last century and a half has been the picture of economic life so skillfully painted by Adam Smith. Within his treatise on the "Wealth of Nations" are contained the fundamental concepts which run through most modern thought. Though adjustments in his picture have been made by later writers to account for new conditions, the whole has been painted in the colors which he supplied. Private property, private enterprise, individual initiative, the profit motive, wealth, competition,—these are the concepts which he employed in describing the economy of his time and by means of which he sought to show that the pecuniary self-interest of each individual, if given free play, would lead to the optimum satisfaction of human wants. Most writers of the Nineteenth Century built on these logical foundations, and current economic literature is, in large measure, cast in such terms.

Yet these terms have ceased to be accurate, and therefore tend to mislead in describing modern enterprise as carried on by the great corporations. Though both the terms

9. Except under the most unusual conditions as for instance in case of a proxy fight, when the bulk of the stockholders play the role of the populace supporting or refusing to support a palace revolution.

and the concepts remain, they are inapplicable to a dominant area in American economic organization. New terms, connoting changed relationships, become necessary.

When Adam Smith talked of "enterprise" he had in mind as a typical unit the small individual business in which the owner, perhaps with the aid of a few apprentices or workers, labored to produce goods for market or to carry on commerce. Very emphatically be repudiated the stock corporation as a business mechanism, holding that dispersed ownership made efficient operation impossible. "The directors of such companies . . . ," he pointed out, "being the managers rather of other people's money than of their own, it cannot well be expected that they should watch over it with the same anxious vigilance with which the partners in a private copartnery frequently watch over their own. Like the stewards of a rich man, they are apt to consider attention to small matters as not for their master's honour, and very easily give themselves a dispensation from having it. Negligence and profusion, therefore, must always prevail, more or less, in the management of the affairs of such a company. It is upon this account that joint stock companies for foreign trade [at the time he was writing the only important manifestation of the corporation outside of banks, insurance companies, and water or canal companies] have seldom been able to maintain the competition against private adventurers. They have, accordingly, very seldom succeeded without an exclusive privilege, and frequently have not succeeded with one. Without an exclusive privilege they have commonly mismanaged the trade. With an exclusive privilege they have both mismanaged and confined it."

Yet when we speak of business enterprise today, we must have in mind primarily these very units which seemed to Adam Smith not to fit into the principles which he was laying down for the conduct of economic activity. How then can we apply the concepts of Adam Smith in discussing our modern economy?

Let us consider each of these concepts in turn.

## Private Property

To Adam Smith and to his followers, private property was a unity involving possession. He assumed that ownership and control were combined. Today, in the modern corporation, this unity has been broken. *Passive property,*—specifically, shares of stock or bonds,—gives its possessors an interest in an enterprise but gives them practically no control over it, and involve no responsibility. *Active property,*—plant, good will, organization, and so forth which make up the actual enterprise,—is controlled by individuals who, almost invariably, have only minor ownership interests in it. In terms of relationships, the present situation can be described as including:—(1) "passive property," consisting of a set of relationships between an individual and an enterprise, involving rights of the individual toward the enterprise but almost no effective powers over it; and (2) "active property," consisting of a set of relationships under which an individual or set of individuals hold powers over an enterprise but have almost no duties in respect to it which can be effectively enforced. When active and passive property relationships attach to the same individual or group, we have private property as conceived by the older economists. When they attach to different individuals, private property in the instruments of production disappears. Private property in the share of stock still continues, since the owner possesses the share and has power to dispose of it, but his share of stock is only a token representing a bundle of ill-protected rights and expectations. It is the possession of this token which can be transferred, a transfer which has little if any influence on the instruments of production. Whether possession of active property,—power of control over an enterprise, apart from ownership,—will ever be looked upon as private property which can belong to and be disposed of by its possessor is a problem of the future, and no prediction can be made with respect to it.[10] Whatever the answer, it is clear that in dealing with the modern corporation we are not dealing with the old type of private property. Our description of modern economy, in so far as it deals with the quasi-public corporation, must be in terms of the two forms of property, active and passive, which for the most part lie in different hands.

## Wealth

In a similar way, the concept "wealth" has been changed and divided. To Adam Smith, wealth was composed of tangible things,—wheat and land and buildings, ships and merchandise,—and for the most people wealth is still thought of in physical terms. Yet in connection with the modern corporation, two essentially different types of wealth exist. To the holder of passive property, the stockholder, wealth consists, not of tangible goods,—factories, railroad stations, machinery,—but of a bundle of expectations which have a market value and which, if held, may bring him income and, if sold in the market, may give him power to obtain some other form of wealth. To the possessor of active property,—the "control"—wealth means a great enterprise which he dominates, an enterprise whose value is for the most part composed of the organized relationship of tangible properties, the existence of a functioning organization of workers and the existence of a functioning body of consumers.[11] Instead of having control over a body of tangible wealth with an easily ascertainable market value, the group in control of a large modern corporation is astride an organism which has little value except as it continues to function, and for which there is no ready market. Thus, side by side, these two forms of wealth exist:—on the one hand passive wealth,—liquid, impersonal and involving no responsibility, passing from hand to hand and constantly appraised in the market place; and on the other hand, active wealth,—great, functioning organisms dependent for their lives on their security holders, their workers and consumers, but most of all on their mainspring,—"control." The two forms of wealth are not different aspects of the same thing, bur are essentially and functionally distinct.

10. Such would be the case, for instance, if by custom the position of director became hereditary and this custom were given legal sanction.

11. The concept of the consumer as a functioning part of a great enterprise is one which may at first be difficult to grasp. Yet, just as a body of members is essential to the continued existence of a club, so a body of consumers is essential to the continued existence of an enterprise. In each case the members or consumer are an integral part of the association or enterprise. In each case membership is obtained at a cost and for the purpose of obtaining the benefits. The advertising slogan, "Join the Pepsodent Family," is perhaps unintended recognition of this fact.

## Private Enterprise

Again, to Adam Smith, private enterprise meant an individual or few partners actively engaged and relying in large part on their own labor or their immediate direction. Today we have tens and hundreds of thousands of owners, of workers and of consumers combined in single enterprises. These great associations are so different from the small, privately owned enterprises of the past as to make the concept of private enterprise an ineffective instrument of analysis. It must be replaced with the concept of corporate enterprise, enterprise which is the organized activity of vast bodies of individuals, workers, consumers and suppliers of capital, under the leadership of the dictators of industry, "control."

## Individual Initiative

As private enterprise disappears with increasing size, so also does individual initiative. The idea that an army operates on the basis of "rugged individualism" would be ludicrous. Equally so is the same idea with respect to the modern corporation. Group activity, the coordinating of the different steps in production, the extreme division of labor in large scale enterprise necessarily imply not individualism but cooperation and the acceptance of authority almost to the point of autocracy. Only to the extent that any worker seeks advancement within an organization is there room for individual initiative,—an initiative which can be exercised only within the narrow range of function he is called on to perform. At the very pinnacle of the hierarchy of organization in a great corporation, there alone, can individual initiative have a measure of free play. Yet even there a limit is set by the willingness and ability of subordinates to carry out the will of their superiors. In modern industry, individual liberty is necessarily curbed.

## The Profit Motive

Even the motivation of individual activity has changed its aspect. For Adam Smith and his followers, it was possible to abstract one motive, the desire for personal profit, from all the motives driving men to action and to make this the key to man's economic activity. They could conclude that, where true private enterprise existed, personal profit was an effective and socially beneficent motivating force. Yet we have already seen how the profit motive has become distorted in the modern corporation. To the extent that profits induce the risking of capital by investors, they play their customary role. But if the courts, following the traditional logic of property, seek to insure that all profits reach or be held for the security owners, they prevent profits from reaching the very group of men whose action is most important to the efficient conduct of enterprise. Only as profits are diverted into the pockets of control do they, in a measure, perform their second function.

Nor is it clear that even if surplus profits were held out as an incentive to control they would be as effective an instrument as the logic of profits assumes. Presumably the motivating influence of any such huge surplus profits as a modern corporation might be made to produce would be subject to diminishing returns. Certainly it is doubtful if the prospect of a second million dollars of income (and the surplus profits might often amount to much larger sums) would induce activity equal to that induced by the prospect of the first million or even the first hundred thousand. Profits in such terms bear little relation to those envisaged by earlier writers.

Just what motives are effective today, in so far as control is concerned, must be a matter of conjecture. But it is probable that more could be learned regarding them by studying the motives of an Alexander the Great, seeking new worlds to conquer, than by considering the motives of a petty tradesman of the days of Adam Smith.

### Competition

Finally, when Adam Smith championed competition as the great regulator of industry, he had in mind units so small that fixed capital and overhead costs played a role so insignificant that costs were in large measure determinate and so numerous that no single unit held an important position in the market. Today competition in markets dominated by a few great enterprises has come to be more often either cut-throat and destructive or so inactive as to make monopoly or duopoly conditions prevail. Competition between a small number of units each involving an organization so complex that costs have become indeterminate does not satisfy the condition assumed by earlier economists, nor does it appear likely to be as effective a regulator of industry and of profits as they had assumed.

In each of the situations to which these fundamental concepts refer, the Modern Corporation has wrought such a change as to make the concepts inapplicable.[12] New concepts must be forged and a new picture of economic relationships created. It is with this in mind that at the opening of this volume the modern corporation was posed as a major social institution; and its development was envisaged in tends of revolution.

## Chapter IV: The New Concept of the Corporation

Most fundamental to the new picture of economic life must be a new concept of business enterprise as concentrated in the corporate organization. In some measure a concept is already emerging. Over a decade ago, Walther Rathenau wrote concerning the German counterpart of our great corporation:

"No one is a permanent owner. The composition of the thousand-fold complex which functions as lord of the undertakings is in a state of flux.... This condition of things signifies that ownership has been depersonalized.... The depersonalization of ownership simultaneously implies the objectification of the thing owned. The claims to ownership are subdivided in such a fashion, and are so mobile, that the enterprise assumes an independent life, as if it belonged to no one; it takes an objective existence, such as in earlier days was embodied only in state and church, in a municipal corporation, in the life of a guild or a religious order.... The depersonalization of ownership, the

12. It is frequently suggested that economic activity has become vastly more complex under modern conditions. Yet it is strange that the concentration of the bulk of industry into a few large units has not simplified rather than complicated the economic process. It is worth suggesting that the apparent complexity may arise in part from the effort to analyze the process in terms of concepts which no longer apply.

objectification of enterprise, the detachment of property from the possessor, leads to a point where the enterprise becomes transformed into an institution which resembles the state in character."

The institution here envisaged calls for analysis, not in terms of business enterprise but in terms of social organization. On the one hand, it involves a concentration of power in the economic field comparable to the concentration of religious power in the mediaeval church or of political power in the national state. On the other hand, it involves the interrelation of a wide diversity of economic interests,—those of the "owners" who supply capital, those of the workers who "create," those of the consumers who give value to the products of enterprise, and above all those of the control who wield power.

Such a great concentration of power and such a diversity of interest raise the long-fought issue of power and its regulation—of interest and its protection. A constant warfare has existed between the individuals wielding power, in whatever form, and the subjects of that power. Just as there is a continuous desire for power, so also there is a continuous desire to make that power the servant of the bulk of the individuals it affects. The long struggles for the reform of the Catholic Church and for the development of constitutional law in the states are phases of this phenomenon. Absolute power is useful in building the organization. More slow, but equally sure is the development of social pressure demanding that the power shall be used for the benefit of all concerned. This pressure, constant in ecclesiastical and political history, is already making its appearance in many guises in the economic field.

Observable throughout the world, and in varying degrees of intensity, is this insistence that power in economic organization shall be subjected to the same tests of public benefit which have been applied in their turn to power otherwise located. In its most extreme aspect this is exhibited in the communist movement, which in its purest form is an insistence that *all* of the powers and privileges of property, shall be used only in the common interest. In less extreme forms of socialist dogma, transfer of economic powers to the state for public service is demanded. In the strictly capitalist countries, and particularly in time of depression, demands are constantly put forward that the men controlling the great economic organisms be made to accept responsibility for the well-being of those who are subject to the organization, whether workers, investors, or consumers. In a sense the difference in all of these demands lies only in degree. In proportion as an economic organism grows in strength and its power is concentrated in a few hands, the possessor of power is more easily located, and the demand for responsible power becomes increasingly direct.

How will this demand be made effective? To answer this question would be to foresee the history of the next century. We can here only consider and appraise certain of the more important lines of possible development.

By tradition, a corporation "belongs" to its shareholders, or, in a wider sense, to its security holders, and theirs is the only interest to be recognized as the object of corporate activity. Following this tradition, and without regard for the changed character of ownership, it would be possible to apply in the interests of the *passive* property owner the doctrine of strict property rights, the analysis of which has been presented above in the chapter on Corporate Powers as Powers in Trust. By the application of this doctrine, the group in control of a corporation would be placed in a position of trusteeship in which it would be called on to operate or arrange for the operation of the corporation for the *sole* benefit of the security owners despite the fact that the latter have ceased to have power over or to accept responsibility for the *active* property in which they have an interest. Were this course followed, the bulk of American industry might soon be operated by trustees for the sole benefit of inactive and irresponsible security owners.

In direct opposition to the above doctrine of strict property rights is the view, apparently held by the great corporation lawyers and by certain students of the field, that corporate development has created a new set of relationships, giving to the groups in control power which is absolute and not limited by any implied obligation with respect to their use. This logic leads to drastic conclusions. For instance, if, by reason of these new relationships, the men in control of a corporation can operate it in their own interests, and can divert a portion of the asset fund of income stream to their own uses, such is their privilege. Under this view, since the new powers have been acquired on a quasi-contractual basis, the security holders have agreed in advance to any losses which they may suffer by reason of such use. The result is, briefly, that the existence of the legal and economic relationships giving rise to these powers must be frankly recognized as a modification of the principle of private property.

If these were the only alternatives, the former would appear to be the lesser of two evils. Changed corporate relationships have unquestionably involved an essential alteration in the character of property. But such modifications have hitherto been brought about largely on the principle that might makes right. Choice between strengthening the rights of passive property owners, or leaving a set of uncurbed powers in the hands of control therefore resolves itself into a purely realistic evaluation of different results. We might elect the relative certainty and safety of a trust relationship in favor of a particular group within the corporation, accompanied by a possible diminution of enterprise. Or we may grant the controlling group free rein, with the corresponding danger of a corporate oligarchy coupled with the profitability of an era of corporate plundering.

A third possibility exists, however. On the one hand, the owners of passive property, by surrendering control and responsibility over the active property, have surrendered the right that the corporation should be operated in their sole interest,—they have released the community from the obligation to protect them to the full extent implied in the doctrine of strict property rights. At the same time, the controlling groups, by means of the extension of corporate powers, have in their own interest broken the bars of tradition which require that the corporations be operated solely for the benefit of the owners of passive property. Eliminating the sole interest of the passive owner, however, does not necessarily lay the basis for the alternative claim that the new powers should be used in the interest of the controlling groups. The latter have not presented, in acts or words any acceptable defense of the proposition that these powers should be so used. No tradition supports that proposition. The control groups have, rather, cleared the way for the claims of a group far wider than either the owners or the control. They have placed the community in a position to demand that the modern corporation serve not alone the owners or the control by all society.

This third alternative offers a wholly new concept of corporate activity. Neither the claims of ownership nor those of control can stand against the paramount interests of the community. The present claims of both contending parties now in the field have been weakened by the developments described in this book. It remains only for the claims of the community to be put forward with clarity and force. Rigid enforcement of property rights as a temporary protection against plundering by control would not stand in the way of the modification of these rights in the interest of other groups. When a convincing system of community obligations is worked out and is generally accepted, in that moment the passive property right of today must yield before the larger interests of society. Should the corporate leaders, for example, set forth a program comprising fair wages, security to employees, reasonable service to their public, and stabilization of business, all of which would divert a portion of the profits from the owners of passive property, and should the community generally accept such a scheme as a logical and human solution of industrial difficulties, the interests of passive property owners would have to give way. Courts would almost of necessity be forced to recognize the result, justifying it by whatever of the many legal theories they might choose. It is conceivable,—indeed it seems almost essential if the corporate system is to survive,—that the "control" of the great corporations should develop into a purely neutral technocracy, balancing a variety of claims by various groups in the community and assigning to each a portion of the income stream on the basis of public policy rather than private cupidity.

In still larger view, the modern corporation may be regarded not simply as one form of social organization but potentially (if not yet actually) as the dominant institution of the modern world. In every age, the major concentration of power has been based upon the dominant interest of that age. The strong man has, in his time, striven to be cardinal or pope, prince or cabinet minister, bank president or partner in the House of Morgan. During the Middle Ages, the Church, exercising spiritual power, dominated Europe and gave to it a unity at a time when both political and economic power were diffused. With the rise of the modern state, political power, concentrated into a few large units, challenged the spiritual interest as the strongest bond of human society. Out of the long struggle between church and state which followed, the state emerged victorious; nationalist politics superseded religion as the basis of the major unifying organization of the western world. Economic power still remained diffused.

The rise of the modern corporation has brought a concentration of economic power which can compete on equal terms with the modern state—economic power versus political power, each strong in its own field. The state seeks in some aspects to regulate the corporation, while the corporation, steadily becoming more powerful, makes every effort to avoid such regulation. Where its own interests are concerned, it even attempts to dominate the state. The future may see the economic organism, now typified by the corporation, not only on an equal plane with the state, but possibly even superseding it as the dominant form of social organization. The law of corporations, accordingly, might well be considered as a potential constitutional law for the new economic state, while business practice is increasingly assuming the aspect of economic statesmanship.

## Louis Brandeis
## *Shall We Abandon the Policy of Competition?*
## Reprinted from *The Curse of Bigness* (1934)

Shall we abandon as obsolete the long-cherished policy of competition, and accept in its place the long-detested policy of monopoly? The issue is not (as it is usually stated by advocates of monopoly), "Shall we have unrestricted competition or regulated monopoly?" It is, "Shall we have regulated competition or regulated monopoly?"

Regulation is essential to the preservation and development of competition, just as it is necessary to the preservation and best development of liberty. We have long curbed physically the strong, to protect those physically weaker. More recently we have extended such prohibitions to business. We have restricted theoretical freedom of contract by factory laws. The liberty of the merchant and manufacturer to lie in trade, expressed in the fine phrase of *caveat emptor*, is yielding to the better conceptions of business ethics, before pure-food laws and postal-fraud prosecutions. Similarly, the right to competition must be limited in order to preserve it. For excesses of competition lead to monopoly, as excesses of liberty lead to absolutism. The extremes meet.

The issue, therefore, is: Regulated competition versus regulated monopoly. The policy of regulated competition is distinctly a constructive policy. It is the policy of development as distinguished from the destructive policy of private monopoly.

It is asserted that to persist in the disintegration of existing unlawful trusts is to pursue a policy of destruction. No statement could be more misleading. Progress demands that we remove the obstacles in the path of progress; and private monopoly is the most serious obstacle.

One has heard of late the phrases: "You can't make people compete by law." "Artificial competition is undesirable."

These are truisms, but their implication is false. The suggestion is not that traders be compelled to compete, but that they be prevented from killing competition. Equally misleading is the phrase, "Natural monopolies should not be interfered with." There are no natural monopolies today in the industrial world. The Oil Trust and the Steel Trust have been referred to as natural monopolies, but they are both most unnatural. The Oil Trust acquired its control of the market by conduct which involved flagrant violations of law. Without the aid of criminal rebating, of bribery and corruption, the Standard Oil would never have acquired the vast wealth and power which enabled it to destroy its small competitors by price-cutting and similar practices.

The Steel Trust acquired control not through greater efficiency, but by buying up existing plants and ore supplies at fabulous prices. It is believed that not a single industrial monopoly exists today which is the result of natural growth. Competition has been suppressed with by ruthless practices or by an improper use of inordinate wealth and power. If the law prohibiting such practices is clearly defined and enforced, as it is the purpose of the La Follette Bill to accomplish, no similar trust will arise in the future.

The only argument that has been seriously advanced in favor of private monopoly is that competition involves wastes, while the monopoly prevents waste and leads to efficiency. This argument is essentially unsound. The wastes of competition are negligible. The economies of monopoly are superficial and delusive. The efficiency of monopoly is at the best temporary.

Undoubtedly competition involves waste. What human activity does not? The wastes of democracy are among the greatest obvious wastes, but we have compensations in democracy which far outweigh that waste and make it more efficient than absolutism. So it is with competition. The waste is relatively insignificant. There are wastes of competition which do not develop, but kill. These the law can and should eliminate by regulating competition.

It is true that the unit in business may be too small to be efficient. It is also true that the unit may be too large to be efficient, and this is no uncommon incident of monopoly.

Whenever trusts have developed efficiency, their fruits have been absorbed almost wholly by the trusts themselves. From such efficiency as they have developed, the community has gained substantially nothing.

The proposed Government commission to fix prices would not greatly relieve the evils attendant upon monopoly. It might reduce a trust's profits, but it would fail materially to reduce the trust's prices; because the limitation of the monopoly's profits would, by lessening this incentive, surely reduce the monopoly's efficiency.

To secure successful management of any private business, reward must be proportionate to success. The establishment of any rule fixing a maximum return on capital would, by placing a limit upon the fruits of achievement, tend to lessen efficiency.

No selling price for monopoly products could be set constitutionally at a point lower than that which would allow a reasonable return on capital. And in the absence of comparative data from any competing businesses producing the same article at less cost, it would be virtually impossible to determine that the cost should be lower.

The success of the Interstate Commerce Commission has been invoked as an argument in favor of licensing and regulating monopoly.

But the Interstate Commerce Commission has been effective principally in preventing rate increases and in stopping discrimination. In those instances where the Commission has reduced rates (as distinguished from preventing increases) the Commission rested its decisions largely on the ground that existing rates amounted to discriminations against particular places or articles, or the lower rates were justified by a comparison with other rates of the same or other companies. Price-fixing of that nature applied to industrial trusts would afford little protection to the public.

In the second place, there is a radical difference between attempts to fix rates for transportation and similar public services, and fixing prices in industrial businesses. Problems of transportation, while varying infinitely in detail, are largely the same throughout the whole country, and they are largely the same yesterday, today, and tomorrow. In industry we have, instead of uniformity, infinite variety; instead of stability, constant change.

In the third place, the problems of the Interstate Commerce Commission, relatively simple as they are, already far exceed the capacity of that or any single board. Think of the infinite questions which would come before an industrial commission seeking to fix rates, and the suffering of the community from the inability of that body promptly and efficiently to dispose of them.

Every business requires for its business health the *memento mori* of competition from without. It requires likewise a certain competition from within, which can exist only where the ownership and management, on the one hand, and the employees, on the other, shall each be alert, hopeful, self-respecting, and free to work out for themselves the best conceivable conditions.

The successful, the powerful trusts, have created conditions absolutely inconsistent with these—America's—industrial and social needs. It may be true that as a legal proposition mere size is not a crime, but mere size may become an industrial and social menace, because it frequently creates as against possible competitors and as against the employees conditions of such gross inequality, as to imperil the welfare of the employees and of the industry.

In the midst of our indignation over the unpardonable crimes of trade-union leaders, disclosed at Los Angeles, would not our statesmen and thinkers seek to ascertain the underlying cause of this widespread, deliberate outburst of crimes of violence? What was it that led men like the McNamaras to believe really that the only recourse they had for improving the condition of the wage-earner was to use dynamite against property and life?

Certainly it was not individual depravity. Was it not because they, and men like them, believed that the wage-earner, acting singly, or collectively, is not strong enough to secure substantial justice? Is there not a causal connection between the development of these huge indomitable trusts and the horrible crimes now under investigation? Are not these irresistible trusts important contributing causes of these crimes—these unintelligent expressions of despairing social unrest? Is it not irony to speak of the equality of opportunity, in a country cursed with their bigness?

The right of labor to organize and to deal collectively with its employers should not be curtailed.

There is not the slightest danger that labor will assume control of industry. It has become exceedingly difficult for the unions to maintain themselves because of the constant inflow of foreign labor and the great number of non-union men. This maintains a state of competition, which, did it exist in the industrial and financial business of the country, would make unnecessary any change in existing laws.

The only right claimed by the labor unions is that of collective bargaining, and this right employers also should have and exercise. It would be perfectly proper for independent competing employers to form employers' organizations, and to deal with the labor unions upon exactly the same footing as is the case with unions—that is, collectively.

Nothing has been done to improve the conditions under which men labor, that has not increased their efficiency. Shorter hours often lead to greater production; and there is economy in high wages.

## The Regulation of Competition Against the Regulation of Monopoly

A large part of the American people realize today that competition is in no sense inconsistent with large scale production and distribution. They realize that the maintenance of competition does not necessarily involve destructive and unrestrained competition, any more than the maintenance of liberty implies license or anarchy. We learned long ago that liberty could be preserved only by limiting in some way the freedom of action of individuals; that otherwise liberty would necessarily lead to absolutism and in the same way we have learned that unless there be regulation of competition, its excesses will lead to the destruction of competition, and monopoly will take its place.

A large part of our people have also learned that efficiency in business does not grow indefinitely with the size of the business. Very often a business grows in efficiency as it grows from a small business to a large business; but there is a unit of greatest efficiency in every business at any time, and a business may be too large to be efficient, as well as too small. Our people have also learned that these profits are not due in the main to efficiency but are due to control of the market, to the exercise by a small body of men of the sovereign taxing power. Nothing has helped so much to make this clear to our people as an incident in the life of the Tobacco Trust. When the Spanish War came on and we needed additional revenue, Congress properly increased the tax on tobacco products. Three years later, when our country no longer needed that additional revenue, Congress sought to remove the burden which it had placed upon the people, but Congress found itself powerless to remove the burden it had imposed. And when Congress reduced the tax, the effect was merely to transfer, from the Treasury of the United States to the treasury of the Trust, the several millions of dollars a year which represented the reduction in the tax; because the tobacco-products market was controlled by the Trust, which held the selling price practically unchanged.

The history of the Tobacco trust also showed in the history of its detailed operations how control made for profit, for the degree of control exercised by that great Trust was very different in the various departments of its business and, as the commissioner of corporations found, the ratio of profit was ordinarily in direct relation to the ratio of control. Where the trusts had a high degree of control, the profits were great;

where they had a small degree of control the profits were small. In the cigar business, in which the Trust had no control of the market, in which it was merely a large concern, doing perhaps one-eighth of the cigar business of the country, the Trust's profits were not only small, but they were very much smaller than would be satisfactory to the ordinary manufacturer. In the same year in which some of the subsidiary corporations of the Trust were earning fifty, sixty, eighty, or one hundred percent upon the tangible assets, the Trust was earning in its cigar department only four to six percent, although the ultimate management of all departments of the Trust's business rested with the same able men and was supplied with the same great resources. Such facts as these have made men realize that while trusts are sometimes efficient, it is not their efficiency but the fact that they control the market, that accounts for the huge profits of trusts.

And people have learned also another fact of perhaps even greater importance. They have come to realize the effect of monopoly in arresting progress, arresting that advance in industry without which a great industrial future is unattainable.

What America needs is not that we do anything for these, our fellow citizens, but that we keep open the path of opportunity to enable them to do for themselves. When these Americans come to do for themselves they find this situation: The trust is not merely a capitalistic control of men. It is the worst form of capitalistic control. One hundred and fifty thousand persons are said to be interested as stockholders in the Steel Trust. The Steel Trust is a conspicuous instance of ownership separated from responsibility. The Steel Trust presents a condition similar to that which led to the demoralization of Ireland—the condition of absentee landlordism. The managers may be good men and true, but the permanent separation of ownership from control must prove fatal to the public interest. The responsibility of ownership is lacking. If there had been responsibility of ownership in the Steel Trust it would have been impossible that with the huge profits of the corporation—which the commissioner of corporations found to be $650,000,000 in ten years, far in excess of a fair return upon the capital originally invested in that concern—men would have been compelled to work twelve hours a day, seven days in a week, and at such low wages that even if they had worked 365 days in a year, seven days a week, the year's earnings would have been less than was necessary, less than the minimum amount necessary in the city of Pittsburgh for the support of a man, his wife, and three children with the minimum of decency, alas!

## Rexford Tugwell

## *The Industrial Discipline and the Governmental Arts*

## Chapter VIII: Government and Industry

Governments, presumably, are expressions of a social will. That is their excuse for being. but the social will is a vague and elusive thing, difficult to apprehend, more difficult to pin down to specific issues. This was not so when the operating units of society were restricted to a small area and a limited population. The town meeting had a way of expressing itself and of making its governmental machinery responsive. But when the organizations which express our social life grow beyond the scope of any merely local authority and multiply almost to infinity, the sphere of government, as such, becomes more and more difficult to define. Many of the functions of government, indeed, are taken over by these organizations, and we are left confused as to just what the government does or ought to reserve to itself. It was this growing tendency to diffuse the administration of public services among various private organizations as well as governmental agencies, perhaps, which led to the conception of government as a residue of powers which, one after another, were to be given up as they could be taken over by other social bodies. This has by now gone so far that we tend to think of the political unit as having only the function of holding a balance among other groups and having no positive responsibilities of its own.

## 1. The Social Will

The social will is achieved, in such a system, outside the government. If, for instance, it is industry we think of, the government has only the duty of protecting one business against the unfair tactics of others and, when exploitation becomes somewhat outrageous, protecting some other interests such as those of consumers, workers, or farmers. The responsibility of the government is very much lighter than it might be if, for instance, it were specifically charged with the provision of goods for the population. As we all know, however, we depend for this upon individual initiative and the incentives furnished by search among business organizations for profits, hoping that, [somehow] these impulses will prove sufficiently strong as motivation to survive even a good deal of repression and regulation.

Nevertheless, there is a rather persistent popular feeling that the government is more responsible than an analysis of its actual powers would lead a social analyst to expect. A period of depression, for instance, is attributed pretty generally to the national administration which happens to be in power. And, though businesses cling to the ideal of "keeping the government out of business," they expect protection from it whenever disaster threatens. The farmers, for instance, have, in recent years, demanded a good deal more than Republican administrations could concede in the way of favors; and various manufacturers, with greater success, have caused the tariffs to be regulated in their interest. Political parties make claims to responsibility for "prosperity"; and these are widely believed in by the electorate.

There is apparently a good deal of exception to the idea that government ought to be only a regularizing instrument. Indeed, the question is frequently raised whether this regularizing function does not require considerable extension of positive action. How can farmers' distresses be relieved without Federal organization of certain new institutions? How otherwise can workers achieve their ambitions? When the government defines the limits of competition and says what a business may or may not do, just how much responsibility is involved? Suppose businesses refuse to function under the limitations, would the government be obligated to take over their duties? Issues such as these we tend to settle one by one. Each is treated separately and, so far as that can be done, without reference to the general political theory involved; but as practical illustrations of what needs to be done, they are sure to raise the general question: what kind of relations between government and industry are we developing?

If we look at the bare bones of governmental structure, we do not discover much which really helps to answer this question; it is the flesh on the bones which radiates life; but the life cannot be understood without looking into anatomy. The most obvious anatomical characteristic of the American political system is its tripartite nature: local, State, and Federal. Local units we may, for our purpose, disregard. Their controls over industry are, by now, negligible. But the relation of the States to the Federal unit is important. It is defined by our Constitution, but interpreted by the courts; so that it is even more important to know what the Supreme Court says than what the Constitution seems to say. In the instrument itself, all powers not specifically given to the nation are reserved to the States. And, since nothing at all is said about industry, that presumably comes under State jurisdiction if any at all. The single exception is that interstate *commerce* comes within the national purview; our forefathers could hardly have escaped seeing that. This relationship between the States and the nation, as defined by the Constitution, has caused more discussion and legal controversy, perhaps, than any single feature of our constitutional system. For industry, presumably left to be regulated by the States, proceeded immediately to outgrow these conflicts. And because no other jurisdiction was available it has escaped much of any real control. It is not a representative firm, in our time, which does business within anyone State. Perhaps 99 percent of our goods are made by firms which do an interstate business. But is interstate *business* interstate *commerce?* It would be pure invention to attribute any such notion to the writers of our Constitution; interstate businesses did not exist then. But those who wish for some control over industry, and who are plagued with the obvious ineffectiveness of State powers, are reduced to appealing from a restricted view of commerce *as commerce* to a view of it *as industry.* When, on a few occasions, such attempts have been embodied in legislation, another clause of the Constitution—the Fifth Amendment—has invariably been invoked in rebuttal. That clause says that property cannot be taken without due process of law, and has served to obstruct, most effectively, attempts to extend Federal controls to industry. For when a privilege is limited, that seems to be taking property without due process, regardless of the corollary fact that the privilege itself also involves such a taking of property. But we happen to be more shocked when the government does it for the public benefit than when businesses do it for their own benefit.

It should be clear by now that our form of government is fixed in a series of formal relationships so difficult to change that alteration almost never occurs. Matters of deep emotional stress, such as prohibition was, can override all difficulties. And so we get an occasional though infrequent Amendment. But the workaday world is a prosaic affair. The price of bread or the profits of a shoe manufacturer are not charged with emotional content. And so there is no Amendment which relates to industry. If there is a social will in the matter, it is spasmodic, unpersistent, and results in few new institutions. The whole field of industrial regulation is left to the definition of the courts—and they are, to speak very mildly indeed, conservative. Individual and corporate rights are conserved more often than those which may be supposed to belong to the public; in this, of course, they follow the tradition of classical economics. The courts cannot be blamed for orthodoxy or conservatism. That is their function—to conserve. It is not their duty to define what they shall protect; it is the duty of the rest of us.

"But," someone will say, "we control public utilities, and we have broken up the trusts, we have a Clayton Act and a Federal Trade Commission. Surely these are sufficient evidence that the Federal power extends to industry." We may, for the moment, examine this idea.

## 2. Regulation or Control

Laissez faire may have been inherited from Britain, but it found a comfortable home in the hearts of our own nineteenth-century business men. Its welcome is by no means yet outworn. But the free competition which is its distinguishing characteristic had certain intolerable results. Workers suffered under it—hours were long, conditions bad, wages low. It made shoddy goods, contrary to the theory that, in order to sell in competition, they must be good. But what is most paradoxical of all, it led straight to combination and monopoly. And so consumers suffered too, as well as the weaker among the businesses. All these abuses were perfectly evident and required action. We have met the situation by progressive modifications of the freedom to compete, clinging consistently, however, to the central ideal of competition: that a balance among opposed conflicts will result in general welfare. We may have come to the point where the next necessary modification of the prevailing pattern will require drastic reconstruction: of that, more later. First let us look at the modifications which have been made as concessions to the injured interests of workers, consumers, and such others as farmers.

With a governmental system such as ours a question always arises concerning the proper authority for interference, and the interests of the workers have been protected by both the State and Federal governments. We come at once to the police powers. Government may protect "health, morals, and welfare." But what government? Presumably those of the States unless the "interstate commerce clause" can be made to stretch so far. And, as would be expected, what minimum wage legislation, social insurance, limitation of the hours of work, or regulation concerning the maintenance of healthful working conditions has eventuated has come mostly from the States. The Adamson eight-hour law is an exception; but that was sanctioned by the Supreme Court in an hour of national crisis, and its effectiveness as a precedent could probably be evaded. When it came to limiting the labor of children, in spite of the frightful conditions which were shown to exist, the court refused to say that only those goods should be permitted to pass into interstate commerce which had been made without the use of children's work. The commerce clause refused to stretch.

There is a great difference in the lengths to which individual States are willing to go in protecting workers and also some argument about what they are able to do; for it is frequently argued that one State must not go further than others have, lest it ruin its industries by raising the cost of production. This reasoning could result in grading all down to the level of those least willing to do anything. Historically, this has not been absolutely true; but there has been something of this effect. The advantages of protection by the Federal government, since these handicaps to State action exist, are obvious, but the Supreme Court has remained so reluctant that not much has been tried. On the whole, the United States is the most backward among all industrialized nations in these respects.

As to the making of shoddy, misrepresented, or adulterated goods, it has been easier to enlist Federal interference. The Pure Food and Drugs Act stands as a monument. It shows, moreover, what can be done with an extension of the idea of a Federal police power. Why this cannot be stretched to include the protection of other vital interests, admitted to be injured, must be left for explanation to the more subtle minds among constitutional lawyers. Perhaps it is a greater or a different injury when one is forced to buy misrepresented bread or shoddy clothes than it is when one is forced to pay an exorbitant price for them; but to the lay mind, the difference is too narrow to fathom. Ideally, competition is supposed to prevent both; actually, it prevents neither. But one injury we outlaw, and the other we do not.

This last mentioned distinction is extremely important, for it prevents the protection of consumers in their most vulnerable interest. But here we come to the theory underlying the series of antitrust acts culminating in that which set up the Federal Trade Commission. This theory, again, is that there must be fixed levels below which individual enterprises are forbidden to penetrate in their competitive activities; and that competition must be kept operative, must, if necessary, be restored when it has disappeared. If competition is kept alive, and if its levels are fixed, the theory is that consumers and the weaker among our businesses will be protected from the exploitations by the superior market advantages of those concerns which have been more successful. For competition did lead to combination. It was wasteful and inefficient, and small units have, since the middle of the last century, shown a disconcerting persistence in combining. Not only this, but new businesses, such as those in the automobile industry, have grown big and powerful sometimes without combining, but merely through exploiting the possibilities of efficiency in large-scale organizations and mass production.

It will have to be sufficient here to point out that, in general, this policy of restoring conflict and keeping it within bounds has not been altogether successful. Neither the antitrust acts nor the Federal Trade Commission sufficed to keep competition alive or business units numerous and small. The ingenuity of corporate lawyers has outrun that of legislators and administrators—granting, that is, a genuine will to enforce the law among the latter—a rather doubtful assumption in recent years. Associationism has gone on developing; and because the theory of competitive protection was clung to, the police powers have infrequently been resorted to in the attempt to protect the weaker among business firms and consumers in general. In fact, we still lack clear definition of what can or cannot be done under them.

## 3. Governmental Responsibility

But is it only the rather negative regulations, which would protect these interests, for which our Federal government has a responsibility? Is there any burden of responsibility for the continuance or the restoration, for instance, of our American prosperity? Ought the government to act in such a way as to ensure the provision to citizens of any goods and services? The power to regulate, one might say, is the power to destroy. Might it also be the power to provide? Certainly not under the prevailing theory of laissez faire. But is that theory written so deeply into our Constitution that there is no power to act in these ways without violating it? In the interest of the general welfare, might the Federal government encourage one and discourage other activities if that course should promise avoidance of depression, for example, or the relief of unemployment? Or, possibly, the solution of the persistent problems of agriculture? These, it is true, might not involve government assumption of actual industrial functions; but then again in the coal, oil, railroad, or telephone industries it might. Assuming that it would not, but that all we need is such controlling power as would serve to encourage some and discourage other industrial activities, does the government possess it? If the general disposition to involve national administrations in whatever blame or praise arises from depression or prosperity is an indication of social will in the matter, there must be assumed an accompanying willingness in public opinion to allow the government scope for control. True, there may be an entirely inconsistent feeling that depression is attributable to "government meddling" and that, if the administration's hands were kept completely off, everything would be all right. But this reaction is characteristic only of those who happen to be doing well with things as they are; a far wider feeling that "the government might do something" exists.

Certainly, the great task to which America must dedicate itself in the coming years is clear. The world must be made a safe place in which to live. The sources of present insecurity are many. Their challenge to statesmanship is very similar to that challenge we met not so many years ago to make the world safe for democracy. We thought that crisis sufficiently important to call out all our reserves of man power and of administrative skill. For once, the traditional forms of organization were abandoned for those which were plainly necessary to the task at hand.

Every statesman will be forced, in the coming years, to ask himself searching questions which have to do with economic responsibility. The anguish of the wounded on the battlefields of France lay no heavier on the heart of Woodrow Wilson than the sufferings of idle men and women must lie on the hearts of statesmen in the coming years. Theories and traditions weighed very lightly in the scale over against the exigencies of efficiency which might save some lives in the process of establishing victory. Theories and traditions will again be weighed in the balance against the economic insecurity with which civilization has now joined battle. This does not mean that we can abandon our equipment of industry, technique, and methods any more than the imposition of the universal draft could take place by ignoring the American local pride of selection or any more than Liberty Motors could be made without engineers and their familiar materials. We have to start from where we are and to use the materials that we have.

Indeed, it gives us a long start to have developed here the most effective industrial machine ever devised. It gives us a longer start to have behind us a century of popular education and of technical training. Man power, trained intelligence, an efficient factory system, highly developed systems of communication and transport—these, it might be thought, are nearly everything. In fact, they turn out to be merely the materials for something we have yet to achieve. For we have not yet attained the kind of industrial and political organization which enables us to achieve with them the common purpose which animates us.

What is this common purpose? The simpler aspects of it seem to be easy enough to define. And these are our most conspicuous failure. Men and women do not ask much from this world in which they find themselves—not more, at least, than ought to be guaranteed them by our resources and achievements. They ask security—security of access to the goods of simple living, security of employment, security in ill health and old age, security of maintenance and training for their dependents, security in the exercise of technical tasks which involve progress in the ancient struggle to escape labor.

If we ask why it is, with an equipment adequate to this purpose, this provision of a minimum of security still remains conspicuously lacking, the answer must be discovered in the kind of economic and political organization which dominates our industrial machine. The system of unregulated business enterprise has failed us in this respect; it must be modified and regulated to repair the failure. The question is, whether this is to be a governmental task. And if it is, what can government do to furnish the kind of control which will avoid instability?

These are not new questions. Throughout the development of highly integrated industrial enterprises, there have been two extreme views of the duties of government. One held that business should be let alone. Another, that government should take over completely all economic functions. We have proceeded, in our history, on neither of these dogmatic theories. We have, however, leaned toward an extreme of [freedom], and only very reluctantly have we interfered anywhere. In certain instances we have had to—in the case of the railroads, for instance, and, in another way, in the case of the trusts. But these instances differed greatly in principle. Railroads have always been public utilities and so subject to a rigorous and constructive regulation. Other businesses have been considered to be private, and their regulation has stopped short of any constructive suggestion. Our theory has been that if businesses competed, they would be forced to provide fair service at fair prices. For if one did not, another would, and would consequently get the business. In pursuit of this idea, we have been content to define what was fair and what was not fair in competition—to set standards for the competitive process. Beyond that, we have been determined to break down monopoly wherever it could be reached. That was the intent of the Sherman Act and the Clayton Act. In pursuit of these purposes we set up the Federal Trade Commission, whose duties were to investigate competition and, sometimes, to enforce it. The Commission has done its best; our legal machinery has moved again and again to destroy monopolies. But what is the situation today?

Evidently what we have done is not enough. There has never been a more conspicuous disparity between our possibilities and our performances. The question whether we do not need something more than an enforcement of competition and a defining of its standards is being insistently raised. Do we need some kind of compulsion to efficiency, to adhere to common purpose? It seems quite apparent to many theorists that the government must supplement whatever forces there are in private industry which work in this direction; that it must modify its suppression of monopoly where these suppressive efforts interfere with planning for equilibrium. In doing this, it is said, it need not neglect the protection of workers and consumers; indeed, this protection is the reason for a change of policy. It must, for instance, require that wider planning and closer integration among businesses shall not result in so limiting production as to restrict consumers' access to goods. It must also require that working standards and wage levels shall be protected. They can and should be consistently increased as more efficient central organization is achieved.

What is it that the government can and ought to do if this reasoning is followed? The answer to this delicate question is not easy—for reasons one must have seen who knows our Constitution, our complex governmental structure, and our confused attitudes toward industry. It ought to be clear also that with such an interrelated system of business enterprises as we have, proceeding in a voluntary fashion to do what they like, controls inserted anywhere in the system have effects, often unforeseen, in many other places. The control of railway rates may affect the wheat crop, the prosperity of Atlantic ports, the price of chicken feed, or the sales policy of Chicago merchants—and perhaps many other enterprises and relationships. This is one reason why piecemeal regulation tends to widen and why some effort at really national planning becomes a practical issue immediately upon consideration of any planning at all—for presumably any regulation which may be entered on will not be undertaken without some assessment of expected effects.

This and other considerations cause many social theorists to feel that it is a legitimate function of the Federal government to make and execute such a national plan, whether or not all industrial activities are actually to be controlled. It is undoubtedly within the Federal power to prepare such a plan; the difficulties would arise when it came to be put into effect. For what would be undertaken would be, we may suppose, a survey of the nation's needs for goods and services of all kinds and a study of our present arrangements for providing them. Such a study would be the basis for undertaking such a rearrangement of present industries or such a control over their actions as would meet the criteria of our plan. We have, at present, too great a dearth of knowledge to anticipate just what would need to be done and, for this reason, we cannot say which of them would be constitutionally permissible, if Congress should undertake the passage of enabling legislation. But there are a few requirements which seem sufficiently clear to be considered in the broad aspects.

If industries were to be controlled, incorporation of business enterprises would need, in effect, to be transferred from the States to the nation, though some subterfuge might need to be employed; the flow of new capital into different uses would need to be supervised; prices would have to be controlled; and some vital interests, now partly or wholly neglected, would need to be protected. These last would include the weaker businesses, consumers, workers, farmers, and technicians, all of which suffer now from disadvantages and discriminations which are too obvious to be denied. All these seem, from the present point of vantage, necessary elements of a scheme which would give the Federal government powers commensurate with the responsibilities widely laid at its doorstep. There are, we may repeat, two important ways of looking at such a scheme: is the opinion which blames the government when things go wrong or praises it when they go well a mere hazy desire to shift to wider shoulders burdens which are sought to be evaded; and, even though such a program could be shown to be necessary to governmental effectiveness in this area, would opinion respect it when its specific items came to standing out in bold relief? Those who denounce in certain terms the utter failure of laissez faire and the miserable chaos of affairs—especially economic ones—which, they say, has followed insidiously upon its decline, are willing to work for such a change in opinion as will lead the public to accept the logic of its own attitudes, to substitute the specific and the practical for the general and the futile.

That victory is still to be won; but there seems sufficient probability of final acceptance, at least, to warrant further exploration of possibilities. There are those who will say that what the public actively desires, it will find ways to achieve; but it is worth noting that such achievements are easier if some scouting is carried on ahead of the event, if possibilities are explored and experimented with in the imagination. One possibility is constitutional amendment. But that seems far off indeed. Are there ways in which existing institutions can be used to attain the same results? On the whole, it is better to make use, so far as that can be done, of familiar instruments; it is easier to persuade people to acceptance if what is to be done can be shown to involve, not something new and untried, but merely the extension of present half recognized and feebly used means. With this in mind, and quite conditionally, it may be valuable to cast up the situation presented by the problems of controlling the allocation of capital and of fixing prices.

## 4. The Allocation of Capital

The question immediately arises in considering such a long forward step as is suggested by the direction of investment: do we actually need this instrument? We must first say why, therefore, capital allocation under Federal authority seems, to those who propose it, needed. We may first recall the fact that industries, at present, are, many of them, overequipped: they have plant, machinery, materials, and men enough to produce more than they do now—sometimes twice as much. Somehow, they have been able to get hold of enough investment funds to build more plants and install more machinery than they ever use.

In order to gather up the implications of this main obviously appearing phenomenon, some other circumstances have to be kept in mind. First, there is never overproduction *in general;* for that would mean that everyone had all the products of industry for which he has any desire. This is never true. The more accurate statement is that consumers have all of particular kinds of goods they feel they can afford *at the price which is charged.* Usually they would take more if the price were lower or if their incomes were higher. At any rate, they would buy more of *something.*

This leads directly to the question: why are prices so high or incomes so low that they cannot buy what they wish? This evidently cannot be answered completely, but even a partial explanation seems to involve reference to our inexpert allocation of capital. For this in itself involves high costs which must be covered in selling prices. This is because unused plant and machinery are, whether or not they are used, an almost constant expense; and these "overhead costs" are necessarily distributed *over the whole product,* not just part of it. If equipment is used to capacity, the overhead costs will be charged to more units of products than they will if it is not used to capacity. In the one case prices which meet costs can be lower than in the other.

If there were a system of planning, it is therefore said, which allocated to specific industries capital sufficient to produce an amount of goods which would be taken by consumers at the price possible with capacity production, and no more, prices could be lower than they are at present. The surplus investment capital could then be assigned to other industries, and because less of each individual's income was required to buy good number 1, he could buy more of number 2, 3, and so on.

We are asked to consider coal as an example. If the mines, men, plants, machinery, and marketing facilities were reduced by something over one-third, the mining equipment of the country could still produce as much coal as ever has been used in any given period. But the cost of keeping up one-third of the plant would be eliminated. The coal actually produced would be the same as now, but its cost would be enormously reduced. When it is remembered that coal enters into the cost of nearly all other manufactured goods, it is seen that this reduction in cost might spread itself throughout the economic system. And it is undoubtedly true that if the argument is allowed as to coal, the same considerations are relevant to many other industries.

Capital allocation would depend on knowledge, from some planning agency, of how much for a measured future period ought to be put to one use rather than to another. Given this information, the first step in control would be to limit self-allocation. This is the first great problem in this field. Industries, because of their past and present successes, regardless of temporary luck, grow overconfident of the future and expand their own activities beyond all reason. Witness, for instance, the automobile industry. But along with this is another problem. In each industry there are many businesses. There is not only the problem of knowing what the industry's output will be or ought to be, but also that of knowing how much of the business will go to each firm involved. But this touches another phase of such a general problem. Combination and association to the point of having each industry closely articulated would be the function of another sort of administration. It is certainly true that until substantial articulation throughout each industry could be achieved, the regulation of capital would be very difficult. These would need to be developed side by side. In the meantime, while there were still numerous independent concerns operating in the same industrial field, some principle of apportionment would have to be adopted. It might, for instance, be done on the basis of present size, or present contribution to the national output; or there might be some recognition of the superior efficiency of one over others. But this problem is too intricate to be discussed in advance in any detailed way; at least the forecast has not, up to now, run in more detailed form.

Assuming, however, that each industry had its various firms either combined or sufficiently closely associated for practical action, how then would the problem be attacked? In general the principle invoked would be to drive corporate surpluses into the open investment market; for most of the trouble comes from self-allocation occurring strictly within a single organization. It is overoptimistic internal expansion and the use of funds, earned in the past, to commit the concern to increased activity which cause the problems of surplus which yearly grow more acute.

To meet this problem it is frequently suggested that a tax be imposed on funds, over and above replacement, which are kept for expansion purposes. If taxation forced these funds into distribution as dividends, they would have to seek reinvestment through the regular channels, and a concern's plans for expansion would be subject to check in the investment market. It might be said incidentally, also, that a salutary check upon present practices in issuing stock dividends and concealing earnings for manipulative purposes would follow. Once all funds were forced into the investment market, however, some other means of supervising their uses would be needed. This might be done through the Federal incorporation of businesses. For new capital issues, then, revision of original charters would be necessary.[1]

If funds were thus forced into the open investment market, and if there were control of new capital issues, the problem would be as adequately met as seems necessary to the advocate of the general idea. For funds from the other sources we have mentioned—individual savings, investment trusts, insurance companies, savings institutions, etc.—would come into the investment market in any case. There is no danger from self-allocation in these. The revenues of the government are, also, normally subject to public supervision for expenditure. They might be better used than they have been in the past, to regularize industrial activity; but this is not a question of breaking ground for a new policy. It will be seen, then, that the control of investment is not so complex a matter, at least in principle, as it might at first seem. The principles involved would be only two: the forcing of all investment funds into an open market, and the regulating of new capital issues. Neither of these seems impossible if we grant (1) the substitution of Federal for State incorporation, and (2) the correctness of using the taxing power to force surpluses into the market. The scheme is recommended as eminently practical by those who put it forward; certainly it would have far-reaching effects; it rests, however, upon an extension of Federal authority upon which we have, until now, been unwilling to venture.

1. An alternative to this sometimes suggested is a tax on unused capacity, which those who argue for it believe would achieve many of these same results.

## 5. The Encouragement of Integration

It is said alternatively, however, that the encouragement of integration might not be necessary, in any positive way, if we should remove discouragements such as the antitrust laws are. Given permission, the patterns of industry might assume, more rapidly and normally, the shape they are working toward now with so much difficulty. It needs to be said, perhaps, in this connection, that there would be several sources of opposition. There is, in the first place, that which would come from believers in laissez faire as a politico-economic philosophy; there is also that which would come from convinced protectors of States' rights against Federal encroachment, for such permission would clearly indicate a need for Federal control; and lastly, there is the opposition which could be counted on from a number of vested interests, such as constitutional lawyers, corporation advisors, and others of the legal profession who find their most lucrative field of activity in the devious attempts of business to evade the present laws. These would contemplate the change with extreme disfavor. Small business men may also be said to have a vested interest in antitrust legislation, though this might not be nearly so formidable a source of opposition as the lawyers.

But those who believe in planning are not satisfied to go only so far. A nation, they say, which was venturing into an economic field must go further and actually encourage integration in the interest of coordinated efficiency. Fear of the strength of these coordinated interests would, of course, dictate numerous safeguards. This fear is a legitimate one, and the dangers it points to would need to be covered in initial organization.

## 6. Price Control

The dangers and difficulties of price control have been dwelt on by many critics. It is usually assumed, however, that a system of control, if it were entered on at all, would be begun and pursued in piecemeal fashion, being extended only to those commodities which could be shown to be somehow like those which we now regulate as public utilities. It seems clear enough that there are many of these in which consumers' interests need protection. But we are here considering the possibility, however remote it may be, of a *system* of industrial control, consciously entered upon and pursued by a number of means, price control being only one of them. This alters the problem considerably. There are to be considered two kinds of prices: those paid by consumers for finished or consumption goods and those paid by businesses for raw or semi finished materials. In the one field, price control is protective, but indirectly, through a lowering of the costs of production. It may be thought of further as protecting the interests of business buyers as against business sellers. The great constitutional difficulty running throughout this field is that when a price is controlled, the act of control takes property away from one individual and bestows it upon another "without due process of law." For the due process clause of the Constitution to be held in suspension in favor of regulation, it is necessary to show that the price being considered is one which is "affected with a public interest." This last means that there must be a continuing market disadvantage to one party to the bargain. Such a situation most conspicuously arises (1) when businesses develop unequally and one gains an advantage over others because of size and power, or (2) when consumers are under compulsion to take a price or leave it, when leaving it would involve obvious and distressing hardship. There would seem some logic in saying that competition does not fix a fair price in either of these cases. And price control, by the same logic, could remedy the discrepancy. Whether the Supreme Court is prepared to accept the consequences of the reasoning thus attributed to it and to permit a far-reaching control, no one can say. Its attitudes have hitherto been somewhat contradictory and uncertain. The most that can be done at this stage by one who is trying to understand this new point of view is to point out the reasons for the invention of such a device without forecasting the details of its administration. Certainly greater concentration and increase of power among businesses is likely to be used for private advantage rather than the public good if some such device is not used. We have seen the argument for the abandonment of antitrust compulsions, but we must recognize that it is only made in anticipation of a wide control of prices. Still, whether these forms of legislation are abandoned or not, we are told that concentration is bound to go forward in some way and, if this is so, price control will be found necessary for protecting the public interest. Abandoning the antitrust acts is only the recognition of something which has, in effect, already happened in important instances even if in devious ways. It may be essential that price controls should be set up in any case. It is doubly essential if we admit that added efficiency is to be had by further concentration and if we seek to encourage it. For otherwise the advantages of efficiency will result in corporate profits, but not in lower prices.

Congress, when its committees examined the industrial situation before deciding to authorize the Federal Trade Commission, saw clearly that the choice lay between the enforcement of competition and the institution of a series of controls which would include prices. The latter was talked about very freely. It was decided that the time had not yet come. But the years of experience which have passed since have allowed the situation to clarify. The patterns of industry are now more obvious; and the failure of all attempts to control by not controlling is also more obvious. The Federal Trade Commission has not succeeded in doing more than to throw light upon the situation; no betterment has resulted. A similar examination by Congress now would, one must conclude, leave that body much less certain that competition is the correct organizing principle.

If the time comes for a genuine consideration of price control as part of a new social policy, there will be considerable experience to draw upon. The reports of the war-time Price Fixing Committee will assist; the experience of State Public Utility Commissions will be available; and the Interstate Commerce Commission will furnish something of a pattern for modes of control in other industries. The rough outline of procedure is apparent: (1) a survey of normal needs for the commodity, (2) a survey of the means of producing it and the costs involved, and (3) the setting of a price calculated to bring just enough of it into the market.

The protection of buyers who are final consumers and of buyers who are to make use of goods in further production, also, as we have noted, fall into different categories. Consumers' prices would have to be fixed locally by agencies of a control board working through regional administrations. The prices of producers' goods—raw and semi-finished materials—would be part of the effort to prevent more powerful firms from exploiting weaker ones, and of regularizing interbusiness relations. It might be done, however, on a national scale from Washington by fixing maximums and differentials as was done with wheat in war time. These matters would have to be worked out in conjunction with careful factual surveys of situations; and facts cannot be anticipated. Because we have not seriously considered national self-control, the materials are lacking for an examination of the necessary administrative machinery. In any case, what have first to be considered are the policies of transition.

## 7. The Administration of Industry in Transition

What we need to do, in effect, is to furnish a means through which American business can achieve the purposes for which it is allowed to exist. But this mechanism must be surrounded by entirely adequate safeguards to ensure the full protection of those public interests which are likely to be neglected in business plans. Such a scheme is not, in its details, something that can be formulated easily and quickly. Those who have attempted it must be credited with this cautionary attitude. They recognize fully that difficult legal and administrative problems have to be met, and that the devices have to be of a sort to which business men will at first voluntarily agree and which at the same time contain no threat to the public.

A scheme formulated with these ends in view seems to anticipate that some governmental agency—for instance, the Federal Trade Commission or some agency of the Department of Commerce—should be empowered to issue certificates of convenience and necessity to industrial organizations on presentation of evidence of the affiliation of a certain percent of the productive facilities of any single industry.[2] The Commission or the Department, suitably organized for this purpose, would need to set up a classification of industries and to maintain a survey of consumption and production throughout the country as well as an estimate of probable markets abroad and needed imports.

The associations thus authorized would be expected to set up their own planning boards and central management devices for maintaining standards of competition and for controlling maximum prices and minimum wages. Ordinarily this management would function without outside interference except that on affiliation of several industrial groups a central organization of these associations would be set up to function as a mediating and integrating body for the coordination of the several industries' plans and policies respecting production, prices, division of markets, working conditions, and the like. This central body might be called the United States Industrial Integration

2. This is a substitute for Federal incorporation which may achieve most of the advantage without raising all of the problems, especially constitutional ones.

Board, and those for each industry the (Blank) Integration Association. On the central Board, consisting of directors suitably distributed among the affiliated industries, representatives of the government would sit.

The controlling body, it is conceived, would have powers of investigation and review of association policies with respect to security issues and prices. It would need to require common accounting systems, simplification of security issues, and the maintenance by the industry of fair prices, adequate wages, and decent working conditions; and what is equally important, it could impose arrangements for patent-pooling and for the conservation of efficiency. Subject to review by the courts, it would have the power to lay fines on corporations or members deductible from balances in the Industrial Reserve Fund. As a last resort, it might be able to require expulsion of members of associations or the revocation of enabling certificates.

The Industrial Reserve Fund, just mentioned, would be built up by an excise tax laid on the products of industry—say of 3 percent. The Fund would be administered by a Board having representatives from government fiscal authority as well as the controlling agency. The Fund would be divided annually into three parts: one-third would be returned to those industries which had adhered to the plan, in proportion to the tax yield from their products; one-third would be retained in the Fund until its size equaled perhaps twice the paid-in capital of the member industries, after which it could be drawn on for the payment of dividends to shareholders—and for that purpose only; one-third would be transferred to a wage-reserve fund set up separately, to be returned proportionately to those States which had set up schemes for unemployment insurance.

Each of these has a purpose. The first is to reward compliant industries and to compel adherence; the second is to furnish a safe and convenient substitute for the menacing reserve funds modern corporations have set up so extensively for themselves, and whose existence must necessarily defeat the general purpose for which they are set up; the third is intended to furnish a wider general base for unemployment reserves than can be attained by the State schemes which will probably be the first American approach to insurance. Aside from these thirds, there ought to be deducted from the fund, before division, the estimated budget of the control authority for a year ahead, thus removing this item of government expense from general appropriation.

Obviously the controlling body would need to learn much from its experience with the relations to be set up between itself and the associations under its jurisdiction. It ought not to be hampered in its work by too close definition of procedures and standards. It remains true, however, that in such a scheme, in two areas at least, there would need to be a public advocate: the allocation of capital and the regulation of prices. How far these two vital controlling functions could be left to the management of the associations themselves, it is so difficult to foresee that no suggestion seems to be offered. It is clear, however, that public representatives would need to have a part in shaping such policies as these. When necessary, they ought to have the final word.

In order to insure action in the public interest rather than against it, it is suggested that the three representatives of the controlling body sitting on the United

States Industrial Integration Board ought to have special powers and duties. Their duties would consist in the clear and definite transmission to the Board of the general plans for industry which are worked out by the government itself. These would concern consumption, production, the necessary allocation of capital, and prices. It would be the function of the Board to gather up and reconcile the plans of the various affiliated industries and to reconcile this general design with the independent one transmitted by the government through its representatives on the Board. Their powers would consist in recommendations of action. In instances of irreconcilability, the representatives would transmit information of the instance to the controlling body, which would then consider the invoking of appropriate sanctions, which would include publicity, fines, and expulsion.

In this way the initiation of planning would come up through affiliates to the Board of each association. Most of the work would take place in these central offices. Expansion and contraction, price policies, standards of wages, and working conditions would be worked out there in budgetary fashion quarterly. These proposed policies would be sent on to the Integration Board and there reconciled with each other and with the plan of the government. They would then be returned to the association Boards with appropriate changes on approval. These in turn would transmit information as to policies to be pursued to the affiliated businesses.

It is, I believe, a good educational principle that we learn by doing. In this matter of industrial integration and the persuasion of industries to function with longtime plans for themselves and for the public in view, what is more needed than anything else is a sufficiently adequate device so that a new beginning can be made. Given a start, a method of procedure, we can, unless we are dogmatic about administrative details, and unless we prove unwilling to compromise on unessentials, discover ways to achieve a balance of production and consumption and to protect all interests with a legitimate stake. This will not be a short and easy transition. But if it should be undertaken with energy and with an eye to escape from the distressing insecurities of the present, we should be able to see it through. It is not necessary, for preliminary analysis, to approve of any definite schemes. I have thought it useful, however, to explore one possible approach to a problem which most social theorists believe we are about to face. There is no commitment involved in exploration.

## 8. Public Policy

At the present stage of the development of our public policy, nothing is to be gained by going further into details. Perhaps enough has been said to indicate that the first long step to be made is the decision whether policy must be revised. Even this necessity has not yet become clear to Americans, partly because they have not understood the developments in technique which have been going on all around them, and partly because there are powerful and vociferous interests which do not favor change. Once this decision has been taken, however, there seems reason to believe that, by using already familiar instruments, what is necessary to be done will be readily possible. Our ingenuity has simply not been brought to bear on problems of control.

The simplification and generalization of our developing industrial technique for readier popular assimilation is much needed. Just to see that the dominant design of industrial patterns is an immense growth in the scale of operations, in correlation with a double concentration and elaboration of processes, brings the problem into sharper relief. And if we set over against this the dominant design of our public policy, which is the attempted enforcement of the universal petty conflict which was once characteristic of small-scale, one-man business, the separation of theory and reality becomes apparent. The reality is industry; the theory is public policy. We, who are interested in government as an instrument for making what we hope may be a better workers' world, will continue to press for an adjustment of theory to reality. What is of value to the human spirit lies somewhere beyond the limits of a scheme for achieving generally greater incomes. But these are bridges to the unknown.

We are forced to recognize, of course, that one of the first requisites of a good instrument is that it should have a certain double relevancy: (1) to the conditions in which it operates, and (2) to the purposes sought to be achieved. Neither of these has been conspicuously present in our political administration. The instrument with which we have to work is, to begin with, poorly suited to its purpose. A government made up as ours is, with the residual powers—upon which we must depend for control of industry, since no specific powers are granted to Washington in the instrument itself—vested in the States, must present especially difficult problems of a constitutional nature when industry overflows the State jurisdictions. This industry has done. The State cannot control; the nation is not permitted to do so. Such a situation is ideally suited to the defensive purposes of those who want nothing done. And the problem is made doubly difficult for those who do. For not only does the desirability of doing it have to be demonstrated, but also the ways in which it can be done, without constitutional limitations. Our reformers are faced with the necessity of using an antiquated instrument to accomplish their ends. This is the reason for what sometimes seem rather devious approaches to simple problems.

What is required in view of the nature of industry is a recognition of the desirability of large scale and of concentration correlated to elaboration. Such a recognition would cause us to abandon attempts to prevent association and to enforce conflict. But what is equally necessary is that the new powers which an industry, strengthened by this encouragement, would have must be assimilated to the public interest rather than used against it. It would also involve the protection of a number of vital interests which have been enumerated as consumers, weaker businesses, workers, farmers, and technicians. Some of these would be protected adequately with capital and price controls; but some, such as workers, farmers, and technicians, might need specially devised administrative bodies to care for their further and more specific interests.

Control, in this sense, would undoubtedly require that the Federal government should make good its superiority by knowing more about industry than industrialists do. This brings out a distinction it seems necessary to keep in mind: that there is a difference here between the individual sphere and the social sphere. Control bodies would not need to know more about a specific process than do those who are engaged in it;

that would be manifestly impossible. They need only to know more about the industry in general and about the relationships among industries than anyone business can. And since this is the field in which business has registered its greatest failure, we might reasonably expect to find it done better by some other agency. An industrial administration of some sort, being supreme in this field, might use its superior knowledge and power to devise a system of affairs in which each unit would be complementary to each other one, in which cooperation, rather than, as at present, conflict, should be the organizing principle. There are numerous contemporary thinkers who believe that only by such means can we ever achieve a favorable medium for the normal, untortured growth of the industrial arts, for the achieving of something approximating justice in industrial affairs, and for the acceptance of a governmental responsibility, already widely acknowledged, for the maintenance of living levels and the reconstruction of work.

## Thurman W. Arnold

## *The Bottlenecks of Business*

## I. The Basic Problem of Distribution

The purpose of this book is to explain to the consumer what can be done for him to increase the distribution of goods under our existing laws and by pursuing our traditional ideals of an economy of free and independent enterprise. It is written on the assumption that there is no substantial political group in the United States which will support drastic changes in our economic structure. We are committed to a system of distribution of goods through private enterprise. The success of that system depends upon the ability of the consumers of America to use the instruments of government which they have at hand to get the maximum distribution of goods in a free market.

The problem of the American consumer, who depends on private enterprise to give him goods at competitive prices, is intensified by the crisis in national defense. That crisis has created a gigantic new consumer, coming into our market with mass buying power and artificial credit, to compete with the ordinary American who wants food, clothes, and houses. It would appear, for the present at least, that we have plenty of goods to satisfy this new giant. He will cause men to be employed and purchasing power to be increased and some organizations may gain unprecedented riches. Yet if we do not understand the situation, or if we are unprepared to meet it, this new purchasing power and these new riches may hinder instead of help the American consumer. They may even create a permanent dislocation of our economy of distribution for the next twenty-five years.

What happened to the ordinary consumer in the boom which followed the outbreak of the war in 1914? When the war first broke out there was a drop in prices and general distress. Then came the war inflation which robbed productive industry for war boom industry, resulting in complete unbalance of prices. We were confronted with the spectacle of the Southern farmer going hat in hand to the newly-created millionaires and asking them for charity's sake to buy a bale of cotton.

There were no controls. Real wages went down one-third while thousands of new fortunes were made. Wilfred I. King estimated that in the United States alone enough money was transferred from the pockets of labor and consumers to the pockets of manufacturers and promoters to make forty thousand new millionaires.

There is no reason, in the nature of things, why this need happen again. We have somewhere around ten million unemployed—more men than in the entire Allied armies. We have vast reservoirs of idle capital. This is a colossal waste. Putting this labor and capital to work at anything, at least until there is an actual shortage of labor and productive capacity, should raise instead of lower the standard of living in this country, at 1east until there is an actual shortage of labor and productive capacity.

It is cheaper for the country to put idle labor and idle capital to work at something rather than to permit them to rot away through disuse. Skills disappear and capital is destroyed when we fail to put them to work. Therefore, the necessity of preparation for national defense, regrettable though it may be as compared to an ideal alternative, does have the hint of a silver lining, provided war industry is not permitted to destroy peace-time industry.

The problem we face on the eve of great expenditures for national defense is, therefore, not essentially different from the problem we faced during the depression when we had to spend huge amounts for relief and subsidies. We must see that these expenditures are made in a free market. We must see that the distribution of peace-time necessities of life, which are now produced by private industry, is not handicapped. More than ever today the American consumer needs protection against fixed prices and inefficient non-competitive methods of distribution. More than ever we need to guard against the private seizure of power over a free market. In order to better understand the problem that is ahead, and how to meet it, we should be familiar with the pattern of restraints that have been clogging the market in the past.

Most of the books in the past on the antitrust laws have been written with the idea that they are designed to eliminate the evil of bigness. What ought to be emphasized is not the evils of size but the evils of industries which are not efficient or do not pass efficiency on to consumers. If the antitrust laws are simply an expression of a religion which condemns largeness as economic sin they will be regarded as an anachronism in a machine age. If, however, they are directed at making distribution more efficient, they will begin to make sense, and, incidentally, they will also solve the problem of bigness wherever bigness is blocking the channels of trade.

A nation's economic wealth consists of its productive capacity. Its income consists of the goods and services which it is capable of getting around to consumers. When farmers and laborers cannot get goods, national income goes down. When national income goes down, it is harder to live in peace and it is also harder to prepare for national defense. National income is ordinarily given in terms of dollars, but this dollar value can only be given to goods or services that people can buy. Idle productive capital has no dollar value; it is a liability because it requires upkeep. Idle labor cannot produce national income; it is a liability because it requires relief. Goods which are unsalable lose their dollar value, and those who possess them become bankrupt. No one gets these dollars that the owner of the goods has "lost"; they simply go out of existence. At the same time the manufacturing plants which produce the goods that cannot be sold lose their dollar value. Their owners also become bankrupt. And the farms that produce the food which no one can buy become worth less than the mortgages even though they are better farms than they used to be.

The economic problem that faces an industrial democracy, therefore, in both war and peace is whether private enterprise is able to distribute to consumers the food, clothes, houses, and other commodities which they need. Theoretically, private enterprise can do it because competition always will force prices down to meet purchasing power. This theory is called the law of supply and demand. Let us see how it has been working since the great depression.

The Brookings Institution estimated that during the twelve-year period from 1922 to 1934 this country could have produced in goods and services $248 billion more than it did produce. This means that $8,000 in goods and services were withheld from each of our thirty million families. This is more than ninety percent of them could save in a lifetime. Such a situation seems senseless. It is a dangerous kind of waste because it advertises to the ordinary man in the street that our industrial economy is not efficiently distributing the goods which our engineers and technicians are able to produce through modern methods of mass production.

The history of distribution of goods in the United States since 1850 may be pictured by the following chart [omitted—eds.]. It shows the national income expressed in dollars which have been weighted against fluctuations in currency value. It is, therefore a shorthand way of expressing the amount of goods and services distributed each year since 1850.

This chart shows a constant increase in the material income of the American people from 1850 to the depression. The lines on the chart prior to the year 1920 do not show the intervening ups and downs because they have been figured in ten-year periods. The chart indicates that at the end of each of these ten-year periods the American people had more material income than in the preceding decade. During the war the income rose enormously in spite of the fact that war is supposed to be wasteful. It continued to rise until the depression. Then, for the first time in the history of America, in the face of plenty, national income dropped. The end of the chart shows our national income below the level of 1920 in spite of the fact that we have a much larger population and a greater productive capacity than we had twenty years ago. The chart gives us a picture of a system of distribution that has somehow gone wrong—that is not operating the way it used to operate. It is from such charts that radical economic planners get ammunition to support sweeping changes.

The same thing may be illustrated in another way by presenting a picture of the distribution of income among our thirty million families. The following chart [omitted—eds.], prepared by Theodore J. Kreps from figures compiled by the National Resources Committee, represents the best available data regarding the distribution of income with government aid eliminated. There is no way of checking the figures on this chart with anything approaching absolute accuracy. They represent the best guess that skilled men can make. But assuming that they are fifty percent inaccurate, the income distribution picture still looks like the Eiffel Tower.

The minimum on which a family of three can purchase a fair share of the goods advertised over the radio and in our better magazines is approximately $2,500 a year. Families with that income or over comprise only thirteen percent of our population, or about the population of the State of New York! The chart, therefore, shows that our productive plant, equipped to make goods for a country of 130 million people, can distribute its production only to thirteen percent of that population without some form of government aid. Under these circumstances it is not surprising that, when the wheels of industry start turning, it is only a short time before goods pile up on shelves and the wheels have to stop.

Figures and charts of this kind are compiled in abundance in the first volume of the hearings of the Temporary National Economic Committee. The general observations set out here are proved there with elaborate detail by distinguished economists. Ten years of experience since the beginning of the great depression have demonstrated that we have made extraordinary strides in invention and in the efficiency of organized production. It is the economic machinery of distribution which is stalled. And this raises the problem which puzzles American consumers today. To sum up, these charts show an economic machine which is either in reverse or which has brakes that are stronger than its engine.

Some people think that we can throw the machine away and buy a new one. The trouble with that notion is that there do not seem to be any new machines on the market in which the American people like to ride. There is nothing about the European models that appeals to us. Therefore, we are faced with the absolute of making our own machine run. We have got to fix it with the tools presently at hand.

## The Basic Problem

Broadly speaking, human society has found only two ways of distributing goods and services. One is the army system, by means of which a commanding officer passes out the goods in the supply house to the troops in proportion to their needs. The other is by a system of exchange in a free market. As organization increases, free exchange necessarily becomes more limited, so that neither the army system nor the free market system of distribution ever entirely disappears from any society. Even in the most pioneer society the State always has to distribute some goods and services to its citizens. And, on the other hand, even in the most highly organized army, the soldiers can trade their pocketknives and buy whiskey with their pay.

In a society where individual freedom is the prevailing ideal, the main method of distributing goods and services must be by free exchange in a free market. It is not a particularly orderly process. It is not a planned economy. Nevertheless, it is the only process which relies on the independence of the individual as a person rather than on his efficiency as a cog in a machine. It is the only process which does not become static by freezing at the top a dynasty of men who have the means of keeping new enterprise from coming to the surface. It is the American ideal because the existence of industrial democracy is the only basis on which political democracy can rest.

The maintenance of a free market, therefore, becomes the first concern of every political democracy. It is not a difficult problem in an agricultural economy where men can obtain the necessities of living by their own hard work and where each farm is an independent unit. It becomes more difficult in a machine age as mass production and distribution of necessities develop. The reason for this is that when industry becomes highly organized, it gains the power to control prices which the people must pay. The exchange of raw materials and services by unorganized groups for the products of organized industry becomes more and more a one-sided bargain. When this happens a farm problem always arises because the farmers cannot buy. Then an unemployment problem becomes acute because the manufacturers cannot sell. Then an investment problem appears because no one wants to put money in an enterprise that cannot sell its goods. Then the unorganized groups, who cannot exchange their raw materials and services for necessities of decent living, have to demand that the government buy these necessities for them. Then a budget-balancing problem takes the center of the stage and people begin to worry about taxes to pay for subsidies.

This has happened in every business civilization whenever prices were fixed by great industrial organizations so high that consumers could not buy. The bread and circuses given to the poor in Rome were the same kind of thing as relief and WPA theater projects are today. They were not given because politicians foolishly followed wrong economic principles. Government subsidies have poured out and always will pour out when the free exchange of goods and services for manufactured products breaks down.

This is what is happening in America today. Let us examine the economic situation which is back of farm subsidies and relief. The great mass of our population sell their goods, services, and labor in a competitive market. They buy their necessities in a controlled market. Thus our economic structure consists of two separate worlds. The first is a world of organized industry; the second is a world of small unorganized business men, farmers, laborers, and consumers. In the first world, there is the power to maintain high prices no matter how much the demand for the product falls off. When this power is exercised, purchasing power is curtailed, production drops, men are laid off, and this in turn lowers purchasing power and makes demand drop still further. A vicious downward spiral is set in operation. In the second world, unlimited competition still exists and cannot be controlled. In this world live the farmers, retailers, and small business men who supply the consumers with both goods and labor. Here, when the supply increases or the demand falls off, prices drop to the bottom, but the people go right on producing as much as the conditions of the market will permit. In the first world we have concentrated control, which makes possible high and rigid prices. These, in turn, lead to restriction of production and wholesale discharge of labor. In the second world, we find competition, low flexible prices, large production and labor standards often at starvation levels.[1]

1. The dividing line between these two worlds is not necesarily between big and little business. Small groups in little business often succeed in organizing to raise their own prices at the expense of distribution. The cumulative effect of a lot of little price-fixing organizations is as bad as a few big ones.

The trouble with the system is that the first of these worlds works at cross-purposes with the second. In the first world, organizations, great and small, keep up prices and layoff labor. The labor so laid off has no power to purchase the consumers goods furnished by the second world, but that world is not organized to restrict production and maintain high prices in the face of falling demand. Unmarketable surpluses therefore pi1e up.

In the business decline of 1937, our troubles were bid to the accumulation of huge inventories which could not be distributed. Industries had speeded up production and enlarged their productive capacity without any realization that price policies should be inextricably linked with productive capacity. Productive capacity was planned on a ten-year basis. Price policies were planned on a three-month basis. With the expanding market, most industries attempted, by raising their prices, not to distribute the most goods but to obtain the largest share of that expanding purchasing power. The result was that we became choked with our own wealth. We are coming to realize the absurdity of people going without goods because inventories of these very goods have become too large.

So, today, we are forced to face the price and distribution problem because the organizing genius of the American people will not tolerate a series of depressions which are caused principally by the fact that we have too much undistributed wealth. The American people will not submit to going without goods which they see piled up on every side of them simply because industrial management is unable to distribute the wealth which industrial technicians are able to produce in such quantities. We have the materials, the factories, the men and the money. The problem now is to unleash the productive forces for the benefit of consumers without taking the short and easy road to industrial autocracy.

The ordinary man has little understanding of economic structures. He can only understand what he sees in front of him. When he observes an industrial management which for no understandable reason is unable to distribute the goods that it makes, he turns to the government. Here, at least, there is practical relief, and he feels that he has nothing to lose. Preaching and denunciation of totalitarian systems of industrial control is as useless to stop this process as preaching against disease.

There are two ways of running industry to capacity and distributing all of its product. One is to establish conditions under which competitive independent industries can maintain themselves. The other is for the state to regulate the centralized industrial power which has been allowed to develop. The former method is represented by an economy like that of Sweden, where the government function is concerned with the means of giving the privileges of free and unrestrained competition to independent business. The latter method is represented roughly by the model of the collective states of Europe in which centralized industry is controlled by the iron hand of government and effective distribution of goods is thus insured.

The inevitable result of the destruction of competitive domestic markets by private combinations, cartels, and trade associations is illustrated by Germany today. Prior to the First World War that country had no antitrust law, but industrial self-regimentation was counterbalanced by a strong centralized government, ready to adopt necessary socialistic legislation. There was a practical compromise that worked.

In the depression that followed the war, a weak government in Germany permitted the self-regimentation of industries to proceed without restriction. That system of industrial concentration without public responsibility failed disastrously. Public discontent forced the enactment in 1923 of a decree similar in purpose to our antitrust laws. But unfortunately for Germany its tradition of free enterprise was too weak. The law was never enforced. The year 1927 witnessed the last gasp of free enterprise in Germany. An economic commission was appointed to study the monopoly problem. It sat for three years and produced nearly forty volumes. The activities of this commission are interesting because the arguments for the cartel system were identical with the arguments now being used to oppose enforcement of our antitrust laws. First, there was the theory that enforcement of the antitrust laws created uncertainty in business. Then the socialist planners of Germany argued that out of their enforcement no planned economy could result. The trade associations insisted on protection against the chiseler. The unions believed that higher wages would come from large and prosperous cartels. So the commission ended on the note of letting business combinations alone.

With this encouragement German business regimentation drifted to its logical conclusion. Industrial Germany became an army with a place for everyone, and everyone was required to keep his place in a trade association or a cartel. Here was arbitrary power without public control and regimentation without public leadership. That power, exercised without public responsibility, was constantly squeezing the consumer. There was only one answer. Germany was organized to such an extent that it needed a general and Hitler leaped into power. Had it not been Hitler it would have been someone else. When a free market was destroyed, state control of distribution had to follow.

In discussing these questions we should remember that there is nothing new about this problem of restraints of trade. It is as old as business civilization. From the days of ancient Corinth down through the business empires of Venice and Florence to modem times, the disappearance of a free market for consumers has been the first step in the decline of every business civilization,—the beginning of its absorption into a centralized government.

Inventory booms and artificial surpluses in times of real scarcity are not new. They have been intensified by the machine age, but they can be observed in the decadence of business civilization long before mechanized production was dreamed of. They appear whenever private monopoly chokes off its home markets. The most convenient modern illustration is again found in Germany. Prior to Hitler, food was relatively scarce in Germany. Manufactured products were relatively plentiful. Indeed, at one time it was feared that the German industrial machine would flood the world with cheap goods under pressure to pay reparations. Yet in this situation of plentiful manufactured products and scarce food, a farm problem developed. The farmer found that he could not exchange his produce on a parity basis for the products of industry which he needed. An unemployment problem followed in spite of the fact that there was a vast reconstruction job to do and not enough labor to do it to. The consumers of Germany woke up, and there is much evidence of their activity during the decade from 1923 to 1933 to establish competitive prices in a free internal market.

But the movement failed, perhaps because there were so many economic planners in Germany—so many believers in the rationalized state—that it was impossible to gain wide acceptance for the idea of forcibly preventing the growth of the great cartel, or to devise any method of checking it.

The disappearance of competitive enterprise in Germany and the rise of a powerful industrial autocracy occurred under pressures which we have never had to face in this country. And yet we can observe a few disquieting symptoms of the same sort of process in this country. In 1920 the American farmer got 50¢ of each dollar spent by the American consumer. He was spending that 50¢ to buy manufactured products. Today he gets only 30¢ of each consumer's dollar. He cannot buy the same proportion of manufactured goods. He has lost forty percent of his proportionate purchasing power. That loss expressed in dollars is $1,800,000,000 each year. The manufacturer did not get this money. It has simply disappeared. This means that the farmer cannot buy so many goods, and therefore less manufactured products will be distributed to farmers. How is the farmer making up that loss? He is getting a $1,000,000,000 subsidy from the government. But he is still $800,000,000 short if we keep to these rough figures. And the budget is unbalanced. And everyone is beginning to worry about the government taking over the distribution of goods which should be the function of private enterprise.

At this point the economic thinker can go in one of two directions. He can begin to talk about a general planned economy and start the long struggle with private enterprise, which naturally does not wish to subject itself to government dictation. The result of that struggle will be the chaos of last ditch battles when general economic planning is thrown against the stubborn resistance of private enterprise. He will be in for years of struggle, legislative sabotage, judicial controversies, and the bitterness of extreme theoretical positions. We have been going through much of that chaos in the past eight years. If, however, limited planning for specific industrial problems is thrown against a broad background of free enterprise, he can argue its merits in terms of the particular need of a particular industry. Some planning is unquestionably necessary. We are getting used to the idea that in certain areas the State must step in and perform functions which private enterprise cannot effectively do. But this limited planning for particular needs can only be made to work if competitive forces are freely allowed to distribute the maximum of the goods and services on which we live.

## II. How Restraints on Trade Affect Your Standard of Living

### Restraints of Trade in Peace Time

Generalizations about a free market and restraints of trade have become a drug on the market. What consumers really want to know more concretely is how the evils of monopoly affect their daily lives. The best way of presenting that picture is by giving a kaleidoscopic series of actual examples. In this way the reader may observe the cumulative effects of such restraints in destroying free trade between the states. He can see how the unbalance of prices which they cause creates the need for relief and subsidies. He will understand how government spending, imposed on a controlled market, ends by raising prices still higher and thus compels more spending.

Let us start with the distribution of automobiles. Here is the industry which has been the most competitive in its growth and, therefore, the most efficient of any in our economy in distributing goods to the consumer. It has made the automobile a more widely distributed product than decent houses. It has changed motor fuel from a luxury to a necessity. Let us examine how a series of growing restraints in the field of motor distribution can hamper the distribution of other commodities such as food.

We will begin with the man who lives across the road from my house just outside Washington. He has been having a hard time for the past few years. He has a few acres, but he is always behind on the rent because he has no cash income. His cow and pigs do not give him a balanced diet. His children are not getting an even start in this world. His family is poorly clothed and his house is in bad condition. He is a burden on the State because from time to time he has to rely on relief or on charity.

For a while he was fortunate enough to have a job on a construction project. He saved fifty dollars. One day I was astounded to find that he had paid fifty dollars down on a shiny, new, second-hand car, priced at $400. The balance was on installments. I felt indignant at such improvidence. If the poor act like this how can they expect the taxpayers to help them? I therefore considered it my duty as a citizen and a taxpayer to tell him what I thought.

He replied, "I had to buy that car because I am losing my job." This answer seems absurd until we analyze what is back of it. When he lost his job he had to apply for relief. He told me that he would be willing enough to save his fifty dollars for a rainy day if he could use it to eke out the miserable standard of food and clothing for people on relief. "But they won't let me on relief so long as I have fifty dollars," he explained. "They will let me on relief if I have a car that isn't paid for. Anyway, I can get more for my fifty dollars by buying this car than if I buy anything else."

Of course he will never pay for that car. Sooner or later it will be taken back, when there is some other place to put it. It will absorb this man's fifty dollars and such installments as he can pay. Then it will take up someone else's thirty dollars and next a third person's twenty-five dollars. On its way to the junk yard it will act like a piece of blotting paper, soaking up money that should go to the producers of food and clothing, competitive industries which are trying to sell their goods in an organized market.

But how is it possible for a man who can't pay for a car to buy one? The answer is that great finance companies issue a kind of fiat currency, called installment paper, which can be discounted at banks. Back of this paper is a long procession of cars on their way to the junk yard, but each individual car is so far away from the promissory note which it secures that nobody knows or cares who has it. The second-hand cars support the automobile installment currency just as the gold buried in the Kentucky hills supports the national currency.

Everybody believes it is there—and that confidence is sufficient.

There is another important angle. Suppose you offer cash for one of these second-hand cars. You will find that ability actually to pay for the car gives you no advantage over the man who cannot pay for it. There is practically no competitive market in second-hand cars for those who want to buy. The whole machine is geared to keep up the price of second-hand cars. Installment telling is an important factor in keeping up the price of second-hand cars. If the cars had to be sold for cash, obviously prices would have to come down to move them. Installment sales at high prices are desired by the industry in preference to cash sales. The reason is that if second-hand cars were sold at really competitive prices they would sell so low that they would compete with new cars. This would mean that the prices of new cars would have to come down or else the automobile companies would have to get out a cheaper and more efficient car—a new "tin lizzie" that would get you there and get you back with less fuel.

Reliable automobile engineers tell me that it is possible to make an excellent light car to sell for $300 which will go forty miles on a gallon of gasoline. Such a car would give the consumer cheaper transportation. It would also give the farmer a greater portion of the consumer's dollar (because consumers would then have more money to spend for things the farmer raises), so that it would take less government subsidies to keep the farmers afloat. But such a free market would cause a loss of millions to the great automobile Manufacturers by forcing them to change their present highly organized processes in order to put out the $300 car.

Therefore, it is only natural that the automobile manufacturers should try to put a floor under the price of second-hand cars so that they will not absorb the cash which goes into new cars.

I do not wish to raise here any question as to the legality of combinations which have secured for automobiles such strategic advantages in the national market that the poor go without proper diet and housing to buy them.[2] Nor do I wish to blame the automobile for a situation which no one in the industry intentionally created. (Railroads are now selling vacation tickets on installments.) I use the automobile industry only to illustrate how domination of the market in the distribution of one important product may finally reach a state where it unbalances our entire distribution system. The automobile industry has grown up under free competitive forces. That growth has been marked by efficiency of production and distribution. It is now in a position of power where the balance wheel of competition has become less effective. General Motors, today, is reaching out toward market domination in every type of automobile, in refrigerators, and in motor fuel. This constant expansion is accompanied by a like increase of its already vast powers over consumer finance. It is taking mortgages on the consumers'

2. The question of the legality of the control of finance companies by automobile manufacturers was raised indirectly in the criminal prosecution in which Ford, Chrysler, and General Motors were indicted on the charge of coercing dealers to use exclusively the finance company affiliated with the manufacturer. Ford and Chrysler entered into a decree in which they agreed to abandon their control of financing under certain protections against impositions by loan sharks. General Motors declined to enter into such a decree. It was convicted of violating the antitrust laws at South Bend, Indiana. The case is now on appeal. If a conviction is sustained, the Government expects to bring a suit to dissolve the combination of General Motors and the General Motors' finance company. Until the Supreme Court decides the case, it is impossible to state the law with any finality.

dollars of the future. How many such mortgages may be taken without unreasonably restraining trade?

The determination of that question is the function of the antitrust laws. In this situation an antitrust investigation would compel a choice between two policies. The first policy would be to attack in court as unreasonable the power over consumer finance now exercised which gives the motor industry such advantages over distribution. The second policy would be to refer the situation to Congress in order to develop consumer finance in other lines so that home building would be on a competitive basis with automobiles. Because it compels that choice, an antitrust investigation is the best method for focusing attention upon an industry whose power is approaching the danger point. It compels us to devise remedies for such situations not in the abstract but case by case in the light of the particular facts of each industry.

But there is another reason why even the efficient and reasonable use of enormous size and power must be watched, and that is to prevent others from using such an industry as the springboard from which to exploit the consumer. With this in mind, let us look at the oil industry from which the man across the road must immediately buy since after he has once bought his car gasoline becomes a necessity.

Therefore, when gasoline becomes a necessity control of the market is in effect the power to tax. The poor will go without a proper diet in order to ride. The lords of the gasoline market can take away cash income from the farmer and send him to the government begging for subsidies (which he must spend for more gasoline), simply putting a floor under the price of motor fuel.

Suppose, therefore, we examine the marketing of motor fuel which the man across the road must buy. We find that the distribution of 85 percent of all the motor fuel in the United States has been controlled by a combination of the Ethyl Corporation and the refiners. Here we may speak more positively about the illegality of the combination (in which General Motors had a part) because it has been recently condemned by the Supreme Court of the United States. It was worked in the following way:

The Ethyl Corporation was jointly owned by the Standard Oil Company of New Jersey, the General Motors Corporation, and the Du Pont interests. It had a patent on a fluid called "Ethyl" which made gasoline much more efficient for high compression engines. To make ordinary anti-knock motor fuel (called regular gasoline) required only one gallon of this patented fluid for forty-two hundred gallons of unpatented gasoline.

The Ethyl Corporation got its profits by selling the fluid, but it also had a patent on the motor fuel made by mixing the patented fluid with ordinary gasoline. Thus it was able to control the distribution of 4200 gallons with one gallon of Ethyl fluid. Under this patent it gave away free of charge to 123 refiners the right to make and sell this motor fuel. The refiners agreed in return that they would sell only to persons who were licensed by the Ethyl Corporation. The Ethyl Corporation then followed a policy of refusing to license those who did not allow the "marketing policies and posted prices" of the major oil companies or their market leaders. Thus was the system of distribution controlled.

There was also direct price fixing. The refiners agreed that they would establish a fixed differential of two cents per gallon in price between regular and high test gasoline. The difference in cost is much less than that. In this way the patent was used to maintain an open price-fixing scheme which took away money which might have been spent for farm products and gave it to the refiners.

The decision declaring that the patent licensing system of the Ethyl Corporation was illegal had far reaching effects because the same method of eliminating competitors was familiar throughout American industry. Patents were used to fix prices and control the whole distribution of a commodity. There are 153 patents on one type of wallboard used in building houses. The American Telephone and Telegraph Company controls 15,000 patents. The General Electric Company controls between 8,000 and 9,000 patents. The money which the government spends for war materials is spent in a series of industries where prices are controlled by a similar use of patents.

Let us see how this same type of patent control works in another field—the spectacle industry. There is a patent on a spectacle frame which is in common use. Through that patent the price to the consumer of both frames and lenses is controlled. The device was the same as that used by the Ethyl Corporation, i.e., to refuse to license distributors who want to cut prices.

There is no economic reason why the ten-cent stores should not sell spectacles. The argument is made that it is necessary to the health of the public that good optometrists be employed. However, Woolworth's is in as good a financial position to hire a good optometrist as is anyone else. The fact is that merchants who are willing to distribute spectacles cheaply have been unable to get hold of the best type of product. The only spectacles which they could sell were made from inferior Japanese lenses with inferior frames.

Spectacles are a necessity. It is estimated that 21 million people in the United States need them. The tax on low income groups by fixing the price of spectacles is enormous. And again it is also a tax on the farmer because the family of $1,500 a year who pays $10 too much for a pair of spectacles must take it out of the budget for diet or for clothes.

It seems a far cry from spectacles to Ethyl gasoline. Yet the decision of the case against the Ethyl Corporation led directly to a reduction of the cost of spectacles in Washington. The story is told in two full-page advertisements which appeared in the Washington Daily News on April 19 and June 3, 1940 shortly after the decision in the Ethyl Case.

The first advertisement [offered eyeglass frames for "$7.50 complete. You pay no more than this low price."].

A week after this advertisement, the dealer received a call and was told to stop cutting prices. He complained to the Department of Justice. Shortly after that four indictments were handed down. Then followed a second full-page advertisement [which declared "'SENSATIONAL EXPOSE' BY U.S. GOVERNMENT Verifies Claim That Here You Get the Best Glasses and Pay only $7.50."].

Such situations are easy to deal with if there is an organization in the Antitrust Division able to take care of complaints, and to watch the distribution of the principal necessities of living. If that organization is on the job ripples of one antitrust investigation will spread in all directions. Offhand there seems to be as little connection between the price of gasoline and the price of hosiery as there was between gasoline and spectacles, and yet the revolutionary decision of the Supreme Court of the United States in the Ethyl Case had the following interesting results in the distribution of hosiery.

The Du Pont interests are one of the principal owners of the Ethyl Corporation. They have also developed a new thread called Nylon which they control by patents. It is supposed to make a better stocking than has ever been made before. At the time the Ethyl decision was handed down, Du Pont was proposing by a patent licensing system to control the price at which stockings made from Nylon would be sold. If Nylon hose fulfills expectations, it may revolutionize the stocking industry. Other processes may become obsolete. Capital will be lost. Men will lose their jobs. Such technological change in the long run will work to distribute more goods provided the savings of the new process are passed, on to the consumer. It may mean a temporary loss of capital and wages in the industry made obsolete by the new product, but the farmer and the laborer will gain in the long run because a smaller proportion of the dollars consumers spend will go for stockings. Therefore, the man across the road can get a better diet and make his house warmer for the winter even though his wife insists on silk stockings. Unorganized industry will have a better chance to get a part of the consumer's dollar than before the invention was made.

But suppose that Nylon does succeed in destroying the manufacturers of other stockings without distributing the savings to consumers. The farmer will still have to pay almost as much for his wife's stockings. He won't have any extra money to buy her a new dress. And the people who made the old type of stockings and have been put out of business can no longer buy his farm products. This is exactly what the Du Pont Company proposed to do. After the Ethyl decision and at the suggestion of the Department of Justice the Du Pont Company voluntarily dropped its proposed plan of control. It was a simple case of policing economic traffic without the necessity of calling anyone to court, made possible because the Antitrust Division had an economic section on the job, watching the development of key industries. Suppose that these men had not been available. On the 15th of May, 1940, the licenses would have gone into effect. If complaint had been made years later, after the lines of control had been consolidated and vested interests had become entrenched, innocent investors might have suffered. The moving picture cartel grew up under government neglect. It is going to take years of expensive litigation and loss to stockholders to straighten it out.

But there is another aspect to price fixing which few people realize. It does not necessarily mean more profits because it creates wasteful and more expensive distribution. When great organizations succeed in putting a floor under prices, they still compete with each other for the greatest share of the market, without dropping prices.

The competition takes the form of adding unnecessary luxuries to the distribution system. This raises its cost. It forces a luxury system of distribution on low income groups.

Take the oil companies as an example. The major oil companies aided by the Ethyl Corporation had put a floor under prices. There is no difference in motor fuels because they had become standardized. Competition has become a race to see which company could put out the most expensive hokum. Millions have been spent in advertising different brands that were in fact one and the same. Filling stations more luxurious than the homes of most of the customers appeared on every corner. Maps were given away free. Unnecessary services were added. Men were hired to smile at poor customers and say "Happy Motoring." All this meant that a greater share of the customer's dollar was going into gasoline. The government relief checks filled the gap and helped pay for that hokum.

The effect on the efficiency of distribution was this:—On an average throughout the country major costs of both refining and transportation have been 6 cents a gallon. The average cost of getting the gas through ten feet of hose into your car has been 6 cents a gallon. Thus the savings from an efficient technological process were all absorbed by a wasteful system of distribution.

They were not passed on to the consumer.

Take tobacco as another example. There is no price competition among the companies dominating the industry. There is plenty of competition at rigid prices. This means that most tobacco advertising is expensive hokum. Cigarettes have become a necessity. Yet the ten-cent cigarette packet cannot get a foothold in a market where half the family incomes are under $1,000 a year.

Let us turn from the things the man across the road must buy and look at an example of a great new enterprise trying to get a chance to sell more modern and better equipment in a controlled market.

Within the last few years the design of sleeping cars has improved enormously, partly through the ideas of a new competitor of Pullman, the Budd Manufacturing Company. In a competitive market Pullman would have been compelled to scrap its old equipment in order to compete with Budd. But Pullman has a virtual monopoly on the operation of sleeping cars, and it is able to force the railroad to use its old equipment by threatening withdrawal of all sleeping car service if the railroads themselves buy new equipment from Budd.[3] This is a familiar monopoly device. It resembles block booking in movies, or full line forcing in the liquor industry. It was effective in keeping Pullman cars of obsolete design in service. However, we are concerned here with the economic effect of throttling a new competition in the car field. The continuance of the old equipment made it unnecessary for the Pullman Company to manufacture new cars until the old ones had worn out. It prevented Budd from hiring more labor to make better cars. It relieved Pullman of the necessity

3. In July 1940 an antitrust proceeding was begun against the Pullman Company in the United States District Court in Philadelphia charging generally the facts set out in this paragraph.

of hiring more labor to build cars to compete with Budd. The labor that was not hired could not buy houses or food. Taxpayers had to dig up to keep it on WPA projects or relief.

This is only a single example of the kind of thing that happens over and over again in great industries. Let the reader use his imagination as to the cumulative effect of the repetition of this kind of restraint of trade throughout our economy. It is easy to prevent if there is an adequate force to patrol the road—but if it is let alone it grows like weeds in a tropical garden.

# 7

# Antitrust After Populism

## Introduction

BY HERBERT HOVENKAMP

One paradox of antitrust history was that just as it attained greater power as a regulator of industry structure and conduct it largely fell out of the public focus. The early decades of federal antitrust enforcement were characterized by popular outcries against monopoly and big business, and by presidential platforms such as those in the 1912 election that included antitrust reform as a major plank. Antitrust promised to preserve a vision of American life that valued small business, free labor, and local control. During the late nineteenth and early twentieth centuries antitrust was not simply the expression of an economic policy. It also channeled public moral outrage against vast aggregations of power, maldistribution of wealth, unfair business conduct, and what appeared to be the declining fortunes of the laboring class. In an earlier era the same moral fervor had propelled political rage against the steamboat, bridge, slaughterhouse, and railroad monopolies, as well as state corporation laws obsessed with keeping business corporations under close state control. The same popular outrage also led the Progressives to their black-and-white depictions of big business that persisted all the way through the history writing of the 1960s and 1970s. The Progressives characterized the industrialists of the Gilded Age, such as John D. Rockefeller, Andrew Carnegie, Jay Gould, J. P. Morgan, and Leland Stanford as "robber barons." The journalists who exposed them were called "muckrakers," and they called New Jersey the "traitor state" for succumbing to the wishes of national corporations. Skilled politicians such as Theodore Roosevelt and Woodrow Wilson, and later Franklin Delano Roosevelt, picked up on these concerns. Many of the great early antitrust cases were brought against robber baron companies, including Standard Oil, U.S. Steel, American Tobacco, and many railroads.

The fervor of the popular antitrust movement was also characterized by a great deal of technical ambiguity and a stunning lack of visible achievement.[1] The populists and later the

1. See, e.g., Walter Adams, "Dissolution, Divorcement, Divestiture: The Pyrrhic Victories of Antitrust," 27 *Ind.L.J.* 1 (1951).

Progressives tended to see maldistribution of wealth, small business failures, unfair practices, impure food and drugs, low wages and harsh working conditions all as manifestations of the same problem, namely, big business. This moral urge explains the early antitrust preoccupation with moral categories drawn from tort law, such as intent. By the end of World War II, however, Judge Learned Hand could proclaim that the law of monopolization should "disregard any question of intent," looking only at technical analysis of market power and anticompetitive effects.[2]

More fundamentally, however, the American hostility against big business and defense of small business gave way to other realities. Many more Americans came to work for large firms. For the most part, bigger companies paid more and provided better benefits. Although the owners of small business may still prefer more antitrust aggressiveness against bigger companies, they constituted a shrinking portion of the political landscape.[3]

Richard Hofstadter (1916–1970), one of the greatest American social and intellectual historians in the middle twentieth century, wrote an obituary for the antitrust movement in the mid-1960s.[4] Ironically, at the time of his writing the U.S. government enforcement agencies and the Supreme Court were setting out on the most expansive antitrust agenda in the history of the antitrust laws, with an aggressive policy against even relatively minor mergers, virtual per se illegality for vertical restraints, and broad enforcement of the Robinson-Patman Act against even minor price discriminations in industries where monopoly was hardly possible.[5] For the most part, however, the Supreme Court was not responding to a public campaign against big business. Rather, it was giving effect to the economic ideology of structuralism, which offered a much more technical rationale for limiting the power of large firms. As Hofstadter observed, we had gone from a movement without antitrust prosecutions to antitrust prosecutions without a movement. Antitrust became much more important as an economic movement than as a social and political movement.

Like many great American reform movements, including gold vs. silver, immigration, prohibition, tariffs, and more recently health care, what starts out as a popular movement ends up being woven into the enormous fabric of American government policy and bureaucracy. More often than not it functions much better in that position, largely invisible to most of the public. That development may not be so ironic. Once the public believes that a problem has been solved or has become irrelevant, public fervor naturally subsides. In this case, Hofstadter argued, two things happened. First, by the 1950s big business had come to fit much more comfortably into the landscape of American public opinion than it had during

2. *United States* v. *Aluminum Co.*, 148 F.2d 426, 431 (2d Cir. 1945).

3. See Wyatt Wells, *Antitrust and the Formation of the Postwar World* (2002).

4. Richard Hofstadter, "What Happened to the Antitrust Movement," in *The Paranoid Style in American Politics and Other Essays* 188 (1967). The essay originally appeared under the title "What Happened to the Antitrust Movement: Notes on the Evolution of an American Creed," in *The Business Establishment* 113 (Earl F. Cheit, ed., 1964).

5. E.g., *Northern Pacific Railway Co.* v. *United States*, 356 U.S. 1 (1957); *Brown Shoe Co.* v. *United States*, 370 U.S. 294 (1962); *United States* v. *Loew's, Inc.*, 371 U.S. 38 (1962); *Utah Pie Co.* v. *Cont'l Baking Co.*, 386 U.S. 685 (1967). See generally Thomas E. Kauper, "The 'Warren Court' and the Antitrust Laws: of Economics, Populism, and Cynicism," 67 *Mich.L.Rev.* 325 (1968).

the populist and Progressive eras, and even between the wars. Second, antitrust became much more technical and began to speak the language of economists. He was clearly right. By the time Hofstadter wrote, antitrust talk in political speeches and campaign platforms had greatly diminished, but economists had moved from a position of broad skepticism at the turn of the century to considerable aggressiveness, as recognized in the structuralism of the 1950s and 1960s.[6]

Since Hofstadter wrote, several significant things have happened. First, antitrust has pulled back from the enforcement aggressiveness of the 1960s, thanks in part to the influence of the Chicago School but perhaps even more to a generally more conservative Supreme Court. Second, writing in the 1960s Hofstadter proclaimed private antitrust enforcement to be largely a failure, but he was in fact standing at the beginning of a dramatic expansion of antitrust, particularly of private antitrust actions. Third, Hofstadter was able to describe antitrust as a uniquely American institution, but today under the name "competition law" it has achieved popularity and even the quality of a popular movement in nations around the world, from Western Europe to former Soviet bloc countries and China.

Fourth, Hofstadter's essay tends to describe the antitrust movement as a conflict between big business and small business, a rhetoric that has largely disappeared from antitrust discourse. Today antitrust rhetoric is all about the welfare of consumers vis-à-vis sellers large and small who seek high prices by monopoly or collusion. Although a few of us are owners of large businesses and many more own small businesses, *all* of us are consumers. Ironically, the public lost its fervor just as antitrust was about to develop "consumer welfare" as its defining purpose.

## Richard Hofstadter

## What Happened to the Antitrust Movement?

[Note: This essay, which at first carried the subtitle "Notes on the Evolution of an American Creed," was written for a conference on the political and social environment of American business, made possible by the Ford Foundation and held on the Berkeley campus of the University of California in January 1964. The papers, written for the conference by a half-dozen authors, were published in *The Business Establishment* (New York, 1964), edited by Earl Cheit, who organized the conference. The version that appears here is substantially revised. A portion appeared also in *Commentary*, August 1964.]

### I

The antitrust movement is one of the faded passions of American reform. Historians have always been interested in the old romance, but with remarkable unanimity and an uncharacteristic lack of realism, they have neglected to tell us what happened when it was over. The writers of our general history books deal with the antitrust issue when

6. See Chapter Ten of this volume and Daniel A. Crane, "Technocracy and Antitrust," 86 *Tex.L.Rev.* 1159 (2008).

they tell of the rise of the great corporations and the passing of the Sherman Act and then, again, in discussing antitrust sentiment in the Progressive era and the enactment of further regulatory laws. Most of them touch on it briefly once more when they take up the New Deal antitrust revival, Thurman Arnold, and the T.N.E.C. [Temporary National Economic Committee]. Then, for the most part, they drop the subject; the student or the general reader must study law, economics, or business administration to become aware that the antitrust enterprise has more significance in contemporary society than it had in the days of T.R. or Wilson, or even in the heyday of Thurman Arnold.

Presumably the historians drop the subject of antitrust at or around 1938 not because they imagine that it has lost its role in our society but because after that point it is no longer the subject of much public agitation—in short, because there is no longer an antitrust movement. The intensity of public concern is, of course, a poor guide for historians, but here their neglect embodies a certain self-protective wisdom. They ignore antitrust for the same reason the public ignores it: it has become complex, difficult, and boring. In any case, the intricacies, both legal and economic, of regulating monopoly and competition are intricacies of a sort the historian is ill equipped to handle. It is simpler for him to sweep the whole thing under the carpet, and retire, along with the general public, from the baffling maze of technical refinements which the lawyers and economists have created.

Perhaps, at the risk of oversimplifying a little, the source of the problem can be put in this paradox: once the United States had an antitrust movement without antitrust prosecutions; in our time there have been antitrust prosecutions without an antitrust movement. In its day the antitrust movement had such consequences for our political and intellectual life that no historian who writes about the period 1890–1940 can safely ignore it. But the antitrust enterprise, as an institutional reality, now runs its quiet course without much public attention, and we lose sight of it. In failing to take more cognizance of its work, the historians are missing one of the most delicious minor ironies of our reform history and one of the most revealing facets of our institutional life. In the very years when it lost compelling public interest the antitrust enterprise became a force of real consequence in influencing the behavior of business.

For a long time liberal historians held to a kind of mythological history of the antitrust experience which, though it was not entirely false at any point, ended somehow in being entirely misleading. Antitrust, as an ideology and a movement of reform, always contrasted so sharply with its actual achievements in controlling business that it tempted our powers of satire. The conventional history went something like this: In 1890, as a largely meaningless and cynical gesture to appease public sentiment, an ultra-conservative Congress passed the Sherman Antitrust Act. The act was couched in such vague terms as to confirm our doubts that those who passed it expected that it could ever be enforced. Its early history fully warranted such doubts. From the beginning it was rendered a dead letter by administrative neglect and judicial hostility. Though it had little effect on the big business firms that were supposed to be its main object, it was used with greater success against labor unions. By the time Theodore

Roosevelt took office, when the Sherman Act was little more than ten years old, it had become all too clearly a charade behind which the consolidation of big business, notably accelerated between 1898 and 1904 went on apace. It was easy and amusing to debunk the reputation of T.R. as a trustbuster when one considered the infrequency and superficiality of his prosecutions, as well as his own doubts about the value of the whole enterprise, and to compare his robust rhetoric with the comic and pathetic image of the Antitrust Division of the Justice Department sallying out against the combined might of the giant corporations with a staff of five lawyers and four stenographers.

Subsequent statutory efforts under Wilson to strengthen regulation of monopolistic conduct, whatever one is to say of their value and the intent behind them, had to be recounted by the historians with a full sense of the denouement in mind. And the denouement required us to say that the antitrust effort went down the drain with the attempt to organize industry for the First World War; that the ensuing saturnalia of reaction during the 1920's, another period of business consolidation, undid the Wilsonian reforms—indeed, that the Federal Trade Commission was converted from an agency to control business into an agency controlled by business. Finally the revival of antitrust under F.D.R., the creation of the Temporary National Economic Commission, and the installation of Thurman Arnold's reforms seemed to be largely a movement of desperation, a return to the old antitrust charade, on the part of an administration which had exhausted its capacity to reform and was having indifferent results in its efforts to bring about recovery. The very appointment of Thurman Arnold as head of the Antitrust Division—a man whose books had effectively ridiculed the antitrust laws as a facade behind which the concentration of American industry could go on unimpeded—seemed to underline perfectly the whole comedy of the antitrust enterprise. And here, for the most part, as I have observed, the standard history of antitrust breaks off, perhaps with a few words about the difficulties Arnold confronted, and how his honest efforts were circumvented during the Second World War.

Without attempting to subvert the elements of truth in this version of antitrust history, it seems important to take account of certain additions to the story. First, it seems fair to say that while there was some impatient cynicism present in 1890 when the Sherman Act was passed, there was puzzlement as well, an honest if ineffectual concern with the problems of size and monopoly, and genuine doubts about the proper means of solving them. The general language of the Sherman Act may be looked upon as a broad enabling measure, which at least some men hoped would be followed by statutory and administrative advances. What has customarily been said of the lax enforcement that followed needs little qualification, except to add that the difficulties involved were the difficulties inherent in the subject as well as in the relatively conservative and circumspect attitudes taken by the Progressive Presidents and their advisers. They were living in a society that wanted to reap the benefits of large-scale enterprise, as well as to prevent the evils of monopolization; and on the whole, despite the confident pronouncements they found it desirable to make in political campaigns, men like T.R. and Wilson were aware that they did not know how to arrive at a quick and satisfactory solution to the problem. Whatever else may be said about all the seemingly empty and futile rhetoric about monopoly and bigness in the Progressive era, it did serve to keep alive the salutary American fear of excessive market power.

Something more must also be said about the antitrust revival under Franklin Roosevelt and Thurman Arnold. Viewed in a very fiat time perspective, Roosevelt's 1938 message on monopoly capitalism, the T.N.E.C., and Arnold's prosecution may be set down as having originated out of administrative desperation and may be regarded as substantial failures. But, in the longer perspective, they mark the true beginning of effective antitrust action, for it was the efforts begun at this time—not to speak of new personnel Roosevelt brought into the federal judiciary—that created the social and legal climate in which something could be done. The 1940's can be seen retrospectively as a watershed in the history of antitrust jurisprudence. Today, anybody who knows anything about the conduct of American business knows that the managers of the large corporations do their business with one eye constantly cast over their shoulders at the Antitrust Division, and that the antitrust enterprise has gone far to make up for its inability to reverse business concentration by considerable successes in affecting business conduct. Antitrust has won its spurs as a useful approach to the problems of large-scale enterprise, and in the Western world as a whole it is gaining acceptance. Its successes in America have aroused some emulation since the Second World War both in Britain and in France, and antitrust enforcement has reached a rudimentary stage in the Common Market.

## II

The history of antitrust may be divided into three phases. In the first, from about 1890 to 19l4—the era of the founding fathers of antitrust—the opening steps were taken, in statutes and in the courts, to define what form the antitrust efforts of the federal government might take and to see how they would work. The great outburst of business consolidation quickened antitrust sentiment, which was strong throughout the Progressive era. Often a common hostility to big business was the one link that bound together a variety of interest groups that diverged on other issues. The Progressive era, which culminated in 1914 with the passing of the Clayton Act and the creation of the Federal Trade Commission, probably marks the high point of anti-big-business sentiment in our history. As a movement, though hardly as an administrative reality, antitrust was in high gear.

The second phase, lasting from the First World War to about 1937, might be called the era of neglect. Efforts at prosecution during the 1920's were almost minimal, and even the New Deal in its opening years suspended the antitrust laws to accommodate the N.R.A. [National Recovery Administration] codes. The present phase, which may be dated from 1937, is the phase of revival, opened by the New Deal's reactivation of the Antitrust Division and the T.N.E.C. investigation. The sharp legal and administrative activity of this period has taken place without any corresponding revival of public sentiment against big business, indeed in the face of a growing public acceptance of the large corporation. Antitrust has become almost exclusively the concern of small groups of legal and economic specialists, who carry on their work without widespread public interest or support.

Whereas the first of these three phases was marked by tentative efforts at enforcement with nearly negligible results, and the second by minimal or token enforcement, the comparative vigor of the third may be measured roughly by the number of prosecutions. During all the years from 1891 to 1938, the government instituted an average of 9 cases a year. The peak years of this barren half-century were 1912 and 1913, with 29 and 27 prosecutions respectively. For about thirty years after 1913 the typical load was about 12 cases, often considerably fewer, and the objects chosen for prosecution were not often vital points in American industry. In 1940, with the Roosevelt-Arnold revitalization well on its way, the number of cases jumped to 85—only two less than the number instituted during the entire first two decades of the Sherman Act. Thereafter the number of cases, though still fluctuating, stayed at a level considerably higher than that maintained before 1938. In 1962 the Antitrust Division, employing 300 lawyers and working with a budget of $6,600,000, instituted 92 cases. Figures, of course, are crude, but a qualitative analysis of the legal victories of the antitrust revival would show that the decisions it has won from the courts, particularly since 1940, have greatly amplified the possibility of enforcement. Despite the collapse of antitrust feeling both in the public at large and among liberal intellectuals, antitrust as a legal-administrative enterprise has been solidly institutionalized in the last quarter-century.

The antitrust movement and its legislation are characteristically American. Perhaps this is attributable to the particularly flagrant form that monopoly took in America during the early years of its development. It may also be said that, except for the Canadians, no other people has taken the principle of economic competition so earnestly as to try to underwrite it by statute, until recently when some European countries began to show interest in the American approach to the subject. The idea of competition as a means of social regulation—as an economic, political, and moral force—has grown stronger roots in the United States than elsewhere, partly because it has had little to compete with in the way of aristocratic, militaristic, or labor-socialist theories. Founded to some degree in the common-law tradition, whose injunctions against restraint of trade proved an inadequate basis for the protection of competition, the antimonopoly tradition also rested intellectually upon classical economic theory and upon the pluralism of American democratic thought. But in America competition was more than a theory: it was a way of life and a creed. From its colonial beginnings through most of the nineteenth century, ours was overwhelmingly a nation of farmers and small-town entrepreneurs—ambitious, mobile, optimistic, speculative, anti-authoritarian, egalitarian, and competitive. As time went on, Americans came to take it for granted that property would be widely diffused, that economic and political power would be decentralized. The fury with which they could be mobilized against any institution that even appeared to violate these expectations by posing a threat of monopoly was manifest in the irrational assault on the Bank of the United States during Jackson's presidency. Their most respected thinkers habitually assured them that their social order was God-ordained or natural, and they probably thought it would last forever.

Then, with extraordinary rapidity as historical time is reckoned, that order was overwhelmed by the giant corporation. In the last three decades of the nineteenth century a wholly new economy came into being. An American born in 1828, the year of Jackson's election, came of age in a society in which the old small-enterprise economy, however dynamic and expansive, had kept its fundamental pattern more or less intact. But in his mature years he would have seen that economy fast becoming obsolete, and if he lived as late as 1904, he would have seen industry concentrated to a degree inconceivable not only to his fathers but even to him during most of his adult life. This economic transformation happened so fast that the mind could not easily absorb it. An entire people could hardly be expected to cease overnight to dream the dreams of the small entrepreneur. In 1900 the problem of big business and the threat of monopoly were still so new that it was hard to get one's bearings. Bigness had come with such a rush that its momentum seemed irresistible. No one knew when or how it could be stopped.

It is hardly surprising that the men of the first antitrust generation made some frightening projections into the future. In 1890, and even in 1914, bigness had not yet been domesticated either as a force in the economic world or as a factor in the American imagination. A nation that had gone so fast from competitive small enterprise to corporate giantism might readily go with equal speed from corporate giantism to a system of monopolistic tyranny. Hence, discussions of big business in the last decades of the nineteenth and the opening decade of the twentieth century are full of dark prognostications, most of them plausible enough at the time, however little they have been realized.

Since it had been widely assumed that competition, being "natural," would be largely self-perpetuating, the classical theory had not reckoned with the possible "necessity" of underwriting competition by statute. But by the 1880's the old confidence in the self-sustaining character of competition was dead, and there seemed no adequate protection for competition in existing law. As soon as it became clear that the common-law tradition against restraints of trade had ceased to have any force and that state laws on the subject were altogether inadequate to the purpose, the demand for federal action arose. George Gunton thought in 1888 that "the public mind has begun to assume a state of apprehension almost amounting to alarm," and that the social atmosphere was "surcharged with an indefinite but almost inexpressible fear of trusts."[1] Senator Sherman warned his colleagues that "the popular mind is agitated with problems that may disturb the social order," singling out inequities of wealth and the formation of combinations of capital so great that they threatened to produce "a trust for every production and a master to fix the price for every necessity of life." "Congress must heed the appeal of the voters," he said, "or be ready for the socialist, the communist, and the nihilist. Society is now disturbed by forces never felt before."[2] Historians,

1. G. W. Stocking and M. W. Watkins, *Monopoly and Free Enterprise* (New York, 1951), p. 157.

2. *Congressional Record*, 51st Cong., 1st sess. (March 21, 1890), p. 2460. "Although this body is always conservative," Sherman said hopefully, "yet, whatever may be said of it, it has always been ready to preserve not only popular rights in their broad sense, but the rights of individuals as against associated and corporate wealth and power."

like contemporaries, have differed as to how imperative the demand for federal action was. In a careful survey of articulate opinion on the "trust" problem in 1890, Hans B. Thorelli concludes that public demand, though perhaps less than an irresistible tide, was too strong to be ignored by the politicians.

Was the Congress of 1890 cynically offering a sop to public sentiment? The plutocratic character of that Congress lends some credence to this view, as does the observation of Senator Orville Platt, at one point in the debate, that the conduct of the Senate during the previous days was "not in the line of honest preparation of a bill to prohibit and punish trusts" but was merely an effort "to get some bill headed 'A bill to punish trusts' with which to go to the country."[3] These circumstances of its origins have helped to confirm many historians in their suspicion that antitrust was, from beginning to end, only a charade.

But there is also reason to believe, on the contrary, that most congressmen thought of the competitive order in business as being the cornerstone of the whole democratic way of life and that they considered themselves to be making the first tentative step in formulating a policy for the control of trusts, which, if it could be put on sound constitutional footing, might serve as the basis for corrective litigation and perhaps subsequent statutory changes. Admittedly, they were breaking new ground. Senator Hoar said that Congress was entering a wholly new field of legislation and that "the opinions of Senators themselves, of able and learned and experienced lawmakers, were exceedingly crude in this matter."[4]

It is true, of course, that Congress emerged with a statute written in the most general terms, which for many years was emasculated by judicial decisions and administrative lethargy.

But it is very likely that, with its broadly worded prohibition of conspiracies in restraint of trade and of efforts to monopolize, Congress was attempting to lay down a general declaration of policy that would serve as a guide to future action in much the same flexible way as the Constitution itself had served the country after 1787. Many congressmen doubtless believed that the self-enforcing features of the law would be far more effective than they actually became—that is, that the triple-damage suits authorized for victims of restraints of trade would cause businessmen themselves to carry on a good deal of the policing of the economy. Perhaps the problem confronting Congress can be reconstructed with greater sympathy if we try to imagine whether a drastically different and significantly more effective law would have been passed by a wholly populistic and militantly anti-big-business Congress, and whether such a law could have been expected to receive a more successful implementation than the Sherman Act in the hands of the subsequent administrative officers and judges.

3. Hans B. Thorelli, *The Federal Antitrust Policy* (Baltimore, 1955), p. 198. There is a mass of information about the antimonopoly aspects of the American tradition in Arthur P. Dudden's unpublished doctoral dissertation, "Antimonopolism, 1865–1890," University of Michigan (1950). On contemporary views, see also Sanford D. Gordon: "Attitudes towards Trusts prior to the Sherman Act," *Southern Economic Journal*, XXX (October 1963), 156–167.

4. Congressional Record, 51st Cong., 1st sess. (April 8, 1890), p. 3146.

One may say with reasonable assurance that the confusion of Congress over the economic significance of antitrust mirrored a more general confusion in American society. The goals of antitrust were of three kinds. The first were economic; the classical model of competition confirmed the belief that the maximum of economic efficiency would be produced by competition, and at least some members of Congress must have been under the spell of this intellectually elegant model, insofar as they were able to formulate their economic intentions in abstract terms. The second class of goals was political; the antitrust principle was intended to block private accumulations of power and protect democratic government. The third was social and moral; the competitive process was believed to be a kind of disciplinary machinery for the development of character, and the competitiveness of the people—the fundamental stimulus to national morale—was believed to need protection.

Among the three, the economic goal was the most cluttered with uncertainties, so much so that it seems to be no exaggeration to regard antitrust as being essentially a political rather than an economic enterprise. A fundamental difficulty in economic thought, troubling from the very start, arose over the relative claims of combination and competition. The Sherman Act was framed and debated in the pre-expert era, when economists as a professional group were not directly consulted by the legislators. But even if they had been, they would have given mixed and uncertain advice. The profession was split. A few years earlier the American Economic Association had been founded by men in revolt against the classical tradition and laissez-faire doctrines, although, of course, many economists of the older school were still ensconced in universities and colleges. Economists were familiar with the argument that the competitive order, far from being fixed in a permanent, beneficent, self-sustaining equilibrium, might have a strong tendency toward self-liquidation through the disappearance of weaker competitors. One of the early historicists, E. Benjamin Andrews, argued in 1893 that laissez-faire was no more than a systematized expression of anarchy, and the following year warned:

> Bills have been brought before half the legislatures of the Union to free competition by making trade syndicates absolutely illegal. To my mind there is no question that such legislation will be vain. The age of competition as we have known it is gone forever. As well try to waken the dead.[5]

The more influential voice of Richard Ely was also raised in protest against the ideal of pure competition. He was among those who insisted that size should not be equated with monopoly, and long before Thurman Arnold he held that antitrust legislation was not only futile but actually encouraging to monopoly, because it caused business leaders to replace "soft" combinations by "hard" combinations in the form of mergers.[6]

5. Thorelli, op. cit., pp. 112 n. 1, 316.

6. Id., pp. 314–315.

No consensus was to be had on the proper line of governmental action on trusts or on the kind of law Congress should pass. Nearly all economists believed that attempts simply to prohibit combinations by law would be futile. There was a growing disposition to consider that both competition and combination needed some measure of control and that neither could be eliminated by law. In this sense, as William Letwin has pointed out, the counsel that was available from the economists, however much attended to or ignored, shared the ambiguity that the legislators themselves could feel as lawyers:

> The economists thought that both competition and combination should play their parts in the economy. The lawyers saw that the common law permitted combination in some instances and prohibited it in others. Congressmen seized on this hidden agreement, and set out to construct a statute which by the use of common-law principles would eliminate excesses but allow "healthy" competition and combination to flourish side by side.[7]

If one gives due regard to the uncertainties of the matter and to the improbability that any attempt at a quick solution would be effective, one may arrive at a more charitable judgment of the Congress of 1890. Its members were probably trying to lay down general guidelines by means of which their successors might evolve a policy that would give society the advantages of both competition and combination. As Senator Sherman said, "All that we, as lawmakers, can do is to declare general principles."[8] These principles could hardly have been enunciated in more sweeping language than that used in the Sherman Act. Presumably, many congressmen hoped that the courts would find a way of striking at the notoriously unfair methods of competition that had already been used to build such companies as Standard Oil and the National Cash Register Company, without barring useful consolidations or even such restrictive agreements as were intended to eliminate intolerably rigorous competition.

This original uncertainty about the economic rationale for antitrust continued to haunt well-intentioned Progressives in the years before the First World War. The vagueness and inconsistency so often expressed by intelligent and relatively candid political leaders during this era must be taken as a reflection not on the caliber of the leadership but rather on the intrinsic difficulty of the problem.

Theodore Roosevelt represents, on this count, a maximum of shrewdness combined with a minimum of anxiety. With the exception of railroad regulation, Roosevelt was not profoundly interested in the economic issues that agitated the American public during his presidency; indeed, he was quite candid in confessing his reluctance to tackle them head on. When in difficulties, as in 1907, he was disposed

7. William Letwin, *Law and Economic Policy in America: The Evolution of the Sherman Antitrust Act* (New York, 1965), p. 85; see, in general, Ch. 3 on the intentions of Congress.

8. *Congressional Record*, 51st Cong., 1st sess. (March 21, 1890), p. 2460. Sherman was here conceding the difficulty of defining in law the precise difference between legal and illegal combinations, and expressing a preference for leaving such decisions to the courts in particular cases.

to trust to the judgment and the political and financial leadership of the conservatives in the Senate or the economic powers in Wall Street. However, he saw the trust problem as something that must be dealt with on the political level; public concern about it was too urgent to be ignored. He understood how important it was to assure the public that the government of the United States had the will and the power to assert its authority over large corporations. Accordingly, his antitrust prosecutions, although few, were in some cases appropriately spectacular. When he assessed the significance of the Northern Securities case, he did not say that it would open the way to a general assault on bigness, but rather that it was important for showing that "the most powerful men in this country were held to accountability before the law." His fundamental solution for the problem—that bigness must be accepted as a part of the modern industrial and social order, and that its behavior should be subjected to administrative control under full publicity—comes somewhat closer than the views of most of his political contemporaries to anticipating the future course of antitrust procedure.

Roosevelt was accompanied, or perhaps followed, by a school of liberal publicists—among them Charles R. Van Hise, Herbert Croly, and Walter Lippmann—who accepted his conviction that the Sherman Act philosophy was the product of what he called a "sincere rural Toryism" long since outgrown. Lippmann, in one of the most penetrating attacks on the antitrust philosophy, characterized it as the philosophy of "a nation of villagers." This school of Progressives saw the Western world as entering upon a new era of organization and specialization for which the old competitive philosophy was hopelessly retrograde. Some of them, notably Croly and Van Hise, also saw small-scale business as inadequate to the task of competing in the world's markets, which they believed to be a necessity of the American situation. In retrospect, they appear more sophisticated and prophetic than those who put great stock in the Sherman Act as a force for actual dissolution. They foresaw the decline of antitrust as a movement, and in some instances recognized that if the Sherman Act persisted it would be as a basis for occasional ad hoc regulatory suits rather than as an instrument for dismantling the corporate economy.

Woodrow Wilson spoke more feelingly for the "rural Toryism" and the village democracy which seem to have been at the center of popular antitrust feeling; but by the same token he illustrated more clearly than Roosevelt their intellectual difficulties. Speaking in the campaign of 1911, which afforded a full-dress display of the differences between the two schools of thought on trusts, he asserted that he too was not against size as such. He was all for bigness as an inevitable and natural growth, whenever it was the outcome of superior efficiency. But he was against "the trusts," which had grown out of illicit competition. He was never very successful, however, in explaining why a business that had become large through legitimate methods might not become just as menacing to competition as one that had grown large through illicit competition. His statement "I am for big business and I am against the trusts" seems hardly more than an unsatisfactory attempt to evade the argument that there is a self-liquidating threat inherent in competition.

## III

The political and social arguments against monopoly were pressed with greater clarity than the economic argument and with hardly less fervor. Antitrust must be understood as the political judgment of a nation whose leaders had always shown a keen awareness of the economic foundations of politics. In this respect, the Sherman Act was simply another manifestation of an enduring American suspicion of concentrated power. From the pre-Revolutionary tracts through the Declaration of Independence and *The Federalist* to the writings of the states' rights advocates, and beyond the Civil War into the era of the antimonopoly writers and the Populists, there had been a perennial quest for a way of dividing, diffusing, and checking power and preventing its exercise by a single interest or by a consolidated group of interests at a single center. Hence, the political impulse behind the Sherman Act was clearer and more articulate than the economic theory. Men who used the vaguest language when they talked about "the trusts" and monopolies, who had not thought through the distinction between size itself and monopolistic practices, who had found no way of showing how much competition was necessary for efficiency, who could not in every case say what competitive acts they thought were fair or unfair, or who could not state a rational program that reconciled their acceptance of size with their desire for competition, were reasonably clear about what it was that they were trying to avoid: they wanted to keep concentrated private power from destroying democratic government.

One of the glories of the competitive model had been that it purported to solve the question of market power by denying that such power had any particular location. The decisions of the market were beautifully impersonal, since they were only the averagings of the decisions of thousands of individuals, none of whom enjoyed any decisive power. The market mechanism suggested that power was not really exercised by anyone. With the perfect impersonality of Adam Smith's "invisible hand," the market made decisions that ought not be vested in the hands of any particular man or body of men. Hence, the market mechanism met the desire for the diffusion of power and seemed to be the perfect economic counterpart of American democratic pluralism.

Where power must be exercised, it was agreed that it should be located in governmental and not in private hands. But the state governments were inadequate; in sheer mass, business enterprises already overshadowed them. Charles William Eliot pointed out as early as 1888 that the large corporations, considered as units of economic organization, had already begun to tower over the states. A Boston railroad company, for example, employed 18,000 persons and had gross receipts of about $40,000,000 a year, whereas the Commonwealth of Massachusetts employed only 6,000 and had receipts of only $7,000,000. Even individually, some corporations were big enough to dominate state governments, and if they should combine among themselves, they might come to dominate the federal government as well.

The existence of the industrial combinations and the threat that under one auspice or another—perhaps that of the investment bankers—there would come about some day a combination of the combinations that would be stronger than civil government itself, provoked a fear that haunted the minds of the writers of the industrial era, including many whose social views were as conservative as Eliot's. The fundamental fear of private power was well put by William Jennings Bryan, in a speech delivered at the Chicago Conference on Trusts in 1899:

> I do not divide monopolies in private hands into good monopolies and bad monopolies. There is no good monopoly in private hands. There can be no good monopoly in private hands until the Almighty sends us angels to preside over the monopoly. There may be a despot who is better than another despot, but there is no good despotism.[9]

And the general sense that the dire economic and political consequences of monopoly were as one was incorporated in the Democratic platform of 1900:

> Private monopolies are indefensible and intolerable.... They are the most efficient means yet devised for appropriating the fruits of industry to the benefit of the few at the expense of the many, and unless their insatiate greed is checked, all wealth will be aggregated in a few hands and the Republic destroyed.[10]

The most articulate expression of the Progressives' case against the political power of monopoly was made by Woodrow Wilson in 1912. It was the burden of his argument, against T.R., that once the existence of large-scale combinations is accepted, regulation of them by government becomes impossible, because the political power of business combination will be great enough to nullify all attempts at controlling it. Wilson played artfully on the fears and suspicions of the small entrepreneurs. Even some very powerful men, he said, knew that "there is a power somewhere so organized, so subtle, so watchful, so interlocked, so complete, so pervasive, that they had better not speak above their breath when they speak in condemnation of it.... They know that somewhere, by somebody, the development of industry is being controlled."[11] He pictured concentrated capital as being already in control of the government: "The masters of the government of the United States are the combined capitalists and manufacturers of the United States.... The government of the United States at present is a foster-child of the special interests."[12]

Of necessity this would continue to be the state of affairs until the combinations not only were unseated by the people but also were dissolved—until "this colossal 'community of interest'" was disentangled. It was a thing that the laws must "pull apart, and gently, but firmly and persistently dissect." Otherwise, under Roosevelt's plan for accepting and regulating monopolies, there would only be a union between

9. Thorelli, op. cit., p. 336.

10. Kirk H. Porter and Donald B. Johnson, *National Party Platforms* (Urbana, Ill., 1956), p. 114.

11. Wilson, op. cit ., p. 140.

12. Ibid., pp. 57–58.

monopoly and government: "If the government controlled by the monopolies in its turn controls the monopolies, the partnership is finally consummated." "If monopoly persists, monopoly will always sit at the helm of the government. I do not expect to see monopoly restrain itself. If there are men in this country big enough to own the government of the United States, they are going to own it."[13]

The third objective of antitrust action, hardly less important than the others, was psychological and moral. It sprang from the conviction that competition has a disciplinary value for character, quite aside from its strictly economic uses. America was thought to have been made possible by the particular type of character that was forged by competitive individualism, a type that had flourished in the United States because competitive opportunities had been so widespread that alert men could hardly fail to see them, to grasp and use them, and hence, to be shaped by them. The American male character we believed to have been quickened and given discipline by the sight and pursuit of opportunity. For this process to take place it was important that business be carried on fairly—the sporting vocabulary was never far below the surface—and that newcomers be able to enter the game as entrepreneurs on reasonably open terms.

The significance of this faith that competition could be relied upon to form character can be fully grasped only if we bear in mind the Protestant background of our economic thinking. Economists themselves had not been in the habit of analyzing economic relationships in purely mechanical and secular terms, and what may be said of them on this count can be said with greater force about laymen, when they thought about economic issues. Behind the American way of thinking there lay a long Protestant tradition, which tended to identify economic forces with religious and moral forces and which regarded economic processes from the standpoint of their contribution to the discipline and development of character. The economic order was not merely an apparatus for the production of goods and services; it was a set of rules for forging good conduct. Everyone is familiar, I believe, with the proposition that some of the concepts of classical economics were shaped under the influence of a kind of prudential morality in which savings and abstinence were not merely instruments of economic analysis but moral sanctions. In our time we have heard conservatives frankly condemn government fiscal policy that deviates from the prudential rules suitable to a family budget by appealing to the Puritan tradition. Such critics are the legitimate heirs of the men of the nineteenth and the early twentieth century who saw the protection of competition and its incentives as a safeguard of national morale, as a means for mobilizing and rewarding the industrious and the prudent and for penalizing those whom William Graham Sumner called "the poor and the weak, the negligent, shiftless, inefficient, silly, and imprudent . . . the idle, intemperate, and vicious."[14]

13. Ibid., pp. 118, 207, 286. For a later statement of this view see the dissenting opinion of Mr. Justice Douglas in *U.S.* v. *Columbia Steel Co.*, 334 U.S. 495 (1948).

14. William Graham Sumner, *What Social Classes Owe to Each Other* (New Haven, 1925), p. 21.

Here again one looks to Woodrow Wilson for the most articulate expression of this emphasis on the economic foundations of character and especially to the masterful speeches in 1912 in which he expressed his concern for "the beginner," "the man with only a little capital," "the man on the make," upon whose genius he thought the country had always been built. "The treasury of America," he argued, "lies in those ambitions, those energies that cannot be restricted to a special favored class." It rests upon the inventiveness and the energy of "unknown men" and would lose its force if the economic order ceased to stimulate such inventiveness and energy. It was possible, he hinted, that under large-scale organization the country would turn its back on its past, which he evoked in poignant terms:

> ... the ancient time when America lay in every hamlet, when America was to be seen in every fair valley, when America displayed her great forces on the broad prairies, ran her fine fires of enterprise up over the mountainsides and down into the bowels of the earth, and eager men were everywhere captains of industry, not employees; not looking to a distant city to find out what they might do, but looking about among their neighbors, finding credit according to their character, not according to their connections, finding credit in proportion to what was known to be in them and behind them, not in proportion to the securities they held that were approved where they were not known.[15]

The prospect that these "fine fires of enterprise" were about to be quenched suggested that the old kind of character would be destroyed, that the old America was about to die—a reason even more imperative than mere industrial efficiency for seeking out the possibilities of antitrust action.

The inherited belief that small property and opportunity for small business have forged the American character, which might well lose its form without the discipline imposed by a particular variety of entrepreneurial competition, is one that has never died out. Near the end of the Second World War the Small Business Committee of the Senate put this faith clearly when it said that the pursuit of opportunity by the small business owner

> has been a great motive force among our people. It stimulates expression of the fundamental virtues of thrift, industry, intelligence, schooling, home ties, and family pride-in short, those fireside virtues which have counted for so much in developing our strength and character.[16]

The preservation of opportunities for small business, as a member of the S.E.C. put it in 1945, is more important than any economic goal; it is "a goal which transcends

15. Wilson, op. cit., pp. 18–19.

16. Quoted in John H. Bunzel, *The American Small Businessman* (New York, 1962), p. 84.

economic and political forms and processes as such, and remains fundamentally concerned with the character of the men and women who comprise the nation."[17]

## IV

There are two salient differences between the problem of bigness as it was perceived about sixty years ago and the problem as it is perceived now; the first is that it is no longer a new problem, and the second is that the economy has performed in a way hardly dreamed of before the Second World War. In 1965 we are as remote in time from the passage of the Sherman Act as the men of 1865 were from the first term of George Washington. The public has had almost three-quarters of a century of experience in living with big business, and analysts of the big-business problem no longer make the same frightening projections as to its future dangers that could be made with entire plausibility sixty or seventy years ago. At the same time, the public is hardly unaware that the steepest rise in mass standards of living has occurred during the period in which the economy has been dominated by the big corporation. Whatever else may be said against bigness, the conception of monopolistic industry as a kind of gigantic, swelling leech on the body of an increasingly deprived and impoverished society has largely disappeared.

About the change in public attitudes from those prevailing sixty years ago we can make only an educated guess. Today we can check our impressions of the public mind against opinion polls; for the earlier era we have impressions alone. But it is very difficult for anyone who reads widely in the political literature of the period 1890–1914 to believe that public concern today over big business has anything like the sense of urgency that it had then. In 1951 the Institute of Social Research of the University of Michigan published the results of an illuminating survey, *Big Business as the People See It*. Its findings show some residues of the old popular suspicion of bigness, but the noteworthy thing is public acceptance. Americans have always had to balance their love of bigness and efficiency against their fear of power and their regard for individualism and competition. The survey indicates that this ambivalence has been largely resolved in favor of the big business organization.

A quarter of the population, as represented in the Institute's national sample, showed some concern over big business and an awareness that it had an important effect on their lives. But a substantial majority reacted favorably to big business. Asked to give a general characterization of its social effects, the respondents answered as follows:

| | |
|---|---|
| The good things outweigh the bad things | 76% |
| They seem about equal | 2 |
| The bad things outweigh the good things | 10 |
| Don't know | 5 |
| Confused; evaluation not ascertainable | 7 |
| | 100% |

17. Rudolph L. Weissman, *Small Business and Venture Capital* (New York, 1945), p. 164.

Plainly, big business was no longer a scare word to the public at large. Eighty-four percent of those polled reacted without apparent emotion to the question, and only a small minority reacted unfavorably. Questioned on particulars, respondents spoke with especial favor of the productive powers of big business and its ability to give jobs and keep prices down. The most critical responses about big business dealt mainly with its effect on "the little man" and the destruction of competition. Very little concern was expressed about the power of big business over its workers (it is commonly regarded as a good employer) and surprisingly little about its influence on government.

Whereas fifty years before, fear of an indefinitely continued increase in the political power of big business was commonplace, the typical expectation expressed in the poll of 1951 was that the power of big business would decline, and properly so. As in the Progressive era, there was a strong preference for a balance of power and a conviction that wherever there must be a clear preponderance of power it should rest in governmental and not private hands. But the existing state of business power was not widely considered to be dangerous. In fact, big-business power was ranked third among five forces—behind national government and labor unions and ahead of state governments and smaller business. Stronger feeling was shown against labor unions than against big business. There was a fraction of the public that saw big business as more powerful than labor unions and would have liked to see the situation reversed; but there was a fraction almost twice as large that saw the unions as more powerful and would have preferred to see the situation reversed.[18]

The findings of the Michigan group were not widely at variance with those of Elmo Roper, who a few years earlier had collated the responses of the public over a span of fifteen years to questions about business. Roper found that "the public has mixed feelings about big business. There is pride over the achievements of big business but some apprehension over the possible abuses of power inherent in big business." The public was disposed to want a watchdog set upon the amoral and greedy elements in business, but only about a fourth of the respondents were found to believe that the disadvantages of bigness overshadow whatever advantages there might be.[19]

To what can we attribute this public acceptance of big business? Not much, I believe, to the efforts that big-businessmen have made to cultivate a favorable "image" for the large corporation. As the fate of the postwar campaign to sell "free enterprise" suggests, such efforts can miscarry badly when they represent nothing more than an attempt to make the public take seriously the blather with which big business sometimes comforts itself.[20] What has really made bigness palatable more than anything else is the remarkable performance of the economy since the beginning of the Second World War. Something too must be credited to the emergence of countervailing bigness in government and labor, whose effects on public attitudes emerge clearly from

18. Burton R. Fisher and Stephen B. Withey, *Big Business as the People See It* (Ann Arbor, 1951), passim.

19. Elmo Roper, "The Public Looks at Business," *Harvard Business Review* XXVII (March 1949), 165–174.

20. William H. Whyte, Jr., is eloquent on the failure of one such campaign in *Is Anybody Listening?* (New York, 1952).

the Michigan survey. Moreover, anyone who is aware of the historical circumstances under which hostility to big business flourished must be aware that big business has not lived up to the horrifying billing that it got in the age of the muckrakers. It is not merely that no business treats competitors today as they were treated in the early days of the National Cash Register Company or Standard Oil. What is important is that a whole range of fears that existed in the Progressive era, based largely upon a preoccupation with an unknown future, has vanished. We now live in that future, and although it has fears of its own—nightmarish beyond anything anticipated in the days of Bryan and Wilson—they are of a wholly different origin. Probably the worst of the Populist-Progressive nightmares was the notion expressed in the Pujo Committee's inquiry, in Brandeis's *Other People's Money*, in Wilson's speeches, and in Jack London's *The Iron Heel*—of the formation, under the auspices of the investment bankers, of a giant syndicate, a combination of the combinations, which would rule the country with a tyrannical grip. The self-financing character of the great corporations, the survival of competition in investment banking, and the failure of investment banking to remain a power of the first order after the crash of 1929 have set this specter to rest.

If no sinister central syndicate had to be feared, it did at least seem reasonable at the turn of the century to anticipate a steadily growing concentration of industry that would eventually deprive the country of every advantage of competition. And here, insofar as the antitrust enterprise was directed against size itself or against concentration, it was beaten before it ever got started; American industry was already highly concentrated in 1904, when T.R. was boasting about the lessons of the Northern Securities case. But insofar as the Progressives were worried about what the economists later came to call "workable competition" in industry, they might well have been reassured as time went on. The investigations of such economists as M. A. Adelman, G. Warren Nutter, and George J. Stigler have cast considerable doubt on the idea that either the scope of monopoly or the degree of concentration has, in fact, grown since early in the century. "The extent of concentration," Adelman concluded in an important study, "shows no tendency to grow, and it may possibly be declining. Any tendency either way, if it does exist, must be at the pace of a glacial drift."[21] Measuring monopoly is an undertaking of considerable complexity and the issues are controversial. But it is at least safe to say that no one who has due regard for the difficulties of the problem can any longer raise alarmist cries about the rapid growth of monopoly or concentration without flying in the face of much formidable testimony.

21. M. A. Adelman, "The Measurement of Industrial Concentration," *Review of Economics and Statistics* XXXIII (November 1951), 269–296. See also the discussion by Adelman and others, ibid. XXXIV (May 1952), 156 ff.; G. Warren Nutter, *The Extent of Enterprise Monopoly in the United States, 1899–1939* (Chicago, 1951); and George J. Stigler, *Five Lectures on Economic Problems* (London, 1949), pp. 46–65. However, on the identity of the largest firms and the mobility of firms into positions of leadership, see Norman R. Collins and Lee E. Preston, "The Size Structure of the Largest Industrial Firms," *American Economic Review* LI (December 1961), 986–1003. Fritz Machlup, *The Political Economy of Monopoly* (Baltimore, 1952), pp. 469–528, is instructive on the difficulties of the subject. See also Edward S. Mason, *Economic Concentration and the Monopoly Problem* (New York: Atheneum ed., 1964), pp. 16–43.

Another cause of concern, very real to many men in the Progressive era and rather quaint from today's perspective, had to do with the progress of industry. "Monopoly," warned Wilson in 1912, "always checks development, weighs down natural prosperity, pulls against natural advance." In the past, he said, competitive America had produced or developed the steamboat, the cotton gin, the sewing machine, the reaper, the typewriter, the electric light, and other great inventions, but the day was at hand when monopoly might end all this. "Do you know, have you had occasion to learn, that there is no hospitality for invention nowadays? There is no encouragement for you to set your wits at work.... The instinct of monopoly is against novelty, the tendency of monopoly is to keep in use the old thing, made in the old way." Only a restoration of freedom could unleash American inventiveness again: "Who can say what patents now lying, unrealized, in secret drawers and pigeonholes, will come to light, or what new inventions will astonish and bless us, when freedom is restored?"[22] To two generations that since 1912 have been astonished and blessed almost to death by inventions, such rhetoric can no longer be alarming or inspiring; it is merely a curiosity. Today the public needs no persuading that it is the large corporations, with their programs of research, that are technologically progressive. As Galbraith has remarked, the showpieces of American industrial progress are, in the main, those dominated by a handful of large firms, and "the foreign visitor, brought to the United States by the Economic Cooperation Administration, visits the same firms as do attorneys of the Department of Justice in their search for monopoly."[23]

Another typical fear expressed in Progressive writing was that the possibility of individual advancement would be frozen out, that the upward social mobility that had refreshed and inspired American development in the past would come to an end, when the business of the country was fully dominated by the large corporation. I know of no very certain information on how the American public regards the prospects for social mobility today, although our concerted scramble for educational position and advantage suggests that the middle-class public, and even much of the working-class public, is rather well aware that mobility still exists; it is also aware of the educational machinery through which it can be pursued. What can be said with greater confidence is that informed observers no longer speak so glibly of the decline of mobility or opportunity.

Indeed, there is strong evidence that the opportunity of middle- or lower-class men to rise to top positions in business has somewhat increased over what it was fifty or sixty years ago, and there is some reason to believe that the increase, or at least the persistence, of occupational opportunity has, in fact, impressed itself on the public mind. In fact, the modern corporation has proved to be a better medium fur social mobility and opportunity than the old system of individual and family entrepreneurship, whose openness in this respect was always much exaggerated. Oddly enough,

22. Wilson, op. cit., pp. 265–266, 270.

23. John Kenneth Galbraith, *American Capitalism* (Boston, 1952), p. 96; cf. Joseph A. Schumpeter, *Capitalism, Socialism, and Democracy* (New York, 1947), pp. 81–82.

the concentration of capital and the divorce of ownership from the entrepreneurial function may prove in the long run to be more conducive to the lowering of social tensions and to political stability than used ownership. The ways of achieving occupational advancement and economic success have changed; individual entrepreneurship is a much less sure and satisfactory path as compared with bureaucratic careers. The acquisition of specialized skills has become more important, and with it the seizure and exploitation of educational opportunities.

I do not mean to suggest that the old ideal of self-employment or the old confidence in the entrepreneurial path to success has been entirely abandoned in favor of the bureaucratic career. Although the incidence of self-employment and the number of those who actually live by the competitive ideal have shrunk very considerably in the three-quarters of a century since the Sherman Act, most of this is attributable to the numerical decline of family farmers, who in 1890 still comprised nearly half the population and today comprise about a tenth. The farmers, with their dependence on subsidies and government-administered prices, can hardly be looked upon any more as vigorous exponents of the competitive way of life. But the dream of self-employment that dominated the agrarian-entrepreneurial society of the nineteenth century is still alive. It has been estimated that about 20 to 30 percent of the American working force has been at some time or other self-employed.[24] The growth of small businesses over the past dozen years or so has roughly kept pace in numbers with the growth of the adult population, and the aspirations of small business have been institutionalized in Senate and House committees as well as in some antitrust activities.

But although small business holds its place as an occupational segment of the economy itself, its role as a sector of society committed to the entrepreneurial ideal has declined. Small business can no longer be idealized for its independence and hardihood or its devotion to competitive principles. It, too, looks to government intervention for sustenance, whether in the form of resale price maintenance, anti-chainstore legislation, or the Small Business Administration. Small business, which used to be, as one writer put it,[25] "a symbol of opportunity, enterprise, innovation, and achievement" and of "an independent way of life," has been driven largely into the marginal areas of economic life, where it often tries to maintain itself by waging its own assaults upon the competitive principle. Various segments of small business, in their pressure for support for the Robinson-Patman Act of 1936 and the Miller-Tydings Amendment of 1937, have shown how quickly they can be rallied against competition, when it impinges upon their own interests. Vigorous advocates of the Sherman and Clayton acts where big business is affected, they turn their backs on competitive virility when it suits their purposes. If there is anything rarer than a small-businessman who will question the merits of competition as a principle, it is one who can understand and abide competition when it really afflicts him as a fact.

24. Lipset and Bendix, op. cit., pp. 102–103.

25. Theodore O. Yntema, in the Foreword to A. D. H. Kaplan, *Small Business: Its Place and Problems* (New York, 1948), p. vii.

Not only can the small-businessman not purport, in the eyes of any well-informed observer, to be a vigorous and consistent exemplar of the competitive ideal; he can no longer be idealized by progressive-minded men from other walks of life, as he could, say, in the era when Woodrow Wilson waxed rhapsodical about the new men out of "unknown homes" who had really made America. In the United States and elsewhere, liberal intellectuals now cock a suspicious eye at him, if not as a potential stronghold of support for fascist movements, at least as the backbone of the reactionary wing of the Republican party. An occasional big-business leader may stand out for his enlightenment and urbanity, as compared with the small-businessman, who more often than not proves to be a refractory anti-union employer, a parochial and archaic opponent of liberal ideas, a supporter of vigilante groups and of right-wing cranks. As a figure in our economic society, the small-businessman still plays a part of some considerable importance, but as a partner in the American liberal coalition, he has all but disappeared, and with him has gone much of the pristine anti-bigness feeling of the Progressive tradition.

Still, the conviction that American democracy will survive only if small-business enterprise survives to sustain the American character has not disappeared. It has been inherited from the Progressives of yesterday by the conservatives of today. It appears to be, as we shall see, a conviction that flourishes less among the young than among the old, who are often troubled that they cannot persuade their juniors of its importance. "For the development of self-reliance," say two authors of a manual for small-business operation, "for making men as well as money, small business excels."[26] In 1936, when the Robinson-Patman Act was under consideration, this effort to underwrite the middleman was touted by the chairman of the House Committee on the Judiciary as a potential bulwark of the democratic order: "There are a great many people who feel that if we are to preserve democracy in government, in America, we have got to preserve a democracy in business operation.... We must make some effort to *maintain the yeomanry in business*."[27]

During the 1940's and 1950's there was evidence of a widespread uneasy conviction that years of war, depression, and bureaucratic expansion had finally drained away the old regard for entrepreneurship among the young, and that the spirit that animated the old competitive ideal had finally succumbed to the world of the large corporation. The signs and portents are numerous, but a memorable article of 1949 in Fortune may be taken as a landmark. Surveying "The crass of '49," Fortune's editors pointed out that it was perhaps the most significant college graduating class in our history. It was one of the largest, most mature (with a high proportion of veterans) and responsible; but its distinguishing feature was its aversion to risk, its passion for security. "The class of '49," the editors reported, "wants to work for somebody else—preferably somebody big. No longer is small business the promised land. As for the idea of going into business

26. Pearce C. Kelley and Kenneth Lawyer, *How to Organize and Operate a Small Business* (Englewood Cliffs, N.J., 1949), p. II.

27. Quoted in Merle Fainsod, Lincoln Gordon, and Joseph C. Palamountain, Jr., *Government and the American Economy* (New York, 1959), p. 549; italics added.

for oneself, the idea is so seldom expressed as to seem an anachronism." Only in the Southwest, which seems socially and intellectually to lag behind the rest of the country, was there any sign of significant exceptions to this generalization. The generation which had been impressionable children during the depression and which had come of age in the shadow of the war rendered a firm verdict in favor of security, service, and the good life (measured in modest income expectations) rather than risk, self-assertion, and the big prizes. The emergent young man, the editors reported, "is not afraid of bigness; where his father of the twenties, fearful of anonymity, was repelled by hugeness in an organization, he is attracted."[28]

This was the response of a generation raised in an economy of giant corporations, educated very often in universities with thousands of students, "disciplined by army life, and accustomed to the imperatives of organization, mass, and efficiency." No doubt they often saw in big businesses the promise of laboratories and market research to which the atmosphere of the universities had already accustomed them. Because of its army experiences, the class of 1949 may have been unusually security-minded, but there is no reason to doubt that its acceptance of large organization represented a secular trend. Not long after the Fortune piece appeared, the Youth Research Institute Survey put to 4,660 high school and college seniors, recent college graduates, and veterans the question: "Do you feel that you will be able to achieve all of your economic desires by working for someone else?" In reply, 61.1 percent said yes, 20.4 percent no, and 18. 5 percent were uncertain.[29] In his essay "The Found Generation," an analysis of the expressed life ideals of the class of 1955, David Riesman found not only a bland acceptance of the large corporation as a place in which to do one's life work but also a depressing complacency about the terms and rewards of the corporate life. The class of 1949 had at least been aware of making a somewhat difficult choice in which their individuality might be at stake. The class of 1955 took the bureaucratic career for granted.[30]

It is this acceptance of the bureaucratic career that, more than anything else, tells us why there is no longer an antitrust movement. It is far more revealing than the law cases or the books on the control of monopoly. It is also a perfect illustration of how the problems of yesterday are not solved but outgrown. Only a few people today are concerned about how to make the large corporations more competitive, but millions are concerned about how they are going to live inside the corporate framework. The existence and the workings of the corporations are largely accepted, and in the main they are assumed to be fundamentally benign. What is questioned, when anything is questioned, is matters of personal style: What can be salvaged, of either individualism or individuality, in an age in which the big corporation has become a way of life? It is this concern that marks the transition from an age in which *The Curse of Bigness* and *Other People's Money* voiced the prevailing anxieties to one in which everyone reads *The Lonely Crowd* and *The Organization Man*.

28. "The Class of '49," *Fortune* (June 1949), pp. 84–87.

29. William H. Whyte, Jr., *The Organization Man* (New York, 1957), p. 79 n.

30. David Riesman: "The Found Generation," in *Abundance for What?* (New York, 1964), pp. 309–313.

Long-prevailing systems of values do not usually go under without a fight, and along with the new acceptance there is a good deal of uneasiness about the corporate life. The young may be losing the concern of their elders with the virile prerogatives of enterprise. Certainly they are now much more disposed to ask of the economic order not whether it is raising a nation of enterprising and hardy men but more matter-of-factly whether it is maintaining an adequate level of employment and producing a sufficient increase in the Gross National Product. But there is also a persistent uneasiness, which has its manifestations both on the left and on the right. The left, if it can be called that, rebels in the name of nonconformity and opts out of the whole bourgeois world in the manner of the beatnik and the hipster. The right (in the manner of Barry Goldwater and his enthusiasts) rebels in the name of the older individualism, which believed that economic life should inculcate discipline and character. Though they would hate to admit it, they are both bedeviled in different ways by the same problem; each of them is trying to make its variety of nonconformism into a mass creed—which is a contradiction in terms. The beats opt out of corporate uniformity in their own uniforms and erect themselves into a stereotype. The rightwingers sing their praises of individualism in dreary, regimented choruses and applaud vigilantes who would kill every vestige of genuine dissent.

In politics, of course, it is the right-wingers who really count—it is they who have the numbers, the money, the political leverage. They can also invoke the old American pieties and can appeal to the kind of old-fashioned American who believes that federal fiscal policy is just like the family budget. Much of our conservative writing echoes with concern over the decline of the older kind of economic morale, which it identifies with small entrepreneurship. But conservatives understandably fear to make the large corporation the object of their criticism; this smacks too much of subversion. They have a safer and more congenial outlet for their animus against the organization of modern life in the form of denunciations of big government. In this way, the large corporation escapes its proper share of odium. But, historically, it was the giant corporation far more than government policy that eclipsed the old-fashioned economic morality.

Here conservatives and liberals have all but reversed their former positions. In the main it is conservatives who are disgruntled with the style of contemporary economic life, while liberals complete the paradox by springing to its defense and, in particular, to the defense of bigness. As we have seen, there were always a number of Progressive intellectuals who preferred to accept corporate organization and to whom the possibilities of rationalization and order were more appealing than the competitive ideal. Today it is men of such views who seem to have inherited what is left of American liberalism. Of course, big business still holds a place as a negative symbol in the liberal creed, and the liberal creed still gives a certain ritualistic compliance to the anti-big-business sentiment that was once very close to the heart of progressivism. But by and large, as Carl Kaysen has remarked, "today's liberals have abandoned the symbol of competition without much struggle."[31]

31. Carl Kaysen, "Big Business and the Liberals, Then and Now," *The New Republic* (November 22, 1954), pp. 118–119.

Some of the most striking efforts to reconcile us to the business structure have been written in recent years by liberals who derive from the New Deal tradition. If, in 1953, one read a paean to big business asserting, among other things, that the emotional antagonism to which it was subject was based on "abuses long since corrected"; that the big-business leader is "a man with a strong and practical sense of responsibility to the public, and an awareness of the ethics of present day business competition"; that "big business has performed economic wonders with one hand tied behind its back"; that it has actually increased competition and multiplied small enterprises; that "size is our greatest single functional asset"; that big business nourishes diversity; that "we are living in what is probably the most highly competitive society men have ever known"; that big-business research has multiplied opportunities for small-business enterprise; that ill-considered antitrust prosecutions have "grave implications for national security"; and that "in Bigness we have the material foundation of a society which can further the highest values known to men, values we describe as spiritual"[32]—one no longer expected to find that one had been reading a speech by a General Motors or A. T. & T. director and was not at all surprised to learn that the author was David E. Lilienthal, once one of the most outspoken democratic idealists of the New Deal bureaucracy and a former disciple of Brandeis.

Lilienthal's innocent rhapsodies to big business may perhaps be taken as the effusions of one who had been reshaped by his experiences in giant public enterprises like the T.V.A. and the A.E.C. But there is also A. A. Berle, Jr., another New Dealer, who held his first job in Brandeis's office and whose public career was marked by friendships with Robert La Follette, George Norris, and Franklin D. Roosevelt. In his most recent works Berle has been speculating about the possible development of a corporate conscience and arguing that the contemporary business power system is governed by public consensus. In his *Power Without Property* he urged liberals to reconsider their former, and historically justified, antipathy to big business and to judge it in the light of its achievements in increasing income and distributing property.[33] Finally, there is John Kenneth Galbraith, whose book *American Capitalism* has probably done as much as any other work to reconcile the contemporary liberal mind to the diminished role of competition as a force in modern economic society by offering, as an alternative account of the mechanism by which market power is controlled in the public interest, the principle of countervailing power. Of course, neither Berle nor Galbraith advocates doing away with the antitrust laws—Galbraith, in fact, argues that, in the main, federal antitrust policies have helped to produce countervailing power, where it has not emerged spontaneously[34]—but the net effect of their view of our society is to lower the premium on competition and to turn attention to other economic and social mechanisms that promise to control excessive market power.

32. David E. Lilienthal, *Big Business: A New Era* (New York, 1953), pp. 5, 7, 17, 33, 36, 47, 190, and passim.

33. A. A. Berle, Jr., *Power Without Property* (New York, 1959), pp.11–16.

34. Galbraith, op. cit., p. 151.

To be sure, liberal intellectuals have not ceased to be critical of business civilization or, on occasion, of big business. But a variety of other issues—foreign policy, urban development, civil rights, education, and the like—have become more central, and where these issues are concerned, liberals do not always find themselves in a simple antagonistic confrontation with big business, as they did in the past. Their criticisms of business civilization now rest more on cultural than economic grounds. The last thing they are interested in is the restoration of competition as the solution to the evils that they see. Even a scandal like the General Electric affair, although it confirms their view of what may be expected from businessmen, no longer excited them very much. In short, that gale of creative destruction about which Joseph Schumpeter wrote so eloquently, when he described the progressive character of capitalist technology, has driven both the liberal and the conservative ideologies before it.

## V

It is easier to account for the decline of the antitrust movement as a matter of public sentiment than it is to explain the persistence and growth of the antitrust enterprise as a legal and administrative fact. But the fate of antitrust is an excellent illustration of how a public ideal, vaguely formulated and often hopelessly at odds with stubborn realities, can become embodied in institutions with elaborate, self-reserving rules and procedures, a defensible function, and an equally stubborn capacity for survival. Institutions are commonly less fragile than creeds.

The antitrust revival originated in the closing phases of the New Deal. It was a response to the recession of 1937–8, which itself brought about a crisis in the thinking and the political strategy of the New Dealers. The recession gave to the Brandeis liberals, who had always been present in New Deal councils, a chance to reassert their ideas about competition and their suspicion of big business. In 1934, long before the cartelization of the N.R.A. was abandoned, the economist Gardiner C. Means, then economic adviser to the Secretary of Agriculture, had prepared a memorandum on administered prices that provided the economic rationale for a new approach to the depression. Early in 1935 this memorandum was published by the Senate.[35] Means contrasted market prices, which were made and remade in the market as the result of interactions between buyers and sellers in the fashion of traditional economic theory, with administered prices, which were set by administrative action and held constant for a considerable period of time. Market prices are flexible and respond readily to a fall in demand; administered prices are rigid. Means considered the disparity

35. Gardiner C. Means, *Industrial Prices and Their Relative Inflexibility*, Senate Document No. 13, 74th Cong., 1st sess. Parts of this document, along with later papers on the same theme, are reprinted in Means's *The Corporate Revolution in America* (New York, 1962). For a critique and some reflections on later interest in the theory, see Richard Ruggles, "The Nature of Price Flexibility and the Determinants of Relative Price Changes in the Economy," in *Business Concentration and Price Policy* (Princeton, 1955), esp. pp. 443–464, and the conflicting views expressed by economists before the Kefauver Committee: Administered Prices, Hearings before the Subcommittee on Antitrust and Monopoly of the Committee on the Judiciary, United States Senate (Washington, 1957).

between flexible and rigid prices to be an important aggravating force in the depression. Although he did not identify administered prices with monopoly, he focused attention once again on those industries in which market power was sufficiently concentrated to make administered prices possible. Some of his contemporaries seized upon the conception as a rationale for stepping up antitrust activity, and Franklin D. Roosevelt invoked it in his message of 1938, calling for the creation of the T.N.E.C. At the same time, other New Deal theorists, notably Assistant Attorney General Robert Jackson, who was then head of the Antitrust Division of the Department of Justice, and Secretary of the Interior Harold L. Ickes, became convinced that the organized power of big business was attempting to sabotage reform through a "strike of capital" and that a new assault on business power must be undertaken as a basis for further attempts at recovery. The old argument that business power was a threat to democratic government itself thus entered into Roosevelt's T.N.E.C. message.

The new attack on business power took two forms; the first was the elaborate, if inconclusive, T.N.E.C. investigation, which yielded a mass of factual information, much of it new, but no programmatic proposals in which the investigators themselves had any confidence. The second was the stepping up of antitrust activity under the leadership of Thurman Arnold, the new chief of the Antitrust Division. Congress doubled appropriations for Arnold's division in 1939 and then doubled them again in 1940. Between 1938 and 1943 its staff grew almost fivefold.

In retrospect it is instructive to see what results came from uncertain and, at times, ill-considered beginnings. Today the Jackson-Ickes view of the recession seems quite partisan and fanciful; the T.N.E.C. investigation, for all the information it gathered, was from a pragmatic point of view a fiasco; the value of Means's emphasis on administered prices is highly controversial among economists; and Thurman Arnold's experiment with antitrust enforcement can be judged, at least from one angle of vision, a substantial failure. And yet, as in the case of so many of the gropings of the New Deal, there was a valuable outcome, which in this case can best be got at by looking at the core of success wrapped up in Thurman Arnold's frustration.

Arnold's story is replete with ironies. He had written of the antitrust enterprise with a devastating note of mockery, and the appointment of a man with such views, especially by an administration that had only recently resorted to the wholesale cartelization of the N.R.A., was looked at askance by antitrust-minded senators as a possible effort to sabotage the Antitrust Division. But Arnold proceeded to recruit and inspire a splendid staff and to rehabilitate the entire antitrust function. His goal was not to attack bigness or efficient mass production or efficient marketing, but rather to discipline the pricing policies of business at the vital points where abuses seemed most important. Antitrust was thus to become an instrument of social and economic policy, aimed to stop firms from setting prices above reasonable levels, to prevent businesses from holding new processes off the market, and to reduce unemployment. All this was to be achieved not so much by isolated cases or by responding to this or that complaint, but rather by systematic action against whole industries—motion pictures, petroleum, radio broadcasting, drugs, housing.

From a short-run point of view, Arnold's regime could be judged a failure. His program for housing was spiked when the Supreme Court made it impossible to act effectively against the labor unions, which constituted a linchpin of restraint of trade in that industry; his plan for the food industry lost its point during the war; his program for transportation was put off by the War Production Board.[36] He could not wholly reform a single industry, much less bring about important general structural changes in the economy. And yet he succeeded in demonstrating the usefulness of the antitrust laws. In actually using the Sherman Act, thanks to the enlarged staff that Congress had given him, he showed for the first time what it could and could not do. Although it could not alter the fundamental character of the economy or make it less liable to cyclical instability (as Arnold had promised it would in his book *The Bottlenecks of Business*), it could significantly affect the conduct of business within the framework of the existing structure. Arnold's division soon won a number of decisions from the courts—particularly in the Alcoa case of 1945 and the American Tobacco case of the following year—which opened new possibilities for enforcement. It won from Congress a permanent reversal of the former policy of niggardly support. And finally, it put the antitrust enterprise on such a footing that it could flourish under both Democratic and Republican regimes.

The return of the Republicans under Eisenhower did not bring a remission of efforts to use the Sherman Act or a retrenchment of the Antitrust Division. Instead, the Eisenhower administration set up the Attorney General's National Committee to Study the Antitrust Laws, which in 1955 returned a unanimous judgment in favor of antitrust policy and of the current state of case law, under which enforcement had been tightened. Although the Committee did not make any dramatic recommendations for more rigorous enforcement, the effect of its work was to reaffirm the bipartisan character of the antitrust commitment by ratifying the achievements of Democratic administrations in the preceding fifteen years.[37] Nor should we forget that the most spectacular and revealing case involving a criminal price conspiracy—the General Electric case—took place during the Eisenhower administration.

What makes it possible to institutionalize antitrust activities at the higher plateau that has been maintained since 1938 is not a consensus among economists as to its utility in enhancing economic efficiency, but a rough consensus in society at large as to its value in curbing the dangers of excessive market power. As in the beginning, it is based on a political and moral judgment rather than economic measurement or even distinctively economic criteria. "It must be recognized," says Edward S. Mason, "that there is an element of faith in the proposition that maintaining competition substantially improves the efficiency of resource use." The option for a minimal level

36. See Corwin D. Edwards, "Thurman Arnold and the Antitrust Laws," *Political Science Quarterly* LVII (September 1943), 338–355.

37. Report of the Attorney General's National Committee to Study the Antitrust Laws (Washington, 1955). For a critique, see Mason, op. cit., pp. 390–401.

of competition to be underwritten by public policy, although it can be backed by substantial economic arguments, "rests basically on a political judgment," write Carl Kaysen and Donald F. Turner in their inquiry into trust policy: "In our democratic, egalitarian society, large areas of uncontrolled private power are not tolerated." "We found," write J. B. Dirlam and A. E. Kahn in their book *Fair Competition*, "that the decisions [of courts and commissions] could not be fully understood or fairly appraised by economic standards alone. Hence we concluded that the appropriate question for economists to ask about antitrust policy is not whether this is the most efficient way of structuring or reorganizing the economy, but the inverted one: Does antitrust seriously interfere with the requirements of efficiency?" "The rationale of antitrust," writes A. D. Neale, a British student of the American experience, "is essentially a desire to provide legal checks to restrain economic power and is not a pursuit of efficiency as such." "For most Americans," concludes John Kenneth Galbraith, "free competition, so called, has for long been a political rather than an economic concept."[38]

In any case, the state of antitrust enforcement seems to correspond with a public consensus. Economists and lawyers differ profoundly on how effective the antitrust laws have been and on how effective they could be if they were more amply enforced, but there is hardly a major industry that has not seen a significant lawsuit or two, and in most industries in which intervention might be thought desirable, government action has had more than negligible effects. It is also one of the strengths of antitrust that neither its effectiveness nor its ineffectiveness can be precisely documented; its consequences rest on events of unknown number and significance that have not happened—on proposed mergers that may have died in the offices of corporation counsel, on collusive agreements that have never been consummated, on unfair practices contemplated but never carried out. Liberals can support it because they retain their old suspicion of business behavior, and conservatives support it because they still believe in competition and they may hope to gain an additional point of leverage in the battle against inflation. No one seems prepared to suggest that the antitrust enterprise be cut back drastically, much less abandoned, and Congress has consistently supported its enlarged staff. The existing state of enforcement conforms to the state of the public mind, which accepts bigness but continues to distrust business morals. Even business itself accords to the principle of antitrust a certain grudging and irritated acceptance, and largely confines its resistance to the courts. Visitations by the Department of Justice are a nuisance, lawsuits are expensive, and prosecution carries an odious stigma, but the antitrust procedures can be considered an alternative to more obtrusive regulation such as outright controls on prices. At any rate, big business has never found it necessary or expedient to launch a public campaign against antitrust enforcement; the pieties at stake are too deep to risk touching.

38. Edward S. Mason in the Preface to Carl Kaysen and Donald B. Turner, *Antitrust Policy* (Cambridge, Mass., 1960), p. XX; ibid., p. 5; J. B. Dirlam and A. E. Kahn, *Fair Competition* (Ithaca, 1954), p. 2; A. D. Neale, *The Antitrust Laws of the U.S.A.* (Cambridge, Eng., 1962), p. 487; Galbraith, op. cit., p. 27.

A final element in antitrust enforcement rests on the fact that the government itself is now a major consumer, and the points of exposure of industrial prices to official concern and reaction have been multiplied. One of the reasons for the antitrust revival in 1938 was the irritation of government officials over the prevalence of what seemed to be collusively priced bids. Thurman Arnold's hope that consumers could be mobilized behind the new antitrust enforcement was out of keeping with the historical passivity and disorganization of American consumers. But the presence of the government as a consumer may supply some of the leverage he was looking for.

Antitrust reform is not the first reform in American history whose effectiveness depended less upon a broad movement of militant mass sentiment than upon the activities of a small group of influential and deeply concerned specialists. In ceasing to be largely an ideology and becoming largely a technique, antitrust has taken its place among a great many other elements of our society that have become differentiated, specialized, and bureaucratized. Since no layman can any longer concern himself with the enormous body of relevant case law or with the truly formidable literature of economic analysis and argument that has come to surround the issue, the potentialities of antitrust action have become almost exclusively the concern of a technical elite of lawyers and economists. Indeed, the business of studying, attacking, defending, and evaluating oligopolistic behavior and its regulation has become one of our lively small industries, which gives employment to many gifted professional men. No doubt this is another, if lesser, reason why antitrust has become self-sustaining: it is not our way to liquidate an industry in which so many have a stake.

If all this is taken as the preface to some unduly optimistic conclusion, my intention will have been misunderstood. My concern is not to suggest that the old problem of market power is on the verge of being solved; it is merely to illustrate how expectations and creeds can change, and how a particular reform, after two generations of noisy but seemingly futile agitation, has been quietly and effectively institutionalized. But it is one thing to say that antitrust has at last begun to fulfill a function, and another to forget how modest that function is. Although the full range of evils anticipated seventy-five years ago from concentration and monopoly has not materialized, the traditional American fear of concentrated power seems hardly less pertinent today. The American economy, whether or not its concentration is still significantly increasing, is extremely concentrated as it stands, and its business structure has brought into being a managerial class of immense social and political as well as market power. This class is by no means evil or sinister in its intentions, but its human limitations often seem even more impressive than the range of its powers, and under modern conditions we have a right to ask again whether we can ever create enough checks to restrain it. The economy over which it presides has had remarkable successes in increasing its production of goods and services, and yet the urban mass society in which these are produced is still not freed from widespread poverty and impresses us again and again with the deepness of its malaise, the range of its problems that stand unsolved, even in some cases pitifully untried. Today our greatest domestic danger lies not in our failure to produce enough goods because we do not have enough competition, but in our failure to render certain humane, healing, humanly productive and restorative social services that are not comprehended at all in the ethos of competition. At its best, big business will not perform such services. At its worst, it can sustain a class of men who will prevent them from being performed.

# 8

# Ordoliberalism and the Freiburg School

## Introduction

BY DANIEL CRANE

Although the primary focus of this book is the currents of Anglo-American intellectual history that paralleled the development of U.S. competition law and policy, we turn in this chapter to the leading continental influence of the post-War period: German ordoliberalism. The ordoliberal school provides an illuminating point of comparison to the increasingly technical-economic trend in Anglo-American theory in the second half of the twentieth century. It also helps to explain some of the reasons for the apparent divergences between European Union and U.S. antitrust policy, which have appeared prominently at various moments during the last quarter century.

Ordoliberalism has its roots in pre–World War II Germany. Franz Böhm, Walter Eucken, and Hans Grossmann-Doerth, professors at Freiburg, penned their *Ordo Manifesto* in 1936 amid the rise of National Socialism. The ordoliberals suffered some Nazi repression, but of a comparatively minor degree for the times. For example, Böhm lost his professorship in 1938 because of his liberal, anti-Nazi views but regained it after the war.[1]

One of the reasons that ordoliberalism has been poorly understood outside of the continent is that it was far broader than a philosophy of competition. Methodologically, the ordoliberals reacted to the positivistic, relativistic, and fatalistic bent of nineteenth-century German legal scholarship associated with intellectuals such as Friedrich von Savigny. They also lamented the compartmentalization of academic disciplines, particularly economics. According to Eucken, "during the nineteenth century economic thought gradually had become isolated, and economists had lost sight of both the political and social contexts of economic issues."[2] As a result, the liberal tradition had become narrowly associated with *laissez faire* political ideology. The ordoliberals sought to promote moralistic and humane

1. For a comprehensive account of the rise of ordoliberal thought, see David J. Gerber, *Law and Competition in Twentieth Century Europe: Protecting Prometheus* 232–265 (1998).

2. Id. at 237.

values by fusing economic and legal understanding into a comprehensive account of a just and liberal social order.

Competition entered the ordoliberal framework not merely as instrumental to achieving consumer or social welfare, but as a fundamental requirement of social justice and a well-functioning society. Free economic participation by all citizens was the primary channel for achieving liberal and humane values. Market power by individuals or firms stood in the way of this goal. Accordingly, the state had an affirmative obligation to promote market competition in order to secure liberal goals.

A major point of difference between ordoliberalism and mainstream Anglo-American traditions is that the Freiburg School conceived of competition principles as bedrock constitutional principles operating on both the state and private actors. Although the U.S. Supreme Court has described the Sherman Act as the "magna carta of free enterprise,"[3] the U.S. antitrust laws are not understood as constitutional in any meaningful sense. The government has no affirmative obligation to protect any private firm or individual from monopolistic oppression. It may, and frequently does, exempt large actors from antitrust scrutiny and, more generally, make judgments about what degrees of market power are tolerable or intolerable insofar as they promote or retard efficiency.

By contrast, the ordoliberals understood the promotion of individual economic freedom as a core obligation of the state. Freedom, in this lexicography, meant the absence of arbitrary control by private actors. Even if concentrations of market power could advance economic efficiency, the government could not permit such concentrations without compromising the liberal interest in personal freedom. As Böhm explains in the selection ahead, "[i]f we want freedom, we have no option but to sacrifice some advantage which we could obtain only by employing concentrated power."

Although the ordoliberal tradition clashes in obvious ways with the "law and economics" approach of the Chicago School that has dominated U.S. antitrust theory for the last quarter century, the ordoliberal vocabulary and values should not be altogether unfamiliar to the American reader. For example, one can see important parallels to the atomistic competitionist views of the Brandeisians—in their belief in antitrust law as creating a level playing field and economic opportunity, and that large concentrations of economic power are undesirable despite their possible efficiencies. Americans who react to the narrowing of antitrust goals toward efficiency and innovation values often cite greater comfort with the "European approach," without fully comprehending its ordoliberal roots.

Indeed, the ordoliberal tradition may even resonate with some on the populist-libertarian right. Friedrich von Hayek, who is revered by American libertarians, maintained close intellectual connections to the Freiburg School and made frequent contributions to the ORDO journal.[4] Although Hayek saw less of a need for the state to play a major role in promoting competition, he concurred with the ordoliberals about the centrality of competition to economic and personal freedom.[5]

3. *U.S.* v. *Topco Assoc.*, 405 U.S. 596, 610 (1972).

4. Gerber, at 237.

5. Id.

Partly owing to its lineage as an anti-Nazi ideology and its proponents' anti-Nazi credentials, ordoliberalism grew in favor during the postwar era. With West Germany's meteoric economic growth paralleling the rise of European integration and the creation of antitrust principles across Europe, ordoliberalism was poised to become an important—perhaps the dominant—European antitrust ideology.[6] As David Gerber has explained, "[o]rdoliberal ideas were well suited to the goal of pursuing European integration through the creation of a common market. This task called for establishing a new community centered on the operation of a market economy…and this corresponded to the central objective of ordoliberal thought."[7] Ordoliberalism is thus central to understanding the development of European competition law and its contrasts to parallel developments in the United States.[8]

In recent years, the European Commission's stated goal of moving away from a "form-based" approach to an "effects-based" approach to competition issues may spell a decline in ordoliberalism's influence across Europe.[9] Nonetheless, pockets of support for an ordoliberal approach remain throughout Europe, and much controlling European Court of Justice case law bears its imprints. As with most of the intellectual currents studied in this book, it would be unwise to declare ordoliberalism's central impulses permanently discarded.

## Franz Böhm, Walter Eucken, and Hans Grossman-Doerth *The Ordo Manifesto of 1936*[1]

## (*In Germany's Social Market Economy: Origins and Evolution,* Alan Peacock and Hans Willgerodt, eds.[2])

Nowadays complaints are widespread that law and political economy are lagging behind events, that they do not make any formative contribution and that they no longer constitute an intellectual force. To disregard such criticism is to fail completely to appreciate the gravity of the situation, for it is true that in Germany these two sciences no longer exercise any appreciable influence on fundamental decisions of a politico-legal and economic nature. Anyone who asserts that this has always been the case

6. Id. at 263–265.

7. Id. at 264.

8. Nicola Giocoli, "Competition Versus Property Rights: American Antitrust Law, the Freiburg School, and the Early Years of European Competition Policy," 5 *J. Competition L. & Econ.* 747, 773 (2009).

9. See, e.g., Christian Ahlborn and David S. Evans, "The Microsoft Judgment and Its Implications for Competition Policy Toward Dominant Firms in Europe," 75 *Antitrust L. J.* 887, 889–890 (2009) (contrasting Court of First Instance's ordoliberal-influenced form-based approach in *Microsoft* with the commission's proposals for reforms in direction of effects-based analysis); cf. Pierre LaRouche, "The European Microsoft Case at the Crossroads of Competition Policy and Innovation: Comment on Ahlborn and Evans," 75 *Antitrust L. J.* 933, 962 (2009) (disagreeing with Ahlborn and Evans's characterization of CFI *Microsoft* decision, but agreeing with characterization of ordoliberalism as influencing form-based antitrust approach).

1. In the original version, there were no notes and references. These have been added by the editors in the translated version insofar as it has been possible to identify them.

2. This article has been translated from the original article that appeared in a series entitled *Ordnung der Wirtschaft*, publication 2 (Stuttgart and Berlin: W. Kohlhammer), published in 1936, under the title "Our Task." This essay was an introduction to a series of publications edited by the three authors.

is mistaken. Law and political economy were once formative forces which exercised considerable influence—for instance, on the reconstruction of the legal and economic system which has taken place in all civilized countries since the end of the eighteenth century. Only in the course of the nineteenth century and the early twentieth century did they gradually forfeit their leading positions.

## Decline in Economic Science

There is now no possible doubt that the consequences of this dethronement of the two sciences have been extremely harmful. Men of science, by virtue of their profession and position being independent of economic interests, are the only objective, independent advisers capable of providing true insight into the intricate interrelationships of economic activity and therefore also providing the basis upon which economic judgments can be made. They are also the only ones who, on the strength of their intimate knowledge of those interrelationships—a knowledge which is constantly being expanded and refined by the continuing penetration of new ideas—are capable of forming an objective judgment, independent of their own immediate economic interests, about economic measures appropriate in particular circumstances.

If men of science relinquish this role or are deprived of it, then other less competent advisers take over—the interested parties. They are certainly expert in the technical details of their professional field, but equally certainly they are not, nor can they be, competent to assess overall economic interrelationships. Moreover, they are incapable of divorcing themselves from their own economic interests which, as a rule, inevitably results in the welfare of their own professional field being confused with that of the national economy as a whole. If the state follows the advice of such interested parties, then politico-economic and legal decisions, which are based on a precise knowledge of the great organising principles of economic activity and which fit into this general system and derive their importance from it, are replaced by decisions which run counter to systematic analysis of the economy and reduce a well-regulated system to chaos. "What we are experiencing today throughout the entire world," wrote Albrecht Forstmann in 1935, "is simply nothing more than a virtually unmistakable declaration of bankruptcy of the method of those who claim to solve the most extensive political-economic problems from the wormseye view of private-economic experiences."[3]

Accordingly, the authors consider that the most urgent task for the representatives of law and political economy, is to work together in an effort to ensure that both disciplines regain their proper place in the life of the nation. This is not only for the sake of science but, more important, in the interests of the economic life of the German nation.

3. Albrecht Forstmann, *Der Kampf um den Internationalen Handel* (Berlin: Haude & Spenersche Buchhandlung, 1935) p. 5. The author adhered first to National Socialism but changed his mind comparatively early. This book was a somewhat peculiar hidden attack on National Socialism, with the author using phrases that seemingly praised the regime. After a while, Forstmann was put into a concentration camp, but he survived and became professor of economics in Berlin.

Yet how can this goal be reached? What must be done in order to restore these two sciences to their former status? The real answer is contained in the series itself. A scientific programme is no substitute for detailed work on the subject in hand. The statement contained in these words of introduction concerns not so much the content of the work as the intellectual attitude with which the task must be approached. To be clear about this, it must first be realised why law and political economy ceased to be guiding influences in the life of the German nation.

In Germany during the nineteenth century law and political economy were affected by that intellectual movement which permeated the whole of scientific and non-scientific thought: historicism. Although historicism has attracted waves of criticism, it has prevailed until the present day. Historicism is much more than a scientific point of view—it denotes a specific scientific attitude. Romanticism and the school of historicism have destroyed the belief in a natural system in both law and political economy. In their entirely justifiable endeavour to comprehend reality and life itself they were bound to come across the changing nature of all human institutions, concepts and ideas. The idea of evolution penetrated these sciences also. There can be no disputing the fact that an understanding of law and political economy based on their historical development considerably extended scientific horizons. It is undeniable that credit must be given for this to men such as Friedrich von Savigny, Friedrich List and others. The historicist movement also exposed the two sciences to grave dangers, however, which were initially felt only slightly, later much more, and which now pose a serious threat to their status—indeed, to their very existence. It might be said that they lost the Archimedean Point from which reality can be comprehended.

"The law grows," said Savigny, "with the nation, develops along with it and finally fades away in the same way as the nation loses its specific identity."[4] The law should be further developed "by inner silent forces, not at the discretion of a legislator." By saying this Friedrich von Savigny denied that in his own time and, for that matter in any other age, there was any need for professional legislators.

This confidence in the inner silent forces seemed innocuous but, in reality, as later events demonstrated, it proved extremely dangerous. Relativism and fatalism were nurtured by it and were to determine the politico-legal attitude of many generations of German lawyers right up to the present.

## Relativism and Fatalism

Legal historicism gradually lost its hold. It could only observe historical change in the substance of the law and without further ado ultimately arrived at the view that the idea of the law followed the substance of the law. In this way, the idea of the law also became relative and thereby lost its dignity. The "inner silent forces" which, in Savigny's opinion, had the right to fashion the law, fundamentally changed in nature in the course of

4. Friedrich Carl von Savigny, *Vom Beruf unserer Zeit fur Gesetzgebung und Rechtswissenschaft*, 1st ed., 1814. Reprint of the third edition of 1840 (Freiburg im Breisgau: J. C. B. Mohr [Paul Siebeck, 1892), pp. 7 and 9.

the nineteenth century. Massive economic power groups emerged on the grandest of scales and these power groups fashioned the law in an entirely one-sided manner. One example is the way such power groups created conditions for delivery and payment which invalidated important sections of the current Law of Obligations for broad sectors of the economy. Apart from a few exceptional cases, legal science and the concept of legal jurisdiction succumbed to this extremely harmful development. This self-made law governing economic relationships seemed (of necessity) to grow out of historical development and it was, and still is, professed by skilful and expert business lawyers. How could a legal system which made historical development into an absolute and which, moreover, no longer acknowledged any fundamental standards—how could such a system not recognise such deformities for what they were? All genuine legal criticism from men of science was bound to waste away, confronted with relativism such as this.

The other danger to which the school of historicism and also that of legal sociology fell victim was fatalism. In his fight against supporters of natural rights, Savigny had repeatedly asserted that the views and will of the lawyer were bound by the views and living conditions of his people and of his era. History shows that in this respect he was partly, though only partly, correct. In times when jurisprudence was in decline as, for instance, in the post-Diocletian Roman Empire, the lawyers did in fact fail to display any creative force. In eras when it was strong, however, as in the first two centuries AD, it was precisely the Roman lawyers who shaped the legal views and institutions of their era and also of their people, thereby exercising a profound influence on their living conditions.

Savigny's legal fatalism, however, was in keeping with the spirit of his own times of the century to follow. In particular, economic conditions appeared to the lawyers of this era as ineluctable facts, to which the law had to adapt itself. The prevailing view was that "the private law in force at any given time, as the system of private interrelationships between citizens, represents at all times the spirit of the prevailing social and economic situation." The politico-legal task of science can only ascertain in each case the most recent social and economic situation and make recommendations as to how the law should adapt itself to this situation. Confronted with such a fatalistic attitude the lawyer can only adjust to the economic conditions. He does not feel that he has the strength to shape them. The formation of cartels, for instance, was accepted by the Imperial Court as an unalterable fact since the indicative and fateful decision of February 4, 1897. No attempt at all was made to formulate a law controlling cartelisation by using the principles embodied in the commercial code. Alternatively, one need only think of the company law which enabled economic power groups virtually to ignore the stringent constitutional law. This subversion of company law, the dire consequences of which the German nation subsequently had to bear, was only possible because legal science and its jurisdictional principles took it for granted that actual economic development must be accepted as a datum.

"Capitalism has at all times found ways and means of succeeding, *de lege, praeter lagem et contra legem*." With these words Werner Sombart gave expression, as he so often did, to the widespread mood of the times. He was speaking as a political economist. Historicist thought in Germany also penetrated political economy and engendered a fatalist-relativist attitude in many generations of scholars. Viewed in more precise terms, there was and still is, within historicist political economy, one group which is more strongly influenced by fatalism and a second one which is characterised more by relativism. These two groups, however, overlap with each other in many respects.

## Karl Marx and Fatalism

The former group received its greatest inspiration from Karl Marx, even though he was certainly not its founder. Marx believed in a law of development in modern society and in his thinking historicism and naturalism intermingle. As he states in the Preface to *Das Kapital*:

> Even when a society has discovered the natural law regulating its own movement, the final purpose of this work is to reveal the economic law of motion of modern society—it can neither leap over nor sweep aside natural phases of its development. It can, however, shorten and alleviate birth pangs.

The aim was to establish the developmental tendencies which are necessarily at work in capitalism, to facilitate their success and thereby hasten the death of capitalism—neither science nor politics can achieve more than this. It was not only Marx who helped such a fatalist belief in development or in decline to gain widespread victory. Even today many regard such a belief as the obvious foundation for their thinking, up to and including the "Tat-Kreis" which before 1933 had such a strong impact on younger generations. To perceive early the symptoms of new trends pressing towards a breakthrough then to await the future and pave the way for this future, even if it may look unpleasant, it is the only acknowledged task. This fatalistic view of history gives rise to an attitude of wary resignation which nevertheless frequently embraces the heroic gesture. "To anticipate which path fate has chosen for it" is regarded by Oswald Spengler for instance as the final great task of western culture. Fatalism and scepticism are always close to one another. Such a fundamental attitude makes it seem pointless or foolish to pit oneself against the relentless course of events or to stand up for an idea.

We are historians enough to take historicist fatalism for what it really is: a sign of weakness on the part of certain intellectuals. Feeling their intellect to be insecure, they can no longer summon up the strength to tackle the job of shaping events and consequently, they retire to the role of observer. In their attempts to justify their attitude they regularly work with historical constructions and doctrines which are totally unrealistic. Above all, they fail to appreciate the huge variety of forces which shape history. It is therefore no coincidence that the prognoses upon which the fatalists focus all their thoughts and wishes almost always prove to be false.

Totally inadmissible simplifications of the pattern of history have already been perpetrated by Marx, who was only able to arrive at his fatalist doctrine of development by regarding technico-economic development as the sole determinant of all historical progress. The whole of social, political, and intellectual life then appears as "superstructure." Consequently, Marx also exercised an influence extending far beyond the circle of his closest disciples. Thus Werner Sombart wrote:

> ... now we must realise that political events generally do not determine the course of economic development, but that the development of capitalism in particular is almost totally independent of the great political revolutions of the last centuries.

Certainly, this thesis is historically incorrect. It reveals an astounding blindness to the impact of political desiderata. For instance, in the times of Napoleon I, Reichsfreiherr vom Stein and Count von Bismarck, up until World War I and the peace treaties which ended it, structural changes in government, foreign and domestic political events have decisively influenced the course of economic development. A non-doctrinaire and truly universal view of history, however, is essential in order to observe correctly the interactions of political and economic events and to discern that they take on different forms in different countries and at various times, depending on the strength of the forces which were and still are active in the areas of both government and the economy. An historicism prone to arbitrary simplification is incapable of perceiving such things. Truly, its fatalism cannot be justified on the basis of historical experience. Unfortunately, it undermines the power of science to be a life-force. How can the intellect shape events when it accepts them as inevitable?

## Influence of Gustav Von Schmoller

In respect of political economy, German historicism also developed, as has already been indicated, another stronger stem which was earlier referred to briefly as relativistic. At the head of its supporters was Gustav von Schmoller. Both directly and through his pupils, he has exercised a lasting influence on the economic thought of broad and important sections of the German nation until the present day. Schmoller's professional interests lay in political economy and social policy. He wanted to make political economy into a moral science. He pronounced, *inter alia*, on the labour problem, the reform of the industrial code, the housing problem and the protective tariff problem. He did not believe that the course of history was inevitable and that no one can successfully intervene. Frequently, he was disposed to call for state intervention. Nevertheless, he certainly did not fulfil the needs of his time. Schmoller must take a considerable portion of the blame for the fact that, in Germany, political economy lost its former power as a truly formative influence. It must now be asked how this came about.

First, when in 1872 at Eisenach, Schmoller and his friends developed their programmes for social policy in response to the increasing gravity of the labour problem, it was still the great issue of the fundamental conflict with the prevailing conditions that guaranteed them power and influence. The entire social system formed the subject of discussion. The courage to pose questions of principle, however, soon vanished. For instance, one need only read Schmoller's speech on the reform of the industrial code of 1877 in which he takes particular issue with free competition. His chief concern was to eschew any decision of principle; each issue would be decided on its merits. At this time fundamental thinking seemed to him doctrinaire, a mistake which caused serious damage. The immense diversity of historical development and historical facts made such an impression on him that, as a realist, he believed he had to avoid coming to general conclusions. Nor is he by any means alone in this respect, either in his own times or ours. Almost everywhere general lines of thought were gradually superseded by questions and thoughts on specific points. Thereby Schmoller and his disciples believed that they were assuming a realistic attitude and were paving the way for realistic policies.

In reality, they were destroying the basis from which political economy specialists are able to comment in realistic terms upon the major issues of practical economic policy. Even the identification of the problems involved became too narrow. Typical, for instance, is the attitude assumed by Schmoller and his school towards the formation of monopolies which had been growing in the German economic system at an increasing rate since the closing decades of the nineteenth century. The fundamental and, at the same time, practical question as to whether the overall system of the economy is destroyed by the formation of monopolies was touched upon but not seriously posed. Had this been done, then they would have realised what the permeation of the economy by private power groups means. Workable politico-economic measures could have been proposed, the entire discussion could have been elevated to another level and much serious damage which later became apparent could have been foreseen. Science would then have fulfilled its duty. The Historical School yielded, however, by its genuinely relativistic opportunism, to the established fact of the existence of monopolies; the crucial question was avoided and issues were dealt with at a superficial level. It is therefore no accident that the last 50 years in Germany are rich in the growth of monopoly organisations but lacking in useful radical scientific questioning of this tendency.

It is precisely the effort of posing questions which clearly distinguishes science from everyday thinking. By forgetting how to ask fundamental questions, this Historical School was essentially no longer capable of transcending everyday experience.

Second, in his efforts to comprehend historical reality, while never losing sight of continual change, Schmoller did not know how to use the abstract thinking apparatus of political economy. He did not see that unless this apparatus is utilised it is impossible to arrive at any true understanding of the interdependencies within the economic system. There are admittedly several, frequently cited utterances of his which show his respect for theoretical research, but what matters is not statements such as these but only the research itself. The disastrous thing was that under his leadership German political economists forgot how to apply theory, how to improve it and how to carry out economic analyses. For that reason, they also forgot how to understand the working of the complex economic system. In short, they lost touch with reality and committed precisely that mistake which they most abhorred, for reality is not an accumulation of unrelated facts. Thus a German economist emerged whose type is still prevalent today. He strives to find economic reality, but does not know how to do so. He respects theoretical research but does not know what to do with it. He wants to help shape the economy, but is unable to do so, because he does not understand economic interrelationships. Such a view of political economy was bound to fail once the great problems of economic life such as, for instance, the German inflation or the transfer problem had to be faced.

The political economy of the Schmoller variety had not discerned that, all-in-all, relativism was cutting the ground from under its own feet. Consciously or unconsciously, the widespread belief in general progress gave it some support. It was no accident that Schmoller concluded his greatest work, *Grundriss der allgemeinen Volkswirtschaftslehre*, with a solemn acknowledgement of a general belief in progress. "Man has made infinite physical intellectual and moral progress," he stated, thereby showing how much he, as a child of his time, under-estimated the demonic passions and egotistic instincts of mankind, which any economic policy has to take into account. Eras of decline, so he believed, would also be merely transitory in the future. He did not perceive the dangers of chaos. In the final analysis, all opportunism is to be explained by this fundamental belief in progress, according to which the actual development of the economic system and the economic process ultimately and necessarily leads to something better.

In both sciences, therefore, in jurisprudence and political economy, a similar drama was and is still being enacted in Germany. As historicism gains ground they are losing their foothold. The idea of law and the idea of truth are becoming relative concepts, being adapted readily to changing facts and opinions. Thereby each of them is ceasing to be an intellectual and ethical force. They are becoming satellites and so economic power groups are able to pursue their interests with ever-increasing success. The views of science are wont to penetrate gradually via the universities to the wider circle of judges, administrative officials and others, who were now becoming affected by this opportunistic, non-fundamental attitude of the scholars. The two sciences maintained self-confidence and efficiency only in so far as they offered resistance to historicism. This must be emphasised all the more, as the criticism to which the two sciences have been subjected in Germany of late derives partly from the spirit of historicism and is therefore worthless.

## Our Programme

The task before us may be defined as one involving critical analysis. We need only to turn our criticism into a positive force in order to identify clearly the lines along which we must work if we are to return law and economics to their proper place.

First, we note the conviction that rational thought and creative action are irreconcilable opposites, that thought impedes the energy and thereby also the success of the deed. This idea has had ever-increasing currency since Friedrich Nietzsche formulated his doctrine of the superman and his creative primitive instincts. Nietzsche wishes the person who acts heroically to be "ever unknowing and also unscrupulous." Blind to rational deliberation, he should give himself up to the demon of his passion.

This antithesis is entirely false. It has no historical foundation. It is bound to have a disastrous effect. A Frederick the Great would have dismissed as totally absurd the idea that it was possible for the statesman or general to see things too clearly. Indeed, he was troubled whenever he was unable to grasp things sufficiently clearly and to discern causal connections. All major figures in the political and military history of the world have been just like this. They became great precisely because their irrational force of will and their force of reason together overcame difficulties which appeared insuperable. Only the inwardly weak man sees reason as a threat, becomes uncertain and divided within himself because of it and, out of fear of the sober world of established facts and reason, rushes headlong into the intoxication of the irrational, into feverish ecstasy. The strong man, however, feels his strength increase whenever he is able to apply reason to illuminate the darkness surrounding the acting agent and to the exercise of his powers. Using this conviction as our point of departure, which is based on historical experience, we wish to bring scientific reasoning, as displayed in jurisprudence and political economy, into effect for the purpose of constructing and reorganising the economic system.

Second, we set against historicism which, as already described in detail, has failed with its relativist and non-committal attitude, our fundamental principle. This consists in viewing individual economic questions as constituent parts of a greater whole. Since all sectors of the economy are closely interconnected, this fundamental approach is the only one which does justice to the subject. The treatment of all practical politico-legal and politico-economic questions must be keyed to the idea of the economic constitution. In this way relativist instability and fatalist acceptance of facts are overcome.

Third, radical rejection of historicism, which is entirely beyond redemption in any shape or form, does not mean that we disregard historical facts. It is precisely by approaching history with fundamental questions that we shall understand it better, penetrate deeper and learn more from it than historicism has. The historical experience of the last decades and centuries must be our starting point. "History will have nothing to do with those gentlemen who will have nothing to do with history."

We must push forward through the mist of intangible ideologies to the constituent facts and the requirements of the subject matter. Ideologies of economic prophets and dogmas which violate the facts, ingenious edifices of ideas which defy rational control, are just as impracticable as the ideologies of interested parties which they not infrequently touch upon. All conceptual speculations which, today more than ever, play an important part in law and also in political economy, have a disastrous effect because they lure us into becoming doctrinaire and unrealistic. Facts and not legal or economic concepts must be studied. The problems that must be solved are practical ones. Fear of reality, which Bismarck scoffed at, must be overcome in our field more than any other. The problems of the economic system can be comprehended and brought to a solution, if realism and fundamental thought are combined, difficult though that might be.

Fourth, the economic constitution must be understood as a general political decision as to how the economic life of the nation is to be structured. Adherence to this idea alone provides the means of acquiring truly reliable and conclusive rules for interpreting many aspects of public or private law. This applies not only to the basic laws, but also particularly to special laws relating to economic matters. Hitherto, for instance, the Bankruptcy Act was treated chiefly from the perspective of the law of procedure. This point of view, however, is undoubtedly one-sided and certainly does not reveal the full sense of the law. On the contrary, it is absolutely essential to understand Bankruptcy Law as a part, indeed an important part, of the economic constitution which determines when and how enterprises are eliminated from the prevailing exchange economy. Only when the structural principles of this economy have been understood is it possible to comprehend Bankruptcy Law, the stipulations and administration of which in turn are extremely important for the functioning of the entire economic constitution and for the regulation of production. The same applies, *mutatis mutandis* to the law of obligations, real estate law, family law, labour law, administrative law, and all other parts of the law. Similarly, in the development of further legislation, the basic idea of the economic constitution must be borne in mind.

The problem of understanding and fashioning the legal instruments for an economic constitution, however, can only be solved if the lawyer avails himself of the findings of economic research. If, for example, the legal practitioner or legal scientist has to deal with a question of unfair competition, then it is certainly not enough for him to investigate the ethical views of the commercial profession and, proceeding from the "sense of propriety of all fair and just-minded people" to declare one group to be just within the law and another as just outside it. On the contrary, it is imperative, particularly in this instance, to reason out the problem in accordance with the provisions of the economic constitution, for free competition is an essential structural principle of the present-day German economy. Free competition must not be stopped on the erroneous grounds of alleged unfair practice. On the other hand, it must not be allowed to degenerate into truly unfair competition either. How the line is to be drawn between unfair and permissible competition, whether there is free competition or not, whether competition is restricted, whether competition is efficient or obstructive, whether or not price-cutting contradicts the principle of the system—all these issues can only be decided by investigations conducted by economists into the various states of the market. The collaboration of the two sciences, which in this respect still leaves much to be desired, is clearly essential.

Complaints about the specialisation of the individual sciences are levelled at the sciences of yesteryear. There are strong forces at work everywhere which are overcoming this problem of specialisation. Indeed, it is the work being carried out on the problems themselves and not unhelpful methodological reflection, which is linking the individual sciences together again at a new level. Today physics, chemistry, mineralogy, physiology and other natural sciences no longer stand apart from one another. On the contrary, the physiologists are now compelled to employ the methods and results of chemistry, and the mineralogists and chemists those of physics. In the wide area of the humanities also a process of reconciliation on the part of the individual sciences is taking place everywhere. The division of the humanities into political, economic, intellectual, ecclesiastical and art history has proved to be untenable. The deeper the historian digs historically, the more he is forced to adopt a universal view of history. The sciences of law and economics are also involved at various points in such a process of reconciliation. Those problems which form the subject of the papers in our series demand that the methods of reasoning and research of both sciences be used, but not in the sense that we let "their boundaries merge into each other," to use Immanuel Kant's words. Kant was quite correct when he expected this to produce "not a propagation but a disfiguration of the Sciences." Each must preserve its individuality if it is to achieve anything. But whenever the subject demands the use of both, then this must be done. We hope to follow the dictates of true science by doing the same.

## Franz Böhm

## *Democracy and Economic Power in Cartel and Monopoly in Modern Law*[1]

### I

It was not always so, but to-day at any rate it is a fact that any nation which operates a free market economy, also has an antitrust legislation. If we want to know the reasons for this development, we shall probably be told that a free market economy constitutes an economic system, which, although it is incompatible with economic power, nevertheless engenders economic power and cannot get rid of it of its own volition. Consequently special laws will have to be enacted either to liberate the free market economy from economic power or to place the holders of economic power under the control of the state and thus prevent them from abusing their dominant position.

To begin with, there are two conclusions in this answer, which are absolutely indisputable, firstly that the free market economy engenders economic power, and secondly that it is incapable of eliminating such power once it has been established.

However, we should like to question the third conclusion that the free market economy constitutes an economic system, which is incompatible with economic power.

In order to judge, whether this statement is true we must first of all come to an understanding as to what is meant by the term "free market economy" and what demands we can make on it. By a free market economy we usually mean an economic system that dispenses with any official control and instead entrusts control of the interplay of economic forces to a mechanism—the market price system—which discharges its control functions automatically. If we proceed from this conception of a free market economy, it will obviously be wrong to argue that this system is incompatible with economic power. On the contrary, the market price system controls the interplay of economic forces automatically even if some market prices are manipulated by economic power. Admittedly, the production and consumption programmes realized in

1. Reports on supranational and national European and American Law, presented to the International Conference on Restraints of Competition at Frankfurt on Main, June 1960, vol. 1, Karlsruhe: Verlag C. F. Muller, 1961.

this case will differ to some extent from those that would be put into practice if all prices were strictly competitive. Incomes will be distributed in another way and the factors of production combined in a rather different manner. However, the automatic control mechanism of the free market economy will be able to co-ordinate the entire operational and consumption plans even under such circumstances. In an economy ruled by monopolistic prices the reacting process develops in exactly the same way as in an economy ruled by competitive prices. Those who hold no economic power regard both the competitive and the monopolistic price as a fact which they have to accept as it is. Each price modification causes the participants in the market to change their economic dispositions, and it makes no difference, whether this change is due to the influence of competition or to the deliberate decision of a monopolist guided by considerations of market strategy. Most participants in the national economy, in particular the consumers, are not in the least interested in how the prices they are charged are determined, whether such prices are competitive or monopolistic or fixed by the government. To them price is price; what matters is that prices are low and, if possible, will decline still further.

In short, whatever the case may be, whether all markets are competitive, or whether some of them are monopolistic, the free market economy operates automatically in both instances. The competitive and the monopolistic price are equally capable of controlling the productive process. Whether this control will lead to more reasonable results if prices are monopolistic, remains to be seen. For the moment all that matters in this respect is that even a monopoly-ridden free market economy is automatically controlled by the price mechanism.

Consequently we shall have to revise our original hypothesis that the free market economy is incompatible with economic power. This—as we said—incorrect hypothesis must be replaced by the following question: Does it make a difference to or is it irrelevant for the logical content of a free market economy system, whether economic power establishes itself in a number of markets? Does a free market economy, in which all markets are competitive ensure a higher degree of economic efficiency than a free market economy, in which any markets are more or less monopolised? Is the distribution of incomes in a strictly competitive economy more reasonable and economically fair than in a monopoly-ridden free market economy? Does a strictly competitive economy make better provision for affording all those participating in it an equal amount of freedom than a free market economy, in which the holders of economic power exercise an estimable permanent influence on market price determination and are capable of manipulating the degree of shortage of supply or demand in a unilateral manner?

The answer to all these questions is not immediately available, but can only be the result of exact study and deliberation. We cannot even know whether the answer to each of these three questions will be similar. It might be possible, for instance, that the question as to the highest degree of efficiency cannot in any way be answered conclusively, in other words, that we shall find that both the unrestricted and the monopoly-ridden economy have their specific advantages and that it is a matter of taste which of these advantages we prefer. The answer to the other two questions will then perhaps be that the fully competitive economy is the only system of free market economy that meets the requirements of social justice and freedom.

However, if we decide in favour of a competitive economy, then, of course, the proposition that the competitive system of economy is incompatible with economic power can be stated with complete certainty. It would follow already ex definitione, for a competitive economy is a free market economy, in which competition is unrestricted in any market either with regard to supply or to demand. The freedom of movement of a supplier or a prospective customer, however, who is not exposed to any competition or only to a limited amount of competition is identical with just that condition which we call economic power.

Once we have decided in favour of a competitive economy, then we shall in fact also be obliged to spare no effort in order to prevent the rise of economic power and to eliminate any economic power already established. It has already been stated at the outset that the automatic operation of the free market economy will be incapable of effecting such prevention and elimination of power. Hence we shall have no option but to avail ourselves of the possibilities offered by the legislation and the political executive. And in the event that these means, too, will be unable to effect the complete prevention and elimination of economic power, we shall have to decide whether to put up with the still remaining rest of economic power as a tribute to the inevitable imperfection of all human systems and to be satisfied with the automatic control of the free market economy or whether to prefer charging our government with the control of monopolized markets by a deliberate economic policy of official interventions if it should prove that automatic control through the market price mechanism fails to furnish the expected results.

## II

Of the three reasons, which argue in favour of opposing economic power and encouraging competition, insofar as this is at all possible, the economic reason has played the most important part, both outwardly and officially. It has been argued that monopolies impair the economic efficiency of the free market economy system and result in the factors of production being imperfectly combined. Monopolies operate like sand in the control mechanism of the free market economy. This at least was the reason, which most governments advanced in order to justify the enactment of antitrust laws and laws against restraints of competition. For it is obvious that governments which espouse a free market economy, but nevertheless regard it as necessary to interfere in the natural developments of the economic process, do not wish to commit such a violation of the dogma without the blessings of the established economic theory.

This, however, does not in any way alter the fact that the real motives behind the enactment of antitrust laws were of a completely different, a more popular nature, if I may say so. It was not economic efficiency and the effectiveness of economic control, but social justice and civil liberties which were held to be threatened by monopolies. In other words, the government was guided by the short-term and perpetually recurring effects of the monopolists' actions on those immediately concerned. In this case, however, already a primitive consideration, which does not require much knowledge of economic theory, will be sufficient to discover a disquieting fact, namely that some of the many changes in the earning and income prospects of those participating in the market—which in a free market economy constantly occur and which must be and usually are accepted by everybody concerned—are caused by deliberate actions of certain individuals or groups. Normally the quantity of a commodity supplied or demanded at a certain price is a factor to which many persons on both sides of the market contribute their share without any of them considering the possibility of setting the market price in motion by an increase or reduction of their supply or demand. Each of them acts as if he had not the slightest influence on the total size of the supply or demand, although he knows, of course, that this total size is composed of the individual supply and demand. But since none of them has even an approximate knowledge of the possible dispositions of the others, nor any chance of influencing such re actions on their part, the future price must necessarily remain completely unknown to them. If there is any change in the current price, which has determined their supply and demand dispositions, they will find themselves compelled to alter their future supply and demand dispositions, but this compulsion is caused by an event which was completely inaccessible to the manipulating arbitrariness of the individual parties concerned. That is why this event—the price modification—is accepted by everybody engaged in commerce as fate, as force majeure, the submission and adaptation to which does not detract from the self-confidence of free human beings. For nobody in his senses is likely to interpret individual freedom as freedom from nature or freedom from the law or legitimate commands of legitimate constitutional authorities or freedom from the helpful or restrictive effects, which the existence, the planning, the actions and omissions of all his fellow human beings in their entirety exercise on the scope of his own development. Each of them is convinced to be at the mercy of these natural, political and social facts without being able or permitted to keep them away from himself. By freedom he understands no more than the chance and the right to react to such facts according to his own decision and through such reactions—each of them having the choice between several kinds of reactions—to contribute one of those grains of sand, which will form the future pattern of society.

However, it is a completely different matter, if the social facts to which we must submit are deliberately manipulated by some of our fellow-beings, in other words, if their condition has to be attributed to the will of some of our fellow-beings. In this case it is no longer a fate for which nobody is responsible, that knocks at our door, but the action of an individual who dares to play fate and to roll a rock in front of our feet, whose existence affects our personal development, our chances as consumers, our professional chances, as well as our income. We are not at all willing to accept as fate such social facts created by spontaneous human actions, all the more when they exercise a detrimental effect on our existence and our expectations from life. To argue with real fate would be stupid and hopeless, since there is no responsible perpetrator whom we can call to account. But where some individuals plant a fate of their own creation before our eyes, it is responsible perpetrators of flesh and blood, whom we are dealing with and whom we can charge for the damage inflicted on us, unless they had the right to act in this way under our constitution and our laws.

Under the constitutions of free countries only those subjects have the right to manipulate social facts which are expressly legitimized to form the volonté générale or to execute the already formed volonté générale, and these are none but the constitutional political authorities, and each of them again within the scope of its constitutional competence and function. Only such social facts can claim to be recognized as fate whose realization is attributable to an event we can describe as being caused by the volonté de tous, in other words, an event consisting in the fusion of many individual wills, which are independent of each other, provided always that the result of this fusion cannot be clearly attributed to any of these spontaneous individual acts involved. This is true at least of such social facts, which are typical ones, since they are continuously manipulated over longer periods of time by decisions attributable to the same persons and considerably affect the scope of development and expectations from life of many people.

If, now, it happens that such typical dominant positions develop in the hands of persons who are not counted among the constitutional political authorities, in other words, that such dominant positions have been conferred on them neither by the political constitution nor by any other law, and if the law and the government are unable or unwilling to prevent the development of such dominant positions, and if such positions are used by their holders without due regard to the will of the people for any kind of purpose, most of all, however, for their own exclusive material benefit, and nobody exists who can compel them or is competent to compel them to exercise their powers with due regard to the will of the people, then we shall be faced with a situation, which every sensible citizen may consider and must consider a threat to social justice and civil liberties. Such a situation has all the characteristics of an arbitrary system, a system of anarchic warfare. Mere accidental external circumstances decide, who is to hold power, and the will of those who happen to hold power influences the course and arrangement of production. The question as to who has access to economic activities and to which of them, if any, and which income he will derive from such activities, depends only to some extent on the possession of productive qualities and for the rest on plain arbitrariness and the talents displayed in the struggle for the survival of the fittest or in economic guerilla warfare.

The specifically economic power is unique insofar as it developed on the soil of private law, in other words, within the framework of a system which regulates the contractual and extracontractual relationships between powerless persons, in other words, which presupposes the lack of power of those involved in such relationships and whose rules and institutions will lose much of their regulating and justice-engendering force if certain groups among the subjects of private law acquire a permanent and typical ascendancy over the other subjects of private law, and be it only on a few markets. It is just as strange that this power is acquired by using the means, the rights and the liberties, which private law provides for any purpose except this one. In the beginning one proceeds not by force, but merely by cunning. The free market economy, as already stated, is controlled by an automatically working control mechanism, the market price system. Thus the scope of development, the chances of professional success, the level of income, depend on the control of this anonymous force which can neither be flattered nor intimidated. Consequently those, who are not content to accept the chances of fortune allotted to them as if by fate, but instead wish to succeed more quickly and easily without observing the general rules of the game, have no other choice but to act like the manipulators of slot machines, by securing access to the mechanism of this machine, in order to influence the result of the process through a corresponding manipulation of the clockwork and lever system. Since the mechanism of the price system resembles a plebiscite, all that matters is to manipulate such plebiscite by getting control of the numerous wills participating in it.

For this purpose two ways are offered by private law, a primitive and direct one, and a complicated and indirect one. The direct way would be that all those participating in the plebiscite or at least nearly all of them make a mutual agreement, under which they arrange how to cast their votes. Whether they come to a direct agreement on their quotations or on the quantities of each party's supply or demand, in both cases the machine will produce other prices than it would have done without such manipulation of the votes polled by all the participants. The complicated way would be that one participant tries to accumulate, exclusively for himself, such a large quota of the total supply or demand that his isolated disposition as regards such supply or demand will itself already constitute the contents of the whole plebiscite. The first way consists in forming cartels by means of making agreements in restraints of competition between all or practically all competing suppliers or prospective customers. The second way consists in expanding capacity, in founding large enterprises or combines with a uniform control of operations. In this case, however, it will be insufficient to conclude just a single agreement of relatively simple contents. A multitude of agreements with all possible suppliers, bankers, workers and customers will be required as well as numerous extra-contractual transactions, in particular, competitive acts. The contents of the cartel agreement differ in a most significant and alarming manner from those of all other agreements usually made by any participants in the market. The agreements and actions, however, which a participant in the market must employ in order to increase his personal market share in a monopolistic, partially monopolistic or oligopolistic manner, differ in no way from any agreements and actions to be employed by enterprises without any market power, that wish to remain fully competitive. This, however, implies—to state it already at this stage—that the legislature can prohibit cartel agreements without having in the least to worry about the success of a free market economy. If it does so, it will destroy exactly what it wants to destroy and nothing else. It is a clean surgical operation completely harmless to the entire economy.

On the other hand, the legislature cannot prohibit agreements or means and ways and actions used to accomplish an exclusive monopoly of individuals or combinations, since they are the daily bread even of those participants in the market, who dare not think or hope of ever acquiring a quota of the total supply or demand likely to influence the market as a whole.

To state it briefly: Either one sees to it that all users of an automatic machine will use it in a manner, which has been fully concerted in advance, or one arranges to be the only supplier or prospective customer, who can use such machine. The system of private law offers legal possibilities for applying both methods, possibilities, which the ordinary civil lawyer adores so passionately that he will defend them with his last ounce of blood, even if they are used for cheating the entire system of private law of its content of order and justice. This infatuation of legal scholars, judges and lawyers with the harmonious marvels of the microcosm of private law and their strange indifference towards the macrocosm of private law, that is to say, the system of private law in its entirety, this lack of interest in the connexion between the design of the system of private law as a whole and the designs of its individual components, has considerably facilitated the rise of economic power within the framework of the free market economy system. For long periods of time lawyers have failed to notice how fundamentally a social control system can be changed and deprived of its meaning by the fact that those controlled by it place coins sanctioned by civil law in a slot machine also sanctioned by civil law, once they have understood the mechanism of this machine. Practically all economic power is accomplished by a cardsharper trick within the sphere of civil law.

If we consider the phenomenon of economic power from this viewpoint, the question that arises will differ entirely from any question that would arise if we concerned ourselves exclusively with the problem whether the reorientation of the economic process caused by the emergence of economic power results in a plus or a minus or just an aliud [Civil law term meaning "something completely different from"—eds.] of economic efficiency. In this case there will be only one question, namely: "Does economic power, if viewed from the angle of our political constitution and from the order content of our system of private law constitute legitimate power or not? Can it be justified from considerations of social justice, as well as the distribution of political rights in accordance with the way of life of a free people to expose the citizens to the interferences by the holders of such power, just as if the changes in the scope of their development, their professional chances and their incomes caused by such interferences were the result of a fate, for which nobody is responsible or the result of a legitimate decision by legitimate political authorities? Can the fact that human power is at work in this case, be simply ignored as civil lawyers have done for generations? Or can it be tacitly legitimized in its entirety just as if this had been laid down in our constitution, in response to demands on the part of those who derive or hope to derive advantage from the possession of such power?"

It is obvious that the answer to this question is completely independent of whether on balance and in the final analysis the possession and use of such economic power will result in economic advantages or disadvantages and whether, if both should be the case, the advantages outweigh the disadvantages or vice versa, or whether they approximately cancel each other out. On the contrary, we must ask ourselves "Shall we, as citizens of a democratic state and members of a free system of society based on the rights of the individual hand over such power to some of our fellow-citizens? What consequences is this going to have for our liberties and for the content of social justice inherent in our system of government and society?" If it should prove that serious dangers to freedom and justice will ensue, we must resolve to place any conceivable obstacle in the way of the establishment of economic power, and must not allow ourselves to be deterred from this resolution by any regard for the possible useful effects of this power any more than we would waver in our resolution to defend our democratic system, should anybody try to show us how many wonderful projects could be realized if only we decided to replace our democracy by a totalitarian dictatorship. Nothing in this world can be had without paying for it, including freedom. If we want freedom, we have no option but to sacrifice some advantage which we could obtain only by employing concentrated power.

On the other hand, we are fortunate enough insofar as the results obtained from the research in our economic theory have shown that a more fully competitive system of economy also produces greater economic efficiency than a free market economy pervaded by considerable elements of economic power, which cannot provide any legal and political protection for competition. In this case, therefore, our love of freedom is even rewarded by economic benefits, which otherwise providence would not usually bestow on us. Thus, the advocates of a fully competitive economic system will have no trouble in confronting those who regard the interest of the state as the cardinal value, including, for instance, our historians, who are in the habit of taking a sceptical attitude towards all other principles, in particular ethical ones, and would just love to banish anybody with an interest in systems of state and society from the historical arena, and to accommodate him on the spectators' grandstand.

The problem of economic power is synonymous with the problem of private power. The latter, however, is by nature a strictly constitutional problem. Right at the beginning of this study we had to realize that private power does not in any way fit into a constitutional democracy. It has no legitimate standing either in the system of government or the system of society of a constitutional democracy. Our system of government cannot tolerate it, because it knows no other than constitutionally assigned power with a political purpose. Such power, in turn, is conferred in accurately determined proportions on specific constitutional authorities, which as regards the use they make of it are bound not only by limitations and duties, but also burdened with constitutional responsibility and subject to control by the people. Here there is no power in private hands, which could be used with the kind of freedom enjoyed by private individuals as long as they move in the private sphere. The private sphere, however, that is to say the system of private law, knows no power at all. Even the state authorities must leave their power and authority in the "cloakroom," if they want to move in the private sphere, be it as buyers or sellers, proprietors or patentees. Within the private sphere each typical and permanent position of power constitutes a serious element of trouble, since the possession of power is completely incompatible with the practically immeasurable freedom of movement and action which the system of private law allows its subjects on the understanding that they just hold no power at all, but are controlled, and this in a very effective way, by their very lack of power.

This problem of constitutional policy, however, is the problem, which in the subject of this formal address has been expressed in the words "Democracy and Economic Power."

## III

On the Continent the term "democracy" is frequently used in a narrow sense by confining it strictly to the state, and then it signifies a principle under which the whole authority of the state is to issue from and to be transferred to the sovereign people. It is obvious, however, that this narrow conception of democracy does not answer the purposes of our study. On the contrary, democracy should be interpreted in a wider sense as a system embracing both state and society, in other words, we should try to see the principles of our political constitution and the principles ruling our society, which is founded on the rights of the individual, side by side and in their interplay and to conceive all processes in state and society as a comprehensive functional whole.

In doing so we shall be in step with that great occidental movement, which led to the rise of our modern democracy. For this movement, too, had in no way confined itself to transforming the absolute or limited monarchy into a democratic state, but in addition had set itself two wider aims, on the one hand to replace the feudal society by a society ruled entirely by the rights of the individual, and secondly to fix the relationship between society and state in quite a specific way, by regarding a society regulated by certain laws and conventions as a perfectly healthy and sound organisation, which, if necessary, could manage quite well without any executive power and authorities, but would nevertheless want to equip itself with such machinery of government in order to employ its services for a few additional purposes while at the same time being afraid of it because the relationship between master and servant could be reversed only too easily, if the servant were armed and the master unarmed.

This third aim—the restriction of the state, in other words the specifically political society to the role of a mere auxiliary institution for regulating the everyday relationships between different human beings—had been described at a very late period in history by a special term, when it was referred to as the principle of government by law. This principle had previously been developed, under the influence of doctrines from the 18th Century philosophy of natural law, from the unlimited natural wealth of rights of the individual and the social contract entered into between the individual and society. However, during the constutional [sic] struggles, which took place in England in the 13th Century and in which for the first time in the history of the occident the rule of government by law was actually contested and legalised, it was not the natural individual rights of men that people had in mind, but rather the venerable world of a society ruled by the common law and its relevant principles, usages and judicial precedence, and besides, of course, those numerous feudal titles, which, too, constituted the system of society of that time. It was this self-supporting system of society, which was to be protected against the arbitrary power and portentous political caprices of the kings.

Rule of the people within the state, rule of private law within the society and rule of law as link between society and state—these are the three great political principles which together constitute democracy in the Western sense.

## IV

If, however, it is a fact that the society which is based on the rights of the individual is joined to and actually supports the democratic state and that the freedom enjoyed by the citizen, which enables him to exercise his right to vote, as well as his other rights of political co-determination within the democratic state, originates in the main from the free system of society based on the rights of the individual, then it will be obvious that democracy is threatened from inside principally by two dangers—firstly that the democratic legislature and the democratic government will in time overextend their functions and competences to the prejudice of the private sphere, and secondly that developments will be started within the private sphere, which considerably restrict the scope of freedom of entire groups of citizens and, in addition, create typical and permanent dependencies.

Thus we are faced with the question whether economic power as it is to be found in our modern industrial society is likely to create a situation where some of its members will be permanently and perceptibly dependent on others. Another question is whether such a development might involve the danger that the democratic legislature and the democratic government could feel themselves compelled or tempted to interfere increasingly in the social processes within the private sphere in order to set up permanent barriers against the establishment of power, or to protect the dependent members of society against the arbitrariness of the economically more powerful ones, or finally because the economically powerful members of society acquire a political influence on the mind of the authorities and use this influence in order to strengthen and to obtain political legitimation for their purely economic dominant positions with the aid of the law and the executive.

It is obvious that any important shift in the distribution of power within the private sphere is bound to be followed by a shift also in the distribution of political power within the democratic society of citizens, and that this other distribution of power within the people must be reflected in the composition of the parliaments and governments. Power will always be respected.

If I had to apply a suitable term to the danger that might arise in this respect, I would call it the danger of a refeudalization of society. A society might develop which gradually loses its ability to support a democratic state. The state, on its part, would then change its nature, that is to say the legislature and executive powers would no longer be exercised in accordance with principles founded on the rule of law, nor with the tendency of neutrality towards any social systems.

The constitutional authorities would feel less and less obliged to counteract the emergence of private power, but make it their business to stabilize such dominant positions by political means and to transform them into individual and group titles of a political character. Such changes in the structure of society would affect even the political ideologies. The sciences which attach great importance to the knowledge of structural connections would have to yield their influence to sociological, historical and psychological approaches, which interest themselves in laws of historical developments, and—if I may say so—want to hear the historical grass grow. However, the converse is probably true to an even greater extent. The emergence of doctrines, which place the main emphasis on the laws of historical developments will encourage tendencies towards concentration of power, while the occupation with structural connections rather tends to encourage tendencies towards greater freedom. At least this is the view that impresses itself on us, if we follow the history of 19th Century ideas and relate them to our own experiences during the 20th Century, as suggested by Ludwig von Mises, who once said that if we wished to understand contemporary events, we would do well to read the books written some 20 or 30 years ago. However, the distance of time would probably have to be a little longer than this.

## V

Economic power arises within the private sphere. It is established with the means provided by private law and exercises an effect primarily within the private sphere. The constitution of the democratic state will only be indirectly affected by the organisational changes within the private sphere. Hence we would have to examine, first of all, whether the shifts in freedom that have occurred within the private sphere due to the increase in dominant economic positions are so extensive as to permit us to talk of a feudalizing process which poses a serious threat to democracy.

Personally I am inclined to question this insofar as only the use of already existing economic power for the purpose of attaining maximal monopolistic profits is concerned. Where a supplier's monopoly is involved the monopolist will charge higher prices and restrict the supply much more than he would do if competition were available. Those who desire his specific commodity will then be compelled by this act—an act committed and answerable by a human being—to make changes in their demand dispositions which are prejudicial to their own interests, and these modified demand dispositions would, in turn, cause shifts, partly favourable and partly unfavourable, in the incomes and chances of an indefinite additional number of participants in the market. All this would happen only because one of the participants in the market has economic power. The distribution of incomes and chances would be different, if he did not hold such power. To this extent all participants in the market who are affected by the difference between the monopolistic and the competitive price are dependent on the monopolist. This dependence is confined only to a single commodity and will probably be felt only in very rare instances as a permanent social dependence of really large proportions. A serious interference with the economic conditions of customers might exist, where a monopolist changes his marketing system from one day to the other, that is to say, where he eliminates practically the entire wholesale trade. Moreover, the yoke of monopolistic domination, set up by such use of economic power, is too light as to give us serious cause for calling to mind any feudal conditions.

Besides, a monopolist who does no more than this will simply provoke competition. The mere fact that he restricts his production, raises his prices and simultaneously realizes considerable profits, is bound to make operations in this field of trade and industry appear to be extremely lucrative. Since the monopolist realizes his profits through a conduct which is detrimental to his customers, he makes it very easy for potential competitors to earn money by appearing on the same market with a slightly more favourable offer. That, in fact, is what monopolists upbraid outsiders for with a great deal of emotion, when they accuse them of transacting easy business in the shadow of cartels and monopolies, but they conveniently forget that nobody compels our cartels and market dominating enterprises to cast any shadow. If economic power, therefore, were something that a few enterprises in industries with large undertakings could acquire almost automatically, so to speak, the legislature could perhaps justify leaving such economic power to its own imperiled fate and to the control of the free market economy system, which is still effective even when competition has ceased to operate in a few markets. Good reasons could be advanced for abandoning the enactment of special antitrust laws under such circumstances, in particular, antitrust laws, which provide for a divesture and break-up even of perfectly sound enterprises and combinations of enterprises and thus burden the courts and state authorities with an extremely difficult task, besides providing them with means of intervention, which are none too harmless.

## VI

In reality, however, economic power operates in a much more dramatic way. The conventional idea that monopolists, partial monopolists or oligopolists are people who thoroughly enjoy their monopolistic income, as long as a benevolent fortune empties its cornucopia over them, is probably not very flattering from a human point of view, but politically harmless, if not idyllic. If the activities of holders of considerable market power were to confine themselves to exploiting such power to the very limit so as to realize a momentary profit and to tap the purchasing power of those directly or indirectly dependent on them, these people would hardly constitute any serious threat to our civil and political liberties. Their existence would be no obstacle worth speaking of to the civil and political order of democracy, but only affect its moral prestige, if any. The monopoly capitalists have always been the proverbial villains of our middle class democracy, and it is, in particular, the political dictators of the 20th Century who never tire in drawing the attention of the general public to the sinister activities of these modern "slaveholders and éminences grises."

The real menace to our liberties, our social and political system issuing from the possession of economic power, however, lies in the fact that monopolistic power is not only exploited, but desired, contested, defended and expanded with ruthless vehemence. Monopolistic power is constantly menaced in a free market economy. Those who want to enjoy economic power must first conquer and then defend and protect it. It is not the monopoly that exploits its power, but the monopoly that fights for it, which really gives us serious cause for worrying about our civil and political liberties, our system of society and government. The monopolist who exploits his monopoly will at least also do quite a number of useful things. The monopolist who engages in economic warfare, however, causes nothing but damage and destruction. He not only exploits, but also subjugates and oppresses others and forces them against their own interest into his never ending campaigns against outsiders, against existing and merely potential competitors. It is not the possession of a monopoly, but only the fight for it that throws our system of society out of gear and threatens to corrupt the constitutional life of our democracy. Not until this war has actually begun will the whole legal cynism of the attacking holders of power and the whole servility of those who are menaced by and afraid of such power, disclose itself. And this corruption does not by any means confine itself to the parties directly involved in this war, but is spreading also to the ranks of the legal and economic advisers and even to the ranks of the principal ideologists in our contemporary literature.

The brunt of these destructive forces must be sustained by our system of private law. For it is the fundamental absolute rights of the individual, in particular private property and patent rights, but also the rights to trade-marks, firm names and other names, it is the party autonomy and freedom of contract established by our law of contract, it is the liberties to which the subject of our private law is entitled in extracontractual transactions and in industrial competition together with all the institutions of private law pertaining to these rights, which to a larger or smaller extent will be hopelessly corrupted in fraudem legis, as soon as they are used by holders of economic power in order to establish, expand, defend and stabilize such power.

From an economic point of view these destructions of values caused by such warfare—to mention only the waste and misdirection of productive energies, occurring in supply and delivery stoppages, in aimed or global cut-throat price wars, cornering and patronage rebate campaigns—constitute the costs of establishing and maintaining monopolies, costs which, as a rule, are shifted entirely to foreign shoulders, although, in case of extreme necessity, especially price wars, they are even shouldered by the monopolist himself, at least to a major extent. Thus, if already the peaceful use of economic power is likely to impair the efficiency of a free market economy, we must add to such economic damage the total cost of the fight for economic power, which is not only unproductive, but also affects and curtails production, in order to estimate the total economic damage caused by this detrimental development. This aspect of the problem has in my opinion been neglected to an excessive degree both in the economic and the legal discussion.

Still more extensive is the damage which such monopolistic warfare inflicts within the sphere of the system of private law, since the regulating capacity and the logical content of all civil rights and institutions depends on the fact that the subjects of private law using them have no power and for that reason find themselves compelled when using their rights and liberties to give most careful consideration to the interests of their fellow-creatures. Is it not astonishing to see, how millions of private individuals with no influence whatever make available, day after day, without any legal compulsion and quite spontaneously, their property, their working power and a large proportion of their income to the economic production process, in most cases even with a remarkable devotion and intelligence? Is it not evident that the striving for individual advantage induces such persons to conduct themselves in a public-spirited manner, and that it does so in a better and more effective way than the harshest coercive measure and the most munificent rewards on the part of the authorities could do? All this will be changed fundamentally, as soon as these rights and liberties pass into the hands of holders of economic power and are used by them for purposes of economic warfare. No matter whether property, patents, freedom of contract, the right to refuse completion of a contract, advertising, possibilities offered by the stock corporation laws or price competition are involved, all these instruments of exercising the rights of the individual transform themselves from that very hour into injurious weapons, means of starvation and paralysation, methods of subjection, dispossession and exploitation of other subjects of private law, into real instruments of extortion and machinery for the destruction of values. The contract, this classic bond between free and autonomous individuals changes into an exquisite instrument for dominating human beings; competition whose purpose in society is to serve as a peaceful and systematic selective process to be carried out by means of displaying a superiority in productive qualities, transforms itself into a war of plain force, obstruction, injury and deliberate dispossession in which the damage sustained by the loser is not the consequence of his defeat, but his defeat the consequence of previously inflicted destruction and injuries.

A further and quite serious threat issuing from this transformation of the law of contract, as well as the transformation of competition lies in the fact that such transformation extends to the establishment and development of enterprises. The size of the enterprises is increased beyond the limit that appears to be optimal from an economic point of view. Not only does an enterprise desire to select a size likely to give it a dominant position on a specific market, but the size is also calculated in such a way that it permits the market dominating enterprises to protect their dominant economic positions against potential competition, in other words, to conduct economic warfare. This applies not only to the scope and size of single enterprises, it applies in particular to combinations of enterprises, in other words, to the concentration of enterprises in the form of trusts. It is obvious that here the initial aim is to carry out a horizontal concentration. Apart from the cartel method, a partially monopolistic or oligopolistic market quota will in many fields of industry and commerce be attainable not by a mere expansion of an enterprise, but by the absorption in a trust of similar, hitherto competing enterprises. In most cases, however, this horizontal concentration will be regarded as insufficient. In order to conduct monopolistic warfare, it is necessary to have reliable assistants and allies in the fields to be found in front and in the rear of industry. Trusts, therefore, also absorb undertakings on the supplier and customer level, in particular such enterprises which have monopolised a specific article and are thus able to exert pressure on firms outside the main enterprise. Here, the optimum which would be expedient merely from considerations of profitability is well exceeded. In this case, therefore, it is no longer technical reasons which account for the urge to form gigantic enterprises and combines, but the requirements of the monopolistic war strategy which are at the back of the establishment of vertically concentrated trusts organised from consumer to producer level, if not exclusively though nevertheless and quite noticeably as an additional and highly effective contributory motive.

The reason for the extremely dangerous character of this development is that it will be impossible to prohibit the means employed for effecting a vertical concentration in the same way as, for instance, cartel enterprises can be prohibited, because these same means are widely used in industry also for thoroughly useful and necessary objectives. The subsequent deconcentration of such trusts will be just as difficult. This development, therefore, urges the legislative, administrative and judicial defence against the establishment of economic power into efforts, which, if they are to be effective, require an expenditure that will become increasingly disproportionate to the success likely to be accomplished as well as into interventions in the freedom of enterprises which are frequently less alarming to the monopolistic horizontal and vertical combinations threatened by them than to the legislature, the cartel authorities and the judges who have to use these heavy and none too harmless guns, bombs and rockets.

With vertically concentrated trusts we usually find that the considerable amount of economic power accumulated by any of them for a specific product is not so particularly impressive at all, and that the trust managements are frequently not in a position to exploit the monopolistic position of some of their enterprises on certain markets in a reprehensible manner. Frequently this is not at all the actual reason why such trusts constitute a menace. The real reason for alarm and anxiety lies in the fact that most of the vertically concentrated trusts holding any kind of dominant position on specific markets are completely erratic protagonists of the monopolistic cold or hot war. They need not actually go to war. Their mere presence intimidates competition on practically all markets on which they operate, even on those in which they hold little economic power.

It is not the material enjoyment, the exploitation of economic power as such, but only the struggle involved in establishing, maintaining, consolidating and expanding such power that turns the resultant disturbance of our system of society, which is based on the rights of the individual, into a thorough denaturing process. Economic power invariably proves to be also a means to be used for defending and expanding power. Thus we actually have two denaturing processes. On the one hand our system of private law is being denatured already by the exploitation of economic power, and on the other, it is being purposely denatured and corrupted in order that economic power may establish, maintain and consolidate itself.

## VII

This, however, is undoubtedly a process, whose effects cannot be confined to the sphere of the system of private law, but will affect also the constitution of the democratic state. The legislature's obligation to intervene in this development, therefore, is an elementary one. Moreover, it becomes increasingly evident that we cannot stop at attacking those methods of establishing power and conducting monopolistic warfare which are more primitive and easy to prevent, but that one day, whether we like it or not, we must decide to attack the far more difficult problem of combinations.

The establishment and the use of economic power affect the constitution of the democratic state and the constitutionally balanced relationship between the private and the public sphere; the same is true of the manner in which a democratic country attempts to counteract the danger of economic power by legislation and governmental policy.

It is from this specific viewpoint that we must first examine the two possibilities of a solution which offer themselves in this respect. One of them consists in the prophylactic prevention of the establishment of economic power already in its incipient stages with all the means at our disposal and in taking care that already established economic power is eliminated or reduced. The only possibility which may lead to success in this respect consists in favouring and activating competition and eliminating any obstacles obstructing its progress. Competition is the most remarkable and ingenious instrument for reducing power known in history. All we have to do is to evoke it, and it will do any other work automatically. Besides, in order to reduce economic power, it will by no means be necessary that such competition should conform to the requirements which the modern doctrine of market systems has established for so-called "full competition." On the contrary, any competition whose effects will be felt by the holders of economic power, will suffice. And even if the struggle between a partial monopolist and any outsiders or between duopolists or oligopolists does not in any way have the regulating and controlling power characteristic for competition on really competitive markets, it nevertheless has the effect of weakening existing dominant positions and preventing their reinforcement. This effect, however, is so beneficial that for its sake we can easily put up with a certain dose of economic disorder. Competition acts like a "strike-breaker" in relation to the establishment of economic power; as such it should be employed unhesitatingly by the law and the government, regardless of whether it operates in a somewhat clumsy and unorthodox manner, as far as its economic controlling power is concerned.

This means of preventing and destroying monopolies by promoting competition has the advantage of conforming to private law and democracy. It activates the self-controlling power of the free market economy system and the workability of the system of private law and simultaneously relieves the machinery of government of official control duties and freedom-restricting interventions.

The other possibility consists in subjecting economic power to the control of constitutional state authorities. Its use leads to intervention in the economy in two stages. In the first stage private holders of economic power intervene in the processes of the free market economy, whereas in the second stage the state steps in as higher authority and corrects the private interventions by means of official interventions.

This procedure causes a paralysation of the system of private law, an overburdening of the machinery of government and an entanglement of an unbalanced private sphere with an equally unbalanced public sphere threatened by corruption. A feudalizing process takes place within the private sphere which compels the state to reconcile the feudal titles in society with one another by way of a compromise and thus renders it incapable of impartial government.

The result will be a system of society with a reduced content of justice and freedom, obscured by indistinct dependent relationships, an unbalanced anarchy of various groups of social interests, and on top of this denatured society a weak state which—to quote a statement by Carl Schmitt, Professor of Public Law—can no longer cope with its responsibilities and meddles in everything. And this interference necessarily proceeds in an amateurish and arbitrary manner with a great deal of well-meant hustle by the authorities and parliament, but little efficiency, with a punctilious attention to detail, but a supreme lack of an overall conception.

Many national antitrust laws provide for a mixed system. The main instrument to be used is the prophylactic prevention of power by activating competition, while the principle of state control is applied only to those remaining positions of economic power, which competition is unable to eliminate. However, even such a mixed system is not harmless, since the dangers I referred to are inherent in the principle of state control even if this principle is used only as a subsidiary means, as ultima ratio. We could even dispense with this final completion of antitrust policy without risking that any really effective dangers will arise from the rest of economic power still unconquered. For even in those cases, in which competition fails and the chances for restoring it are exhausted there is still one final automatic control left, namely the control exercised by the interdependence of all markets within the system of a free market economy. And although this control does not operate as exactly, as accurately and, above all, as promptly as the control exercised by competition within a specific market, it nevertheless makes itself felt to a still remarkable degree.

However, it is exactly when we decide to dispense with an administrative control of monopolistic behaviour that we must try with redoubled energy to carry out to the very limit the policy of the prophylactic prevention and reduction of economic power. We must create a climate in which all available competitive energies feel like getting political and ideological encouragement. Where such a climate exists, there will be no fertile soil for the establishment and maintenance of economic power.

Moreover, experience has taught us that nothing will contribute more effectively towards creating such a favourable climate than the enactment of a law against restraints on competition or an antitrust law, no matter whether it is good or bad, severe or mild, whether it favours competition or provides for state Intervention, for as soon as such a law exists, public opinion will begin to occupy itself with the problem of economic power by directing its attention not only to theoretical doctrines and doctrines of social policy on this subject, but also to practical events currently occurring on specific markets. For laws of this kind have the strange effect that as soon as they have come into force, the sources of the facts will begin to flow—not below the surface as before, but above ground so that every passer-by can see them. Once these facts have become the subject of discussion, we may be sure that within a few years' time the idea of competition will gain in popularity to a noticeable extent.

This, as I said, has been the case thus far everywhere in the world, at least in the free world. And if this statement should still require any proof—one look into this room, at this International Conference on Antitrust Law held in Frankfurt am Main in the year 1960, will be sufficient to furnish this proof. The fact that so many of the most important practitioners and theoreticians of antitrust policy from the different countries of the world have gathered here during these days is, if I may say so, an event which all of us feel and are firmly convinced, has something to do with democracy and freedom.

# 9

# Competition and Innovation

## Introduction

### BY HERBERT HOVENKAMP

Today most economists believe that innovation contributes far more to economic growth than does the movement of resources from more monopoly to less. Neither Joseph Schumpeter nor Kenneth Arrow, whose writings are excerpted in this chapter, would dispute the proposition. That fact alone, however, does not tell us anything about how policies about competition and innovation should relate to each other. It may be, as Schumpeter argued, that there is an inverse relationship between the two: one gets more innovation only by having less competition. Or it may be, as Arrow argued a generation later, that more competition results in more innovation. This argument has significant consequences for antitrust policy in innovation-intensive markets. For example, if Schumpeter is correct then antitrust policy and patent policy must continuously be balanced, with the nod given to innovation in most cases. By contrast, if Arrow is correct then at least to some extent antitrust can pursue a policy of making markets more competitive and increase innovation in the process.

Joseph Schumpeter (1883–1950) wrote *Capitalism, Socialism and Democracy* just prior to and during World War II. Chapter 7, on "The Process of Creative Destruction," reprinted below, is one of the great classics in the economics of innovation. In his characteristic maverick form, Schumpeter looked back at a half-century of academic economics as a series of lamentations about the decline in competitiveness—oligopoly theory, product differentiation and monopolistic competition theory, and the theory of monopoly. However, even as these writers were lamenting the loss of competitiveness that seemed to characterize industrial production, real standards of living had increased by several magnitudes. This inspired Schumpeter to two of the most important and controversial assertions of midcentury economics, first that innovation contributes much more to economic development than simple competitiveness under constant technology, and second that monopoly is the market structure most conducive to innovation. The first of these propositions has weathered extremely well. Building on Schumpeter's intuitions, Robert M. Solow developed the neoclassical growth model in the 1950s, and since then an array of studies have indicated that constant savings of capital and improvements in price competition cannot explain more than a small percentage of economic growth. The balance, or "residual," is a result of increased productivity, or innovation.[1]

Schumpeter's second thesis relating innovation positively with monopoly has been much more controversial. "Creative destruction"—an idea that Schumpeter borrowed from Marx—refers to an ongoing cycle in which one technology is developed and triumphs, only to be violently displaced when a superior technology comes along. This process, much more than competition among many small firms, drives progress. In the subsequent chapter on "Monopolistic Practices," Schumpeter then explained that only dominant firms have the resources and the freedom from competitive pressure to be able to afford to undertake significant innovation.

Kenneth Arrow (1921–) responded to Schumpeter with an argument that today has considerably more support, although Arrow's argument probably goes too far toward the other extreme. Briefly, Arrow argued that Schumpeter severely underestimated the impact of competitive pressure in inducing innovation. The monopolist who faces no rivals is just as likely to look for the "quiet life," in the words of Judge Wyzanski, as to want to innovate.[2] The monopolist who has a heavy investment in existing technology will be reluctant to displace it, thus losing its investment. By contrast, the competitor knows that if it does not innovate, someone else will; the only question is whether it will be the cause or the victim of the creative destruction that innovation brings about. As a result, the *incremental* gains to innovation are likely to be larger for the competitor than the monopolist, and the incremental risks of not innovating are likely to be larger as well.

The Schumpeter-Arrow debate has produced an enormous theoretical and empirical literature in economics.[3] The debate has spilled over into the antitrust literature as well. Although methodologies and conclusions differ, most of the current literature finds that the relation between innovation and competitive market structure is best expressed by an "inverted U" shaped curve.[4] Both absolute monopoly and atomistic competition tend to produce a low rate of innovation. The highest rate of innovation occurs in the middle, mainly in moderately concentrated markets. This conclusion picks up part of both Schumpeter's and Arrow's arguments. Atomistically competitive markets with tiny firms do not innovate a great deal because prices are continuously being driven to short run marginal cost, with substantial resources not remaining for innovation. At the other end, the Arrovian argument against monopoly applies. The firms most likely to innovate are in markets where the four largest firms tend to have aggregate market shares of 50 percent or more. In these markets prices are typically above cost, giving the firms some discretionary surplus. At the same time,

1. See Robert M. Solow, "Technical Change and the Aggregate Production Function," 39 *Rev. Econ. Stat.* 312 (1957); and Elhanan Helpman, *The Mystery of Economic Growth* (2004).

2. *United States* v. *United Shoe Machinery Co.*, 110 F.Supp. 295, 347 (D.Mass. 1053), aff'd mem., 347 U.S. 521 (1954) ("Some truth lurks in the cynical remark that not high profits but a quiet life is the chief reward of monopoly power").

3. See Wesley Cohen and Richard Levin, "Empirical Studies of Innovation and Market Structure" in 2 *Handbook of Industrial Organization* 1059–1107 (Richard Schmalensee and Robert Willig eds., 1989) (empirical literature on relationship between industry structure and innovation is the largest in the field of industrial organization).

4. For a recent statement, see Philippe Aghion, Nick Bloom, Richard Blundell, Rachel Griffith, and Peter Howitt, "Competition and Innovation: an Inverted-U Relationship," 120 *Q. J. Econ.* 701, 704–708 (2005).

the Arrovian threat applies: if firm A does not innovate, then, absent collusion, it can expect one of its rivals to do so.

There is also some reason for thinking antitrust rules that increase competitiveness in industries with a given market structure also tend to foster innovation. For example, an antitrust policy of keeping high market concentration in check in order to further price competition very likely furthers innovation competition as well.[5] Cartels often find it necessary to fix the "quality" of a product as well as its price. In a cartel, price-cost margins are high, so each member has an incentive to "cheat" by capturing more sales. If the cartel member cannot surreptitiously cut the price, it may very well try to increase its own output by improving the desirability of its product. As a result, cartels may intentionally suppress innovation.

This suggests several principles for antitrust in innovation-intensive markets. First, properly designed "structural" antitrust relief in a market with a monopolist or high degree of concentration need not generally be feared on grounds that it will undermine innovation. For example, an injunction against a merger in a market with, say, four firms is at least as likely to promote innovation as to discourage it, even though our principal reason for condemning the merger is to prevent coordination of prices. Second, the antitrust concern with restraints on innovation is greater in concentrated markets than in more competitive ones, for it is in concentrated markets that innovation is most likely to occur and where restraining it is most profitable to established firms that have a commitment to their older technologies. Third, the relationship between competition, innovation, and market structure is much more relevant when we consider specific situations rather than structure generally. For example, an efficiency defense in a merger case has importance when the postmerger firm is able to undertake and capitalize on innovation more efficiently than the two firms prior to the merger. Largely the same thing is true of antitrust policy toward joint ventures, whose antitrust legality depends on both the underlying market structure and on the venture's particular elements. Although it is clear today that the legal policy that will best encourage innovation is highly specific to the market or technology at issue, the IP laws for the most part do not take structural variations in various industries into account. As a result, incentivizing innovation by policing market structure falls mainly to the antitrust laws.[6]

## Joseph A. Schumpeter
## *Capitalism, Socialism and Democracy*
## Chapter VII: The Process of Creative Destruction

The theories of monopolistic and oligopolistic competition and their popular variants may in two ways be made to serve the view that capitalist reality is unfavorable to maximum performance in production. One may hold that it always has been so and that all along output has been expanding in spite of the secular sabotage perpetrated by the

5. See Jonathan Baker, "Beyond Schumpeter and Arrow: How Antitrust Fosters Innovation," 74 *Antitrust L.J.* 575, 586 (2007).

6. See Christina Bohannan and Herbert Hovenkamp, *Creation Without Restraint: Promoting Liberty and Rivalry in Innovation*, Ch. 1 (2012).

managing bourgeoisie. Advocates of this proposition would have to produce evidence to the effect that the observed rate of increase can be accounted for by a sequence of favorable circumstances unconnected with the mechanism of private enterprise and strong enough to overcome the latter's resistance. This is precisely the question which we shall discuss in Chapter IX. However, those who espouse this variant at least avoid the trouble about historical fact that the advocates of the alternative proposition have to face. This avers that capitalist reality once tended to favor maximum productive performance, or at all events productive performance so considerable as to constitute a major element in any serious appraisal of the system; but that the later spread of monopolist structures, killing competition, has by now reversed that tendency.

First, this involves the creation of an entirely imaginary golden age of perfect competition that at some time somehow metamorphosed itself into the monopolistic age, whereas it is quite clear that perfect competition has at no time been more of a reality than it is at present. Secondly, it is necessary to point out that the rate of increase in output did not decrease from the nineties from which, I suppose, the prevalence of the largest-size concerns, at least in manufacturing industry, would have to be dated; that there is nothing in the behavior of the time series of total output to suggest a "break in trend"; and, most important of all, that the modern standard of life of the masses evolved during the period of relatively unfettered "big business." If we list the items that enter the modern workman's budget and from 1899 on observe the course of their prices not in terms of money but in terms of the hours of labor that will buy them—i.e., each year's money prices divided by each year's hourly wage rates—we cannot fail to be struck by the rate of the advance which, considering the spectacular improvement in qualities, seems to have been greater and not smaller than it ever was before. If we economists were given less to wishful thinking and more to the observation of facts, doubts would immediately arise as to the realistic virtues of a theory that would have led us to expect a very different result. Nor is this all. As soon as we go into details and inquire into the individual items in which progress was most conspicuous, the trail leads not to the doors of those firms that work under conditions of comparatively free competition but precisely to the doors of the large concerns—which, as in the case of agricultural machinery, also account for much of the progress in the competitive sector—and a shocking suspicion dawns upon us that big business may have had more to do with creating that standard of life than with keeping it down.

The conclusions alluded to at the end of the preceding chapter are in fact almost completely false. Yet they follow from observations and theorems that are almost completely[1] true. Both economists and popular writers have once more run away with some fragments of reality they happened to grasp. These fragments themselves were mostly seen correctly. Their formal properties were mostly developed correctly. But no conclusions about capitalist reality as a whole follow from such fragmentary analyses.

1. As a matter of fact, those observations and theorems are not completely satisfactory. The usual expositions of the doctrine of imperfect competition fail in particular to give due attention to the many and important cases in which, even as a matter of static theory, imperfect competition approximates the results of perfect competition. There are other cases in which it does not do this, but offers compensations which, while not entering any output

If we draw them nevertheless, we can be right only by accident. That has been done. And the lucky accident did not happen.

The essential point to grasp is that in dealing with capitalism we are dealing with an evolutionary process. It may seem strange that anyone can fail to see so obvious a fact which moreover was long ago emphasized by Karl Marx. Yet that fragmentary analysis which yields the bulk of our propositions about the functioning of modern capitalism persistently neglects it. Let us restate the point and see how it bears upon our problem.

Capitalism, then, is by nature a form or method of economic change and not only never is but never can be stationary. And this evolutionary character of the capitalist process is not merely due to the fact that economic life goes on in a social and natural environment which changes and by its change alters the data of economic action; this fact is important and these changes (wars, revolutions and so on) often condition industrial change, but they are not its prime movers. Nor is this evolutionary character due to a quasi-automatic increase in population and capital or to the vagarities [sic] of monetary systems of which exactly the same thing holds true. The fundamental impulse that sets and keeps the capitalist engine in motion comes from the new consumers' goods, the new methods of production or transportation, the new markets, the new forms of industrial organization that capitalist enterprise creates.

As we have seen in the preceding chapter, the contents of the laborer's budget, say from 1760 to 1940, did not simply grow on unchanging lines but they underwent a process of qualitative change. Similarly, the history of the productive apparatus of a typical farm, from the beginnings of the rationalization of crop rotation, plowing and fattening to the mechanized thing of today—linking up with elevators and railroads—is a history of revolutions. So is the history of the productive apparatus of the iron and steel industry from the charcoal furnace to our own type of furnace, or the history of the apparatus of power production from the overshot water wheel to the modem power plant, or the history of transportation from the mail-coach to the airplane. The opening up of new markets, foreign or domestic, and the organizational development from the craft shop and factory to such concerns as U.S. Steel illustrate the same process of industrial mutation—if I may use that biological term—that incessantly revolutionizes[2] the economic structure *from within*, incessantly destroying the old one, incessantly creating the new one. This process of Creative Destruction is the essential fact about capitalism. It is what capitalism consists in and what every capitalist concern has got to live in. This fact bears upon our problem in two ways.

index, yet contribute to what the output index is in the last resort intended to measure—the cases in which a firm defends its market by establishing a name for quality and service for instance. However, in order to simplify matters, we will not take issue with that doctrine on its own ground.

2. Those revolutions are not strictly incessant; they occur in discrete rushes which are separated from each other by spans of comparative quiet. The process as a whole works incessantly however, in the sense that there always is either revolution or absorption of the results of revolution, both together forming what are known as business cycles.

First, since we are dealing with a process whose every element takes considerable time in revealing its true features and ultimate effects; there is no point in appraising the performance of that process *ex visu* of a given point of time; we must judge its performance over time, as it unfolds through decades or centuries. A system—any system, economic or other—that at *every* given point of time fully utilizes its possibilities to the best advantage may yet in the long run be inferior to a system that does so at no given point of time, because the latter's failure to do so may be a condition for the level or speed of long-run performance.

Second, since we are dealing with an organic process, analysis of what happens in any particular part of it—say, in an individual concern or industry—may indeed clarify details of mechanism but is inconclusive beyond that. Every piece of business strategy acquires its true significance only against the background of that process and within the situation created by it. It must be seen in its role in the perennial gale of creative destruction; it cannot be understood irrespective of it or, in fact, on the hypothesis that there is a perennial lull.

But economists who, *ex visu* of a point of time, look for example at the behavior of an oligopolist industry—an industry which consists of a few big firms—and observe the well-known moves and countermoves within it that seem to aim at nothing but high prices and restrictions of output are making precisely that hypothesis. They accept the data of the momentary situation as if there were no past or future to it and think that they have understood what there is to understand if they interpret the behavior of those firms by means of the principle of maximizing profits with reference to those data. The usual theorist's paper and the usual government commission's report practically never try to see that behavior, on the one hand, as a result of a piece of past history and, on the other hand, as an attempt to deal with a situation that is sure to change presently—as an attempt by those firms to keep on their feet, on ground that is slipping away from under them. In other words, the problem that is usually being visualized is how capitalism administers existing structures, whereas the relevant problem is how it creates and destroys them. As long as this is not recognized, the investigator does a meaningless job. As soon as it is recognized, his outlook on capitalist practice and its social results changes considerably.[3]

The first thing to go is the traditional conception of the *modus operandi* of competition. Economists are at long last emerging from the stage in which price competition was all they saw. As soon as quality competition and sales effort are admitted into the sacred precincts of theory, the price variable is ousted from its dominant position. However, it is still competition within a rigid pattern of invariant conditions, methods of production and forms of industrial organization in particular, that practically monopolizes attention. But in capitalist reality as distinguished from its textbook picture, it is not that kind of competition which counts but the competition from the new commodity, the new technology, the new source of supply, the new type of organization (the largest-scale unit of control for instance)—competition which commands a

3. It should be understood that it is only our appraisal of economic performance and not our moral judgment that can be so changed. Owing to its autonomy, moral approval or disapproval is entirely independent of our appraisal of social (or any other) results, unless we happen to adopt a moral system such as utilitarianism which makes moral approval and disapproval turn on them *ex definitione*.

decisive cost or quality advantage and which strikes not at the margins of the profits and the outputs of the existing firms but at their foundations and their very lives. This kind of competition is as much more effective than the other as a bombardment is in comparison with forcing a door, and so much more important that it becomes a matter of comparative indifference whether competition in the ordinary sense functions more or less promptly; the powerful lever that in the long run expands output and brings down prices is in any case made of other stuff.

It is hardly necessary to point out that competition of the kind we now have in mind acts not only when in being but also when it is merely an ever-present threat. It disciplines before it attacks. The businessman feels himself to be in a competitive situation even if he is alone in his field or if, though not alone, he holds a position such that investigating government experts fail to see any effective competition between him and any other firms in the same or a neighboring field and in consequence conclude that his talk, under examination, about his competitive sorrows is all make-believe. In many cases, though not in all, this will in the long run enforce behavior very similar to the perfectly competitive pattern.

Many theorists take the opposite view which is best conveyed by an example. Let us assume that there is a certain number of retailers in a neighborhood who try to improve their relative position by service and "atmosphere" but avoid price competition and stick as to methods to the local tradition—a picture of stagnating routine. As others drift into the trade that quasi-equilibrium is indeed upset, but in a manner that does not benefit their customers. The economic space around each of the shops having been narrowed, their owners will no longer be able to make a living and they will try to mend the case by raising prices in tacit agreement. This will further reduce their sales and so, by successive pyramiding, a situation will evolve in which increasing potential supply will be attended by increasing instead of decreasing prices and by decreasing instead of increasing sales.

Such cases do occur, and it is right and proper to work them out. But as the practical instances usually given show, they are fringe-end cases to be found mainly in the sectors furthest removed from all that is most characteristic of capitalist activity.[4] Moreover, they are transient by nature. In the case of retail trade the competition that matters arises not from additional shops of the same type, but from the department store, the chain store, the mail-order house and the supermarket which are bound to destroy those pyramids sooner or later.[5] Now a theoretical construction which neglects this essential element of the case neglects all that is most typically capitalist about it; even if correct in logic as well as in fact, it is like *Hamlet* without the Danish prince.

4. This is also shown by a theorem we frequently meet with in expositions of the theory of imperfect competition, viz., the theorem that, under conditions of imperfect competition, producing or trading businesses tend to be irrationally small. Since imperfect competition is at the same time held to be an outstanding characteristic of modern industry we are set to wondering what world these theorists live in, unless, as stated above, fringe-end cases are all they have in mind.

5. The mere threat of their attack cannot, in the particular conditions, environmental and personal, of small-scale retail trade, have its usual disciplining influence, for the small man is too much hampered by his cost structure and, however well he may manage within his inescapable limitations, he can never adapt himself to the methods of competitors who can afford to sell at the price at which he buys.

# Chapter VIII: Monopolistic Practices

What has been said so far is really sufficient to enable the reader to deal with the large majority of the practical cases he is likely to meet and to realize the inadequacy of most of those criticisms of the profit economy which, directly or indirectly, rely on the absence of perfect competition. Since, however, the bearing of our argument on some of those criticisms may not be obvious at a glance, it will be worth our while to elaborate a little in order to make a few points more explicit.

1. We have just seen that, both as a fact and as a threat, the impact of new things—new technologies for instance—on the existing structure of an industry considerably reduces the long-run scope and importance of practices that aim, through restricting output, at conserving established positions and at maximizing the profits accruing from them. We must now recognize the further fact that restrictive practices of this kind, as far as they are effective, acquire a new significance in the perennial gale of creative destruction, a significance which they would not have in a stationary state or in a state of slow and balanced growth. In either of these cases restrictive strategy would produce no result other than an increase in profits at the expense of buyers except that, in the case of balanced advance, it might still prove to be the easiest and most effective way of collecting the means by which to finance additional investment.[6] But in the process of creative destruction, restrictive practices may do much to steady the ship and to alleviate temporary difficulties. This is in fact a very familiar argument which always turns up in times of depression and, as everyone knows, has become very popular with governments and their economic advisers—witness the NRA. While it has been so much misused and so faultily acted upon that most economists heartily despise it, those same advisers who are responsible for this[7] invariably fail to see its much more general rationale.

Practically any investment entails, as a necessary complement of entrepreneurial action, certain safeguarding activities such as insuring or hedging. Long-range investing under rapidly changing conditions, especially under conditions that change or may change at any moment under the impact of new commodities and technologies, is like shooting at a target that is not only indistinct but moving—and moving jerkily at that. Hence it becomes necessary to resort to such protecting devices as patents or temporary secrecy of processes or, in some cases, long-period contracts secured in advance. But these protecting devices which most economists accept as normal elements of

6. Theorists are apt to look upon anyone who admits this possibility as guilty of gross error, and to prove immediately that financing by borrowing from banks or from private savers or, in the case of public enterprise, financing from the proceeds of an income tax is much more rational than is financing from surplus profits collected through a restrictive policy. For some patterns of behavior they are quite right. For others they are quite wrong. I believe that both capitalism and communism of the Russian type belong in the latter category. But the point is that theoretical considerations, especially theoretical considerations of the short-run kind, cannot solve, although they contribute to the solution of, the problem which we shall meet again in the next part.

7. In particular, it is easy to show that there is no sense, and plenty of harm, in a policy that aims at preserving "price parities."

rational management[8] are only special cases of a larger class comprising many others which most economists condemn although they do not differ fundamentally from the recognized ones.

If for instance a war risk is insurable, nobody objects to a firm's collecting the cost of this insurance from the buyers of its products. But that risk is no less an element in long-run costs, if there are no facilities for insuring against it, in which case a price strategy aiming at the same end will seem to involve unnecessary restriction and to be productive of excess profits. Similarly, if a patent cannot be secured or would not, if secured, effectively protect, other means may have to be used in order to justify the investment. Among them are a price policy that will make it possible to write off more quickly than would otherwise be rational, or additional investment in order to provide excess capacity to be used only for aggression or defense. Again, if long-period contracts cannot be entered into in advance, other means may have to be devised in order to tie prospective customers to the investing firm.

In analyzing such business strategy *ex visu* of a given point of time, the investigating economist or government agent sees price policies that seem to him predatory and restrictions of output that seem to him synonymous with loss of opportunities to produce. He does not see that restrictions of this type are, in the conditions of the perennial gale, incidents, often unavoidable incidents, of a long-run process of expansion which they protect rather than impede. There is no more of paradox in this than there is in saying that motorcars are traveling faster than they otherwise would *because* they are provided with brakes.

2. This stands out most clearly in the case of those sectors of the economy which at any time happen to embody the impact of new things and methods on the existing industrial structure. The best way of getting a vivid and realistic idea of industrial strategy is indeed to visualize the behavior of new concerns or industries that introduce new commodities or processes (such as the aluminum industry) or else reorganize a part or the whole of an industry (such as, for instance, the old Standard Oil Company).

As we have seen, such concerns are aggressors by nature and wield the really effective weapon of competition. Their intrusion can only in the rarest of cases fail to improve total output in quantity or quality, both through the new method itself—even if at no time used to full advantage—and through the pressure it exerts on the preexisting firms. But there are aggressors so circumstanced as to require, for purposes of attack and defense, also pieces of armor other than price and quality of their product which, moreover, must be strategically manipulated all along so that at any point of time they seem to be doing nothing but restricting their output and keeping prices high.

On the one hand, largest-scale plans could in many cases not materialize at all if it were not known from the outset that competition will be discouraged by heavy capital

8. Some economists, however, consider that even those devices are obstructions to progress which, though perhaps necessary in capitalist society, would be absent in a socialist one. There is some truth in this. But that does not affect the proposition that the protection afforded by patents and so on is, in the conditions of a profit economy, on balance a propelling and not an inhibiting factor.

requirements or lack of experience, or that means are available to discourage or checkmate it so as to gain the time and space for further developments. Even the conquest of financial control over competing concerns in otherwise unassailable positions or the securing of advantages that run counter to the public's sense of fair play—railroad rebates—move, as far as long-run effects on total output alone are envisaged, into a different light;[9] they *may* be methods for removing obstacles that the institution of private property puts in the path of progress. In a socialist society that time and space would be no less necessary. They would have to be secured by order of the central authority.

On the other hand, enterprise would in most cases be impossible if it were not known from the outset that exceptionally favorable situations are likely to arise which if exploited by price, quality and quantity manipulation will produce profits adequate to tide over exceptionally unfavorable situations provided these are similarly managed. Again this requires strategy that in the short run is often restrictive. In the majority of successful cases this strategy just manages to serve its purpose. In some cases, however, it is so successful as to yield profits far above what is necessary in order to induce the corresponding investment. These cases then provide the baits that lure capital on to untried trails. Their presence explains in part how it is possible for so large a section of the capitalist world to work for nothing: in the midst of the prosperous twenties just about half of the business corporations in the United States were run at a loss, at zero profits, or at profits which, if they had been foreseen, would have been inadequate to call forth the effort and expenditure involved.

Our argument however extends beyond the cases of new concerns, methods and industries. Old concerns and established industries, whether or not directly attacked, still live in the perennial gale. Situations emerge in the process of creative destruction in which many firms may have to perish that nevertheless would be able to live on vigorously and usefully if they could weather a particular storm. Short of such general crises or depressions, sectional situations arise in which the rapid change of data that is characteristic of that process so disorganizes an industry for the time being as to inflict functionless losses and to create avoidable unemployment. Finally, there is certainly no point in trying to conserve obsolescent industries indefinitely; but there is point in trying to avoid their coming down with a crash and in attempting to turn a rout, which may become a center of cumulative depressive effects, into orderly retreat. Correspondingly there is, in the case of industries that have sown their wild oats but are still gaining and not losing ground, such a thing as orderly advance.[10]

9. The qualification added removes, I think, any just cause for offense that the above proposition might conceivably cause. In case that qualification is not explicit enough, I beg leave to repeat that the moral aspect is in this case, as it must be in every case, entirely unaffected by an economic argument. For the rest, let the reader reflect that even in dealing with indubitably criminal actions every civilized judge and every civilized jury take account of the ulterior purpose in pursuit of which a crime has occurred and of the difference it makes whether an action that is a crime has or has not also effects they consider socially desirable. Another objection would be more to the point. If an enterprise can succeed only by such means, does not that prove in itself that it cannot spell social gain? A very simple argument can be framed in support of this view. But it is subject to a severe *ceteris paribus* proviso. That is to say, it holds for conditions which are just about equivalent to excluding the process of creative destruction—capitalist reality. On reflection, it will be seen that the analogy of the practices under discussion with patents is sufficient to show this.

10. A good example illustrative of this point—in fact of much of our general argument—is the postwar history of the automobile and the rayon industry. The first illustrates very well the nature and value of what we might call

All this is of course nothing but the tritest common sense. But it is being overlooked with a persistence so stubborn as sometimes to raise the question of sincerity. And it follows that, within the process of creative destruction, all the realities of which theorists are in the habit of relegating to books and courses on business cycles, there is another side to industrial self-organization than that which these theorists are contemplating. "Restraints of trade" of the cartel type as well as those which merely consist in tacit understandings about price competition may be effective remedies under conditions of depression. As far as they are, they may in the end produce not only steadier but also greater expansion of total output than could be secured by an entirely uncontrolled onward rush that cannot fail to be studded with catastrophes. Nor can it be argued that these catastrophes occur in any case. We know what has happened in each historical case. We have a very imperfect idea of what might have happened, considering the tremendous pace of the process, if such pegs had been entirely absent.

Even as now extended however, our argument does not cover all cases of restrictive or regulating strategy, many of which no doubt have that injurious effect on the long-run development of output which is uncritically attributed to all of them. And even in the cases our argument does cover, the net effect is a question of the circumstances and of the way in which and the degree to which industry regulates itself in each individual case. It is certainly as conceivable that an all-pervading cartel system might sabotage all progress as it is that it might realize, with smaller social and private costs, all that perfect competition is supposed to realize. This is why our argument does not amount to a case against state regulation. It does show that there is no general case for indiscriminate "trust-busting" or for the prosecution of everything that qualifies as a restraint of trade. Rational as distinguished from vindictive regulation by public authority turns out to be an extremely delicate problem which not every government agency, particularly when in full cry against big business, can be trusted to solve.[11] But our argument, framed to refute a prevalent *theory* and the inferences

"edited" competition. The bonanza time was over by about 1916. A host of firms nevertheless crowded into the industry afterwards, most of which were eliminated by 1925. From a fierce life and death struggle three concerns emerged that by now account for over 80 percent of total sales. They are under competitive pressure inasmuch as, in spite of the advantages of an established position, an elaborate sales and service organization and so on, any failure to keep up and improve the quality of their products or any attempt at monopolistic combination would call in new competitors. Among themselves, the three concerns behave in a way which should be called co-respective rather than competitive: they refrain from certain aggressive devices (which, by the way, would also be absent in perfect competition): they keep up with each other and in doing so play for points at the frontiers. This has now gone on for upwards of fifteen years and it is not obvious that if conditions of theoretically perfect competition had prevailed during that period, better or cheaper cars would now be offered to the public, or higher wages and more or steadier employment to the workmen. The rayon industry had its bonanza time in the twenties. It presents the features incident to introducing a commodity into fields fully occupied before and the policies that impose themselves in such conditions still more clearly than does the automobile industry. And there are a number of other differences. But fundamentally the case is similar. The expansion in quantity and quality of rayon output is common knowledge. Yet restrictive policy presided over this expansion at each individual point in time.

11. Unfortunately, this statement is almost as effective a bar to agreement on policy as the most thoroughgoing denial of any case for government regulation could be. In fact it may embitter discussion. Politicians, public officers and economists can stand what I may politely term the whole-hog opposition of "economic royalists." Doubts about their competence, such as crowd upon us particularly when we see the legal mind at work, are much more difficult for them to stand.

drawn therefrom about the relation between modern capitalism and the development of total output, only yields another *theory,* i.e., another outlook on facts and another principle by which to interpret them. For our purpose that is enough. For the rest, the facts themselves have the floor.

3. Next, a few words on the subject of Rigid Prices which has been receiving so much attention of late. It really is but a particular aspect of the problem we have been discussing. We shall define rigidity as follows: a price is rigid if it is less sensitive to changes in the conditions of demand and supply than it would be if perfect competition prevailed.[12]

Quantitatively, the extent to which prices are rigid in that sense depends on the material and the method of measurement we select and is hence a doubtful matter. But whatever the material or method, it is certain that prices are not nearly as rigid as they seem to be. There are many reasons why what in effect is a change in price should not show in the statistical picture; in other words, why there should be much spurious rigidity. I shall mention only one class of them which is closely connected with the facts stressed by our analysis.

I have adverted to the importance, for the capitalist process in general and for its competitive mechanism in particular, of the intrusion of new commodities. Now a new commodity may effectively bring down the preexisting structure and satisfy a given want at much lower prices per unit of service (transportation service for instance), and yet not a single recorded price need change in the process; flexibility in the relevant sense may be accompanied by rigidity in a formal sense. There are other cases, not of this type, in which price reduction is the sole motive for bringing out a new brand while the old one is left at the previous quotation—again a price reduction that does not show. Moreover, the great majority of new consumers' goods—particularly all the gadgets of modern life—are at first introduced in an experimental and unsatisfactory form in which they could never conquer their potential markets. Improvement in the quality of products is hence a practically universal feature of the development of individual concerns and of industries. Whether or not this improvement involves additional costs, a constant price per unit of an improving commodity should not be called rigid without further investigation. Of course, plenty of cases of genuine price rigidity remain—of prices which are being kept constant as a matter of business policy or which remain unchanged because it is difficult to change, say, a price set by a cartel after laborious negotiations. In order to appraise the influence of this fact on the long-run development of output, it is first of all necessary to realize that this rigidity is essentially a short-run phenomenon. There are no major instances of long-run rigidity of prices. Whichever manufacturing industry or group of manufactured articles of any importance we choose to investigate over a period of time, we practically always find

12. This definition suffices for our purposes but would not be satisfactory for others. See D. D. Humphrey's article in the *Journal of Political Economy,* October 1937, and E. S. Mason's article in the *Review of Economic Statistics,* May 1938. Professor Mason has shown, among other things, that contrary to a widespread belief price rigidity is not increasing or, at all events, that it is no greater than it was forty years ago, a result which in itself suffices to invalidate some of the implications of the current doctrine of rigidity.

that in the long run prices do not fail to adapt themselves to technological progress—frequently they fail spectacularly in response to it[13]—unless prevented from doing so by monetary events and policies or, in some cases, by autonomous changes in wage rates which of course should be taken into account by appropriate corrections exactly as should changes in quality of products.[14] And our previous analysis shows sufficiently why in the process of capitalist evolution this must be so.

What the business strategy in question really aims at—all, in any case, that it can achieve—is to avoid seasonal, random and cyclical fluctuations in prices and to move only in response to the more fundamental changes in the conditions that underlie those fluctuations. Since these more fundamental changes take time in declaring themselves, this involves moving slowly by discrete steps—keeping to a price until new relatively durable contours have emerged into view. In technical language, this strategy aims at moving along a step function that will approximate trends. And that is what genuine and voluntary price rigidity in most cases amounts to. In fact, most economists do admit this, at least by implication. For though some of their arguments about rigidity would hold true only if the phenomenon were a long-run one—for instance most of the arguments averring that price rigidity keeps the fruits of technological progress from consumers—in practice they measure and discuss primarily cyclical rigidity and especially the fact that many prices do not, or do not promptly, fall in recessions and depressions. The real question is therefore how this short-run rigidity[15] may affect the long-run development of total output. Within this question, the only really important issue is this: prices that stay up in recession or depression no doubt influence the business situation in those phases of the cycles; if that influence is strongly injurious—making matters much worse than they would be with perfect flexibility all round—the destruction wrought each time might also affect output in the subsequent recoveries and prosperities and thus permanently reduce the rate of increase in total output below what it would be in the absence of those rigidities. Two arguments have been put forth in favor of this view.

In order to put the first into the strongest possible light, let us assume that an industry which refuses to reduce prices in recession goes on selling exactly the same quantity

13. They do not as a rule fall as they would under conditions of perfect competition. But this is true only *ceteris paribus,* and this proviso robs the proposition of all practical importance. I have adverted to this point before and shall return to it below (§ 5).

14. From a welfare standpoint, it is proper to adopt a definition different from ours, and to measure price changes in terms of the hours of labor that are currently necessary to earn the dollars which will buy given quantities of manufactured consumers' goods, taking account of changes of quality. We have already done this in the course of a previous argument. A long-run downward flexibility is then revealed that is truly impressive. Changes in price level raise another problem. So far as they reflect monetary influences they should be eliminated for most of the purposes of an investigation into rigidity. But so far as they reflect the combined effect of increasing efficiencies in all lines of production they should not.

15. It should, however, be observed that this short run may last longer than the term "short run" usually implies—sometimes ten years and even longer. There is not one cycle, but there are many simultaneous ones of varying duration. One of the most important ones lasts on the average about nine years and a half. Structural changes requiring price adjustments do in important cases occur in periods of about that length. The full extent of the spectacular changes reveals itself only in periods much longer than this. To do justice to aluminum, rayon, or motorcar prices one must survey a period of about forty-five years.

of product which it would sell if it had reduced them. Buyers are therefore out of pocket by the amount to which the industry profits from the rigidity. If these buyers are the kind of people who spend all they can and if the industry or those to whom its net returns go does not spend the increment it gets but either keeps it idle or repays bank loans, then total expenditure in the economy may be reduced thereby. If this happens, other industries or firms may suffer and if thereupon they restrict in turn, we may get a cumulation of depressive effects. In other words, rigidity may so influence the amount and distribution of national income as to decrease balances or to increase idle balances or, if we adopt a popular misnomer, savings. Such a case is conceivable. But the reader should have little difficulty in satisfying himself[16] that its practical importance, if any, is very small.

The second argument turns on the dislocating effects price rigidity may exert if, in the individual industry itself or elsewhere, it leads to an additional restriction of output, i.e., to a restriction greater than that which must in any case occur during depression. Since the most important conductor of those effects is the incident increase in unemployment—unstabilization of employment is in fact the indictment most commonly directed against price rigidity—and the consequent decrease in total expenditure, this argument then follows in the tracks of the first one. Its practical weight is considerably reduced, although economists greatly differ as to the extent, by the consideration that in the most conspicuous cases price rigidity is motivated precisely by the low sensitiveness of demand to short-run price changes within the practicable range. People who in depression worry about their future are not likely to buy a new car even if the price were reduced by 25 percent, especially if the purchase is easily postponable and if the reduction induces expectations of further reductions.

Quite irrespective of this however, the argument is inconclusive because it is again vitiated by a *ceteris paribus* clause that is inadmissible in dealing with our process of creative destruction. From the fact, so far as it is a fact, that at more flexible prices greater quantities could *ceteris paribus* be sold, it does not follow that either the output of the commodities in question, or total output and hence employment, would actually be greater. For inasmuch as we may assume that the refusal to lower prices strengthens the position of the industries which adopt that policy either by increasing their revenue or simply by avoiding chaos in their markets—that is to say, so far as this policy is something more than a mistake on their part—it may make fortresses out of what otherwise might be centers of devastation. As we have seen before, from a more general standpoint, total output and employment may well keep on a higher level with the restrictions incident to that policy than they would if depression were allowed to play havoc with the price structure.[17] In other words, under the conditions created by capitalist evolution, perfect and

16. The best method of doing this is to work out carefully *all* the assumptions involved, not only in the strong case imagined but also in the weaker cases that are less unlikely to occur in practice. Moreover, it should not be forgotten that the profit due to keeping prices up may be the means of avoiding bankruptcy or at least the necessity of discontinuing operations, both of which might be much more effective in starting a downward "vicious spiral" than is a possible reduction in total expenditure. See the comments on the second argument.

17. The theorist's way to put the point is that in depression demand curves might shift downwards much more violently if all pegs were withdrawn from under all prices.

universal flexibility of prices might in depression further unstabilize the system, instead of stabilizing it as it no doubt would under the conditions envisaged by general theory. Again this is to a large extent recognized in those cases in which the economist is in sympathy with the interests immediately concerned, for instance in the case of labor and of agriculture; in those cases he admits readily enough that what looks like rigidity may be no more than regulated adaptation.

Perhaps the reader feels some surprise that so little remains of a doctrine of which so much has been made in the last few years. The rigidity of prices has become, with some people, the outstanding defect of the capitalist engine and—almost—the fundamental factor in the explanation of depressions. But there is nothing to wonder at in this. Individuals and groups snatch at anything that will qualify as a discovery lending support to the political tendencies of the hour. The doctrine of price rigidity, with a modicum of truth to its credit, is not the worst case of this kind by a long way.

4. Another doctrine has crystallized into a slogan, viz., that in the era of big business the maintenance of the value of existing investment—conservation of capital—becomes the chief aim of entrepreneurial activity and bids fair to put a stop to all cost-reducing improvement. Hence the capitalist order becomes incompatible with progress.

Progress entails, as we have seen, destruction of capital values in the strata with which the new commodity or method of production competes. In perfect competition the old investments must be adapted at a sacrifice or abandoned; but when there is no perfect competition and when each industrial field is controlled by a few big concerns, these can in various ways fight the threatening attack on their capital structure and try to avoid losses on their capital accounts; that is to say, they can and will fight progress itself.

So far as this doctrine merely formulates a particular aspect of restrictive business strategy, there is no need to add anything to the argument already sketched in this chapter. Both as to the limits of that strategy and as to its functions in the process of creative destruction, we should only be repeating what has been said before. This becomes still more obvious if we observe that conserving capital values is the same thing as conserving profits. Modern theory tends in fact to use the concept Present Net Value of Assets (= capital values) in place of the concept of Profits. Both asset values and profits are of course not being simply conserved but maximized.

But the point about the sabotage of cost-reducing improvement still calls for comment in passing. As a little reflection will show, it is sufficient to consider the case of a concern that controls a technological device—some patent, say—that use of which would involve scrapping some or all of its plant and equipment. Will it, in order to conserve its capital values, refrain from using this device when a management not fettered by capitalist interests such as a socialist management could and would use it to the advantage of all?

Again it is tempting to raise the question of fact. The first thing a modern concern does as soon as it feels that it can afford it is to establish a research department every member of which knows that his bread and butter depends on his success in devising improvements. This practice does not obviously suggest aversion to technological progress. Nor can we in reply be referred to the cases in which patents acquired by business concerns have not been used promptly or not been used at all. For there may be perfectly good reasons for this; for example, the patented process may turn out to be no good or at least not to be in shape to warrant application on a commercial basis. Neither the inventors themselves nor the investigating economists or government officials are unbiased judges of this, and from their remonstrances or reports we may easily get a very distorted picture.[18]

But we are concerned with a question of theory. Everyone agrees that private and socialist managements will introduce improvements if, with the new method of production, the total cost per unit of product is expected to be smaller than the prime cost per unit of product with the method actually in use. If this condition is not fulfilled, then it is held that private management will not adopt a cost-reducing method until the existing plant and equipment is entirely written off, whereas socialist management would, to the social advantage, replace the old by any new cost-reducing method as soon as such a method becomes available, i.e., without regard to capital values. This however is not so.[19]

Private management, if actuated by the profit motive, cannot be interested in maintaining the values of any given building or machine any more than a socialist management would be. All that private management tries to do is to maximize the present net value of total assets which is equal to the discounted value of expected net returns. This amounts to saying that it will always adopt a new method of production which it believes will yield a larger stream of future income per unit of the corresponding stream of future outlay, both discounted to the present, than does the method actually in use. The value of past investments, whether or not paralleled by a bonded debt that has to be amortized, does not enter at all except in the sense and to the extent that it would also have to enter into the calculation underlying the decisions of a socialist management. So far as the use of the old machines saves future costs as compared with the immediate introduction of the new methods, the remainder of their service value is of course an element of the decision for both the capitalist and the socialist manager; otherwise bygones are bygones for both of them and any attempt to conserve the value of past investment would conflict as much with the rules following from the profit motive as it would conflict with the rules set for the behavior of the socialist manager.

It is however not true that private firms owning equipment the value of which is endangered by a new method which they also control—if they do not control it, there

18. Incidentally, it should be noticed that the kind of restrictive practice under discussion, granted that it exists to a significant extent, would not be without compensatory effects on social welfare. In fact, the same critics who talk about sabotage of progress at the same time emphasize the *social* losses incident to the pace of capitalist progress, particularly the unemployment which that pace entails and which slower advance might mitigate to some extent. Well, is technological progress too quick or too slow for them? They had better make up their minds.

19. It should be observed that even if the argument were correct, it would still be inadequate to support the thesis that capitalism is, under the conditions envisaged, "incompatible with technological progress." All that it would prove is, for some cases, the presence of a lag of ordinarily moderate length in the introduction of new methods.

is no problem and no indictment—will adopt the new method only if total unit cost with it is smaller than prime unit cost with the old one, or if the old investment has been completely written off *according to the schedule decided on before the new method presented itself.* For if the new machines when installed are expected to outlive the rest of the period previously set for the use of the old machines, their discounted remainder value as of that date is another asset to be taken account of. Nor is it true, for analogous reasons, that a socialist management, if acting rationally, would always and immediately adopt any new method which promises to produce at smaller total unit costs or that this would be to the social advantage.

There is however another element[20] which profoundly affects behavior in this matter and which is being invariably overlooked. This is what might be called *ex ante* conservation of capital in expectation of further improvement. Frequently, if not in most cases, a going concern does not simply face the question whether or not to adopt a definite new method of production that is the best thing out and, in the form immediately available, can be expected to retain that position for some length of time. A new type of machine is in general but a link in a chain of improvements and may presently become obsolete. In a case like this it would obviously not be rational to follow the chain link by link regardless of the capital loss to be suffered each time. The real question then is at which link the concern should take action. The answer must be in the nature of a compromise between considerations that rest largely on guesses. But it will as a rule involve some waiting in order to see how the chain behaves. And to the outsider this may well look like trying to stifle improvement in order to conserve *existing* capital values. Yet even the most patient of comrades would revolt if a socialist management were so foolish as to follow the advice of the theorist and to keep on scrapping plant and equipment every year.

5. I have entitled this chapter as I did because most of it deals with the facts and problems that common parlance associates with monopoly or monopolistic practice. So far I have as much as possible refrained from using those terms in order to reserve for a separate section some comments on a few topics specifically connected with them. Nothing will be said however that we have not already met in one form or another.

(a) To begin with, there is the term itself. Monopolist means Single Seller. Literally therefore anyone is a monopolist who sells anything that is not in every respect, wrapping and location and service included, exactly like what other people sell: every grocer, or every haberdasher, or every seller of "Good Humors" on a road that is not simply lined with sellers of the same brand of ice cream. This however is not what we mean when talking about monopolists. We mean only those single sellers whose markets are not open to the intrusion of would-be producers of the same commodity and of actual producers of similar ones or, speaking slightly more technically, only those single sellers who face a given demand schedule that is severely independent of their own action as well as of any reactions to their action by other concerns. The traditional Cournot-Marshall theory of monopoly as extended and amended by later

20. There are of course many other elements. The reader will please understand that in dealing with a few questions of principles it is impossible to do full justice to any of the topics touched upon.

authors holds only if we define it in this way and there is, so it seems, no point in calling anything a monopoly to which that theory does not apply. But if accordingly we do define it like this, then it becomes evident immediately that pure cases of long-run monopoly must be of the rarest occurrence and that even tolerable approximations to the requirements of the concept must be still rarer than are cases of perfect competition. The power to exploit at pleasure a given pattern of demand—or one that changes independently of the monopolist's action and of the reaction it provokes—can under the conditions of intact capitalism hardly persist for a period long enough to matter for the analysis of total output, unless buttressed by public authority, for instance, in the case of fiscal monopolies. A modern business concern not *so* protected—i.e., even if protected by import duties or import prohibitions—and yet wielding that power (except temporarily) is not easy to find or even to imagine. Even railroads and power and light concerns had first to create the demand for their services and, when they had done so, to defend their market against competition. Outside the field of public utilities, the position of a single seller can in general be conquered—and retained for decades—only on the condition that he does not behave like a monopolist. Short-run monopoly will be touched upon presently.

Why then all this talk about monopoly? The answer is not without interest for the student of the psychology of political discussion. Of course, the concept of monopoly is being loosely used just like any other. People speak of a country's having a monopoly of something or other[21] even if the industry in question is highly competitive and so on. But this is not all. Economists, government agents, journalists and politicians in this country obviously love the word because it has come to be a term of opprobrium which is sure to rouse the public's hostility against any interest so labeled. In the Anglo-American world monopoly has been cursed and associated with functionless exploitation ever since, in the sixteenth and seventeenth centuries, it was English administrative practice to create monopoly positions in large numbers which, on the one hand, answered fairly well to the theoretical pattern of monopolist behavior and, on the other hand, fully justified the wave of indignation that impressed even the great Elizabeth.

Nothing is so retentive as a nation's memory. Our time offers other and more important instances of a nation's reaction to what happened centuries ago. That practice made the English-speaking public so monopoly-conscious that it acquired a habit of attributing to that sinister power practically everything it disliked about business. To the typical liberal bourgeois in particular, monopoly became the father of almost all abuses—in fact, it became his pet bogey. Adam Smith,[22] thinking primarily of

21. These so-called monopolies have of late come to the fore in connection with the proposal to withhold certain materials from aggressor nations. The lessons of this discussion have some bearing upon our problem by way of analogy. At first, much was thought of the possibilities of that weapon. Then, on looking more closely at it, people found their lists of such materials to be shrinking, because it became increasingly clear that there are very few things that cannot be either produced or substituted for in the areas in question. And finally a suspicion began to dawn to the effect that even though some pressure can be exerted on them in the short run, long-run developments might eventually destroy practically all that was left on the lists.

22. There was more excuse for that uncritical attitude in the case of Adam Smith and the classics in general than there is in the case of their successors because big business in our sense had not then emerged. But even so they

monopolies of the Tudor and Stuart type, frowned on them in awful dignity. Sir Robert Peel—who like most conservatives occasionally knew how to borrow from the arsenal of the demagogue—in his famous epilogue to his last period in office that gave so much offense to his associates, spoke of a monopoly of bread or wheat, though English grain production was of course perfectly competitive in spite of protection.[23] And in this country monopoly is being made practically synonymous with any large-scale business.

(b) The theory of simple and discriminating monopoly teaches that, excepting a limiting case, monopoly price is higher and monopoly output smaller than competitive price and competitive output. This is true provided that the method and organization of production—and everything else—are exactly the same in both cases. Actually however there are superior methods available to the monopolist which either are not available at all to a crowd of competitors or are not available to them so readily: for there are advantages which, though not strictly unattainable on the competitive level of enterprise, are as a matter of fact secured only on the monopoly level, for instance, because monopolization may increase the sphere of influence of the better, and decrease the sphere of influence of the inferior, brains,[24] or because the monopoly enjoys a disproportionately higher financial standing. Whenever this is so, then that proposition is no longer true. In other words, this element of the case for competition may fail completely because monopoly prices are not necessarily higher or monopoly outputs smaller than competitive prices and outputs would be at the levels of productive and organizational efficiency that are within the reach of the type of firm compatible with the competitive hypothesis.

There cannot be any reasonable doubt that under the conditions of our epoch such superiority is as a matter of fact the outstanding feature of the typical large-scale unit of control, though mere size is neither necessary nor sufficient for it. These units not only arise in the process of creative destruction and function in a way entirely different from the static schema, but in many cases of decisive importance they provide the necessary form for the achievement. They largely create what they exploit. Hence the usual conclusion about their influence on long-run output would be invalid even if they were genuine monopolies in the technical sense of the term.

Motivation is quite immaterial. Even if the opportunity to set monopolist prices were the sole object, the pressure of the improved methods or of a huge apparatus would in general tend to shift the point of the monopolist's optimum toward or beyond the competitive cost price in the above sense, thus doing the work—partly, wholly, or

went too far. In part this was due to the fact that they had no satisfactory theory of monopoly which induced them not only to apply the term rather promiscuously (Adam Smith and even [Nassau William] Senior interpreted for instance the rent of land as a monopoly gain) but also to look upon the monopolist's power of exploitation as practically unlimited which is of course wrong even for the most extreme cases.

23. This instance illustrates the way in which the term keeps on creeping into illegitimate uses. Protection of agriculture and a monopoly of agrarian products are entirely different things. The struggle was over protection and not over a nonexistent cartel of either landowners or farmers. But in fighting protection it was just as well to beat up for applause. And there was evidently no simpler means of doing so than by calling protectionists monopolists.

24. The reader should observe that while, as a broad rule, that particular type of superiority is simply indisputable, the inferior brains, especially if their owners are entirely eliminated, are not likely to admit it and that the public's and

more than wholly—of the competitive mechanism,[25] *even if restriction is practiced and excess capacity is in evidence all along*. Of course if the methods of production, organization and so on are not improved by or in connection with monopolization as is the case with an ordinary cartel, the classical theorem about monopoly price and output comes into its own again.[26] So does another popular idea, viz., that monopolization has a soporific effect. For this, too, it is not difficult to find examples. But no general theory should be built upon it. For, especially in manufacturing industry, a monopoly position is in general no cushion to sleep on. As it can be gained, so it can be retained only by alertness and energy. What soporific influence there is in modern business is due to another cause that will be mentioned later.

(c) In the short run, genuine monopoly positions or positions approximating monopoly are much more frequent. The grocer in a village on the Ohio may be a true monopolist for hours or even days during an inundation. Every successful corner may spell monopoly for the moment. A firm specializing in paper labels for beer bottles may be so circumstanced—potential competitors realizing that what seem to be good profits would be immediately destroyed by their entering the field—that it can move at pleasure on a moderate but still finite stretch of the demand curve, at least until the metal label smashes that demand curve to pieces.

New methods of production or new commodities, especially the latter, do not per se confer monopoly, even if used or produced by a single firm. The product of the new method has to compete with the products of the old ones and the new commodity has to be introduced, i.e., its demand schedule has to be built up. As a rule neither patents nor monopolistic practices avail against that. But they may in cases of spectacular superiority of the new device, particularly if it can be leased like shoe machinery; or in cases of new commodities, the permanent demand schedule for which has been established before the patent has expired.

Thus it is true that there is or may be an element of genuine monopoly gain in those entrepreneurial profits which are the prizes offered by capitalist society to the successful innovator. But the quantitative importance of that element, its volatile nature and its function in the process in which it emerges put it in a class by itself. The main value to a concern of a single seller position that is secured by patent or monopolistic

the recording economists' hearts go out to them and not to the others. This may have something to do with a tendency to discount the cost or quality advantages of quasi-monopolist combination that is at present as pronounced as was the exaggeration of them in the typical prospectus or announcement of sponsors of such combinations.

25. The Aluminum Company of America is not a monopoly in the technical sense as defined above, among other reasons because it had to build up its demand schedule, which fact suffices to exclude a behavior conforming to the Cournot-Marshall schema. But most economists call it so and in the dearth of genuine cases we will for the purposes of this note do the same. From 1890 to 1929 the price of the basic product of this single seller fell to about 12 percent or, correcting for the change in price level (B.L.S. index of wholesale prices), to about 8.8 percent. Output rose from 50 metric tons to 103,400. Protection by patent ceased in 1909. Argument from costs and profits in criticism of this "monopoly" must take it for granted that a multitude of competing firms would have been about equally successful in cost-reducing research, in the economical development of the productive apparatus, in teaching new uses for the product and in avoiding wasteful breakdowns. This is, in fact, being assumed by criticism of this kind; i.e., the propelling factor of modem capitalism is being assumed away.

26. See however *supra*, § 1.

strategy does not consist so much in the opportunity to behave temporarily according to the monopolist schema, as in the protection it affords against temporary disorganization of the market and the space it secures for long-range planning. Here however the argument merges into the analysis submitted before.

6. Glancing back we realize that most of the facts and arguments touched upon in this chapter tend to dim the halo that once surrounded perfect competition as much as they suggest a more favorable view of its alternative. I will now briefly restate our argument from this angle.

Traditional theory itself, even within its chosen precincts of a stationary or steadily growing economy, has since the time of Marshall and Edgeworth been discovering an increasing number of exceptions to the old propositions about perfect competition and, incidentally, free trade, that have shaken that unqualified belief in its virtues cherished by the generation which flourished between Ricardo and Marshall—roughly, J. S. Mill's generation in England and Francesco Ferrara's on the Continent. Especially the propositions that a perfectly competitive system is ideally economical of resources and allocates them in a way that is optimal with respect to a given distribution of income—propositions very relevant to the question of the behavior of output—cannot now be held with the old confidence.[27]

Much more serious is the breach made by more recent work in the field of dynamic theory (Frisch, Tinbergen, Roos, Hicks and others). Dynamic analysis is the analysis of sequences in time. In explaining why a certain economic quantity, for instance a price, is what we find it to be at a given moment, it takes into consideration not only the state of other economic quantities at the same moment, as static theory does, but also their state at preceding points of time, and the expectations about their future values. Now the first thing we discover in working out the propositions that thus relate quantities belonging to different points of time[28] is the fact that, once equilibrium has been destroyed by some disturbance, the process of establishing a new one is not so sure and prompt and economical as the old theory of perfect competition made it out to be; and the possibility that the very struggle for adjustment might lead such a system farther away from instead of nearer to a new equilibrium. This will happen in most cases unless the disturbance is small. In many cases, lagged adjustment is sufficient to produce this result.

All I can do here is to illustrate by the oldest, simplest and most familiar example. Suppose that demand and *intended* supply are in equilibrium in a perfectly competitive market for wheat, but that bad weather reduces the crop below what farmers intended to supply. If price rises accordingly and the farmers thereupon produce that quantity of wheat which it would pay them to produce if that new price were the equilibrium price, then a slump in the wheat market will ensue in the following year. If now the farmers

27. Since we cannot enter into the subject, I will refer the reader to Mr. R. F. Kahn's paper entitled "Some Notes on Ideal Output" *(Economic Journal* for March 1955), which covers much of this ground.

28. The term dynamics is loosely used and carries many different meanings. The above definition was formulated by Ragnar Frisch.

correspondingly, restrict production, a price still higher than in the first year may result to induce a still greater expansion of production than occurred in the second year. And so on (as far as the pure logic of the process is concerned) indefinitely. The reader will readily perceive, from a survey of the assumptions involved, that no great fear need be entertained of ever higher prices' and ever greater outputs' alternating till doomsday. But even if reduced to its proper proportions, the phenomenon suffices to show up glaring weaknesses in the mechanism of perfect competition. As soon as this is realized much of the optimism that used to grace the practical implications of the theory of this mechanism passes out through the ivory gate.

But from our standpoint we must go further than that.[29] If we try to visualize how perfect competition works or would work in the process of creative destruction, we arrive at a still more discouraging result. This will not surprise us, considering that all the essential facts of that process are absent from the general schema of economic life that yields the traditional propositions about perfect competition. At the risk of repetition I will illustrate the point once more.

Perfect competition implies free entry into every industry. It is quite true, within that general theory, that free entry into all industries is a condition for optimal allocation of resources and hence for maximizing output. If our economic world consisted of a number of established industries producing familiar commodities by established and substantially invariant methods and if nothing happened except that additional men and additional savings combine in order to set up new firms of the existing type, then impediments to their entry into any industry they wish to enter would spell loss to the community. But perfectly free entry into a *new* field may make it impossible to enter it at all. The introduction of new methods of production and new commodities is hardly conceivable with perfect—and perfectly prompt—competition from the start. And this means that the bulk of what we call economic progress is incompatible with it. As a matter of fact, perfect competition is and always has been temporarily suspended whenever anything new is being introduced—automatically or by measures devised for the purpose—even in otherwise perfectly competitive conditions.

Similarly, within the traditional system the usual indictment of rigid prices stands all right. Rigidity is a type of resistance to adaptation that perfect and prompt competition excludes. And for the kind of adaptation and for those conditions which have been treated by traditional theory, it is again quite true that such resistance spells loss and reduced output. But we have seen that in the spurts and vicissitudes of the process

29. It should be observed that the defining feature of dynamic theory has nothing to do with the nature of the economic reality to which it is applied. It is a general method of analysis rather than a study of a particular process. We can use it in order to analyze a stationary economy, just as an evolving one can be analyzed by means of the methods of statics ("comparative statics"). Hence dynamic theory need not take, and as a matter of fact has not taken, any special cognizance of the process of creative destruction which we have taken to be the essence of capitalism.

It is no doubt better equipped than is static theory to deal with many questions of mechanism that arise in the analysis of that process. But it is not an analysis of that process itself, and it treats the resulting individual disturbances of given states and structures just as it treats other disturbances. To judge the functioning of perfect competition from the standpoint of capitalist evolution is therefore not the same thing as judging it from the standpoint of dynamic theory.

of creative destruction the opposite may be true: perfect and instantaneous flexibility may even produce functionless catastrophes. This of course can also be established by the general dynamic theory which, as mentioned above, shows that there are attempts at adaptation that intensify disequilibrium.

Again, under its own assumptions, traditional theory is correct in holding that profits above what is necessary in each individual case to call forth the equilibrium amount of means of production, entrepreneurial ability included, both indicate and in themselves imply net social loss and that business strategy that aims at keeping them alive is inimical to the growth of total output. Perfect competition would prevent or immediately eliminate such surplus profits and leave no room for that strategy. But since the process of capitalist evolution these profits acquire new organic functions—I do not want to repeat what they are—that fact cannot any longer be unconditionally credited to the account of the perfectly competitive model, so far as the secular rate of increase in total output is concerned.

Finally, it can indeed be shown that, under the same assumptions which amount to excluding the most characteristic features of capitalist reality, a perfectly competitive economy is comparatively free from waste and in particular from those kinds of waste which we most readily associate with its counterpart. But this does not tell us anything about how its account looks under the conditions set by the process of creative destruction.

On the one hand, much of what without reference to those conditions would appear to be unrelieved waste ceases to qualify as such when duly related to them. The type of excess capacity for example that owes its existence to the practice of providing capacity for the cyclical peaks of demand would in a regime of perfect competition be much reduced. But when *all* the facts of the case are taken into consideration, it is no longer correct to say that perfect competition wins out on that score. For though a concern that has to accept and cannot set prices would, in fact, use all of its capacity that can produce at marginal costs covered by the ruling prices, it does not follow that it would ever have the quantity and quality of capacity that big business has created and was able to create precisely because it is in a position to use it "strategically." Excess capacity of this type may—it does in some and does not in other cases—constitute a reason for claiming superiority for a socialist economy. But it should not without qualification be listed as a claim to superiority of the perfectly competitive species of capitalist economy as compared with the "monopoloid" species.

On the other hand, working in the conditions of capitalist evolution, the perfectly competitive arrangement displays wastes of its own. The firm of the type that is compatible with perfect competition is in many cases inferior in internal, especially technological, efficiency. If it is, then it wastes opportunities. It may also in its endeavors to improve its methods of production waste capital because it is in a less favorable position to evolve and to judge new possibilities. And, as we have seen before, a perfectly competitive industry is much more apt to be routed—and to scatter the bacilli of depression—under the impact of progress or of external disturbance than is big business. In the last resort, American agriculture, English coal mining, the English textile industry are costing consumers much more and are affecting *total* output much more injuriously than they would if controlled, each of them, by a dozen good brains.

Thus it is not sufficient to argue that because perfect competition is impossible under modem industrial conditions—or because it always has been impossible—the large-scale establishment or unit of control must be accepted as a necessary evil inseparable from the economic progress which it is prevented from sabotaging by the forces inherent in its productive apparatus. What we have got to accept is that it has come to be the most powerful engine of that progress and in particular of the long-run expansion of total output not only in spite of, but to a considerable extent through, this strategy which looks so restrictive when viewed in the individual case and from the individual point of time. In this respect, perfect competition is not only impossible but inferior, and has no title to being set up as a model of ideal efficiency. It is hence a mistake to base the theory of government regulation of industry on the principle that big business should be made to work as the respective industry would work in perfect competition. And socialists should rely for their criticisms on the virtues of a socialist economy rather than on those of the competitive model.

## Kenneth J. Arrow

## *Economic Welfare and the Allocation of Resources for Invention*

### I. Introduction

Invention is here interpreted broadly as the production of knowledge. From the viewpoint of welfare economies, the determination of optimal resource allocation for invention will depend on the technological characteristics of the invention process and the nature of the market for knowledge.

The classic question of welfare economics will be asked here: to what extent does perfect competition lead to an optimal allocation of resources? We know from years of patient refinement that competition insures the achievement of a Pareto optimum under certain hypotheses. The model usually assumes among other things that (a) the utility functions of consumers and the transformation functions of producers are well-defined functions of the commodities in the economic system, and (b) the transformation functions do not display increasing returns (more strictly, the transformation sets are convex). The second condition needs no comment. The first seems to be innocuous but in fact conceals two basic assumptions of the usual models. It prohibits uncertainty in the production relations and in the utility functions, and it requires that all the commodities relevant either to production or to the welfare of individuals be traded on the market. This will not be the case when the commodity for one reason or another cannot be made into private property.

We have then three of the classical reasons for the possible failure of perfect competition to achieve optimality in resource allocation: increasing returns, inappropriability, and uncertainty. The first problem has been much studied in the literature under the heading of marginal-cost pricing and the second under that of divergence between social and private benefit (or cost), but the theory of optimal allocation of resources under uncertainty has had much less attention. I will summarize what formal theory exists and then point to the critical notion of information, which arises only in the context of uncertainty. The economic characteristics of information as a commodity and in particular of invention as a process for the production of information are next examined. It is shown that three of the reasons given above for a failure of the competitive system to achieve an optimal resource allocation hold in the case of invention. On theoretical grounds a number of considerations are adduced as to the likely biases in the misallocation and the implications for economic organization.[1]

## II. Resource Allocation Under Uncertainty

The role of the competitive system in allocating uncertainty seems to have received little systematic attention.[2] I will first sketch an ideal economy in which the allocation problem can be solved by competition and then indicate some of the devices in the real world which approximate this solution.

Suppose for simplicity that uncertainty occurs only in the production relations. Producers have to make a decision on inputs at the present moment, but the outputs are not completely predictable from the inputs. We may normally describe the outputs as determined by the inputs and a "state of nature" which is unknown to the producers. Let us define a "commodity-option" as a commodity in the ordinary sense labelled with a state of nature. This definition is analogous to the differentiation of a given physical commodity according to date in capital theory or according to place in location theory. The production of a given commodity under uncertainty can then be described as the production of a vector of commodity-options.

This description can be most easily exemplified by reference to agricultural production. The state of nature may be identified with the weather. Then, to any given set of inputs, there corresponds a number of bushels of wheat if the rainfall is good and a different number if rainfall is bad. We can introduce intermediate conditions of rainfall in any number as alternative states of nature; we can increase the number of relevant variables which enter into the description of the state of nature, for example adding temperature. By extension of this procedure, we can give a formal description of any kind of uncertainty in production.

1. For other analyses with similar points of view, see R. R. Nelson, "The Simple Economics of Basic Scientific Research," *Journal of Political Economy*, Vol. LXVII (1959): 297–306; and C. J. Hitch, "The Character of Research and Development in a Competitive Economy," P-1297, RAND Corporation, 13 May 1958.

2. The first studies of which I am aware are the papers of M. Allais and myself, both presented in 1952 to the Colloque International sur le Risque in Paris; see M. Allais, "Généralisation des théories de l'équilibre économique général et du rendement social au cas du risque," and K. J. Arrow, "Rôle des valeurs boursières pour la repartition la meilleure des risques," both in *Économetrie*, Colloques Internationaux du Centre National de la Recherche Scientifique, Vol. XL, Paris: Centre National de la Recherche Scientifique, 1953. Allais' paper has also appeared in *Econometrica*, 21(1953): 269–290. The theory has received a very elegant generalization by G. Debreu in *Theory of Values*, New York: Wiley, 1959, Ch. VII.

Suppose, and this is the critical idealization of the economy, we have a market for all commodity-options. What is traded on each market are contracts to buy or sell prescribed quantities of a given commodity *if* a certain state of nature prevails. For any given set of inputs, the firm knows its output under each state of nature and sells a corresponding quantity of commodity-options; its revenue is then completely determined. It may choose its inputs so as to maximize profits.

The income of consumers is derived from their sale of supplies to firms, including labor, and their receipt of profits, which are assumed completely distributed. They purchase commodity-options so as to maximize their expected utility given the budget restraint imposed by their incomes. An equilibrium is reached on all commodity-option markets, and this equilibrium has precisely the same Pareto-optimality properties as competitive equilibrium under certainty.

In particular, the markets for commodity-options in this ideal model serve the function of achieving an optimal allocation of risk-bearing among the members of the economy. This allocation takes account of differences in both resources and tastes for risk-bearing. Among other implications, risk-bearing and production are separated economic functions. The use of inputs, including human talents, in their most productive mode is not inhibited by unwillingness or inability to bear risks by either firms or productive agents.

But our economic system does not possess markets for commodity-options. To see what substitutes exist, let us first consider a model economy at the other extreme, in that no provisions for reallocating risk-bearing exist. Each firm makes its input decisions; then outputs are produced as determined by the inputs and the state of nature. Prices are then set to clear the market. The prices that finally prevail will be a function of the state of nature.

The firm and its owners cannot relieve themselves of risk-bearing in this model. Hence any unwillingness or inability to bear risks will give rise to a sub-optimal allocation of resources in that there will be discrimination against risky enterprises as compared with the optimum. A preference for risk might give rise to misallocation in the opposite direction, but the limitations of financial resources are likely to make underinvestment in risky enterprises more likely than the opposite. The inability of individuals to buy protection against uncertainty similarly gives rise to a loss of welfare.

In fact, a number of institutional arrangements have arisen to mitigate the problem of assumption of risk-bearing. Suppose that each firm and individual in the economy could forecast perfectly what prices would be under each state of nature. Suppose further there were a lottery on the states of nature, so that before the state of nature is known any individual or firm may place bets. Then it can be seen that the effect from the viewpoint of any given individual or firm is the same as if there were markets for commodity-options of all types, since any commodity-option can be achieved by a combination of a bet on the appropriate state of nature and an intention to purchase the commodity in question if the state of nature occurs.

References to lotteries and bets may smack of frivolity, but we need only think of insurance to appreciate that the shifting of risks through what are in effect bets on the state of nature is a highly significant phenomenon. If insurance were available against any conceivable event, it follows from the preceding discussion that optimal allocation would be achieved. Of course, insurance as customarily defined covers only a small range of events relevant to the economic world; much more important in shifting risks are securities, particularly common stocks and money. By permitting individuals to shift freely their proprietary interests among different firms, they can to a large extent bet on the different states of nature which favor firms differentially. This freedom to insure against many contingencies is enhanced by the alternatives of holding cash and going short.

Unfortunately, it is only too clear that the shifting of risks in the real world is incomplete. The great predominance of internal over equity financing in industry is one illustration that securities do not completely fulfill their allocative role with respect to risks. There are a number of reasons why this should be so, but I will confine myself to one, of special significance with regard to invention. In insurance practice, reference is made to the *moral factor* as a limit to the possibilities of insurance. For example, a fire insurance policy cannot exceed in amount the value of the goods insured. From the purely actuarial standpoint, there is no reason for this limitation; the reason is that the insurance policy changes the incentives of the insured, in this case, creating an incentive for arson or at the very least for carelessness. The general principle is the difficulty of distinguishing between a state of nature and a decision by the insured. As a result, any insurance policy and in general any device for shifting risks can have the effect of dulling incentives. A fire insurance policy, even when limited in amount to the value of the goods covered, weakens the motivation for fire prevention. Thus steps which improve the efficiency of the economy with respect to risk-bearing may decrease its technical efficiency.

One device for mitigating the adverse incentive effects of insurance is *co-insurance*; the insurance extends only to part of the amount at risk for the insured. This device is used, for example, in coverage of medical risks. It clearly represents a compromise between incentive effects and allocation of risk-bearing, sacrificing something in both directions.

Two exemplifications of the moral factor are of special relevance in regard to highly risky business activities, including invention. Success in such activities depends on an inextricable tangle of objective uncertainties and decisions or the entrepreneurs and is certainly uninsurable. On the other hand, such activities should be undertaken if the expected return exceeds the market rate of return, no matter what the variance is.[3] The existence of common stocks would seem to solve the allocation problem; any individual stockholder can reduce his risk by buying only a small part of the stock and diversifying his portfolio to achieve his own preferred risk level. But then again the actual managers no longer receive the full reward of their decisions; the shifting of the risks is again accompanied by a weakening of incentives to efficiency. Substitute

3. The validity of this statement depends on some unstated assumptions, but the point to be made is unaffected by minor qualifications.

motivations, whether pecuniary, such as executive compensation and profit-sharing, or non-pecuniary, such as prestige, may be found, but the dilemma of the moral factor can never be completely resolved.

A second example is the cost-plus contract in one of its various forms. When production costs on military items are highly uncertain, the military establishment will pay, not a fixed unit price, but the cost of production plus an amount which today is usually a fixed fee. Such a contract could be regarded as a combination of a fixed-price contract with an insurance against costs. The insurance premium could be regarded as the difference between the fixed price the government would be willing to pay and the fixed fee.

Cost-plus contracts are necessitated by the inability or unwillingness of firms to bear the risks. The government has superior risk-bearing ability and so the burden is shifted to it. It is then enabled to buy from firms on the basis of their productive efficiency rather than their risk-bearing ability, which may be only imperfectly correlated. But cost-plus contracts notoriously have their adverse allocative effects.[4]

This somewhat lengthy digression on the theory of risk-bearing seemed necessitated by the paucity of literature on the subject. The main conclusions to be drawn are the following: (1) the economic system has devices for shifting risks, but they are limited and imperfect; hence, one would expect an underinvestment in risky activities; (2) it is undoubtedly worthwhile to enlarge the variety of such devices, but the moral factor creates a limit to their potential.

## III. Information as a Commodity

Uncertainty usually creates a still more subtle problem in resource allocation; information becomes a commodity. Suppose that in one part of the economic system, an observation has been made whose outcome, if known, would affect anyone's estimates of the probabilities of the different states of nature. Such observations arise out of research, but they also arise in the daily course of economic life as a by-product of other economic activities. An entrepreneur will automatically acquire a knowledge of demand and production conditions in his field which is available to others only with special effort. Information will frequently have an economic value, in the sense that anyone possessing the information can make greater profits than would otherwise be the case.

It might be expected that information will be traded in, and of course to a considerable extent this is the case, as is illustrated by the numerous economic institutions for transmission of information, such as newspapers. But in many cases, the problem of an optimal allocation is sharply raised. The cost of transmitting a given body of information is in many cases very low. If it were zero, then optimal allocation would obviously call for unlimited distribution of the information without cost. In fact, a given piece of information is by definition an indivisible commodity, and the classical problems of

4. These remarks are not intended as a complete evaluation of cost-plus contracts. In particular, there are, to a certain extent, other incentives which mitigate the adverse effects on efficiency.

increasing returns or indivisibilities appear here. The owner of the information should not extract the economic value which is there, if optimal allocation is to be achieved; but he is a monopolist, to some small extent, and will seek to take advantage of this fact.

In the absence of special legal protection, he cannot however simply sell information on the open market. Any one purchaser can destroy the monopoly, since he can reproduce the information at little or no cost. Thus the only effective monopoly would be the use of the information by the original possessor. This however will not only be socially inefficient, but may not be of much use to the owner of the information either, since he may not be able to exploit it as effectively as others.

With suitable legal measures, information may become an appropriable commodity. Then the monopoly power can indeed be exerted. However, no amount of legal protection can make a thoroughly appropriable commodity of something so intangible as information. The very use of the information in any productive way is bound to reveal it at least in part. Mobility of personnel among firms provides a way of spreading information. Legally imposed property rights can provide only a partial barrier, since there are obviously enormous difficulties in defining in any sharp way an item of information and differentiating it from other similar-sounding items.

The demand for information also has uncomfortable properties. In the first place, the use of information is certainly subject to increasing returns; the use of information about production possibilities, for example, need not depend on the rate of production. In the second place, there is a fundamental paradox in the determination of demand for information; its value for the purchaser is not known until he knows the information, but then he has in effect acquired it without cost. Of course, if the seller can retain property rights in the use of the information, this would be no problem, but given incomplete appropriability, the potential demander will base his decision to purchase information on less than optimal criteria. He may act, for example, on the average value of information in this class as revealed by past experience. If any particular item of information has differing values for different economic agents, this procedure will lead both to a sub-optimal purchase of information at any given price and also to a sub-optimal allocation of the information purchased.

It should be made clear that from the viewpoint of efficiently distributing an existing stock of information, the difficulties of appropriating information are an advantage, provided there are no costs of transmitting information, since then optimal allocation calls for free distribution. The chief point made here is the difficulty of creating a market for information if one should be desired for any reason.

It may be added that it follows from the preceding discussion that costs of transmitting information create allocative difficulties which would be absent otherwise. Information should be transmitted at marginal cost, but then the demand difficulties raised above will exist. From the viewpoint of optimal allocation, the purchasing industry will be operating under increasing returns, with all the usual difficulties; and we still leave unsolved the problem of the purchaser's inability to judge the value of the information. There is a strong case for centralized decision-making under these circumstances.

## IV. Invention as the Production of Information

The central economic fact about the processes of invention and research is that they are devoted to the production of information. By the very definition of information, invention must be a risky process in that the output (information obtained) can never be predicted perfectly from the inputs. We can now apply the discussion of the preceding two sections.

As a risky process, there is bound to be some discrimination against investment in inventive and research activities. In this field, especially, the moral factor will weigh heavily against any kind of insurance or equivalent form of risk-bearing. An insurance against failure to develop a desired new product or process will surely very greatly weaken the incentives to succeed. The only way, within the private enterprise system, to minimize this problem is the conduct of research by large corporations with many projects going on, each small in scale compared to the net revenue of the corporation. Then the corporation acts as its own insurance company. But clearly this is only an imperfect solution.

The deeper problems of misallocation arise from the nature of the product. As we have seen, information is a commodity with peculiar attributes, particularly embarrassing for the achievement of optimal allocation. In the first place, any information obtained, say a new method of production, should, from the welfare point of view, be available free of charge (apart from the cost of transmitting information). This insures optimal utilization of the information but of course provides no incentive for investment in research. In an ideal socialist economy, the reward for invention would be completely separated from any charge to the users of the information.[5] In a free enterprise economy, inventive activity is supported by using the invention to create property rights; precisely to the extent that it is successful, there is an underutilization of the information. The property rights may be in the information itself, through patents and similar legal devices, or in the intangible assets of the firm if the information is retained by the firm and used only to increase its profits.

The first problem, then, is that in a free enterprise economy the profitability of invention requires a sub-optimal allocation of resources. But it may still be asked whether or not the allocation of resources to inventive activity is optimal. The discussion of the preceding section makes it clear that we would not expect this to be so; that, in fact, a downward bias in the amount of resources devoted to inventive activity is very likely. Whatever the price, the demand for information is below optimal for two reasons: (1) since the price is positive and not at its optimal value of zero, the demand is bound to be below the optimal; (2) as seen before, at any given price, the very nature of information will lead to a lower demand than would be optimal.

In addition, as already remarked, the inventor will have in any case considerable difficulty in appropriating the information produced. Patent laws would have to be of an unimaginable complexity and subtlety to permit such appropriation on a large

5. This separation is in fact the case in the Soviet Union, according to N. M. Kaplan and R. H. Moorsteen, RAND Corporation (oral communication).

scale. Suppose, as the resu lt of elaborate tests, some metal is discovered to have desirable properties, say resistance to high heat. Then of course every use of the metal for which this property is relevant would use this information and would be made to pay for it. But, even more, if another inventor is stimulated to examine chemically related metals for heat resistance, he is using the information already discovered and should pay for it in some measure; and any beneficiary of his discoveries should also pay. One would have to have elaborate distinctions of partial property rights of all degrees to make the system at all tolerable. In the interests of the possibility of enforcement, actual patent laws sharply restrict the range of appropriable information and thereby reduce the incentives to engage in inventive and research activities.

These last considerations bring into focus the interdependence of inventive activities, which reinforces the difficulties in achieving an optimal allocation. Information is not only the product of inventive activity, it is also an input—in same sense, the major input apart from the talent of the inventor. The school of thought which emphasizes the determination of invention by the social climate as demonstrated by the simultaneity of inventions in effect emphasizes strongly the productive role of previous information in the creation of new information. While these interrelations do not create any new difficulties in principle, they intensify the previously established ones. To appropriate information used as a basis for further research is much more difficult than to appropriate its use in producing commodities; and the value of information for use in developing further information is much more conjectural than its use in production and therefore much more likely to be underestimated, so that if a price is charged for the information, the demand is even more likely to be sub-optimal.

Thus basic research, the output of which is only used as an informational input into other inventive activities, is especially unlikely to be rewarded. In fact, it is only likely to be of commercial value to the firm undertaking it if other firms are prevented from using the information obtained. But such restriction on the transmittal of information will reduce the efficiency of inventive activity in general and will therefore reduce its quantity also. We may put the matter in terms of sequential decision-making. The *a priori* probability distribution of the true state of nature is relatively flat to begin with. On the other hand, the successive *a posteriori* distributions after more and more studies have been conducted are more and more sharply peaked or concentrated in a more limited range, and we therefore have better and better information for deciding what the next step in research shall be. This implies that at the beginning, the preferences among alternative possible lines of investigation are much less sharply defined than they are apt to be later on and suggests, at least, the importance of having a wide variety of studies to begin with, the less promising being gradually eliminated as information is accumulated.[6] At each stage the decisions about the next step should be based on all available information. This would require an unrestricted flow of information among different projects which is incompatible with the complete decentralization of an ideal free enterprise system. When the production

6. The importance of parallel research developments in the case of uncertainty has been especially stressed by B. Klein; see his "A Radical Proposal for R. and D.," *Fortune*, May 1958: 112 ff.; and Klein and W. H. Meckling, "Application of Operations Research to Deve lopnent Decisions," *Operations Research*, Vol. 6 (1958): 352–363.

of information is important, the classic economic case in which the price system replaces the detailed spread of information is no longer completely applicable.

To sum up, we expect a free enterprise economy to underinvest in invention and research (as compared with an ideal) because it is risky, because the product can be appropriated only to a limited extent, and because of increasing returns in use. This underinvestment will be greater for more basic research. Further, to the extent that a firm succeeds in engrossing the economic value of its inventive activity, there will be an underutilization of that information as compared with an ideal allocation.

## V. Competition, Monopoly, and the Incentive to Innovate

It may be useful to remark that an incentive to invent can exist even under perfect competition in the product markets, though not, of course, in the "market" for the information contained in the invention. This is especially clear in the case of a cost-reducing invention. Provided only that suitable royalty payments can be demanded, an inventor can profit without disturbing the competitive nature of the industry. The situation for a new product is not very different; by charging a suitable royalty to a competitive industry, the inventor can receive a return equal to the monopoly profits.

I will examine here the incentives to invent for monopolistic and competitive markets, that is, the potential profits from an invention which will be compared with the costs. The difficulty of appropriating the information will be ignored; the remaining problem is that of increasing returns in use, an inherent property of information. By the competitive situation will be meant one in which the industry produces under competitive conditions, while the inventor can set an arbitrary royalty for the use of his invention. In the monopolistic situation, it will be assumed that only the monopoly itself can invent. It will be argued that the incentive to invent is less under monopolistic than under competitive conditions but even in the latter case it will be less than is socially desirable.

We will assume constant costs both before and after the invention, the unit costs being $c$ before the invention and $c' < c$ afterwards. The competitive price before invention will therefore be $c$; let the corresponding demand be $x_c$. If $r$ is the level of unit royalties, the competitive price after the invention will be $c' + r$, but this cannot of course be higher than $c$, since firms are always free to produce with the old methods.

It is assumed that both the demand and the marginal revenue curves are decreasing. Let $R(x)$ be the marginal revenue curve. Then the monopoly output before invention, $x_m$, would be defined by the equation

$$R(X_m) = c.$$

Similarly, the monopoly output after invention is defined by

$$R(_m) = c'.$$

Let the monopoly prices corresponding to outputs $x_m$ and $x'_m$, respectively, be $P_m$ and $P'_m$. Finally, let $P$ and $P'$ be the monopolist's profits before and after invention, respectively.

What is the optimal royalty level for the inventor in the competitive case? Let us suppose that he calculates $P'_m$, the optimal monopoly price which would obtain in the post-invention situation. If the cost reduction is sufficiently drastic that $P'_m < c$, then his most profitable policy is to set $r$ so that the competitive price is $P'_m$, i.e., let

$$r = P'_m - c'.$$

In this case, the inventor's royalties are equal to the profits a monopolist would make under the same conditions, i.e., his incentive to invent will be $P'$.

Suppose, however, it turns out that $P'_m > c$. Since the sales price cannot exceed $c$, the inventor will set his royalties at

$$r = c - c'.$$

The competitive price will then be $c$, and the sales will remain at $x_c$. The inventor's incentive will then be $x_c(c - c')$.

The monopolist's incentive, on the other hand, is clearly $P' - P$. In the first of the two cases cited, the monopolist's incentive is obviously less than the inventor's incentive under competition, which is $P'$, not $P' - P$. The pre-invention monopoly power acts as a strong disincentive to further innovation.

The analysis is slightly more complicated in the second case. The monopolist's incentive, $P' - P$, is the change in revenue less the change in total cost of production, i.e.,

$$P' - P = \int_{x_m}^{x'_m} R(x)dx - c'x'_m + cx_m$$

Since the marginal revenue $R(x)$ is diminishing, it must always be less than $R(x_m) = c$ as $x$ increases from $x_m$ to $x'_m$ so that

$$\int_{x_m}^{x'_m} R(x)dx < c(x'_m + x_m)$$

and

$$P' - P < c(x'_m - x_m) - c'x'_m + cx_m = (c - c')x'_m$$

In the case being considered, the post-invention monopoly price, $P'_m$, is greater than $c$. Hence, with a declining demand curve, $x'_m < x_c$. The above inequality shows that the monopolist's incentive is always less than the cost reduction on the post-invention monopoly output, which in this case is, in turn, less than the competitive output (both before and after invention). Since the inventor's incentive under competition is the cost reduction on the competitive output, it will again always exceed the monopolist's incentive.

It can be shown that, it we consider differing values of c', the *difference* between the two incentives increases as $c'$ decreases, reaching its maximum of P (pre-invention monopoly profits) for $c'$ sufficiently large for the first case to hold. The *ratio* of the incentive under competition to that under monopoly, on the other hand, though always greater than 1, decreases steadily with $c'$. For $c'$ very close to $c$ (i.e., very minor inventions), the ratio of the two incentives is approximately $x_c/x_m$, i.e., the ratio of monopoly to competitive output.[7]

The only ground for arguing that monopoly may create superior incentives to invent is that appropriability may be greater under monopoly than under competition. Whatever differences may exist in this direction must of course still be offset against the monopolist's disincentive created by his pre-invention monopoly profits.

7. To sketch the proof of these statements quickly, note that, as $c'$ varies, $P$ is a constant. Hence, from the formula for $P' - P$, we see that

$$d(P'-P)/dt = dP'/dt = R(x'_m)(dx'_m/xc') - c'(dx'_m/xc') - x'_m = -x'_m$$

since $R(x'_m) = c'$. Let $F(c')$ be the difference between the incentives to invent under competitive and under monopolistic conditions. In the case where, $P'_m \leq c$ this difference is the constant $P$. Otherwise,

$$F(c') = x_c(c - c') - (P' - P)$$

so that

$$dF/dc' = x'_m - x_c.$$

For the case considered, we must have $x'_m < x_c$ as seen in the text. Hence, $dF/dC' < 0$, so that $F(c')$ increases as $c'$ decreases.

Let $G(c')$ be the ratio of the incentive under competition to that under monopoly. If $P'_m \leq c$, then

$$G(c') = P'/(P' - P)$$

which clearly decreases as $c'$ decreases. For $p' > c$, we have

$$G(c') = x_c(c - c')/(P' - P)$$

Then $dG/dc' = [-(P'-P)x_c + x_c(c-c')x'_m]/(P'-P)^2$.

Because of the upper bound for $P' - P$ established in the text, the numerator must be positive; the ratio decreases as c' decreases.

Finally, if we consider $c'$ very close to $c$, $G(c')$ will be approximately equal to the ratio of the derivatives of the numerator and denominator (L'Hopital's rule), which is, $x_c/x'_m$, and which approaches $x_c/x_m$ as c' approaches $c$.

The incentive to invent in competitive circumstances may also be compared with the social benefit. It is necessary to distinguish between the *realized* social benefit and the *potential* social benefit, the latter being the benefit which would accrue under ideal conditions, which, in this case, means the sale of the product at post-invention cost, $c'$. Clearly, the potential social benefit always exceeds the realized social benefit. I will show that the realized social benefit, in turn, always equals or exceeds the competitive incentive to invent and, *a fortiori*, the monopolist's incentive.

Consider again the two cases discussed above. If the invention is sufficiently cost-reducing so that $p'_m < c$, then there is a consumers' benefit due to the lowering of price which has not been appropriated by the inventor. If not, then the price is unchanged, so that the consumers' position is unchanged, and all benefits do go to the inventor. Since by assumption all the producers are making zero profits both before and after the invention, we see that the inventor obtains the entire realized social benefit of moderately cost-reducing inventions but not of more radical inventions. Tentatively, this suggests a bias against major inventions, in the sense that an invention, part of whose costs could be paid for by lump-sum payments by consumers without making them worse off than before, may not be profitable at the maximum royalty payments that can be extracted by the inventor.

## VI. Alternative Forms of Economic Organization in Invention

The previous discussion leads to the conclusion that for optimal allocation to invention it would be necessary for the government or some other agency not governed by profit-and-loss criteria to finance research and invention. In fact, of course, this has always happened to a certain extent. The bulk of basic research has been carried on outside of the economic system, in universities, in the government, and by private individuals. One must recognize here the importance of non-pecuniary incentives, both on the part of the researchers and on the part of the private individuals and governments, who have supported research organizations and universities. In the latter, the complementarity between teaching and research is, from the point of view of the economy, something of a lucky accident. Research in some more applied fields, such as agriculture, medicine, and aeronautics, has consistently been regarded as an appropriate subject for government participation, and its role has been of great importance.

If the government and other non-profit institutions are to compensate for the under-allocation of resources to invention by private enterprise, two problems arise: how shall the amount of resources devoted to invention be determined, and how shall efficiency in their use be encouraged? These problems arise whenever the government finds it necessary to engage in economic activities because increasing returns prevents the private economy from performing adequately (highways, bridges, reclamation projects, for example), but the determination of the relative magnitudes is even more difficult here. Formally, of course, resources should be devoted to invention until the expected marginal social benefit there equals the marginal social benefit in alternative uses, but in view of the presence of uncertainty, such calculations are even more difficult and tenuous than those for public works. Probably all that could be hoped for is the estimation of future rates of return from those in the past, with investment in invention being increased or decreased accordingly as some average rate of return over the past exceeded or fell short of the general rate of return. The difficulties even of *ex post* calculation of rates of return are formidable though possibly not insuperable.[8]

The problem of efficiency in use of funds devoted to research is one that has been faced internally by firms in dealing with their own research departments. The rapid growth of military research and development has led to a large-scale development of contractual relations between producers and a buyer of invention and research. The problems encountered in assuring efficiency here are the same as those that would be met if the government were to enter upon the financing of invention and research in civilian fields. The form of economic relation is very different from that in the usual markets. Payment is independent of product; it is governed by costs, though the net reward (the fixed fee) is independent of both. This arrangement seems to fly in the face of the principles for encouraging efficiency, and doubtless it does lead to abuses, but closer examination shows both mitigating factors and some explanation of its inevitability. In the first place, the awarding of new contracts will depend in part on past performance, so that incentives for efficiency are not completely lacking. In the second place, the relation between the two parties to the contract is something closer than a purely market relation. It is more like the sale of professional services, where the seller contracts to supply not so much a specific result as his best judgment. (The demand for such services also arises from uncertainty and the value of information.) In the third place, payment by results would involve great risks for the inventor, risks against which, as we have seen, he could hedge only in part.

There is clear need for further study of alternative methods of compensation. For example, some part of the contractual payment might depend on the degree of success in invention. But a more serious problem is the decision as to which contracts to let. One would need to examine the motivation underlying government decision-making in this area. Hitch has argued that there are biases in governmental allocation, particularly against risky invention processes, and an excessive centralization, though the latter could be remedied by better policies.[9]

One can go further. There is really no need for the firm to be the fundamental unit of organization in invention; there is plenty of reason to suppose that individual talents count for a good deal more than the firm as an organization. If provision is ade for the rental of necessary equipment, a much wider variety of research contracts with individuals as well as firms and with varying modes of payment, including incentives, could be arranged. Still other forms of organization, such as research institutes financed by industries, the government, and private philanthropy, could be made to play an even livelier role than they now do.

8. For an encouraging study of this type, see Z. Griliches, "Research Costs and Social Returns: Hybrid Corn and Related Innovations," *Journal of Political Economy*, Vol. LXVI (1958): 419–431.

9. *Op. cit.*

# 10

# Structuralism

## Introduction

### BY DANIEL CRANE

Few schools of antitrust thought have enjoyed such temporal success as the structuralist school, which came to become known as the Harvard School because of its association with Harvard professors Carl Kaysen, Donald Turner, and Phil Areeda; and Joe Bain, a Harvard-trained economist who spent the bulk of his career at the University of California at Berkeley.[1] The Harvard School heavily influenced U.S. antitrust policy from the 1950s to the early 1970s.

Structuralism's core (and elegant) tenet was that a strong, deterministic relationship exists between a market's structure, conduct, and performance (thus giving rise to the structure-conduct-performance, or just S-C-P, paradigm). Concentration was the most significant component of structure. Thus, a highly concentrated market inexorably led to anticompetitive firm behavior, and such behavior inexorably led to poor market performance, expressed as higher prices and lower quality. The upshot was that the government could directly attack concentrated market structures without worrying about the specific mechanisms (conduct) that led from that structure to poor market performance.

At a theoretical level, structuralism rested on four broad theoretical and empirical propositions. First, the structuralists assumed a strong link between the number of firms in a market and the propensity of prices to rise above cost. This claim rested principally on strong assumptions, formalized by the nineteenth century French mathematician Augustin Cournot, that oligopoly behavior would increase as the number of firms decreased. As we shall see in the readings ahead, the structuralists claimed that the Cournot assumptions were borne out by empirical studies showing that firms in concentrated industries earned higher profits than those in more competitively structured industries.

Second, echoing a theme from Brandeis, the structuralists rejected the notion that large aggregations of capital were necessary to achieving economies of scale. Although economies

1. See generally Leonard W. Weiss, "The Structure-Conduct-Performance Paradigm and Antitrust," 127 *U. Pa. L. Rev.* 1104 (1979); Herbert Hovenkamp, "United States Competition Policy in Crisis: 1890–1955," 94 *Minn. L. Rev.* 311, 350–354 (2009).

of scale did exist, in many markets the firms were far larger than minimum efficient scale demanded; such markets could be "deconcentrated" by breaking up large firms without causing significant production inefficiencies.

Third, the structuralists claimed that barriers to entry were high in many industries, but particularly in those with a large fixed-cost component. The Harvard School's broad definition of entry barriers would raise a strong challenge from the Chicago School, which gave a much narrower definition to entry barriers—with the implication that far fewer markets would be considered difficult to enter.

Fourth, Kaysen-Turner argued that, given the close link between Cournot theory and maximizing behavior, poor performance in highly concentrated markets was inevitable. As a result, antitrust should focus on structure and pay relatively less attention to conduct.

Given the difficulties of ferreting out "bad behavior" on the part of oligopolists or monopolists, it is not difficult to understand the S-C-P paradigm's appeal to government officials and courts. Instead of worrying about whether "conscious parallelism" amounts to collusion[2] or whether a particular price level was predatory, the antitrust agencies could simply direct their efforts at ensuring deconcentrated markets—whether by breaking up oligopolies or monopolies or preventing their occurrence through merger. Hence, during the 1960s especially, some academics began to question the need for ferreting out "fault" in antitrust cases. Identifying poor structures might suffice.

In late 1967, President Lyndon Johnson secretly asked Phil Neal, dean of the University of Chicago Law School, to lead a commission of distinguished economists and lawyers to report on the state of competition in the United States and recommend potential changes to the antitrust laws.[3] Johnson intended to use the report as part of his reelection campaign, but he eventually decided not to seek reelection because of the unpopularity of the Vietnam War.[4] Nonetheless, the commission concluded its work and released its report, which we examine here in part.

The report represents the high water mark of structuralist thinking. It proposed a Concentrated Industries Act that would give the attorney general a mandate to "search out" oligopolies and order divestiture to the point that no firm would end up with a market share exceeding 12 percent. It also proposed a much stronger structuralist presumption in horizontal merger cases, condemning any merger in which the four-firm concentration ratio

2. The "conscious parallelism" question gave rise to a historically ironic exchange between Turner and Richard Posner. Although the Harvard School is generally assumed to be far more interventionist than the Chicago School, when it came to the meaning of Section 1 of the Sherman Act's agreement ("contract, combination, or conspiracy") requirement, Turner advocated a more restrictive view than Posner. Donald F. Turner, "The Definition of Agreement Under the Sherman Act: Conscious Parallelism and Refusals to Deal," 75 *Harv. L. Rev.* 655 (1962); Richard A. Posner, "Oligopoly and the Antitrust Laws: A Suggested Approach," 21 *Stan. L. Rev.* 1562 (1969). Because Turner believed that firms in oligopolies were virtually predestined to price above competitive levels, he found it troubling to condemn them criminally for price fixing when all they had done was follow their unavoidable instincts to engage in Cournot behavior. Posner rejected the deterministic link between structure, conduct, and performance and was therefore more willing to find "agreement" in conscious parallelism situations, on the grounds that the firms had the free will to behave otherwise.

3. Herbert Hovenkamp, "Introduction to the Neal Report and the Crisis in Antitrust and a Reprint of the Neal Report," 5 *Comp. Pol'y Intl'l* 217 (2009).

4. Id.

exceeded 50 percent and one of the firms involved in the merger had a market share exceeding 10 percent.

None of the report's recommendations was adopted into law. Not only did Richard Nixon's election kill off its immediate political prospects, but as discussed in the following chapter, by the early 1970s the Chicago School was rapidly eroding structuralism's theoretical and empirical assumptions. In the 1970s, Turner underwent a self-described "conversion experience" in which he accepted many of the Chicago School critiques of the S-C-P paradigm.[5] Vestiges of structuralist thinking appeared as late as 1979, when Jimmy Carter's National Commission to Review Antitrust Law and Procedures recommended adoption of a no-fault monopolization statute and in various iterations of the Justice Department and Federal Trade Commission's Horizontal Merger Guidelines, but the fire had long since gone out of the S-C-P paradigm.

The decline of the structuralist school did not spell the end of Harvard's influence on antitrust policy. One enduring legacy of the Harvard School is the *Antitrust Law* treatise launched by Areeda and Turner and currently in the custody of Herbert Hovenkamp. Early editions of the treatise were perceived as reflecting structuralist influences,[6] but later editions began to move in a less structuralist direction.[7] Over time, a new "Harvard School" has emerged, one less associated with structural presumptions and more associated with the administrability of antitrust principles. In addition to Areeda and Turner, the new Harvard school is heavily associated with Stephen Breyer, who as a federal appellate judge and now Supreme Court justice has articulated a restrained approach to antitrust enforcement that takes into account the limitations of judges and juries in deciding complex economic questions. An emerging literature traces the new Harvard School's conjunctions and divergences with the Chicago School.[8] It is an important story, but one that has little to do with the old style structuralism.

## Joe Bain
## *Industrial Organization*
## Chapter 10
## The Relation of Market Structure to Market Performance

Having reviewed salient aspects of the market structure, conduct, and performance of American industries, we turn to our most crucial analytical question: To what extent are the market structure and conduct of industries related to their market performance? This inquiry is stimulated by popular beliefs and theoretical hypotheses that market

5. Herbert Hovenkamp, *The Antitrust Enterprise: Principle and Execution* 37 (2005).

6. See, e.g., Thomas C. Arthur, "Farewell to the Sea of Doubt: Jettisoning the Constitutional Sherman Act," 74 *Cal. L. Rev*. 263, 320 n. 312 (1986) (describing the Areeda-Turner treatise as reflecting Harvard School structuralism).

7. Hovenkamp, *The Antitrust Enterprise*, at 37.

8. See, e.g., Einer Elhauge, "Harvard, Not Chicago: Which Antitrust School Drives Recent U.S. Supreme Court Decisions?" 3 *Comp. Pol'y Int'l* 59 (2007); William E. Kovacic, "The Intellectual DNA of U.S. Competition Law for Dominant Firm Conduct: The Chicago/Harvard Double Helix," 1 *Colum. Bus. L. Rev*. (2007); Daniel A. Crane, "*LinkLine*'s Institutional Suspicions," 111 *Cato. Sup. Ct. Rev*. (2009).

structure and conduct are in a significant degree determinants of market performance. With each of several different sorts of market structure and/or conduct, that is, we might expect a specific different sort of market performance, or, variations in structure or conduct should be associated with corresponding variations in market performance.

A first reason for empirical testing—to find to what extent and in what sense the preceding is true—is the simple desire to contribute to scientific knowledge by establishing, from evidence, what structure-conduct-performance associations probably exist. This endeavor may take the form of testing a priori predictions about such associations, or of more or less pragmatic experimentation with data, aimed at discovering associations inductively.

Second there is the desire to acquire factual information which should be useful in formulating public regulatory policies toward industry. Although the market performance of industries is the ultimate test of how well they fulfill their social function of enhancing material welfare, and though the aim of public regulatory policy should be to improve performance in those instances in which it is "unworkable," actual public policy in a capitalist economy cannot feasibly proceed by directly regulating or dictating the character of market performance in most or all "miscreant" industries. Such direct regulation, especially if it is widely applied, tends to impair essential enterprise incentives or profit motivations, to induce and to protect inefficiency, to engender "evasive" behavior on the part of enterprises, to stimulate endeavors by the regulated firms to capture or control the public agencies set up to regulate them, and to induce other undesirable economic consequences. Performance is crucial, but it does not follow that extensive direct public regulation of performance is consistent with the maintenance of a viable capitalist economy.

On the other hand, a feasible way of exercising regulatory influence on market performance is to impose restrictive regulations or requirements on market structures and possibly on market conduct, to the end of creating or preserving market situations and patterns of conduct which are conducive to good enterprise performance. The distinction here is one, for example, between on the one hand insisting on a relatively unconcentrated market structure and prohibiting express collusion, but otherwise leaving sellers free to compete according to their own discretion, and on the other hand requiring each enterprise to produce a certain output and sell at a certain "fair" price sufficient to yield a minimal profit. The former procedure is feasible in the sense of being consistent with maintaining adequate enterprise incentives and drives for efficiency; the latter is not.

This being the case, an essential body of knowledge for the governmental policy-maker concerns the character of the association of market structure and conduct to market performance. For it is only on the basis of such knowledge that the policy-maker can know what patterns of market structure and conduct are associated respectively with poor and good performance, and can therefore know what sorts of revisions of existing structure and conduct he should seek in order to eliminate indirectly poor performance as it is found. We therefore must push for as complete as possible a knowledge of what are the necessary structure-conduct conditions for good market performance on the part of our numerous industries, as a guide to policymaking action. It is desirable, moreover, to establish these things as far as possible on the basis of empirical evidence, especially in the light of the frequently inconclusive or uncertain indications of relevant *a priori* hypotheses.

We thus turn to empirical evidences of associations between market structure and conduct on the one hand, and market performance on the other, noting that such findings as are available refer mainly to the relation of market structure to market performance. As indicated in Chapter 8, our ability to measure and classify actual patterns of market conduct is ordinarily insufficient to provide a sound basis for empirical determination of the relation of conduct to performance.

## A. The Relationship of Market Structure to Efficiency

A first question concerns the relationship of the market structure of the industry in such dimensions as the degree of seller concentration, the condition of entry, and the degree of product differentiation, to the efficiency performance of the industry as affected by the scales of plants and firms and the relation of capacity to demand. Efficiency in the sense designated is an important aspect of industry performance, and a study of manufacturing industries has suggested that there is a significant minor incidence of inefficiency due to insufficient scale of plant or firm in most industries, and a lesser and more scattered incidence of inefficiency due to chronic excess capacity. Further, the extent of inefficiency attributable to unduly small plants and firms varies considerably among the industries sampled.

Are some market structures more conducive to efficiency in scale of plant and firm than others? On this point we are not without ad hoc hypotheses, two of the more popular of which might read as follows. First, higher seller concentration may reflect the growth of firms to relatively larger sizes and thus tend to reduce the incidence of inefficiently small plants and firms, so that industries of relatively high concentration should tend to be more efficient than industries of relatively low concentration. Second, industries to which entry is exceptionally easy are more likely to attract and maintain a substantial group of inefficiently small plants and firms, and be less efficient than industries protected by substantial barriers to new entry. These hypotheses indicate that low seller concentration and easy entry are conducive to relatively poor efficiency in the matter of plant and firm scales. On the other hand, they are contradicted by a third ad hoc hypothesis to the effect that low seller concentration and easy entry both are conducive to more intense price competition, that such competition should tend to force efficiency in scale on surviving competitors (to a degree that it does not with high concentration and difficult entry), and that therefore industries of higher concentration and more difficult entry should tend to be less efficient in the matter of plant and firm scales. In brief, theoretical indications on this point arc indefinite and inconclusive, and empirical evidence is badly needed.

The only available empirical test for a structure-performance relationship with reference to efficiency in scale refers to our sample of twenty manufacturing industries, and since the sample is small and only manufacturing is covered, the results of the test must be viewed as extremely tentative. For what they are worth, the indications of this test are generally either negative or inconclusive, to the following effect: (1) There is no evident association of the degree of seller concentration to the relative size of the fringe of inefficiently small plants and firms. Whatever the degree of concentration among the larger firms supplying the bulk of industry output, a fringe of inefficiently small plants and firms seems to persist, and in a degree not systematically related to high-level seller concentration. Further, the incidence of this sort of inefficiency does not seem to be systematically related to the importance of scale economics as measured by the percentage of the market supplied by one plant or firm of minimum optimal scale. (2) There is no evidence associating the height of the barrier to entry to an industry to the incidence of inefficiency due to uneconomically small scales. The occurrence and the size of an inefficient fringe of small plants and firms seems as likely to occur with difficult entry conditions to the industry as with easy ones. It would thus be impossible to affirm, on the basis of such evidence as is available, that seeking either higher or lower seller concentration or more difficult or easier entry for our industries would have a significant effect on the aspect of efficiency performance in question.

The only tentatively positive indication regarding the association of market structure to efficiency in plant and firm scale is that industries with the largest fringes of inefficiently small firms are usually industries with high degrees of product differentiation among established sellers. This tentative finding is consistent with another ad hoc hypothesis—that a pattern of strongly developed consumer preferences for various company names, brands, or product designs is more likely to afford a number of inefficiently small firms limited markets at favorable prices, than is a pattern in which consumer preferences as among competing products are weak. Even in industries with relatively slight product differentiation, however, some fringe of inefficiently small plants and firms usually finds a means of surviving.

Some minor part of the continued survival of inefficiently small sellers is apparently attributable to the fact that they supply odd "corners" of the market, by providing special products or supplying regions geographically remote from the main producing centers, in which case their "inefficiency" may be more apparent than real. But a major part of this survival is attributable to two things: the ability of inefficiently small firms in some industries to make normal profits in competition with larger rivals who set their prices so as to earn considerable excess profits; and the almost endless supply (in some other industries) of small enterprises willing to succeed each other in the unenviable position of incurring net losses and ultimately going broke, only to have their ranks filled by new candidates for financial destruction. Thus, monopolistic pricing policies by large firms and excessive or unwise entry by small firms are both crucial factors.

One qualification may be offered to our generalization that the relative size of the fringe of inefficiently small plants and firms does not appear to be much related to the degree of seller concentration in the industry. The generalization should be taken to mean that the size of the inefficient fringe seems unrelated to the "high-level" seller concentration within the industry, as measured by the proportion of industry output supplied by the largest few firms (three or four or eight) in the industry. As this measure of concentration varies among industries, the proportion of output supplied by inefficiently small plants and firms does not seem to vary systematically in response. On the other hand, it will generally be true that, if there is some fringe of inefficiently small firms, "overall" seller concentration will be too low for efficiency, in the sense that consolidation of the operations of the several or many smallest firms into fewer firms would permit their output to be produced under more efficient scale conditions. In this restricted sense, seller concentration is generally too low, and in greater degree as the relative size of the inefficient fringe is larger.

A remaining question concerns the incidence of chronic excess capacity in relation to demand, and whether this is related to market structure. The principal available hypothesis here is that such excess capacity is most likely to occur in industries with perceptible but relatively low barriers to entry, provided that established sellers develop enough concentration to make oligopolistic price-raising feasible. In this setting, they might find it unattractive to set prices low enough to forestall new entry, and attractive instead to raise prices enough ultimately to induce excessive entry and excess capacity.

As indicated in the preceding chapter, systematic evidence on the incidence of chronic excess capacity is very scanty. It may be worth noting, however, that in all three of the twenty manufacturing industries sampled in which there was reasonably clear evidence of chronic excess capacity (flour, shoes, and cement) the structural conditions were roughly those described in the hypothesis above. In brief summary, such tests as have been made fail to reveal any statistically significant relation of efficiency in scale or capacity to the market structure of the industry, except that fewer and larger "small" firms would usually lead to improved efficiency. The impact of market structure on performance is probably found in the main with respect to dimensions of performance other than efficiency.

## B. The Relationship of Market Structure to Price-Cost Margins of Profits

It has been possible to make somewhat more extensive tests for the relation of price-cost margins or profit rates to market structures. The excess of price over average cost in an industry, roughly and indirectly measured by the ratio of accounting profits to owners' equity, represents a strategic dimension of the market performance of an industry. Chronic excess profits are symptomatic of monopolistic output restriction and price raising, and thus of a lack of sufficient or "workable" competition; chronic net losses are generally indicative of the failure of even intense competition to force a desirable limitation of supply in relationship to demand.

Determination of the relation of market structure to the incidence and magnitude of excess profits is important for three reasons. First, we should like to know what structural situations are conducive, or more conducive than others, to unworkable performance in the form of potentially monopolistic excess profits. In particular, we should like to test the theoretical prediction that high seller concentration and high barriers to entry tend to lead to monopolistic excess profits. Second, if such a qualitative prediction is valid (that "high" concentration is conducive to substantial excess profits but that "lower" concentration is not) we need to give the qualitative prediction a quantitative or numerical implementation. This we may do, for example, by discovering how high seller concentration can become before severe excess profits tend to be encountered, or how low it needs to be in order to effect a "workably competitive" market structure. Third, determination of whether or not observed high excess profits occur typically in structural situations which would theoretically be expected to produce monopolistic excess profits should provide a crucial clue to the extent to which these observed excess profits are indeed monopolistic in origin (and thus undesirable), as opposed to having their origin in windfalls, retards to innovation, and the like. A comparable set of reasons exists for ascertaining the relationship of market structure to the incidence of chronic net losses.

The tests which have been made for the association of market structure to profit rates or margins, far from complete or comprehensive, refer to the relationship of seller concentration to the rate of profit (after taxes) on equity for firms in 42 manufacturing industries in the 5-year period 1936–1940, and to the relationship of both seller concentration and the condition of entry to the comparable profit rate for firms in 20 of these industries in the two 5-year periods 1936–1940 and 1947–1951. As a preamble to a review of findings from these tests, the following should be pointed out. First, for the sample of industries chosen, there is no significant incidence of net losses (returns lower than a basic interest return on equity) on the average for any group as classified according either to seller concentration or to condition of entry. Thus, practically nothing is revealed about the structural conditions which may be conducive to chronic net losses; the main findings refer to the structural conditions for excess as opposed to relatively normal profits. Second, in all categories of industries sampled—whether distinguished on the basis of seller concentration or on that of the condition of entry—there is apparent at least some small average margin of excess profits. We are thus in effect expressly engaged in distinguishing the structural conditions which are conducive respectively to higher and lower excess profits, rather than distinguishing the condition for some excess profits as opposed to no excess profits at all. (This circumstance may result from the fact that the great bulk of the industries sampled evidence a sufficient degree of seller concentration to be classified as, in one sense or another, oligopolistic. For example, 38 of the 42 industries in the 1936–1940 sample had 30 percent or more of industry output supplied by the largest 8 firms in the industry.) On this background, let us briefly review the findings.

A first indication is that there is a definite relationship of the degree of seller concentration in manufacturing industries to the size of the profit rate, such that high seller concentration tends to be connected with substantially higher rates of excess profit than does moderate or low seller concentration. This relationship does not appear to be of a smooth "linear" form, however; there is no steady and regular upward progress of the profit rate with successive small increases in concentration. Rather, there appears to be some critical degree of seller concentration above which industry profit rates on the average are higher, and below which on the average they are lower. Industries thus fall generally into two groups (a dichotomy), though within either of these two concentration groups there is not in evidence any significant variation of profit rates in response to variation in concentration. In the sample of 42 industries examined for the period 1936–1940, the dividing line between the two groups seemed to fall at about 70 percent control of the market by the largest 8 firms in the industry. In 21 industries in which the largest 8 sellers supplied more than 70 percent of industry output, average annual profit rates were substantially higher (11.8 percent of equity was the average of industry average 5-year profit rates), than in 21 industries in which the largest 8 sellers supplied less than 70 percent of industry output (where the average of industry average profit rates was 7.5 percent),

In the "high-concentration" group the percentage controlled by the largest 8 firms ranged from 71 up to 100 percent; in the "lower-concentration" group it ranged from 68 down to 8 percent, but within either group the profit rate was not significantly related to concentration. Industries with 80 percent control by 8 firms did not have significantly different profit rates than those with 9.5 percent control by 8 firms, and industries with 60 percent control by 8 firms did about as well as those with 30 percent control. The main effect of concentration on profit rate was observed as we distinguished such rates for all industries with more and with less respectively than roughly 70 percent control by the largest 8 firms. There was, of course, a substantial variation among individual-industry profit rates in each of the two concentration groups, but standard statistical tests indicated that the observed intergroup difference in profit rates was "significant," or attributable to the different characteristics (concentration) of the two groups, and had almost no chance of being due to a sampling or other statistical accident.

A less extensive check for 20 of these industries for the relation of seller concentration to profit rate for 1947–1951 (based on the profits of the largest 2, 3, or 4 firms in each industry) indicated that the same general relationship continued to hold after the Second World War as held before it: above some critical concentration level in the neighborhood of 70 percent control by 8 firms, industry profit rates were on the average significantly higher than they were below this level of seller concentration.

These findings may be tentatively interpreted as follows. First, the appearance of a significant association between the rate of profits and the degree of seller concentration in the industry—such that substantial excess profits on the average occur mainly in a relatively high concentration range—strongly suggests, on the basis of underlying theory, that observed high excess profits are, on the average, in large part identifiable as monopolistic excess profits, rather than windfalls, rewards to innovation, and the like. This identification of their origin is at any rate the most obvious explanation of their association with high seller concentration.

Second, on the average, the tendency toward substantial monopolistic excess profits seems to be found mainly in industries of relatively high seller concentration. These were tentatively identified in the tests in question as industries in which 70 percent or more of output is supplied by the largest 8 firms. Because of a certain downward bias in the concentration ratios used (from census calculations), we might suspect that the "true" dividing line, in terms of concentration ratios calculated for theoretical industries, would lie slightly higher, in the neighborhood perhaps of 75 or even 80 percent control of the market by the largest 8 firms in the industry. Wherever the line lies, there is a tentative indication that there may be in the economy two sorts of oligopolies: those sufficiently concentrated that monopolistic pricing policies usually are successful and produce substantial excess profits; and those sufficiently unconcentrated that a moderately close approximation to competitive pricing and profits is likely to ensue. In terms of the concentration classification set forth in Chapter 4, industries of "very high" and "high" seller concentration appear to have undesirable monopolistic tendencies; those of "low-moderate" and lesser concentration seem to be relatively free of these tendencies; those of "high-moderate" concentration are somewhere on the borderline. The preceding may provide some tentative guides in the search for the structural conditions for workable competition.

A second general indication from our tests is that the condition of entry, as well as the degree of seller concentration, is significantly related to the profit rate of the industry. In brief, it was found for the sample of 20 manufacturing industries in the periods 1936–1940 and 1947–1951, that industries with "very high" entry barriers (such that established firms might elevate price above minimal average cost by 10 percent or more without attracting new entry) had distinctly higher average profit rates than industries protected by lower barriers to entry. (No significant distinction could be found between the profit rates of industries with "medium" and "low" barriers to entry; the lack of a smooth linear relation of structure to performance again was suggested.) This finding tends further to confirm the suspicion that observed substantial excess profits tend to be of monopolistic origin, and identifies extreme barriers to entry as a structural characteristic which is generally conducive to poor performance in the dimension of price-cost relationships.

A third indication is that the condition of entry (height of entry barrier) exercises an influence on profit rates which is distinguishable and separate from the influence of seller concentration. It is conceivable, of course, that high concentration and high entry barriers could be "intercorrelated" to such an extent that any industry that had one also had the other, so that we could only say that high concentration and difficult entry *in combination* were conducive to high profit rate. This, fortunately, is not the case, since among industries with "high" seller concentration (above 70 percent control by 8 firms), we can identify industries protected by very different heights of entry barrier. For example, 12 of the 20 industries sampled for both 1936–1940 and 1947–1951 had high "seller" concentration (above the 70 percent line), but only 5 of them had "very high" entry barriers, the remaining 7 having "medium" or "low" barriers. Investigation of this restricted sample of 12 highly concentrated industries, moreover, revealed that in both 1936–1940 and 1947–1951, the 5 industries with very high entry barriers had substantially higher profits than the 7 industries, of comparably high seller concentration, which had lower barriers to entry. The tentative indication is, therefore, that very high entry barriers provide an independent, contributing structural cause for monopolistic excess profits, and that the conjunction of high seller concentration and extreme entry barriers provides a less desirable structural situation than high concentration alone. Extremes both of seller concentration and of difficulty of entry may be tentatively viewed as at least quasi-independent characteristics of market structure which are conducive to unworkable performance in the matter of profits.

A fourth observation is that the industries in our sample of 20 with the highest average excess profit rates over the two 5-year periods—industries with both high seller concentration and very high barriers to entry—are also all industries with very high degrees of product differentiation (those producing automobiles, liquor, cigarettes, typewriters, and quality fountain pens). It is uncertain *a priori* how much of the effect of extreme product differentiation is registered in impeding entry, and how much in moderating competition among firms within the industry. But this indication does tend to cast a shadow of doubt on frequently repeated assertions that strong product differentiation is conducive to a more workable competition. The reverse may well be true.

One interesting hypothesis which we have so far been unable to test systematically is that the conjunction of high buyer concentration with high seller concentration, effecting a situation of "bilateral oligopoly," or "countervailing power" of sellers and buyers, will tend to result in less monopolistic restriction and a better profit performance than high seller concentration alone. A few individual instances might be adduced in support of this proposition, but we are unable to confirm or disconfirm it with organized and impartially selected evidence. We will thus dismiss the matter here with the observation that the hypothesis is reasonable though not axiomatic, and substantially untested.

The search for empirical generalizations concerning the association of market structure to price-cost margins or profit rates has produced some suggestions concerning the structural conditions for workable competition, so far as the latter is revealed by profit performance. Monopolistic pricing and profits are favored both by high seller concentration and by high entry barriers, and are especially likely to be acute if these two structural conditions exist together in the same industry. The adverse consequences of high seller concentration, in terms of monopolistic price and profit tendencies, are likely to be mitigated significantly if the barriers to new entry (the force of potential competition) are only moderate or low. And, oligopoly with seller concentration only in the moderate range or lower, and with no more than moderate entry barriers, may well usually provide a reasonably competitive performance in the matter of pricing, or at any rate a good deal better performance than is provided by highly concentrated industries with high entry barriers. The implied suggestions for a public policy are obvious.

## C. The Relationship of Market Structure to Performance in Other Dimensions

Although systematized evidence on the relation of market structure to other dimensions of performance is generally deficient or unavailable, we may submit certain impressions, based on casual observation, concerning the association of structure to performance in the matters of selling cost, product, progressiveness, and conservation.

A first and unsurprising regularity observed is that selling costs tend to be greater in industries with higher degrees of product differentiation among established sellers and higher product-differentiation barriers to entry. This type of relationship seems to hold fairly well, for example, in the sample of 20 manufacturing industries previously referred to. Industries with slight product differentiation (such as copper, cement, steel, meat packing, and standard canned goods) have small or negligible selling costs; industries with "medium" product differentiation (such as rubber tires, tin cans, and higher-priced men's shoes) have middle-sized selling costs; those with extreme product differentiation (including cigarettes, liquor, and automobiles) have high costs of sales promotion.

This finding, however, is not only unsurprising but also not very meaningful. It is at least equally appropriate to say that industries *develop* more extreme product differentiation and higher product differentiation barriers to entry because selling costs are high, as to say that extreme product differentiation and high product-differentiation barriers lead to high selling costs. Since the relative seniority of the chicken and the egg is not readily established, we end up at this level with little more than the observations that (*a*) high selling costs are where we find them, and (*b*) that they are usually accompanied, at least as much by way of result as by way of cause, by a high degree of product differentiation.

To get further with this issue, it is necessary to go behind the superficial characteristic of market structure (degree of product differentiation) to the basic structural characteristics of an industry which determine how attractive it is for firms to incur large selling costs and thus strongly differentiate their products—to refer, that is, to the basic conditions for profitable "differentiability" of products.

Some rough indications concerning these basic conditions follow. First, the opportunities for profit from extreme product differentiation and large selling costs are particularly good in the case of products which are "prestige," "conspicuous consumption," or "gift" goods. In each of these instances price tends to be a relatively less important consideration than product reputation, "glamor," or asserted quality, all of which can be successfully built by concerted promotional efforts. (Quality fountain pens, liquor, and automobiles all fit this description.) Second, extreme product differentiation and high selling costs tend to go well with products which, because of their complexity or other characteristics, consumers are unable really to evaluate or appraise, even after repeated use, thus becoming dependent on product reputations to protect themselves against unwise purchases. (Pharmaceutical products and, again, automobiles, would qualify for inclusion in this class.) Third, the same opportunities for intensive differentiation via selling costs are present for very durable consumers goods which are purchased infrequently and with large unit outlays, so that the consumer has at best very limited opportunities to experiment by purchasing and comparing different brands of the same product. (Most consumers' durable goods fall in this class.) Conversely, the best basic settings for slight product differentiation and low selling costs are found for goods which are purchased for their basic or functional utility, which the consumer can easily evaluate and appraise, and which, being nondurable, are purchased frequently and in small amounts, allowing the consumer a maximum opportunity for experimentation with the comparison of alternatives. Most food and many clothing products clearly fit into this category.

These structural conditions for various sorts of selling-cost performance are indeed so basic that, for purposes of public policymaking, they must also be viewed as relatively immutable and not in any important degree "remediable," although programs for consumer education and grade-labelling, as well as direct regulations of the volume and content of promotional activity, might remedy the more adverse situations somewhat. It may be noted in conclusion that not every industry with high selling costs has the basic characteristics outlined above; we are at a loss to explain, for example, in terms of the preceding argument, the very high level of selling costs which persists in the soap industry. More empirical and theoretical investigation is thus indicated.

The structural conditions for various sorts of product performance are at present far from clear. Some *a priori* theorizing has been done on this issue, but its results are inconclusive. The same applies to empirical findings, where the added difficulty of substantial inability really to measure or appraise product performance is also encountered. About the most that can be said is that a relatively broad range of product-performance alternatives is found mainly in the realm of large, complex, durable goods, and that it is in this area that there is a maximum opportunity for significant aberrations from a good or "workable" product performance.

The situation is similar when we turn to the putative relationship of market structure to technological progressiveness. Theoretical indications on the issue are extremely inconclusive and ambivalent, and empirical exploration for structure-performance associations is fatally hampered by difficulties both of definition (of adequate progressiveness) and of measurement (of what progressiveness has been relative to alternatives). We must be aware, of course, of popular ad hoc hypotheses that relate high seller concentration and connected high profits to rapid progressiveness, and low concentration cum low profits to inadequate progressiveness. Neither theory nor observation really supports such hypotheses, except to the extent that industries with chronic subnormal profits or net losses—possibly in some degree connected with atomistic market structures and very easy entry—frequently appear to evidence some technological backwardness. This is perhaps attributable to a chronic lack of funds for research. development, and innovation. Putting aside these extreme cases, no regularity of association of technological progressiveness to market structure is either in evidence or predictable, given the existing state of empirical research and theorizing.

The structural conditions for good and poor conservation performance have not been adequately explored on either the theoretical or the empirical level, but some general observations are in order. Poor resource conservation by enterprise, as we have noted, generally results from choice of poor techniques of exploitation, from undue "shortsightedness" of private enterprises in balancing present against future resource yields and earnings, and from the unwillingness or inability of enterprises to make appropriately large current investments or other cost outlays in the interest of enlarging or sustaining future production. The only obvious link of market size to such aberrations from satisfactory conservation performance involves the potentially adverse effects of atomism, or very low concentration among producer-sellers engaged in exploiting a natural resource. This is not to say that atomistic resource exploitation is always bad in its conservation effects, but it may be bad in two ways.

First, competitive exploitation of *a single common resource deposit or unit* by several or (worse yet) many individual producers in a setting wherein each competing firm can capture more or less of the yield of the common resource deposit depending on how quickly it extracts or captures output from the deposit is generally conducive to (*a*) adoption of inferior techniques of exploitation, and (*b*) extreme shortsightedness on the part of individual producers, such that the effect of present outputs and techniques upon future yields is substantially neglected. A convenient but inadequate simile that comes to mind involves the situation in which each of twenty competitive children is given as many straws as desired with which to suck from a single 5-gallon container of ice-cream soda, each being able to drink as much soda as he can get before the container is emptied. The possibilities of unduly rapid use of the resource, consequent indigestion, wasteful use of straws, and later regrets are obvious.

In a more realistic vein, we may consider the results of giving several or many antagonistic interests a common right to exploit a single natural resource deposit, such as a single underground oil (petroleum) pool or a single forest, under conditions in which each may enlarge his own share of the output of common oil pool or forest by drilling more oil wells or using more lumbermen, axes, or other equipment. The results in such situations are usually (a) elevation of costs without corresponding increase in yields, as each producer vies to capture the common resource before his competitors do; (b) consequent adoption of production techniques which are generally injurious to future yields, or yield-cost ratios, since no one producer can attach much importance to the future; and (c) a general disposition to discount heavily or overlook future yields in comparison to present yields, in the general race to capture present yields before someone else does. (These tendencies are well substantiated in the histories of the American petroleum and lumber industries.) This is not to say that competition or atomism in the exploitation of resources necessarily has injurious effects on conservation performance. Such injurious effects emerge when there is competitive and antagonistic exploitation of a common resource deposit or unit by antagonistic interests. For exploitation of a single resource unit, single-firm or monopolistic exploitation promises the best conservation results. But if there are enough such units of the same sort, an effective competition among monopolistic producers exploiting different units would still be possible.

Second, atomistic market structure may be "bad for conservation" if it leads to, or is partly responsible for, a chronically excessive or destructive competition which leaves producers so short of funds (or credit facilities) that they are financially unable to pursue good conservation practices involving current cost outlays to enhance future yields. (This difficulty has evidently been encountered at times in various agricultural industries, with reference to soil conservation.) This is simply to say that destructive competition, marked by chronic net losses to enterprise, has adverse effects on conservation performance.

Such destructive competition is usually associated with atomistic market structures, but a majority of such atomistic structures evidently are not plagued with truly destructive competition. We will refer to this matter further in the following chapter.

## D. The Relationship of Market Conduct to Structure and Performance

Since many comments were made in Chapter 8 concerning both the predicted and the verifiable associations of market conduct to either structure or performance, a very brief review of this issue will suffice here.

With respect to market conduct of enterprise in the matter of price output determination (or "price policy") we have noted that there is available a substantial body of *a priori* hypotheses concerning the sorts of market conduct which are likely to emerge from various sorts of market structure, and the sorts of market performance which will result from different sorts of conduct. On a theoretical level, therefore, market conduct represents a necessary and logical link between structure and performance, being systematically associated to the structure as its "cause" and to performance as its "effect." We have also noted, however, first that certain analytically essential characteristics of the pattern of market conduct in determining prices, referred to by the received theory, involve the effective principles of price calculation which are applied; and second that the superficial character of the devices of interseller coordination employed are not of crucial importance and should not even hypothetically be expected to have a definite and systematic association to structure or to performance. Finally, we have noted that what can actually be determined by empirical observation of market conduct patterns in the matter of price determination refers almost entirely to devices of interseller coordination, and that the essential information on principles of price calculation employed is not independently ascertainable in any significant degree. Therefore, we are in effect unable to establish empirically any meaningful associations of market conduct in this aspect to structure or to performance, or to attribute much analytical importance to what we can ascertain about patterns of market conduct in price determination. For purposes of empirical study, we thus retreat to attempts to establish links between market structure and performance, leaving the question of just how conduct forms the bridge between structure and performance to the realm of abstract theorizing.

Market conduct in the determination of selling costs and products is studied only with equal difficulty, again in large part because of the relative impossibility of ascertaining independently what principles are guiding the various observed promotional and product policies of sellers. In fact, it is fair to say that most of what can be learned about promotional and product policies is simply what can be inferred from observations of performance in the matter of selling costs and product behavior. Market conduct in these aspects is thus not independently ascertained or evaluated, and the relation of conduct to structure or performance cannot in fact be empirically tested. We retreat again to the search for direct structure-performance relations.

The one main aspect of market conduct with respect to which it is possible to establish some empirical association to structure and performance involves predatory and exclusionary tactics. There are more easily observed and evaluated than other aspects of conduct, and their effects on structure and performance more visible in actual cases. From a relatively unorganized scattering of observations, it is possible to conclude first that actual predation and exclusion frequently have been effective in developing and maintaining more highly concentrated market structures, and markets to which new entry is more difficult, than would develop in the absence of such tactics. Predacious attack on small competitions or prospective entrants, as by price wars, discriminatory price cutting, or aggressive pre-emption of necessary resource deposits or other materials, obviously has these effects when it occurs, although such attack is most seriously discouraged by existing interpretations of the federal antitrust laws. More important in fact are subtler exclusionary practices and devices, many of which will be defended by their users as "normal and prudent" business practices. Pre-emption of distributive channels through integration or exclusive-dealing contracts with retailers, and refusal by integrated firms to furnish nonintegrated competitors either with material supplies or with market outlets on favorable terms, are important phases of exclusionary practices which influence market structures. In these respects, there is a clear and identifiable influence of market conduct on market structure—an influence which is very appropriate subject-matter for consideration by public regulatory authority.

By influencing market structures directly (that is, by developing higher seller concentration and more difficult entry), predatory and exclusionary conduct may of course influence market performance indirectly, so far as higher concentration and more strongly impeded entry are conducive to a more monopolistic performance. The extent of these indirect effects will depend on the actual impact of the practices in question on market structures, and on the general relationship which holds between such structure and performance. About the most that can be said on this point is that there is evidence concerning a number of individual industries in which "successful" predation and exclusion have had substantial direct effects on structure and indirect effects on performance.

The necessary and sufficient original structural bases for the emergence of predatory and exclusionary tactics in important degree are not entirely clear. It might be suggested, however, that favoring structural conditions include the following: (*a*) dependence of the industry on a natural resource which is largely restricted in its geographical distribution to one or a few locations, facilitating the development of concentrated ownership of control of the necessary resource; (*b*) durability and complexity of the good, requiring the existence of specialized distributive-service outlets, this facilitating the development of integrated or exclusive chains of such outlets by individual manufacturers; and (*c*) dependence of producers or distributors of the good on specialized transport facilities (for example, oil pipelines) which require huge investments and are conveniently integrated by firms engaged in production and/or distribution. In industries with one or more of these characteristics, exclusionary conduct seems especially likely to develop almost as a matter of course, the law permitting.

## E. The Structural Conditions for Workable Competition

The available empirical findings on the relationship of market structure to market performance are incomplete and based only on rather small samples, so that definitive statements cannot be made concerning those conditions of market structure which are and are not conducive to a reasonably good or "workable" performance.

First, "high" or "very high" seller concentration in an industry generally seems to be conducive to poor performance in the crucial matter of price-cost relations or profits, without evidently bestowing offsetting advantages in other dimensions of market performance. Tentative indications are that if seller concentration exceeds that in which the largest 8 sellers supply from two-thirds to three-fourths of the output of an industry (the number and sizes of smaller sellers occurring as they usually do in these cases), there is a strong disposition toward significant monopolistic price-raising and excess profits. On the other hand, in industries where seller concentration is "moderate" or less, so that, for example, the largest 8 sellers supply less than two-thirds of the output of an industry (the number and sizes of smaller sellers occurring as they usually do in these cases), there is on the average a disposition toward much slighter excess profits and a much closer approximation to a competitive price-cost-output adjustment. At the same time, performance in other respects is not evidently poorer on the average than it is in highly concentrated industries.

Thus, as a matter of public policy, it would be salutary to preserve and as necessary create market structures which are no more than moderately concentrated on the sellers' side. This rule is applicable, at any rate, to all industries except those in which economies of large-scale production are so great as to require high or very high seller concentration in order to secure plants and firms of optimally efficient scale. (It appears from evidence that this sort of exception will arise only in a very small minority of cases. In these exceptional cases, of course, high seller concentration may have to be accepted and dealt with in order to secure efficiency, and there is a fundamental impossibility of securing a market structure which is conducive to good performance in all important respects.)

It is not evident from available findings that market performance in industries with low seller concentration or relatively atomistic structures tends to be systematically better or worse than that in industries of moderate concentration. That is, moderately concentrated oligopolies seem to tend toward desirably competitive performance about as well as industries of relatively atomistic structure. The important structural distinction is not between atomistic and oligopolistic industries, but rather between highly concentrated oligopolies and all others, the "all others" including both moderately concentrated oligopolies and relatively atomistic industries.

On the other hand, it is not evident that very low seller concentration, where it occurs and is consistent with efficiency in scale, is generally inferior in its performance tendencies to somewhat higher degrees of concentration. It is, however, possible that very low concentration has undesirable performance tendencies in certain settings, such as in industries engaged directly in natural resource exploitation, and also that very low seller concentration may in some industries aggravate the adverse performance tendencies basically attributable to other causes. In such instances, atomistic structure may in some sense be practically an inferior alternative to moderate seller concentration, but these are more or less special cases and require special treatment. We will refer to them further in the following chapter.

There are some theoretical but very few and indistinct empirical indications that the adverse performance tendencies of high seller concentration tend to be mitigated if there is at the same time relatively high buyer concentration on the "receiving end" of the market. Because the theoretical indications are inconclusive in substantial degree, and because the counterbalancing of concentrated selling with concentrated buying is a practical alternative at best in only a small minority of cases, it seems unrealistic to view the establishment of buyer concentration to oppose seller concentration as an important alternative way of securing workable market structures. High buyer concentration alone (not conjoined with high seller concentration) seems in general to be an undesirable structural development, to be opposed on grounds similar to those on which high seller concentration is opposed.

A second suggestion is that high barriers to entry tend to have an adverse effect on market performance, as compared to moderate and low barriers to entry to the industry. This shows up at least among highly concentrated industries, in which nearly all cases of extreme barriers to entry are understandably found. Highly concentrated industries protected by very high entry barriers seem to perform worse in general than highly concentrated industries to which entry barriers are more moderate. The worst structural situation is usually one of quite high seller concentration combined with very high barriers to entry, and high seller concentration alone seems generally less noxious if its potential effects are tempered by a considerable threat of new competition.

In the same vein, moderate seller concentration in oligopolistic industries probably is associated with more desirable market performance partly because it is generally linked with no more than moderate barriers to entry. Lowered concentration and lowered entry barriers in fact typically interact to effect a reasonably competitive market performance. The policy implications of this finding are clear. Reduction of high entry barriers, as feasible, should produce structural conditions for a more workable competition in both highly concentrated and moderately concentrated industries, and the overall aim should be to secure or preserve both moderate or lower seller concentration, and moderate or lower barriers to entry simultaneously. The reduction of existing barriers to entry, however, may in practice be difficult to accomplish, especially so far as the impediments to entry inhere mainly in the product-differentiation advantages of established firms.

There is a remaining question as to possible adverse effects of "unduly easy" entry. (We have already had occasion to refer to the extreme case in which there is an essential chronic oversupply of new-entrant enterprises which continue to crowd into an already overcrowded industry without regard to the fact that, statistically, their major prospect is for net losses and ultimate bankruptcy, the end results being a maintenance of chronic overcapacity and a high rate of enterprise "turnover" and of business mortality in the industry.) This sort of "condition of entry" is in general undesirable, though it seems more attributable to lack of knowledge or judgment on the part of entrant enterprises than to any basic structural condition. The appropriate character of remedies may be suggested by this fact, although public or other programs to eliminate the physical redundancy of obsolete plant or of immobile labor force attached to the particular industry plagued with excessive entry might often go far to lessen the inducement to such entry.

A more subtle difficulty may arise in industries where entry is quite easy but where nevertheless a substantial oligopolistic concentration among established sellers develops. Then established sellers, finding it relatively unprofitable to set prices low enough to forestall entry, may elevate them for immediate profits and subsequently attract excessive entry and excess capacity. A few instances of this apparent tendency have been noted in our sampling of manufacturing industries. In such cases, the creation of a moderate as distinct from a very low entry barrier would probably be conducive to better industry performance over time. But a superior practical alternative may be deconcentration to secure a more moderately concentrated and more competitive market structure among established sellers.

A final characteristic of market structure to be evaluated from the standpoint of "workability" is the degree of product differentiation. Although some degree of product differentiation within the industry is frequently an essential device for providing buyers with a desirable variety of product alternatives, high degrees of product differentiation, as they occur or sui generis, are generally inimical to good market performance. As high degrees of product differentiation develop, they do not appear to augment progressively the real variety of product alternatives available, but rather to emphasize the determination of buyer choices among closely similar products on the basis of persuasion, reputation, and the like. On the other hand, extreme product differentiation (or the effort to create it) is generally linked with wastefully high selling costs and with the creation of excessive barriers to new entry, so far as established sellers succeed in creating strong buyer preferences for their products as distinct from new-entrant products. It is thus difficult to accept at face value, or even at a 50 percent discount, the often-repeated assertion that strong product differentiation is a circumstance tending to make competition more "workable" than it otherwise would be. The empirical indications are contrary. On the other hand, it is extremely hard to devise practicable ways of remedying existing situations of undue and undesirable product differentiation, and this difficulty poses a major dilemma for public regulatory policy. If product differentiation is excessive in certain cases, by what psychologically, economically, and politically practicable means can we really lessen it?

We have spoken above of the structural conditions for workable competition, but not of the conduct conditions—of the sorts of market conduct which are and are not conducive to good performance. The reasons for this omission should be clear from our earlier discussions; although on an abstract theoretical level we can specify some conduct conditions for good performance, these conditions are not operational in the light of our powers empirically to observe and appraise actual conduct. So long as we are practically able to ascertain only the superficial forms of interseller coordination in market conduct, and unable to ascertain independently the principles of price calculation or of promotional-and-product-policy calculation employed by sellers, we are also unable to establish any operationally useful or practically applicable norm of desirable (as distinct from undesirable) observed market conduct. We cannot honestly say, for example, that collusive conduct of one variety or another is bad as compared to noncollusive conduct, until we are able to distinguish the numerous different principles of calculation potentially applied under the myriad subvarieties of both collusive and noncollusive conduct. The view just stated is not traditional, but it is supported by our analysis of market conduct in Chapter 8 above. We eschew, therefore, any general attempt to state an operational criterion of the conduct conditions of workable competition, and adhere in the main to a suggestion only of structural conditions.

The only significant exception to this position involves predatory and exclusionary conduct. In general predation and exclusion—except as occasionally justified on grounds that they are necessary adjuncts to realizing actual efficiencies such as those of vertical integration—tend to be at least indirectly inimical to good performance, and their elimination should be one of the conditions for workable competition.

## Carl Kaysen and Donald F. Turner

## *Antitrust Policy: An Economic and Legal Analysis*

## III: A Policy for Antitrust Law

## The Policy Goals

Almost any policy proposal resolves itself into a statement of a hierarchy of ends, ordered to indicate which should prevail in situations where they conflict. In proposing that the primary goal of antitrust policy be the limitation of market power, we do not make it our sole goal; we also give great weight to the achievement of desirable economic performance. Indeed, in so far as reduction of market power is incompatible with efficiency and progressiveness, we subordinate the first goal to the second. If, for example, the efficient scale of operation in a particular market is so large in relation to the size of the market that efficient firms are so few in number as to make their possession of market power likely, and the reduction of market power cannot be achieved except at the cost of a substantial loss in efficiency, our policy would call for no action against the power itself. But where market power exists and can be reduced without sacrifices in performance, then such action is desirable without reference to the question of how good over-all performance may have been.

The other two of the broad classes of goals—promoting "fair" business conduct and the redistribution of social power between large and small business—occupy a much lower position in our hierarchy of policy aims. We expect that some degree of regulation of business conduct in the interest of "fair dealing" may be necessary. As we have already indicated, the policy of limiting market power will not be pressed to the point of reducing it to negligible dimensions everywhere (and indeed, this is not possible, even if it were viewed as desirable). Thus there may be some case for limiting the way in which residual market power is used. To the extent that some methods of using market power will be controlled on grounds that they are likely to contribute to the perpetuation of market power or to its increase, the area of regulation on pure "fair dealing" grounds will be correspondingly narrowed. But some kinds of conduct which will require such regulation do exist, and where it can be achieved without too high a price in efficiency, we deem it desirable. The following is a brief summary of our recommendations.

## Limitations of Market Power

1. We propose statutory authorization for the reduction of undue market power, whether individually or jointly possessed; this to be done normally by dissolution, divorcement, or divestiture. We would except market power derived from economies of scale, valid patents, or the introduction of new processes, products, or marketing techniques.
2. We suggest, in the alternative, that the program be either (a) a permanent feature of antitrust policy, thus applying both to existing concentrations of market power and to concentrations that may later arise through inadequacies in the law, or in enforcement of the law, concerning conduct; or (b) a program limited to the time required to deal with existing undue concentrations of market power.
3. With respect to either of the above alternatives, we suggest that the policy might be carried out either (a) under a statute in which market power is defined in general terms, requiring a fairly extensive economic inquiry for determination of each case; or (b) under a statute in which market power is more arbitrarily defined, which would facilitate the disposition of cases and more clearly identify the "targets," but could possibly be applied to firms that, in fact, lacked market power.

## Limitations on Conduct Contributing to Market Power

1. *Mergers.* Particularly if the proposals as to market power are deemed unwise or undesirable, and perhaps in any event, we propose tightening the law on mergers. Some means of making enforcement more effective than it now is seems of paramount importance. We propose, as one step in this direction, a requirement of advance reporting of all mergers involving firms of more than a certain absolute size in assets or more than a certain share of any market in which they operate. We also suggest the possibility of a more arbitrary standard for illegality, in line with the similar suggestion as to market power stated above.
2. *Price-fixing or price-influencing agreements.* Regarding trade association and similar collective activities, we propose specific statutory prohibition of agreements:
   (a) to abide by reported list prices,
   (b) to report offers at which no sales are made,
   (c) to inform each other of the individual buyers and sellers in all transactions,
   (d) to refuse to make reports, submitted to each other, available to buyers or buyers' trade associations,
   (e) to submit books and accounts to the inspection of any member of the group or representative thereof; or
   (f) to report transactions to each other, or to a representative of the group, within a period of seven days or less after said transactions take place.
3. *Collective refusals to deal.* Apart from those incidentally resulting from productive joint ventures, we would make collective refusals to deal illegal per se.
4. *Patents and patent licensing.* Proceeding on the basic premise that patentees' realizable rewards can be lowered without significantly reducing the flow of useful inventions and innovations, we propose:
   (a) that the patent laws be revised to create a class of "petty" patents, with monopoly rights for five years only, and to raise the standard of invention for seventeen-year patents;
   (b) that on restrictive clauses in patent licensing agreements,
      (1) price-fixing clauses be made illegal per se,
      (2) clauses providing for grant-backs of new patents or exclusive licenses thereunder be made illegal per se,
      (3) covenants not to contest patent validity be invalid in any licensing agreement containing restrictions in addition to a uniform royalty provision,
      (4) cross-licensing and pooling agreements contain no restrictions beyond that for a uniform royalty charge on each patent from all licensees (except that the owner may restrict the use), and
      (5) all licensing agreement be registered with the Federal Trade Commission (but not made public);
   (c) that Section 7 of the Clayton Act be revised to cover acquisitions of patents from individuals as well as from corporations.

5. *Price discrimination*. We propose that the Robinson-Patman Act be repealed, in favor of a statute dealing separately with (a) price discrimination directed against competing sellers and (b) price discrimination that harms particular buyers. In each case, we would make some substantive changes in the existing law. In both cases, we would liberalize the "cost" defense and specifically exclude from the law all geographic price discrimination that is accounted for entirely by differences in transportation cost.

## Procedural and Related Recommendations

1. We propose that criminal penalties be limited to the so-called per se offenses.
2. We propose that treble damages also be limited to the per se offenses; that no private suit be maintainable under a market power statutory provision; and that judgment under the market power provision would not constitute prima facie proof of anything under Section 5 of the Clayton Act.
3. We suggest the creation of a special court for adjudicating monopoly cases and other Sherman Act cases in which divestiture is part of the relief sought. For an extended program against undue market power, we propose a special court, with the prosecuting function placed in the hands of a new administrative agency. We also propose certain procedural steps designed to clarify and speed the trial of economic issues of fact.

Our reasons for giving primary emphasis to the fourth of the general goals of policy stated above and for making the above recommendations are partly positive and partly negative. Our positive reasons rest ultimately on a value judgment. The most important aspect of the competitive process is that it is self-controlling with regard to private economic power. For all the important qualifications and limitations of the doctrine of the invisible hand which modern economic analysis has produced, that doctrine remains the basic political justification for an enterprise economy in which major economic decisions are compelled and coordinated through the market. It is the fact that the competitive market compels the results of its processes which is the ultimate defense against the demand that economic decisions be made or supervised by politically responsible authorities. Without such market compulsion, that demand appears ultimately irresistible in a society committed to representative government. It is our preference for the kind of autonomy in economic life which a market-organized society makes possible that forms the particular judgment we make.

Our negative reasons are more objective, and less subject to dogmatic acceptance or rejection. In essence, they amount to the proposition that the alternative standards present definitional and administrative problems of such magnitude that consistent and sensible enforcement would be well-nigh impossible. While similar difficulties would attend the carrying out of a market power standard, we conclude that they would be much less severe. Moreover, we believe it is possible to formulate arbitrary tests designed to reduce administrative problems under a market power standard with considerably more confidence in the results than if similar steps were taken in order to carry out the other designated goals.

We now turn to a detailed discussion of the workability of policy standards that we substantially reject.

## Standards Other Than Market Power

[Note: In this section, which is omitted, the authors consider and reject antitrust approaches that would seek to limit the power of big business, directly regulate the performance of big business, or mandate "fair dealing."]

## Limitations of Market Power: Definitions, Analysis, and Problems

We have stated that our primary policy goal is one of curbing undue market power, whether individually or jointly possessed, to the extent consistent with the achievement of desirable economic performance. We would therefore make no direct attempt to eliminate market power derived from economies of scale, valid patents, or the introduction of new processes, products, or marketing techniques, nor would we impose the remedy of dissolution where for these or other limited reasons the performance costs would be too great. In addition, we recognize the need for considerable regulation of the conduct of firms, to control attempts to achieve or maintain market power, to control practices that are likely to create or maintain such power, and to control the use of such power that our policy would deem "reasonable."

Having disposed of alternative policy goals on the principal ground that they pose definitional and hence administrative problems of a quite unmanageable nature, we wish to repeat at the outset of this discussion that a market power standard is by no means immune to difficulties on this score. Indeed, one of the purposes of our discussion is to point out just what, and how serious, those difficulties are; and the existence of these difficulties, though we believe them much less severe than those inherent in alternative policy aims, leads us eventually to consider the desirability of adopting some arbitrary tests of "market power," and of limiting any direct program against undue market power to a fixed period of time.

### Market Performance, Market Structure, and Market Power

Our interest in the operation of markets involves two elements: certain specified results, which we have called desirable economic performance, especially those of efficiency and progressiveness; and the character of the market processes themselves, in particular the scope of decision for the firms in it, and the extent to which the market compels the particular performance actually observed.

Antitrust policy, however, cannot operate directly either on performance or on processes: we cannot conceive of an effective order which says, be efficient, or, be competitive. Rather, policy operates directly on market structure and on firm conduct in order to affect processes and performance. "Market structure" we use to mean those conditions external to the firm which are relatively permanent or which change only slowly, and which affect, if they do not determine, the way the firm operates. Such features of a market as the numbers of buyers and sellers, the techniques of production and marketing, the geographic distribution of production and demand, the character of demand for the product, are all elements of market structure. "Conduct" comprises aspects of the market which are the result of specific decisions of firms and which are, at least conceivably, alterable in relatively short periods of time. Patent-pooling arrangements, the use of exclusive dealerships, basing point pricing formulas, are examples of market conduct. Crudely put, conduct is subject to alteration by injunction; change in structure requires some more drastic reorganization measures of the dissolution, divestiture, and divorcement type. But this is a crude distinction, and the line between what is called structure and what is called conduct is not always an easy one to draw. In particular markets, there is an intimate association between certain lines of conduct and certain structural features of the market which makes a sharp separation artificial. Thus in a market with a very small number of sellers and closely similar products, such as the cigarette market, the phenomenon of price leadership typical of such markets may be classified as "conduct," or viewed simply as a correlate of the structural features of small numbers and closely similar products. Application of the policy criterion would lead to the classification of price leadership under structure since, in this situation, it would be impossible to alter it merely by injunction. Conversely, we can think of examples of conduct which, when persisted in, alter structure. Thus a policy of exclusive dealing maintained by many firms in a particular market may over time limit the kind of distributors who are able to carry the product in question, and thus make this aspect of market structure different than it would have been without the exclusive distribution policy. Thus it is not useful to attempt to maintain too rigid a distinction between structure and conduct; structure in a broad sense can be taken to include both structure proper and conduct. In this broad sense, the structure of a market, from the point of view of a particular firm, comprises the circumstances external to that firm which condition its decisions, including the characteristic conduct of other firms in the market.

Ideally, we should like to make a complete analytical chain from market structure (including conduct) to processes to performance. We would then be able both to deduce present performance from observation of present structure, and to predict what alterations in performance would result from particular changes in structure. Further, we would be able to say to what extent any observed pattern of performance was compelled by the structure of the market, and to what extent it was the result of policy choices by firms, which could well have been other than they were. The theoretical model of the perfectly competitive market provides an example of such a one-to-one correspondence of structure, processes, and performance. In practice, our analytic apparatus is inadequate to the task of providing such correlations in the study of actual markets, and the prospects of speedy improvement in it are not bright. We can neither predict market performance from market structure, nor can we tell from structure alone how competitive the processes of the market are. A major consequence of the gaps in our knowledge is that our conclusions about the functioning of any concrete market depend on the joint study of both structure and performance. We cannot determine what structure is without examining certain aspects of performance. Our problem then is to trace out the underlying structure both by direct observation and by inference from the behavior of certain performance variables in the known circumstances of the past.

Thus, for example, a conclusion that barriers to entry in some markets are high may be based in part on an examination of the size of the smallest efficient production unit, the nature of distribution channels, the existence of a closed patent pool, etc. In part, however, it will rest on the observation of continued high profits and non-price rationing of output among customers in periods of high demand. In general, we would not be able to draw a confident conclusion on this point on the structural evidence alone, but would require confirmation from past performance consistent with our inference on structural evidence. Each thorough industry study does something to close the gap in our knowledge of the associations between structure and performance, but their number is still far too few.[1]

Our inability to predict performance from structure is not the only serious gap in our knowledge. We are only somewhat better off in predicting the relations between the various individual aspects (or dimensions) of performance, and the ultimate results, in terms of the whole economy, which we view as desirable. Efficiency and progressiveness are the results we seek that are closely related to the functioning of markets. We can define efficiency with some precision, and characterize the dimensions of performance which measure its various aspects in detail. The same cannot be said of progressiveness: we lack both a standard against which the observed measures of progress can be tested and knowledge of the relations between measures of progressiveness and measures of efficiency. Ideally, a standard of performance for any particular performance dimension should reflect the relation of that aspect of performance to the achievement of both efficiency and progressiveness. Thus, for example, a standard of profit performance should depend not only on the result of efficiency, which by itself requires that the long-run profit in excess of the supply price of capital and entrepreneurship be zero, but also on the result of progressiveness, which conceivably might call for higher profits in any industry deemed capable of innovating. In practice, though, our knowledge does not permit us to discuss what the profit standard should in fact be, if progressiveness as well as efficiency are taken into consideration. We may be able to say something about profits in a particular industry, in the context of a detailed examination of that industry, but we lack the basis in either theory or experience for making any generalized statements about profit standards which reflect the relation of profits to all the desirable results we seek to achieve.

1. For evidence of certain kinds of structure-performance associations see J. S. Bain, "Relation of Profit Rate to Industry Concentration, American Manufacturing, 1936–40," *Quarterly Journal of Economics* (August 1951); "Workable Competition in Oligopoly," *American Economic Review* (May 1950); and *Barriers to New Competition* (1956).

The consequence of our ignorance is that performance standards fall into two classes: those concerned with the efficiency aspects of performance, which derive from the competitive model and are mutually interrelated in definite ways; and those concerned with progressiveness and other aspects of performance, which rest on no corresponding theoretical structure. The functioning of any market must be tested against these two classes of performance standards separately, and then some ad hoc evaluation of the possible consistency or inconsistency between them must be made, since a general statement of their relationship cannot be made.

(1) Efficiency aspects of performance. The efficiency aspects of performance divide, in turn, into three classes: relations between prices and costs; relations among output, capacity, and demand; and technical efficiency.

(a) Prices and costs. Price-cost relations are measured for individual firms, and they refer to average behavior over a long period. Ideally, we are looking for information on the behavior of prices with respect to long-run average costs; averages of prices and costs over a period long enough to include at least one complete business cycle, and preferably several cycles, serve as an approximation to this ideal. In conditions of stationary demand, with output constant, on the average, price should approximate cost, including some measure of normal profit. Where demand and output are declining in the long run, prices should fall short of costs as long as output is declining faster than productive capacity. Since capacity can be adjusted only slowly, over the average, prices for products with declining demands should fall short of long-run average costs (including normal profits). With long-run rising demand and with output continually pressing on capacity, price should on the average exceed cost (including normal profits).

[Note: Here the authors discuss relevant measures of cost for large and small firms.]

The competitive model, which defines economic efficiency, tells us that prices should equal costs, product by product, in long-run equilibrium. Translated into observational terms, when demand is stationary, substantial departures from price-cost equality, on the average of a period of years, indicate the existence of noncompetitive performance. When demand is growing, we expect excess profits or margins. Stated crudely, we can say that these are of the appropriate order of magnitude if (1) the excess profits do not persist when the expansion of capacity and output ceases or (2), where growth is continuous, the excess profits are on the order of the rate of growth of capacity. If either of these conditions is violated, then we can conclude that price-cost behavior differs from efficient behavior as defined by the competitive model.

* * *

(b) Output, capacity, and demand. The second set of performance dimensions relevant to efficiency are the relations among output, capacity, and demand. An efficiently functioning industry shows no excess capacity at the cyclical (or cyclical-seasonal) peaks in production. In measuring excess capacity, allowance must be made for the existence of obsolete equipment, kept for stand-by purposes, which is occasionally brought into use at seasonal peaks in demand but is not regularly utilized. Again, we are interested in long-run excess capacity, and the appropriate measurement is an average over several peak periods. Excess capacity is compatible with efficiency if it is accompanied by losses, and by declines in capacity which tend to reduce the excess. In local or regional market industries where there have been regional shifts in demand (e.g., cement or gypsum), excess capacity and losses in some regions may be observed along with profits and growing capacity in others, consistent with economic efficiency. But persistent excess capacity not accompanied by losses is a mark of inefficiency and of undue market power.

Excess capacity is usually a phenomenon of declining demand. The corresponding problem in situations of rising demand is the expansion of capacity to meet growths in demand. Persistent lags of capacity behind demand, indicated either by nonprice "rationing" of output at demand peaks or by sudden spurts in prices at periods of high demand, show a maladaptation of capacity to demand. In examining the relation of capacity to demand in any particular industry, allowance must be made for the time taken to build new plants and, where it exists, for any unusual variability of demand.

(c) Technical efficiency. The requirements of technical efficiency are three: production must be by efficient methods ("on" the cost curve), in plants of efficient scale, and at efficient locations. The first point is largely an engineering matter, but it also means that firms should show no obvious internal inefficiencies in terms of knowledge of costs, accounting procedures, and the like. The second point is also primarily a matter of engineering judgment, but in judging the appropriateness of plant scales, allowance must be made for lags in the adaptation of new techniques, and for the persistence of production in existing plants of old design even in competitive conditions, so long as variable costs are recovered. Similarly, in judging the efficiency of plant location, shifts in demand and the persistence of production at existing locations must be taken into account. Both judgments—that of efficient scale and that of efficient location—thus are applicable rather to new or recently built plants than to the whole industry, especially in situations where demand and technology are both changing rapidly.

When these three sets of conditions are met, production is efficient in the sense that no reorganization of inputs would lead to greater outputs from the given bundle of resources. The equilibrium of the competitive model, in which all industries are perfectly competitive, is efficient in this sense, and it is of course for this reason that we deduce the efficiency conditions from it. In practice, of course, we cannot observe industries in equilibrium. But we can observe the extent to which changes in external circumstances are met by responses moving toward equilibrium, and whether or not these movements are rapid or relatively slow. Such observations can lead us to a judgment on whether or not industry performance is efficient.

(2) Other aspects of performance. The second group of performance dimensions include progressiveness and selling costs. What they have in common is the purely negative attribute that we have no ideal standard against which to measure them in the

same way that we can measure efficiency against the standards provided by the competitive model. In discussing them, we can add little to what we have already said.

Progressiveness, the more important of the two, includes the introduction of new end-products, and the introduction of new techniques of production which reduce costs, so that a given bundle of inputs yields more outputs than it could previously. Observed progress in reduction of costs and creation of new goods is not difficult to record. It is, however, difficult to measure in any comparative or analytical sense. We know that relatively new technologies—those of oil, chemicals, electronics—appear to provide more scope both for the development of new products and for cost reduction than relatively mature technologies—those of meat packing, textile production, garment manufacture. But sometimes a revolutionary enough discovery turns an "old" into a "new" technology, and the boundaries between them are to a large degree arbitrary. Further, it is not clear to what extent we are trying to measure "absolute" progressiveness, to what extent progressiveness in relation to the opportunities offered. In general, we can say that the more progressiveness, the better, but even this may not always be true. While the addition of new products to a previous range of choice unequivocally makes consumers no worse off, the same cannot be said if new products displace old. When a new product becomes "fashionable," and a corresponding old product ceases to be offered, consumers may or may not be better off. Cost reduction presents no such paradox; any cost-reducing innovation is worth what it saves, and no more than this will knowingly be expended in achieving it.

While we can talk in abstract terms about the relation of the costs of innovation to the returns from it, in a fashion similar to the general notion of the equalization of costs and returns by market processes, we can find little concrete guidance for the analysis of innovation in practice. This is in part because of possibly remediable ignorance, in part because of deeper difficulties which we have already indicated above.

[Note: In the omitted portion, the authors discuss the effect of competition on product promotion.]

All in all, with respect to both progressiveness and excessive selling costs, we are left with some general guides, and the task of applying them, ad hoc, to particular industries in the light of such information as appears relevant.[2]

(3) *Structure*. When we turn from performance to structure, we can be briefer without being less clear. The structure of a market, broadly defined, consists of those stable features of the environment of a business firm which determine or condition the firm's decisions. They are more or less stable, in the sense that in any short-run period,

2. There is a third aspect of performance of much less significance which also falls in this class: the adequacy or superfluity of product variety. In part, this is an efficiency problem, and the production of too much product variety, in the sense of producing products for which prices do not cover costs, is covered by the efficiency criterion. On the other hand, the problem of insufficient product variety is not. The nonproduction of a potentially remunerative product cannot generally be detected: it is really an aspect of progressiveness, and of the introduction of new products. In the competitive model, all products whose costs could be covered by their prices would be produced. Conceivably some products could be produced under discriminatory pricing whose costs would not be covered under simple competitive pricing. Traditionally, the need for discriminatory pricing to cover costs has been viewed as an indicator of the need for government regulation, since some degree of monopoly is necessary for the successful practice of discrimination. We do not think that much more can usefully be said on this point.

the structure can be viewed as given, although in the long-run market structures do change. In examining market structure, we seek ultimately to determine whether or not the structure is such as to compel or conduce to competition by the firms in the market, where competition means, as we have several times said, both certain kinds of economic results and a certain kind of process which leads to them. Since the markets of experience do not show any simple one-to-one correspondence between a single structural configuration and the processes and results of the market, such as characterizes the perfectly competitive market model, our examination of structure is inevitably incomplete in its answer to the question. But we can say something about whether particular aspects of a given market structure, in the context of the other aspects of that structure, probably do or do not conduce to competition in the market.

The major elements of market structure can be divided into five classes: (1) the breadth of the market and the character of demand, (2) the number and size distribution of sellers and buyers, (3) the conditions of entry for new sellers and expansion for existing sellers, (4) the character and importance of product differentiation, and (5) the degree of independence of action among sellers and buyers.

The first element of market structure involves the delimitation of the market and the cataloguing of the major characteristics of the demand for what is traded in it. Delimitation of the market involves tracing out the geographic area and the group of products within which sellers' offers are substitutes for each other in meeting the demands of buyers. In examining the geographic and product boundaries of the market, it is necessary to consider both how they are drawn under the present price and transport cost regime, and how they have fluctuated and would fluctuate with changes in prices (including the prices of the relevant substitutes) and in transport costs. The economic character of the product—durable, semidurable, perishable, consumers' good, producers' good, and the time pattern of demand—the character of seasonal and cyclical fluctuations, its long-term growth, stability, or decline, are the most important attributes of demand to be examined.

The number and relative size distribution of both sellers and buyers—their market shares—both currently and over time form the next major element of market structure. In general, numbers and size distribution on the selling side can be summarized into one of four patterns: large numbers and no relatively large firms—atomistic structure; a small number (less than twenty) of firms supplying 75 percent of the market, with no one supplying more than 10–15 percent and a fringe of smaller firms supplying the rest—loose oligopoly; a very small number (eight or fewer) firms supplying 50 percent of the market, with the largest firm having a 20 percent or higher share, and with or without a fringe of small suppliers—tight oligopoly; and a single large firm supplying 60 percent or more of the market, with no other single seller supplying a significant proportion of the demand—dominant firm, or partial monopoly. A similar classification can be applied to the buying side. Relative size distributions must be viewed in the perspective of time: the structural element we seek is the average situation over a long period rather than that existing at any particular moment. Of course, persistent changes in market shares are also important, and any movement toward greater or less concentration as well as the average picture of the whole period of study must be taken into account.

The third element of market structure on our list is the set of conditions affecting the entry of new sellers into the market and the expansion of existing sellers. In part these overlap, in part they are distinct. The first of the conditions affecting entry is the optimum scale of the plant and firm in relation to the size of the market, and the actual scales of existing sellers in comparison with the optimum. Entry is usually difficult where the optimum scale is relatively large, the cost disadvantages of suboptimal scale are significant, and existing sellers are at optimal scale. Large absolute optimum size (as well as large size relative to the market) adds to the difficulty of entry because of the large capital requirement for an optimum firm or plant. These conditions are also important in respect to the expansion of existing firms, although optimum plant size may be more important and optimum firm size less important than in the case of new entrants.

Barriers preventing free access to technology are a second important class of conditions affecting entry and the expansion of existing firms. Patents are one form such barriers take, and such patent practices as the freedom of licensing, the existence of pools, and the like, as well as the intrinsic importance of the patented technology, determine how high these barriers are and how they operate with respect to existing and new firms in the market. But patents are not the only kind of barriers to technology. Secret know-how or "corners" on scarce trained personnel may be equally important. Third, access to factor supplies may not be possible on equal terms to established firms and new entrants, or to all established firms. The pattern of ownership of scarce factors—mineral deposits, naturally favorable sites, and the like—is important in this respect. Where such factors are tied to some existing firms, would-be entrants and other existing firms may not be able to buy as much of the resource as they want at any price. In general, the labor market does not present similar features, but in special instances it might, such as in the case of specially skilled or talented persons mentioned above. Every new firm—as opposed to a new entrant into a particular market which is an established firm in some other market—finds it usually has access to capital on less favorable terms than its established rivals. This is partly because new firms are usually small, and capital is available more cheaply to large than to small enterprises, partly because newness itself is a disadvantage in the eyes of suppliers, since it is associated with a higher risk of failure than prevails for similar "seasoned" firms. Markets for fabricated inputs may show customary supplier-buyer relations, or long-term supply contracts, which put newcomers at a disadvantage. Access to markets, like access to factor supplies, may not be available on equal terms to new entrants and existing sellers, or to all existing sellers. The character of distribution channels, the existence of forward integration into distribution, the existence of quasi-integration through such practices as exclusive dealerships, requirements contracts, long-term leases, and the like, all determine how the new entrant will fare in disposing of his product. Similarly, where expansion of sales means expansion of distribution outlets, some of the same circumstances will bear on the ability of existing sellers to expand. In general, the organization of the buying market is an important feature of market structure for the selling market.

The fourth element of market structure is the character of product differentiation—advertising, selling costs, promotional efforts, design variation, etc.—and its importance in the market. Logically, this might be seen as another element in the conditions of entry, but it is important enough to warrant distinction. The existence of important product differentiation, with "loyal" customers of particular sellers who view the products of other sellers as poor substitutes, usually involves many elements: product variation, heavy advertising expenses, other heavy selling expenses. Where these exist they make entry for a new firm difficult in that it must overcome the established good will of existing sellers. Since this good will is a function not only of the current outlays of existing firms on selling and advertising, but of the sum of such outlays over many years, the magnitude of the new entrant's handicap can be considerable, and may be overcome only after an unprofitable period of years—an investment in creating good will. Where product differentiation is important, the whole character of entry may change, in that the would-be entrant can offer only a rather different product than existing sellers. In the extreme, the publisher of a new weekly picture magazine, for example, would not be selling the same product as *Life* or *Look*, in the sense that the new steel producer would be selling the same product as U.S. Steel or Bethlehem.

Finally, the degree of independence of action of existing sellers in the market is an important element of market structure. The existence of collusive agreements, trade association arrangements for price reporting, pricing formulas, market sharing arrangements, all come under this head. So does the existence of a well-defined system of price leadership, or other observable nonindependent action, even though it is not crystallized in institutional form.

As we have repeatedly warned, it is not generally possible to evaluate the significance of individual elements of market structure, taken alone, for particular markets. But we can broadly, and with exceptions, distinguish what is likely to be more and what is likely to be less conducive to competition, on the average. The broader the market, the less important product differentiation and promotional efforts, and the more independence of action among sellers and buyers both, the more will the market structure probably be one which is conducive to competition.

(4) *Market power*. As a result of this long excursion into the meaning of market performance and market structure, we are now in a position to define market power more fully than we have heretofore. A firm possesses market power when it can behave persistently in a manner different from the behavior that a competitive market would enforce on a firm facing otherwise similar cost and demand conditions. When the "can" in this definition is emphasized, we see that the concept of market power is basically a structural concept. We ask, does the market permit or constrain firms to behave in such-and-such a way, or not? But, although the concept is one of structure, we do not rely on the examination of the elements of market structure alone in making judgments about market power. Because of our inability to correlate structure and performance with precision, we look at performance directly, taking what the firm's performance has

been as the best evidence of what it can be. Since we are interested in the future as well as in the past, we look at structure as well as performance, in order to correlate as well as we can the observed performance with the observable features of market structure, and thus be able to predict the probable relation of future to past performance. Further, since we are interested in antitrust policy, and action of antitrust type operates immediately on conduct and structure and only indirectly on performance, the correlation of performance with structure is a necessary step in the application of antitrust policy to concrete cases. Only the efficiency dimensions of performance can be evaluated in terms of the competitive standard, and thus an examination of the efficiency dimensions of performance can tell us whether or not performance has been consistent with the absence of market power. Thus an examination of whether or not a firm has market power involves an examination of both the market structure in which it operates and the efficiency dimensions of its performance.

Our definition of market power, strictly construed, is consistent with a notion of "unexercised market power," which would exist when a firm could, but did not, behave differently than would a firm in an otherwise similar competitive market. Logically the existence of unexercised market power is inconsistent with profit maximization. A firm which had the power to increase its long-run price-cost margins, for example, and did not do so would be sacrificing income it could earn; the same would be true for other dimensions of performance. However, we cannot rely on firms engaging in profit-maximizing behavior even where it is well defined, and this is not always the case, so we may say that the existence of unexercised market power is a real possibility. To detect it, however, we would be forced to rely on structural information alone since, by hypothesis, it would not be reflected in past performance. In general, then, we may say that unexercised market power is not readily detectible, though in specific circumstances the structure of a particular market might point so strongly to the existence of market power that we might be willing to infer that it exists unexercised even in the absence of noncompetitive performance. In practice, the problem is unlikely to arise, since most firms with market power wish to benefit from it in some way.

We have spoken so far of the market power of a firm in the singular. This is strictly appropriate only for markets with dominant firms—monopolies or partial monopolies. In the more typical market structures of oligopoly, market power is possessed not by one but by a group of firms and is dependent on the mutual interrelations of their behavior. In such situations, we can speak loosely of the market power of a particular firm in the market, but we must do so with the realization that this is shorthand for a situation in which market power is the collective attribute of a number of firms whose several actions have certain interrelations, and that, strictly speaking, one firm alone might not possess the power.

In the long run, the maintenance of market power, whether by a single firm or by a group, implies the existence of significant barriers to entry into the market by new sellers. Without such barriers, the attempt to exercise power would in general attract new sellers, whether the attempt took the form of maintaining high price-cost margins, either in general or for particular products, or of rationing output in periods of high demand without raising prices. But the converse proposition is not true; the existence of substantial barriers to entry in a particular market may not lead to the possession of market power by any of the sellers in it. The behavior of existing sellers may be such as to leave none with significant power. In most cases, it is also a condition of a firm's possession of market power that it be one of the major sellers in a structurally oligopolistic market—that it have a small number of important competitors and a relatively large share of its market, or else, of course, that it be a dominant firm. There are exceptions: markets of atomistic structure in which overt agreements and restrictive practices function effectively enough to limit competition persistently. But they are not frequent; typically, the successful cartel is in a small—rather than a large—numbers market. Oligopoly structure, like blockaded entry, is not a sufficient condition for the existence of market power, nor is a combination of the two. As we have already indicated, we cannot in general state sufficient conditions applicable to all markets.

(5) *Unreasonable market power*. Our primary policy goal is the limitation of market power, not its entire abolition. We recognize that it is impossible to reduce to zero the market power of firms in most markets: economies of scale limit the possible number of efficient sellers in many markets; the facts of geography and transport costs limit the size of many markets; advertising, other kinds of promotional effort, and consumer desires for product variety are real and permanent and thus product differentiation cannot be wished away; the advantages of established sellers over newcomers are persistent and often significant; and there are inevitable limitations on entrepreneurial knowledge, on entrepreneurial rationality, and on factor mobility which can lead to significant imperfections in particular markets. Our standard of limitation, then, must leave us content with some positive quantum of power in most markets. Let us call what we will accept a "reasonable degree of market power," and what we judge exceeds that, "unreasonable market power." We can then phrase our goal as the abolition of "unreasonable market power."

In defining unreasonable market power, we look to two different kinds of criteria: one of magnitude and one of source. We certainly wish to draw some lower limit to the degree of market power which is worth noticing; and we must recognize that some kinds of market power may not be avoidable, except at costs—say in efficiency—which we are not prepared to pay.

Any market power which is persistent we deem sufficiently great in magnitude to warrant notice. Persistent we define in terms of a period of at least a decade—long enough to reflect behavior over more than one cycle, not long enough so that underlying conditions of demand and technology will typically show radical changes. But since we have already defined market power so as to incorporate the notion of persistence, we can dispense with repetition, and say that any market power which is perceptible is of great enough magnitude to be worthy of notice.

Market power resting on certain bases we consider "reasonable," because we think it either undesirable or impossible to eliminate them. First, where economies of scale are such that only a very small number of efficient sellers can survive in a market, a substantial degree of market power in these sellers may be inevitable. It could be reduced only at the cost of producing at higher costs in inefficiently small units; this price we do not desire to pay. In small markets and geographically segmented markets, this limitation may be of considerable importance. Second, where market power rests solely on barriers to entry arising from the legal use of basic patents, it is likewise to be considered reasonable. The policy of the antitrust law must be accommodated with the policy of the patent law: this is a minimum accommodation. This exception is probably not of great quantitative importance. Typically, market power which involves patent barriers to entry rests on patent pooling, licensing arrangements, and other practices, and further barriers than those provided by patents alone. But some examples which would come under it can be found, for example, nylon during the life of the basic patents. We speak of basic patents because effective market power could not rest solely on patent protection of relatively minor features of technology; where no important technical improvements are involved, the market power must be supported by other means, and thus falls without the exception. Third, where market power rests on the introduction of new processes, products, or marketing techniques, it also falls within the exception of reasonableness. Again, although this is probably a quantitatively unimportant category of exceptions, examples can be found. One kind is the production of a superior product, not based on patented technology, which other firms simply fail to imitate. The skilled or fortunate producer may then achieve persistently high margins over costs which are not competed away by his rivals, and thus show market power as we have defined it. Perhaps *Life* or *Look* or the *Saturday Evening Post* exemplifies this in some degree in the field of weekly magazines. Of the three bases of market power which we consider reasonable, only the first—economies of scale such as permit only few efficient firms in the market—is likely to be of substantial quantitative importance in practice.

If we wish to eliminate unreasonable market power, we must in general move toward less concentrated markets in which there are more sellers with smaller shares. An increase in the number of competitors and a decrease in the relative market positions of the larger of them is usually a sufficient condition for the reduction of market power in any market. The maximum increase in numbers consistent with efficiency represents the practicable limit to the reduction of market power. But though an increase in numbers and a decrease in concentration is usually a sufficient condition for making markets more competitive, it is not generally a necessary one. In many markets, practices of one kind or another—price reporting arrangements, patent pools, exclusive dealing contracts, etc.,—are indispensable buttresses to the power of leading firms; without them, a sharp reduction in that power would take place over time. Even so, it is clear that a policy of eliminating unreasonable market power will involve a much more widespread use of dissolution and divestiture remedies than has been the case in the past. Up till now, these were measures of last resort, to be used only when no other remedy which promised any relief appeared practicable, and, even then, more often in the case of defendants whose offenses had been aggravated by predatory conduct or conspiracy. Under the proposed policy, programs for reducing the relative size of firms large in particular markets will occupy a preferred position, to be invoked, in general, unless other remedies promise to do a thorough job.

But this preferred status requires one important qualification: dissolution or divestitures are not to be carried out at any substantial cost in terms of economic performance. The first implication of this proviso is that the size of existing plants sets a lower limit to any dissolution proposal, even where they are bigger than the size needed to achieve minimum costs. The obvious costs involved in the division of any existing technical unit preclude such measures. Second, the plan of divestiture must contemplate the creation of viable firms with reasonable prospect for survival. Third, any absolute advantages of existing units must be taken into account in reorganizing market structures: the specific advantages that are peculiar to existing firms should not be cast away without consideration. In particular, though the progressiveness dimensions of performance play no part in evaluating the existence of market power or its reasonableness, no change in market structures which will significantly lower the level of performance in this respect should be made. Here again our interest in limiting market power is controlled by our interest in securing desirable economic performance. Considerations of fairness may further limit the scope of desirable reorganizations of market structure. Since the interests of customers, suppliers, and smaller competitors must be taken into account to some extent, at least the speed with which any going market arrangements can be changed will be limited.

The result of considering the costs of reducing market power as well as its reasonableness is to make possible, at least logically, a situation in which we condemn a firm as possessing unreasonable market power, and yet are unwilling to take measures to reduce it. In practice, again, this should not prove an important problem: partly because business practices are frequently important elements in noncompetitive market structures, and these can usually be changed without losses in performance; partly because, typically, the largest firms in the larger markets are multiplant firms well beyond the optimum firm size, and operating many optimum-sized plants.

Moreover, with respect both to claims that market power is "reasonable" in terms of defined exceptions, and to claims that structural reorganization would entail substantial performance losses, we would place the burden of proof on the defendants. In short, we would resolve doubts in favor of reducing market power rather than maintaining performance. One reason for this is a practical one: the relevant information is in defendants' hands or can be more readily obtained by them than by the government. The other reason is an unprovable but plausible judgment that reduction of market power is more likely to improve performance than to worsen it, an assumption we shall shortly examine more thoroughly.

* * *

## Power Versus Performance: How Much Conflict?

In our proposed standard of policy we have given primacy to the limitation of market power over the promotion of desirable economic performance. We limit the possible loss in performance that might be caused by its application in particular situations by subjecting reductions in market power to the proviso that they should sacrifice neither efficient scale nor progressiveness. However, our allocation of the burden of proof in justifying market power as reasonable or rejecting reorganization proposals as too costly is such as to resolve doubts in favor of reducing power, rather than in maintaining performance. Can we say how important the conflict between the two kinds of goals is in fact?

The limitation of market power may conflict with the achievement of desirable performance in two ways. Since the progressiveness dimension of performance is not taken directly into account either in defining unreasonable market power or in seeking to reduce it where it exists, there might be a direct conflict between reducing market power and achieving a high rate of technical progress. The efficiency dimensions of performance do enter directly into the definition of market power, and thus a similar direct conflict is not possible. Nonetheless, indirect conflict may be even more important. Efficiency and progressiveness both depend ultimately on vigorous entrepreneurship, which constantly seeks to better existing methods and push business to the utmost pitch of efficiency. Competitive market structures themselves will not produce the substance of competition if all entrepreneurs are slackly content with the quiet life and traditional ways:[3] Conceivably, a policy of reducing market power could have serious unfavorable repercussions on the motivations of entrepreneurs and, thus, indirectly on economic efficiency and progressiveness. We examine these two possibilities in turn, noting that in both cases we will be better furnished with speculation than with well-grounded empirical knowledge.

The idea that monopoly in some degree might be an important prerequisite of a high rate of progressiveness was first formulated by Schumpeter, for whom it was one aspect of his general theory of the "perennial gale of creative destruction" which was at the heart of the capitalist process. His central notion was that some degree of market power provided both the finance and the "breathing space" which made possible the risky investments in innovation, and also provided the rewards, the big prizes in the lottery, which were necessary to stimulate others to innovate. These ideas have been repeated—if not improved—in the recent literature of the "new competition." In general, it is not unfair to say that the writings cited contain more assertions than they do evidence, but together with other evidence they do provide some basis for the belief that there may be substantial economies of scale involved in the process of research, development, and promotion of new products and processes. These arise

3. The competitive model assumes away this problem, because it assumes perpetual striving after maximum profits. In actual markets, managerial ignorance and inertia are important sources of inefficiency. It is, of course, one of the virtues of a competitive market that it does not permit some entrepreneurs to be lazy: if some are vigorously pursuing profits, the rest will be forced to follow. "The greatest of all monopoly profits is a quiet life."

from several causes. First, uncertainty about the way in which the results of particular research endeavors will prove to be useful means that the firm which produces a wider rather than a narrower range of products will be able to profit from more of the results of its research efforts. Second, since research is a slow process with long-deferred yields, and a research organization must operate fairly steadily to be good, it cannot readily be expanded and contracted. This points to advantages for a firm large enough to be able to finance research at a reasonably steady level and with enough confidence in its own future to be willing to invest in slowly maturing projects. Third, the benefits of exchange of ideas and experience and of pooling men with different types of training and temperaments, given the necessary restrictions of commercial secrecy which keep such an exchange within the firm, point to some minimum size for an effective research unit. Fourth, equipment requirements in some kinds of research are heavy, and in themselves lead to need for substantial scale.

Further, it is clear, aside from these arguments, that the atomistic firm of the competitive swarm might have neither incentive nor ability to invest in research. Incentive would be lacking because of the high turnover of firms, which would make any individual firm loathe to spend on benefits which might come too late for it to reap and which, in many cases, may be quickly copied by all rivals without cost to them. Ability might be lacking simply because funds for speculative investments of this type might not readily be provided by outside investors, and the profits of the atomistic competitor would be too meager to do the job. In areas such as the chemical, oil, and electronic industries, for example, where large investments and current outlays are required for research, organized research might disappear under atomistic conditions.

But neither this argument, nor the probably correct conclusions on the existence of some economies of scale in research and development activities, is helpful in settling our problem. Since we are talking only in terms of business units at least as large as those necessary for efficient production and distribution, the problems of competitive atomism are irrelevant. In crude terms, our problem is to distinguish between the ability of the $500 million to $5 billion firms to contribute to a high rate of progress, and that of the $50 million to $500 million firms. Firms which are big enough to be technically and managerially efficient in most of the oligopolistic industries are big enough to fall outside the area of obvious disability in research and development; whether they are as efficient as their bigger brothers is not shown by presently available evidence.

On the other hand, competition is clearly a stimulus to innovation. It is precisely when old products made by old processes yield only meager returns that the economic stimulus to discover new products or cheaper processes is strongest. Thus reduction of market power may not impair the capacity for innovation, and it will certainly increase the incentive to it. Further, not all innovation is the fruit of large-scale organized research and development effort. Much of it takes place in industries where such activity is minimal, and flows from the work of the engineer, the skilled foreman, and the factory superintendent. Here the effects of competition on incentive may be far more important than the effects of high and secure profits in contributing to the finance of industrial research.

This discussion is necessarily inconclusive, since the fundamental information we require for an adequate discussion is lacking. But it hardly justifies the anticipation of a widespread and serious direct conflict between the reduction of market power and the maintenance of a high rate of progress, given the exceptions to the main direction of policy which are available whenever such conflict can be demonstrated.

Our second possible conflict is more serious. If energetic enforcement of a policy designed to limit market power produces a significant diminution of the vigor of entrepreneurship, the policy will not be worth while. After all, we wish to achieve our results without great costs in terms of desirable economic performance and if we cannot, we must abandon the proposed policy. The essential danger arises from the fact that an attack on market power that relies heavily on dissolution and divestiture is an attack on achieved growth, and may be viewed as a threat against further growth. In our economy, growth is the badge of entrepreneurial success, and the achievement of growth is an important stimulus to entrepreneurial effort. Any limitation of growth may thus have wide repercussions on the general efficiency of enterprise far beyond the firms directly affected by particular antitrust proceedings.

It is clear that the proposed policy will limit certain kinds of growth, and—as seen by those on the receiving end of the policy—it will penalize growth achieved in the past. Any firm which is large relative to some market in which it operates or any large firm which is growing substantially relative to some market in which it operates will certainly be open to scrutiny and perhaps to action under the antitrust law. Some firms will be dissolved or lose part of their holdings because they are large relative to the markets in which they operate. While the policy involves no limitations on the absolute size of firms, as distinguished from their relative size in particular markets, it will close certain routes of growth—such as merger—to firms that are already very large.

Other kinds of growth possibilities will remain open, however. A firm which grows in absolute size by diversification purely through internal growth without mergers, and does so without becoming large relative to any market, will not come within the scope of the ban on unreasonable market power. But typically, the large firm today, though diversified, is fairly heavily concentrated in a few markets in which it does occupy a relatively large position. At the very least, therefore, our proposal will require some shift in past growth patterns if continued growth is to be attained. Further, by increasing the degree of competition, it will tend to make growth somewhat more difficult. In general, the most important limitation on the size of firms is the limitation on their growth imposed by the "crowding" of other firms competing for customers. The stronger the competition, the more stringent the limitations on growth, especially on growth at a rate faster than the growth of total demand. Despite this, however, we are not inclined to consider as probable the danger that a significant decline in entrepreneurial vigor will be the consequence of our policy proposal. Our view rests in part on what we consider relevant, though indirect, evidence from recent economic history, in part on more speculative grounds. The New Deal and Fair Deal, apart from their verbal thrusts at the power and prestige of "big business," imposed many substantial limitations on the freedom of business decision, especially in labor relations and financial policy. The verbal reaction was pained and eloquent. But there is no convincing evidence that the vigor of business effort was in any way impaired. Recovery from the depression may have been slow, but there is little indication that a more sympathetic administration would have revived business any faster.

[Note: In the omitted portion, authors discuss relevant impact of taxation policies.]

The motivations which conduce to effective entrepreneurship and management are apparently built deep into American society. They do not operate merely at the level of visible economic rewards, or even at the level of current symbols of business achievement in terms of size and growth. Rather they stem from the whole structure of American society—its emphasis on occupational achievement, its drive toward universal egalitarianism, its great geographical and occupational mobility, the relative unimportance of family ties. Radical changes in fundamental aspects of the social structure would be prerequisite to a significant change in the efforts of American businessmen toward effective management and entrepreneurship. That the scope of our own policy proposals is more modest need hardly be said.

All in all, we consider it unlikely that the negative effects of the proposed policy on good economic performance will reach significantly beyond the specific firms that are brought within its reach. When its impact on them in this respect promises to be serious, it would be taken into account.

## The Regulation of Conduct

Our program of limiting market power would require some regulation of business conduct as well as the reshaping of situations of market power. Regulation of business conduct would be of two kinds: that which rests basically on market power criteria and that which rests basically on criteria of fairness.

Our goal dictates the regulation of business conduct which may lead to an increase in market power, or contribute to its maintenance, where it has in fact produced that effect or where it has a strong probability of so doing. In other words, we would, as under present law, seek to control actual or incipient restraints on competition. Some kinds of conduct are two-sided in that they have important business justifications other than their potentially restrictive effects, and their potentially restrictive effects vary with the market context in which they occur. Regulation of such conduct requires fairly complete investigation of the market situation in which it occurs, though it may not be necessary to have as complete an investigation as is required for a proposal aimed at reorganizing market structure. Conduct which falls into this category includes mergers, requirements contracts, exclusive dealing arrangements, and patent licensing and pooling arrangements. Another class of conduct comprises practices whose sole or major aim is restraint of competition, and which are probably harmful whatever the market context in which they appear. Such practices can be regulated by per se rules without the necessity for an examination of their actual effects in particular circumstances.

Typically, neither the direct attack on market power nor the control of business conduct on market power criteria will reduce market power to zero. Indeed, in many markets the economic limitations on reorganization which we mentioned will result in the persistence of significant degrees of power in some firms. Thus some scope will remain for the regulation of the exercise of residual power in terms of fairness. The nonoppressive use of power in business transactions, as they are viewed by the weaker participants in them, is the substantive aim of policy in such situations. One class of examples arises where buyers or sellers in national markets deal with sellers or buyers in narrower regional or local markets. The power of any particular buyer, let us say, in the national market may be small, or it may be reduced to the minimum. Yet, in regard to the transactions with a particular local, market supplier, the national buyer may possess great bargaining power. This reflects essentially the imperfection of the market and the immobility of the local supplier. The bargaining power of the buyer is measured by the costs to the seller of getting in touch with other customers whom he has never served, or otherwise spending resources to dispose of his output through different channels, as well as the risk that he may fail to sell as much in this way as he has sold to his big customer in the past. Ultimately, the buyer can pay the seller as little as he is willing to take and still remain in business as a supplier. From an economic point of view, the full exploitation of the seller by the buyer, through payment of the lowest possible price at which he will continue to serve, represents an appropriation by the more powerful firm of rents which might otherwise accrue to the less powerful one. This appropriation is possible with little or no impact on efficiency or on market structure because of the imperfections of the market and the immobility of the entrepreneur in the local firm. The prevention of such exploitation is thus not an aspect of promoting the competitive process but rather an end in itself, given the inevitable limitations on factor mobility and information in nearly every market, no matter how competitive.

Another class of examples to which the same observations apply is furnished by situations in which large firms operate as partial suppliers of capital to small firms which are their customers, through leasing expensive capital equipment or sites to them, as in the case of relations between gasoline refiners and service stations. The prevalence of capital rationing, and the risks involved in cutting loose from existing sources of capital, tie particular customers closely to their supplier in a way which creates much opportunity for exploitation. This opportunity is relatively invariant, within wide margins, with varying degrees of competition in the supplying market.

Possibilities of this sort provide an important rationale for statutes like the Robinson-Patman Act, independently of the effects of the practices it forbids on competition. To be sure, in concrete cases it is not always possible to draw a firm line between what is done on grounds of fairness and what is done on grounds of preventing the incipient development of market power. Some practices are both unfair and contributory to the growth of market power. Analytically, however, the separation is worth making.

## How Significant Would the Changes Be?

The standard of unreasonable market power we have defined is in terms a standard of business situation rather than of business conduct. In this respect, it differs from what has traditionally been a major element in the policy of the antitrust laws throughout their history—the element of intent or fault.[4] The Sherman Act is a criminal statute, and it is to be expected that it should ban some kind of conduct which conceivably the offender could have eschewed. It is hardly in the spirit of our legal tradition to apply criminal sanctions to some one because of a situation in which he finds himself willy-nilly. In form then, the change we propose is a serious one, and indeed we would abandon criminal sanctions as a method of enforcing it. Is the change equally serious in substance? In light of the exceptions which we allow as for "reasonable" market power, it might appear that we exempt those who find market power innocently thrust upon them and hence are merely saying the same thing the law now says but in different words. We believe the proposal would be more than that.

Application of our proposed policy, with the reduction of market power as a central goal, would result in four significant changes in the present policy of the law. First, the direct regulation of conduct would be guided by the goal of limiting market power; practices would be viewed primarily, though not entirely, in terms of their effect in creating or maintaining market power. This would result in a shift of attention by the agencies of enforcement from the history of individual commercial transactions, viewed as evidence of illegal intent, to a stronger focus on the economic functioning of the market, the role of particular firms in it, and the possibilities of improving its function. Such a shift would contribute to a more rational selection of cases for action by enforcement agencies, and a more meaningful trial of issues in the adjudication process.

Second, the relation between judgments on market power and evaluations of market performance in the administration of the law would be defined in entirely different terms than it now is. As our quick survey in Chapter I of the important recent cases shows, it is difficult to state in any specific way the relative importance now attached to judgments on structure and judgments on performance. The cases point to a situation in which the original trier of fact will have considerable latitude in assigning weights to these two sorts of judgments, both in respect to finding liability and prescribing remedies. In the nature of the situation, there can be little reliance on precedent to guide the trier within the scope of his discretion. Defendants will always press a performance standard; our previous discussion indicates the difficulties the trier will have in assessing their claims. Thus the present pattern of decisions points to a considerable variation in the standards of decision from case to case, whenever something more than conspiracy in the crude sense and conduct traditionally deemed predatory are involved—in other words, in the typical big case involving counts under

4. See, for example, the definition of monopolization given in the *Report of the Attorney General's National Committee Study of the Anti-Trust Laws* (1955), pp. 43–56, especially p. 55, where monopolization is described as monopoly power plus an element of deliberateness.

both Section 1 and Section 2 of the Sherman Act. Such variation can be avoided either by rejecting the new elements which have entered into the administration of the antitrust law and returning to earlier standards in which conduct and intent were central, or by pressing on to define the ways in which finding market power and evaluations of market performance should enter into determinations in antitrust law. Our proposal goes in the latter direction.

Third, certain kinds of noncompetitive oligopoly situations now lie without the reach of the law. Where a very small number of rival sellers sell somewhat different products, or highly specialized and complex products, so that price identity is difficult to define, and their noncompetitive conduct manifests itself in no overt market division scheme, pricing formula, or the like, their conduct probably is not subject to the present law.

On a standard of intent, or deliberateness, it is difficult to find such conduct illegal, consistently with the usual meaning of the terms intent and deliberate. To be sure, intent can be read to mean that any firm with market power intends to have it and use it, and therefore any firm with market power violates Section 2 of the Sherman Act. But this is a strained construction, and projection of the rationale of cases like *Alcoa* and *Tobacco* to sustain it appears unwarranted. Our standard would cover situations of this kind.

Fourth, remedy proposals involving structural reorganization of firms—dissolution, divestiture, and divorcement—would occupy a much larger place in antitrust policy than they do now. There would be many situations in which the maintenance of market power depended heavily on patterns of conduct, and thus market power could be limited without reorganizing firms. But in many situations of tight oligopoly, significant reduction of the power of the dominant firms demands an increase in numbers and decrease in concentration. In such cases, and in the case of dominant firms, the presumption would be in favor of reorganization remedies.

* * *

## Phil C. Neal, William F. Baxter, Robert H. Bork, Carl H. Fulda, William K. Jones, Dennis G. Lyons, Paul W. MacAvoy, James W. McKie, Lee E. Preston, Richard E. Sherwood, and S. Paul Posner

## *The Neal Report (1967)*

[Note: Report of the White House Task Force on Antitrust Policy, *2 Antitrust Law and Economics Review* 11 (1968–69). In December 1967, President Johnson appointed a Task Force on Antitrust Policy and asked it to complete its report and recommendations by June 30, 1968. The task force consisted of three practicing lawyers, three economists, five professors of law, and the chairman, Phil

C. Neal, dean of the Law School, University of Chicago. Initially a "secret" task force, the group's Report to the President of July 5, 1968, was not released until early 1969.]

Five major recommendations are made by the Task Force, four of them calling for either new legislation or a substantial overhaul of existing laws.

**1. Concentrated Industries Act.** The Task Force recommended the enactment of a new statute entitled the "Concentrated Industries Act," one under which the Attorney General would be directed to affirmatively search out all "oligopoly industries" in the United States (defined as industries having sales of $500 million or more and in which the four largest firms have held 70 percent or more of the market for a prescribed number of years) and bring legal proceedings against all "oligopoly firms" in those industries (defined as those having 15 percent or more of the market in question) aimed at achieving, "within a reasonable period of time not in excess of four years, a reduction of concentration such that the market share of each oligopoly firm in such oligopoly industry does not exceed 12 percent." The statutory objective, in short, is to "reduce the four-firm concentration ratio below 50 percent and the market shares of individual firms below 12 percent." Limitations on advertising expenditures and other such forms of supplementary relief would also be available. (The full text of this proposed statute, including the explanatory Comments on it provided by the Task Force, is set forth in Appendix A, below, page 65.)

A special procedure is recommended, one in which these divestiture cases would be brought not in the regular federal district courts but before a "Special Antitrust Court" composed of judges selected specifically for the assignment by the Chief Justice of the Supreme Court. Special provision is also made for the designation of "one or more economists or other persons to serve as expert witnesses to be called by the court."

Priorities are to be established: "Since the Attorney General and the FTC do not have unlimited resources at their disposal, they would necessarily have discretion in establishing priorities. In exercising this discretion, it is assumed that they would first investigate those industries which are of most fundamental importance in the economy and in which concentrated market structure, not dictated by economies of scale, has had the most pronounced effect in producing market behavior at variance with competitive norms."

Several limitations are provided. For example, a decree could not "require a firm to take steps which would result in substantial loss of economies of scale," i.e., the statute would "preclude divestiture reducing a firm below minimum efficient size or creating new entities below minimum efficient size." In short, "the court would not ordinarily divide an oligopoly firm into firms smaller than that indicated by experience to be necessary for survival in the industry." The burden of proof on this issue is on the firm.

**2. Merger Act.** The Task Force also proposes a new "Merger Act," one that would prohibit any "large firm" from acquiring or merging with any "leading firm," these two terms being defined, respectively, as (a) a firm with assets of $250 million or sales of $500 million, and (b) a firm with 10 percent or more (and among the four largest firms) of a relevant market with sales of $100 million or more in which the four largest have 50 percent or more of its total sales, "Since the [Merger] Act prevents future acquisitions, unlike the Concentration Act, which undoes existing concentration, a four firm concentration ratio was picked which was at the lower end of the spectrum in which concentration leads to market performance departing from the competitive norm."

**3. Revision of the Robinson-Patman Price Discrimination Law.** The Task Force recommends a major revision of the existing price discrimination statute, the Robinson-Patman Act, a revision based on the group's conclusion that, while it "is possible for price discrimination to adversely affect competition," in practice "such instances are exceptional." In the view of the Task Force, "most" price discrimination is affirmatively beneficial to competition and should therefore be encouraged. The revised statute recommended by the group would prohibit only those instances of price discrimination that satisfy a number of stated criteria, these centering around such factors as (a) the duration of the discriminatory pricing, (b) the depth or magnitude of it, (c) the breadth of it, and (d) its effects in terms of whether it tends to eliminate competitive entities whose existence is essential to the maintenance of effective competition in the relevant market.

**4. Patent Legislation.** The Task Force recommends a new patent law, one that would require (a) a filing of all patent licenses, (b) diligent enforcement, and (c) nondiscriminatory licensing of all comers requesting it once any licenses have been granted, i.e., a prohibition of "exclusive" licensing. This latter requirement "is intended to minimize the possibility that license agreements can confer a share of patent monopoly profits on licensees. In general, such an arrangement suggests that the patent is either legally vulnerable or not economically valuable. In such cases, patent licenses can serve to neutralize those who are most likely to launch a successful attack on the patent, and they may serve as a pretext for cartelization."

**5. Availability of Economic Data.** The Task Force recommends the formation of a standing Committee to develop techniques and procedures for improving the collection and dissemination of economic data by the Census Bureau and other government organizations, with special emphasis on more refined definitions of "markets" and on profit figures (reported by corporate divisions and product lines) and other data having special "antitrust significance."

The full text of the Report is set forth below, including the separate statements of three of its individual members and the text and comments of the group on its proposed "Concentrated Industries Act." (The text and notes on the other proposed statutes, while too lengthy for presentation here, are available from the Government Printing Office, Washington.)

# Summary

## Oligopoly Legislation

### Importance of Industry "Structure"

1. *We recommend specific legislation on the subject of oligopolies, or highly concentrated industries.*

The purpose of such legislation would be to give enforcement authorities and courts a clear mandate to use established techniques of divestiture to reduce concentration in industries where monopoly power is shared by a few very large firms. Up to now such measures have been employed only in the rare instances where the monopolistic structure of an industry takes the form of a single firm with an overwhelming share of the market. Specific legislation dealing with entrenched oligopolies would rectify the most important deficiency in the present antitrust laws.

Effective antitrust laws must bring about both competitive behavior and competitive industry structure. In the long run, competitive structure is the more important since it creates conditions conducive to competitive behavior. Competitive structure and behavior are both essential to the basic concern of the antitrust laws—preservation of the self-regulating mechanism of the market, free from the restraints of private monopoly power on the one hand and government intervention or regulation on the other. In one important respect, the antitrust laws recognize the necessity for competitive market structures: the 1950 amendment to section 7 of the Clayton Act has effectively prevented many kinds of mergers which would bring about less competitive market structures. Our proposed remedy, which would deal with existing noncompetitive market structures, is a necessary complement to section 7.

### Size of the Oligopoly Sector

Highly concentrated industries represent a significant segment of the American economy. Industries in which four or fewer firms account for more than 70 percent of output produce nearly 10 percent of the total value of manufactured products; industries in which four or fewer firms account for more than 50 percent of output produce nearly 24 percent. An impressive body of economic opinion and analysis supports the judgment that this degree of concentration precludes effective market competition and interferes with the optimum use of economic resources. Past experience strongly suggests that, in the absence of direct action, concentration is not likely to decline significantly.

While new legal approaches might be developed to reduce concentration under existing law—a result which should be encouraged—the history of antitrust enforcement and judicial interpretation do not justify primary reliance on this possibility. For this reason, we recommend a specific legislative remedy directed to the reduction of concentration. Our proposed Concentrated Industries Act, which appears in Appendix A to the Report, establishes criteria and procedures for the effective reduction of industrial concentration.

## Merger Legislation

### "Leading Firm" Role

2. *We recommend additional legislation prohibiting mergers in which a very large firm acquires one of the leading firms in a concentrated industry.*

This legislation would supplement section 7 of the Clayton Act, which prohibits mergers which may tend substantially to lessen competition. The primary impact of the new legislation would be on diversification or "conglomerate" mergers. Under section 7 of the Clayton Act, such mergers may be prevented if adverse effects on competition can be anticipated. But the detection of such effects frequently depends on factual and theoretical judgments that are highly speculative. As a result, some mergers with potentially adverse effects on competition may escape attack and mergers which will not harm competition will be prohibited because the effects cannot readily be predicted. Because of the inherent limitations of the competitive standard of section 7, the recently published Merger Guidelines [of the Justice Department] do little to resolve these difficulties.

### Deflecting Mergers into Desirable Channels

Our proposed legislation would prevent some possibly anticompetitive mergers which might have gone unchallenged because of the difficulty of applying section 7 standards, and thus would act as an effective supplement to existing policy. In addition, the proposed legislation would have affirmative aspects in channeling merger activity into directions likely to increase competition. If large firms are prevented from acquiring leading firms in concentrated industries, they will seek other outlets for expansion which may be more likely to increase competition and decrease concentration.

This policy of deflecting conglomerate mergers into desirable channels is preferable to any rule that would limit mergers without regard to considerations of market structure. Although the number of conglomerate mergers has increased sharply in recent years, there is only a moderate tendency toward increase in the overall concentration of manufacturing assets in American industry. Nor does the present merger movement threaten to reduce the aggregate number and proportion of smaller firms. Remedial measures based on size alone would constitute a radical innovation in our antitrust policy and no rationale is available for determining the appropriate upper limit on the size to which a single firm may grow.

We therefore believe that restrictions on mergers should continue to be based on considerations related to competitive market structure. The policy we recommend would permit the continued growth of firms by diversification as well as by internal expansion but would, we believe, promote the development of more competitive market structures.

A draft of the Merger Act, implementing our recommendation, appears in Appendix B to the Report. [Not reproduced in this volume—eds.]

# Price Discrimination Legislation

## Anticompetitive Effects of Present Law

3. *We recommend a thorough revision of the Robinson-Patman Act to remove features that unduly restrict the free play of competitive forces.*

It has long been recognized that many aspects of the Robinson-Patman Act in its present form have serious anticompetitive effects. The course of enforcement and interpretation of the Act have in many instances aggravated those effects. In addition, the ambiguities and complexities of the statute as written have posed unusual difficulties of compliance. Experience with the Act and the extensive criticism to which it has been subjected provide the basis for a general revision that will make it consistent with the major aims of antitrust policy. In our view such a revision is long overdue.

## Goal of Price Discrimination Law

The central purpose of the Robinson-Patman Act is to eliminate price discrimination that unduly favors national over local sellers or confers unjustified advantages on large purchasers merely because of their size. But not all price differentials represent discrimination and not all discrimination is undesirable. Some price discrimination does have anticompetitive effects, but in other cases price discrimination improves the functioning of the competitive system. A statute designed to restrict price discrimination should therefore be narrowly drawn, so that the important benefits of competition as evidenced in price differentials will not be lost in an excessive effort to curb limited instances of harm. Our proposed revision is intended to leave room for price behavior which is related to the improved functioning of the competitive system.

The Robinson-Patman Act contains several prohibitions supplementing the price-discrimination prohibition. These prohibitions should be repealed. They accomplish little that could not be accomplished by a properly drawn price-discrimination prohibition. In their present form, they often impair competition; they discourage legitimate transactions; and they promote irrational distinctions.

A proposed revision of the price-discrimination provisions of the Robinson-Patman Act appears in Appendix C to the Report. [Not reproduced in this volume—eds.]

# Patent Legislation

## Nondiscriminatory Licensing

4. *We recommend legislation to establish the principle that a patent which has been licensed to one person shall be made available to all other qualified applicants on equivalent terms.*

Patents are one of the principal sources of monopoly power, since they confer upon the patentee the right to exclude others from the field covered by the patent. An important goal of antitrust policy is to prevent the use of a patent by the patentee in collaboration with others to create a monopoly broader than the patent itself. That goal will be served by denying the patentee the right to confine use of the patent to a preferred group and requiring that if the patent is licensed it shall be open to competition in its application. Such a principle does not prevent the owner of a valid patent from fully exploiting the monopoly conferred by the patent. Our proposal does not fix or limit the royalty to be charged by the patentee, nor does it involve compulsory licensing. It merely requires that if the patentee chooses to license others rather than exploiting the patent himself he shall make such licenses available on nondiscriminatory terms to as many competitors as may desire it.

### Public Filing—Nondiscriminatory Enforcement

Supplementary provisions in our proposal would require the public filing of all patent license agreements and would bar enforcement of a patent against particular infringers if the patent owner has not taken reasonable steps to enforce the patent against others.

We believe that each of these measures has some independent value in deterring misuse of patents and that they could be adopted independently of the requirement of nonexclusive licensing.

## Economic and Financial Data Gathering

### New Standing Committee

5. *We recommend that steps be taken to improve the quality and availability of economic and financial data relevant to the formulation of antitrust policy, the enforcement of the antitrust laws, and the operation of competitive markets.*

Specifically, we recommend formation of a standing committee of representatives of the Census Bureau and other Government agencies which gather or use economic information to consider (1) improving the gathering and presentation of economic information within the statutory limits on disclosure of information on individual firms; (2) new interpretations of existing law or, eventually, new legislation to minimize restrictions on disclosure of types of information which are not highly sensitive from the point of view of individual firms but are of great value in the formulation of policy and the application of law; and (3) machinery for developing information on the competitive structure of relevant economic markets, because such markets do not necessarily coincide with Census industry and product classifications. These recommendations could be implemented immediately, without new legislation or appropriations.

### Financial Reporting

In addition, the role of financial information in the operation of competitive markets should be reflected in the formulation of financial reporting requirements by the Securities and Exchange Commission. These requirements are now imposed pursuant to the Securities Exchange Act of 1934, which is oriented to investor protection. We recommend that the Act be amended to recognize the role of financial information in the operation of a competitive economy, and to require that the SEC consult with antitrust enforcement agencies in formulating reporting requirements.

Pending adoption of this recommendation, the antitrust enforcement agencies should be requested to consider submitting recommendations to the SEC in connection with the current divisional reporting inquiry.

### Additional Recommendations

*6. We have a number of additional recommendations for further action or further study.*

These include advance notification of mergers and a reasonable statute of limitations on lawsuits attacking mergers; a limit on the duration of antitrust decrees; an examination of the effects of the income tax laws on merger activity and market concentration; a review of the extent to which competition may be substituted for regulation in the regulated industries; and the abolition of resale price maintenance.

# I. Introduction

## Role of Competition

### Consumer Welfare—Economic Freedom

The antitrust laws reflect our Nation's strong commitment to economic freedom and the material benefits that flow from this freedom. The antitrust laws are based on the recognition that optimum use of economic resources and maximum choice and utility for consumers can best be obtained under competition. Moreover, they assume that the preservation of a large number and variety of decision-making units in the economy is important to ensure innovation, experimentation and continuous adaptation to new conditions. While consumer welfare is thus in the forefront of antitrust policy, important corollary values support the policy. Not only consumers, but those who control the factors of production—labor, capital and entrepreneurial ability—benefit when resources are permitted to move into the fields of greatest economic return; competition induces such movement and monopoly inhibits it. Antitrust policy also reflects a preference for private decision-making; a major value of competition is that it minimizes the necessity for direct Government intervention in the operation of business, whether by comprehensive regulation of the public utility type or by informal and sporadic interference such as price guidelines and other ad hoc measures.

The function of the antitrust laws in the pursuit of these goals is twofold: they are concerned both with preventing anticompetitive behavior and with preserving and promoting competitive market structures. Our Task Force has understood its assignment to be to examine the antitrust laws in broad perspective and consider ways in which they might be made more effective in this dual role.

### Behavioral Problems

In relation to the principal kinds of anticompetitive behavior, such as price-fixing, market division and other forms of collusive action among independent firms, we believe the present laws are generally adequate. Their effectiveness depends principally upon vigilance to provide sufficient enforcement resources and the vigorous use of enforcement power. We have identified three areas, however, in which modification of present laws would assist the effort to maximize competitive behavior. First, it is important to ensure that laws aimed at preserving competition do not themselves unduly restrict the free play of market forces. The Robinson-Patman Act in its present form has such effects and we recommend its revision to eliminate its anticompetitive tendencies. Second, patents are susceptible of being used to facilitate collusive arrangements in ways difficult to disentangle from legitimate exploitation of the patent monopoly. We recommend certain restrictions on patent licensing that are designed to discourage such use. Third, we share the view that the provisions of law permitting resale price maintenance encourage anticompetitive practices and we favor the repeal of these provisions.

## Role of Market "Structure"

Our consideration of the present state of the antitrust laws focuses to a considerable extent on problems of market structure. The principal laws presently concerned with competitive market structure are section 7 of the Clayton Act, dealing with mergers, and section 2 of the Sherman Act, which is addressed to cases of monopoly. We believe these laws can he made more effective by certain additional legislation on mergers and on oligopoly industries.

### Relationship Between Concentration and Price

Market structure is an important concern of antitrust law for two reasons. First, the more competitive a market structure (the larger the number of competitors and the smaller their market shares) the greater the difficulty of maintaining collusive behavior and the more easily such behavior can be detected. Second, in markets with a very few firms effects equivalent to those of collusion may occur even in the absence of collusion. In a market with numerous firms, each having a small share, no single firm by its action alone can exert a significant influence over price and thus output will be carried to the point where each seller's marginal cost equals the market price. This level of output is optimal from the point of view of the economy as a whole.

### Oligopolistic Restriction of Output—Raising of Prices

Under conditions of monopoly—with only a single seller in a market—the monopolist can increase his profits by restricting output and thus raising his price; accordingly, prices will tend to be above, and output correspondingly below, the optimum point. In an oligopoly market—one in which there is a small number of dominant sellers, each with a large market share—each must consider the effect of his output on the total market and the probable reactions of the other sellers to his decisions; the results of their combined decisions may approximate the profit-maximizing decisions of a monopolist. Not only does the small number of sellers facilitate agreement, but agreement in the ordinary sense may be unnecessary. Thus, phrases such as "price leadership" or "administered pricing" often do no more than describe behavior which is the inevitable result of structure. Under such conditions, it does not suffice for antitrust law to attempt to reach anticompetitive behavior; it cannot order the several firms to ignore each other's existence. The alternatives, other than accepting the undesirable economic consequences, are either regulation of price (and other decisions) or improving the competitive structure of the market.

We believe that the goals of antitrust policy require a choice wherever possible in favor of attempting to perfect the self-regulating mechanism of the market before turning to public control. It is for this reason that we favor steps that will increase the effectiveness of the antitrust laws in promoting competitive market structure. Such steps are desirable, not only because the problem of concentrated industries is significant in economic terms, but because the existence of such concentration is a continuing (and perhaps increasing) temptation for political intervention. In a special sense, therefore, our recommendations have preventive as well as corrective purposes.

### Alternative Approaches—"Intent" and "Performance" Factors

In devising antitrust measures for such purposes, alternative techniques or approaches may be considered. Under one approach, general standards expressed in terms of broad policy goals require the trier of fact to make ad hoc judgments as to the relevant scope of inquiry in any case. The general effect of such an approach is to require consideration of a wide range of complex and difficult issues, some of them of marginal significance. Such issues may include economic issues which are beyond our present capacity to gather and evaluate economic information; they may include issues such as motive and intent, which are both elusive and of marginal relevance to the central issue of market structure; and they may include an indirect measurement of competitive behavior or structure through an evaluation of performance, an approach requiring judgments more appropriate to regulation than to antitrust policy. Such an approach generally expands the scope and complexity of lawsuits and makes decisions less useful as precedents.

The other approach uses rules which are based on easily ascertainable criteria and avoids individualized consideration of complex factors which would be unlikely to affect the outcome. This approach simplifies litigation. More importantly, it provides businessmen and law enforcement officials with a better idea of what will be lawful and what will be unlawful.

The judgment of members of the Task Force is that it is virtually impossible to gather all the data relevant to any particular case, and even the best of judges could not properly take account of all such data. Therefore, we believe that carefully drawn rules yield results superior to highly general admonitions to weigh all relevant factors. Accordingly, our proposals generally rely on fairly closely articulated rules. They are drafted to reflect general economic experience and theory, and they make allowance for factors which may be significant in individual cases. But they do not call for proof of an exactness beyond the present limits of economic knowledge. Of necessity, they are predicated not on rigorously proven theorems, but on a consensus of informed economic judgment which admittedly fragmentary economic knowledge tends to confirm.

## II. Oligopoly or Concentration in Particular Markets

### Costs of Monopoly

#### Reduced Output—Higher Prices—Less Innovation

The evils of monopoly are well known and the antitrust policy of the United States has sought from its beginning to provide safeguards against them. But those evils are not confined to situations conforming to the literal meaning of monopoly, i.e., an industry with but a single firm. In the years since the Sherman Act was adopted there has been growing recognition that monopoly is a matter of degree. A firm with less than 100 percent of the output of an industry may nevertheless have significant control over supply, and thus be in a position to impose on the economy the losses associated with monopoly: lower output, higher prices, artificial restraints on the movement of resources in the economy, and reduced pressure toward cost reduction and innovation. Likewise, a small number of firms dominating an industry may take a similar toll, either because the small number makes it easier to arrive at and police an agreement or because, without agreement, each will adopt patterns of behavior recognizing the common interest.

#### Competition and the Number of Firms

In general it may be said that the smaller the number of firms in an industry—at least where that number is very small or where a very small number is responsible for the overwhelming share of the industry's output—the greater the likelihood that the behavior of the industry will depart from the competitive norm.

These propositions have found general acceptance in economic literature in the past 25 or 30 years. They have also found recognition in the policy of the antitrust laws: a major aim of section 7 of the Clayton Act, as amended in 1950 and as interpreted by judicial decisions, and the new Merger Guidelines, is not merely to prevent monopolies but also to prevent all combinations of business firms that significantly increase market concentration or reduce the number of firms in an industry.

### The Monopoly Case Law

#### "Mere Possession of Economic Power"

Interpretation of the Sherman Act itself, however, has lagged behind these developments. Early cases involving giant firms emphasized the purposes and methods by which a firm was created as the basis of illegality, and looked for evidence of predatory or abusive exercise of power rather than the power of a firm or group of firms to control prices and output. Decisions affecting market concentration were confined to instances, such as the old *Standard Oil* and *American Tobacco* cases, where a single firm commanding nearly the entire market had been assembled by mergers of many previous competitors. Even such major combinations as United States Steel Corporation, United Shoe Machinery Company, and the International Harvester Company escaped condemnation by the Supreme Court. An important advance was registered when Judge Learned Hand announced in the *Alcoa* case that a single firm, not resulting from a merger, might be guilty of "monopolizing" merely by acquiring a sufficiently large market share and retaining its market share over a substantial period of time, if that market share was not the inevitable result of economic forces. That holding adopted and extended Judge Hand's early insight, in the *Corn Products* case of 1916, that "it is the mere possession of economic power, acquired by some form of combination, and capable, by its own variation in production, of changing and controlling price, that is illegal." The *United Shoe Machinery* decision of 1953 applied and reinforced the new doctrine represented by the *Alcoa* case. In both of those cases, however, the monopoly section of the Sherman Act was invoked against a single firm with a predominant share of the market. While Judge Hand had intimated that a share as low as 65 percent might suffice, no subsequent case has tested that proposition or explored the limits of the *Alcoa* doctrine. Nor has any case yet provided a basis for treating as illegal the shared monopoly power of several firms that together possess a predominant share of the market, absent proof of conspiracy among them.

### Gap in the Present Law

Thus a gap in the law remains.[1] While section 7 of the Clayton Act provides strong protection against the growth of new concentrations of market power in most instances, existing law is inadequate to cope with old ones.

## The "Oligopolized" Sector

### 24 Percent of American Manufacturing

This gap is of major significance. Highly concentrated industries account for a large share of manufacturing activity in the United States. The accompanying table shows the percentage of manufacturing shipments and of value added by manufacturing accounted for by four-digit industry groups and five-digit product classes in which the aggregate market share of the four firms with the largest market shares (the "four-firm concentration ratio") equalled or exceeded selected levels. These figures are based on 1963 Census figures, and on Census industry and product classifications. Census classifications do not necessarily reflect relevant markets; in general, the four-digit classifications are probably broader and the five-digit classifications are probably narrower

1. This gap has been recognized by noted authorities. See, e.g., Kaysen and Turner, *Antitrust Policy: An Economic and Legal Analysis* (1959), at 44; Stigler, "The Case Against Big Business," *Fortune* (May 1952), reprinted in Mansfield (ed.), *Monopoly Power and Economic Performance*, (1964), at 3; *cf.* Galbraith, *The New Industrial State* (1967).

| | Four-Digit Industries | | Five-Digit Product Classes |
|---|---|---|---|
| **Four-Firm Concentration Ratio Equal to or Greater Than** | **Percent of Total Manufacturing Shipments** | **Percent of Total Value Added by Manufacturing** | **Percent of Total Manufacturing Shipments** |
| 90% | 1.56 | 2.33 | 5.69 |
| 80% | 2.95 | 3.59 | 10.53 |
| 70% | 9.35 | 14.53 | 15.85 |
| 60% | 13.47 | 19.98 | 22.55 |
| 50% | 23.88 | 33.41 | 31.32 |

*Source:* Computed from *Concentration Ratios in Manufacturing Industry* (1963), Tables 2, 3 and 4.

than relevant product markets, so that, if only national markets are considered, figures for concentration with which we are concerned probably fall somewhere in between the two sets of figures shown in the table. If regional instead of national markets were considered, concentration figures would probably be considerably higher in many industries.

Percent of Manufacturing Shipments and Value Added by Manufacturing in 1963.

The highly concentrated industries reflected in this table include such major and basic industries as motor vehicles, flat glass, synthetic fibres, aircraft, organic chemicals, soap and detergents, and many others, as well as a host of smaller but nevertheless significant industries.

### No "Erosion" of Concentration over Time

If competitive pressures could be relied on to erode concentration in the reasonably foreseeable future, the direct reduction of concentration would be less urgent. But concentration does not appear to erode over time; rather, the evidence indicates that it is remarkably stable. In those industries with value of shipments greater than $100 million and four-firm concentration ratios by value of shipments greater than 65 percent in 1963, average concentration ratios were stable or declined insignificantly—by less than half a percentage point. Even though section 7 of the Clayton Act has generally been effective in forestalling increases in concentration through mergers and by other means, the antitrust laws and economic forces have not brought about significant erosion of existing concentration. The problem is not one which will disappear with time.

## Costs of Tight Oligopoly

### Excess Profits—Restricted Output

The adverse effects of persistent concentration on output and price find some confirmation in various studies that have been made of return on capital in major industries. These studies have found a close association between high levels of concentration and persistently high rates of return on capital, particularly in those industries in which the largest four firms account for more than 60 percent of sales. High profit rates in individual firms or even in particular industries are of course consistent with competition. They may reflect innovation, exceptional efficiency, or growth in demand outrunning the expansion of supply. Above-average profits in a particular industry signal the need and provide the incentive for additional resources and expanded output in the industry, which in due time should return profits to a normal level. It is the persistence of high profits over extended time periods and over whole industries rather than in individual firms that suggests artificial restraints on output and the absence of fully effective competition. The correlation of evidence of this kind with the existence of very high levels of concentration appears to be significant.

## Imperfect Knowledge—Inaction as a "Policy"

We recognize the need for further refinement of economic evidence of this type and for additional knowledge, theoretical and empirical, about the behavior of oligopolistic industries. It would be less than candid to pretend that economic science has provided a complete or wholly satisfactory basis for public policy in this field. But public policy must often be made on the basis of imperfect knowledge, and the failure to adopt remedial measures is in itself the acceptance of a policy. The judgment of most of the members of the Task Force is that enough is known about the probable consequences of high concentration to warrant affirmative government action in the extreme instances of concentration. Moreover, as we have noted, such action does not require acceptance of a new premise for public policy. A conviction that concentration is undesirable underlies the present stringent policy toward horizontal mergers. The same premise supports a policy of attempting, within conservative limits, to improve the competitive structure of industries in which concentration is already high and apparently entrenched.

## Scale Economies—Rate of Innovation

Endorsement of such a policy implies a judgment that the potential gains from reducing market shares and increasing the number of competitors in an industry will not be offset by losses in efficiency. We think there is little basis for believing that significant efficiencies of production are dependent on generally maintaining existing high levels of concentration.

There is little evidence that economies of scale require firms the size of the dominant firms in most industries that are highly concentrated. Evidence to the contrary is the fact that in most such industries very much smaller firms have survived in competition with the large firms. On the basis of studies covering a large number of industries, Professor Stigler concluded that: "In the manufacturing sector there are few industries in which the minimum efficient size of firm is as much as 5 percent of the industry's output and concentration must be explained on other grounds." [George J.] Stigler, *The Theory of Price* (3rd ed., 1966), p. 223. Similarly, there is no evidence of any correlation between size or market concentration and research and development activities.

### Transferability of Non-Scale Efficiencies

The success of very large firms may, of course, be explained on the basis of efficiencies other than economies of scale, such as superior management talent or other unique resources. To the extent that such efficiencies exist, however, they may ordinarily be transferred and thus would not necessarily be lost by reorganization of the industry into a larger number of smaller units. The same is true of advantages that inhere in legal monopolies, such as an accumulation of patents. It must also be borne in mind that efficiencies belonging to or achieved by a firm with some degree of monopoly power may be reflected only in higher profits rather than lower prices. Reduction of concentration would increase the chance that such efficiencies would be passed on to consumers through competition; indeed, a net gain from the consumer standpoint might result even though some efficiencies were lost in the process of reducing concentration.

## The "Concentrated Industries Act"

### "Survivor Test" as Limit on Divestiture Orders

The statute we propose would, however, take account of possible adverse effects on efficiency resulting from divestiture by forbidding relief that a firm establishes would result in substantial loss of economies of scale. It would be expected that a court would consider, among other factors relevant on this issue, the minimum size that experience has indicated is necessary for survival in the industry.

### Advantages of Legislative Approach

For the foregoing reasons we conclude that remedies to reduce concentration should be made available as part of a comprehensive antitrust policy. To assist in translating that conclusion into workable legislation we have drafted in some detail a proposed statute embodying our views. That statute, entitled the Concentrated Industries Act, is attached to this Report as Appendix A. While we believe, as hereafter noted, that some relief against concentration might be obtained through new interpretations of the Sherman Act, we also think that a statute such as the one we propose has several distinct advantages over reliance on existing law: (1) it would provide a clear determination of legislative policy and establish clear criteria for the application of that policy; (2) it would establish appropriate special procedures; and (3) it would limit the policy to remedial ends.

### Criteria: Four-Firms 70 percent—Important Industries

The Act establishes clear criteria for its application. It applies only to those industries in which four or fewer firms have accounted for 70 percent or more of industry sales, and it provides for steps to reduce the market shares of firms with 15 percent market shares in such industries. The Act contains other provisions to limit its application to industries which are of importance in the economy as a whole and in which concentration has been high and stable over considerable periods of time. The criteria laid down in the Act are designed to minimize the likelihood that output levels over a short period of time will affect the applicability of the Act. Moreover, even if the Act does apply, there are no penalties but only prospective relief. Thus, the possibility is minimized that corporations will resort to output-restricting strategies in order to avoid application of the Act.

### Improved Procedures—Specialized Court

The Act also lays the basis for defining relevant markets in terms that are more closely related to economic realities than are the definitions developed under existing antitrust laws. By and large, the Act limits the scope of inquiry to facts which are of relevance to its primary concern, the reduction of concentration, and which may be determined with reasonable precision. For these reasons, litigation under the Act should be relatively simple.

The Act establishes special procedures appropriate to the reduction of concentration. Under existing law, complex antitrust actions may be conducted by judges who have had little opportunity to become familiar with the kinds of questions involved, and who must rely on expert testimony offered by the parties. Expanding on the recently enacted provisions of 28 U.S.C. section 1407, the Act would establish a special panel of district judges and circuit judges to conduct deconcentration proceedings. In addition, it would enable the court to draw on the specialized knowledge and experience of its own economic experts. This feature of the Act should be of importance in arriving at appropriate market definitions. In addition court appointed experts would assist in evaluating the probable effect of proposed decrees.

### Limitations in Proposed Statute—Prospective Relief Only

Finally, the Act is limited to prospective relief designed to reduce concentration. Unlike existing law, it makes no provision for criminal penalties or for private actions seeking treble damages. The absence of these collateral effects makes the Act a more appropriate tool for reducing concentration.

Those who support the proposed Concentrated Industries Act believe, in varying degrees, that more can be done about concentration than has been done under existing law. We recommend that the Attorney General be encouraged to develop appropriate approaches under existing law and to bring carefully selected cases to test those theories.

### Expanded Enforcement of Present Law

Under existing law, three statutory provisions might be brought to bear. Section 2 of the Sherman Act prohibits monopolization or attempts to monopolize any part of interstate or foreign commerce. Section 1 of the Sherman Act prohibits any contract, combination, or conspiracy in restraint of interstate or foreign commerce. Section 7 of the Clayton Act prohibits acquisitions which may tend substantially to lessen competition. While existing precedents and the history of antitrust enforcement do not justify widespread use of these statutes against concentrated industries, we believe that appropriate precedents might be developed which would be useful in some cases.

Courts may be reluctant to expand the scope of these statutes, because their application would expose defendants to criminal penalties and treble damage liability. Moreover, existing law does not readily lend itself to the establishment of sufficiently clear and workable criteria. While expanded enforcement efforts might make some inroads in reducing concentration, they would not preclude the need for new legislation.

# III. Conglomerates or Large Diversified Firms

## Current Merger Movement

### Changes in Structure of Economy

The initial mandate establishing the Task Force reflected concern with the current rate of merger activity, particularly diversification or "conglomerate" mergers. Current data confirm that the number and scale of mergers, and particularly of conglomerate mergers, have been accelerating rapidly and continue to accelerate. Individual firms have achieved spectacular growth in this way. There is no comparable trend toward reduction in corporate size through spinoffs of assets. The current rate and pattern of mergers is causing significant and apparently permanent changes in the structure of the economy, and the long-run impact of these changes cannot be readily foreseen.

A variety of legal and economic factors have contributed to the conglomerate merger movement. Relatively clear legal prohibitions on horizontal and vertical mergers, set forth in section 7 of the Clayton Act and recently articulated in the Antitrust Division's Merger Guidelines, have channeled merger activity away from these more traditional forms while leaving conglomerate mergers relatively free from antitrust restraints. Although the Merger Guidelines identify some types of conglomerate mergers as likely candidates for antitrust attack and some conglomerate mergers have been successfully attacked on antitrust grounds, the antitrust laws leave relatively wide latitude for conglomerate mergers. This latitude reflects the fact that existing knowledge provides little basis for forecasting adverse effects on competition that support application of the merger prohibition of section 7.

### Motives for Conglomerate Mergers

The economic forces encouraging conglomerate mergers are numerous and complex, and are not easy to identify in particular cases. These appear to include the desire of owners of smaller firms to convert their holdings into more readily marketable securities; the desire of management of large firms for growth for its own sake apart from or in addition to growth in profits; the opportunity to bring more efficient management personnel or techniques to smaller or less successful firms; the possibility of reducing costs or increasing sales by meshing product lines or processes or methods of distribution; the desire to diversify business activities and reduce risks; the possibility of using one firm's cash flows or credit in another firm with limited access to capital; the tax advantages of direct reinvestment of earnings by corporations instead of distribution to stockholders for reinvestment through the general capital market; and the opportunity for speculative gains through mergers that immediately increase the per-share earnings of the surviving firm.

## "Merger Market"

Whatever the causes, it is clear that many conglomerate mergers are not explainable in terms of obvious efficiencies in integrating the production or marketing facilities of the firms involved. The merger movement has contributed to and is furthered by a specialized "merger market" in business firms as such; merger candidates and independent experts actively seek out favorable opportunities to acquire or dispose of businesses through conglomerate mergers. The existence of such a market is not a sinister symptom; it merely emphasizes the volume and complexity of merger activity and its underlying causes. Indeed, an active merger market suggests a healthy fluidity in the movement of resources and management in the economy toward their more effective utilization. The existence of such a market may serve as a significant incentive for the establishment of smaller firms. It may partially overcome imperfections in the capital market which are not readily susceptible to other effective remedies. In many cases, merger activity may replace proxy fights as an effective means for changes in corporate control.

## Objectives to Conglomerate Mergers

There are two types of possible antitrust objections to the current increase in merger activity: (1) mergers may have adverse effects on competitive structure and behavior in particular markets; (2) the volume and scope of merger activity may result in concentration of overall economic activity in a few large organizations and may substantially reduce the number of significant decision-making units within the economy.

## Effect on "Aggregate" Concentration—"Social" Issues

As to the second point, the possibility that economic activity might become unduly concentrated in a few large firms would raise difficult and far-reaching questions of social policy. Fortunately, such a development is not now imminent. In spite of the high and increasing rate of merger activity, concentration of aggregate economic activity (which should not be confused with concentration in particular markets, referred to in part II of this Report) has changed only slowly over time. Preliminary FTC data show that the share of total corporate manufacturing assets held by the 100 largest manufacturing firms has grown from 45.8 percent in 1957 to 47.7 percent in 1967; the share of the 200 largest has increased from 55.0 percent to 58.7 percent in the same period. Mergers have contributed somewhat to this trend; indeed, if no mergers had occurred, the shares of the largest firms would have declined somewhat during parts of the period. Nevertheless, it is clear that mergers are not solely responsible for the continued growth of the largest units in the economy, and have accounted for only a minor portion of such growth. Indeed, among the largest firms, the net effect of mergers has been to expand the size of smaller large firms relative to the top few. Further, the merger movement does not seem likely to cause the disappearance of smaller firms. The numbers of manufacturing firms with assets of $5 million to $10 million, $10 million to $25 million, and $25 million to $50 million have remained steady or increased somewhat during the period of greatest merger activity. Indeed, the numbers of non-manufacturing firms have increased significantly.

In any event, the level of economy-wide concentration and numbers of firms that would be incompatible with the maintenance of a competitive market system is not known. Even very large firms may continue to grow as a result of desirable response to changing economic circumstances, and mergers—including conglomerate mergers—may result in important economic benefits. We are therefore not persuaded of the need to establish specific limits to the growth of large firms, either by merger or otherwise. Thus, we do not endorse the suggestion put forward at one time by Donald F. Turner, former Assistant Attorney General in charge of the Antitrust Division, that further expansion of larger firms by merger be prohibited.

### Competitive Effects in Particular "Markets"

Conglomerate mergers may affect competition in particular markets. Three possible types of anticompetitive effects of conglomerate mergers have been identified and are reflected in the new Merger Guidelines: (1) elimination of "potential competition" by a firm which, but for its acquisition of another firm, might have entered the latter firm's market in a way that would have increased competition in that market; (2) the creation of opportunities for "reciprocal dealing" relationships between the merged firm and other firms that may foreclose competitors of the conglomerate firm; and (3) the addition of large resources to a firm already dominant in a market, possibly insulating its position from erosion through competition.

## Dangers in Case-by-Case Analysis

The detection of these effects rests, in general, on factual and theoretical judgments that are more speculative than the findings usually relied upon in section 7 cases; but to the extent that specific effects can be clearly identified in individual merger cases, present law and enforcement policies appear adequate. There are, however, two dangers in basing conglomerate merger policy entirely on the case-by-case substantiation of specific anticompetitive effects.

### The "Too Much"–"Too Little" Dilemma

1. These or similar objections to conglomerate mergers may be pressed beyond the point where they are well founded, perhaps because of quite different objections, such as fear of the growth of individual large firms or of concentration of assets in very large firms, which are not explicitly recognized in the merger prohibition. The existence of these different objections may also lead to other distortions; for example, market definitions may be distorted to treat a conglomerate merger as horizontal and therefore subject to a more easily established prohibition. Such distortions would result in uncertainties in enforcement and unfairness to those affected.

2. Potentially anticompetitive mergers may be allowed to proceed because economic theory and analytical foresight are inadequate to predict anticompetitive effects in specific cases, even though there may be good reason for believing that some classes of mergers, considered in the aggregate, are harmful to competition.

### Need for a Simpler Prohibition

Because of these difficulties, and because the incentives that have produced the current conglomerate merger movement can and should be directed to increase competition, we propose a statutory prohibition to supplement the merger prohibition of section 7 of the Clayton Act. Such a prohibition should be clear and not rely on conjectural judgments of likely competitive effect in particular cases; it should prohibit or discourage mergers most likely to have anticompetitive consequences, and in doing so lessen reliance on extended and contrived interpretations of section 7; and it should seek to direct the force of conglomerate merger activity into channels that will improve competitive structure to the maximum extent possible.

## The "Leading Firm Rule"

We propose that this be accomplished by forbidding mergers between very large firms and other firms that are already leading firms in concentrated markets significant in the national economy. A draft of a proposed statute embodying this recommendation, together with explanatory notes, is attached to this Report as Appendix B. [Not reproduced in this volume—eds.]

Such a rule satisfies our criteria for a supplementary prohibition. Unlike the Merger Guidelines applicable to conglomerate mergers, which rely on the difficult and conjectural questions referred to above, the proposed rule would provide clear criteria based solely on data as to market shares and sales or assets. It would apply to a large number of conglomerate mergers which might be attacked under existing law or under the law which might be developed in suits brought in accordance with the *Guidelines*.[2] The existence of this simpler prohibition will lessen the pressure on enforcement agencies and courts to engage in the distorted extensions to which section 7 lends itself. At the same time, the simpler prohibition will make enforcement simpler, and will prevent some mergers which would have gone unchallenged under section 7 even though careful analysis or subsequent developments might have indicated a violation of section 7.

### "Channeling" Merger Activity Toward Smaller Firms

In addition to these negative aspects of discouraging anticompetitive mergers, the proposed rule would have affirmative aspects in that it would channel merger

2. In the interests of certainty, the proposed rule would apply whether or not a merger could be characterized as purely conglomerate. We have not given detailed consideration to vertical or horizontal mergers or to the *Guidelines* as applied to such mergers. However, our proposed rule appears unlikely to add significantly to existing prohibitions on horizontal mergers or vertical mergers, except in the case of a vertical merger involving a leading firm in an industry which is concentrated but which has not been extensively vertically integrated. We conclude that the benefits of certainty override any conjectural losses in efficiency.

activity into directions likely to improve competition. The proposed rule rests on the assumption that if large firms are prevented from acquiring leading firms in concentrated industries, they will seek other outlets for expansion. If the rule is adopted, a large firm wishing to expand into a particular concentrated industry may acquire a small firm with a view to enlarging its capacity and market share, or it may construct wholly new facilities in the industry. Either of these alternative courses of action is more likely to increase competition and to decrease concentration in a concentrated industry than if the large firm simply acquired a leading firm in the industry and settled for maintaining or modestly increasing the market share of that firm.

## Role of Mergers in Reducing Concentration

As large firms become more diversified and more interested in further diversification, they become "potential entrants" into more and more industries. Although the probability that any one firm will enter any particular industry is extremely small, the probability that a substantial number of large diversified firms will enter a substantial number of concentrated industries is undoubtedly higher. The *Guidelines* and present enforcement based on the potential competition doctrine focus on the first probability alone, and must, therefore, be ineffectual or dependent on fictitious premises contrary to fact in many instances. If the potential competition doctrine under section 7 is expanded to the extent indicated by the *Guidelines* and current enforcement policy, such firms may well be disqualified from expanding by merger into many markets, including some in which they might make contributions of general benefit to the economy. These contributions might take the form of new technology and competitive innovation, reduced costs, or simply the introduction of new and forceful competitive pressures. Our proposal focuses on the second probability, that a substantial number of large diversified firms will enter a substantial number of concentrated industries, and is intended to channel the potential competition of large firms along lines that are conducive to reducing levels of concentration in the American economy.

## Preserving Conglomerate "Efficiencies"

Thus, the rule has both negative and affirmative aspects that tend to strengthen competition. Members of the Task Force who support this proposal assess somewhat differently the relative values of the negative and affirmative effects of the rule, depending on their differing judgments about the likelihood that mere size and superior financial resources will confer unwarranted advantages on an acquired firm. They are agreed, however, as to the net beneficial effect of such a rule. Since the rule would leave even a very large firm free to enter a new market by acquiring a going concern in the new market, it would preserve wide opportunity for diversification and for exploitation of efficiencies that may be inherent in conglomerate mergers.

# IV. The Robinson-Patman Act

## Anticompetitive Effects of Present Law

The Robinson-Patman Act has been the subject of extensive and well-earned criticism. Enacted in 1936 to tighten and supplement the price-discrimination prohibition in section 2 of the Clayton Act, the Robinson-Patman Act was intended to curb price discrimination that unduly favors national over local sellers and to protect independent merchants from unfair competition from large buyers obtaining the benefits of price discrimination.

### Preventing Desirable Price Reductions

Over the years, the Robinson-Patman Act has come to have unintended anticompetitive effects. The price-discrimination prohibition has discouraged types of price differentials which might have improved competition by lessening the rigidity of oligopoly pricing or by encouraging new entry:

1. In highly concentrated markets, prices may be rigid and a seller may hesitate to announce price reductions which would be met immediately by competitors, thus minimizing the seller's increase in sales. But he may be prepared to make concessions to make sales to particular buyers. Where such price reductions are sporadic and not part of a systematic pattern favoring large purchasers, they may be the first step toward more general price reductions.

2. A new or potential entrant to a market may find it necessary to reduce prices below those of his competitors in particular cases in order to overcome the inertia of established trade relationships. But the prospective seller may be reluctant to do so if he must make corresponding reductions to all other purchasers, and he may decide not to enter.

### Preventing More Efficient Distribution

The Robinson-Patman Act has impaired competition and the development of new methods of distribution in numerous other respects: by discouraging sellers from passing on cost savings to buyers, it has impaired experimentation with possibly more efficient methods of distribution integrating wholesale and retail functions; by requiring proportionally equal treatment in certain promotional practices, it has discouraged experimentation with price-cutting methods which are equivalent to desirable types of price differentials; by prohibiting sellers from paying brokerage to customers or their agents, it has erected an artificial protective barrier around independent brokers and inhibited integration of brokerage functions.

## Proposed New Price Discrimination Law

### "Most" Price Discrimination Not Harmful

We conclude that the Robinson-Patman Act requires a major overhaul to make it consistent with the purposes of the antitrust laws. A suggested revision of the price discrimination provisions is set forth, together with explanatory comments, in Appendix C to this Report. [Not reproduced in this volume—eds.] We recommend that the other provisions of the Robinson-Patman Act be repealed.

In its present form, the Robinson-Patman Act contains three major prohibitions. Sections 2 (a), (b) and (f) impose broad prohibitions on price discrimination in the sale of commodities. Sections 2 (c), (d) and (e) establish prohibitions dealing with the payment of brokerage, payment to customers for services rendered by them, and the furnishing of services to customers. Section 3 imposes criminal prohibitions which partly overlap the civil prohibitions of section 2.

Many of the reasons for price discrimination are related to the improved functioning of the competitive system. Price discrimination has an adverse effect on competition only in exceptional cases. Therefore, a statute restricting price discrimination should be narrowly drawn, to avoid losing the important benefits of price discrimination in an excessive effort to curb limited harm.

## Magnitude and Duration of the Discrimination—Cost Justification

Our proposed revision of the Act would make numerous changes in substance and in detail, and would eliminate many features of the present Act which forfeit the benefits of price discrimination in a competitive system. Two major changes are as follows:

1. Section 2 (a) of the present law makes unlawful a discrimination which may "injure, destroy, or prevent competition with any person...," as well as a discrimination the effect of which "may be substantially to lessen competition or tend to create a monopoly...." The reference to injury to competition with specific persons has focused the attention of courts and enforcement authorities on the plight of individual competitors, and *enforcement designed to preserve competitors is generally at odds with the working of a competitive system.* The proper focus is the effect on competition in the market as a whole. Our proposed revision specifies in some detail the kinds of competitive effects which make a discrimination unlawful; in doing so, it narrows and clarifies the law and avoids misconceived protection of competitors as distinguished from competition. Among other changes, the proposed language requires in general that a discrimination be *substantial in amount* and *persistent in duration.* The language of the proposed Act is carefully tailored to avoid prohibiting those differentials which are manifestations of more effective competition.

2. Under present law, a price differential is not unlawful if it makes only due allowance for cost differences. Enforcement authorities and courts have required these cost differences to be shown with extreme exactitude. The proposed revision permits price differentials approximating actual cost differences or based on reasonable estimates of cost differences or based on a reasonable system of classification.

## Brokerage—Promotional Arrangements

The prohibitions of section 2 (c), (d) and (e), unlike the basic price discrimination prohibition, do not depend on any showing of injury to competition and are not subject to the defense of cost-justification. We recommend that these sections be repealed, and that only such practices continue to be unlawful as are unlawful under the revised price discrimination provisions of section 2 (a).

Section 2 (c) has been interpreted to prohibit any payment of brokerage by a seller to a customer or to any agent of the customer, even though the customer has performed the services of a broker. Thus, the performance of brokerage services by customers has been penalized, even though it may be more efficient than the use of independent brokers. Section 2 (c) has also been held to prohibit an independent broker from reducing the commission to be paid to him by the seller in order to enable the seller to offer a lower price to the buyer, thereby directly interfering with price competition at both the seller and the broker level.

Section 2 (d) makes it unlawful for a seller to pay a customer for services or facilities furnished by the customer in connection with the processing or sale of any product manufactured or sold by the seller unless the payment is available on proportionally equal terms to all customers competing in the distribution of such product. Section 2 (e) makes it unlawful for any seller to discriminate in favor of one customer against another customer by furnishing any services or facilities in connection with the processing or sale of a commodity on terms not accorded to all customers on proportionally equal terms. These sections have been interpreted to require that some form of service or allowance be made available to every customer, even in cases where customers can be separated into distinct groups which are only marginally in competition with each other, and even if factors peculiar to a particular market make it difficult to furnish equivalent services to all customers.

The prohibitions in section 2 (c), (d) and (e) were designed to prevent conduct which, in its more blatant forms, might be viewed as equivalent to price discrimination. Under our proposal, such conduct could still be challenged as price discrimination, subject to the same defenses as any other price discrimination. Because violations of these subsections are relatively easy to establish, they have attracted a disproportionate amount of enforcement activity and have had substantial anticompetitive effects, suppressing many legitimate transactions.

## "Knowing" Price Discrimination—Motive and Intent

Section 3 of the Robinson-Patman Act establishes criminal penalties, but no private right of action, for three distinct offenses:

1. Knowingly entering into a sale transaction which discriminates against competitors of the purchaser;
2. Selling or contracting to sell goods in any part of the United States at prices lower than those exacted elsewhere in the United States, for the purpose of destroying competition or eliminating a competitor.
3. Selling or contracting to sell goods at unreasonably low prices for the purposes of destroying competition or eliminating a competitor.

The first prohibition very largely overlaps the basic price discrimination prohibition in sections 2(a) and (f) of the Robinson-Patman Act, but it differs in several important respects. Section 3 applies only to like quantities, has no requirement of competitive injury and is not subject to a cost justification defense. Even if a criminal penalty is justified for violation of the price discrimination prohibition, there is no justification for a criminal prohibition broader than the civil prohibition. We recommend that the criminal prohibition be dropped altogether.

The other two prohibitions of section 3 are designed to reach particular instances of predatory price cutting with adverse effects on competition in the seller's market. We have taken account of the purposes of these prohibitions, to the extent they are justified and have reflected them in the basic price discrimination prohibition in the body of section 2 of the Robinson-Patman Act. We recommend that they be dropped from section 3, since there is no justification for a criminal prohibition inconsistent with or broader or less specific than the civil prohibition of section 2.[3]

# V. The Patent Laws

## Nondiscriminatory Licensing

### Broadening the Patent Monopoly

We recommend new legislation to curtail certain practices which, under color of the patent laws, undermine the purposes of the antitrust laws. Such legislation would not prevent the owner of a valid patent from fully exploiting the monopoly conferred by his patent, and it would not involve any changes in the structure of the patent law. A draft of such legislation and our comments on it is attached to this Report as Appendix D. [Not reproduced in this volume—eds.]

We recommend that, in general, a patent owner who has granted a license with respect to his patent must license all qualified applicants on equivalent terms. This proposal does not involve compulsory patent licensing. A patentee may decline to issue any licenses at all, or he may issue licenses in some fields of use and reserve to himself the practice of the patent in other fields.

Ordinarily, it is unnecessary for a patent owner to grant an exclusive license to obtain the full reward for his patent. A rational patent owner can exact the full monopoly reward of the invention by setting appropriate royalties, and that reward will be greatest if the patented invention is exploited under competitive conditions. The grant of an exclusive license to a single licensee or a small group of licensees generally puts the licensee or licensees in a position to exact a monopoly profit. In effect, the patent owner is sharing his monopoly profit with the licensees. This will generally be to the patent owner's advantage only if the patent is vulnerable or if the arrangement

3. Dennis G. Lyons and George D. Reycraft believe that the latter two prohibitions of section 3 should not be repealed.

creates a monopoly broader than the patent.[4] That is, a patent licensing arrangement with limited membership may be nothing more than a device by which prices are fixed or markets shared.

### Increasing Number of Licenses

These effects can be avoided by a requirement that, if a license has been granted, a license on the same terms must be made available to all qualified applicants. Then, a licensee will be unable to obtain more than a reasonable profit for his role in exploiting the patent. Our proposed remedy will not require that courts or administrative agencies determine what are reasonable royalties; royalties would continue to be bargained between patent owners and initial licensees. To the extent that this proposal increases the number of licensees during the life of a patent, it may also result in more effective competition in the practice of the patent after expiration.

## Filing of License Agreements

We also recommend that copies of license agreements be filed with the Commissioner of Patents and be freely available to all, including antitrust enforcement officials. This provision is essential to effective operation of the nondiscriminatory licensing requirement, and it is similar to the requirement of existing law that interference settlements be filed. Even if the nondiscriminatory licensing requirement is not enacted, we recommend enactment of the filing requirement. Such a requirement would materially aid the enforcement of the antitrust laws to the extent that they now apply to license agreements or might be interpreted to apply to license agreements in the future. No legitimate interest would be sacrificed by exposing such agreements to the light of day.

## Nonenforcement Penalty

Finally, we recommend that a patent be unenforceable if the patent owner has not consistently taken reasonable steps to enforce his patent. This provision is necessary to avoid tacit or covert agreements not to enforce patents; such agreements would undermine the purposes of the nondiscriminatory licensing requirement and the filing requirement. The provision also has independent value, since it would recognize the obsolescence of patents which are of little commercial value or questionable validity and are not worth litigation, but which nevertheless serve to discourage entry into the field covered by the patent.[5]

4. In some few cases, the grant of an exclusive license may be a necessary inducement to the licensee to undertake the commercial risk of exploiting an innovation to an extent beyond the patent owner's financial capabilities. This possibility is reflected in the proposed statute. Many members doubt that such cases will arise.

5. We have not given detailed consideration to the desirability of permitting license restrictions on pricing, field of use, or territories. Members of the Task Force have expressed varying views on different types of restrictions.

# VI. Problems of Information

## Role of Economic Data in Antitrust

### Structure-Performance Data

In the course of preparing this *Report*, we have been struck by the need for improved collection, organization and availability of financial and economic data. Such information plays several roles in antitrust law. First, it is essential in the formulation of antitrust policy. Second, it may be essential in the application of the antitrust laws, in facilitating observance of the law by businessmen and enforcement of the law by the government. Third, it may have an effect on the operation of competitive markets and thus have direct antitrust implications.

### Census Bureau's "Secrecy" Policy

The formulation of economic policy requires a variety of financial and economic information. Such information may, for example, cast light on the competitive structure of industries, on the relation between prices and costs, on industry performance, on merger activity and plant construction, and on numerous other facts of obvious relevance in the formulation of economic and antitrust policy. Much of this information is already in the files of the Census Bureau. The Census Bureau operates under a statutory mandate not to disclose information with respect to individual firms, even if such information is not particularly sensitive or has already been made public in another form. The only way an individual researcher can have access to this information is by being sworn in as a Census employee and accepting the Census Bureau restrictions on disclosure of information; even government agencies attempting to obtain such information, such as the Federal Trade Commission, are subject to similar restrictions.

Current Census Bureau practice also requires that computer programming be done by Census Bureau personnel and that Census Bureau computers be used. Yet in contrast with its practice on population information, the Census Bureau has not established efficient procedures for furnishing specialized economic information to other government agencies. The result is that researchers and government agencies very often choose to forego the benefits of Census Bureau information and to gather less detailed information by dissemination of questionnaires or to use public sources.

## Proposed Interagency Coordinating Group

### Making Census Data More "Accessible"

We recommend establishment of an interagency group consisting of representatives of the Census Bureau, Securities and Exchange Commission, Internal Revenue Service and other agencies which gather information; the Council of Economic Advisers, Federal Trade Commission, Justice Department and other agencies which use information; and the Office of Statistical Standards in the Bureau of the Budget. This group could also include experts from outside the government. The group would consider how, within the framework of existing restrictions on disclosure, information for policy-making and research may be made more readily accessible to policymakers and researchers. In addition, the group would assist the Census Bureau and other information-gathering agencies in setting up procedures and facilities, along the lines of those presently set up for population census information, for responding to requests for economic information.

### Legislative Restrictions: Interpretation and Modification

The group would also consider the extent to which new interpretations of existing legislation and, eventually, new legislation are feasible and desirable to modify the effect of restrictions on disclosure. We recognize that the Census Bureau depends in large part on voluntary compliance with its reporting requirements, and that the assurance of confidentiality is an important ingredient in obtaining that compliance. Therefore, any modification of disclosure restrictions would be limited to those types of information which are highly significant for antitrust policy and either are not highly sensitive or are similar to other information which has been publicly disclosed.

## Data of "Antitrust Significance"

### Market Definitions—Market Shares

The application of our legislative proposals, as well as existing antitrust law, requires economic information such as market shares and sales in specific markets. Information prepared by the Census Bureau is based on industry and product classifications which do not necessarily coincide with relevant national and regional markets. We recommend that the interagency group recommended above establish procedures for developing and publishing information of antitrust significance, such as studies of important markets, including those in which deconcentration proceedings might be appropriate and those in which merger activity has been high. In many cases such information could be made available without disclosing information on industrial firms. The group also could coordinate and evaluate requests for information to the Census Bureau and other information-gathering agencies.

### Divisional Reporting of Profit

We recommend that the provisions of the Securities Exchange Act of 1934 authorizing the SEC to specify the details of financial reports "for the protection of investors and to ensure fair dealing" in the securities markets be expanded to recognize the impact of profit and loss information on the operation of competitive markets, and to require that the SEC issue regulations implementing these provisions after consulting with the Justice Department and the Federal Trade Commission. Pending adoption of this recommendation, the Justice Department and the Federal Trade Commission should be requested to consider submitting recommendations to the SEC, within the existing statutory framework, for regulations providing for disclosure of profit and loss information desirable from an antitrust viewpoint. Such recommendations should be submitted as soon as possible, since the SEC is currently considering divisional reporting requirements.

### Disclosure of Profits as Aid to Competition

Information as to the profitability of operations in particular economic markets should be widely available to facilitate the operation of a competitive economy. Above-normal profits in an industry should attract investment by new entrants or additional investment by existing suppliers. Thus, in the long run, output will be brought up to the level optimum from the point of view of the economy as a whole. In addition, new entry into a market in response to profit opportunities may reduce concentration in that market. The availability to stockholders of information as to the profitability of particular operations or transactions might encourage closer scrutiny of the advisability of such operations and transactions. The availability of profit information may lessen any temptation for large or diversified firms to use their superior financial resources and staying power to drive smaller rivals out of business.

## VII. Additional Recommendations

### Premerger Notification and Related Matters

The Department of Justice and the Federal Trade Commission must presently rely primarily upon public sources of information in the enforcement of statutory prohibitions on mergers. We endorse proposals for mandatory premerger notification and have set forth a proposed statute in Appendix E. [Not reproduced in this volume—eds.] Under the proposed statute, the Attorney General would be empowered to make regulations, subject to certain restrictions designed to keep reporting from becoming too onerous. At the same time, we recommend a reasonable statute of limitations, such as ten years, on government actions against mergers. We oppose a requirement that actions be brought prior to consummation of mergers, since this might prove too much of a strain on enforcement resources. Such a requirement might also hamper legitimate mergers by encouraging enforcement authorities to bring actions which, upon more complete investigation, might not have been brought.

Our proposal, coupled with the clear standards of our proposed legislation to deal with mergers, would make it possible to resolve many merger actions prior to consummation of mergers. Under those standards, it would be possible to obtain preliminary injunctions in cases where mergers appeared to be unlawful.

### Duration of Decrees

Many decrees under the antitrust laws, including consent decrees, are of long or indefinite duration. The effects of these decrees may change with the passage of time. Such decrees may turn out to be ineffective or anticompetitive. We recommend a general provision limiting the duration of antitrust decrees, including consent decrees, to a relatively short period, such as ten years, but permitting the court to extend decrees in original or modified form for additional ten-year periods. Provisions along these lines are built into our proposed legislation to deal with concentrated markets and our proposed revision of the Robinson-Patman Act. A draft of suggested language is set forth in Appendix E to this Report. [Not reproduced in this volume—eds.]

## Income Tax Laws

Some features of the income tax laws may have effects on market concentration or merger activity. We recommend that the income tax laws be reexamined to see whether these effects exist and whether they can be neutralized without significant harm to the purposes of the income tax laws.

The reorganization provisions of the Internal Revenue Code provide that, in certain kinds of acquisitions, the selling stockholders recognize no gain. The reorganization provisions, alone or in conjunction with other provisions of the tax laws, may provide significant incentives to stockholders to make their companies available for acquisition. On the other hand, there are offsetting disadvantages to the acquiring corporation, and the reorganization provisions may affect primarily the form rather than the number of acquisitions. The justification for and effect of these provisions deserve reconsideration in preparing a tax reform program.

Corporations and their stockholders are generally taxed separately, and stockholders are not taxed on earnings which are retained rather than distributed as dividends. The effect of this provision may be to channel investment funds through existing corporations rather than independent or new enterprises. Thus, corporations may grow larger than they otherwise would, and some of this expansion may serve to maintain or increase their market shares in industries in which they already have large market shares. In addition, this aspect of the law may encourage acquisitions for cash or acquisitions of corporations which will require the investment of additional capital.

We recommend that the competitive effects of this feature of the tax laws be examined in preparing a tax reform program.

## Antitrust Laws and the Regulated Industries

In the regulated sector of the economy, the bias of policy and its enforcement is overwhelmingly against competition. This bias manifests itself in more permissive policies toward mergers and exemption of mergers from antitrust standards; in restrictions on entry; and in regulation of minimum rates for the protection of competitors and competing industries, in addition to more traditional regulation of maximum rates for the protection of consumers. We believe that this bias is contrary to the public interest in many cases. We recommend further study of regulated industries to determine the extent to which competition and the competitive standards of the antitrust laws can be substituted for at least some aspects of regulation.

## Resale Price Maintenance

The Miller-Tydings Act and the McGuire amendment to section 5 (a) of the Federal Trade Commission exempt certain resale price maintenance arrangements from the antitrust laws where States have enacted so-called "fair trade" laws. The case against resale price maintenance has been made so often and persuasively that we think no further elaboration is necessary. We recommend repeal of antitrust exemptions for resale price maintenance.

# 11

# The Chicago School

## Introduction

### BY HERBERT HOVENKAMP

The Neal Report excerpted in the previous chapter proved to be the swan song of structuralism. Just two years later a competing report, commissioned by President Nixon and chaired by University of Chicago economics professor George J. Stigler, called virtually every one of its recommendations into question.[1] Among the other members of the Stigler commission were Ward S. Bowman, Jr., Ronald H. Coase, and Richard A. Posner, indicating just how important the "Chicago School" of economics had become for antitrust policy.

The Chicago School of antitrust analysis developed mainly in reaction to two interrelated themes in the economics and antitrust policy of the midtwentieth century: structuralism and the "leverage" theory of monopoly expansion. As we saw in the last chapter, structuralism was in fact an elegant, heavily empirically tested theory that developed several themes that dominated industrial organization economics and antitrust policy. To recap, first was the assumption of a strong link between the number of firms in a market and the propensity of prices to go above cost. This theory rested mainly on strong Cournot assumptions that oligopoly behavior would increase as the number of firms decreased. It was evidenced in numerous studies that tended to show that firms in concentrated industries earned higher profits than those in more competitively structured industries. Second was a perception that, even though economies of scale did exist, in many markets the firms were far larger than minimum efficient scale demanded; such markets could be "deconcentrated" by breaking up large firms without causing significant production inefficiencies. Third, barriers to entry were high in many industries, but particularly in those with a large fixed-cost component. Fourth was the Kaysen-Turner view that, given the close link between Cournot theory and maximizing behavior, poor performance in highly

1. "Stigler Report," 2 *Antitrust Law and Economics Rev.* 13 (1969). See Herbert Hovenkamp, "The Neal Report and the Crisis in Antitrust," 5 *Competition Policy Int'l* 217 (April 30, 2009); Daniel A. Crane, *The Institutional Structure of Antitrust Enforcement* 56–63 (2011).

concentrated markets was inevitable. As a result, antitrust should focus on structure and pay relatively less attention to conduct.[2]

In addition, vertical integration in concentrated markets was thought to be bad for three reasons: (1) it often required new entrants to enter markets at two levels rather than one, thus increasing entry barriers; (2) it locked up markets by dedicating suppliers and buyers to one another, making it more difficult for unintegrated rivals to compete; and (3) it permitted firms to "leverage" monopoly profits from one market level to another. The leverage theory, which manifested itself in many situations involving multimarket firms, vertical mergers, or vertical contractual practices such as tying, held that a firm with monopoly power in one market could "expand his empire" into vertically related or complementary markets.[3]

Other parts of the status quo did not fit quite as cleanly into the pure structuralist model. For example, Chamberlin's theory of monopolistic competition had generally assumed large numbers of firms and easy entry. As a result the theory was in some tension with oligopoly theory, which depended on a small number of firms, high entry barriers and, typically, a fungible product. Bain himself had found product differentiation to be a highly indeterminate factor that could point both ways.[4] But within antitrust policy, product differentiation tended to be regarded with considerable suspicion and was strengthened by the commonly held view that consumers were unsophisticated and easily misled by advertising claims.

All of these views were dismantled by Chicago School writers, who argued with great effectiveness that the link between high concentration and high prices was greatly overstated. Firms had incentives to compete even in highly concentrated markets. The task for antitrust policy was not to pursue structure for its own sake but rather to ensure that firms did not adopt practices that would facilitate collusion. Further, the studies tending to show higher accounting rates of return in concentrated industries were deeply flawed for two reasons. First, they confused accounting profits with economic profits, often understating the effect of high fixed costs. Second, the studies actually tended to show that the larger firms in many industries were more efficient than smaller firms, thus explaining the higher profits.[5]

Chicago School writers also argued that barriers to entry were much less of a factor in American industry than Bain believed. Capital markets were efficient and as a result any firm with good prospects should be able to borrow to get in. As a result, the only real barriers resulted from differential risk, or costs that a new firm would encounter that previous entrants had not encountered.

2. Carl Kaysen and Donald F. Turner, *Antitrust Policy: An Economic and Legal Analysis* (1959). For further development of these views, see Herbert Hovenkamp, "United States Competition Policy in Crisis: 1890–1955," 94 *Minn.L.Rev.* 311 (2009); Herbert Hovenkamp, "The Law of Vertical Integration and the Business Firm, 1880–1960," 95 *Iowa L.Rev* 863 (2011). Turner went on to be head of the Antitrust Division of the Department of Justice in the late 1960s and is largely responsible for the first set of government Merger Guidelines, which were issued in 1968. Thereafter he returned to Harvard Law School and (with Phillip E. Areeda) began the *Antitrust Law* treatise (1978–).

3. E.g., *United States* v. *Griffith*, 334 U.S. 100, 108 (1948) (from one geographic market to another); *Northern Pac. Ry. Co.*, v. *United States*, 356 U.S. 1, 14 (1958) (vertical expansion by tying).

4. See Joe S. Bain, *Industrial Organization* 215–218 (1959).

5. E.g., Harold Demsetz, "Barriers to Entry," 72 *Am.Econ.Rev.* 47 (1982); Demsetz, "Industry Structure, Market Rivalry, and Public Policy," 16 *J.L. & Econ.* 1 (1973).

The Chicago School assessment of vertical integration was so radically different from the structuralist assessment as to be unrecognizable. Chicago School economists believed that the structuralists seriously underestimated the impact of production and distribution efficiencies that served to reduce a vertically integrated firm's costs. Chicago School writers drew from Ronald Coase's seminal articles on "The Nature of the Firm" (1937) and "The Problem of Social Cost" (1960) to argue that a great deal of vertical integration is related to savings in transaction costs.[6] Coase had argued that use of the market itself is costly, and that a firm in equilibrium produces or distributes for itself whenever the net cost of doing so is lower than the cost of relying on the market. One of these costs was the cost of imperfections in vertically related markets, such as might occur when these markets were subject to either oligopoly or collusion. Chicago theory relied on a robust model of "double marginalization" to explain why both the firm itself and consumer are better off when a firm's vertical integration eliminates a second markup in a vertically related market. The result of such integration would be lower prices and higher output, even if vertical integration did not result in any production efficiencies.

Another thing that the Chicago School gave to antitrust was the rhetoric of consumer welfare. A great deal of pre-Chicago antitrust policy saw antitrust as a device for protecting small business from larger rivals. Although the rhetoric of monopoly was always present in this talk, much of the time the very "evil" that antitrust policy targeted was low prices that might injure smaller competitors.

The selections that follow trace these developments. Aaron Director and Edward Levi's *Law and the Future* (1956) presented a number of qualms that the authors had with then-reigning structuralism and the leverage theory. This article ranks next to Ward Bowman's article on leverage as one of the great early Chicago School critiques of the prevailing antitrust policy.[7] George J. Stigler's collection of articles published in 1968 as *The Organization of Industry*, together with his book on price theory, became definitive statements of the Chicago School attack on structuralism.[8] Robert Bork began his career as an antitrust scholar at Yale Law School, with articles written in the 1950s and 1960s attacking the dominant view of vertical integration and promoting the view that from the very beginning the framers of the Sherman Act believed that economic efficiency should be the exclusive goal of antitrust enforcement.[9] He collected and updated these views in his immensely popular book *The Antitrust Paradox: A Policy at War with Itself* (1978). Finally, Richard A. Posner's highly influential article about the Chicago School of antitrust was published in 1979. It is the best summary of the issues that divided structuralism from the Chicago School.

6. Ronald H. Coase, "The Nature of the Firm," 4 *Economica* 386 (1937); Coase, "The Problem of Social Cost," 3 *J.L.& Econ.* 1 (1960).

7. Ward S. Bowman, Jr., "Tying Arrangements and the Leverage Problem," 67 *Yale L.J.* 19 (1957).

8. George J. Stigler, *The Organization of Industry* (1968); Stigler, *The Theory of Competitive Price* (1942), subsequently enlarged and published as *The Theory of Price* (1946; 3rd ed. 1966).

9. E.g., Robert H. Bork, "Legislative Intent and the Policy of the Sherman Act," 9 *J.L. & Econ.* 7 (1966); Robert H. Bork, "Vertical Integration and the Sherman Act: The Legal History of an Economic Misconception," 22 *Univ. Chi.L.Rev.* 157 (1954).

## George J. Stigler

## *The Organization of Industry*

# Chapter 13: A Note on Profitability, Competition, and Concentration

The firms in a competitive industry expect to earn at least as much in the industry as they could earn elsewhere, or they would leave the industry. They will not expect to earn more because if earnings were higher their rivals would expand (if there were no diseconomies of scale) or new firms would enter. A monopolistic firm has the same minimum rate of earnings—it too can migrate to another industry! If competition is leashed, however, the firm may earn a higher than competitive rate of return for a time or permanently. If investments are guided by reasonably good foresight, the average rate of return should be higher in monopolistic than in competitive industries.

Rates of return will also differ among industries for a second reason: industries are not always in equilibrium. Presumably, if our data on rates of return cover enough industries and time, the effects of disequilibrium (which can go in either direction) will become small, but the obscuring effect of such disturbances is usually substantial. If the impact of disequilibrium upon rates of return is as large as the impact of monopoly, the coefficient of correlation between rates of return and monopoly is reduced by 30 percent.

All empirical studies are plagued also by imperfections in the data on rates of return. Three important examples will suffice to illustrate limitations. Inflation makes historical costs, and depreciation based upon historical costs, obsolete. The returns in industries which have relatively durable assets, and in industries with relatively old assets, will be overstated relative to industries with the opposite characteristics. Again, certain expenditures—chiefly on research and advertising—yield returns over a period of years but are commonly charged off completely in the year in which they are made, so income and assets are both understated. If these expenditures are steady at a level just maintaining the assets (so expenditures equal depreciation), then assets are too small and reported rates of return too high. Finally, in small corporations which are owned by the officers, it is to their advantage to withdraw income as wages rather than as dividends because no corporation income tax need be paid on the wages (and the personal income tax is the same on wages and dividends). This third factor is associated with concentration (as the other imperfections may not be) because these small companies are important only in unconcentrated industries.

On a different footing is the problem that the data on profits may be *too* good. If I create, by shrewdness or luck, a monopoly which yields 20 percent on my original investment, it is really worth twice its original cost if the appropriate rate of return is 10 percent. If I sell the monopoly, the buyer will earn only 10 percent upon *his* cost and there will appear to be no monopoly return. Accountants do not generally record such changes in valuation—they are opposed to including intangibles such as monopoly

TABLE 1 **Distribution of Rates of Return on Capital in Unconcentrated Manufacturing Industries, 1955–57* (*N* = 55)**

| Rate of Return (%) | Number of Industries 1955 | 1956 | 1957 | Average 1955–57 |
|---|---|---|---|---|
| -4 to -3 | | | 1 | |
| -3 to -2 | | | — | |
| -2 to -1 | 1 | 1 | — | |
| -1 to 0 | 1 | — | 1 | 1 |
| 0 to 1 | 1 | 1 | — | 1 |
| 1 to 2 | — | — | 4 | 2 |
| 2 to 3 | 1 | 2 | 4 | 3 |
| 3 to 4 | 7 | 8 | 11 | 9 |
| 4 to 5 | 9 | 11 | 9 | 8 |
| 5 to 6 | 10 | 7 | 8 | 7 |
| 6 to 7 | 7 | 8 | 9 | 10 |
| 7 to 8 | 11 | 6 | 5 | 9 |
| 8 to 9 | 6 | 8 | 2 | 4 |
| 9 to 10 | 1 | 2 | 1 | 1 |
| 10 to 11 | | — | | |
| 11 to 12 | | 1 | | |
| Mean | 5.63 | 5.74 | 4.68 | 4.66 |
| Standard deviation | 2.24 | 2.35 | 2.32 | 2.02 |

* Data from George J. Stigler, Capital and Rates of Return in Manufacturing Industries (New York, 1963), Appendices B-1 and C-2.

power and goodwill among the assets—but to the extent that they allow such perfectly valid market prices of assets, monopoly profits vanish.

The translation into numbers of the proposition that under competition there is a tendency for the rate of returns to approach equality is not a simple task. We have listed two reasons why, at any given time rates of return may differ among competitive industries: the industries may be in disequilibrium (because it takes time to learn of rates of return and to leave one field and enter another), and the rates of return may be improperly reported. A third reason may be added: the rates of return that should approach equality allow for all advantages and disadvantages, so if industry A is much riskier than B, and men dislike risk, they must earn a higher average rate in A than B to compensate.

The average rates of return in unconcentrated manufacturing industries in 1955, 1956, and 1957 are in Table 1.[1] The average of the three years is of course more compact

1. An industry is defined as unconcentrated if it has a national market and a concentration ratio (for the four largest firms) under 50 percent, or a regional market and a concentration ratio under 20 percent.

than that of any one year, but even if we lengthened the period to a hundred years the dispersion among rates of return would not vanish. Quite aside from deficiencies in the data, there is no assurance that the entrepreneurs in each industry will on average predict correctly all the changes in supply and demand conditions. If the distribution were, say, bimodal (with two concentrations of industries around 5 or 10 percent) we would reject the classical proposition on rates of return approaching equality, but dispersion alone will not support a rejection.

A more illuminating way to look at the classical proposition is to ask: how long does it take, on average, for differences, in rates of return among industries to vanish? Suppose we know the rates of return in the manufacturing industries of Table 1 in 1955. Will this pattern help to explain the pattern of rates among industries in 1956? Surely yes: differences in rates due to disequilibrium will not be removed immediately, it may require several years for firms in broad wool goods (who *lost* 1.51 percent on capital in 1955) to shift to dyeing and finishing of textiles (which earned 5.85 percent in 1955). In fact, the correlation of 1955 with 1956 rates was .80 and of 1956 with 1957 rates it was .78. But if competition is doing its work, on average these patterns will disappear after a time. The quicker the correlations go to zero, the greater the mobility of resources in response to differences in profitability. On average the correlations are close to zero after about five years: on average with a knowledge only of the rates of return in year $t$, one can explain more than half the variation in rates of return among industries in year $(t + 1)$ (i.e., $r^2 > .5$) but one can explain less than one-tenth of the variation in rates in year $(t + 5)$ (i.e., $r^2 < .1$). Hence the period within which given inequalities in rates of return among industries are essentially eliminated is perhaps five years—but of course varies with the cost of movement of capital.

A substantial number of investigations have been made of the relationship between concentration and rates of return. The results are surprisingly consistent in two respects: a positive relationship is always found, and it is usually weak: not more than one half, and often less than one fifth, of the variance of rates of return among in industries is accounted for by differences in concentration. The similarity of results is of course partly due to the use of the same or closely related data in the various studies. The disquieting feature is the fact that profitability is better correlated with crude industry measures (food) than with more sharply defined industries (canned fruits and vegetables).

Our theory of oligopoly suggests that for a given level of concentration, the probability of successful collusion is smaller, the fewer the buyers. A loose test of this is provided for manufacturing industries in Table 2. The industries had national markets, and their 1954 concentration ratios (four leading firms) were over 50 percent. The number of buyers was generally determined by whether the commodity was a producer or consumer good (automobile tires were one exception: the automobile manufacturers and major retailers [such as mail order businesses] are major customers). The results are timidly helpful (although they do not meet the usual tests of significance): no high rate of return industries dealt with few buyers.

TABLE 2 **Percentage Rates of Return, 1953–55, and Number of Buyers**

| | **Under 6** | **6–8** | **Over 8** |
|---|---|---|---|
| Many buyers | Distilled liquor | Tobacco except cigarettes | Cereal preparations |
| | Sugar refining | Soaps and detergents | Motor vehicles |
| | Carpets, yarn | Office machinery | Glass |
| | Agricultural machinery | | |
| | Motorcycles and bicycles | | |
| Few buyers | Tires and tubes | Tin cans | |
| | Smelting nonferrous metals | Automotive electric equipment | |
| | Railroad equipment | Industrial chemicals | |
| | Miscellaneous electric goods | Engines and turbines | |

*Source:* George J. Stigler, *Capital and Rates of Return in Manufacturing Industries* (New York, 1963).

## Aaron Director and Edward H. Levi

## *Law and the Future: Trade Regulation*

In this note we do not attempt to predict the future of the antitrust laws. Rather we wish to direct attention to certain problem areas for study. We assume for the purposes of this discussion that an over-riding belief in both free enterprise and in competition will prevail over future possible NRA attempts. We assume also that despite the extension of government regulation of one form or another, there will still be a place for regulation by competition. The ability of the antitrust laws in weathering NRA and government regulation attempts in the past provides a basis for assuming the laws will continue. The durability of the antitrust laws is perhaps their main characteristic. In large measure, this is a common law durability, built on a case by case development, and exhibiting that flexibility which is the strength of the common law. But this flexibility is now limited by particularizing legislation enacted to accompany the Sherman Act. Throughout its history, indeed, the Sherman Act has exhibited the twin tendencies of flexibility and ambiguity, on the one hand, and a drive for certainty and automaticity, on the other. At the moment, the drive for certainty and automaticity seems paramount, but not without criticism and reaction. Much of this drive for certainty rests not so much on the concept of fair warning, which is inherent in any idea of the rule of law, but rather more on the belief that new and automatic applications of the laws will catch objectionable conduct and effects in their incipiency. The idea of incipiency seems to rest on economic doctrines, or, conclusions drawn from experience. Because of these doctrines or conclusions, certain types of conduct are deemed harmful in themselves, although the harm in the particular case may not be visible. Economic theory or experience thus substitutes for an observed effect.

In no area, of course, is the law self-contained, that is, completely independent of the teachings of other disciplines or the assumptions, which may change, of underlying philosophy. The common law, itself, provides the mechanism for moving from doctrines outside the law into felt distinctions which make the law. As much as any field of law, and more than most, the antitrust laws in their evolution have exhibited an explicit interdependence with economic and political thought. Many of the cases, of course, reflect the law's skepticism for economists and economics. But the antitrust laws have been greatly influenced by economic doctrine. At times the legal and economic theory have appeared to be the same. New problems for the antitrust laws are therefore created if it can be shown that, in terms of present day situations, much of the reliance on economic doctrine is unjustified. Even if this can be shown, it is possible, perhaps probable, that the law will continue on its own, for the law is not economics. The main lines of the law, then, may remain the same, but the statement of reasons for the law may change, and this in itself should have an interstitial effect in the cases. Indeed, there is uncertainty whether the dominant theme of the antitrust laws is to be the evolution of laws of fair conduct, which may have nothing whatever to do with economics, or the evolution of minimal rules protecting competition or prohibiting monopoly or monopolizing in an economic sense. But this uncertainty only becomes meaningful as the issues concerning the underlying economic doctrines are sharpened.

We believe the conclusions of economics do not justify the application of the antitrust laws in many situations in which the laws are now being applied. We conclude, therefore, that there are new problems for the antitrust laws, and that the future perhaps will be occupied, at least in part, with their resolution. The new problems for the antitrust laws have to do with size, the concept of abuse, and with the application of the idea of collusion. They exist, therefore, in the central field of antitrust enforcement.

The problems are new. The earlier history of the Sherman Act involved its enforcement against units of great relative size which had acquired that position largely through mergers and acquisitions and which, in most cases, had engaged in conduct which was characterized as abusive. Under this analysis, there were three elements combined in the cases. First, there was great relative size. Since the relative size which was reached, although not always maintained, was sufficiently great, the firm could be characterized with some assurance as a monopoly, and its behavior in an important respect could be predicted. Second, this size was obtained through acquisitions. Great importance could be attached to this method of growth. A perennial fear in the application of the Sherman Act is that it will cut down units which have grown to great size only because of the economies of large scale, that is, in response to the demands for efficiency. But during this earlier period, the means of growth used by monopolies in many industries were mergers or acquisitions. It could be argued, although not without some doubt, that, presumptively, growth because of the economies of large scale would not take the form of merger or acquisition in so many industries. The underlying rationale behind this presumption is that it would strain credulity to believe that in so many industries the ideal arrangement for one firm would be merely the collection into one ownership unit of factories which were originally justified as parts of separate firms. In the reasoning of the law, the method of growth through mergers or combination thus could be used as some evidence of intention to monopolize, and as an answer to the efficiency argument. Third, there was present also conduct frequently described as abusive. There were instances of price cutting, exclusive arrangements or tying clauses, the receipt of rebates, and full line forcing. Perhaps this conduct was important because it colored the origin of the monopoly. Perhaps it was important because it characterized the way the monopoly was used. But since the abuses accompanied great relative size acquired through combination, no really separate decision had to be made as to whether it was these abuses which caused illegality. The abuses might have been merely incidental features of monopolies which were illegal because they had arrived at such size without the justification of efficiency.

The old *Standard Oil* case reflects this union of size, combination, and abuses. It was the "unification of power and control over petroleum and its products which was the inevitable result of the combining in the New Jersey corporation... aggregating so vast a capital" which gave rise "in the absence of countervailing circumstances, to say the least, to the prima facie presumption of intent and purpose to maintain the dominancy over the oil industry...." And this presumption was then made conclusive by considering conduct and results. This analysis left unanswered the question of the importance of the abuses in determining illegality. Specifically, it was not settled whether given sufficient size acquired through combination, an injury through abuses of that power would have to be shown to spell out a violation of the Sherman Act. As Judge Hand wrote in the *Corn Products* case, "perhaps it is yet an open question whether or not the test is to be found only in the combination of enough producing capacity to control supply and fix prices, or whether it must be shown that the combination had injured the public in the exercise of that power."

But the combination of factors made it unnecessary to decide this question in *Corn Products.* There was also an open question as to the status of power less than monopoly but acquired through past abuses. This was the question which might have been reached in the *United States Steel Corporation* case, if past abuses had been found. But the *Steel Corporation* case, itself, marks a turning point. It is the beginning of the modern period for the Sherman Act when, with few exceptions, industrial combines are not monopolies. Some of the firms indeed might have been monopolies in the past, but there was little likelihood for most of them that such large relative size would be acquired again.

Today the industrial pattern is far different than it was at the beginning of the century. It is much less common than it was to have an industry in which one firm has seventy or more percent control over productive capacity or sales. There are likely to be at least three or four units of considerable relative size in an industry. The absolute size of these firms may be much greater than that once possessed by any single dominating firm. And large absolute size, of course, carries with it a power of its own. But it confuses concepts to call this monopoly power. And there is an additional change. The role of combination appears to be different. Whatever the ultimate conclusion may be, it has not yet been shown that such industrial concentration as exists is due in any widespread way to recent mergers or acquisitions. And this cannot be shown, of course, merely by counting the number of mergers or acquisitions which occur annually. The application of the antitrust laws to firms of less than monopoly size or to firms which acquired their size without combination presents new problems for the antitrust laws.

The *Aluminum Co.* case hits one of these problems head on. The big step taken in *Alcoa* was to find illegality, perhaps without abuses, but in any event without recent combination. This finding of monopolizing without combination raises a serious question as to the application of the antitrust laws to monopolies born solely out of efficiency. The presence of combinations in the older cases was supposed to provide the necessary presumption that the growth in the form taken was not due to the drive towards efficiency and appropriate scale. Mergers thus appeared to minimize the point raised in *Alcoa* that monopoly may "have been thrust upon" the firm, and thus to satisfy, as Judge Hand indicates, the older cases on the question of "natural" or "normal" conduct, or on the question of intent. Absent combination and abuses, it is possible to decide, as *Alcoa* appears to do, that monopoly as such is illegal as monopolizing. This means that the law has decided that monopoly behavior is not dependent on the circumstances which gave rise to the monopoly, and that perhaps even with access to an industry open, and without collusion, monopoly is not sufficiently self correcting. If stated without qualification, this would mean that a firm which grew to monopoly size because of the economies of large scale nevertheless would be illegal. The consequences of the law would be a less efficient system of production. This would not necessarily be a decisive criticism of the law, for, as Hand tells us, the Sherman Act has other objectives. The Congress which passed the statute, he reminds us, "was not necessarily actuated by economic motives alone. It is possible, because of its indirect social or moral effect, to prefer a system of small producers, each dependent for his success upon his own skill and character, to one in which the great mass of those engaged must accept the direction of a few." And this maintenance of an organization of industry in small units was to be "in spite of possible cost." Yet despite this language, the *Alcoa* opinion attempts to carve out a place for the argument of efficiency as a defense.

The *Alcoa* position on efficiency as a defense is somewhat complicated. The "successful competitor," we are told, "having been urged to compete, must not be turned upon when he wins." The opinion draws a distinction between monopoly which has been "achieved" and monopoly which has been "thrust upon" the firm. Persons "may unwittingly find themselves in possession of a monopoly, automatically, so to say; that is without having intended either to put an end to existing competition, or to prevent competition from arising when none had existed; they may become monopolists by force of accident." Three illustrations are given:

> A market may, for example, be so limited that it is impossible, to produce at all and meet the cost of production except by a plant large enough to supply the whole demand. Or there may be changes in taste or in cost which drive out all but one purveyor. A single producer may be the survivor out of a group of active competitors, merely by virtue of his superior skill, foresight and industry.

The language appears to give full consideration to the requirements of efficiency. But there is balancing language on the other side. The issue for Alcoa is posed in this fashion: "The only question is whether it falls within the exception established in favor of those who do not seek, but cannot avoid, the control of a market." On this issue, Judge Hand writes:

> It was not inevitable that [Alcoa] should always anticipate increases in the demand for ingot and be prepared to supply them. Nothing compelled it to keep doubling and redoubling its capacity before others entered the field. It insists that it never excluded competitors; but we can think of no more effective exclusion than progressively to embrace each new opportunity as it opened, and to face every newcomer with new capacity already geared into a great organization, having the advantage of experience, trade connection and the elite of personnel. Only in case we interpret 'exclusion' as limited to maneuvers not honestly industrial, but actuated solely by a desire to prevent competition, can such a course, indefatigably pursued be deemed not 'exclusionary.'

Perhaps, then the successful competitor can be turned upon when he wins, because he has been told not to compete.

Judge Wyzanski, in his opinion in the *United Shoe Machinery* case, describes the doctrine announced by Judge Hand in *Alcoa* as determining that "one who has acquired an overwhelming share of the market 'monopolizes' whenever he does business... apparently even if there is no showing that his business involves any exclusionary practice." "But," Judge Wyzanski's opinion continues, "it will also be recalled that this doctrine is softened by Judge Hand's suggestion that the defendant may escape statutory liability if it bears the burden of proving that it owes its monopoly solely to superior skill, superior products, natural advantages (including accessibility to raw materials or markets), economic or technological efficiency (including scientific research), low margins of profit maintained permanently and without discrimination, or licenses conferred by, and used within, the limits of law (including patents on one's own inventions, or franchises granted directly to the enterprise by a public authority)." Perhaps, then, so far as efficiency is concerned, *Alcoa* only shifts the burden to the firm to justify its growth. It seems clear that *Alcoa,* in any event, has not settled the question of the weight to be given to the requirements of efficiency. In the enforcement of a regulatory statute, this issue might be less troublesome, but it is different for a statute intended to remove restraints to enterprise as a means of fostering competition. For the artificial limitation on the growth of a firm is of as much concern as the artificial growth through combination in order to monopolize. This is a major unsolved problem in the field of antitrust.

Whatever difficulties the doctrine of *Alcoa* may have with the application of the law to growth because of efficiency, the case, since it deals with undoubted monopoly size, has a strong underlying basis for its assumption that this size carries with it the power to fix prices. In the case of the assured monopoly, one may predict a restriction on production because this restriction will be sensible from the standpoint of the firm. To be sure, even then the firm will wish to take into account problems of good will and the threat of governmental intervention. This restriction on production may provide adequate justification for a law which carries the burden of limiting economic expansion. But the application of the monopolizing concept of the law to units of lesser relative size raises special difficulties. For with units of lesser relative size, it cannot be said that there will be inevitably a restriction in production. If it is granted that there will be more competition if additional units are fashioned in the industry, this may not be an adequate basis to justify the application of the law. This is particularly true in terms of both the state of economics and of the history of the Sherman Act. For the Sherman Act, as has often been said, is directed against restraints and monopoly or monopolizing. It was not intended to compel all possible competition. The act arose out of an antipathy towards monopoly, and those restraints which were thought to have the consequences of monopoly. And it is in the identification and the prediction of the consequences of monopoly that economics has the most to contribute. There is much greater uncertainty about the consequences of imperfect competition. The application of the monopoly concept to industries with three or four large units leads to curious anomalies. Thus what is deemed adequate relief for one industry, as, for example, the three firms in aluminum, may be the starting point for bringing a case against another industry, such as tobacco. It is in connection, with the application of the antitrust laws to firms of less than clear monopoly size, that the concepts of collusion and abuses have been expanded.

Perhaps it can be said that what is emerging is a law limiting the uses of size. As Justice Holmes wrote in his dissent in *Northern Securities,* "it has occurred to me that it might be that when a combination reached a certain size it might have attributed to it more of the character of a monopoly merely by virtue of its size than would be attributed to a smaller one." But since the units themselves do not have that position which would condemn them as monopolies, instead the law has developed to prohibit for them certain types of conduct deemed collusive or abusive. Thus without a finding of monopoly, collaborative efforts accompanied by the exclusion of others for competitive reasons are deemed unlawful in the case; integration becomes unlawful in the motion picture industry, although vertical integration per se is not illegal; tying arrangements are found illegal when based upon what is called a monopoly or dominant position, although the position in itself may be deemed lawful. This places the concepts of collusion and abuses in a new light.

The concept of abuses is illustrated in Justice Douglas' opinion in *United States v. Griffith.* The *Griffith* case is one of a sequence of antitrust cases dealing with the motion picture industry. In *Griffith,* affiliated exhibitors used a common agent or agents to negotiate with distributors. The exhibitors therefore "were concededly using their circuit buying power to obtain films." Moreover, "their closed towns were linked with their competitive towns." These practices apparently were decisive in finding a conspiracy in violation of both section one and section two of the Sherman Act. Justice Douglas explains that "anyone who owns and operates the single theatre in a town, or who acquires the exclusive right to exhibit a film, has a monopoly in the popular sense," although it is not necessarily illegal. Then, "if he uses that strategic position to acquire exclusive privileges in a city where he has competitors, he is employing his monopoly power as a trade weapon against his competitors. It may be a feeble, ineffective weapon where he has only one closed or monopoly town. But as those towns increase in number throughout a region, his monopoly power in them may be used with crushing effect on competitors in other places.... When the buying power of the entire circuit is used to negotiate films for his competitive as well as his closed towns, he is using monopoly power to expand his empire." This is "a misuse of monopoly power under the Sherman Act. If monopoly can be used to beget monopoly, the Act becomes a feeble instrument indeed." There could be no doubt that the monopoly power of the circuit "had some effect on their competitors and on the growth" of the circuit.

The doctrine of abuses sees them as exclusionary devices useful for getting a monopoly, or expanding it, or for moving from one monopoly to the creation of another. Thus when vertical integration is concerned, the inquiry is often as to the "leverage" of the device. When a tying clause is annexed to a patent, the courts regard this as an attempt to expand the scope of the patent, or as an attempt to create a new monopoly using the leverage of the patent monopoly. So in the *Griffith* case, buying power which joins the competitive with the closed towns, is a use of monopoly power to beget monopoly. It is natural that as the antitrust laws are applied to firms with less than assured monopoly size, new emphasis should be placed upon these exclusionary devices or abuses. Since the firms have not achieved positions which are regarded as illegal in themselves, it becomes important to see if their conduct threatens to bring to them greater monopoly power. The rule of *Griffith,* then, in contrast to *Alcoa* which dealt with assured monopoly size, emphasizes these exclusionary practices which are viewed as the means of achieving greater monopoly power and therefore as an illicit use of the power already possessed. New importance therefore must be attached to the concept of abuses. In addition, the history of related legislation since the Sherman Act is to give independent status to these abuses. The abuses represent conduct which is thought to create monopoly and these are the practices to be caught under the Robinson-Patman Act, under section three and, to some extent, seven of the Clayton Act, and under section five of the Federal Trade Commission Act. The practices are to be caught in order to prevent monopoly in its incipiency.

We are not sure of the basis or the justification for the concept of abuses. Insofar as the practices involved are covered in special legislation, perhaps it may be suggested that all that is involved is a legislative determination that the conduct should be banned. These enactments have introduced a certain automaticity into the law; to some extent they preclude or make unnecessary separate inquiry in each of the cases as to the effects, advantages, or disadvantages of the banned practices. But even so the enactments must be supposed to rest upon conclusions drawn from experience and supportable in general, even though they may not be true of an exceptional case. Moreover the interrelationship between the Sherman Act and the amendatory acts suggests that no one of the special statutes is completely insulated from a pervasive concern with the doctrines of economics in the field of competition and monopoly. Indeed the attempt to apply the legislative standard with strictness has provoked criticism. The report of the Attorney General's Committee on section three of the Clayton Act, relating to exclusive dealing, for example, seems to prefer "full factual analysis of significant market data," and here as elsewhere it appears to favor incorporation of advances in economic teaching into the case law. We may conclude that to an undefined extent it is of interest to the law to know whether the abuses in fact do create monopoly.

The economic teaching gives little support to the idea that the abuses create or extend monopoly. Firms that are competitive cannot impose coercive restrictions on their suppliers or their customers as a means of obtaining a monopoly. They lack the power to do this effectively. Firms which have some monopoly power over prices and output can impose coercive restrictions on suppliers and customers. In the normal case, however, they will lose revenue if they do impose such restrictions, and this casts some doubt on how prevalent or continued the practice would be. Such firms would lose revenue because they cannot both obtain the advantage of the original power and impose additional coercive restrictions so as to increase their monopoly power. The coercive restrictions on customers are possible only if the price which would be charged without the restriction is reduced. The restrictions therefore would not be sensible except as a means of price discrimination. If used as a means of price discrimination, the restrictions might be considered more an enjoyment of the original power than an extension of it. In point of fact even a firm with complete monopoly power over prices and output cannot both get the advantage of such power and impose additional coercive restrictions on suppliers and customers. At most such a firm, and of course one with only some monopoly power, can decide to impose additional costs upon itself for the sake of a restriction. Such a restriction might be valuable if the effect of it would be to impose greater costs on possible competitors. But except for this special case, there is no clearly apparent advantage to a firm with monopoly power as against one without such power.

We realize that it is sometimes said that the restrictive practices support or extend monopolies because they can impose large capital requirements on existing or potential competitors. But this argument seems to require clarification and study. It is not evident whether the argument is based on an imperfection in the capital market, on the reluctance to assume the consequent risks, on the economies associated with raising large amounts of capital, or on the less efficient scale imposed on rival firms.

To a certain extent the economic analysis of the effect of the abuses may be relevant only to an interpretation of the meaning of the language of the law. We have suggested that in most instances the supposed abuses neither support nor enlarge monopoly power. Yet we realize that in the typical patent tying clause case, for example, the courts speak of the device as an attempt to expand the patent monopoly. In the *Carbice* case, for example, where the patent was "for a particular kind of package employing solid carbon dioxide in a new combination," but not on the package nor on the dry-ice, the use of the patented combination was tied to the purchase of dry-ice. Justice Brandeis stated that "relief is denied because the Dry Ice Corporation is attempting, without sanction of law, to employ the patent to secure a limited monopoly of unpatented material used in applying the invention." This was beyond the "scope of the patentee's monopoly." In the *Mercoid* case, the use of a combination patent on a heating system was tied to the purchase of stoker switches used in the combination. Justice Douglas stated that the case was "a graphic illustration of the evils of an expansion of the patent monopoly by private engagements." The practice in both of these cases could be described as an administrative device for collecting revenue from patents assumed to be valid.

The *Carbice* and *Mercoid* cases are perhaps exceptional in the tying clause field because they involve combination patents. The usual reference in this area would be to the practices as portrayed in the *Dick, International Business Machines Corporation,* and the block booking portions of the motion picture cases. In the *Dick* case the use of the mimeograph machine was tied to the purchase of the supplies for it. The restriction was impliedly upheld, but Chief Justice White in dissenting wrote, "I have already indicated how, since the decision in the Button Fastener Case, the attempt to increase the scope of the monopoly granted by a patent has become common by resorting to the devices of license restrictions manifested in various forms, all of which tend to increase monopoly and to burden the public in the exercise of their common rights. My mind cannot shake off the dread of the vast extension of such practices which must come from the decision of the court now rendered." In the *International Business Machines* case, the use of the machines was tied to the cards utilized with it. Justice Stone characterized the effect of the condition as one "whose substantial benefit to the lessor is the elimination of business competition and the creation of monopoly...." Block booking is described in the *Paramount* case as the "practice of licensing, or offering for license, one feature or group of features on condition that the exhibitor will also license another feature or group of features released by the distributors during a given period." The result was said "to add to the monopoly of the copyright in violation of the principle of the patent cases involving tying clauses." Nevertheless, we believe that the practices in each of the three cases can be explained best as methods of charging different prices to different customers and not as extensions of monopoly to other areas.

There are three remaining types of restrictive practices to which reference is frequently made. They are: (1) joint buying power linking open and closed situations as in the *Griffith* case; (2) exclusive arrangements as in the *Standard Fashions* or *Standard Oil of California* cases; and, (3) vertical integration. The joint buying power arrangement assumed to exist in *Griffith* includes within that power the strength of the monopoly of the theatres in the closed towns. This monopoly by itself is assumed to be lawful. If it is a monopoly, the owner will be enabled to obtain better prices from the suppliers than could be obtained by each of several independent exhibitors in that market. As we have suggested, it would seem that in order to impose additional coercive restrictions on the suppliers, as, for example, on the supplies for competitive markets, the monopoly owner would have to pay the suppliers for these additional restrictions. Nor would it seem to be in the interest of the suppliers to encourage the growth of monopoly among the exhibitors. Perhaps it could be argued and shown that the monopoly of the theatres confers larger resources upon the owner, but otherwise the monopolist has no obvious advantage for competitive areas over any other competitor who sets out to establish a monopoly. It would seem therefore that the method of buying supplies for a monopoly and a competitive market through a single source cannot be assumed to be effective as a means for extending a monopoly without additional evidence. There is no necessary effect on competitors. The case is not necessarily different from where the single source buys for many competitive theatres.

In the exclusive arrangement cases, the firm which is assumed to have some monopoly power imposes a cost upon itself in order to obtain the restriction forbidding its customer from handling the goods of others. There is an obvious monopoly problem if control over all the possible outlets were thus obtained, but most of the cases do not involve such control, nor would it be clear that a firm with a monopoly over the supply would wish to obtain a monopoly over the outlets. Its monopoly over the supplies is not increased through its monopoly over the outlets, unless it can be said that the restrictions on the outlets impose greater costs on potential competitors than they do on the monopoly company itself. This may have been the situation in the *Standard Fashion* case. There a firm with widespread control over a variety of patterns for garments entered into exclusive arrangements with a multitude of outlets. A competitor with less control over the variety of patterns might, through this arrangement, have a greater cost imposed upon it to secure outlets. The reason for this is that there may well be economies for an outlet in handling a variety of patterns. But the *Standard Oil of California* case seems less justified on this basis. In that case no one firm had such a dominion over the products, and a single outlet handling the gasoline of a competitor would appear to have the same economies open to it as were open to Standard's stations. The vertical integration cases appear similar to the exclusive arrangement situations. Vertical integration, however, often appears explainable as a method of price discrimination. It will be said that vertical integration like exclusive arrangements and tying clauses increases a competitor's capital requirements, and so places him at a disadvantage. We have already indicated our belief in the need for further exploration and clarification of that line of argument.

If, then, there is doubt as to the economic support for the conclusions of law with respect to the effect of abuses, this does not mean that the law will change. When the courts speak of expanding a monopoly, or of attempting to secure a monopoly through various exclusionary means, the language used may point to matters about which economics has little to say. For example, the scope of the monopoly conferred by a patent is a matter of law. Perhaps a combination patent cannot be enjoyed if the only means of collecting for its use is through the sale of one of the parts. Perhaps, also, the enjoyment of a patent is to be cut short to prevent price discrimination through the use of a tying device. Having conferred a monopoly in one area, the courts may feel that the incidents of that monopoly must be confined. Thus a restriction imposed on the use of products with a patented machine would have an effect upon the producers of the products. Moreover, even if the restriction does not bring a new monopoly into existence, it can be regarded as a restraint. The important point, however, is that the restrictions or abuses will not in most cases carry with them the normal incidents of monopoly. They will not in the normal case carry with them any decrease in production, nor, except for price discrimination, any increase in revenue, nor any increase in price. They may in fact, in some cases of price discrimination, result in an increase in production. In the language of the Robinson-Patman Act and of the Clayton Act, the abuses do not in most cases either tend to substantially lessen competition or tend to create a monopoly. If this were agreed upon, the law might not change, but its objectives would be clarified. The law would be seen as having less to do with competition and monopoly and more to do with merely a set of rules of fair conduct, perhaps emphasizing the protection of smaller firms. Clarification of the economic basis thus presents the opportunity of choice for the law.

The problem of collusion has always been central to the antitrust laws. Price-fixing agreements operate to affect the market price when they result in restriction in output which affect the market supply. It is difficult to provide an economic basis for a law against price-fixing agreements when the market price is unaffected. Moreover, price-fixing agreements, when adherence to them cannot be compelled through coercion or penalties, might be self-correcting either through the defection of members, which would be rewarding to the individual firm, or through the advent of new firms. But if a price-fixing agreement occurs between members of an industry controlling a substantial share of the market, then, when seen as in reality an agreement to control output, the consequences of this behavior may be predicted with some certainty. It becomes unnecessary to examine the consequences in the individual case in order to determine whether the resulting prices are different than competitive. Adopting the standard of competition, it becomes unnecessary to embark on what Judge Taft called a sea of doubt where reasonableness of the prices is in issue. Accordingly, there is an economic foundation for the illegality of price fixing in itself when market price is affected. There is less foundation when it cannot be shown that the members of the arrangement control a substantial share of the market. And despite the repetition of the slogan that price fixing is illegal per se, the cases as yet do not hold, save possibly for resale price control, that price-fixing agreements without power to affect the market price are illegal. The clarification which economics can contribute at this point is to emphasize the importance of examining the effect of the agreement on production and the market supply. Yet surely the law may conclude on its own that if the participants believe the agreement to be worthwhile for them, then there is sufficient likelihood market supply is affected so that a general prohibition is justified. The extension of the Sherman Act into the remoter nooks and crannies of commerce, because of the broadened view of commerce among the states, however, may be thought to raise some question as to the worthwhileness of a prohibition of all forms of price fixing regardless of market effect.

But the serious problem of collusion is to determine what conduct is to be characterized as the equivalent of an agreement to control output. A facet of this problem concerns allowable trade association activities and the proper scope to be permitted to the uses of knowledge. The relative merits of knowledge and ignorance are not well defined in legal or economic doctrine. The counterpart of efficient scale in the size problem is the improvement of the market where collusion is concerned. Behavior designed to achieve these improvements cannot be readily isolated from behavior which can be interpreted as characterizing monopoly or effective agreements to control output. For example, dissemination of real or assumed knowledge as to pending market changes can bring about a restriction in output in the industry. The magnitude of the change for the individual firm, however, must be based on a prediction by that firm of the behavior of other firms in the industry. It would appear to be extremely difficult and unwise for the law to assume that action taken on general knowledge implies a concert of action equivalent to collusion, conspiracy or agreement, and yet the result may be the same as that which follows from an agreement. It seems unworkable to suggest that illegality in such cases should be reserved for those instances where the restriction in individual output goes beyond the point justified by a common reaction and reaches that further restriction of output characteristic of a monopoly. This problem concerns also the application of the law to industries with several large firms when the attempt is made to deal with them as jointly monopolizing because of common patterns of behavior. Here it cannot be said that economic doctrine indicates with certainty that there will be collusion among the firms; it cannot be said that there will be inevitably a restriction in production.

The central problems in the field of antitrust as yet unsettled and pressing for solution concern size, abuses and collusion. We do not mean to suggest that there are simple economic or legal answers. The problems are difficult, and the law is not likely to meet them directly. Nor do we mean to suggest that the law must of necessity conform to the prescriptions of economic theory, let alone move within the confines of changing fashions in such theory. The law indeed can have a life of its own. But in this field of law more than any other, the general presumptions are of such a character that they cannot be readily isolated from the corresponding presumptions which dominate economic theory. We do suggest that in the future there may well be a recognition of the instability of the assumed foundation for some major antitrust doctrines. And this may lead to a re-evaluation of the scope and function of the antitrust laws.

## Robert H. Bork

## *The Antitrust Paradox: A Policy at War with Itself*

### Introduction: The Crisis in Antitrust

Improbable as the statement may seem, antitrust today is almost an unknown policy. It is ubiquitous: Antitrust constitutes one of the most elaborate deployments of governmental force in areas of life still thought committed primarily to private choice and initiative. It is popular: There is some intellectual but almost no political opposition to its main features. And it is even exportable: This supposedly peculiarly American growth has spread to and taken at least equivocal root in Europe and even in Asia. Yet few people know what the law really commands, how its doctrines have evolved, or the nature of its ultimate impact upon our national well-being. Even among the specialized and elite corps of lawyers who operate the antitrust system there is remarkably little critical understanding of the policy.

This state of affairs is curious, and certainly unfortunate, but perhaps it is understandable. Antitrust is a subcategory of ideology, and by the time a once militant ideology triumphs and achieves embodiment in institutional forms, its adherents are likely long since to have left off debating first principles. "The antitrust movement," as Professor Richard Hofstadter remarks, "is one of the faded passions of American reform." But Hofstadter goes on, and probably it is not a paradox—"the antitrust enterprise has more significance in contemporary society than it had in the days of T.R. or Wilson, or even in the heyday of Thurman Arnold." The very nearly simultaneous "collapse of antitrust feeling both in the public at large and among liberal intellectuals" and our arrival at a state of affairs in which "the managers of the large corporations do their business with one eye constantly cast over their shoulders at the Antitrust Division" are probably to be explained, though Hofstadter does not quite make the causality explicit, by the fact that "antitrust as a legal-administrative enterprise has been solidly institutionalized in the past quarter-century." The waning of fervor with the growth of organization, bureaucracy, and effective power is a familiar occurrence in both secular and religious movements.

But the ideology remains, and its inner logic drives the antitrust enterprise—lawyers, economists, judges, and legislators—inexorably toward the conclusions implicit in the premises. This phenomenon, along with a modest resurgence of antitrust feeling, accounts for the current round of litigation and proposed legislation designed to dissolve many of America's most successful corporations. In all kinds of political weather the machinery of antitrust enforcement grinds steadily on, mindlessly reproducing both the policy triumphs and disasters of the past. Even when public and political enthusiasm for the harassment of business is at an ebb, the enforcement bureaucracy and the residual potency of the antitrust symbol remain strong enough to prevent the law's mistakes from being retracted.

The full range of modern rules that significantly impair both competition and the ability of the economy to produce goods and services efficiently is discussed in detail in the remainder of this book. Generally, these rules ignore the obvious fact that more efficient methods of doing business are as valuable to the public as they are to businessmen. In modern times the Supreme Court, without compulsion by statute, and certainly without adequate explanation, has inhibited or destroyed a broad spectrum of useful business structures and practices. Internal growth to large market size has been made dangerous. Growth by merger with rivals is practically impossible, as is growth by acquisition of customers or suppliers. Even acquisitions for the purpose of moving into new markets have been struck down, as the law evolves a mythology about the dangers of conglomerate mergers. Cooperative ventures between independent businesses are outlawed through a misapplication of the sound policy against price fixing and market division. The Court has destroyed the most useful forms of manufacturer control over the distribution of products, requiring higher-cost modes of reaching the public. It has needlessly proliferated rules about pricing behavior that have the effect of making prices higher and markets less effective allocators of society's resources. The Court has done these things, moreover, on demonstrably erroneous notions of the economics that guide the law.

So far as the Supreme Court is concerned, we appear at the moment to be between cycles of antitrust expansion. Extensions of old doctrine to new fields have been relatively infrequent the last half dozen years or so, but there is scant comfort in that. The situation will not last. A position based not upon settled ideology but rather upon an accidental equilibrium of forces is unlikely to prove stable. Unless the theory of antitrust is understood and the law brought into line with it, the law will surely move on again, becoming even more unnecessarily restrictive of business freedom. A majority of the current Supreme Court has recently taken a significant step toward reforming a part of antitrust, and prospects for an intelligible, proconsumer law may now be brighter than they have been for several decades. Still, there is a very long way to go. Existing case law incorporates principles that have not been extended to the full reach of their internal logic. Law grows by analogizing new situations to old, and antitrust may move still further away from a policy of competition simply by realizing the potentialities inherent in the principles it now espouses.

But there is more to fear than that, for the courts are of course not the sole generators of antitrust policy. A new era of antitrust expansion seems likely to begin in Congress, which is influenced by popular moods. There has always existed in this country a populist hostility to big business, a hostility that is currently reinforced by the suspicion that major corporations are somehow to blame for hardships that have their origin elsewhere, in the politics of OPEC, in federal regulation of natural gas prices—or in bad weather, for that matter.

The direction of new legislation is determined by the prevailing tone of public discourse. That discourse has in recent years been almost uniformly in favor of fresh antitrust assaults on business. Ralph Nader, though rather more voluble than most, expresses not untypical attitudes. "Antitrust," Mr. Nader informed us a few years back, "is going to erupt into a major political issue because it is not just an esoteric issue for lawyers." Rather, it is "going modern and will shed more and more of its complexities." He was a true prophet: shortly thereafter, a Nader Study Group filed a report on something called "The Closed Enterprise System" which shed the complexities of antitrust so completely that the reader is given no hint of their existence. Indeed, both the tone and the message of the report are best paraphrased by Professor Richard Posner as suggesting "that if we would only stop thinking so much about the problem and throw the book at the bastards our monopoly problem would be solved."

Nader's essentially nihilistic attitude might perhaps be little to the point except that he and his Study Group are by no means alone, and some of their company is quite distinguished. I have heard an eminent professor of antitrust law argue that the economic problems of antitrust are too difficult and that the government should, for that reason, eschew policy analysis and just keep bringing lawsuits in order to keep businessmen "shook up." Several hundred lawyers at a meeting of the Antitrust Section of the American Bar Association listened to a nationally prominent attorney, who subsequently became an Associate Justice of the Supreme Court, contend that it was fruitless to worry about antitrust's intellectual problems. Antitrust, the attorney said, is in the good old American tradition of the sheriff of a frontier town: he did not sift evidence, distinguish between suspects, and solve crimes, but merely walked the main street and every so often pistol-whipped a few people.

Such attitudes have, of course, found reflection in Congress. Recently, for example, Congress enacted legislation allowing each state to sue on behalf of all persons residing within its borders for triple the damage done them by antitrust violations. The same legislation made mergers more difficult by requiring advance notification to government, and greatly expanded government's power to compel information without resort either to a lawsuit or a grand jury investigation. The Petroleum Industry Competition bill, which won astonishingly wide support in the Senate in 1976, was designed to destroy vertical integration in the major oil companies by requiring that each company confine itself to one of three phases of the industry: production, transportation, or refining and marketing. That bill is, as of this writing, scheduled for reintroduction, along with other bills that would prevent oil companies from entering or remaining in any other energy field, such as coal or solar energy. There is no reason to believe that the destruction of national wealth involved in the enactment of these bills or other recent proposed legislation would be compensated by any social gain.

We are urged, then, by persons in and out of Congress, to throw the antitrust book at business in order to improve the quality of American life. One could wish that those who want to throw the book had taken the time to understand it. In the pages that follow, I attempt to contribute to that necessary understanding by reading the antitrust book in light of the disciplines of law and economics, in order to show that the policy is not what it seems. Antitrust presents itself as a body of developed knowledge and principle worked out over years of investigation, thought, and litigation. That image is misleading. Antitrust is not all of a piece.

Because antitrust's basic premises are mutually incompatible, and because some of them are incorrect, the law has been producing increasingly bizarre results. Certain of its doctrines preserve competition, while others suppress it, resulting in a policy at war with itself. During the past twenty years or so, the protectionist, anticompetitive strain in the law has undergone a spectacular acceleration, bringing to pass what Ward Bowman and I have termed the "crisis in antitrust." The resolution of this crisis will determine antitrust's future. The law must either undergo a difficult process of reform, based upon a correct understanding of fundamental legal and economic concepts, or resume its descent to the status of an internal tariff against domestic competition and free trade.

Given the pace and direction of its development, the overriding need of antitrust today is a general theory of its possibilities and limitations as a tool of rational social policy. Yet there exists among those professionally concerned with antitrust a surprising lack of agreement concerning the most basic questions. The disagreement, though variously phrased, is finally about two issues: (1) the goals or values the law may legitimately and profitably implement; and (2) the validity of the law's vision of economic reality. I have attempted in this book to resolve both of those issues. A consideration of the virtues appropriate to law *as* law demonstrates that the only legitimate goal of antitrust is the maximization of consumer welfare. Current law lacks these virtues precisely because the Supreme Court has introduced conflicting goals, the primary one being the survival or comfort of small business.

A consumer-oriented law must employ basic economic theory to judge which market structures and practices are harmful and which beneficial. Modern antitrust has performed this task very poorly. Its version of economics is a mélange of valid insights and obviously incorrect—sometimes fantastic—assumptions about the motivations and effects of business behavior. There are many problems here, but perhaps the core of the difficulty is that the courts, and particularly the Supreme Court, have failed to understand and give proper weight to the crucial concept of business efficiency. Since productive efficiency is one of the two opposing forces that determine the degree of consumer well-being (the other being resource misallocation due to monopoly power), this failure has skewed legal doctrine disastrously. Business efficiency necessarily benefits consumers by lowering the costs of goods and services or by increasing the value of the product or service offered; this is true whether the business unit is a competitor or a monopolist. When efficiency is not counted, or when it is seen as a positive evil, it appears that no business structure of behavior has any potential for social good, and there is consequently no reason to uphold its legality if any remote danger can be imagined. The results could not have been worse, and would probably have been better, if the Court had made the opposite mistake and refused to recognize any harm in cartels and monopolies. Yet neither mistake need have been made. The hopeful development in the current Supreme Court's approach to antitrust, referred to a few pages back, is a single case weighing in favor of a business practice its capacity to create efficiency. That approach seems obvious, but against the background of the jurisprudence of the last two decades it appears revolutionary. Applied generally, it could save antitrust as useful and respectable policy. It is too soon to tell whether the Court will follow up its new beginning.

This book attempts to supply the theory necessary to guide antitrust reform. Such an attempt assumes that reasonable certainty concerning basic issues is possible. I believe it is. Because the issues of goals and of economic means must both be faced, antitrust is necessarily a hybrid policy science, a cross between law and economics that produces a mode of reasoning somewhat different from that of either discipline alone. I use the words "science" and "discipline" deliberately. Basic microeconomic theory is of course a science, though like many other sciences it is by no means complete in all its branches. Were it not a science, rational antitrust policy would be impossible. We are too little accustomed, however, to thinking of law as a science, and indeed in current practice there is little enough to suggest the concept. Yet it should be obvious that the very idea of the rule of law requires some degree of certainty and logical rigor. Though its theory is not, and cannot be, nearly so highly developed as that of economics, law does have requirements that are distinctively its own. When these are ignored, as they increasingly have been in antitrust adjudication, law that is bad as law, quite apart from its substantive content, necessarily results.

* * * *

## Chapter 4: Business Behavior and the Consumer Interest: Some Rudiments of Theory

Antitrust is about the effects of business behavior on consumers. An understanding of the relationship of that behavior to consumer well-being can be gained only through basic economic theory. The economic models involved are essential to all antitrust analysis, but they are simple and require no previous acquaintance with economics to be comprehended. Indeed, since we can hardly expect legislators, judges, and lawyers to be sophisticated economists as well, it is only the fact that the simple ideas of economics are powerful and entirely adequate to this field that makes it conceivable for the law to frame and implement useful policy.

Consumer welfare is greatest when society's economic resources are allocated so that consumers are able to satisfy their wants as fully as technological constraints permit. Consumer welfare, in this sense, is merely another term for the wealth of the nation. Antitrust thus has a built-in preference for material prosperity, but it has nothing to say about the ways prosperity is distributed or used. Those are matters for other laws. Consumer welfare, as the term is used in antitrust, has no sumptuary or ethical component, but permits consumers to define by their expression of wants in the marketplace what things they regard as wealth. Antitrust litigation is not a process for deciding who should be rich or poor, nor can it decide how much wealth should be expended to reduce pollution or undertake to mitigate the anguish of the cross-country skier at the desecration wrought by snowmobiles. It can only increase collective wealth by requiring that any lawful products, whether skis or snowmobiles, be produced and sold under conditions most favorable to consumers.

The role of antitrust laws, then, lies at that stage of the economic process in which production and distribution of goods and services are organized in accordance with the scale of values that consumers choose by their relative willingness to purchase. The law's mission is to preserve, improve, and reinforce the powerful economic mechanisms that compel businesses to respond to consumers. "From a social point of view," as Frank H. Knight puts it, "this process may be viewed under two aspects, (a) the assignment or *allocation* of the available productive forces and materials among the various lines of industry, and (b) the effective *coordination* of the various means of production in each industry into such groupings as will produce the greatest result."

These two factors may conveniently be called *allocative efficiency* and *productive efficiency*. (When, for convenience, the word "efficiency" alone is used, productive efficiency is meant.) These two types of efficiency make up the overall efficiency that determines the level of our society's wealth, or consumer welfare. The whole task of antitrust can be summed up as the effort to improve allocative efficiency without impairing productive efficiency so greatly as to produce either no gain or a net loss in consumer welfare. That task must be guided by basic economic analysis, otherwise the law acts blindly upon forces it does not understand and produces results it does not intend.

## The Nature of Allocative Efficiency

Both economics and law generally link business behavior to consumer welfare through the concepts of "competition" and "monopoly." But the two disciplines mean quite different things by those terms, and when the differences go unremarked—or, worse, when various common-speech meanings are inserted without notice—debate grows more and more heated and less and less illuminating. The economist's models of competition and monopoly are descriptive. The lawyer's, if he thinks of antitrust as designed to preserve competition and destroy monopoly, must be normative. There is a wide gap in practical consequences. The economist builds a pure model in order to clarify thought; such models are indispensable starting places for policy analysis, but they are not prescriptions for policy. They leave out too much. A determined attempt to remake the American economy into a replica of the textbook model of competition would have roughly the same effect on national wealth as several dozen strategically placed nuclear explosions. To say that is not to denigrate the models but to warn against their misuse.

An understanding of the efficient allocation of resources, and hence of the evils of misallocation, is best attained through simple models of firm behavior under differing market structures. I will sketch the most basic aspects of the conventional theories of competition, monopoly, and oligopoly. Each of these terms describes an industry structure. Economic theory attempts to relate structure to performance, and performance to the goal of consumer welfare. The theories are listed in descending order of rigor. The theory of competition states the way in which firms *must* behave if they are to survive when the market is competitively structured. The theory of monopoly states the way in which a firm possessing control of a market *can* behave in order to maximize profits. Conventional oligopoly theory, however, is little more than a guess about the ways in which firms might be able to behave in a market composed of a few sellers.

## Competition

[Note: In the omitted portions, Bork explains how competition drives prices down toward costs and thus creates consumer welfare. He concludes:]

[T]he forces of competition in open markets cause the actual allocation of resources to be ever shifting in pursuit of the constantly moving equilibrium point. And the more closely the economy approximates this limiting condition, the more closely do we approach the maximization of consumer welfare. Indeed, the best practicable approximation to the limiting condition can realistically be called the maximization of consumer welfare.

## Monopoly

We are now in a position to understand the case against monopoly. As we shall see, it is not an absolute case, for though monopoly may interfere with allocative efficiency, it may also rest upon productive efficiency. Whether a particular monopoly is, on balance, beneficial or detrimental to consumer welfare must take both types of efficiency into account. Later on, we shall see how that is done. For the moment, remember that the case made here is entirely in terms of allocative efficiency and is therefore one-sided.

Suppose that our hypothetical 100 widget manufacturers either merge into a single corporation or simply meet and agree to place the power to make output decisions for all firms in a central industry committee. Let us suppose also that neither course of action produces any change in costs. We would have, in one case, a monopolistic horizontal merger or, in the other, a cartel. In either case, the new management would have control of 100 percent of widget output. The new monopolist, whether corporation or committee (I will no longer distinguish, the principles being the same), will perceive at once that its output decisions do affect market price. Since the monopolist is the entire industry, it faces the sloping industry demand curve rather than the competitive firm's flat demand curve. More important, the monopolist does not maximize profits by continuing to run along at the old output rate of 25 million widgets annually. The reason is simple. For the competitor, marginal revenue was always the same at any output rate and always equaled market price. But for the monopolist, marginal revenue is always less than market price because his demand curve slopes. Should he decide to offer an additional 1 million widgets per year, the demand curve shows that he would have to accept a lower price, and the crucial point is that the lower price would apply not just to the additional million but to all his output. He would get less for the first 25 million widgets as well as for the additional million. The additional output has a drag effect upon his marginal revenues all the way along the line.

* * * *

Now the widget monopolist, like the widget competitor and all businessmen under any circumstances, maximizes profits by producing at a rate where marginal cost equals marginal revenue. As may be seen from Figure 1, the intersection of marginal cost and marginal revenue is well to the left of the intersection of marginal cost and demand.

This means that the monopolist will find it profitable to produce fewer widgets annually than did the same industry when competitively structured. This cutback in the rate of production and sale is what economists call a "restriction of output." Here, the lowered rate is 15 million widgets annually. Fewer widgets on the market, the demand curve informs us, means that purchasers will bid a higher price for what is available, in this case $50 each.

* * * *

But the higher price is not the root of the problem, nor is the lower output. Many unobjectionable developments could produce these. An increased demand for housing, and hence for steel, could have made the raw material for widgets more expensive, raising the marginal cost curve, so that even a competitive widget industry might have cut back to an annual production of 15 million, with a resulting $50 widget price. The distinctive feature of the monopoly situation is that the monopolist has created a gap between marginal cost and price, which means that social costs and social desires are no longer equated. Indeed, the monopolist has made his monopoly profit by creating an imbalance between cost and desire. With the restriction in output, moreover, the widget industry no longer needs as many resources as before. The unneeded resources must either lie idle, an obvious social waste, or migrate to other industries where the value of their marginal product will be less than it would be in the monopolized widget industry. The result, of course, is that they contribute less wealth as consumers define wealth, so that consumers would be better off if these resources could return to making widgets.

This is the mechanism by which restriction of output, made possible by monopolistic merger or cartel or any other means of controlling the market, creates a misallocation of resources and thereby makes society poorer. The evil of monopoly, then, is not higher prices or smaller production (though these are its concomitants) but misallocated resources, or allocation inefficiency.

It is a common misconception that a monopolist's increased efficiency redounds only to the monopolist's benefit. The preceding figure should dispel that notion. If marginal cost is lowered, the intersection with marginal revenue moves to the right, indicating a larger output and a lowered price. That benefits consumers as well as the monopolist.

One important caveat should be stated here. As the monopolist pushes the price of widgets higher, consumers may suddenly switch to a product that was not considered a substitute at lower prices. That is to say, the demand curve may suddenly approach the horizontal at some point. If this occurred at a price of $40 per widget, for example, the monopolist would not misallocate resources to the same extent as supposed here. This limitation may often be important and, as will be discussed, is probably important in the case of monopoly gained by superior efficiency.

## Oligopoly

Almost none of the markets with which antitrust law must deal resemble the atomized or monopolistic models just outlined. For the vast majority of actual markets, therefore, we may not automatically assume that business behavior has the effect upon resource allocation predicted by either model. To this intermediate range of market structures has been applied the theory of oligopoly, which attempts to predict the behavior of firms in markets where rivals are "few." The lack of rigor in that theory may be suggested by the observation that there appear to be about as many oligopoly theories as there are economists who have written on the subject. In fact, it is a most unsatisfactory branch of economic theory, and as I will attempt to show in Chapter 8, there is no very good reason to think that so-called "concentrated" markets behave in a less satisfactory manner than more fragmented ones.

The dominant, but by no means universal, opinion among economists and antitrust commentators holds that markets with few rivals (there is very little agreement as to how many firms may still be "few" enough for the theory to apply) will perform poorly because the firms will, without overt agreement, recognize their mutual self-interest and restrict output in order to behave, so far as possible, as if they had formed an actual cartel.

Now in their desire to achieve cartel results, though without collusion, the firms in a concentrated industry differ not at all from those in a fragmented industry. Rather, it is their ability that differs; this, the theory holds, is chiefly a matter of numbers and the effect of individual firm behavior on the market. The 100 widget manufacturers of our hypothetical competitive industry know as well as any economist that they would make more money if they could all restrict output and take higher prices. If businessmen did not know this principle, they would not form cartels. Being barred by law from agreeing explicitly, they would like to get the same results by each behaving as if he were in a cartel. That is, mutual forbearance in rivalry could approach a situation in which industry marginal cost and industry marginal revenue are equated, so that each firm takes 1 percent of a monopoly profit instead of 1 percent of a lower competitive return. No one thinks that will happen in a fragmented industry, for a variety of reasons: each firm will be severely tempted to take more sales at the higher price, letting the others make the sacrifice of holding price up by holding back on sales; costs will differ, so that the firms will not arrive at the same judgment as to the most profitable price; costs and demand will change, increasing the probability of differing responses; and so on.

But the situation is thought by many persons to be different if the industry becomes concentrated. Suppose that in the fragmented widget industry, over time, some firms grow and others decline, many leaving the industry altogether, so that eventually there remain only four firms. One of these has 50 percent of actual sales, another 30, a third 15, and the fourth is struggling somewhat at 5 percent. Almost all economists would describe such an industry as "oligopolistic" or "concentrated," and perhaps most would predict that its structure would cause it to behave noncompetitively. The basis for that prediction is the concept of *oligopolistic interdependence.* Each firm is aware that its price and output decisions are no longer insignificant with respect to total industry price and output. Sellers no longer face an impersonal market price but one they can, to a greater or lesser degree, affect.

This much is true. If the 50 percent firm, which, let us suppose, now makes 12,500,000 widgets annually, expanded its output by 10 percent, perhaps because it lowered its costs, to 13,750,000 widgets per year, the market price would drop initially from $30 to under $28 per widget. If the other firms adjusted by reducing output to equate marginal cost with the new price, the price would rise somewhat and after a series of adjustments would settle down perhaps above $28 but below $30. The point of all this is that the widget makers would be aware of their power over price and might separately decide to try raising it. The 50 percent firm might begin by announcing a new $35 widget price. If the others did not follow, the higher price would not last long. The theory supposes, however, that the 30 percent firm's management will realize that undercutting the largest firm is short-sighted, since that firm will drop its price and all firms will be back where they began. Why not follow the price up? If the other two firms reason similarly, all will be getting $35, a price above the competitive level, though not at the monopoly level. By such a process the rivals may work themselves up to the monopoly price (and the restricted output necessary to raise the price), jointly maximizing their profits, without ever once meeting surreptitiously at a country club or leaving the telltale evidence of long-distance calls to one another in the telephone company's records.

Devotees of oligopoly theory rarely claim that businesses' maneuvers and reactions will be adroit enough for the oligopolists to arrive at the monopoly output and price that a single firm occupying the entire industry would choose. Changing conditions of demand and technology will continually alter the profit-maximizing solution, and four firms are most unlikely to read an uncertain and fluid situation in an identical way. When costs differ, as they always do, the best price and degree of restriction will differ for each firm, making tacit cooperation still more difficult. When products are not identical, and particularly when product descriptions change, so that prices must vary, yet another unsettling factor is introduced. Moreover, there will always be a temptation to "cheat," to pick up a very profitable piece of extra business with a small price cut. Purchasers can play sellers against each other to break down the oligopoly price.

It will be urged, however, that the theory does not demand perfect formation flying. If oligopolists cannot achieve the complete monopoly solution, that does not mean they will necessarily arrive at the complete competitive solution with prices at marginal cost. No, it does not. But nothing in the theory compels the conclusion that oligopolists do not behave as competitors. The whole thing is speculation about how firms may or may not be able to behave. The theory has nothing like the definiteness and rigor of the theories of competition and monopoly. We will examine it more closely and attempt to gauge its usefulness for antitrust policy in Chapter 8.

The models described so far constitute the rudiments of the theory of allocative efficiency. So far as consumer welfare is concerned, they are only half the story. We turn next to the other half.

## The Nature of Productive Efficiency

Productive efficiency is a simple, indispensable, and thoroughly misunderstood concept. Not one antitrust lawyer in ten has a remotely satisfactory idea of the subject, and the proportion of economists who do, though surely higher, is perhaps not dramatically so. The situation has deteriorated so badly that one can hear it hotly denied that efficiency has anything to do with antitrust. There even appears to be an impression among the more zealous antitrust enforcers that efficiency does not exist but is some sort of trick thought up by unscrupulous defense attorneys. Yet, as Frank Knight points out, this form of efficiency is one of the two that enter into the organization of production to meet consumer preferences, and it follows that antitrust policy cannot be rational unless productive efficiency is understood and weighed in the law's processes.

Productive efficiency is any activity by a business firm that creates wealth. The concept is symmetrical with that of allocative efficiency. Productive efficiency, like allocative efficiency, is a normative concept and is defined and measured in terms of consumer welfare. Since a free market system assumes that consumers define their own welfare, it follows that productive efficiency consists in offering anything, whether products or services, that consumers are willing to pay for. (The caveat that the goods or services concerned must not be ones that society outlaws for other reasons—addictive drugs or prostitution, for example—is obvious.) The relative efficiency of firms is therefore measured by their relative success in the market.

Attention must be focused on this definition of productive efficiency rather than on the wide variety of factors that contribute to it. Economies of scale, specialization of function, ability to obtain capital, management skill—all of these and many more are elements that contribute to the firm's ability to please consumers, but they are causes rather than manifestations of efficiency. Efficiency is at bottom a value concept, not a description of mechanical or engineering operation. As Knight points out:

> There is a common misconception that it is possible to measure or discuss efficiency in purely physical terms. The first principles of physics or engineering science teach that this is not true, that the term efficiency involves the idea of value, and some measure of value as well. It is perhaps the most important principle of physical science that neither matter nor energy can be created or destroyed, that whatever goes into any process must come out in some form, and hence as a mere matter of physical quantity, the efficiency of all operations would equal one hundred percent. The correct definition of efficiency is the ratio, not between "output" and "input" but between *useful* output and total output or input. Hence efficiency, even in the simplest energy transformation, is meaningless without a measure of usefulness or value. In any attempt to understand economic efficiency, the notion of value is more obviously crucial since most economic problems are concerned with a number of kinds both of outlay and of return, and there is no conceivable way of making comparisons without first reducing all the factors to terms of a common measure.

In antitrust the required common denominator is provided by the goal or value of consumer welfare. In a system which permits consumers to define their own welfare by their purchases, it follows, that, with an important reservation to be mentioned shortly, a firm's efficiency is shown by its success. It is useless, for antitrust purposes, to study the minimum efficient size of the firm by studying the engineering efficiencies of the plant and production line because the important factor is consumer response to what comes off the production line.

* * * *

Considerations such as these, perhaps, led George Stigler to define efficiency simply as "competitive effectiveness." That will do as well as any other brief definition, but it must be remembered that competitive effectiveness or productive efficiency is not a concept coterminous with profitability. A firm may be profitable because it forms a cartel, merges to monopolistic size, or employs predatory tactics successfully. Profitability based upon such tactics is not evidence of productive efficiency because consumer welfare is lessened rather than increased. Profitability in such cases is based upon the disruption of allocative efficiency rather than the enhancement of productive efficiency. The methods of distinguishing efficiency from mere profitability are discussed in Chapter 6, and their application takes up much of the remainder of this book.

It may be objected that I have created a false dichotomy by assuming that the effects of business behavior are always classifiable with respect to allocative efficiency or productive efficiency. There are other problems in the world; among them are income distribution, externalities, and the purchase of goods that society does not want consumers to have. Quite right. If it were asserted that all of society's concerns with business behavior can be summed up as the effect on allocative and productive efficiency, the dichotomy would be false. The claim, however, is only that the dichotomy is proper for the specialized purposes of antitrust law. The classification is not merely proper, for we shall see in Chapter 6 that it is essential to reasoning about antitrust.

This definition of productive efficiency—competitive effectiveness—must necessarily be left without more content at this stage. As we go along we shall see in a variety of contexts some of the elements that go to produce efficiency.

## Chapter 5: The Consumer Welfare Model

We can now be more explicit about the factors that are included in antitrust's consumer welfare calculus and those that must be excluded from it. We may usefully illustrate the basic reckoning involved with a graph [Figure 1] employed by Oliver Williamson to represent the trade-off problem in a merger that both creates power to restrict output and cuts costs.

Williamson's graph . . . compares the "dead-weight" loss (the amount above costs that consumers would be willing to pay for the lost output) to the gains to all consumers of cost reductions resulting from the merger. Cost reductions mean that the saved resources are freed to produce elsewhere in the economy.

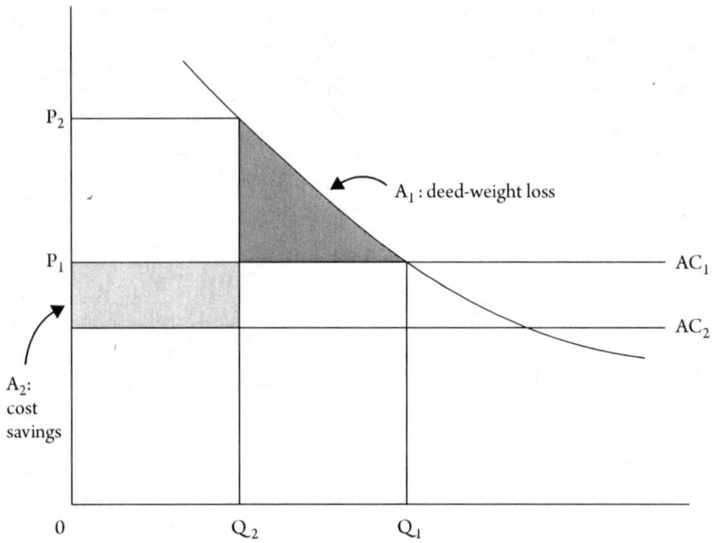


FIGURE 1 Effects on Consumer Welfare of a Merger That Restricts Output and Cuts Costs

The diagram assumes that the merger reduces the long-run average costs of the two firms from $AC_1$ to $AC_2$ but that the increased market power created by the merger results in a restriction of output so that the rate moves from $Q_1$ to $Q_2$. We then see that consumers have lost output—for which they would have been willing to pay an amount above cost equal to the area labeled $A_1$—and have gained in resource savings an amount equal to the area *A2*. Obviously, if $A_2$, the cost savings, is larger than $A_1$, the dead-weight loss, the merger represents a net gain to all consumers. If $A_1$ is larger than $A_2$, a net loss results.

This diagram can be used to illustrate all antitrust problems, since it shows the relationship of the only two factors involved, allocative inefficiency and productive efficiency. The existence of these two elements and their respective amounts are the real issues in every properly decided antitrust case. They are what we have to estimate—whether the case is about the dissolution of a monopolistic firm, a conglomerate merger, a requirements contract, or a price-fixing agreement.

But the consumer welfare diagram must not be taken literally, as if one could read correct decisions off the graph paper. It merely illustrates a relationship; it does not quantify it. We do not know the location of any of the sides of the triangular area $A_1$ or of three of the sides of the rectangle $A_2$ (the fourth is merely the price axis), so that we cannot possibly calculate their areas mathematically. We do not know in any actual case the slope of the demand curve, the location of the initial cost curve, the distance (if any) the cost curve will shift, or the amount (if any) the output will change.

It must also be remembered that there need not always be a tradeoff. In most cases, in my opinion, economic analysis will show that one of the areas does not exist, and decision of the case is therefore easy. Some phenomena involve only a dead-weight loss and no, or insignificant, cost savings. That is the case with the garden-variety price-fixing ring. Output is restricted so that $Q_2$ is to the left of $Q_1$, creating the area $A_1$, but there is no downward shift of costs, no line $AC_2$, and hence no area $A_2$. Other phenomena will involve only efficiency gain and no dead-weight loss. Examples of these include most of the mergers the Supreme Court strikes down and the price "discriminations" the Robinson-Patman Act is intended to stamp out. $AC_2$ drops below $AC_1$ creating the rectangle $A_2$, but $Q_2$ does not move to the left of $Q_1$, so there is no triangular area $A_1$. In fact, if the efficiency gain takes the form of a cost savings, $Q_2$ moves to the right of $Q_1$, signifying an increased rate of output due to lowered costs.

That raises a most important caveat which must accompany Williamson's diagram. The area $A_2$ represents only cost savings, and cost savings are but one element or form of increased efficiency. The area $A_2$, therefore, must be taken to symbolize any efficiency gain and not merely the reduction of costs.

Perhaps this representation of the consumer welfare model contains too many traps for the unwary, but I have adopted it because it illustrates so clearly the relationship between allocative and productive efficiencies in determining consumer wealth. It makes plain the error committed by the Supreme Court in holding either that efficiency is irrelevant or that it is actually a reason to strike down a merger. When efficiency is deemed irrelevant, there can never in any case be an area labeled $A_2$. Thus the merger can only be neutral, if no market power whatsoever is created (so that there is no area $A_1$), or harmful (if there is any area $A_1$ at all). When efficiency is deemed harmful, the merger is almost certainly bad, because it will almost certainly create either market power or efficiency. Otherwise, there would be very little reason to merge. The result of ignoring or outlawing $A_2$ is outlandish antitrust law. As Williamson says in arguing that the value of efficiency must be recognized: "if neither the courts nor the enforcement agencies are sensitive to these considerations, the system fails to meet a basic test of economic rationality. And without this the whole enforcement system lacks for defensible standards and becomes suspect."

* * * *

## Income Distribution

The model outlined addresses the total welfare of consumers as a class. It says nothing of how shares of consumption should be allocated through changes in the distribution of income. Yet all economic activity has income effects and, in particular, restriction of output by the exercise of monopoly power has income effects not taken into account by weighing only changes in allocative and productive efficiency. If the reader will look once more at the figure he will see that at the competitive price, $P_1$, there is a large area under the demand curve that lies above the market price. This area represents the amount above the actual price that consumers would be willing to pay rather than go without the product; it is generally called the "consumer's surplus," perhaps on some notion that the consumer gets surplus value for his money.

Those who continue to buy after a monopoly is formed pay more for the same output, and that shifts income from them to the monopoly and its owners, who are also consumers. This is not dead-weight loss due to restriction of output but merely a shift in income between two classes of consumers. The consumer welfare model, which views consumers as a collectivity, does not take this income effect into account. If it did, the results of trade-off calculations would be significantly altered. As Williamson notes, referring to his diagram: "The rectangle... bounded by $P_2$ and $P_1$ at the top and bottom respectively and 0 and $Q_2$ on the sides represents a loss of consumers' surplus (gain in monopoly profits) that the merger produces.... Inasmuch as the income distribution which occurs is usually large relative to the size of the dead-weight loss, attaching even a slight weight to income distribution effects can sometimes influence the overall valuation significantly."

The issue is not crucial, perhaps, since most antitrust cases do not involve a trade-off. The law's mistake has generally consisted of seeing restriction of output where there is none, and in such cases there will be no loss of consumer surplus. But even in cases where the trade-off issue must be faced, it seems clear the income distribution effects of economic activity should be completely excluded from the determination of the antitrust legality of the activity. It may be sufficient to note that the shift in income distribution does not lessen total wealth, and a decision about it requires a choice between two groups of consumers that should be made by the legislature rather than by the judiciary. This argument in its general form was developed in Chapter 3.

This conclusion is reinforced by the recognition that disapproval of the income redistribution could only rest upon a tenuous moral ground. Let us see where the income distribution criterion, if it were employed, would bite. It would never be important in any case in which deadweight loss exceeds efficiency gain, because the business behavior in question would be unlawful on consumer welfare grounds alone. The income distribution criterion would be superfluous. That criterion could only play a role where the behavior under examination—a merger, for example—creates an efficiency gain that is larger than the dead-weight loss, but where dead-weight loss and consumer-surplus loss together are larger than efficiency gain. Such a merger would have the net effect of benefiting consumers, and its legality would turn upon the inclusion or exclusion of income redistribution as a factor. It would be improper to include income redistribution as a factor *because* we disapprove of monopolistic restriction of output, for that would really be to count the dead-weight loss against the merger twice. The dead-weight loss has already been subtracted, and we must now consider whether the remaining net efficiency gain is to be overcome by income redistribution.

Once the issue is refined to that point, it becomes difficult to distinguish between this merger and a merger that creates only efficiency gain. The pure efficiency-gain merger also redistributes income. The new efficiency will divert income to the merged firm from less efficient rivals, and all firms using resources of the type released will gain at the expense of the owners of such resources because the new efficiency means that demand for the resources has declined relative to supply.

I am unable to distinguish the pure efficiency gain merger from the net efficiency-gain merger. Both increase consumer welfare and redistribute income. If income redistribution is not counted against one, why should it be counted against the other? There seems no reason. The impulse to count income redistribution arises from an excessive and uncritical moral aversion to the existence of *any* dead-weight loss, an aversion transferred to income redistribution. There is no basis for that aversion, at least no basis that courts can adopt, when the deadweight loss is inseparable from a greater efficiency gain that benefits society at large.

Williamson suggests that the income transfer could be regarded unfavorably "because it produces social discontent." He means not that it will certainly produce social discontent but that it *may,* and that such a possibility is an appropriate factor to weigh. It certainly is, but the question is what institution should weigh it and in what context. Income redistribution due entirely to increased efficiency may, and often does, produce social discontent, as when computers replace file clerks, but that would not be a reason for a court in an antitrust case to enjoin the progress of automation. The problem of social discontent is one for Congress and not the federal judiciary to address.

Other objections to income redistribution as an antitrust criterion could be elaborated. If income redistribution were to be weighed against cases of net efficiency creation on the ground that consumers are generally poorer than producers (which would be a most dubious ground), then the principle would seem to require that income redistribution be weighed in favor of any economic behavior when producers of a product had generally lower incomes than consumers. This would justify price fixing by poorly remunerated producers. If the criterion is to be taken seriously, moreover, courts really ought to attempt to trace all the income effects as they spread to rival firms and to the owners of competitive and complementary resources. These efforts would introduce horrendous complexities in which it is surely undesirable to mire the processes of antitrust.

There is every reason, therefore, to conclude that courts should ignore income distribution in deciding antitrust cases and stick to the criteria of the consumer welfare model.

[Note: Discussions of costs of gaining and maintaining monopoly, theory of the second best, and externalities omitted.]

## Chapter 6: The Method of Antitrust Analysis

To read antitrust literature or to participate in the numerous conferences convened to discuss policy is to become convinced that antitrust is less a discipline than a buzzing confusion of unrelated opinion. Even agreement on conclusions is usually superficial, papering over fundamental disagreement about reasons. One cause of this eminently unsatisfactory state of affairs lies in a failure to focus and settle the question of the form of reasoning, or argument, proper to the subject matter.

The mode of correct antitrust analysis is determined by the strengths and weaknesses of price theory. Once these are understood and respected, we should achieve greater agreement on substantive issues.

This chapter will advance several related propositions.

First, price theory assures us that economic behavior is not random but is *primarily* directed toward the maximization of profits.

Second, attempts to maximize profits can stand in only three relationships with respect to consumer welfare. Economic behavior is primarily efficiency creating, primarily output restricting, or neutral in its consumer welfare impact.

Third, price theory enables us to identify, with an acceptable degree of accuracy, those activities whose primary effect is output restricting, leading to the inference that all other activity is either efficiency creating or neutral.

Fourth, antitrust must avoid any standards that require direct measurement and quantification of either restriction of output or efficiency. Such tasks are impossible.

Finally, in all cases in which behavior is neutral or in which analysis does not provide a basis for predicting effects upon consumer welfare, tie-breaking considerations indicate that the law should not intervene.

## The Relation Between Price Theory and Antitrust

The basic assumptions and doctrines of conventional price theory will be used throughout this book. To those who object that economics is not a sufficiently certain discipline upon which to rest major policy conclusions, the answer given here is not (though it could be) that they misunderstand the nature and strength of the theory, but rather that such reliance is inevitable. There is no body of knowledge other than conventional price theory that can serve as a guide to the effects of business behavior upon consumer welfare. To abandon economic theory is to abandon the possibility of a rational antitrust law.

Since the argument of this book will disagree rather strongly with some economists, it had better be explained that such disagreement does not of itself contradict my claim to rely upon basic economic postulates. The layman is likely to think that economic theory is what any economist theorizes, but of course it is not. If it were, we should have to believe that there are dozens or hundreds of mutually incompatible versions of economic theory, each as good as any other. Basic economic theory is an intensely logical subject, and much of it consists of a drawing out of the implications of a few empirically supported postulates. When I speak of economic theory, therefore, I mean those statements which, judged by the evidence available and the quality of the argument which supports them, appear to be the most probably correct statements at the moment. That way of stating the matter may make some theory appear more tentative than it really is. In many cases the theory is so well grounded that we can be certain, or virtually so, of its reliability. Economists differ on particular subjects for a variety of reasons, some of which it would be invidious to discuss. To mention a few of the others, it is quite easy to make mistakes in the process of creating and applying a detailed logical system, and it is particularly easy in fields where emotions and political and social attitudes vie with reason to control men's beliefs. There are, moreover, special difficulties in applying theory to business practices. It is easy to overlook the existence of alternative theoretical explanations for a single practice, or to neglect a seemingly minor aspect of behavior that will not fit the theory being imposed.

All of this means that the judge, legislator, or lawyer cannot simply take the word of an economist in dealing with antitrust, for the economists will certainly disagree. Unless we would be driven to a sterile agnosticism, therefore, we must work through the arguments and make up our own minds. And we will find that on most subjects there is a better view which we ought to accept until fresh analysis provides yet a superior position.

Several of the first principles of antitrust methodology derive from an aspect of the market system that has often been expressed in the analogy to the Darwinian theory of natural selection and physical evolution. The familiarity of that parallel, and the overbroad inferences sometimes drawn from it, should not blind us to its important truths. The environment to which the business firm must adapt is defined, ultimately, by social wants and the social costs of meeting them. The firm that adapts to the environment better than its rivals tends to expand. The less successful firm tends to contract—perhaps, eventually, to become extinct. The Stanley Steamer and the celluloid collar have gone the way of the pterodactyl and the great ground sloth, basically for the same reasons. Since coping successfully with the economic environment also forwards consumer welfare (except in those cases that are the legitimate concern of antitrust), economic natural selection has normative implications that physical natural selection does not have. At least there seems to me more reason for enthusiasm about the efficient firm than about the most successful physical organisms, the rat and the cockroach, though this view is, no doubt, parochial.

A key factor in evolution is death, and that holds true in economic as in physical evolution. The firm has an advantage over the animal because it can consciously change not just its behavior but its structure and so avoid or postpone death, but the threat is there and it becomes an actuality for many firms every year. There is in the literature much loose talk by people who should know better to the effect that the large modern corporation can escape the forces of the market through internal financing. Internal financing may often be a means of lowering the costs of acquiring capital, but it does not insulate the firm from the demands of the market. To expand, or even to survive, every firm requires a constant flow of capital for employees' wages, raw material, capital investment, repairs, advertising, and the like. When the firm is relatively inefficient over a significant time period, it represents a poorer investment and greater credit risk than innumerable alternatives. If the firm is dependent upon outside capital, the firm must shrink and, if no revival in its fortunes occurs, die. That fate cannot be averted by financing out of retained earnings. There is, in the first place, no reason for a firm to throw its own money into a losing proposition rather than invest elsewhere. Even if one postulated a management that did so, and also postulated an ability to escape stockholder revolts, takeover bids, and so forth, internal financing could only delay the end. The firm would be incurring expenses that were not recovered, and it could continue only so long as it was willing and able to go on giving away its capital to consumers. There is no theoretical, empirical, or intuitive reason to suppose that such conduct is at all common.

The need to make profit produces the search for it. Profit motivation is patently ubiquitous and overwhelming, and it matters little whether we view it as entirely a conscious motivation, merely the type of behavior selected for survival by the economic environment from random forms of behavior, or, perhaps most realistically, as something of each. It is a common observation of biologists that whenever the physical environment provides a niche capable of sustaining life, an organism will evolve or adapt to occupy the place. The same is true of economic organisms, hence the fantastic proliferation of forms of business organization, products, and services in our society. We turn out everything from the most sophisticated electronic equipment to chartreuse compact cars to hair sprays, from business executives to field goal specialists to psychiatrists for disturbed household pets to rentable conversationalists for sagging dinner parties. The yellow pages of the telephone book do not begin to tell the story. The strength of the driving force that sends persons and firms into every crevice capable or even just possibly capable of sustaining profitable economic activity can hardly be overestimated.

This assumption of price theory is so crucial—and yet so insistently misunderstood by, among others, businessmen and antitrust lawyers—that elaboration may not be amiss. It is commonly objected that businessmen are not purely, or perhaps even primarily, rational profit seekers, that they could not in any case master and apply the complex calculations that such a goal requires, and that they employ guidelines to behavior that are inconsistent with profit maximization. None of these is a valid objection. Though if required I should not hesitate to impute conscious profit maximizing to businessmen—experience with businessmen and, even more, with antitrust lawyers and consulting economists should convince anyone that profit is a goal not only consciously but constantly borne in mind—price theory requires no such assumption. The validity of its tenets depends upon their success in predicting behavior, and the basic tenet of price theory, as Milton Friedman points out, states that businessmen generally behave *as if* they were engaged in maximization, just as a theory of physical science might state that leaves position themselves on trees "as if each leaf deliberately sought to maximize the amount of sunlight it receives."

Thus, "firms behave *as if* they were seeking rationally to maximize their expected returns... and had full knowledge of the data required...; *as if,* that is, they knew the relevant cost and demand functions, calculated marginal cost and marginal revenue from all actions open to them, and pushed each line of action to the point at which the relevant marginal cost and marginal revenue were equal."

Friedman uses an analogy that effectively disposes of the objections both that profit maximization is too complicated a goal and that businessmen often do not talk like profit maximizers:

> Consider the problem of predicting the shots made by an expert billiard player. It seems not at all unreasonable that excellent predictions would be yielded by the hypothesis that the billiard player made his shots *as if* he knew the complicated mathematical formulas that would give the optimum directions of travel, could estimate accurately by eye the angles, etc., describing the location of the balls, could make lightning calculations from the formulas, and could then make the balls travel in the direction indicated by the formulas. Our confidence in this hypothesis is not based on the belief that billiard players, even expert ones, can or do go through the process described; it derives rather from the belief that, unless in some way or other they were capable of reaching the same result, they would not in fact be *expert* billiard players.
>
> ... Now, of course, businessmen do not actually and literally solve the system of simultaneous equations in terms of which the mathematical economist finds it convenient to express this hypothesis, any more than leaves or billiard players explicitly go through the complicated mathematical calculations or falling bodies decide to create a vacuum. The billiard player, if asked how he decides where to hit the ball, may say that he "just figures it out" but then also rubs a rabbit's foot just to make sure; and the businessman may well say that he prices at average cost, with of course some minor deviations when the market makes it necessary. The one statement is about as helpful as the other, and neither is a relevant test of the associated hypothesis.

Friedman's point is not that firms maximize perfectly, any more than expert billiard players plan and execute every shot correctly. Perfection is the limiting condition to which the more successful come closer than their rivals. As Armen Alchian observes, business success is measured against rivals rather than the ideal: "Realized positive profits, not *maximum* profits, are the mark of success and viability.... Positive profits accrue to those who are better than their actual competitors, even if the participants are ignorant, intelligent, skillful, etc. The crucial element is one's aggregate position relative to actual competitors, not some hypothetical perfect competitors." Profit maximization is the limiting point toward which success tends.

The fact that businessmen talk in terms not always equatable with profit maximization is of no particular importance, though it does mislead those who look no further. There are a variety of explanations: the simplest is that businessmen are no more self-conscious and articulate than the rest of the human race about their real motivations and conduct. Moreover, in a society whose intellectual leaders seem often not to understand the social value of self-seeking business behavior, the ability to talk vaguely about broad "social responsibility" while actually engaged in profit maximizing may be an important adaptive technique. Besides, many businessmen are as confused as other people about the morality of profits. Stigler reports that "in one field study, when [businessmen] were asked whether they maximized profits, they indignantly rejected the suggestion and pointed out that they were sincerely religious, public-spirited, and so on—as if these traits were inconsistent with profit-maximizing. But when the question was reformulated as: would a higher or lower price of the product yield larger profits?, the answer was, usually, no."

The unsophisticated observer may also mistake for irrationality, or as indicating a goal other than profits, those rules of thumb that businessmen use to cope with uncertainty or to avoid the impossible task of rethinking every problem every time it arises. "Thus," according to Alchian, "the urge for 'rough-and-ready' imitative rules of behavior is accounted for. What would otherwise appear to be merely customary, 'orthodox,' nonrational rules of behavior turn out to be codified imitations of observed success, e.g., 'conventional' markup, price 'followship,' 'orthodox' accounting and operating ratios, 'proper' advertising policy, etc." Such rules serve the function that habit and custom perform in other areas of life. Without them, moment-to-moment behavior would pose insuperable complexities. The firm will do better or worse as its rules of thumb prove to have survival value or not, and as it has or lacks the ability to alter them to meet circumstances.

We come now to a crucial point. To carry out its mission, antitrust must classify varieties of behavior with respect to their probable impacts upon consumer welfare. Obviously, only three relationships are possible, and these correspond to three quite different ways of making money. A business firm may seek to increase its profits by achieving new efficiency (beneficial), by gaining monopoly power and restricting output (detrimental), or by some device not related to either productive or allocative efficiency, such as taking a bookkeeping advantage of some wrinkle in the tax laws (neutral).

The task of antitrust is to identify and prohibit those forms of behavior whose net effect is output restricting and hence detrimental. It should, of course, leave untouched behavior that is beneficial or neutral. The available resources of price theory dictate the manner in which this task must be accomplished. The best-developed branch of price theory is the theory of the ways in which firms may profit by interfering with allocative efficiency. Though we know something of the subject, there is no comparably clear, reliable, and general theory of the ways in which they may create productive efficiency. It follows, therefore, that antitrust analysis, if it is to be successful, must proceed primarily by elimination. We must appraise any questioned practice—say, a merger or a requirements contract—in order to determine whether it contains any likelihood of creating output restriction. If it does, and if it also contains the possibility of efficiency, we have a mixed case, which raises problems that will be discussed in a moment. If a practice does not raise a question of output restriction, however, we must assume that its purpose and therefore its effect are either the creation of efficiency or some neutral goal. In that case the practice should be held lawful.

It makes some people uneasy to have to rely entirely upon theory to infer the nature of a reality that is not directly observed. Yet I am convinced both that the theory is good enough to make the task doable and, equally important, that there is no other possible way to proceed. An economist once called this the "Philo Vance approach to antitrust"; he was not, one gathered, one of that detective's greatest admirers. (As a matter of fact, he was probably thinking of Sherlock Holmes's dictum: "When you have eliminated the impossible, whatever remains, *however improbable,* must be the truth.") The characterization is not without justice, but the objection it implies is wide of the mark. Philo (or Sherlock) did not have the advantage of the tight, logical system provided by price theory. If he had, his method of deduction would have been perfectly practical.

This is not by any means to suggest that it is not possible and desirable to go further and to specify the nature of the efficiencies created or intended by various forms of business behavior. Such an effort may serve as a valuable double-check upon conclusions arrived at by the process of elimination, and it is certainly likely to be more persuasive. But it is not logically necessary.

The application of this technique to particular situations will not be completely error free. But that is not a fatal objection. No system of laws is error free. The legal system makes mistakes in perceiving reality in the decision of every kind of case, from torts and contract disputes to homicide prosecutions. To demand perfection is to demand the abolition of law. The question is whether a method of applying the law can give an acceptable degree of accuracy and whether this method is better than any alternative method. The method of reasoning by elimination in antitrust cases passes both these tests. Indeed, no other method of antitrust analysis is even possible, since the only alternative, that of quantifying both efficiency and restriction of output, is well beyond the present powers of economic analysis and is likely forever to remain so.

## Richard A. Posner[1]

## *The Chicago School of Antitrust Analysis*

The use of the term "Chicago" to describe a body of antitrust views to which I, among others, am thought to subscribe is very common. I shall argue in this paper that although there was a time when the "Chicago" school stood for a distinctive approach to antitrust policy, especially in regard to economic questions, and when other schools, particularly a "Harvard" school, could be discerned and contrasted with it, the distinctions between these schools have greatly diminished. This has occurred largely as a result of the maturing of economics as a social science, and, as a corollary thereto, the waning of the sort of industrial organization that provided the intellectual foundations of the Harvard school. More generally, this change can be attributed to the fact that the diversity in fundamental premises among economists studying antitrust questions has substantially diminished. No longer is it such a simple thing to identify a Harvard or a Chicago position on issues of antitrust policy. Partly this is a matter of growing consensus; partly of a shift from disagreement over basic premises, methodology, and ideology toward technical disagreements of the sort that would be found even in a totally nonideological field.

Part I of this paper recounts the development of the Chicago school of antitrust analysis, and, more briefly, of the Harvard school. The sharpest differences between them are assignable to the 1950's and early 1960's. Part II discusses a number of areas in which the positions of the two school have since overlapped, converged, or crossed over, with special reference to predatory pricing. Part III considers the issue in which traces of the traditional Chicago-Harvard confrontation are most conspicuous—the

1. Lee and Brena Freeman Professor of Law, University of Chicago. The helpful comments of Robert Bork, Kenneth Dam, William Landes, George Stigler, and Donald Turner on a previous draft are gratefully acknowledged.

issue whether to break up leading firms in highly concentrated industries. The general conclusion of the paper is that it is no longer worth talking about different schools of academic antitrust analysis.

## I. The Chicago and Harvard Schools: The Foundations

The basic features of the Chicago school of antitrust analysis are attributable to the work of Aaron Director in the 1950's. Director formulated the key ideas of the school, which were then elaborated on by students and colleagues such as Bowman, Bork, McGee, and Telser. These ideas did not, I believe, emerge from a full-blown philosophy of antitrust. Rather, they were the product of pondering specific questions raised by antitrust cases, and only in retrospect did it become clear that they constituted the basis of a general theory of the proper scope of antitrust policy. In summary form the key ideas may be stated as follows:

1. A tie-in (i.e., requiring a buyer to buy a second product as the condition of buying the first) is not a rational method of obtaining a second source of monopoly profits, because an increase in the price charged for the tied product will, as a first approximation, reduce the price that the purchaser is willing to pay for the tying product. A tie-in makes sense only as a method of price discrimination, based on the fact that the amount of the tied product bought can be used to separate purchasers into more or less elastic demanders of the tying product. There is no need to worry about price discrimination, however, because it does not aggravate the monopoly problem. On the contrary, price discrimination is a device by which the monopolist in effect seeks to serve additional consumers, i.e., those having the more elastic demands, who might be deterred by the single monopoly price that would be charged in the absence of discrimination. Thus, price discrimination brings the monopolist's output closer to that of a competitive market and reduces the misallocative effects of monopoly.

2. From the standpoint of the manufacturer imposing it, resale price maintenance is not a rational method of distribution if its effect is to give dealers monopoly profits. Yet manufacturers, if permitted, often will impose it. The explanation is that, by preventing price competition among dealers, resale price maintenance encourages dealers to offer consumers presale services (such as point of sale advertising, inventory, showroom display, and knowledgeable sales personnel) up to the point at which the cost of these services at the margin just equals the price fixed by the manufacturer. Such services, which enhance the value of the manufacturer's product to consumers and hence the price he can charge the dealers, might—because of "free-rider" problems—not be provided if price competition among dealers were permitted.

3. Selling below cost in order to drive out a competitor is unprofitable even in the long run, except in the unlikely case in which the intended victim lacks equal access to capital to finance a price war. The predator loses money during the period of predation

and, if he tries to recoup it later by raising his price, new entrants will be attracted, the price will be bid down to the competitive level, and the attempt at recoupment will fail. Most alleged instances of below-cost pricing must, therefore, be attributable to factors other than a desire to eliminate competition.

These ideas generated others. The tie-in analysis, for instance, was extended to vertical integration in general. To illustrate, it makes no sense for a monopoly producer to take over distribution in order to earn monopoly profits at the distribution as well as the manufacturing level. The product and its distribution are complements, and an increase in the price of distribution will reduce the demand for the product. Assuming that the product and its distribution are sold in fixed proportions, and thus that the price discrimination analysis is inapplicable, the conclusion is reached that vertical integration must be motivated by a desire for efficiency rather than for monopoly.

The analysis of resale price maintenance generalized readily to other restrictions on distribution, such as exclusive territories and exclusive outlets. The predatory-pricing analysis generalized to other methods by which firms were thought to hurt others by hurting themselves—for example, by demanding that purchasers sign longer-term contracts than they desire, in order to deny a market to competing sellers: a rational purchaser would demand compensation for accepting such a disadvantageous term.

From these various analyses, a conclusion of great significance for antitrust policy emerges: firms cannot in general obtain or enhance monopoly power by unilateral action—unless, of course, they are irrationally willing to trade profits for position. Consequently, the focus of the antitrust laws should not be on unilateral action; it should instead be on: (1) cartels and (2) horizontal mergers large enough either to create monopoly directly, as in the classic trust cases, or to facilitate cartelization by drastically reducing the number of significant sellers in the market. Since unilateral action, as I have defined the term, had been the cutting edge of antitrust policy for a great many years, to place it beyond the reach of antitrust law, as Director and his followers seemed to want to do, implied a breathtaking contraction in the scope of antitrust policy.

What was the source of Director's heterodox thinking? Because of Director's close personal and professional associations with Milton Friedman, it is common to think that Director's antitrust analysis was the product of conservative (which is to say, "liberal" in the nineteenth-century sense of the term) antipathy to government intervention in the economy. I question this view. I believe Director's conclusions resulted simply from viewing antitrust policy through the lens of price theory. Each of his ideas was deducible from the assumption that businessmen are rational profit-maximizers, the deduction proceeding in accordance with the tenets of simple price theory, i.e., that demand curves slope downward, that an increase in the price of a product will reduce the demand for its complement, that resources gravitate to the areas where they will earn the highest return, etc. "Simple" and "easy" are not the same thing, however.

Although the analytic tools used by Director were simple, the insights they yielded were extremely subtle. Certainly they were resisted for many years.

Yet it is still fair to ask why the application of price theory to antitrust should have been a novelty. The answer, I believe, is that in the 1950's and early 1960's, industrial organization, the field of economics that studies monopoly questions, tended to be untheoretical, descriptive, "institutional," and even metaphorical. Casual observation of business behavior, colorful characterizations (such as the term "barrier to entry"), eclectic forays into sociology and psychology, descriptive statistics, and verification by plausibility took the place of the careful definitions and parsimonious logical structure of economic theory. The result was that industrial organization regularly advanced propositions that contradicted economic theory.

An example is the "leverage" theory of tie-ins that Donald Turner, a Harvard economist in the Edward Mason and Joe Bain tradition, espoused shortly after Director had developed his price-discrimination theory of tie-ins. The leverage theory held that if a seller had a monopoly of one product, he could and would monopolize its indispensable complements as well, so as to get additional monopoly profits. Thus, if he had a patented mimeograph machine, he would lease the machine at a monopoly price and also require his lessees to buy the ink used in the machine from him and charge them a monopoly price for the ink. This procedure, however, makes no sense as a matter of economic theory. The purchaser is buying a service, mimeographing. The pricing of its components is a mere detail; it is, rather, the total price of the service that he cares about. If the seller raises the price of one component, the ink, the purchaser will treat this as an increase in the price of the service. If the machine is already being priced at the optimal monopoly level, an increase in the price of the ink above the competitive level will raise the total price of the service to the consumer above the optimal monopoly level and will thereby reduce the monopolist's profits.

There was a similar confusion in the concept of a "barrier to entry," a concept that played—and still plays—a large role in thinking about competition. Suppose that it costs $10,000,000 to build the smallest efficient plant to serve some market; then, it was argued, there is a $10,000,000 "barrier to entry," a hurdle a new entrant would have to overcome to serve the market at no disadvantage vis-à-vis existing firms. But is there really a hurdle? If the $10,000,000 plant has a useful life of, for example, ten years, the annual cost to the new entrant is only $1,000,000. Existing firms bear the same annual cost, assuming that they plan to replace their plants. The new entrant, therefore, is not at any cost disadvantage after all.

Advertising presents a similar situation. A new entrant, to get his product accepted in the market, may have to launch it with an expensive advertising campaign. Again, this is a capital expenditure, because the effect of the campaign will not be fully used up in the first year. There is no reason to expect the annual cost of this capital expenditure to be any higher than that of firms in the market. They too must spend money on advertising to keep the consumer interested in their products. Most advertising, in fact, depreciates more rapidly than most plants; therefore, it is a lesser "barrier to entry" than having to build a plant (although in the traditional analysis it was considered a greater one). Neither the plant nor the advertising is a barrier in any useful sense.

The Chicago school's view of advertising is especially noteworthy because of the importance that advertising had assumed in the Harvard thinking on antitrust. Advertising played a dual role in that thinking. First, it was one of the most important barriers to entry. Second, it was used as the riposte to the free-rider argument about why manufacturers imposed resale price maintenance. The Harvard position was that overcoming the free-rider problem and thereby increasing the provision of presale services by the retailer was not a social benefit, because those services were forms of advertising, and advertising enables the manufacturer more effectively to differentiate his brand from competitors' brands, thereby creating or enhancing barriers to entry. The underlying assumption is that consumers are irrational and manipulable, and the Chicago theorist rejects this assumption as inconsistent with the premises of price theory. The rational consumer will pay for advertising (in the form of a higher price for the advertised brand) only to the extent that advertising reduces his costs of search. The services provided by advertising are therefore real services. In fact, they are indistinguishable from those yielded by a better product—and it is never suggested that making one's product genuinely better than those of competitors or potential competitors creates a "barrier to entry."

A clue to the nature of the Harvard school of industrial organization is that its practitioners were so fond of doing studies of competition in particular industries—airlines, tin cans, aluminum, rayon, Douglas firs, etc. These studies exemplified the particularistic and nontheoretical character of the field. The powerful simplifications of economic theory—rationality, profit maximization, the downward-sloping demand curve—were discarded, or at least downplayed, in favor of microscopic examination of the idiosyncrasies of particular markets.

The "kinked demand curve," "workable competition," "cut-throat competition," "leverage," "administered prices," and the other characteristic concepts of the industrial organization of this period had this in common: they were not derived from and were often inconsistent with economic theory, and in particular with the premises of rational profit maximization. They were derived from observation, unsystematic and often superficial, of business behavior. Director's approach was the opposite. He explained tie-ins, resale price maintenance, and other business behavior described in antitrust cases not by studying the practices but by looking for an explanation for them that squared with basic economic theory. When they first began to emerge in the articles written by his colleagues, students, and disciples, Director's ideas made little impact either on scholarly opinion or on policy. In some quarters the Chicago school was regarded as little better than a lunatic fringe. Kaysen and Turner's *Antitrust Policy*, the classic statement of the Harvard school, published in 1959, contains virtually no trace of any influence of the Chicago school.

Twenty years later, the position is dramatically changed. Partly as a result of George Stigler's attacks on the intellectual foundations of traditional industrial organization and partly as a result of the growing sophistication of economic analysis, the traditional industrial organization is becoming discredited in academic circles. The Chicago school has largely prevailed with respect to its basic point: that the proper lens for viewing antitrust problems is price theory. At the same time, some of the specific ideas first advanced by Aaron Director have been questioned, modified, and refined, resulting in the emergence of a new animal: the "diehard Chicagoan" (such as Bork and Bowman) who has not accepted any of the suggested refinements of or modifications in Director's original ideas.

The work of Director and his followers focused on the question when, if ever, a firm can unilaterally obtain or maintain monopoly power. The question when a firm can obtain such power by collaboration with its competitors received less attention. Partly, perhaps, for tactical reasons (not to seem to reject antitrust policy in its entirety), the members of the Chicago school would sometimes denounce price fixing. But it is unlikely that they regarded even price fixing, let alone oligopoly, as a serious problem. In the classical economic tradition running from Smith to Marshall, the tradition in which the Chicago school operates, a clear recognition of the propensity of sellers to attempt collusion was conjoined with a general indifference to, and sometimes an explicit rejection of, the desirability of imposing legal sanctions on collusion. This complacency (if one can call it that) rested on the belief that cartels were, first, highly unstable because of the propensity of members to cheat (so long as the cartel was not legally enforceable), and, second, in the long run futile in the absence of substantial barriers to entry. Collusion might still be attempted frequently if attempting it was cheap, but it would rarely succeed and its overall misallocative effects would be too slight to warrant inevitably costly public proceedings.

Given this tradition, given the Chicago school's rejection of the expansive notion of "barriers to entry," given the lack of any clear theoretical basis for oligopoly theory (and its accouterments such as the kinked demand curve), given Harberger's tiny estimate of the welfare costs of monopoly, given the atheoretical, ad hoc, and unsupported character of the efforts to avoid the implications of Harberger's analysis by ascribing to oligopolists failures of innovation or cost control, it was not to be expected that the Chicago school would attach great importance to vigorous prosecution of colluders. But such enforcement activity, in contrast to that directed against unilateral monopolizing acts, was not deplored.

George Stigler's work in the late 1950's and early 1960's, however, did focus on collusion and thus served to complete the edifice of Chicago antitrust thought. A series of articles chipped away at the apparatus that the traditional industrial organization had constructed to analyze collusion. In its place Stigler proposed a general theory of collusion that embraced oligopoly, i.e., collusion not involving explicit communication, as a special case. He approached the question of collusion by asking, in the manner of a price theorist rather than an industrial-organization man, when the benefits of collusion, in higher profits, exceed the costs (of preventing cheating) to the individual seller. The rate of entry, the elasticity of demand, the concentration of buyers, and other factors were identified. Many of these factors had been noted by the oligopoly theorists; Stigler's contribution was to show that every facet of the collusion question, including tacit collusion or oligopoly behavior, could be analyzed using the tools of price theory.

Stigler's analysis did not deny the possibility of collusion, even of the tacit variety. But it did suggest that tacit collusion would be a problem only at very high levels of concentration, and in so doing cast grave doubt on the necessity for draconian measures, whether under section 7 of the Clayton Act or section 2 of the Sherman Act, for preventing tacit collusion by arresting or destroying concentration.

By 1969, then, an orthodox Chicago position (well represented in the writings of Robert Bork) had crystallized: only explicit price fixing and very large horizontal mergers (mergers to monopoly) were worthy of serious concern.

## II. The Growing Convergence of the Two Schools

The basic tenet of the Chicago school, that problems of competition and monopoly should be analyzed using the tools of general economic theory rather than those of traditional industrial organization, has triumphed. The concepts and methods of traditional industrial organization are increasingly discredited in economics as practiced in the leading universities and this change is beginning to be reflected in the application of economics to antitrust law. The new Areeda and Turner treatise is a notable example of this point, although the treatise, perhaps because it is addressed primarily to practitioners rather than scholars, does not explicitly acknowledge the modification or abandonment of many of Professor Turner's earlier views. At the same time, the application of price theory to antitrust law has not left the pioneering work of Director and his followers untouched.

Let us consider now how the passage of years has affected some of the specific controversies between the Chicago and Harvard schools.

1. Tie-ins. The leverage theory of tie-ins early gave way in Harvard thinking to a barriers-to-entry theory. A tie-in was said to complicate entry because the new entrant would have to produce the tied as well as the tying product. When the motive for tying is price discrimination, however, the producer of the tying product need not assume control over any part of the production of the tied product, let alone produce it all. Instead, all that is required is that he act as an intermediary between the producer and the ultimate consumer so that he can reprice it in accordance with his discriminatory scheme. A new entrant will be able to obtain the tied product from the same source that the existing firm obtains it from.

One element (and an important one) of the Chicago analysis is, however, subject to criticism: the assumption that price discrimination is on the whole socially beneficial because it moves the monopolist's output closer to the competitive level and hence reduces the misallocative effects of monopoly. As Joan Robinson pointed out long ago, if price discrimination is not perfect (and it never is), it may lead to a smaller, rather than a larger, output than single-price monopoly. For example, many of the heavy users of mimeograph machines might be deterred by an ink tie-in that had the effect of raising the price of the machine and the loss of output might not be offset by greater business from small users, even though on balance the monopolist's profits were higher (higher profits, rather than greater output, being the purpose of price discrimination). Even a larger output may not result in a smaller misallocation. The price-discriminating monopolist breaks up his demand curve into a series of separate demand curves for different groups of customers. Within each of these submarkets he sells the output that equates his marginal revenue to his marginal cost. The total misallocation brought about by the price-discriminating monopolist is the sum of the misallocations in each submarket, and may easily exceed the misallocation caused by a monopolist charging a single price and producing a smaller output.

Other criticisms of the Chicago position have also been made. Professor Williamson, for instance, has noted that price discrimination involves extra transaction costs—specifically, the costs of preventing the low-price purchasers from reselling to the high-price purchasers (arbitrage)—which reduce the welfare gains from a higher output—if output is in fact higher. It has also been argued that, by increasing the expected gains from monopolizing, price discrimination increases the investment in monopolizing—which may not be socially desirable. Indeed, the costs of creating and maintaining monopolies may exceed the misallocative costs resulting from the smaller output of monopolized compared to competitive markets.

In the light of such criticism, the original Chicago analysis of the effects of tie-ins now seems a little oversimple. Nevertheless, the conclusion that tie-ins should not be forbidden seems both correct[2] and increasingly influential on academic opinion.

2. Vertical integration. Here too the leverage theory was eventually replaced by a barriers-to-entry theory (the economic analysis of vertical integration being, as I have indicated, symmetrical with that of tie-ins). The thinking was that if, for example, supplier A acquires all of his retail outlets, B, in order to compete, will have to open his own chain of outlets. This, in turn, will make B's entry more costly. The steps in this analysis are illogical, however, and evidence of monopolization by such means scant or nonexistent. A will find it very costly to buy more outlets than he needs. B, on the other hand, will not have to open his own outlets to enter; if his entry is anticipated, the outlets will be there to greet him. Moreover, even if B did have to open his own retail outlets, the higher capital cost of his entry would still be no greater than the (also higher) capital cost to A of being a retailer as well as a manufacturer. The analysis does not depend on whether retail outlets are cheap or expensive to build or acquire or on whether the integration in question is forward into distribution or backward into raw-material, or other, supply. The essential point is that the cost to the monopolist of integrating is prima facie the same as the cost to the new entrant of having to integrate. The validity of this analysis is not affected even if the result of integration is completely to deny the new entrant access to some essential input except by dealing

2. See R. Posner, *Antitrust Law: An Economic Approach* 178–183 (1976).

with the existing firms in the market. The cost to the existing firms is still the same as to the new entrant, although now it is in the form of an opportunity cost. Suppose, for example, that kryptonite is an indispensable input in the manufacture of widgets. A owns all the kryptonite in the universe and also manufactures widgets. He could, of course, refuse to sell kryptonite to B, a prospective entrant into widget production. The cost to A of this refusal is the price B would have been willing to pay. Stated differently, by his control of kryptonite A can extract any monopoly rents available in the widget industry without denying a place in widget manufacture to others' firms. If there is a proper antitrust objection, it is to the kryptonite monopoly rather than to vertical integration.

Yet, despite the force of these arguments, it is incorrect to dismiss entirely the possibility of monopolistic consequences from vertical arrangements. The above arguments assume that, as in the case of the manufacturer-retailer, the relevant inputs, e.g., the manufactured product and its distribution, are combined in fixed proportions to produce the final output (the sale at retail). Suppose, however, that some input is used in variable proportions with other inputs to produce the final output, e.g., uranium and enrichment services in the production of nuclear fuel. If one of the inputs is monopolized, causing its price to rise in relation to those of other inputs, the output manufacturer will seek to reduce the proportion in which he uses this input and, instead, use more of the other inputs. The possibility of such substitution acts as a partial check on the monopoly power of the input monopolist. Assume, however, that the input producer buys the input user. This will eliminate the threat of substitution and so reduce the elasticity of demand for the input in question. Even so, it does not follow that the merger should be prohibited, for one of its effects is that the inputs will now be used in the proportions that minimize the true social costs of manufacturing the output. But it cannot be said that such a merger, merely because it is vertical, cannot possibly increase monopoly. So saying, I do not mean to suggest that such an equivocal and perhaps remote danger warrants reversing the growing support, at least in academic circles, for a permissive policy toward vertical mergers and vertical integration generally.

The change in thinking that has been brought about by the Chicago school is nowhere more evident than in the area of vertical integration. Kaysen and Turner, writing in 1959, advocated forbidding any vertical merger in which the acquiring firm had twenty percent or more of its market.[3] Areeda and Turner, writing in 1978, express very little concern with anticompetitive effects from vertical integration. In fact, as between a rule of per se illegality for vertical integration by monopolists and a rule of per se legality, their preference is for the latter.

3. Restricted distribution. As noted above, the Harvard reply to the Chicago analysis of resale price maintenance was that the benefit that the manufacturer sought to obtain by restricting competition among his distributors, i.e., presale services, was actually a social evil, because these services resulted in "product differentiation," a

3. C. Kaysen and D. Turner, *Antitrust Policy* 133 (1959).

barrier to entry. Facing no close substitutes for his brand because it was differentiated in the consumer's eyes from competing brands, the producer could charge a monopoly price. If the case of fraudulent advertising is put to one side, the conclusion that advertising and related promotional methods create monopoly power, at least in any sense relevant to antitrust policy, cannot be derived from the premises of economic theory. Consumers will not pay more for one brand than for another unless the first is cheaper or better. Advertising can make an advertised brand cheaper by reducing the consumer's search costs by an amount greater than the difference in nominal price between that brand and nonadvertised brands of the same product. The same point can be made with respect to the other presale services, e.g., display, that are encouraged by restricted distribution.

The new industrial organization, which relates advertising to the costs of search, has transformed advertising from a social evil into a social benefit, and in so doing has fatally undermined the Comanor riposte to the Director-Telser theory of resale price maintenance. Although inter-school differences relating to the welfare effects of advertising remain, the position of the Chicago school on restricted distribution has become the orthodox academic position. The decision in *Continental T.V., Inc.* v. *GTE Sylvania Inc.* suggests that it is well on its way to becoming the legal position as well.

4. Predatory pricing. McGee's famous article on the Standard Oil Trust combined the startling empirical finding that the trust, contrary to popular and academic belief, had not engaged in predatory pricing, with theoretical arguments for doubting the rationality of the practice. One of McGee's major arguments—that the trust would not have used predatory pricing because it is cheaper to buy a competitor than to sell below cost—was vulnerable to the criticism of being irrelevant to present-day circumstances, since acquiring a major competitor is clearly and unconcealably unlawful whereas predatory pricing may be difficult to detect. There is, however, a deeper problem with the McGee argument: it neglects strategic considerations. Assume that it is lawful to buy a rival. It does not follow that a firm will never resort to predatory pricing. After all, it wants to minimize the price at which it buys its rivals, and that price will be lower if it can convince them of its willingness to drive them out of business unless they sell out on its terms. One way to convince them of this is to engage in predatory pricing from time to time.

Since classical (or, one might add, modern) economics contains no generally accepted theory of strategic behavior, it is not surprising that the Chicago school should not have been particularly concerned with predatory pricing. Eliminate strategic considerations, and it becomes impossible to construct a rational motivation for predatory pricing without assuming (very uncongenially to a Chicagoan) asymmetric access to the capital markets for financing a period of below-cost selling. But to ignore strategic considerations is not satisfactory. Even without having a well-developed theory of strategic behavior, one can easily imagine circumstances in which predatory pricing, at least in the absence of legal prohibition, would be a plausible policy for a profit-maximizing seller to follow. Suppose that he sells in many markets, and his rivals sell in only one or a few markets each. If he sells below cost in one market, his losses there are an investment that will be recouped with interest in his other markets in the form of more timid competition from the rivals in those markets. Knowing that the multi-market seller can obtain substantial gains from a demonstrated willingness to sell below cost for an extended period of time in one market, the local victim may not think it worthwhile to try to outlast him.

To be sure, the administrative and error costs of trying to prevent this sort of thing may outweigh its dangers to the competitive process. That, however, is a different point. My point is that predatory pricing is not irrational. It is not in the same category with, for example, attempting to get a second monopoly through tying. Bork is able to place predatory pricing in the irrational category only by failing to mention the possibility of strategic behavior.

Additional evidence for the decline of "schools" of antitrust economics is the position that Areeda and Turner (both of the Harvard Law School) have taken on predatory pricing. Their influential article on the subject (and the amplification of the article in their new treatise) is an essay in price theory. Strategic considerations, the sort of thing the traditional industrial organization embraced eagerly, *e.g.*, in oligopoly theory, are not mentioned, and skepticism of the likelihood of predatory pricing is registered. Using the basic premises of classical price theory, Areeda and Turner argue that the only price that should be condemned as predatory is one below short-run marginal cost. Any higher price implies an opportunity to utilize scarce resources more fully by lowering price and expanding output. This is pure textbook price theory unadorned by any of the concepts of traditional industrial organization.

It is not surprising that Professor Scherer, a leading adherent of traditional industrial organization thinking, launched a sweeping attack on the Areeda-Turner article, or that Professor Williamson criticized Areeda and Turner for ignoring strategic considerations in designing a rule against predatory pricing. What is, perhaps, surprising is that I attacked Areeda and Turner as unduly permissive. Unfortunately, my attack bogged down in a terminological dispute. I said that the proper criterion of predatory pricing was selling below long-run rather than short-run marginal cost with intent to destroy an equally or more efficient rival and that short-run marginal cost is lower than long-run marginal cost even when the firm is operating at its full (optimal) capacity, because some of elements of long-run marginal cost are fixed in the short run. Areeda and Turner pounced on the assertion that short-run marginal cost is below long-run marginal cost at full capacity. They pointed out that it would be costlier for a firm already operating at full capacity to expand in the short run than in the long run, for only in the long run could the firm make the adjustments in plant scale, etc., necessary to optimize production at a higher level. I accept this criticism. Although I continue to be troubled by cases, potentially significant in the predatory-pricing context, in which long-run marginal cost might be thought to exceed short-run marginal cost even without excess capacity, these cases can be dealt with by careful definition of the relevant terms.

But this is a side issue that only obscures the serious problems of the short-run marginal cost standard. The lesser problem is that the standard gives the would-be predator an incentive to maintain excess capacity and thereby reduce his short-run marginal costs, an incentive the predator might have anyway in order to make his threat to sell below cost more credible. The greater problem is that the administrative difficulties of basing the legal rule on the concept of short-run marginal cost are so acute as to have led Areeda and Turner themselves to reject short-run marginal cost as the operational standard and instead substitute average variable cost. Yet they continue to defend that standard by reference to the arguments, such as they are, for allowing firms to cut price to short-run marginal cost. Average variable cost could be much below short-run marginal cost. A standard of average variable cost should be defended on its own merits, rather than by reference to a different standard for which it is the crudest possible proxy. But Areeda and Turner do not attempt to defend an average variable cost standard, save as a proxy for short-run marginal cost.

What is the point of having such a low price floor? It would be unusual for a firm that wanted to engage in predatory pricing to set a price equal to or only slightly above zero. It would set a price designed to make its competitors' business unprofitable at minimum cost to itself. Any firm that sells at a price equal to its average variable costs, a price that doesn't cover any of its fixed costs (let alone generate any return on investment), will be unprofitable. Therefore, even if the competitor is somewhat more efficient than the predator, a price equal to the predator's variable costs, and hence close to the competitor's variable costs, should be an effective predatory price. Areeda and Turner allude to this possibility in a cryptic footnote. They write:

> One can posit a case in which (1) one rival has lower variable costs but higher total costs than the other, (2) their joint capacity exceeds the demand at a price that would be profitable to both, and hence (3) marginal-cost pricing by the first rival would drive out the second, which is the more efficient producer in the long run when capital facilities have to be replaced. But even in such a case, the appropriate short-run solution is production by the rival with the lowest variable costs. Obviously, one would not want that firm to replace its facilities, but a rational firm would not do so if the cheaper technique were available to it, or if others could freely enter using that technique.

The last sentence in effect denies the possibility of predatory pricing by asserting that a rational firm would not replace its facilities if the cheaper technique were available to it or if others could "freely enter" with that technique. The first alternative, the availability of the cheaper technique, simply retracts the premise of the discussion—that there is a competitor who is "the more efficient producer in the long run when capital facilities have to be replaced." If a predator is always as efficient in the long run as his competitors, there is little reason to forbid predatory pricing. A more efficient competitor can exclude a less efficient one without pricing below cost and thereby losing money in the short run. To have a rational basis, a rule against predation must assume that firms sometimes want to cling to their markets although they are less efficient than their rivals, i.e., the "cheaper technique" is not available to them.

The second alternative suggested is free entry by firms as efficient as the excluded competitor. There are two ways in which to interpret the meaning of free entry here. One is that there is no need to worry about predatory pricing if there are many potential entrants waiting in the wings: the predator cannot possibly deter them all. If so, there is little reason to have any rule against predatory pricing. Alternatively, Areeda and Turner may be suggesting that predatory pricing is possible only where there are barriers to entry. This, however, neglects strategic considerations, which do not depend on the existence of barriers to entry.

The quoted passage fails to take the problem of predatory pricing seriously. It implies that no rational firm would engage in predatory pricing if its long-run marginal costs were higher than those of its victims. If this is so (which I question on the basis of the strategic considerations suggested earlier), why is it necessary to forbid predatory pricing? Predatory pricing against less efficient firms is not a serious danger since they can be excluded by pricing at or above cost. Areeda and Turner may think that business irrationality is sufficiently common to warrant a rule against predatory pricing. In any event, if there is sufficient danger of predatory pricing to warrant having a legal rule, as Areeda and Turner for whatever reason believe, that danger is triggered when a firm that is less efficient than its rivals cuts its price to its variable costs in order to make it unprofitable for those rivals to enter or remain in the market. Indeed, to repeat an earlier point, it is hard to see why a predator would ever have to price below that level in order to discourage rivals.

Whoever is correct in the debate over predatory pricing, one thing is clear: the debate is no longer one between schools that employ consistently different and ideologically tinged premises to reach predictably opposite results.

## III. Remaining Differences

There is one very important area in which traces of the traditional differences between Chicago price theorists and Harvard industrial organizationists persist: the two schools continue to disagree over the significance of concentration and the wisdom of a policy of deconcentration. Williamson and many other lawyers and economists continue to believe that persistently high concentration in an industry warrants breaking up the leading firms. Brozen, Demsetz, Stigler, Baxter, and others disagree (the last two named, it should be noted, are defectors from the ranks of the deconcentrators). Areeda and Turner, as will be seen, appear to take an intermediate position.

The heart of the difference is not over the strength of the positive correlation, found in many studies, between concentration and profitability but over the explanation for it. The Harvard school, still identifiable as such on this issue, contends that the correlation is explained by the fact that the leading firms in highly concentrated industries employ "conscious parallelism" to avoid price competition and thereby earn abnormal profits. The Chicago school does not deny that concentration is a factor that facilitates collusion of a sort difficult to detect, although it attaches less significance to concentration per se than do the oligopoly theorists. It asks, rather, how it is that excessive profitability can persist without attracting new entry that will cause prices to fall to the competitive level. The Harvard school, after all, wants to restructure only the persistently concentrated industries. If the leading firms in such industries are able, by virtue of concentration, to obtain supracompetitive profits, these profits should act as a magnet to other firms in the economy and their entry will deconcentrate the industry. That is what happened to the steel industry in the years following the formation of U.S. Steel Corporation in 1901. Persistent concentration implies either that the market in question simply does not have room for many firms (economies of scale) or that some firms are able persistently to obtain abnormal profits by cost reductions or product improvements that competitors and new entrants are unable to duplicate. Neither case is an attractive one for public intervention designed to change the market structure.

The Harvard reply is that there is an alternative explanation for persistent concentration in particular industries: barriers to entry. Because Stigler's definition of a barrier to entry, as a cost that differentially affects new entrants compared to firms already in the market, is now generally accepted, the search is for costs having this characteristic. The most sophisticated quester, Oliver Williamson, has found one: the uncertainty of the new entrant's prospects may force him to pay a higher risk premium to obtain capital than existing firms must pay. This is a legitimate point. But it is difficult to believe that such a difference in the cost of capital would be enough to prevent entry if the firms in a market were charging prices substantially above their costs. The risk premium is unlikely to be a large fraction of the new entrant's costs. Interest and profit are rarely more than ten percent of a manufacturing firm's sales price and often they are a much smaller percentage. Thus, even if a new entrant had to pay a ten percent higher interest rate and (expected) return to shareholders to attract the necessary capital, its total costs would be only about one percent higher than those of the firms already in the market. There is no doubt that the differential risk premium is smaller if the new entrant is a well-established firm in other markets, as will typically be the case, and, to the extent that the risk is diversifiable, the risk premium will be still smaller or even disappear entirely. Another important source of new entry, viewing the term functionally rather than lexicographically, is the expansion of the existing small firms in the market. In response to supracompetitive pricing, a fringe of small firms in a market may be able to expand output moderately without incurring significantly higher capital costs than those borne by the larger firms in the market. All in all, it seems far-fetched to base a policy of deconcentration on the allegedly higher borrowing costs of new entrants in concentrated markets.

Williamson has also argued that if a firm once grows big, for whatever reason, there is no reason to expect it to decline as a result of the random shocks to which it and other market participants will be subjected over time. But he neglects a crucial factor. The firm is by hypothesis charging a supracompetitive price as a result of the interdependence or collusion fostered by the concentrated market structure in which it finds itself. That price will attract new firms (or, what amounts to the same thing, expansion by the smaller firms in the market) and the oligopolist will either have to cut price or surrender market share. In the former case, profits will fall and in the latter, concentration will decrease. The persistence of high concentration together with excess profitability remains to be accounted for.

Deconcentration policy, then, is critically dependent upon belief in the existence of substantial barriers to entry in many industries. Once "barrier to entry" was redefined as a differentially higher cost borne by the new entrant, the plausibility of supposing that barriers to entry are common, or commonly substantial, diminished sharply. The deconcentrators are thus arguing from an abandoned premise. This can be seen most clearly by comparing the discussion of barriers to entry in Kaysen and Turner's *Antitrust Policy* and in Areeda and Turner's *Antitrust Law*. Both books are concerned over the anticompetitive consequences of deconcentration, although the latter much more qualifiedly so, and only at much higher levels of concentration. The view of barriers to entry, however, is very different in the two books. To Kaysen and Turner they are numerous and include economies of scale, capital requirements, scarce know-how and inputs, and product differentiation. No rigorous definition of barrier to entry is offered; nor do the authors deduce the concept of barriers to entry from the assumption that business firms act as rational profit maximizers. The important point, however, is that, believing barriers to entry to be numerous and prevalent, the authors have a rational basis for wanting to deconcentrate concentrated markets. Areeda and Turner greatly pare down the list of barriers to entry. Because they utilize Stigler's definition of a barrier to entry, they are led to exclude economies of scale entirely. The related size-of-capital barrier is discarded also and product differentiation is discounted on the basis of a view of advertising that is close to the Chicago view. The only barriers that remain are: (1) the Williamson risk-premium version of the capital barrier and (2) control of scarce input. Thus, Areeda and Turner largely discard the concept of barrier to entry, finding some of the barriers theoretically invalid and others empirically unimportant; such "pure" barriers as remain surely cannot explain much concentration. And although Areeda and Turner do not expressly discuss the dependence of deconcentration theory on the belief in the existence of high and pervasive barriers to entry, they do draw quite different policy implications concerning persistent high concentration from Kaysen and Turner. Whereas the earlier book recommended a policy of deconcentration, the later book recommends remedial action, whether under existing antitrust provisions or new legislation, only where there is proof of noncompetitive performance. There is more than a nuance of difference between these two views. Here, then, is further evidence that even in the most important area where distinctive "Harvard" and "Chicago" approaches remain discernible, the process of convergence is well under way.

## Conclusion

Although this paper has not attempted an exhaustive canvass of rival theories of antitrust analysis, it has, I hope, said enough to persuade the reader that the oldest and most persistent stereotype in antitrust economics, that of the Chicago school, bears little relationship to the current state of academic thinking. Changes of mind within both the Chicago school and its principal rival, which I have called the Harvard school, have produced a steady trend toward convergence. Differences remain, but increasingly they are technical rather than ideological.

# 12

# Transactions Costs Economics and the Post-Chicago Movement

## Introduction

BY DANIEL CRANE

Our final chapter concerns the ongoing progression of ideas about competition policy. We have grouped together two broad "schools" of economic thought—Transaction Cost Economics (or "TCE") and the Post-Chicago school—both of which present challenges to prevailing Chicago School views.

TCE is a broad field with many implications for competition policy and other areas of economic regulation. We offer just a small sampling, with a selection from Oliver Williamson's 1975 *Markets and Hierarchies*. Williamson, a Nobel laureate and economics professor, was a student of Ronald Coase, who is often considered the father of TCE.[1] Williamson, more than anyone else, brought the TCE approach to bear on antitrust problems.

The TCE approach does not neatly fit into either of the two paradigms—structuralism and the Chicago School—that have dominated U.S. antitrust enforcement in the last half century.[2] Williamson served as "special economic assistant" to Donald Turner when Turner headed the Justice Department's Antitrust Division, but he can hardly be counted a structuralist. Williamson has advocated a "total welfare" approach to merger policy[3] and antitrust hospitability to vertical mergers and vertical restraints.[4] But nor can the Chicago School

1. See, e.g., Ronald H. Coase, "The Nature of the Firm," 4 *Economica* 386 (1937).

2. On Williamson's views in relationship to Chicago and post-Chicago thought, see William E. Kovacic, "The Intellectual DNA of Modern U.S. Competition Law for Dominant Firm Conduct: The Chicago/Harvard Double Helix," 2007 *Colum. Bus. L. Rev.* 1, 14 n. 36 (2007).

3. Oliver E. Williamson, "Economies as an Antitrust Defense: The Welfare Tradeoffs," 58 *Am. Econ. Rev.* 18 (1968).

4. Oliver E. Williamson, *Markets and Hierarchies: Analysis and Antitrust Implications* 82–131 (1975).

count Williamson a reliable ally, as he has advocated a much more aggressive approach toward unilateral exclusionary conduct.[5]

Broadly speaking, TCE is the study of how transaction costs affect firm boundaries and firm behavior. The TCE approach can be used to explain why firms might integrate vertically or impose contractual vertical restraints for benign (i.e., not anticompetitive) reasons. But it can also be used to demonstrate market failures. It is this implication of the TCE approach that we survey in this chapter.

As we saw in the last chapter, at the core of the Chicago School approach lies a conviction that markets usually deploy scarce social resources efficiently if freed from governmental interference. In this view, monopolies are inherently unstable and contestable since capital inexorably flows toward the lure of monopoly profits. For Williamson, however, market breakdowns are far more probable and frequent when we understand the transactional impediments to the easy flow of capital toward monopoly profits. The causes of market failure—the transactions costs that impede market self-correction—need not be nefarious. As Williamson explains in the passage ahead, "[c]hance events (uncertainty), unusual business acumen (management idiosyncrasies), and default failures (ineptitude on the part of actual and potential rivals) are the main causative factors which have previously been neglected that can give rise to such [market] breakdowns." Still, once the frailty of markets is recognized, the case for corrective governmental interventions strengthens.

The second school of thought we study in this chapter is loosely called the "post-Chicago School." One may wonder whether such a school really exists—yet. Unlike the Harvard and Chicago schools that were clustered around a few dominant intellectuals centered at Harvard or Chicago, the post-Chicago school has no institutional locus. Nor is it defined by an elegant analytical structure or clear research agenda apart from identifying errors in the Chicago School approach. To be sure, many economists and legal scholars are dissatisfied with Chicago School orthodoxy and have leveled substantial criticisms at the Chicago School's influences on the courts and antitrust agencies.[6] Prominent scholars have marshaled targeted critiques of specific Chicago School tenets.[7] But if "intellectual schools" are defined by a shared analytical approach, a core set of common principles, and a nucleus of intellectuals collaborating on a common research agenda, it is hard to locate the post-Chicago school.

Still, there is much to say about the clusters of scholars who, since the mid-1980s, have been challenging the Chicago School's antitrust approach. Many draw on innovations in game theory implications for industrial strategy or on challenges by behavioralism to the *Homo economicus* rational person model assumed by the Chicago School. Others critique the Chicago School's reductionist assumptions about antitrust's efficiency-maximization

5. Oliver E. Williamson, "Delimiting Antitrust," 76 *Geo. L. J.* 271 (1987).

6. Many criticisms of the Chicago School are collected in Robert Pitofsky, *How the Chicago School Overshot the Mark: The Effect of Conservative Economic Analysis on U.S. Antitrust* (2008).

7. See, e.g., Einer Elhauge, "Tying, Bundled Discounts, and the Death of the Single Monopoly Profit Theory," 123 *Harv. L. Rev.* 397 (2009) (criticizing Chicago School positions on monopoly leverage and tying); Patrick Bolton, Joseph F. Brodley, and Michael H. Riordan, "Predatory Pricing: Strategic Theory and Legal Policy," 88 *Geo. L. J.* 2239 (2000).

goals. Still others criticize the Chicago school as driven more by laissez faire ideology than by "objective" economics.

In this chapter, we present two selections on the post-Chicago school. First, we have an essay by F. M. Scherer, a Kennedy School of Government professor and author of one of the most popular microeconomic textbooks of the last half-century. Scherer seeks to situate Chicago School economics in the stream of twentieth-century conservative economic thought. Scherer argues the differences between strains of conservative economic thought—of which there are many—"stem more from fundamental values and assumptions about human behavior and about the desirability of such phenomena as unequal income distribution than from the choice of one analytic or empirical technique over another." As the progression of ideas in this book has shown, economics is not a dispassionate science free from the ideological preferences of its practitioners.

We conclude with selections from an essay by Herbert Hovenkamp on the challenges of the post-Chicago School. He recounts the major successes of the Chicago School as well as how Chicago School economics were "oversold." He then surveys some of the "perils of post-Chicago economics," which largely have to do with the increasing complexity that antitrust analysis requires when the Chicago School's elegant—perhaps simple—assumptions are relaxed. He reminds us that "anyone who takes the long view should see that 'Post-Chicago' antitrust policy represents little more than another swing in antitrust's ideological pendulum." That statement is a fitting capstone to this book. If there is one thing our survey of competition policy's intellectual history shows, it is that fundamental ideas about monopoly, markets, competition, and the state's regulatory role may cycle in and out, with refinements and modifications, but never go permanently out of fashion.

## Oliver E. Williamson

## *Markets and Hierarchies: Analysis and Antitrust Implications*

### 11. Dominant Firms and the Monopoly Problem

Both this and the following chapter examine structural monopoly issues from a transactional point of view. The evolution of dominant firm industries is considered here; problems of effecting oligopolistic collusion are dealt with in Chapter 12. Whereas a more assertive antitrust policy with respect to the dominant firm industries is encouraged, I am highly skeptical of "shared monopoly" approaches to the oligopoly problem.

The transactional approach to the dominant firm condition that is emphasized here may be contrasted with the more conventional conduct explanation. The implicit assumption of the conduct approach to violations of section 2 of the Sherman Act is that persistent monopoly is not to be expected unless supported by anticompetitive practices, patent protection, or unusual scale economies. This position is challenged here. Not that anticompetitive practices, patents, or unusual scale economies cannot contribute to dominance. But this construes the dominant firm outcome too narrowly. An expanded market failures interpretation of dominance is proposed.

In particular, I argue that dominant firm outcomes are (at least sometimes, perhaps usually) less to be attributed to conduct, patents, or technology than they are to a breakdown of the self-policing properties of markets. Chance events (uncertainty), unusual business acumen (management idiosyncrasies), and default failures (ineptitude on the part of actual and potential rivals) are the main causative factors which have previously been neglected that can give rise to such breakdowns. Whether dominant firm outcomes resulting from market failures of chance event and default types occasion public policy intervention depends in large measure on whether or not unassisted market processes are likely to undo such conditions in any short period of time. Assessing this requires that first-mover advantages, if any, be evaluated.

The chapter proceeds as follows: The current approach to unlawful monopolization is described in Section 1. The proposed market failures interpretation is developed in Section 2. The basis for government intervention under the proposed approach is given in Section 3. The question of remedy is addressed in Section 4, and the structure-conduct controversy is reassessed in the light of this argument in Section 5. The argument is expressly reinterpreted in organizational failures terms in Section 6.

## 1. The Current Approach

Antitrust policy has long been plagued by the problem of continued dominance[1] of an industry by a single firm which has obtained its position by lawful means. Traditional judicial interpretations of the offense of monopolization under section 2 of the Sherman Act[2] have focused on the presence or absence of predatory or exclusionary tactics in obtaining or retaining monopoly power.[3] To be sure, it has been argued that Judge Hand's opinion in Alcoa[4] comes very close to suggesting that a firm may be found to have monopolized unlawfully a market simply by maintaining monopoly power for a period of time substantial enough to indicate that market forces by themselves will be unable to undo the firm's dominant position.[5] But the most recent

1. For the purpose of this chapter dominant firm industries will be defined to be industries for which the output of a single firm has persistently exceeded sixty percent of the relevant market and entry barriers are great. Much higher market shares are required if entry barriers are insubstantial. [If entry can occur frictionlessly, even one hundred percent market share does not imply market power. Cf. Stigler (1968, p. 133).] To be sure, the sixty percent, entry impeded condition is somewhat arbitrary. It has the advantage, however, of focusing attention on a relatively narrow group of industries. If the approach proposed in this chapter can successfully be applied to industries in which the largest firm has consistently maintained a sixty percent market share, consideration can then be given to reducing the cutoff limit. It would seem injudicious, however, to apply the argument immediately to dominant firms with much lower market shares.

2. 15 U.S.C. Sec. 2 (1970). Section 2 provides in part: "Every person who shall monopolize, or attempt to monopolize, or combine or conspire with any other person or persons, to monopolize any part of the trade or commerce among the several States, or with foreign nations, shall be deemed guilty of a misdemeanor."

3. See, for example, *United States* v. *Grinnell Corporation*, 384 U.S. 563, 570–571 (1966): *Standard Oil Company* v. *United States*, 221 U.S. 1, 62 (1911).

4. *United States* v. *Aluminum Company of America*, 148 F.2 d 41 6 (2d Cir. 1945).

5. Turner has recently come out in favor of such an approach (Turner, 1969, p. 1217).

U.S. Supreme Court definition of the offense appears to reject this purely structural approach and to continue to require the presence of abusive conduct before finding unlawful monopolization.[6]

As the law is currently interpreted, dominance does not constitute a section 2 violation if the structure of the industry is attributable to "a superior product, business acumen, or historic accident."[7] A superior product presumably implies a patent monopoly or a cost advantage attributable to scale economies. These are not matters of principal concern here. That dominance due to business acumen or historic accidents should be outside the ambit of section 2 is, however, open to dispute. Indeed, it will be argued that to regard these cases as exempt from section 2 scrutiny is not only unwarranted, but has had the effect of obfuscating legitimate issues and perversely constraining the enforcement agencies to rely on conduct offenses in dealing with the dominant firm industries. Since it is widely felt that dominance ought not to be permitted to continue indefinitely,[8] this has frequently resulted in antitrust suits being brought against these firms on grounds which bear little relation to the structural condition in question.

The implicit assumption in the conduct approach to unlawful monopolization is that competition works—at least in the limited sense that, absent deliberate impairment of competition, actual and potential business competitors can be relied upon to perform self-policing functions by responding appropriately to opportunities for private gain. Except for circumstances in which economies of scale are large in relation to the market (the "natural monopoly" situation) or where the government itself protects a monopoly through the patent system, persistent dominance of an industry by a single firm is not to be expected.[9]

The position taken here is that while considerations of fair play are not to be neglected, the conclusion that structure will take care of itself relies too greatly on average tendencies. That strong competitive instincts normally obtain and that concatenations of chance events do not ordinarily result in dominance are both conceded. But aberrations can and will appear and the implied time horizon for self-policing to be efficacious may be unacceptably long.[10] Indeed, the concession by the Court that

6. "The offense of monopoly under section 2 of the Sherman Ac t has two elements: (1) the possession of monopoly power in the relevant market and (2) the willful acquisition or maintenance of that power as distinguished from growth or development as a consequence of a superior product, business acumen, or historic accident." *United States* v. *Grinnell Corporation*, 384 U.S. 563, 570–571 (1966).

7. Id. at 571.

8. That this is the prevailing attitude is revealed by the positions of the antitrust enforcement agencies and the courts. The Antitrust Division of the U.S. Justice Department regularly scrutinizes dominant firm industries for indications of anticompetitive conduct. Cases are occasionally brought on what appear to be contrived grounds and sympathetic hearings are accorded these in the courts. Since there is no great public outcry against these efforts, the acceptance if not the support of the public might also be presumed.

9. *Standard Oil Company* v. *United States*, 221 U.S. 1,62 (1911) ("monopoly would be inevitably prevented if no extraneous or sovereign power imposed it and no right to make unlawful contracts having a monopolistic tendency were permitted"). Except for allowing for the possibility of scale economies, this is approximately Posner's view also (Posner, 1969, pp. 1596–1597).

10. Posner relies on Brozen's recent finding that a "high-level of concentration in an industry tends to dissipate by natural forces within an average period of ten years," together with the fact that "the average length of a divestiture

business acumen and historic accident may contribute to dominance suggests that competition may not operate smoothly and reveals a possible contradiction between the actual market factors responsible for dominance and the alleged conduct offenses on which dominant firm complaints rest.

## 2. A Market Failure Interpretation of Dominance

The existence of dominant firms which, but for anticompetitive conduct, are apparently immune from the antitrust laws has several undesirable consequences. First, the existence of a dominant firm, whatever its origins, commonly results in resource misallocation—including, but not limited to monopolistic output restriction.[11] Second, as Turner has cogently argued, the inability to deal effectively with established monopoly results in what may sometimes be an excessive expansion of antimerger enforcement (1969, p. 1213). Were the enforcement agencies and courts better able to "correct undue concentration as it appears, there would be less need to prevent mergers which present only remote possibilities of anti-competitive consequences" (Turner, 1969, p. 1214). Third, for structural dominance to remain beyond the reach of section 2 produces charges that antitrust enforcement is a charade (Galbraith, 1966, p. 794; Miller, 1968, p. 136). Whatever its merits in other respects, confidence that an American-style antitrust apparatus can monitor an enterprise system is impaired. Conspicuous, if limited, failures easily become the basis for captious contempt. Finally, dominance in business may be used as an excuse for bigness in other spheres of economic and political activity—to the possible detriment of the public (Stigler, 1952, p.123).

The antitrust enforcement agencies are not unaware of these difficulties. Substantial enforcement resources are accordingly invested in the study of dominant firm industries. Since, however, the admissible grounds for filing a complaint are limited, the main effort is to scrutinize the behavior of dominant firms to discover evidence of offensive business conduct. Considerations of reciprocity, leasing practices, and the like are seized upon to support claims that dominance has resulted from unfair business practices. That, objectively, the conduct in question could not reasonably lead

proceeding in a monopolization case involving a major regional or national market is 8 years" to support his conclusion that "it seems unlikely that administrative methods of deconcentration will work significantly more rapidly than the market" (Posner, 1970, p. 417, n. 50). The Brazen analysis, however, is disputable. See MacAvoy, McKie and Preston (1971). Moreover, even if Brozen's results were to be accepted, Posner relies heavily on average market tendencies which, in the particular cases of high concentration involved here, may be inapposite. Finally, Posner takes prevailing judicial practices as given, despite the fact that various reform proposals are directed to eliminating the delay in antitrust actions. See, for example, the Neal Task Force Report (1969, p. 7).

11. Resource misallocation can take several forms. The usual objection to monopoly is that it results in output restriction with a consequent loss of consumers' and possibly producers' surplus. This may be extended to include losses due to inefficient operations or general lack of aggressive management, but this strand of the argument is not well developed. Monopoly also gives rise to income distribution effects. These, however, are commonly of a much more mixed nature than is usually appreciated. See Caves (1967, pp. 99–100); also Posner (1969, pp. 564–568). Objections to monopoly can also be raised on the grounds that it provides an incentive to distort the durability of goods. See Barro (1972).

to the dominance result is simply disregarded. Attention is focused instead on whether certain practices were employed and, if so, whether they may have had some, however slight, anticompetitive effect. That the process is regarded by outsiders, and even some insiders, as artificial and contrived is only to be expected.

This chapter advances the proposition that the Court's instincts are correct in that dominance is often to be attributed to "business acumen" or "historic accident." However, rather than treat such dominance as exempt from the coverage of section 2, it is argued that frequently it should be regarded as an actionable manifestation of market failure. Under such an interpretation, government intervention to upset this condition seems reasonable, provided only that (1) the dominant firm's market position can be judged to be relatively secure and hence unlikely to be undone by the operation of unassisted market processes, and (2) an efficacious remedy can be devised. Contrived proof of anticompetitive conduct would thereby be made unnecessary in order to obtain relief.

## 2.1 Business Acumen

The usual position on business acumen is that scarcity of decision-making skills is not responsible for dominance. One way of putting this is to state that requisite talent is available in elastic supply. The view expressed by Kaysen and Turner is typical. They assume that not only is there a sufficient supply of first-grade managerial talent to run a few hundred companies, but that such talent is relatively transferable as well. Thus, should any particular firm develop an "advantage in men and methods, rivals can and will copy the methods and hire the men away" (1959, p. 9).

Only recently has this position come under scrutiny. Marschak, in expressing concern over the ready tendency of economists to accept or employ assumptions of fungibility, has offered the following observation on the distribution of talent: "There exist almost unique, irreplaceable research workers, teachers, administrators; just as there exist unique choice locations for plants and harbors. The problem of unique or imperfectly standardized goods...has been indeed neglected in the textbooks" (1968, p. 14). Studies in entrepreneurial history would seem to bear him out: unusual men with exceptional personal force and organizing talent occasionally appear, and their influence has pervasive industry consequences (Chandler, 1966; Chandler and Salisbury, 1971).

Were superlative management the only factor responsible for differential business acumen between firms, the dominant firm that made such a showing might reasonably be exempted from divestiture. If the talent in question is not divisible, much as a scale economy of a technological sort is not, then the firm should be permitted to maintain its size because to do otherwise would result in a nontrivial loss of efficiency. The resulting monopoly power is simply an unhappy by-product of this condition.

Even in light of these considerations, however, the business acumen doctrine may sweep too broadly. For one thing, the management superiority that gave rise to dominance may refer to an earlier period in the firm's history. Often it will have manifested itself through an organizational innovation of a significant sort. The firm may then remain dominant despite the lack of any continuing superior acuity. Displays of unusual organizing ability early in a firm's development that have since lapsed do not obviously support the same policy conclusion reached above. The advisability of placing a time limit on a defense for dominance that relies on management excellence during art earlier period at least warrants consideration.

An even more serious difficulty with the business acumen doctrine is the relative nature of the argument.[12] Dominance does not necessarily imply superiority on any absolute scale. The dominant firm may have displayed no special management expertise but extant and potential rivals, on which the responsibility for self-policing functions devolves, may have been uncommonly inept. Persistent ineptitude of this sort is an indication that the self-policing functions of rivalry have disintegrated. Such discreditable performance on the part of principal rivals during critical formative stages of an industry's development will be referred to as *default failure*.

Management superiority (business acumen) may therefore take either of two forms. First, absolute superiority may have contributed to dominance—although this may have been associated with an early period in the firm's history and may since have lapsed. And second, the advantage of the dominant firm may be attributable to the ineptitude of actual and potential rivals. If, for the reasons given below, unassisted market processes cannot be expected to rectify such dominant firm outcomes in any short period of time, the possibility of eventual government intervention to relieve these conditions ought seriously to be entertained in the second situation, and in the first when the absolute superiority is not both contemporaneous and indivisible.

## 2.2 Historical Accident

Although all of the firms in an industry may have been performing in a fully creditable, but unexceptional, manner, the dominant firm may be thrust ahead of its competitors by an unusual sequence of fortuitous events. Such an outcome will be referred to as *chance event failure*.

It is relevant in this connection to distinguish between defects in the competitive process and dissatisfaction with a stochastic outcome. In order to focus strictly on accidental outcomes, the stochastic generating mechanism will be assumed to operate without defect. Unwanted outcomes thus are to be attributed strictly to the laws of chance intrinsic to the probabilistic process and not to systematic distortions in the mechanism.[13] Even under these conditions, however, probabilistic processes can be expected to generate, with statistical regularity, occasional outcomes that may be

12. As Alchian explains in his discussion of natural selection: "The crucial element IS one's aggregate position relative to some actual competitors.... As in a race, the award goes to the relatively fastest, even if all the competitors loaf" (Alchian, 1950, p. 213).

13. The absence of predatory or exclusionary conduct or of default failure may thus be presumed.

deemed to have "undesirable" properties.[14] The argument is illustrated by the simulation experiment reported by Scherer.

Scherer began with industry of fifty equally sized firms and, for each firm, obtained a series of annual growth rates by sampling repeatedly from a common distribution of growth rates. The growth path of each firm was determined in this way; and industry concentration ratios, at ten-year intervals, were computed. The resulting firm size distributions often revealed high concentration, since "[s]ome firms will inevitably enjoy a run of luck, experiencing several years of very rapid growth in close succession" (1970, p. 127).[15]

Moreover, what is relevant for our purposes, concentration once achieved was not easily undone. "Once the most fortunate firms climb well ahead of the pack, it is difficult for laggards to rally and rectify the imbalance, for by definition, each firm—large or small—has an equal chance of [continuing to grow] by a given percentage amount" (Scherer, 1970, p. 127). Thus, repeated application of the same stochastic mechanism that, within a relatively brief interval, gave rise in some industries to concentration cannot reliably be expected to undo this result in any short period of time.[16] If, during the course of their development, industries typically undergo changes that progressively reduce the frequency and intensity of the random disturbances to which they are exposed, dominant firm outcomes will be all the more secure.

Three stages in an industry's development are commonly recognized: an early exploratory stage, an intermediate development stage, and a mature stage. The first or early formative stage involves the supply of a new product of relatively primitive design, manufactured on comparatively unspecialized machinery, and marketed through a variety of exploratory techniques. Volume is typically low. A high degree of uncertainty characterizes business experience at this stage. The second stage is the intermediate development stage in which manufacturing techniques are more refined and market definition is sharpened; output grows rapidly in response to newly recognized applications and unsatisfied market demands. A high but somewhat lesser degree of uncertainty characterizes market outcomes at this stage. The third stage is that of a mature industry. Management, manufacturing, and marketing techniques all reach a relatively advanced degree of refinement. Markets may continue to grow, but do so at a more regular and predictable rate. More accurate and complete information regarding

14. Consider the following fair coin-tossing experiment described by Alchian (1950, p. 215):

> Suppose two million Parisians were paired off and set to tossing coins in a game of matching. Each pair plays until the winner on the first toss is again brought to equality with the other player. Assuming one toss per second for each eight-hour day, at the end of ten years there would still be, on the average, about a hundred-odd players.... The implications are obvious.... Should one rule out luck and chance as the essence of the factors producing the long-term survival of the enterprise?

The relevance of this argument for our purposes is that luck can contribute not merely to survival but also to dominance.

15. If, in addition, growth rates are serially correlated, as Mansfield's evidence suggests (1962, pp. 1036–1038), concentration outcomes are all the more likely.

16. The argument in the text is illustrated in yet another (if somewhat more artificial) way by the following example. Suppose, as in note 14 above, that the experience of a firm in the market place is likened to the repeated toss of a coin in which heads denote success and tails denote a setback. Assume that the probability of heads on each trial

market developments becomes available. Unanticipated system breakdowns are progressively eliminated as experience accumulates and statistical inference techniques are improved. Plant and equipment are in place; employees with firm-specific experience and attachments are on hand; established connections with customers and suppliers (including capital market access) all operate to buffer changes and thereby to limit large shifts in market shares. Significant innovations tend to be fewer and are mainly of an improvement variety (Kuznets, 1953, pp. 258–267). Circumstances which, at an early stage in an industry's development, would have given rise to considerable dislocation now are attenuated.

Relevant in this connection is Kaysen and Turner's discussion of barriers to entry as a function of the stage of development of an industry (1959, pp. 73–75). As they point out, new entry into a mature industry is impeded by the lack of knowhow, by the difficulty of upsetting established customer connections, and by the absence among would-be entrants of a known performance record to be assessed by factor suppliers (including the capital market). What this argument comes down to, essentially, is this: The potential entrant into a mature industry must not only raise capital sufficient to finance plant and equipment at an efficient scale but must, in addition, have resources sufficient to cover the startup costs which, in a mature industry, may be considerable. Unlike entry at an early stage in an industry's development, where differential experience and reputation effects are, perforce, negligible, cost differences between established firms and new entrants at a mature stage are to be anticipated precisely because these factors now may be considerable. First-mover advantages may be said to favor those firms which, for whatever reason, were there early.[17]

Among the first-mover advantages that warrant special attention are those that are associated with the market for management talent. As noted earlier, Kaysen and

is 0.49 and the probability of tails is 0.51. Suppose further that (1) the title of dominance is conferred on every firm which, from the outset, flips ten or more consecutive heads and (2) once conferred the dominance status is retained so long as the difference between the total number of heads flipped less the total number of tails exceeds eight. Dominance, thus interpreted, will occur infrequently: only eight firms out of 10,000 can expect to achieve dominant firm status. But dominance, once achieved, is also resistant to undoing by the repeated application of the same stochastic mechanism that was responsible for the dominant firm outcome. The expected number of additional trials that will be required for dominance to be "undone" under these circumstances is 100. Cf. Feller (1957, pp. 311–318). Although the system displays self-correcting tendencies (since, as the number of trials increases without limit, dominance will always be undone under the conditions stated), these proceed rather slowly.

17. The argument may be put somewhat more formally as follows: Suppose price at time t is given by $P(t) = k\,AC^{L}$ where $k > 1$ and $AC^{L}$ is the average cost incurred by the lowest cost supplier in the industry at time $t$. Suppose, also, that there is learning-by-doing, but this accrues only through own-experience (there is no interfirm transfer of learning); in particular, assume that the average cost of firm $i$ at time $t$ is given by $AC_i^t = \overline{AC}\,f(t-t_i)$, where $\overline{AC}$ is initial average cost of a new entrant, $t_i$ is the time at which firm $i$ enters, $f(0) = 1$, and $f$⊠ <0, $f$⊠ > 0. Although early entrants into the industry have no cost advantage over later entrants, in the sense that the profile of average costs is any different, the margin profile, $P(t) - AC_i^t$, will differ between early and late entrants—with early entrants having the advantage. Thus, let firms be listed by order of entry, in which case $AC_1^t < AC_n^t$. Depending on the magnitude of $k$ and the time lapse between the entry of firm 1 and firm $n$, it may well be that at the time at which firm $n$ contemplates entry (say $t$⊠), $P(t') - AC_n^{t'} < 0$—in which case firm $n$ will not, at least initially, be able to break even (albeit that $P(t') - AC_1^{t'} > 0$). The argument is plainly oversimple in that both the pricing strategy is arbitrarily imposed and the assumption of no interfirm transfer of learning is too strong (late entrants can ordinarily imitate successes and avoid failures of their predecessors). Also, scale economies are assumed away. Despite these limitations, the model has heuristic merit.

Turner assume the management talent issue away. The argument goes through if the stock of talent is sufficient to staff prospective rivals of the dominant firm, if this talent can be easily identified, and if problems of transferability and interpersonal compatibility are not severe. Of these assumptions, the first two are probably the most plausible. But for the occasional exception of truly gifted entrepreneurs. talent in sufficient numbers and its easy identification will accordingly be taken as given. Problems of interpersonal compatibility and transferability, however, are more formidable.

That managers are imperfectly mobile resources—partly because of personal (including family) preferences and partly because employment contracts commonly include such deterrents to mobility as nonvesting[18]—is obvious. Less evident, but nonetheless important, is the matter of who works well with whom under what circumstances. This is the compatibility issue. Barnard expresses it succinctly as follows: "the question of personal compatibility or incompatibility is much more far-reaching in limiting cooperative effort than is recognized" (1962, p. 146). Efficient adaptation to changing circumstances is impaired "when there is incompatibility or even mere lack of compatibility, [since] both formal communication and especially communication through informal organization become difficult and sometimes impossible" (1962, p. 147). Although team considerations might be overcome by raiding the dominant firm to accomplish the transfer of a coherent group, executing such a transfer poses much more formidable problems than does the hiring of a few key individuals.

The relevance of this condition to the present argument is a temporal one. Thus, it is not that early entrants somehow avoid the costs of assembling the necessary talent but that, given that their cost experience is symmetrical and contemporaneous, none could be said to experience a disadvantage. As between established firms and would-be entrants, however, a contemporaneous cost difference in the respect does exist. To the extent that the prospective entrant's initial costs exceed the steady-state costs of established firms in the industry, a higher price to (steady-state) cost margin will be required to induce entry. *Ceteris paribus*, nontrivial transaction costs in the market for management talent inhibit entry.

Although the industry life cycle stability properties referred to above might be offset if the industry in question is one with a dominant firm, dominance seems more likely to reinforce stability. This obtains for two reasons: the dominant firm is able often to manage variety, and rivalry is apt to be attenuated.[19] The management of variety can take several forms. One of the more important is the supplanting of market tests by engineering and administrative processes. The dominant firm employs an internal selection mechanism to choose among alternative proposals and thereby avoids the unsettling effects of competitive market tests such as would obtain naturally among a group of independently acting firms in a competitive market. Thus, whereas

18. Although nonvesting serves as a deterrent to mobility, it need not be regarded as an imperfection in the market for managerial talent. Nonvesting may be stipulated by fully knowledgeable parties to a labor contract because it encourages investment in firm-specific human capital.

19. Moreover, if dominance is coupled with vertical integration and large absolute size. Still further uncertainty absorption may occur. See Malmgren (1961, pp. 402–403).

in a fully competitive market the independently acting firm is a variety generator in relation to its rivals, the dominant firm absorbs potential variety through internal decision-making processes. In a similar way, the dominant firm may be able to follow a program of contrived depreciation (Barro, 1972).

Rivalry will be further attenuated if extant and potential rivals behave more discreetly in a dominant firm industry than they would otherwise. Potential entrants in particular may recognize that where any significant market share can be secured only at the expense of the dominant firm, there is an especially high risk of economic reprisal. Although extant rivals sometimes enjoy umbrella effects, they may also forego aggressive initiatives, which would be freely undertaken in a less concentrated industry, if these threaten to upset established relationships.

In short, the degree of uncertainty in a mature industry with a dominant firm can be expected to be less than both (1) what the same industry experienced in its intermediate development stage, and (2) what the industry would have experienced in its mature stage but for the presence of a dominant firm. The argument leads to the following proposition: In consideration of the indicated attenuation in the shocks that the system experiences, a position of dominance (achieved by whatever means—including a fortuitous combination of chance events during an industry's intermediate stage of development) is resistant to undoing once the industry has reached an advanced stage of development. To the extent, therefore, that the Court's exemption from section 2 scrutiny of dominance acquired through business acumen or historic accident relies implicitly on the assumption that such dominance will soon be upset by the operation of the market, the doctrine is of dubious merit. The combination of first-mover advantages together with normal variety attenuation and absorption processes in a dominant firm market suggest instead that a doctrine which relies on this line of reasoning ought to be regarded warily.[20]

## 3. Government Intervention and Market Failure

### 3.1 The Problem of Equity and Economic Disincentive

Even if it is conceded that market failures of the types described can lead to dominant firm outcomes which unassisted market forces are unlikely to erode, it might still be argued that government intervention through the antitrust laws is inappropriate in instances where dominance has been achieved through innocent conduct. Antitrust action in these cases might produce severe disincentive effects in the economy as a whole, where the possibilities of outdistancing rivals through superior skill, more consistent, albeit unexceptional, performance, or pure luck operate to induce new entry

20. This position may be contrasted with that expressed by Posner, who argues that, predatory practices and natural monopoly conditions aside, dominance will be secured and maintained only if dominant firms either (1) forego monopoly gains or (2) possess superior skill (1969, p. 1597). Foregone monopoly gain presumably implies that dominant firms earn only competitive returns—which may have been the case with Alcoa but appears not to be the case with IBM. Although the superior skills referred to are presumably of an absolute variety, these may be attributable instead to first-mover advantages that arise from discontinued acumen, historic accident, or default failure—in which case the affirmative defense for monopoly that Posner evidently intends does not obviously obtain.

and to spur existing competitors on to greater efforts. A recent argument to this effect has been made by Marris (1972, p. 113):

> ... trust busting effectively contradicts the most fundamental principle of capitalism. Whatever may be said of the liberty of the individual, capitalism insists on the liberty of the organization. That liberty includes the right to grow. And the system rewards, with growth, the fruits of both good luck and good guidance. I cannot conceive how any political or other mechanism can sustain that principle if it is modified to read "You shall continue to be rewarded for success. But for successive success you shall be punished." I can conceive of some kind of society based on organizational devolution with some effective and inviolable resistance to concentration, but it would not be capitalism, and it certainly could not permit private ownership of the means of production.

Whether considerations of default failure, which are omitted from this statement, would lead Marris and others who adopt this position to conclude otherwise is uncertain. Default failures might, after all, be defended on the grounds that, subject only to rules of fairness, the victor deserves the spoils. The principle is commonly extended to include the proposition that it is even right to reward the tortoise for the indiscretions of the hare; persistence, even though some contestants perform discreditably, nevertheless has merit. But even setting default failure aside, the assertion that the imperatives of capitalism are as described might reasonably be questioned.

A somewhat more flexible position is taken by Turner, who suggests that, insofar as the arguments against intervention in a consolidated dominant firm situation are based on fears that such intervention will either produce a disincentive to future competition or result in an inequitable denial of earned rewards, the real issue is not whether a dominant firm deserves indefinite antitrust immunity, but rather for how long such antitrust insularity should be granted (1969, pp. 1220–1221):

> [D]issolution of a monopoly. Patent monopolies are limited to seventeen years. There is no apparent reason why any firm should have a right to enjoy indefinitely, or even for seventeen years, the fruits of monopoly from sources other than original unexpired patents or economies of scale.

The notion that the government should intervene to upset dominant firms after they have enjoyed their dominance for a certain number of years[21] need not be regarded as a new doctrine, but rather as a simple extension of market failure analysis to embrace a set of issues that has previously been misconstrued—by the courts and economists alike. As interpreted here, dominance attributable to default failure, chance events, or the management excellence of an earlier era constitutes an outcome for which relief, if it can be efficaciously devised, is appropriate. That there is a prima facie case for the government

21. Whatever period is allowed for enjoyment of dominance must be long enough to provide sufficient incentives to entrepreneurs in incipient dominant firms throughout the economy.

to intervene when markets fail is scarcely novel.[22] The reluctance of the government to address the dominant firm outcome in the market failure terms suggested here is not because the dominant firm condition is thought to be innocent—otherwise, the effort to contrive conduct offenses would not be made—but because differential expertise (business acumen) has been misinterpreted and chance events (historic accidents) have been accepted acquiescently.[23] The interpretation proposed here, however, suggests that these can properly be brought within the ambit of market failure analysis and that the usual presumption of government intervention where remediable market failures occur is warranted. Thus, although special problems would be posed were the government to intervene in markets that fail to display self-correcting tendencies by upsetting dominant firm outcomes attributable to chance events, default failures, or discontinued acumen, the underlying rationale for the intervention is not really unfamiliar.

Consequently, section 2 of the Sherman Act should be interpreted by the courts to require a finding that persistent dominance is presumptively unlawful, provided only that the industry can be judged to have reached an advanced stage of development.[24] The latter requirement reflects a judgment that the dominance outcome is unlikely to be undone by unassisted market forces in any short period of time once the industry has reached maturity. The dominant firm charged with a violation would be able to rebut the presumption of unlawful monopolization by demonstrating that its dominance was the result of economies of scale leading to a natural monopoly, of the exercise of an unexpired patent,[25] or of continuing indivisible, absolute management superiority. But dominance attributable to market failures of the types described in Section 2, above, would provide the occasion for government intervention.

## 3.2 Distinguishing Absolute and Relative Superiority

Whether a default failure outcome is more than a hypothetical possibility—to be conceded in principle but not observed in practice—is perhaps to be doubted. Relevant in this connection is the experience of the diesel locomotive industry, where an argument not only can be but has been advanced that the dominance by General Motors of diesel locomotive manufacture is to be explained by default failure among the steam locomotive firms.[26] Although this record needs to be developed and documented more

22. Market failure is not, however, a sufficient condition for intervention to occur. The efficacy of any attempt to intervene needs also to be assessed. That governments often fail in such attempts needs to be appreciated.

23. Thus, considerations of differential expertise seem tacitly to have been taken to imply the absolute and continuing superiority of the dominant firm's management, so that default failure and lapsed expertise were disregarded, while unfavorable stochastic market outcomes were simply to be endured.

24. This requires that a judgment be made with respect to an industry's stage of development. Expert opinion together with statistical tests, for example fitting the industry's development history to a logistic curve, could probably be combined for the purpose of making an overall evaluation.

25. Turner has argued that once a firm's patents expire it should be subject to divestiture if it has attained a position of dominance that is impervious to market forces (1909, pp. 1220–1220). Having allowed the firm to enjoy the fruits of its invention for seventeen years, he sees little reason to allow it to continue to extract monopoly profits on the basis of a position of dominance established during the years of patent protection.

26. See Hearings Pursuant to S. Res. 61 Before the Subcom. on Antitrust and Monopoly of the Senate Comm. on the Judiciary, 84th Cong., 1st Sess., pt. 8, at 3948–3997 (1955) (testimony of C. R. Osborne).

thoroughly, I find the evidence more than suggestive that the dominance of General Motors in this industry was the result of ineptitude on the part of the steam locomotive manufacturers and imperceptiveness among potential rivals.[27] Though more conjectural, IBM's dominance of the electronic computer industry appears in part to be attributable to default failure—first, on the part of Sperry-Rand, in the early 1950's, followed by General Electric a few years thereafter.[28]

An examination of the sequential decision processes of both the dominant firm and its rivals is indicated if default failure is reasonably to be established in a given period. What major options with what expected payoffs were available to each firm during the interval in question? Rather than evaluate firms in terms of realized outcomes, an assessment of the merits of each firm's strategic posture is called for. A reconstruction of *ex ante* opportunities, rather than a recitation of *ex post* realizations, is accordingly needed. While this requires more intensive examination of individual business practices than antitrust specialists have conducted in the past, will frequently require access to internal documents not publicly available, and may sometimes come to naught, dominant firm outcomes would appear to be sufficiently rare, distinctive, and important to warrant an exploratory effort along these lines. The only problem is that academics, who might be prepared to do the studies, may not have access to the necessary data; while enforcement agencies, as currently constituted, lack the staff and resources to make such an assessment.[29]

An indirect test for absolute management superiority is whether the dominant firm has been a leader in developing new management practices, as revealed especially by organizational innovations. Again, General Motors, under the leadership of Alfred P. Sloan, Jr., illustrates a management that appears to have displayed unusual ability in this respect (Chandler, 1966).

From an enforcement point of view, however, the distinction between absolute and relative superiority may often be inessential. What is significant is that if either or both have contributed to a dominant firm outcome for which dissolution will bring efficacious relief, a section 2 suit is warranted. Dissolution would, however, pose problems if (1) the existing management possesses absolute superiority that will be wastefully dissipated were dissolution to be attempted, or (2) the disincentives that the managements of incipient dominant firms would experience would be substantial. Where the superiority in question is that of past, rather than current, management, the first of these problems does not appear. Whether the second is more than conjectural is uncertain.[30] The issue appears in the discussion of remedy below.

27. The steam locomotive manufacturers appear to have been severely disadvantaged by their limited manufacturing experience: no two steam locomotives were ever built exactly alike. Id. at 3957. This job shop tradition must be compared with the approach of General Motors, which involved extensive standardization in the manufacture of diesels. Implementing an organizational innovation of this sort may have been beyond the competence of the management of the steam locomotive firms.

28. For suggestive discussions of defective decision-making in each of these firms, see "Sperry-Rand: Still Merging," *Fortune*, March 1960, vol. 61, pp. 125–132, 160–166, and *Forbes*, "GE's Edsel," April 1, 1967, pp. 21–20.

29. The recent expansion of the economics staff in the Antitrust Division of the U.S. Department of Justice together with the increased budget of the Division may soon overcome this indicated disability.

30. To contend that firms will be greatly discouraged from taking initiatives that might subsequently lead to dominance seems dubious. Unless prospective rewards are mainly very distant, truncating a stream of earnings after

Assuming, as indicated, that management superiority will normally be manifested through organizational innovation, the first test of a contemporaneous absolute superiority claim is whether the dominant firm—whatever the original occasion for dominance—has recently distinguished itself as an organizational innovator. Absent a showing that established dominant firms are especially fecund sources of organizational innovations of a surpassing sort, for which there is no evidence, few firms can expect to qualify at this stage as exceptions. Among those that do, there is a further test of whether dissolution will impair innovative performance. Since the diffusion of important organizational innovations is ordinarily to be encouraged, and as this will commonly be promoted by dissolution, net losses in this respect will presumably be incurred only infrequently. Indeed, considering the difficulties of making a determinative assessment and the indicated low *a priori* probabilities of obtaining an affirmative result, claims of absolute, contemporaneous superiority might be disallowed altogether.

## 4. Remedies for Structural Dominance

The objective of a remedial decree in cases of structural monopoly should be to induce the dominant firm that is found guilty of a section 2 violation to divide itself into competitive parts within some reasonably short period of time after the first finding by a court that a violation has occurred.[31] Unless the dominant firm voluntarily divides itself into two or more viably competitive parts within a stipulated interval, say five years, the government would be entitled to court-ordered divestiture.

Although this proposal is not problem free, it does have several attractive attributes. First, the management itself, which presumably has the requisite expertise, has the incentive to redistribute the firm's assets into coherent, internally efficient and hopefully competitive parts. Only failure by the firm to exercise this option would require the government to intervene—although the proposed division by the firm would be subject to judicial review to determine whether competitive requirements had been met.

Second, a gradual procedure is provided by this method of divestiture. No immediate interruption of activity need occur; the transition can be performed as expansion and plant renewal decisions come up for consideration. The high transition costs that an immediate dissolution order might impose are thereby mitigated.

Finally, both physical and human assets will be reassigned. Often the expertise of a firm's personnel may constitute its most significant resource. While the duplication of physical assets by existing and potential rivals may be relatively easy, the acquisition of management and technical groups possessing the requisite experience can be much

fifteen years does not much impair incentives. With a twenty percent discount rate, the present value of a dollar earned in the fifteenth year is .065.

31. The relief proposals advanced in this section are a variant of those devised by the White House Task Force on Antitrust Policy. A major difference is that the Neal Report (1969) dealt with both industries dominated by a single firm and those dominated by several firms.

more difficult. The discussion of knowhow in Section 3.2 of Chapter 2, in connection with the United Shoe Machinery case, is relevant in this connection. Recall that it was the U.S. Justice Department's contention that affirmative relief required that United Shoe's potential competitors be given "consulting" assistance so that they might acquire "that intuitive knowledge based upon training and experience that is incapable of translation into written form. The employees of United's potential competitors need to be given as much and as detailed help as United's own employees, if not more."[32] Such consulting assistance would be unnecessary if dominant firms were to divide themselves into viable parts, since the requisite expertise and experience (knowhow) would presumably be distributed among the parts in the process.

Requiring dominant firms to undergo divestiture may, however, have undesirable side effects. First, the dominant firm may engage in aggressive monopolistic pricing, thereby encouraging new entry and the eventual erosion of its dominant market position (Turner, 1969, p. 1221). The emerging dominant firm faces a choice between alternative profit streams. It can choose the profit stream associated with continuing dominance and accept the prospect of eventual dissolution; or it can, during the latter part of the industry's intermediate development stage, increase its prices in order to realize greater short-run profits and effect a decline in market share below threshold levels. Although this second course of action would result in transitional welfare losses, these may not be great. I [like Turner (1969, p. 1221)] would be inclined to accept them—in the expectation that, even in these circumstances, a net social gain would commonly obtain from the early dissolution of the emerging dominant position.[33]

Pre-existing dominant firms, however, would not pose these same difficulties. A firm that already qualifies as dominant at the time the proposed policy is adopted should automatically face a dissolution proceeding. Changes in market share during the period of the proceeding would presumably be small and in any event could be disallowed as a basis for release. Indeed, were an increase in price to cost margin to be attempted, an injunction might reasonably be granted to prevent its implementation.

Second, the dominant firm may, in anticipation of a section 2 complaint, undertake programs designed to make the cost of divestiture exceedingly great. Kaysen and Turner, for example, stipulate that "the court shall not approve a plan involving

32. "Brief for the United States on Relief," U.S. Department of Justice, *United States v. United Shoe Machinery Corp* (1952).

33. This assumes that the industry in question will thereafter perform in a more competitive manner and thus realize allocative efficiency gains. There are several reasons to expect that this will occur. For one thing, technical progress is unlikely to be impaired and may well be improved as a result of greater competition. See Turner and Williamson (1971, p. 135). Also, price competition may be enhanced. Weiss, relying on Stigler's treatment of oligopoly, notes that oligopolistic collusion depends for its success on the individual seller's ability to detect nonrandom sales losses due to chiseling; and this "means that we should be very much concerned about the shares of the top one or two firms and that the shares of any firm beyond about the fourth cannot make much difference" (Weiss, 1971, p. 374). But whether or not such effects are realized in each individual instance, the more general social gains described at the outset of the chapter favor the policy in question. There is, nevertheless, one especially troublesome possibility to be considered: where default failure has occurred and new entry is not induced by the monopolistic pricing policy adopted by the prospective dominant firm, the firms that are benefited by the shift of the dominant firm to a high price mode are those hypothetical hares whose discreditable performance is responsible for the prospective dominance condition in question.

division of the assets of a single plant" (1959, p. 269).[34] Dominant firms that are anxious to forestall a dissolution order may be induced on this account to engage in excessive equipment specialization and plant size concentration.[35] A satisfactory deterrent to such behavior is not easy to devise. Perhaps the only realistic policy is to reject the single plant exception unless nontrivial economies of scale can be clearly shown—in which case the relief issue would not be faced since dominance here is permitted.[36]

If this approach is adopted, however, problems in evaluating claims of single plant economies must be anticipated. To the extent that these economies are said to be attributable to technological factors, objective engineering evidence could be required. Since, beyond a certain size, plant replication typically affords economies, for example, by permitting better access to factor markets and by reducing the transportation expense of servicing customers,[37] the demands for a clear showing of technological economies can be relatively strict. In the absence of such a showing, divestiture, despite high transition costs, could be required. Advance announcement of this policy ought to discourage "strategic" investment in single plants.

Third, allowing a firm to produce its own plan of divestiture may lead to a division that creates noncompeting parts, for example, splitting into an industrial division and a consumer products division. Although such a separation would be consistent with stockholder interests, the government would presumably object if alternatives involving active, contemporaneous competition between parts of the firm could be arranged. Where contemporaneous rivalry cannot be obtained, but the nonoverlapping divisions are both viable and enjoy reasonable parity with respect to size, relief may still be partly efficacious: divisions operating in nonoverlapping markets but sharing common knowledge will, when given independent standing, increase the potential for future competition.

Finally, the dominant firm may allow itself to be run in efficiently. Managers and employees may indulge themselves in on-the-job leisure or in other "corporate personal consumption" activities. In these circumstances, rivals presumably can easily overtake the dominant firm. The industry would thus restructure itself, but with considerable transition costs. Uncertainty with respect to the time that the government will file a section 2 complaint, however, should tend to discourage this behavior. Moreover, competition in the capital market, operating primarily through the takeover mechanism,[38] might be regarded more sympathetically as it applies to the dominant firm industries, since this serves as a check on inefficient practices.[39]

34. See, also, *United States* v. *United Shoe Machinery Corporation,* 110 F. Supp. 295, 348 (D. Mass. 1953) (Wyzanski, J.), *aff'd per curiam*, 347 U.S. 521 (1954).

35. There have been suggestions that General Motors has recentralized certain of its manufacturing activities for this reason. *Wall St. J*, Nov. 5. 1968. at p. 8. col. 3.

36. The stipulation of nontrivial economies is essential. Otherwise, the misallocative effects of the resulting market power may well exceed the efficiency gains—in which case the economies defense should be disallowed.

37. See Georgescu-Roegen (1967, pp. 56–62).

38. See Chs. 8 and 9 for a development of this part of the argument.

39. Any successful takeover agent would be expected not merely to reduce slack but also revert to the high price, short-run profit maximization mode described above.

## 5. Application to the Structure-Conduct Controversy

Baldwin, in a recent survey of the structure versus conduct controversy, distinguishes strong from qualified structuralist positions and contrasts these with a conduct approach to enforcement. The strong structuralist position, which he associates with Bain, Caves, and Stigler, is that structure determines conduct, for the most part, and that tinkering with conduct is unlikely to have significant consequences so long as the underlying structural defect remains. The essential distinction is between symptoms and causes, where conduct reflects the former and structure the latter.[40]

The conduct approach relies on the assumptions that competitive instincts in the U.S. economy are strong and that large numbers competition is usually feasible. Given these, advocates of the conduct approach, of which Baldwin appears to be one, contend that (1) the traditional and appropriate concern of the law has been with conduct, and (2) effective competition will obtain if the law prevents the "deliberate impairment, misdirection, or suppression of competition" (Dirlam and Kahn, 1954, p. 28). Structure will take care of itself if fair play is maintained.

Nothing in the argument developed in earlier sections of this chapter suggests that vigilance with respect to fair play ought to be relaxed. But I am apprehensive that an exclusive emphasis on fair play will suffice. It fails to allow for market failure of the chance event variety and dismisses the possibility of dominance by default. Also, it assumes that relief which is restricted to a few conduct practices (such as lease-only contracts in United Shoe) will be efficacious. This imputes high potency to a few practices and assumes, implicitly, that alternative means to accomplish the same end, while conforming to the letter of the law, are unavailable. As Bain points out, however, "as soon as one specific set of collusive practices is found illegal and enjoined, another set may be invented (not nominally violating the first injunction) to accomplish the original purpose" (1959, p. 495).

Moreover, with few notable exceptions, such as perhaps the franchise system in automobiles,[41] it seems unlikely that individual business practices, taken by themselves, are apt to have sufficiently decisive consequences to support the conduct approach. More often, probably, conduct that has exclusionary consequences will rest not on any particular practice but is the result of a systematic strategy employed by the dominant firm or industry in question—which is to say that it is a pervasive set of interrelated practices, rather than any one or a few, that has the anticompetitive effect.

The prospect that narrow conduct remedies taken by themselves will subsequently produce nontrivial structural changes must, on this line of argument, be regarded as dubious. However, this raises the question of why, in the cases cited by Baldwin (United Shoe, Eastman Kodak, and IBM),[42] mainly conduct remedies were,

40. As Baldwin points out (1969, p. 127). Bain and Caves qualify this position to acknowledge that predatory and exclusionary practices can influence the condition of entry. Conduct can in these respects affect structure, but this aspect of the argument has never been extensively developed or its empirical significance assessed.

41. See Bain (1956, pp. 300, 301, 307) for an argument on the effects of auto franchising.

42. *United States* v. *United Shoe Machinery Corporation*, 110 F. Supp. 295 (D. Mass 1953); *United States* v. *Eastman Kodak Company*, 1954 Trade Cas. #67.920 (W.D.N.Y. 1954); *United States* v. *International Business Machines Corporation*, 1956 Trade Cas. #68.245 (S.D.N.Y. 1956).

on subsequent review by the courts, reported to be relatively efficacious in producing the intended structural correction.

Baldwin, in selecting these three cases for consideration, expresses the view that (1969, p. 128)

> ... for the purpose of analyzing the appropriateness and effectiveness of remedies seeking modification of structure indirectly through restraints on conduct, the most helpful cases are those in which the court handing down or approving the decree and jurisdiction also accepted a provision that the effectiveness of the original remedy would be examined after a specified length of time.

If, after an eight- or ten-year period, the court were to find that significant structural change had occurred, Baldwin is of the opinion, apparently, that the success of the conduct remedy is to be presumed.

Two alternative explanations are neglected, however. For one thing, the courts may have employed weak standards of judging efficacy.[43] For another, the prospect of a mandated structural remedy may be so ominous as to induce the dominant firm subject to review to take measures which, collectively, will reduce its market share to acceptable proportions. Thus, power to produce the intended effect is not to be imputed to the conduct remedy per se; indeed, any conduct remedy, however trivial, coupled with a contingent structural review stipulation may be sufficient. On this argument, the economic significance of the decree resides in the latent or expressed threat of subsequent structural change if the weaker (conduct) remedy is ineffective.

This last view is consistent with the position advanced above (and expressed previously by others) that, ordinarily, conduct remedies by themselves cannot be expected to produce significant structural consequences.[44] What is more interesting, perhaps, is that, as interpreted here, the contingent review procedure that the courts have fashioned is not all that different from the relief policy proposed in Section 4 above. The advantage of the approach proposed in this chapter is that it addresses the issues in a relatively unconvoluted way.

## 6. Dominant Firms and the Organizational Failures Framework

The implicit reliance on the organizational failures framework in preceding sections of this chapter will be made explicit here. That chance event and default failures directly relate to the framework is reasonably obvious; the interpretation of business acumen,

43. This is supported by the government's appeal of the United Shoe outcome.

44. *Eastman Kodak,* which involved a tie between color film purchase and processing, may be an exception. [See *United States* v. *Eastman Kodak, Co.,* 1954 Trade Cas. (CCH) ¶67920 (W.D.N.Y. 1954) (consent decree).] The product acceptability of actual and potential film producers could have been impaired for lack of sufficient processing outlets. If the threshold expenses of putting a viable, independent processing program into effect were considerable, the tie would tend to inhibit color film competition.

by contrast, is somewhat more involved. The conduct approach to the enforcement of section 2 of the Sherman Act and the feasibility of fashioning structural remedies can also be interpreted in organizational failure terms. Consider these *seriatim*.

## 6.1 Chance Event Failure

By definition, chance events are attributable to uncertainty. But the mere fact that decisions are made in the face of uncertainty does not establish that failure obtains. Rather, it is chance outcomes which involve a considerable element of "surprise" or are due to an unusual sequence of chance events that pose the problem.

Surprise outcomes are attributable to the conjunction of bounded rationality with uncertainty. Thus, it is not that low probability outcomes with high payoffs carrying only fair (risk adjusted) expected returns have eventuated. The outcomes in question, rather, are those which, in a conscious commitment sense, were completely unanticipated. It is unrealistic and even disingenuous to impute rational choice to participants who plainly lack the capacity to assess and position themselves strategically with respect to the complex situation of which they are a part:[45] where all the participants are severely limited in bounded rationality respects, differential outcomes are explained, to a large extent, by luck.

## 6.2 Default Failures

The assumption that markets have self-policing properties rests implicitly on a large numbers assumption. Where instead the responsibility for effective rivalry falls on a very few actual and potential rivals, the performance of each becomes critical. Should these firms fail to perform in a creditable way and should this failure persist, what might otherwise have been a relatively competitive oligopoly may become a dominant firm industry instead. A small-numbers condition at the outset thus places the assumption of self-policing markets in jeopardy.

What is essential for default failure, however, is not that one or a few firms fail to grasp a single opportunity, but that this failure occurs repeatedly. Persistent failure to discern and/or realize its profit opportunities is involved. That this should ever occur is a reflection of internal ineptitude and failures in the capital market. With respect to the latter, interested outsiders either fail to perceive the foregone opportunities (on account of information impactedness) or are unable to effect takeover except at great cost (because stockholders cannot take representations of ineptitude on the part of the incumbent at face value, on account of the risk of opportunism; because displaying the evidence in a compelling way and getting stockholders or their agents to evaluate it is costly, given bounded rationality; and because incumbent managements may opportunistically throw up a series of obstacles to takeover). Issues of these kinds are familiar from treatments of competition in the capital market in preceding chapters.

45. Tests of two sorts are germane. First, the chance events themselves may be of a sort which are really decisive and of a quite unanticipated sort. (The onset of World War II in the diesel locomotive industry is an example.) Second, it may be possible by examining file documents and interviewing executives to establish that the outcomes in question were never really within the domain of those which the firm anticipated.

## 6.3 Business Acumen

The existence of a business acumen advantage implies a differential distribution of strategic decision-making or organizational talents. Presumably, however, the marginal productivity of high talent experience diminishing returns. Except, therefore, as these talents may be associated with a single, unique individual, what is it that explains the failure of the market to redistribute this talent among rival firms? Put differently, will the market process on which Kaysen and Turner rely for reallocating management talent operate smoothly?

At least two factors impede this. First, there is the problem of discerning who the really talented managers are. Business performance is the result of collective decision-making in what is commonly a complex system. Who is responsible for what? Information incompleteness conditions obtain. Many managers are involved, but the exceptional ones can be discerned only with difficulty.[46] Moreover, this cannot be easily overcome by asking the high talent managers to come forward. For one thing, they may not really know. Also, the less talented can make the same representations (opportunistically) and the market cannot confidently distinguish between them.

Second, there is the problem of team considerations. This is a manifestation of idiosyncratic group experience, as discussed earlier in connection with the employment relationship.... Although recognition that team factors can be important goes back some two hundred years,[47] the issue has been widely disregarded among academic economists.

## 6.4 The Conduct Approach

Whether the reliance by the enforcement agencies on conduct complaints to bring suits against dominant firms should be regarded as opportunistic might be disputed. Given that chance event and default failures are apparently inadmissible grounds upon which to base a section 2 complaint, the enforcement agencies face a dilemma: either the dominant firm condition is outside the reach of the antitrust laws or they must proceed in a contrived way by attributing the dominance condition to unlawful conduct. Following the latter course may then be regarded as simply maximizing enforcement effectiveness subject to constraint. The failure is not one of enforcement; the interpretation by the judiciary of the law is at fault.

46. Witness the frequency with which efforts to revitalize a moribund firm by hiring an executive in a successful firm come to naught.

47. Though he put the argument in terms of craftsmen rather than executives, Benjamin Franklin expressed the team organization issue in the following terms in the 1800's:

> Manufactures, where they are in perfection, are carried on by a multiplicity of hands, each of which is expert only in his own part, no one of them a master of the whole; and if by any means spirited away to a foreign country, he is lost without his fellows. Then it is a matter of extremest difficulty to persuade a complete set of workmen, skilled in all parts of a manufactory, to leave their country together and settle in a foreign land. Some of the idle and drunken may be enticed away, but these only disappoint their employers, and serve to discourage the undertaking. If by royal munificence, and an expense that the profits of the trade alone would not bear, a complete set of good and skillful hands are collected and carried over, they find so much of the system imperfect, so many things wanting to carry on the trade to advantage, so many difficulties to overcome, and the knot of hands so easily broken by death, dissatisfaction, and desertion, that they and their employers are discouraged altogether, and the project vanishes in smoke. [Cited by Stigler (1951, p. 190).]

This, however, implicitly assigns a narrow and passive role to the enforcement agencies. A more ambitious interpretation of their responsibility is to correct judicial failures by bringing good cases supported with good arguments. The court is there to be convinced. At least, therefore, until such an effort has been made and failed, reliance by the enforcement agencies on contrived conduct offenses seems opportunistic.

However, a further question is raised: Why have the agencies been successful in employing the conduct strategy? I submit that bounded rationality and information impactedness are the critical factors. None of the parties—complainant, defendant, or court—has a sufficiently rich model to sort out the quantitative consequences of the conduct in question (which is a manifestation of bounded rationality), and the requisite data in any event are apt to be deeply impacted. Given that the courts regard dominant firm outcomes apprehensively, a showing that certain conduct practices were engaged in and could have had some, however slight, structural effect has been sufficient to prevail.

## 6.5 Remedy

Remedy issues of two types arise in connection with the dominant firm condition. First, will unassisted market processes reliably undo dominant firm outcomes in any short period of time? Second, what problems are presented if the grounds for bringing a dominant firm complaint are expanded in the manner suggested?

That unassisted market processes may not suffice is due in large measure to first-mover advantages. Dominance conditions, once achieved, are for this reason resistant to undoing. But it does not follow that an effort to achieve remedy by dissolution is warranted. This depends on the capacity of the judicial system to address the dominant firm condition in a timely and competent fashion.

As presently constituted, neither the enforcement agencies nor the courts have the manpower and the necessary expertise to assess the issues in a determinative fashion. Institutional reform designed to mitigate these bounded rationality limits ought thus to accompany any effort by the judiciary to address the dominant firm issue along the lines of the suggested market failures argument.

# Conclusion

Although expanding section 2 enforcement to include dominance acquired by discontinued acumen, chance event, and default failure poses numerous difficulties,[48] the approach proposed has the advantage over existing policy of addressing the issue of single-firm dominance in a direct and candid manner. Assigning residual responsibility to the government to intervene in a dominant firm industry that has reached an advanced stage

48. Other problems in implementing this proposal not noted in the text might also be anticipated. For example, the Sherman Act carries criminal, as well as civil, sanctions. However, as Turner has observed: "It would appear wholly inappropriate to impose criminal sanctions for . . . the mere retention of monopoly power for a substantial period of time without objectionable conduct of any kind" (1969, p. 1222). Turner also suggests that dissolution suits of the sort described should be brought only by the government, since monopoly cases should not be undertaken lightly and "private suits are much less likely . . . to reflect a thorough assessment and dispassionate conclusions regarding the public interest" (1969, p. 1224).

of development (within which self-correcting market processes operate only slowly) relieves the need to rely on claims that anticompetitive conduct is the culprit. It thereby allows enforcement to proceed in a more assertive, less contrived way.[49] Dominant firm industries in which a conduct offense was tenuously associated with dominance could be attacked expressly in terms of structural monopoly (or mixed structural-conduct monopoly). Equally important, the reach of antitrust enforcement could be extended to include industries in which dominance cannot be attributed even remotely to predatory or exclusionary business tactics. Industries in which dominance has manifestly resulted from chance event or default failures, and which now enjoy apparent insularity, would thus come within the ambit of section 2 enforcement without strain.

That notions of stochastic and default failures serve to relieve the strain under which conventional analysis labors in treating the dominant firm condition is hopefully evident. That the proposed enforcement policy follows directly, however, might be disputed. Thus, others might be prepared to accept the argument that dominant firm outcomes are commonly explained by chance event and default failures, but then conclude that such dominance is sufficiently rare that it be tolerated as one of the costs that is associated with what, ordinarily, is a well-working, self-policing enterprise system.

Indeed, for those industries in which the degree of dominance falls below the suggested threshold level, toleration is what is proposed here. But rather than accept all monopolistic outcomes, however egregious, with the same degree of equanimity, the more severe cases are put through a dissolution proceeding. Mainly this is because (1) unassisted market processes are least likely to upset the dominance condition in these industries in any short period of time, (2) uncontested dominance runs contrary to prevailing social norms and undermines confidence in an enterprise system, and (3) the side effects of a delimited policy are not judged to be sufficiently serious to offset the prospective economic and social gains.

## F. M. Scherer

## *Conservative Economics and Antitrust: A Variety of Influences*

## In *How the Chicago School Overshot the Market: The Effect of Conservative Economic Analysis on U.S. Antitrust*

## Introduction

Our task, as I interpret it, is to evaluate the influence conservative economics has had on the enforcement and adjudication of antitrust in the United States. I assume it to

49. Mason characterizes the conduct approach as follows: "There is a school of thought that... believes that all undesirable market situations can, in fact, be reached by a rule on restrictive conduct.... But if the undesirability lies primarily in the situation... this procedure somewhat resembles an attack on kidnapping by prosecuting kidnappers for income tax violation" (1959, p. xiv).

be proven, without undertaking the arduous task of providing support, that the economic doctrines underlying the corpus of judicially accepted antitrust law have gravitated during the past half century in a more conservative direction.

This statement of the problem immediately demands a deeper level of analysis. Antitrust is accomplished through enforcement, and what gets done depends in significant measure on the laws Congress passes and how the courts, especially the higher courts, interpret statutes whose implications and intent are often not precisely stated. What gets written into the statutes and how the courts interpret the statutes depends in part upon economic analysis, although to be sure, much else is thrown into the stew. If there has been a change in emphasis over time, the cause may lie in the underlying economics. But it is much more probable, in my opinion, that changes are attributable to how antitrust enforcers and the courts read what economics has to say; that is, on which among conflicting propositions they have placed emphasis and which ones they have downplayed. And those choices depend importantly upon the values the decision-makers—typically, lawyers rather than economists—bring to the table. As Paul Samuelson wisely quipped, "Economists should be on tap, not on top."

No one can deny that there are conflicting economic analyses. That, in my opinion, is an unmitigated blessing. Knowledge advances through the juxtaposition of alternative theories and testing against evidence to determine which ones are more nearly correct. "More nearly correct" is as close as I dare come in characterizing what economics can add to the debate, because economic propositions are among the least provable of those addressed in the various sciences. Economists' subject matter is intrinsically complex, characterized by uncertainty, reciprocal expectations puzzles (the analogue of physicists' three-body conundrum), and incommensurable values. Our data are often deficient and our empirical methodologies less than satisfactory (but improving). Accepting that we cannot conclusively separate what is true from what is untrue, the best one can hope for from economics in informing antitrust enforcement and adjudication is that differences in the findings from economic analyses will be made clear, as will the probable reasons why those differences cannot readily be resolved.

If the above premises are anywhere near correct, we should be thankful for the existence of a so-called Chicago School of economics, which is often (incorrectly, I shall argue) associated with conservative economics. One clear characteristic of the Chicago School—not the only one, to be sure—is what I, as a person born and raised in what *Chicago Tribune* publisher Robert R. McCormick called "Chicagoland," identify as the great Chicago "a'giner" tradition. If the conventional wisdom says X is true, one redoubles one's efforts to find the flaws supporting that inference and perhaps also to show that instead Y is true. Epitomizing this attitude was the role of Aaron Director at the University of Chicago. Director encouraged legal and economic scholars at Chicago to investigate critically the facts, assumptions, and theories underlying important antitrust doctrines. Those investigations often identified weaknesses in the foundations and sometimes showed that the emperor had no clothes. That train of scholarly work has been of enormous benefit to all of us.

It should be recognized too that virtually all professional economists plying their trade in the United States are conservatives, in the sense that we believe in free markets and capitalism as instruments of discovery and engines of progress—views we adopt *inter alia* from Friedrich Hayek—and in markets as relatively efficient allocators of resources. If some of us (not I) once believed in central planning as a superior alternative, we were disabused of that notion by the failure of communism in the Soviet Union and China and the rather more equivocal triumph of capitalism. I believe it was Chicago's George Stigler who once observed that "the study of economics makes a person conservative."

That said, it must be recognized that there are widely varying degrees of conservatism in the economics practiced within the United States (as elsewhere). The differences stem more from fundamental values and assumptions about human behavior and about the desirability of such phenomena as unequal income distribution than from the choice of one analytic or empirical technique over another. It would certainly be a mistake to view Chicago as the citadel of all conservative economics. One could with equal accuracy point to conservative schools with roots at Auburn University (uniquely attached to the pronouncements of Ludwig von Mises), the University of Virginia, George Mason University, the University of Rochester, and Washington University, not to mention minority groups at a host of institutions including my alma mater and employer, Harvard. And for dogmatic differentiation, one would be hard-pressed to match the range of extremes represented by economic think tanks.

## I. The Influence of "Chicago" Economists

As I have indicated, the University of Chicago is often singled out as the leading bastion of conservative economics. This, I believe, is wrong for at least two reasons. First, by digging into and exposing flaws in accepted antitrust doctrines, Chicago has focused and sharpened the debate—a virtue that I identify with enlightened liberal scholarship. But second and more tellingly, Chicago economists and antitrust scholars have been far from monolithic in advocating a retrenchment of antitrust enforcement programs. I mention briefly four of the most prominent counterexamples.

(1) While New Deal politicians were backing off from their ill-fated experience with cartelization under the National Recovery Administration, "conservative" Chicago economist Henry Simons proposed in 1936, among various policy redirections:

> (1) Operating companies must be limited in size, under special limitations prescribed for particular industries by the Federal Trade Commission.... There would be a breaking down of enormous integrations into more specialized firms, with ownership separation among phases of production which are now largely separate in place and management. For horizontal combinations, the policy would require ownership separation among operating units which are now connected by little more than common advertising and selling organizations.

(2) The most sweeping proposals for deconcentration of concentrated industries made by an official governmental commission came in 1968 from the so-called Neal Report, chaired by University of Chicago Law School dean Phil Caldwell Neal, who had co-taught the School's antitrust law course with Aaron Director.
(3) Richard Posner's 1976 book and related articles recommended much more stringent enforcement of the Sherman Act toward jointly acting oligopolies even in the absence of classical conspiracy evidence.
(4) A powerful demonstration of the welfare distortions that can result from tying arrangements in other than fixed-proportions cases was published by John McGee, who was an associate professor of economics at Chicago between 1957 and 1962.

Other better-known work by McGee gravitated in the opposite direction, diluting the presumptions of antitrust violation through predatory pricing In his appreciation of Aaron Director's influence. Sam Peltzman asserts that the largest antitrust change attributable to Director was on the question of predatory pricing. Up to the time of McGee's seminal article, the research for which was suggested by Aaron Director, it was generally assumed that the Supreme Court acted correctly in 1911 when it condemned *Standard Oil* and, in a parallel case, *American Tobacco*, for achieving and retaining their near-monopoly positions, among other things through predatory pricing. Through his analysis of the Standard Oil case facts, McGee challenged this supposition. His work was cited by the Supreme Court in its 1986 dictum that "there is a consensus among commentators that predatory pricing schemes are rarely tried and even more rarely successful."

However, McGee was by no means the only economist writing on predation. Already by the time of the *Matsushita* decision, there was a substantial scholarly literature documenting what should have passed for predation by any reasonable definition and showing the rationality of sharp price-cutting by a dominant firm to discourage new entrants. Since there was a diversity of scholarly views at the time key Supreme Court pronouncements were rendered on predation, the fault for ignoring one side of the scholarship must be attributed to the Court's myopia or (without the obiter dictum) compelling facts, and not to economists' contributions. More recently, a careful analysis has cast doubt on whether McGee's reading of the *Standard Oil* case facts was accurate and brings forward considerable evidence supporting an inference of predation. In a world governed by the canons of scholarship rather than *stare decisis*, one might in some future case expect a renunciation by the Supreme Court of its previous misconceptions.

Reversion from the tough predatory pricing precedents of Standard Oil, 1911, also was influenced by Phillip Areeda and Donald Turner through a journal article, in which they almost certainly intended to influence ongoing cases against IBM alleging predation against plug-compatible computer equipment makers. Areeda and Turner, professors at Harvard Law School, can hardly be characterized as Chicagoans. Yet their article has been cited favorably in subsequent predation cases, including *Matsushita* and the Supreme Court decision in *Brooke Group*. The main novelty of *Brooke Group* was the Supreme Court's emphasis that to be predatory, a strategy required a reasonable prospect (or dangerous probability) that early profit sacrifices would later be recouped despite oligopolistic coordination obstacles. In its opinion, the Court considered a broad array of expert opinions. If there was favoritism, it was not in the economic literature evaluated, but in the weighing of alternative perspectives.

The domain of judicial interpretation most closely associated with University of Chicago doctrines involves vertical restraints such as exclusive franchises, exclusive territorial arrangements, and resale price maintenance. In that area of the law, Sam Peltzman recorded "a partial victory for the analysis inspired by [Aaron] Director." Two key contributions were Lester Telser's 1960 article on free rider problems and Robert Bork's argument that, by providing the wherewithal for demand-expanding merchandising efforts, minimum-price restrictions imposed by manufacturers upon their retailers can be welfare-enhancing. There are three problems with this attribution. First, the sharpest swerve in Supreme Court interpretations concerning the desirability of vertical restraints came in a decision that considered a wide spectrum of scholarly views. Telser's contribution went unmentioned, although the free rider concept entered indirectly through Justice White's concurring opinion, citing an article by Richard Posner, other facets of which were relied upon heavily by the majority. Second, recognition that vertical pricing relationships could cause welfare losses that might be solved by vertical integration had a much longer history, dating back at least to the 1830s. And third, the Bork proof has been shown to be a special case, by no means applicable in all vertical pricing or resale price maintenance situations.

After Peltzman's declaration of "partial victory," the Supreme Court returned to the core of the vertical restraints question and, openly abandoning *stare decisis*, overturned the per se presumption against resale price maintenance embedded for nearly a century in the *Dr. Miles* precedent. Its decision in *Leegin* moving from per se to rule of reason treatment might be considered the "et tu, Brute" in adjudication of vertical restraint questions. Yet one cannot say that the Court's 5–4 decision, with a strong dissent written by Justice Breyer, was one-sided. A broad range of scholarly arguments was evaluated by both the majority and the minority. Numerous amicus curiae briefs were filed, including one arguing for certiorari and eventual rule of reason treatment by 25 economists, only four of whom had graduate study or faculty appointment ties with the University of Chicago, and ten of whom were educated in the MIT-Harvard-Yale-Princeton axis. I co-signed that amicus brief but also, with William S. Comanor, filed a separate amicus brief on the merits.

Believing that a transition from a per se rule was inevitable, Comanor and I had two main objectives: persuading the Court to take a balanced view of the merits and demerits of resale price maintenance, and seeking to simplify rule of reason cases by articulating presumptions under which per se illegality would be retained. We (and other amici) succeeded, I believe, on the first point. Recognizing that both good and bad effects could exist, the majority stated squarely that "the potential anticompetitive effects of vertical price restraints must not be ignored or underestimated." On the second point, success was mixed. The majority recognized that "courts would have to be diligent in eliminating...anticompetitive uses from the market" and stating, as Comanor and I urged, that resale price maintenance was most likely to be harmful when it "spreads to cover the bulk of an industry's output." We failed in persuading the Court to adopt quantitative presumptions paralleling those already accepted for merger adjudication. Rather than engaging in such arguably legislative rule-making, the Court suggested that as the lower courts gained experience with such cases, they could "devise rules over time for offering proof, or even presumptions where justified, to make the rule of reason a fair and efficient way to prohibit anticompetitive restraints and to promote procompetitive ones." The burden passes now to the antitrust enforcement agencies and (with more difficulty) private plaintiffs to see that consumers are not seriously injured. One cannot say that *Leegin* left them without powerful Supreme Court obiter dicta on which to stand.

An even more dramatic pro-conservative swing has been evident in the enforcement and adjudication of mergers. How dramatic it has been is suggested by Figure 1 [omitted—eds.], from various tabulations of the average annual rate of exit through merger from *Fortune* magazine's annual lists of the top 100 U.S. industrial corporations. From the mid-1930s into the late-1970s, exit rates were quite low, but they then soared after 1982. Through the Celler-Kefauver Act of 1950, Congress eliminated previous loopholes in Clayton Act, section 7 with respect to mergers and made clear its intent that the law be enforced vigorously. A series of tough precedents followed, leading Justice Stewart to exclaim in a dissent, "[t]he sole consistency that I can find is that in litigation under Section 7, the Government always wins." A decisive turn toward greater lenience was the 1974 decision in the General Dynamics–United Electric Coal case, which is attributable more to a change in the ideological composition of the Supreme Court than to identifiable intellectual influences. But enforcers' zeal has undoubtedly been dampened to some extent through articles inter alia by Henry Manne and Michael Jensen, leaders of what might be called a Chicago-Rochester axis, stressing the benefits of mergers. A substantial dissenting literature exists on their contributions too. At the enforcement level, the Merger Guidelines of 1982 were shepherded through the antitrust agencies by a Harvard-trained economist, Lawrence J. White, and drew upon Chicago (George Stigler) mainly in choosing the once-mysterious Herfindahl-Hirschman index rather than previously emphasized concentration ratios to measure merger consequences. A significant modification occurred in 1984, when the Merger Guidelines incorporated an efficiency defense whose intellectual basis was a classic 1968 article by Oliver Williamson—not a Chicagoan. However, its implementation has been more Borkian than Williamsonian, emphasizing directly prospective cost-based price reductions to consumers over the freeing of resources to satisfy other consumer wants.

Also noteworthy is the absence of enforcement against jointly acting oligopolies since the Kellogg case of the late 1970s and the tetraethyl lead case of 1983. Diverse economic analyses led to government defeats in both of those cases. Kellogg's principal economist was Harvard-trained and -chaired. Game-theoretic considerations not associated with Chicago (and anticipated in my 1980 textbook edition) were influential in the tetraethyl lead case. But the composition of the Federal Trade Commission had become more conservative under the Reagan Administration. And there may have been some backlash from challenges to accepted oligopoly structure-performance doctrine by Chicagoans Yale Brozen and Harold Demsetz. The intellectual dispute was crystallized at the Columbia Law School *New Learning* conference, whose proceedings were published in 1974, which threw the economics profession into a state of doctrinal disarray. That matters were more complex than a simple flow of causation from concentration to high profits was shown through articles resulting from the Federal Trade Commission's Line of Business program, most notably, by David Ravenscraft. Clearly, as a result of such work, what economics taught about oligopoly was perceived by antitrust enforcers as more mixed, and enforcement became less vigorous. But again, the influences here are complex and point to many locales other than the University of Chicago.

## II. Other Influences

To the extent that there has been significant backtracking in antitrust precedents and enforcement, I suspect that there are two more important root causes, each of which can be identified with conservatism per se, even if not with conservative scholarship and especially economic scholarship.

For one, a foundational belief among many conservatives—not all, to be sure—is that "government is the problem." This was a belief embodied in Henry Simons's approach to monopolies. He recognized that monopolies existed and that they had harmful effects, but he was reluctant to let government agencies regulate them. Instead, he proposed that they be broken up structurally so that they would act competitively without sustained government intervention. His proposal probably underlay Assistant Attorney General William Baxter's readiness to break AT&T into eight fragments in what for at least a while was the greatest monopolization case of the second half of the twentieth century. If I interpret his position correctly, Baxter saw as AT&T's greatest sin the abuse of regulatory processes in order to suppress entry and preserve its monopoly. Judge Greene agreed in his interim decision, suggesting that the Federal Communications Commission "may realistically be incapable of efficiently regulating a company of AT&T's size, complexity, and power." Where this belief goes too far is when it leads to the appointment to key positions in the federal antitrust enforcement and adjudication hierarchy persons who believe it so passionately that they adopt a "do nothing" approach to their jobs. I believe it went too far during the Reagan Administration, and it has clearly gone too far, not only in antitrust but many other federal agencies under the Bush II Administration.

An argument rooted more deeply in conservative perspectives on economics is the assertion by John McGee, whom I have singled out previously as a believer in vertical market failure. At least with respect to merger and monopolization policy, McGee has argued that

> Unless we are dealing with industries into which the State blocks entry, industrial reorganization schemes have very much the same results as simply dictating to consumers what and from whom they can buy. In my view, this is both antieconomic and, to use an old-fashioned word, tyrannical. In sum, I conclude that apart from those industries dominated by State controls, there is the strongest presumption that the existing structure is the efficient structure.

Professor McGee may be extreme in this Panglossian diagnosis (roughly, everything that is, is good), but such views in attenuated form have been held by many of the individuals who have led the antitrust agencies under recent Republican administrations and the jurists appointed by those administrations to the higher Courts. Antitrust policy has almost surely been affected.

Let me add one point in the same general vein. Those who from firmly held conservative or libertarian principles believe that government is the problem, and/or that free markets are unlikely to go astray for more than brief anomalous periods, tend to be fervent in their beliefs. Those like myself who believe that markets do a pretty good job, but on occasion need a corrective nudge, are inclined to be the kinds of economists President Harry Truman deplored—those who equivocate with, "On the one hand, but on the other hand...." When one has such a complex perception of economic reality, one is unlikely to be fervent. And when there is a clash of views, at least in the currently polarized and showmanship-infatuated United States, fervor tends to trump ambivalence. And that, I believe, more than anything else, explains the ascendance of conservative thinking in antitrust law and economics.

## III. Technological Innovation and Patent Antitrust

I turn finally to a matter I have neglected, but that cannot be ignored, because it is far more important than the efficacy of markets in allocating resources and distributing income at any moment in time: the impact of market structure and related institutions on the vigor and pace of technological innovation. A more rapid rate of technological progress can in a relatively short period overwhelm any resource allocation inefficiencies attributable to monopoly, which tend in any event, as shown by Chicagoan Arnold Harberger, to be modest in relation to gross domestic product. The subject is a huge one, and here I must be highly selective.

Joseph A. Schumpeter, a conservative economist teaching at Harvard during the 1930s and 1940s, argued in 1942 that even when markets were monopolized, "creative destruction" would ensure a rapid pace of technological innovation and progress in an advanced capitalistic economy. As I show in a paper written for an American Bar

Association compendium, he was partly right. Competition through creative destruction does work, but sometimes it needs a helping hand, among other things, from antitrusters limiting barriers to competitive entry by firms with superior new ideas.

Here I address a narrower but important point. Half a century ago, antitrust enforcement took a generally skeptical view of restrictive patent agreements. Reviewing the findings of the Temporary National Economic Committee, George Stigler (then at the University of Minnesota, not Chicago) found the patent policies of the Hartford-Empire Company to be "an eloquent example of an evil demanding correction" and concluded that "[t]he case for limitation of restrictive [patient] licensing is surely irrefutable." The antitrust case waged against Hartford-Empire provided an important precedent for tough-minded compulsory licensing of patents used to monopolize industries and sustain their monopolization. In the ensuing decade and a half, more than 100 compulsory licensing orders were issued under antitrust proceedings.

Attempting to ascertain how such governmental intervention, and in particular the 1956 decrees that ordered compulsory licensing of all patents held by innovative giants AT&T and IBM, affected investment in research and development, eight colleagues and I at the (conservative) Harvard Business School interviewed and administered mail questionnaires to 91 companies. We found to our surprise that the decrees had little adverse impact on R&D investment, and more generally, that for established corporations, the expectation of patent protection was in most cases unimportant to R&D commitments. This finding has been validated by several more ambitious studies, among others, Taylor and Silberston in the United Kingdom and (in the U.S. context) by Edwin Mansfield and the current president of Yale University, Richard Levin.

Ignoring this literature but echoing the empirically unsupported arguments in a book by a Chicago-affiliated lawyer, Reagan Administration appointees to the Antitrust Division backpedaled significantly, staking out a broad area in which restrictive patent licensing agreements would not be challenged. Underlying the policy reversal was an assumption that

> Efforts to appropriate as much as possible of the surplus—the social value in excess of marginal cost—lying under the demand curve for patented technology do not harm competition. Indeed, the potential for appropriating those rents is *the* engine [emphasis added] that drives the technology market.

The increased rent appropriation was to be accomplished through a variety of practices extending the duration and (e.g., through tying practices as well as restrictive cross-licensing) the scope of patent grants. This premise is quite inconsistent with the large body of empirical evidence on the conditions under which well-established corporations are willing to invest in innovation. And yet it was used, despite the great Chicago tradition of supporting one's findings with empirical evidence, to justify a substantial policy change.

That the change was more than transitory is evidenced in major statements on the intersection between patent and antitrust policy by the two federal antitrust enforcement agencies and the Antitrust Modernization Commission. Both support the changed presumptions stemming from Department of Justice initiatives in the 1980s and endorse a rule of reason approach to cases in which the exercise of patent rights might conflict with antitrust objectives. Recognizing the complexity of the issues, I concur that a rule of reason approach is appropriate. But ignoring the empirical literature on the incentive effects of patent protection, both reports imply that the expectation of patent protection is a principal basis for investment in new technology. The DOJ-FTC report, for example, opens by stating that "[i]ntellectual property laws create exclusive rights that provide incentives for innovation... [and] prevent others from appropriating much of the value derived from... inventions or original expressions," and that "intellectual property laws protect the ability to earn a return on the investments necessary to innovate." Beginning with a favorable citation to the 1981 Department of Justice statement quoted above, the Antitrust Modernization Commission asserts that "the courts and the antitrust agencies in recent decades have evidenced a greater appreciation of the importance of intellectual property." It goes on to suggest that "[i]ntellectual property may be critical to future innovation in an industry," and (correctly, in the specifically cited pharmaceutical industry case) that "in innovative industries... intellectual property assets are key." Nowhere to be found in either report is more than peripheral recognition of the substantial empirical evidence demonstrating that in most industries (not all), intellectual property plays a relatively unimportant role as a stimulus to R&D investment. If one believes that the expectation of patent rights is the principal inducement to innovation, one will be wrong more often than right in balancing antitrust objectives against intellectual property considerations in rule of reason cases. It is like positioning a 300-pound gorilla on the pro-patent side of the balancing scale when the real-world counterpart is a 35-pound chimpanzee. A correction in the intellectual foundations of U.S. antitrust policy toward intellectual property is clearly needed.

## Herbert Hovenkamp

## *Post-Chicago Antitrust: A Review and Critique*

## I. Introduction: The Post-Chicago School

The Chicago School of antitrust analysis is the most coherent and elegant ideology that antitrust has ever experienced.[1] One must admire its simplicity, as well as its confidence in markets and its optimism. Nevertheless, those who found markets to be somewhat messier and Chicago economics less robust, began in the 1980s to call for a "post-Chicago" antitrust policy that would take the best that the Chicago School had to offer as a point of departure, and then develop an antitrust policy that was more sensitive to market imperfections. This could then enable anticompetitive behavior by

1. The best brief description is Richard A Posner, "The Chicago School of Antitrust Analysis," 127 *U. Pa. L. Rev.* 925 (1979).

dominant firms, that would take the competitive threats of mergers more seriously, and that would acknowledge the anticompetitive potential of at least a few vertical restraints.[2]

In the subsequent decade and a half, academic writers in abundance and courts in smaller numbers have responded with post-Chicago theory and legal doctrine that is certainly impressive in its amount, if not always in its quality. At the same time, a great deal of Chicago antitrust has "stuck"—so much that one gets the impression that for some doctrinal changes there is no turning back. For example, the per se rule against vertical nonprice restraints[3] or maximum resale price maintenance[4] will probably never be revived, no matter how great the triumph of post-Chicago antitrust.

But in any event, that is not what the best of post-Chicago antitrust is all about. Post-Chicago antitrust should not be evaluated as a throwback to an earlier area, but as an attempt to move on. This article seeks to evaluate post-Chicago antitrust from that perspective.

## II. Economics and Antitrust Before Chicago

Contrary to a common perception, the Chicago School was hardly the first time that United States antitrust law confronted economic theory. Antitrust in the United States has seldom suffered from a shortage of economic theories suggesting why certain behavior should be unlawful. Beginning in the decade that the Sherman Act was passed, litigants began to rely on prevailing economic theories to explain why a particular act was or was not anticompetitive. In the 1890s, economists struggling with the first marginalist models in economics[5] had difficulty explaining how a competitive enterprise could ever recover its fixed costs. Finding no adequate explanation, several economists argued that firms with significant fixed costs would be driven to "ruinous competition" that would invariably yield low returns, bankruptcy, and harmful destruction of assets.[6] John Bates Clark, perhaps the most important American economist of his generation, argued in 1887 that certain industries subject to high fixed costs

2. See Herbert Hovenkamp, "Antitrust Policy After Chicago," 84 *Mich. L. Rev.* 213 (1985) (criticizing the Chicago School model of antitrust and describing the increased influence of post-Chicago economics on this area).

3. *Continental T.V., Inc.* v. *GTE Sylvania Inc.*, 433 U.S. 36 (1977) (overruling *United States* v. *Arnold, Schwinn & Co.*, 388 U.S. 365 (1967)).

4. *State Oil Co.* v. *Khan*, 522 U.S. 3 (1997) (overruling *Albrecht* v. *The Herald Co.*, 390 U.S. 145 (1968).

5. That is, models that incorporated such conceptions as marginal cost and marginal revenue. See Herbert Hovenkamp, "The Marginalist Revolution in Legal Thought," 46 *Vand. L. Rev.* 305 (1993) (describing the evolution of marginalism and its early application to economics).

6. The debate began with Henry Carter Adams, "Relation of the State to Industrial Action," 1 Pub., Mf. Econ. Assn. 7, 52, 59–64 (1887) (arguing that in the case of industries with high fixed costs, "no law can make them compete"; further, for industries subject to economies of scale "the only question at issue is whether society shall support an irresponsible, extralegal monopoly, or a monopoly established by law and managed in the interest of the public."). See also George Gunton, *The Economic and Social Importance of the Eight-Hour Movement* (1889) (warning of the general dangers of overproduction in industries exposed to high fixed costs).

and economies of scale[7] were so prone to overproduction that the firms in them must either collude or face "widespread ruin."[8]

The defendants in the earliest Sherman Act cases involving mainly railroad cartels quickly appropriated these theories, arguing that unregulated railroads would face ruinous competition unless given permission to fix their rates. Justice Rufus Peckham, who wrote for the Supreme Court in both the *Trans-Missouri* and *Joint Traffic* cases, did not cite any of the economic literature, but he was completely familiar with the argument.[9]

Nevertheless, he could not find a "ruinous competition" defense in the language of the Sherman Act, which condemned "every" agreement in restraint of trade, whether economically justified or not.[10] Further, a "ruinous competition defense would force the court to decide what a reasonable rate of profit in a particular industry should be," and courts were not up to that task.[11]

But the economic debate over the possibility of ruinous competition continued into the 1920s and 1930s and had a significant influence on antitrust policy making, such as the important United States Steel merger decision in 1920.[12] The theory also

7. An economy of scale is a factor that makes costs lower for firms with higher output. Significant economies of scale generally result in fewer firms in a market and thus fewer rivals.

8. John Bates Clark, "The Limits of Competition," 2 *Pol. Sci. Q.* 45, 55 (1887). *Accord* Arthur Twining Hadley, "Private Monopolies and Public Rights," 1 *Q.J. Econ.* 28 (1886) (under high fixed costs "more goods are produced than the community can pay for at prices which cover the expense to the producers," resulting in ruinous competition); Carroll D. Wright, "The Relation of Production to Productive Capacity," 24 *Forum* 290 (Nov. 1897); Carroll D. Wright, "The Relation of Production to Productive Capacity," 24 *Forum* 671 (Feb. 1898) (second part); U. H. Crocker, *The Depression in Trade and Wages of Labor* (1886).Thus, William M. Collier defended some firms' practice of acquiring rivals and shutting down their plants, as removing unneeded capacity from the market and thus staving off ruinous competition. William M. Collier, *The Trusts: What Can We Do with Them? What Can They Do for Us?* 66–67 (1900).

9. See *United States* v. *Trans-Missouri Freight Assn.*, 166 U.S. 290, 329–330 (1897):

> [The defendants] draw attention to the fact of the peculiar nature of railroad property. When a railroad is once built, it is said, it must be kept in operation; it must transport property, when necessary in order to keep its business, at the smallest price and for the narrowest profit, or even for no profit, provided running expenses can be paid, rather than not to do the work; that railroad property cannot be altered for use for any other purpose, at least without such loss as may fairly be called destructive; that competition while, perhaps, right and proper in other business, simply leads in railroad business to financial ruin and insolvency, and to the operation of the road by receivers in the interest of its creditors...; that a receiver is only bound to pay operating expenses, so he can compete with the solvent company and oblige it to come down to prices incompatible with any profit for the work done....

See also the lengthy discussion of the "ruinous competition" defense in *United States* v. *Joint Traffic Assn.*, 171 U.S. 505, 577 (1898), which ultimately concluded that:

> Whether, in the absence of an agreement as to rates, the consequences described by counsel will in fact follow as a result of competition, is a matter of very great uncertainty, depending upon many contingencies.... An agreement of the nature of this one, which directly and effectually stifles competition, must be regarded under the statute as one in restraint of trade, notwithstanding there are possibilities that a restraint of trade may also follow competition that may be indulged in until the weaker roads are completely destroyed, and the survivor thereafter raises rates and maintains them.

10. The ruinous competition controversy is discussed more fully in H. Hovenkamp, *Enterprise and American Law, 1836–1937,* 308–322 (1991).

11. See *Trans-Missouri,* 166 U.S. at 372–373. See also *United States* v. *Addyston Pipe & Steel Co.*, 85 Fed. 271, 284 (6th Cir. 1898), *aff'd,* 175 U.S. 211 (1899).

12. *United States* v. *United States Steel Corp.*, 223 F. 55 (D.N.J. 1915), *aff'd,* 251 U.S. 417 (1920) (approving merger, inter alia, because of excess production capacity in a distressed industry). Contemporary literature includes

played a significant role in the trade association movement of the 1920s[13] and the movement for voluntary cooperation among firms in the 1930s.[14]

Antitrust's subsequent hostility toward vertical integration[15] was also the product of prevailing economic theory. Arthur R. Burns' influential 1930s book *The Decline of Competition* was a full-scale attack on vertical integration.[16] Burns conceded that "Integration may result from attempts to secure economies in production and marketing. " Nevertheless, he argued, the anticompetitive theories were much more persuasive and robust than the competitive ones." Where little vertical integration occurs the efficiency of producers is checked at a great many points along the chain of operations...; costs of production are separated for each stage and the market facilitates the frequent comparison of costs and utilities." However, if the firms in an industry tend to be vertically integrated, "the market affords opportunity for comparing only the aggregate cost of all stages of production." As a result, inefficiencies would be disguised and firms

Oswald Knauth, "Competition and Capital," 30 *Pol. Sci. Q.* 578 (1915) (arguing that competition is wasteful in industries with high fixed costs and specialized assets); Spurgeon Bell, "Fixed Costs and Market Price," 32 *Q. J. Econ.* 507, 517 (1918) (defending late nineteenth century mergers as necessitated by ruinous competition brought on by high fixed costs).

13. See Arthur J. Eddy, *The New Competition* 82, 121 (1912) (arguing from premise of high fixed costs for the wisdom of trade associations to keep production in check; firms should compete "under conditions that enable each to know and fairly judge what the others are doing."). Accord M. N. Nelson, *Open Price Associations* 45 (1922). Making the same arguments is the National Industrial Conference Board monograph, *Trade Associations: Their Economic Significance And Legal Status* 17–25 (1925); F. D. Jones, *Trade Association Activities and the Law* 30–31 (1922); E. H. Naylor, *Trade Associations* (1921). See also *Maple Flooring Manufacturers Assn.* v. *United States*, 268 U.S. 563 (1925) (approving trade association activities including price information exchanges); *American Column & Lumber Co.* v. *United States*, 257 U.S. 377, 414–418 (1921) (Brandeis, J., dissenting, arguing that even information exchanges about explicit prices could be competitive when firms were small, isolated, and poorly informed about market conditions.).

14. In the 1920s the theory became much less general, and was applied to natural monopoly industries rather than industries that merely had significant fixed costs. See, e.g., Eliot Jones, "Is Competition in Industry Ruinous?" 34 *Q. J. Econ.* 473, 491 (1920) (ruinous competition argument applied to cases of extreme fixed costs, such as railroads, but not to manufacturing generally); Myron Watkins, *Industrial Combinations and Public Policy* 106–107 (1927) (similar; "ruinous competition" theory applies to railroads and natural monopolies, but not to manufacturing generally).

The work that largely brought the controversy to an end was John Maurice Clark, "A Contribution to the Theory of Competitive Price," 28 *Q. J. Econ.* 747 (1914), which argued that manufacturing industries could attain a competitive equilibrium even in the presence of high fixed costs. This work culminated in the now classic J. M. Clark, *Studies in the Economics of Overhead Costs* (1923). John Maurice Clark was the son of John Bates Clark. Also important was Frank Knight's "Cost of Production and Price over Long and Short Periods," 29 *J. Pol. Econ.* 304 (1921), which applied the concept of long-run marginal cost to argue that even industries with fixed costs could attain a competitive equilibrium. Thus F. W. Taussig could argue that ruinous competition was merely a short-run problem:

> [s]ooner or later—perhaps after a considerable interval, if the operations involve large plant—some of the producers will withdraw, supply will lessen, price will rise, and overproduction will cease.

2 F. W. Taussig, *Principles of Economics* 53–54 (3d ed. 1922). Taussig's position that competitive equilibria are possible even in industries with relatively high fixed costs is basically the one that most neoclassical economists hold today.

15. Vertical integration occurs when a firm develops or acquires some input that it formerly purchased from others. For example, an automobile manufacturer might acquire its own steel making resources, an oil refiner its own railroad for making shipments, or a clothing manufacturer its own chain of branded retail stores.

16. A. Burns, *The Decline of Competition* Ch. 9 (1936).

slower to adopt more efficient procedures. Further, "vertical integration may diminish the responsiveness of the firm to changes in knowledge of methods of production."[17]

And in their 1933 watershed book, *The Modern Corporation and Private Property*, Adolf Berle and Gardiner Means concluded that, far from being efficient, vertical integration made firms too large.[18] Vertically integrated firms were actually less efficient than small firms, but the integrated firms were too big and unresponsive to be disciplined by ordinary competitive processes. Thus it was hardly a coincidence that antitrust policy developed hostility toward vertical integration that was unmatched either before or after.[19]

As early as the 1950s Judge Wyzanski hired an economist, Carl Kaysen, as an assistant to help him deal with a complex antitrust case.[20] Kaysen was a member of the Harvard School of industrial economics, which at the time placed a strong emphasis on "case studies."[21] While Kaysen's report to Judge Wyzanski contained a great deal of economic analysis, as well as citations to numerous books and articles, Judge Wyzanski did not cite any of them or even refer to the report itself, regarding such citations as an "extravagant presentation" that trial judges should generally avoid.[22]

17. Id. at 431–432.

18. A. Berle and G. Means, *The Modern Corporation and Private Property* 350–351 (1932). To the same effect is Willis J. Ballinger's TNEC monograph, with Myron Watkins and Frank A. Fetter as principal contributors, *Relative Efficiency of Large, Medium-Sized and Small Business* (TNEC Monograph #13, 1939). The authors concluded that big business is generally less efficient than small and medium sized business. *Id.* at 10.

19. A few of the most important decisions are *United States* v. *Yellow Cab Co.*, 332 U.S. 218 (1947) (noting that vertical merger might be unlawful if upstream firm (taxicab manufacturer) forced downstream firms (taxi companies) to purchase from it at higher prices); *United States* v. *Paramount Pictures*, 334 U.S. 131, 174 (1948) (finding vertical merger of movie production house and movie theater chains unlawful if its purpose is to gain control of "appreciable segment" of downstream market); *Standard Oil Co. of California* v. *United States* (Standard Stations), 337 U.S. 293 (1949) (promulgating a harsh rule condemning apparently efficient exclusive dealing; non dominant refiner forbade its dealers from selling two different brands of gasoline from the same station); *United States* v. *E.I. du Pont de Nemours & Co.*, 353 U.S. 586 (1957) (holding that a vertical merger is unlawful if it gave upstream firm advantage over others in supplying inputs to downstream firm); *Brown Shoe Co.* v. *United States*, 370 U.S. 294 (1962) (prohibiting vertical merger because it would permit post-merger firm to undersell its non-integrated rivals); *United States* v. *Arnold, Schwinn & Co.*, 388 U.S. 365 (1967) (holding that vertical nonprice restraints are unlawful per se).

20. The case was *United States* v. *United Shoe Mach. Corp.*, 110 F. Supp. 295 (D. Mass. 1953), *aff'd per curiam*, 347 U.S. 521 (1954). The episode is discussed in Carl Kaysen, "In Memoriam: Charles E. Wyzanski, Jr.," 100 *Harv. L. Rev.* 713, 713–715 (1987); and Carl Kaysen, "An Economist as the Judge's Law Clerk in Sherman Act Cases," 12 *ABA Antitrust L. Proc.* 43, 45–46 (1958).

21. Kaysen's own book, which resulted from his work on this case, is a good example. Carl Kaysen, *United States v. United Shoe Machinery Corporation: An Economic Analysis of an Antitrust Case* (1956). On the "case study" approach to the economics of industrial organization, see Hovenkamp, *Enterprise and American Law, 1836–1937*, at Ch. 22 (1991). The case study approach to economics at Harvard is represented in the series of "Harvard Economic Studies," which were largely doctoral dissertations published by Harvard University Press. See, e.g., William H. Price, *The English Patents of Monopoly* (1906); Melvin T. Copeland, *The Cotton Manufacturing Industry of the United States* (1909); Arthur S. Dewing, *Corporate Promotions and Reorganizations* (1914) (containing case studies of several business firms). Perhaps the best known was Eliot Jones, *The Anthracite Coal Combination in the United States* (1914).

22. See *United Shoe Machinery*, 110 F. Supp. at 299:

> It is not the Court's duty to make a precise finding on every detail of four decades of an industry. It is not its duty to approach the issues as an historian, an archaeologist (See A. N. Hand, *Trial Efficiency* pp 31, 32, Business Practices Under Federal Anti-trust Laws, 1951 Symposium, N.Y. State Bar Assoc.), an economist, or even a master appointed to settle every factual dispute. A trial judge who undertakes

In sum, one who observed the relative lack of economic citation in antitrust literature before 1980 and its significant increase thereafter would be seriously misled to believe that antitrust first developed an "economic approach" when the Chicago School entered the field. To be sure, Chicago School antitrust has had significant and lasting consequences for antitrust. But it was hardly antitrust's "discovery" of economics. Rather, it represented the adoption of a different economic model, coupled with more explicit recognition of economics in the judicial literature than judges were accustomed to using. This fact hardly distinguishes antitrust from other legal disciplines. For example, the influence of classical political economy on both English and American judges is documented in a large historical literature.[23] But while the influence itself is beyond controversy, in the entire nineteenth century body of case law there are only a few citations to the writing of classical political economists, and these are mainly to Adam Smith's *Wealth of Nations*, a book that was read by many non-economists, including lawyers and judges.[24]

## III. The Perils of Post-Chicago Enthusiasm

The Chicago School offered an elegant, pro-market and largely anti-government vision of antitrust policy.[25] To oversimplify, its advocates believed that markets were far more robust than people had previously imagined, and nearly always work themselves toward the competitive solution. Further, effective competition requires many fewer firms than once believed—in most cases three is sufficient. Even when competition is not sufficient, any attempt at monopoly pricing will be undermined by new entry, and in an efficient capital market such entry will almost always occur. Finally, while markets work themselves pure, government intervention can hardly make that claim. More often than not, court-ordered antitrust fixes actually make markets less rather than more competitive or injure consumers for the benefit of competitors. As a result, the best antitrust policy is one of doing as little as possible, confined to blatant practices such as naked price fixing or market division.

By contrast, "post-Chicago" antitrust has relatively less confidence in markets as such, is more fearful of strategic anticompetitive behavior by dominant firms, and has a significantly restored faith in the efficacy of government intervention. But anyone who takes the long view should see that "Post-Chicago" antitrust policy represents little more than another swing in antitrust's ideological pendulum. This long view is critical if antitrust is to maintain its integrity. Just as the "ruinous competition" arguments of

such tasks will unnecessarily sacrifice the rights of litigants in other cases clamoring for attention. Moreover, he will encourage just that type of extravagant presentation which has come to plague the field of antitrust law.

23. E.g., P. S. Atiyah, *The Rise and Fall of Freedom of Contract* (1979); Morton J. Horwitz, *The Transformation of American Law: 1780–1869* (1978).

24. On the citation practices of nineteenth century judges that excluded citations to economists, see Herbert Hovenkamp, "The Political Economy of Substantive Due Process," 40 *Stan. L. Rev.* 379 (1988). See also Herbert Hovenkamp, "The First Great Law and Economics Movement," 42 *Stan. L. Rev.* 993 (1990) (describing the impact and influence of economic theory on early American law).

25. For fully developed statements of the various propositions asserted in this paragraph, see the summary in Herbert Hovenkamp, *Federal Antitrust Policy: The Law of Competition and Its Practice* § 2.2b (2d ed. 1999);

the early part of the twentieth century and the strategic vertical integration arguments of the 1930s and 1940s, the Chicago School contribution to antitrust did two things. First, it gave us much that was useful. Second, it was oversold.

First, Chicago School economic writings about antitrust gave us some lasting contributions, often by pointing out the economic nonsense upon which many antitrust decisions were based. Among these contributions were the so-called leverage theory of tying arrangements and antitrust's more general hostility toward vertical integration;[26] deep pocket theories about mergers that often ended up condemning pro-consumer, efficient mergers simply because rivals were injured[27]; exaggerated notions of market dominance and monopolization that too often failed to ask whether the defendant monopolized anything that was even capable of being monopolized; and a failure to appreciate that many forms of joint activity other than naked price and market allocation agreements are socially beneficial.[28]

Secondly, however, Chicago antitrust economics was oversold. If markets are not as elegant as Chicago economists assume, if information and switching costs are in fact quite high, if proportions can be varied, if products are durably differentiated, then markets can in fact be anticompetitive over a variety of circumstances that Chicago economists generally disallowed.[29]

The Chicago School was vulnerable on all these points, and the critiques are quite correct. Importantly, however, just as Chicago School antitrust policy became oversold, post-Chicago policy is in danger of becoming oversold as well. The real value of post-Chicago economics is its renewed recognition of the fact that markets are much

Frank H. Easterbrook, "Ignorance and Antitrust," in *Antitrust, Innovation, and Competitiveness* 119 (T. Jorde and D. Teece eds., 1992); Frank H. Easterbrook, "The Limits of Antitrust," 63 *Tex. L. Rev.* 1, 2 (1984); William Landes, "Optimal Sanctions for Antitrust Violations," 50 *U. CM. L. Rev.* 652 (1983); Edward Kitch, "The Fire of Truth: A Remembrance of Law and Economics at Chicago, 1932–70," 26 *J.L. & Econ.* 163 (1983); Posner, "The Chicago School of Antitrust Analysis," 127 *Univ. Pa. L.Rev.* 925 (1979); Robert H. Bork, *The Antitrust Paradox: A Policy at War with Itself* (1978; Rev. ed. 1993); Harold Demsetz, "Barriers to Entry," 72 *Am. Econ. Rev.* 47 (1982).

26. E.g., W. Bowman, "Tying Arrangements and the Leverage Problem," 67 *Yale L.J.* 19 (1957); L. Telser, "Why Should Manufacturers Want Fair Trade?" 3 *J.L. & Econ.* 86 (1960). The leverage theory condemned tying arrangements on the assumption that a firm with a single monopoly, in the tying product, could use tying to create a second monopoly in the tied product, and thus earn two monopoly profits instead of one, while destroying competition in the tied product. See, e.g., *Carbice Corp.* v. *American Patents Dev. Corp.*, 283 U.S. 27 (1931). The theory is false because there is only a single monopoly profit to be earned in any distribution chain. See Hovenkamp, *Federal Antitrust Policy, supra* note 25, § 10.6a.

27. E.g., *Brown Shoe Co.* v. *United States*, 179 F. Supp. 721, 738 (E.D. Mo. 1959), *aff'd*, 370 U.S. 294, 344 (1962) (condemning merger because post-merger firm would be able to make better shoes for the same price as rivals, or else undersell them). For the critiques, see, e.g., H. Demsetz, "Industry Structure, Market Rivalry, and Public Policy," 16 *J.L. & Econ.* 1 (1973); Y. Brozen, *Concentration, Mergers, and Public Policy* (1982) (presenting data that suggests the contemporary doctrine of monopoly "offers a dangerous base upon which to build a business"). Other literature is summarized in Posner, *Chicago School, supra*.

28. E.g.; *United States* v. *Topco Assocs.*, 405 U.S. 596 (1972) (condemning efficient joint venture by grocers who lacked market power). See also Robert H. Bork, "The Rule of Reason and the Per Se Concept: Price Fixing and Market Division (part 2)," 75 *Yale L.J.* 373 (1966).

29. For a more general discussion, including references, see Hovenkamp, *Federal Antitrust Policy*, supra note 25, at §§ 2.2b, e.

more varied and complex than Chicago theorists were willing to admit. As a result, the number and variety of anticompetitive practices are unknown and open ended, particularly in relatively new markets, such as the internet and software licensing, where the opportunities for collusion and strategic behavior by dominant firms may prove to be quite manifold.

The biggest danger presented by post-Chicago antitrust economics is not that the variety and likelihood of anticompetitive practices will be exaggerated, although that has happened as well. Rather, the danger is that antitrust tribunals will be confronted with antitrust solutions that they are not capable of administering. Indeed, the major shortcoming of post-Chicago antitrust analysis is its failure to take seriously problems of judicial or agency administration.

Antitrust is a defensible enterprise only if it can make markets more competitive—that is, if antitrust intervention tends to produce higher prices, larger outputs, or improved product quality. Antitrust is no good at transferring wealth away from rich to poor, or from large firms to small ones, and cannot be defended on that basis in any event.[30] But this constraint places a premium on administrability. It may be relatively easy to see that a big damage award transfers wealth away from a big firm and towards a smaller firm or a group of customers. It is typically not so easy to see whether such a reward has the short or long run effect of making the economy bigger by increasing the value of its goods and services.

Whatever one might think of its ideology or economics, the Chicago School offered antitrust a purity of vision that few legal disciplines ever attain. Its foundational principles were two: first, that markets are extremely robust and competitive outcomes are highly likely to emerge without any significant governmental intervention other those contained in ordinary contract and property rights; second, that government tribunals and agencies are frail and imperfect decision makers.[31] Building on an imposing foundation of neoclassical economics, Chicago School antitrust writers developed well-reasoned arguments that in the long run markets tend to correct their own imperfections,[32] that the history of aggressive judicial intervention has produced many indefensible results,[33] and that tribunals would be well advised to study practices much more thoroughly before deciding that intervention is appropriate.[34]

By contrast, under post-Chicago antitrust analysis, the market has become a far messier place. The post-Chicago economic literature has produced impressive arguments that certain market structures and certain types of collaborative activity are much more likely to have anticompetitive consequences than Chicago School

30. See 1 Phillip E. Areeda and Herbert Hovenkamp, *Antitrust Law* ¶ 100b (2d ed. 2000) [hereinafter "1 Antitrust Law"].

31. On both propositions, see Hovenkamp, "Antitrust Policy After Chicago," 84 *Mich.L.Rev.* 213 (1985).

32. E.g., Easterbrook, "The Limits of Antitrust," 63 *Tex.L.Rev.* 1 (1984) at 2; Ronald Coase, "The Problem of Social Cost," 3 *J.L. & Econ.* 1 (1960).

33. E.g., Bork, *The Antitrust Paradox: A Policy at War with Itself* (1978).

34. Easterbrook, "Ignorance and Antitrust," in *Antitrust, Innovation, and Competitiveness* 119 (T. Jorde & D. Teece, eds., 1992).

antitrust writers imagined. For example, when the proportions of inputs can be varied, vertical integration can be socially harmful.[35] When information is not evenly balanced, anticompetitive strategic behavior is possible.[36] In the presence of specialized assets and economies of scale strategic pricing, even at prices significantly above cost, can be anticompetitive.[37] Network externalities in some markets, such as for computer operating systems or telephone or other networks, can give dominant firms decisive advantages that enable them to defeat even superior technologies.[38] Mergers in product-differentiated markets pose unique threats to competition that are not captured by the traditional collusion model.[39]

It now seems quite clear that Chicago School economic orthodoxy is no longer the best, or certainly not the only, analytic tool for evaluating markets. But the sad fact is that judges have not come close to developing antitrust rules that takes this messier, more complex economics into account. An even sadder fact is that in many instances Judges may not be capable of doing so. As a result, the rather benign Chicago School rule may be the best one for policy purposes even though it does not do the best job of expressing what we know about economic theory.

Indeed, the problem runs deeper than that—a constant complaint about post-Chicago economic theories is that they are not testable in the conventional positivist sense. That is, often all that economists can do is produce data that are minimally consistent with the theory, but often cannot rule out alternative explanations.[40] Where this critique applies, it can prove fatal to the formation of antitrust policy based on post-Chicago rules. When economists do academic work they select markets on the basis of simplicity and susceptibility to conducting the relevant tests. But antitrust plaintiffs select markets based on much different criteria. Further, the fact-finding

35. E.g., Michael A Salinger, "Vertical Mergers and Market Foreclosure," 103 *Q.J. Econ.* 345 (1988); Michael Waterson, "Vertical Integration, Variable Proportions and Oligopoly," 92 *Econ. J.* 129 (1982). See also Roger D. Blair and David Kaserman, *Law and Economics of Vertical Integration and Control* (1983); Michael Katz, "Vertical Contractual Relations," in *Handbook of Industrial Organization*, Chs. 4 and 11 (Richard Schmalensee and Robert Willig eds., 1989).

36. E.g., Jean Tirole, *The Theory Of Industrial Organization* 367–374 (1988).

37. Id.; Oliver E. Williamson, "Predatory Pricing: A Strategic and Welfare Analysis," 87 *Yale L.J.* 284 (1977); see also Patrick Bolton et al., "Predatory Pricing: Strategic Theory and Legal Policy," 88 *Geo. L.J.* 2239 (2000).

38. See Carl Shapiro, "Exclusivity in Network Industries," 7 *Geo. Mason L. Rev.* 673 (1999); Herbert Hovenkamp, "Exclusive Joint Ventures and Antitrust Policy," 1995 *Colum. Bus. L. Rev.* 1.

39. See, e.g., Jonathan B. Baker, "Contemporary Empirical Merger Analysis," 5 *Geo. Mason L. Rev.* 347 (1997); Jonathan B. Baker, "Unilateral Competitive Effects Theories in Merger Analysis," 11 *Antitrust* 21 (Spring 1997); Carl Shapiro, "Mergers with Differentiated Products," 10 *Antitrust* 23, 24 (Spring 1996); see also Christopher A Vellturo, "Evaluating Mergers with Differentiated Products," 11 *Antitrust* 16 (Spring 1997); Jonathan B. Baker and Timothy F. Bresnahan, "The Gains from Merger or Collusion in Product Differentiated Industries," 33 *J. Indus. Econ.* 427, 429 (1985).

40. See, e.g., Bruce H. Kobayashi, "Game Theory and Antitrust: A Post-Mortem," 5 *Geo. Mason L. Rev.* 411 (1997); Sam Peltzman, "The Handbook of Industrial Organization: A Review Article," 99 *J. Pol. Econ.* 201 (1991). The criticism is not unique to post-Chicago antitrust economics, but has been generalized to all of economics. See, e.g., Ronald H. Coase, "How Should Economists Choose?," in *Essays on Economics and Economists* 15 (1994); Deborah A. Redman, *Economics and the Philosophy of Science*, Ch. 9 (1991); Diedre McCloskey, *The Rhetoric of Economics* (1985); *Why Economics Is Not Yet a Science* (Alfred S. Eichner ed., 1983). See also *Foundations of the Economic Approach to Law* (Avery Weiner Kat ed., 1998).

powers of the antitrust tribunal are considerably less than those of the academic economist and her graduate students, particularly when the relevant fact finder is an American jury. There is no reason to think that if economists doing academic work cannot rule out alternative explanations, antitrust tribunals will do any better. They are likely to do far worse.

In order to adjudicate an antitrust case with confidence a tribunal must do better than conclude that the defendant's conduct was consistent with an anticompetitive hypothesis. If antitrust policy goals are to be furthered, the anticompetitive explanation must be substantially more robust than alternative, more benign or procompetitive explanations. Failing this, antitrust policy will operate so as to chill procompetitive conduct. This is implicit in the Supreme Court's *Matsushita* decision, which redefined the role of summary judgment in antitrust cases,[41] as well as its subsequent decisions inviting the courts to become more diligent about scrutinizing expert testimony.[42] Under *Matsushita*, the expert must do more than produce a hypothesis that passes the test of economic positivism that is, which is consistent with an anticompetitive hypothesis. Rather, the expert must provide evidence that tends to exclude the possibility that alternative, more benign hypotheses explain the defendant's behavior.

In the United States, one of the main factors in judicial inability to confront strategic complexity is, of course, the jury system. But that is hardly the entire story. Judges have often done little better than juries in understanding the most basic of antitrust concepts, and until they understand the basics they certainly will not be able to appreciate the subtleties of strategic behavior in complex markets.

When a particular form of behavior is too complex for reliable analysis within a reasonable time, then the only defensible antitrust rule is to let the market—rather than state intervention—control that behavior, at least for the time being. In the longer run, of course, legislative intervention might be appropriate, and further factual developments may give rise to a justiciable antitrust claim.

But the basic rule should be nonintervention unless the tribunal has a high degree of confidence that it has identified anticompetitive conduct and can apply an effective remedy. This rule is the only defensible one because antitrust is an enterprise dedicated to the proposition that markets generally work, and enduring failures are the exception rather than the rule.

In the American system, making such judgments require, first, that a relatively high percentage of antitrust issues be decided as a matter of law—not because the basic issue is not factual in the lay sense, for it often is. Rather, antitrust addresses facts by considering not only what the facts are, but also what are the institutional constraints on

41. *Matsushita Elec. Indus. Co.* v. *Zenith Radio Corp.*, 475 U.S. 574 (1986). See 2 Phillip Areeda et al., *Antitrust Law* ¶ 308 (2d ed. 2000) [hereinafter "2 Antitrust Law"].

42. See *Brooke Group Ltd* v. *Brown & Williamson Tobacco Corp.*, 509 U.S. 209 (1993) (rejecting testimony of economist and giving defendant judgment as a matter of law); *Daubert* v. *Merrell Dow Pharmaceuticals*, 509 U.S. 579 (1993) (developing standards for greater federal judicial control over the testimony of economic experts). On the impact of Daubert and its progeny on expert testimony in antitrust cases, see Herbert Hovenkamp, "Economic Experts in Antitrust Cases," in *Modern Scientific Evidence: The Law and Science of Expert Testimony* (D. Faigman et al., eds., 2001).

managing facts in a constructive way. A good example of this is the current set of legal rules on predatory pricing.[43] The relevant statutes condemn predatory pricing when it threatens to monopolize a market,[44] or to lessen competition substantially.[45] The statutes themselves do not define a cost test or a set of structural conditions under which predation is likely to be anticompetitive. But the Supreme Court, aided by the lower courts, has developed a number of gateway requirements that the plaintiff must satisfy before the fact finder is even entitled to consider a predatory pricing complaint—for example, that the prices complained of be below a certain measure of cost, with the majority suggesting that average variable cost is the right measure;[46] that the market be protected by high entry barriers and otherwise subject to profitable monopolization or oligopoly, and the like.[47]

Significantly, the premise for these legal requirements is *not* that any alternative facts make anticompetitive pricing strategies implausible.[48] Rather, it is that the history of predatory pricing cases reveals that once these requirements are relaxed, antitrust tribunals lack the tools to distinguish anticompetitive predatory pricing from aggressive procompetitive pricing of a kind that antitrust policy should encourage.

To that extent, the reluctance to advocate a general use of post-Chicago economics in antitrust litigation should be regarded as a contingent and temporal rather than as an absolute and permanent truth. In some areas, refined economic analysis has enabled us to identify anticompetitive outcomes with at least as much predictive power as older methodologies gave us. In that case, fashioning of new antitrust rules is not merely appropriate, it is essential. A good example is "unilateral effects" theories of horizontal mergers, which condemns some mergers in product-differentiated markets where traditional Cournot oligopoly analysis would not. When sufficient data are available, the empirical methodologies for predicting the unilateral price increase of two firms in a product differentiated market can actually produce better results than the methodologies relying on Cournot theory to predict the likelihood and magnitude of coordinated pricing.[49] While those methodologies have become quite comfortable to us, their use actually entails a great many assumptions about how firms will behave as

43. See 3 Areeda and Hovenkamp, *Antitrust Law*, Ch. 7C (2d ed. 2001) [hereinafter "3 Antitrust Law"].

44. 15 U.S.C. § 2 (Sherman Act, condemning monopolization and attempt).

45. 15 U.S.C. § 13(a) (primary-line provision of Robinson-Patman Act); see 3 Antitrust Law ¶ 745 (3d ed. 2008).

46. See id., ¶ 740.

47. Id. at ¶¶ 725–726.

48. See id. at ¶ 735a:

> In a world with far better information than we actually have, "cost" would not necessarily be the only baseline for identifying prices as anticompetitive. Economics texts and journals are filled with theories about anticompetitive prices that are above all relevant measures of cost....
>
> The problem with all such strategies is not that we doubt their existence or even their anticompetitive nature. Rather, identifying them in the particular case without chilling aggressive, competitive pricing is far beyond the capacity of any antitrust tribunal.

49. See *infra* discussion accompanying notes 176 to 181.

markets become more concentrated; and these assumptions must be characterized as at least as speculative as those attending the prediction of unilateral price increases.

But in too many instances antitrust tribunals are simply not up to handling post-Chicago theory. Judges do not know enough economics; the economics itself is insufficiently capable of sorting out anticompetitive from competitive or harmless explanations; the American jury system turns complex fact findings into chaos.

## IV. "Post-Chicago" Claims and Summary Judgment

Summary judgment assumes its most fearful dimensions in the United States adjudication process because of the way it allocates the fact finding duty between the jury and the judge. In a private plaintiff damages action the issue is not merely whether the fact findings will be made before or after a trial. Rather, summary judgment often determines whether the essential facts will be determined by a jury or by the judge.[50]

At the grossest level, juries determine facts while the judge determines the law. In reality, the discretion of juries to find facts has been severely limited by an expanding conception of summary judgment. The watershed antitrust case is the 1986 *Matsushita* decision, which held that there was insufficient evidence in a record for a jury to conclude that one particular conspiracy essential to the plaintiffs case had occurred.[51]

Prior to *Matsushita* courts often said that summary judgment must be used sparingly in antitrust cases, emphasizing that such cases often depended on intent, and intent needs to be discerned from the often conflicting testimony of witnesses.[52] The *Matsushita* decision itself is sometimes presented as a kind of Chicago School victory, largely because the impact of more expansive summary judgment in antitrust cases is to minimize the role of intent and expand the use of purely objective market factors.[53]

50. On summary judgment generally, see 10 and 10A C. Wright et al., *Federal Practice and Procedure* (Civil 3d) §§ 2711 *et seq.* (1998); W. Schwarzer, "Summary Judgment and Case Management," 56 *Antitrust L.J.* 213 (1987); W. Schwarzer, "Summary Judgment Under the Federal Rules: Defining Genuine Issues of Material Fact," 99 *F.R.D.* 465 (1984). On special problems of summary judgment in antitrust cases, see 2 *Antitrust Law* ¶ 308 (3d ed. 2007); Steve Calkins, "Summary Judgment, Motions to Dismiss, and Other Examples of Equilibrating Tendencies in the Antitrust System," 70 *Geo. L.J.* 1065 (1986).

51. *Matsushita Elec. Indus. Co.* v. *Zenith Radio Corp.*, 475 U.S. 574 (1986). In brief, the theory of the case was that the defendant's conspiracy to set high prices in Japan produced profits needed to fund conspiratorial predatory pricing in the United States against the plaintiffs; there was ample evidence of the first conspiracy, but not of the second. See 2 Antitrust Law, *supra* note 41, ¶ 308c2.

52. *Poller* v. *CBS*, 368 U.S. 464, 473 (1962):

> We believe that summary procedures should be used sparingly in complex antitrust litigation where motive and intent play leading roles, the proof is largely in the hands of the alleged conspirators, and hostile witnesses thicken the plot. It is only when the witnesses are present and subject to cross-examination that their credibility and the weight to be given their testimony can be appraised.

53. See, e.g., David E.M. Sappington and J. Gregory Sidak, "Are Public Enterprises the Only Credible Predators?," 67 *Univ. Chi. L. Rev.* 271, 275 (2000); Michael S. Jacobs, "An Essay on the Normative Foundations of Antitrust Economics," 74 *N.C. L. Rev.* 219, 266 (1995); Michael S. Jacobs, "The New Sophistication in Antitrust," 79 *Minn. L. Rev.* 1, 24 (1994); William H. Page, "The Chicago School and the Evolution of Antitrust: Characterization, Antitrust Injury, and Evidentiary Sufficiency," 75 *Va. L. Rev.* 1221 (1989).

Whether or not this is true, a clear hallmark of the late 1980s and 1990s is that a much higher percentage of antitrust cases were decided by some form of abbreviated review.[54] In sum, pre-Chicago antitrust cases tended to emphasize intent over structure and objective plausibility, and juries had a relatively broad role. Under the post-Chicago regime the trend is in the reverse direction.

But accompanying the rise of post-Chicago law and economics one also sees a discernible trend toward letting the jury once again decide more issues. Here, of course, the most significant case is the Supreme Court's 1992 *Kodak* decision, which held that summary judgment should not have been granted on the existing record based on the defendant's claim that a firm who lacks significant market power in its primary market (photocopiers) as a matter of law cannot have significant market power in aftermarket parts or service.[55]

This trend toward broadening the jury's role is misconceived. The hallmark of post-Chicago economics is increased complexity, and the worst way to deal with complexity is to throw the issue to the jury. If anything, summary judgment should be even more important in a post-Chicago world than it was under Chicago school analysis. The basis of the pre-*Matsushita* rule, that summary judgment should be used sparingly in antitrust litigation, was that intent was a sufficient substitute for structural evidence, and of course discerning intent has generally been considered an important part of the jury's role.[56]

Critics of the Chicago School have often observed that Chicago style theories of competitive robustness were based on overly simplistic market assumptions, including fixed proportions, good information, and relatively easy entry. Anticompetitive strategic behavior becomes much more plausible when these assumptions are relaxed.[57] But this argument has a flip side: while many post-Chicago school theories admit a greater range of anticompetitive strategic behaviors, most of these occur only under strictly

54. This term refers not only to summary judgment, but also to judgment as a matter of law, which is typically given after trial, and also to motions to dismiss, where Matsushita also has had an effect. See generally 2 Antitrust Law ¶ 307 (3d ed. 2006).

55. *Eastman Kodak Co.* v. *Image Technical Servs.*, 504 U.S. 451 (1992). Other cases permitting "post-Chicago" claims to go to trial are *Concord Boat Corp.* v. *Brunswick Corp.*, 21 F. Supp. 2d 923 (E.D. Ark. 1998), *rev'd*, 207 F.3d 1039 (8th Cir. 2000), *cert. denied*, 121 S.Ct. 428 (2000); *C.R. Bard* v. *M3 Systems*, 157 F.3d 1340 (Fed. Cir. 1998), *cert. denied*, 526 U.S. 1131 (1999); *Collins* v. *Dairy Queen*, 59 F. Supp. 2d 1312 (M.D. Ga. 1999); *Red Lion Med. Safety* v. *Ohmeda*, 63 F. Supp. 2d 1218 (E.D. Ca. 1999).

56. See, e.g., *Poller*, 368 U.S. at 473 ("summary procedures should be used sparingly in complex antitrust litigation where motive and intent play leading roles").

57. E.g., Steven C. Salop and R. Craig Romaine, "Preserving Monopoly: Economic Analysis, Legal Standards, and Microsoft," 7 *Geo. Mason L. Rev.* 617 (1999); Lawrence A. Sullivan, "Post Chicago Economics: Economists, Lawyers, Judges, and Enforcement in a Less Determinate Theoretical World," 63 *Antitrust L.J.* 669 (1995); Michael H. Riordan and Steven C. Salop, "Evaluating Vertical Mergers: A Post-Chicago Approach," 63 *Antitrust L.J.* 513, 515 (1995); Jonathan B. Baker, "Recent Developments in Economics That Challenge Chicago School Views," 58 *Antitrust L.J.* 645, 655 (1989); Eleanor M. Fox and Lawrence A Sullivan, "Antitrust—Retrospective and Prospective: Where Are We Coming From? Where Are We Going?" 62 *N.Y.U. L. Rev.* 936 (1987); Thomas Krattenmaker and Steven C. Salop, "Anticompetitive Exclusion: Raising Rivals' Costs to Achieve Power over Price," 96 *Yale L.J.* 209, 235–262 (1986); Patrick Rey and Jean Tirole, "The Logic of Vertical Restraints," 76 *Am. Econ. Rev.* 921 (1986); Louis Kaplow, "Extension of Monopoly Power Through Leverage," 85 *Colum. L. Rev.* 515 (1985).

defined circumstances. If these circumstances do not exist, then the contemplated strategy will not work. The principal difference between Chicago and post-Chicago economic analysis is *not* that subjective intent once again becomes central; rather, it is that under a more complex set of assumptions about how a market works, anticompetitive outcomes seem more plausible. But if this is the case, then adjudication of post-Chicago antitrust claims hardly calls for more intervention by the jury. On the contrary, it calls for more careful sifting by the judge to determine whether there is a reasonable basis for thinking that the preconditions for anticompetitive outcomes are present. The jury should be held to its traditional technical role of resolving bona fide disputes of fact.

A good example of an overly quick decision to let the jury decide is the *Brunswick* case, involving the sale of inboard and stern drive boat motors.[58] The district court, which was reversed by the Eighth Circuit, permitted a jury to find that Brunswick violated § 2 of the Sherman Act with a program of market share discounts to boat builders who purchased motors from Brunswick rather than its principal rivals OMC and Yamaha. A boat builder could obtain a 3 percent discount on motor prices by purchasing at least 70 percent of its motor needs from Brunswick. These discounts reached a high of 5 percent for someone who agreed to purchase the stated percentage for a two or three year period.[59] Even the fully discounted prices were well above cost; indeed, the action was brought by the boat builders for a monopoly overcharge, which was claimed to be on the order of 30 percent. As the district court put it, "In essence, Plaintiffs have maintained that Brunswick sets an anticompetitive high price for its engines and then offers an attractive discount schedule designed to lock customers in to Brunswick purchases."[60]

A Chicago School scholar would scoff at the idea that one could monopolize a market in which it had one or more substantial rivals by charging a price 30 percent above the competitive level but then giving a 5 percent discount to firms for buying at least 70 percent of their motor needs from this firm. Any rival could steal the entire market by simply charging the competitive price, or even by charging a price 20 percent above the competitive price. But in fact there are scenarios in which quantity or market share discounts can produce anticompetitive results. One that has been condemned by the courts on more than one occasion occurs when the defendant makes multiple products and aggregates its discount across them, while the plaintiff makes a product that competes with only one of the defendant's offerings. In such a case the plaintiff may be able to match the defendant's discount on the particular product that the plaintiff sells, but in purchasing this product from the plaintiff, the buyer also loses the discount on the other products that the plaintiff does not sell. As a result, the plaintiff can win the customer only by offering a much larger per unit discount than the defendant must

58. *Concord Boat Corp.* v. *Brunswick Corp.*, 207 F.3d 1039 (8th Cir. 2000), *cert. denied*, 121 S.Ct. 428 (2000).

59. *Concord*, 207 F.3d at 1044.

60. *Concord*, 21 F. Supp. 2d at 929.

offer.[61] The prohibition of tying in § 3 explicitly references "discounts" conditioned upon bundling.[62]

The second instance, which is closely related, occurs when the defendant distributes in a larger market than the plaintiff. For example, the defendant might sell its product nationwide while rivals sell only locally. The defendant then gives national purchasers a discount based on their aggregated purchases across the country. Local firms could readily match the price charged to buyers in their local area, but they cannot make up for the loss of discount that these buyers would face on their purchases from other areas.[63]

Neither of these scenarios or anything resembling them was present in the *Brunswick* case. The discounts were aggregated across a single product, and both Brunswick and its rivals sold the full range of products in all parts of the country. While the district court mentioned the multiproduct bundling cases,[64] it appeared not to understand the significant differences between those cases and the case at hand. A strategy of market share or quantity discounting is an implausible monopolization device when a firm faces one or more equally efficient rivals with an equivalent product and geographic range. In addition, downstream entry barriers appeared to be very low. Indeed, the named plaintiff had entered the business a few years earlier in his garage, and the boat building market was a revolving door of firms entering, merging, and exiting on a regular basis.

In such a case the judge is not performing her gatekeeping function unless she ascertains that genuine issues of fact are present that could establish the minimum conditions for competitive harm. This requires at the very least that there be a real factual issue establishing the difficulty of downstream entry and the inability of rivals

61. For example, suppose that the defendant sells pharmaceuticals A, B, and C and gives a 10 percent discount for the purchase of 3,000 units in any combination. A buyer purchases 1,000 units of each. A rival makes only an alternative to pharmaceutical A It could profitably match the defendant's discount on product A alone, but in purchasing A from the rival the buyer would also lose the discount on B and C; as a result, the rival would need to offer a 30 percent discount (assuming equal purchases of equally priced pharmaceuticals) in order to win customers for its A. *See SmithKline Corp.* v. *Eli Lilly & Co.*, 427 F. Supp. 1089 (E.D. Pa. 1976), *aff'd*, 575 F.2d 1056 (3d Cir.), *cert. denied*, 439 U.S. 838 (1978) (finding illegality on roughly similar facts); *accord Lepage's* v. *3M*, 1999–1 Trade Cas. P 72538, 1999 WL 346223 (E.D. Pa. 1999) (denying summary judgment on claim that defendant's progressive discounts aggregated across multiple products effectively forced buyers to take defendant's tape; plaintiff, which sold only tape, could match defendant's tape price only by giving a discount that matched the tape discount and compensated buyers for the loss of discount on non-tape products).

62. See 15 U.S.C. § 14: It shall be unlawful…to lease or make a sale…or fix a price charged therefor, or discount from, or rebate upon, such price, on the condition…that the lessee or purchaser thereof shall not use or deal in the goods…of a competitor.On package discounts as tie-ins, see 10 Phillip E. Areeda et al., *Antitrust Law* ¶ 1758 (3d ed. 2010).

63. See Willard K Tom et al., "Anticompetitive Aspects of Market-Share Discounts and Other Incentives to Exclusive Dealing," 67 *Antitrust L.J.* 615 (2000), which uses a comparable product market analogy: suppose that customers have a base, or inelastic demand for the dominant firm's product in 60 percent of their transactions; now the dominant firm gives an additional 6 percent discount across the board for those taking up to 70 percent of their needs from that firm; in this case the buyer will lose the entire discount unless it takes at least 70 percent of its needs from the dominant firm.

64. See *Concord Boat Corp.* v. *Brunswick Corp.*, 34 F. Supp. 2d 1125, 1129 (E.D. Ark. 1998) (discussing *SmithKline Corp.* v. *Eli Lilly & Co.*, 427 F. Supp. 1089 (E.D. Pa. 1976) and *Lepage's* v. *3M*, 1999–1 Trade Cas. P 72538, 1999 WL 346223 (E.D. Pa. 1999)).

to win more business by matching or besting the dominant firms price schedule. The *Brunswick* facts gave no reason why an equally efficient rival could not have lowered its price by ten or fifteen percent and then made a large profit while stealing sales from the defendant. In that case, there was nothing to send to the jury.[65]

[Section V, "Post-Chicago Successes and Failures," omitted—eds.]

## VI. Conclusion

The Chicago School gave antitrust an elegant and simple set of economic models that emphasized the robustness of markets and the frequent futility of government intervention. But the models themselves were often an overreaction to equally strong and sometimes even silly theories of anticompetitive behavior that were prevalent in the 1970s and earlier.

By contrast, post-Chicago methodologies are necessarily more complex, reflecting the greater complexity of observed markets. While they sometimes produce robust economic conclusions, testing them has proven difficult. Further, they are messier and more difficult to use and too often strain the fact-finding power of courts beyond the breaking point.

This problem of administrability is a serious one for antitrust, which is not a justifiable legal enterprise unless it makes markets work better than they would work in the absence of intervention. A more accurate model whose increased complexity increases the rate of error may be a poorer choice than a less accurate model which is nevertheless simple and easy to use.

So the test for a post-Chicago economic model is not merely whether it discovers an anticompetitive strategy that Chicago School theory had not. Policy makers must also be able to devise rules that will recognize such strategies without an unacceptably high incidence of false positives, and then produce remedies that are not more socially costly than the evils that they correct.

Measured by this test, post-Chicago antitrust economics has had only limited success. Perhaps its biggest failure has been the Supreme Court's *Kodak*[66] decision and its aftermath. When that decision was first handed down it threatened to turn many competitive firms with unique aftermarket parts or service into "monopolists" for antitrust purposes. In reality, it has not had that effect but it has burdened the courts with much unnecessary and costly litigation. That experiment should be proclaimed a failure and *Kodak* itself overruled.

65. Without any analysis, the district simply summarized the plaintiff's case as involving a claim that the defendant (1) charged a very high basic price, but (2) then gave a discount from its very high price to those who took a large share of the needs from the defendant. However, even the fully discounted price was at monopoly levels. The court also accepted at face value the expert's testimony that a boat builder would receive the highest discount if it purchased 70 percent of its engines from Brunswick, but progressively lose Brunswick's discount as its market share fell further below 70 percent; but none of this explained why an equally efficient motor seller could not claim all of this buyer's business simply by offering a lower price. See *Concord*, 21 F. Supp. 2d at 932–934.

66. *Eastman Kodak Co.* v. *Image Technical Servs.*, 504 U.S. 451 (1992).

But post-Chicago antitrust has also had some successes that are likely to endure. The theory of Raising Rivals' Costs (RRC) provides a much more robust and convincing explanation of certain exclusionary practices than do the older "foreclosure" theories that provoked so much wrath from the Chicago School. The so-called unilateral effects theory of horizontal mergers has also proven to be a significant litigation success. What is common to both RRC and unilateral effects theories is that they are capable of providing courts with administrable rules for distinguishing anticompetitive behavior from that which is beneficial or merely harmless. They also pose a significant risk of being overused if their limitations are not kept in mind.

# Index